BEBOP

BEBOP

SCOTT YANOW

Miller
Freeman
Books

SAN FRANCISCO

Published by Miller Freeman Books
600 Harrison Street, San Francisco, CA 94105

un Miller Freeman
A United News & Media publication

Distributed to the book trade in the U.S and Canada by
Publishers Group West
1700 Fourth Street, Berkeley, CA 94710

Distributed to the music trade in the U.S. and Canada by
Hal Leonard Publishing
P.O. Box 13819, Milwaukee, WI 53213

Cover design by Rich Leeds
Text design and composition by
Wilsted & Taylor Publishing Services

Front cover photo of Dizzy Gillespie:
Herman Leonard/Michael Ochs Archives
Back cover photo of Thelonious Monk, Howard McGhee,
Roy Eldridge, and Teddy Hill at Minton's Playhouse:
The Wayne Knight Collection

Library of Congress Cataloging-in-Publication Data
Yanow, Scott.
    Bebop / Scott Yanow.
        p. cm. — (Third ear)
    Includes bibliographical references, discographies,
    and index.
    ISBN 0-87930-608-4 (alk. paper)
    1. Bop (Music)—History and criticism.
    2. Jazz musicians.   3. Bop
    (Music)—Discography.   I. Title.   II. Series.

    ML3508 . Y36 2000
    781.65′5—dc21   00-058248

Printed in the United States of America

00 01 02 03 04 05   5 4 3 2 1

CONTENTS

INTRODUCTION

In 1945, World War II was in its final phase with Nazi Germany collapsing and Japan surrendering after being hit by two atomic bombs. Peace (at first euphoric and then uneasy) settled on most of the world even as the United States' Cold War with the Soviet Union began. Other than Franklin Roosevelt's death and Harry Truman succeeding him as 33rd president, the main domestic story of the year was the gradual return of American servicemen to civilian life. The boys were coming home!

With the end of the Depression, the world seemed temporarily to be a brighter place, although a certain amount of disillusionment would soon set in. It would take some time for many military men to get used to the routine of day-to-day life, which seemed so trivial after the life-and-death struggles they had recently gone through. A lot of adjustment would need to take place in domestic relationships, particularly in situations where women had tasted freedom while being paid well in jobs, or where couples had married quickly before they knew each other, only to be separated for a few years. Black servicemen who had helped defeat fascism would soon discover that racism remained a fact of life in the U.S. Considering these various political and social changes and the cultural climate, what had happened to the Swing era and the big bands?

In 1945, the popular music world was rapidly changing and having a revolution of its own. Swing had been a major part of pop music since 1935 but, due to a variety of factors (including a recording strike during much of 1942–44, the effects of World War II, heavy competition from a revival of Dixieland and the rise of rhythm and blues, and the imposition of an entertainment tax that discouraged dancing), it was rapidly declining, at least on a commercial basis. At the peak of its popularity in 1942, Swing would be considered largely dead by 1947, replaced by singers (such as Frank Sinatra, Doris Day, and Perry Como) on the pop charts and by this odd new music called Bebop in the jazz world.

Bop has become such an integral part of the jazz mainstream that it is hard to believe how radical it was considered in the mid-1940s. To fully appreciate how great a leap forward Bebop was, put on a record of Harry James from 1945 (the hit "It's Been a Long Long Time" is a good choice) and follow it with a Dizzy Gillespie/Charlie Parker recording from the same year, such as " 'Shaw Nuff" (which was actually recorded 2½ months earlier). James, a superior swing trumpeter, led the most popular big band in the country at the time, while Gillespie and Parker, virtual unknowns to the general public, were the two most important innovators in Bebop. Whereas James's recording has a straightforward and nostalgic vocal, a warm melodic trumpet solo, and a smooth, danceable rhythm, the Dizzy/Bird selection is full of fire, rapid unisons, and explosive playing. You cannot sing the main theme of " 'Shaw Nuff" until you've heard it many times. "It's Been a Long Long Time," in contrast, is so catchy that it was destined to be played by cocktail pianists and even Muzak orchestras forever.

Bebop, which became the foundation of all modern jazz styles of the past 55 years, is one of the most exciting types of music ever played. To hear virtuosos invent chorus after chorus of fresh ideas over repeating chord changes, often punctuated with humorous song quotes and unexpected phrases, is one of the thrills of listening to jazz, particularly if the musicians approach the brilliant level of a Charlie Parker or a Dizzy Gillespie. However, Bop never stood a chance as pop music, and most of its main players were against its being considered part of the entertainment world anyway. They sought to have jazz recognized as an art form rather than just used as background music for dancers. But, considering Bebop's negative image in the mass media (where it was seen as a crazy and excitable style of music played by black junkies) and the fact that the general public did not have a gradual chance to become accustomed to the new sounds, Bop was doomed to failure commercially. However, artistically it has remained a major influence up to the present time and at its best still sounds quite fresh today.

What is Bebop, where did it come from, how did it evolve, and where is it today? Who have been its main contributors, and what are the best CDs to acquire? This book seeks to answer all of these questions and many more.

As with my swing book in this series, the most difficult part of writing the Bebop book was deciding what to include and how far to stretch the definition of Bop. Virtually every jazz musician since 1950 (other than those committed to Dixieland and classic jazz) has played Bebop at one time or another, and most have recorded at least a few sessions in that idiom. In addition, Bop was the main inspiration for Cool Jazz and Hard Bop, and its vocabulary can be heard even in many avant-garde and fusion recordings, not to mention sessions by mainstream swing players. Where to draw the line?

The main emphasis in this book is on the key players of the 1945–49 period, the era of Classic Bebop. Since there will be other books in this series on West Coast Cool Jazz and Hard Bop, most of the later innovators and their recordings are being left for those studies, including such major artists as Gerry Mulligan, Chet Baker, Stan Getz, Lee Morgan, Horace Silver, and John Coltrane. Musicians who came to prominence during the Bop era have their later recordings discussed in this book, with the exception of several (such as Miles Davis and Max Roach) who evolved into other areas, and Art Blakey, who would symbolize Hard Bop. Some musicians (such as Clifford Brown) fit comfortably into more than one book (in his case, Bebop and Hard Bop) and are discussed in each survey, in the context of the particular style. In addition, musicians who came up after the Classic Bebop era and who have spent most of their lives playing Bop (such as Phil Woods, Richie Cole, Barry Harris, and Tommy Flanagan) are covered here. So, chances are if one of your favorites is missing from Bebop, he or she is probably in another book in this series.

One of course should keep in mind that these stylistic divisions are a bit artificial and mainly for the purpose of achieving a coherent work that focuses on a particular style. The best jazz musicians simply play their own music without sticking to inflexible rules. Calling Thelonious Monk a Bebop musician is as inaccurate as saying that Duke Ellington merely played swing; Thelonious played his own music his own way.

A few comments about the CD reviews. No attempt has been made to list and review every single CD by every single Bebop artist, but hopefully every significant release is covered. Although some European releases are included, the emphasis, with many exceptions, tends to be on available American discs. In addition to the studio recordings of the period, fortunately a large number of radio broadcasts and live performances from the era have been released, and a strong sampling are covered in this book.

I used a ten-point rating system for the CD reviews. Here are what the ratings mean:

*	*Limited edition box set—Most highly recommended for completists and veteran collectors but be careful to get it while you can!*
10	*A gem that belongs in every serious jazz collection*
9	*Highly recommended*
8	*A very good release*
7	*An excellent acquisition*
6	*Good music but not quite essential*
5	*Decent but not one of this artist's more important works*
4	*So-so*
3	*A disappointing effort with just a few worthwhile moments*
2	*A weak release*
1	*Stinks!*

Although I wrote the Bebop book by myself and am responsible for any errors that have crept in, there are several people whom I would like to thank: Dorothy Cox and Matt Kelsey of Miller Freeman for trusting in me and believing in this important project; Brian Ashley, who got me started in the jazz writing business back in 1976 when he formed Record Review; the many much-maligned but invaluable jazz publicists (including Ann Braithwaite, Lynda Bramble, Lori Hehr, and Terri Hinte) who make life much easier for jazz journalists; the owners of the long-departed College Records (a store located near the campus of Cal State Northridge) where I bought my first Bebop album, a $2 LP of Charlie Parker that included his version of "White Christmas" (hey, I know that tune!); and "Bird and Diz" for following their own musical visions despite everything and helping to create this remarkable music. In addition, a special thanks to my wife Kathy and my daughter Melody for their love and patience.

THE STATE OF JAZZ IN 1944

In 1944 the music world seemed stable, but it was about to begin experiencing some major changes. Swing had been king since 1935, with hundreds of big bands working regularly in the United States. Not only were such bandleaders as Benny Goodman, Artie Shaw, Glenn Miller, Harry James, Count Basie, Duke Ellington, Gene Krupa, Tommy Dorsey, Jimmy Dorsey, and Jimmie Lunceford, among others, respected in the jazz world, but they were national celebrities and household names, occasionally even appearing (in the case of the white stars) in Hollywood movies.

And yet in three years, the Swing era would be dead, most of the big bands would be broken up, and the music would be associated with the past rather than the present. Even in 1944, there were trouble signs for swing. A recording strike by the Musicians Union (who wanted the labels to pay a royalty for every disc sold to make up for the loss of work caused by free radio) kept virtually every musician off records from mid-1942 until near the end of 1943. In the case of the larger labels, such as Victor and Columbia, no new records were made for over two years, not until late-1944. During this period, singers (who in most cases had previously been thought only of in terms of adding variety to a big band) began to take over. They were free to record during the strike years. In addition, the public was becoming hungry for soothing and nostalgic ballads as World War II raged on.

Swing, after having been largely unchallenged for nine years, was also receiving heavy competition from other styles of music. In addition to the singers' gradual takeover of the pop charts, Dixieland was making a comeback, rhythm and blues (as typified by Louis Jordan's Tympani Five) was starting to attract the dancing and partying audience, and then there was Bebop.

To veterans returning from overseas in 1945 and expecting to hear Harry James and Benny Goodman, the sounds of Dizzy Gillespie and Charlie Parker were a sudden shock and one that they were not prepared for. Swing fans from outside of New York City were also very surprised when they first heard Bop, because there had been no real prior warning. The recording strike had succeeded in keeping the transitional period between swing and Bop largely off of records. The 1943 Earl Hines Orchestra (which included Dizzy Gillespie and Charlie Parker on tenor) never recorded, small-group dates that might have hinted strongly at Bop while remaining tied to swing were not made, and the result was culture shock. There was just too much difference between the big bands of Benny Goodman and Dizzy Gillespie for the latter to achieve public acceptance very quickly, and the negative coverage (coupled with the larger record labels' attempts to turn Bebop into a fad during 1948–49) resulted in most of the swing audience going elsewhere. Jimmy Dorsey was famous, but who was this Charlie Parker?

And yet, looked at decades later, it seems obvious that Bebop was not so much revolutionary as it was evolutionary. It was a natural extension of swing and part of jazz's 60-year mad rush (1915–75) to freedom. During those six decades, new styles quickly replaced older ones, and the innovators of one era became the conservative defenders of the faith during the next period. Benny Goodman was the symbol for the new swing music in 1935, and yet he was thought of as a bit of a has-been by 1948, when he was still just 39. The same thing would happen to Bebop, which was seen as so radical in 1945 but considered safe and logical by 1959, when Ornette Coleman burst upon the scene.

But all of this was not obvious in 1944. Jazz and swing were a strong part of the American entertainment industry. Each important city had its jazz center (New York's 52nd Street contained a remarkable number of major clubs within an area of just a few blocks, while Los Angeles's Central Avenue was growing), there were regular radio broadcasts of the big swing bands, and the number of smaller jazz combos playing swing-based music were countless. It was an exciting period for music, with swing, Dixieland, and the new Bebop style all coexisting.

WHAT IS THIS THING CALLED BEBOP?

Although there are several theories as to who named the new style "Bebop" (or "Bop" as it would be more infor-mally known), none are definitive. The syllables "Rebop" (an early alternate name for Bebop) and "Bebop" had appeared a decade earlier in scat singing, and the name is really a tribute to the music's rhythmic nature and spontaneity.

In the early 1940s, big band swing was in a bit of a rut. Many of the orchestras had similar sounds and were playing interchangeable (and often commercial) material using predictable chord changes. Most of the sidemen were re-stricted to brief solos, and the more talented ones were hungry to stretch out. After-hours jam sessions, a tradition in jazz since at least late 1920s Kansas City, were an excellent forum for exchanging new phrases and for experimenting. Some of the more adventurous jams of the early 1940s took place at Minton's Playhouse (where pianist Thelonious Monk and drummer Kenny Clarke were in the house band) and Monroe's Uptown House. The musicians jammed on standards, trying out new ideas and unusual chord changes, helping to lead to Bebop.

Bop in its mature form differs from swing in several ways. To simplify one of the differences: In classic jazz, Dix-ieland, and swing, most of the solos are improvised while keeping the melody in mind; one can usually readily identify the song during most of the solos. In Bebop, the solos are based on the chord changes, and often the melody is dis-carded after the first chorus, not to be played again until the end of the song. The emphasis is much more on the soloist's creativity and inventiveness than on the melody or the song itself. There were examples of this approach prior to the Bebop era, such as Coleman Hawkins's famous 1939 recording of "Body and Soul" (which only hinted at the melody during its first four bars)—but that was unusual for the period.

To confuse matters more for the average listener, many of the "originals" composed by the classic Bebop players used the chord changes of standards but tacked on a completely different theme. For example, "How High the Moon" became "Ornithology"; "I Got Rhythm" was the basis for many songs, including "Anthropology"; "Indiana" was transformed into "Donna Lee"; "Just You, Just Me" became "Evidence"; and the blues reappeared as many titles, including "Now's the Time" and "Billie's Bounce." The more original themes, such as "Confirmation," "Yardbird Suite," and "Moose the Mooche," were not as singable (unless one heard them dozens of times) as the usual swing tune, making their commercial potential beyond the jazz world much less than that of the older swing hits.

In Bop, the rhythm section functioned much differently than in the typical swing group, particularly the pianist. In earlier days, jazz pianists played a stride pattern with their left hand, keeping time by alternating between bass notes and chords, striding back and forth between different parts of the piano while the right hand played melodic varia-tions. The later swing pianists (starting with Teddy Wilson and Count Basie and including Nat King Cole) had a lighter left hand and sometimes implied (rather than explicitly stated) the beat, but they still utilized the piano as if it were an independent orchestra. However, in Bebop, starting with Bud Powell, it all changed. Now the left hand "comped," playing chords but not necessarily on the beat and much more irregularly. The right hand, particularly in solos, tended to emphasize long single-note runs as if emulating a horn.

Because of this change, the string bassist became much more of a necessity as a timekeeper in jazz. Unlike, say, the Benny Goodman Trio of 1935 (comprised of the clarinetist, pianist Teddy Wilson, and drummer Gene Krupa), Be-bop combos had to have a bassist to sound complete. Despite the innovations of Jimmy Blanton, most bassists of the classic Bebop era were not all that different than their swing counterparts, playing fairly basic four-to-the-bar bass lines, except that the tempos were often faster and the chords much more complex.

In the early days of the Swing era, drummers often kept time with their bass drum. Jo Jones with the Count Basie Orchestra had a much lighter feel, switching the timekeeping role to the hi-hat cymbal. But for Bebop, Kenny Clarke moved that function to the ride cymbal, utilizing the bass drum and snare drum for commentary on what was going on, which was called "dropping bombs." Although the drummer still kept a 4/4 beat, it was not as obvious as with swing bands; you had to listen closely to the bass to know exactly where the song was, making it a little more difficult for casual listeners to dance to Bop.

The typical Bop performance features a quick and tricky melody played in unison by the horns (without counter-melodies or spontaneous harmonies), a string of solos, and a closing run-through of the theme. Unlike the many orchestras in the Swing era, most classic Bop groups were smaller combos, for a variety of reasons. Even overlooking the economic factors involved and the collapse of the big band business, the desire of Bop soloists to stretch out and the complexity of their music alone would have resulted in the style being dominated by smaller groups. There were some exceptions, most notably the Billy Eckstine Orchestra and especially the Dizzy Gillespie big band, which showed that Bebop could be orchestrated, but most of the important Bop pioneers were players first and composer-arrangers second (other than Thelonious Monk, Tadd Dameron, and a few others).

Another major change was in the attitude that most Bop musicians had toward themselves and their audiences. The swing big bandleaders knew that no matter how important they considered their music, they ultimately had to satisfy a dancing audience, not to mention their label, booking agency, club owners, song pluggers, and promoters. However, the Bop musicians felt that their main allegiance was to the music itself, which they considered an art form rather than merely a part of the entertainment world. In general they were much less communicative with the audience, were less willing to compromise their music, and in some cases were their own worst enemy, particularly the less reliable musicians. Dizzy Gillespie was an exception, because he enjoyed singing, dancing, telling jokes, and talking to his audience, but most other Beboppers wanted to let the music speak for itself. It was quite a change from the past, and the attitude further split jazz from popular music.

Unlike in swing, where the melodies were accessible and there were many "hooks" to draw in listeners (pretty female vocalists, a very danceable 4/4 beat, and showmanship), Bebop musicians expected their audiences to come to their performances as spectators rather than participants, purely to hear the music. Listeners who took the time to come to the music on its own terms were often startled at first, but many were drawn in, having a veritable light bulb go off in their heads when they finally got it, a turning point in becoming a Bebop fanatic! Many would be "addicted" for life.

THE EVOLUTION OF BEBOP: 1937–1944

The exact point in time when Bebop was fully formed is not known, although 1944 was the first year that it began to appear tentatively on records. The music was in its formative stage for several years before that, and important events occurred as early as 1937 that helped lead to Bebop.

1937: This would actually be one of the prime years of the Swing era, with the Count Basie Orchestra emerging in New York, Benny Goodman's Big Band featuring Harry James and Gene Krupa, trumpeter Bunny Berigan heard at the height of his powers, and swing fully taking over as America's popular music. Most relevant to Bebop, Dizzy Gillespie makes his first appearance on records (playing "King Porter Stomp" with Teddy Hill's Orchestra), sounding a great deal like his idol, Roy Eldridge. Seventeen-year-old Charlie Parker joins Jay McShann's big band in Kansas City.

1938: Benny Goodman's Carnegie Hall concert makes history, Gene Krupa goes out on his own as a bandleader, and Artie Shaw's orchestra catches fire. Kenny Clarke, as the drummer with Edgar Hayes's Orchestra, had mastered swing and starts to experiment with his style.

1939: Glenn Miller's band catches on as the most popular of all swing bands, Coleman Hawkins records "Body and Soul," and both Charlie Christian and Jimmy Blanton begin to make strong impressions. Dizzy Gillespie joins Cab Calloway's orchestra for a two-year period. Charlie Parker visits New York for the first time, at one point working as a dishwasher at a restaurant so he can hear Art Tatum play there nightly.

1940: Both Minton's Playhouse and Monroe's Uptown House begin hosting after-hours jam sessions. Minton's house band consists of Thelonious Monk, bassist Nick Fenton, Kenny Clarke, and Joe Guy. Top swing players (including Charlie Christian) sit in on a regular basis. Dizzy Gillespie and Charlie Parker meet for the first time. Bird makes his first recordings for Jay McShann, small-group sides that show his debt to Lester Young but also find the altoist sounding quite original.

1941: Gillespie is fired from Calloway's band, mistakenly accused of throwing a spitball at the leader. Parker records some studio sides with McShann's orchestra, taking brief solos that impress many of the younger musicians, some of whom also hear him taking longer spots with the McShann Orchestra on radio broadcasts.

1942: Dizzy Gillespie spends a short period with Lucky Millinder's Orchestra, taking a solo on "Little John Special" in an arrangement that hints strongly at "Salt Peanuts." The Cootie Williams Orchestra records Thelonious Monk's "Epistrophy." Charlie Parker leaves Jay McShann's band, spending a short period with Noble Sissle's orchestra. Woody Herman's orchestra records Gillespie's advanced arrangement of "Down Under," and Herman suggests to Dizzy that he give up the trumpet and become a full-time arranger!

1943: Gillespie, Parker (on tenor), and Sarah Vaughan join the Earl Hines Big Band, but the recording strike keeps this very early Bebop orchestra completely off records. Bud Powell becomes a member of the Cootie Williams Orchestra. Monroe's Uptown House closes.

1944: Coleman Hawkins leads the first Bebop recording sessions. Thelonious Monk becomes a regular member of Hawk's quartet. The Billy Eckstine Orchestra features Charlie Parker (on alto), Dizzy Gillespie, Dexter Gordon, Gene Ammons, Art Blakey, and many other young modernists. Parker records with Tiny Grimes, and Gillespie makes a record session with Sarah Vaughan, who records Dizzy's "A Night in Tunisia" as a vocal piece called "Interlude." The Boyd Raeburn Orchestra had already cut Gillespie's Bop classic earlier in the year. The Cootie Williams Orchestra (with Bud Powell) records Thelonious Monk's " 'Round Midnight." The first Jazz at the Philharmonic concert includes J. J. Johnson among the soloists. Howard McGhee and Fats Navarro are both in the trumpet section of the Andy Kirk Orchestra. Woody Herman's Herd begins to catch on as jazz's hottest new big band.

Despite all of these events, as 1945 began, few listeners were prepared for the sudden emergence of Bebop.

Influences on the Bop Movement

Although Bebop seemed to many observers of the time to pop up out of nowhere and to be a radical break with the past, in reality it was tied closely to swing. Nearly all of the Bop players had gained important early experience as members of big bands, and the more advanced swing improvisers were their heroes, idols, and main influences, particularly the 26 covered in this section. Not mentioned here but particularly important as innovators in earlier styles of music were Louis Armstrong, Henry "Red" Allen, Jack Teagarden, Johnny Hodges, Sidney Bechet, Fats Waller, Teddy Wilson, and Billie Holiday; all but Waller were still quite active during the rich years of the Bebop era.

The emphasis in the biographies and the CD reviews in this section is on the swing stylists' influence and connection to the Bebop era; most are more fully profiled in the swing book in this series.

COUNT BASIE

b. Aug. 21, 1904, Red Bank, NJ, d. Apr. 26, 1984, Hollywood, CA

Count Basie's orchestra did not arrive in New York until late in 1936, and it had been preceded by Fletcher Henderson, Duke Ellington, and Benny Goodman, among many others. However, Basie's band soon became the most influential of all the swing-era big bands. And, although defining swing, its innovations helped set the stage for Bebop.

The most important aspect of Basie's band was not its great soloists (which in its early days included trumpeters Buck Clayton and Harry "Sweets" Edison, trombonist Dickie Wells, and such tenors as Lester Young, Herschel Evans, and Evans's replacement, Buddy Tate) but its rhythm section. Basie's band redefined the roles of the piano, guitar, bass, and drums.

Prior to the rise of the big bands, most piano players emphasized stride patterns with their left hands and the piano was utilized as if it were an orchestra, rendering the string bass, horns, and the drums as added attractions that were luxuries. Even Teddy Wilson, who had a light touch, made the bass unnecessary when he was a member of the Benny Goodman Trio and Quartet. Count Basie, despite the fact that Fats Waller was his early influence, helped change all that. His style hinted at much more than he actually played, leaving lots of space. Because his sense of time was impeccable, Basie did not need to state every beat with his left hand. His right played little percussive figures, easy to imitate but impossible to top. And, although Bud Powell did not sound like Count Basie, the freeing of the left hand was an important transitional step toward Bebop piano.

Because Basie had pared down the role of the piano, it was necessary for the rest of the rhythm section to adjust. Freddie Green on acoustic rhythm guitar played chords four-to-the-bar, taking over the role of the left hand on the piano. Bassist Walter Page had a more prominent role than most bassists, keeping the rhythm steady with his walking patterns and pushing the ensembles. And drummer Jo Jones, rather than emphasizing the rhythm with the bass drum (which Gene Krupa and Dixieland drummers of the era often did), switched the timekeeping role to the hi-hat cymbal. The net result was that the Basie rhythm section was lighter than its contemporaries yet outswung everyone.

Bill "Count" Basie, after a brief period playing drums, switched permanently to piano. Inspired by Thomas "Fats" Waller, whom he saw playing organ for silent movies in New York in the early 1920s, Basie was originally a stride pianist. He gained experience playing on the East Coast and touring with various revues that performed at theaters throughout the Midwest. A two-year stint with the Gonzelle White Show ended when the revue broke up in Kansas City in 1927, and Count found himself stranded. The location was quite lucky for the young pianist. He had landed in one of the great jazz centers, a wide-open city where Prohibition was completely ignored and jazz bands were constantly in demand for the partying atmosphere. During the next decade, all-night after-hours jam sessions were a fact of life, and Basie was a major part of the scene.

By 1928, Count Basie was a member of Walter Page's Blue Devils, and a year later he joined Bennie Moten's orchestra, considered the top big band of the Midwest. Count has solos on many of Moten's records (starting in 1929), and you can trace his early evolution as he gradually paired down his stride style. After Moten's death in 1935 from a botched tonsillectomy, Basie formed his own orchestra, which soon became the most popular band in Kansas City. Using Moten alumni (including singer Jimmy Rushing, baritonist Jack

Washington, and Walter Page) as the nucleus of his group at first, Basie soon added the innovative cool-toned tenor of Lester Young (whose playing was a striking contrast to Herschel Evans's Coleman Hawkins-influenced tone), Buck Clayton, and Jo Jones. The band's regular series of broadcasts from the Reno Club attracted quite a few talent scouts from the East Coast, including executives from the Decca label (who signed Basie to a record contract), manager Joe Glaser (who lured trumpeter Hot Lips Page away), and producer John Hammond. In late 1936 Basie traveled East and, although it was a bit of struggle for the first year (his band was quickly expanded from nine to 13 pieces, which resulted in the group's head arrangements having to be altered, written down, and relearned), the band eventually became a sensation in the jazz world. "One O'Clock Jump" and "Jumpin' at the Woodside" were new standards, and many of the other big bands emulated the Basie sound as best they could, turning away from the formerly dominant Benny Goodman model. Even BG toyed with the idea of breaking up his band and joining forces with Basie, whose music he loved.

The young modernists who led the Bebop movement considered Count Basie's orchestra to be one of the most progressive of all the swing bands, and they particularly admired the playing of Lester Young and the lightness of the rhythm section. After Young's surprise decision to leave in late 1940 (he returned to Basie for a period in 1943–44), his spot was taken by such important young tenors as Don Byas, Illinois Jacquet, Lucky Thompson, and Paul Gonsalves. Other significant players who were with Basie in the 1940s included altoist Tab Smith, trumpeters Joe Newman and Clark Terry, and trombonist Vic Dickenson. During the Bebop era, the Count Basie band continued working steadily and delighting both swing and Bop fans. However, the decline of the big band scene, the leader's losses at the racetrack(!), and some bad business decisions resulted in Basie having to reluctantly break up his orchestra late in 1949, just as Bebop was beginning to be swept aside. Soon the pianist was leading a combo that included Wardell Gray, Clark Terry, and Buddy DeFranco, playing music that was both Boppish and tied to the swing tradition. Other notables who passed through the group included Harry "Sweets" Edison, Georgie Auld, and Gene Ammons.

Unlike most other swing bandleaders, Count Basie was able to return to the big band scene and have greater success in the post-swing years than he had enjoyed earlier. Altoist

Marshall Royal helped to recruit musicians, and in 1952 the new Count Basie Orchestra was officially born. Keeping the same feel in the rhythm section (Freddie Green was with Count until the end), the band relied much more on arrangements this time around. Its soloists were flexible enough to play both Bop and swing and included such top-notch players in the 1950s as Frank Wess on flute, tenor, and alto, Frank Foster on tenor, trumpeters Joe Newman and Thad Jones, and, during a few periods, Eddie "Lockjaw" Davis on tenor; later key soloists included Eric Dixon on tenor and flute, trombonist Al Grey, Jimmy Forrest on tenor, and drummer Butch Miles. After having a hit with their recording of "April in Paris" and particularly after Joe Williams joined the band (his "Everyday I Have the Blues" became a standard), the Count Basie Orchestra was considered an institution and was greatly in demand whenever a big band was needed. It has continued swinging its way around the world up to the present time, even outlasting Basie's death in 1984, and today (under Grover Mitchell's direction) ranks as the #1 swinging machine.

10 *The Complete Decca Recordings / Jan. 21, 1937– Feb. 4, 1939 / GRP/Decca 3-611*

This three-CD set gives listeners the best collection currently available of Count Basie's orchestra from the Swing era; the slightly later Columbia recordings are available only in piecemeal fashion. The 57 numbers cut by the Basie big band for Decca (plus six alternate takes) are included, and there are many fine examples of the work of Lester Young, Herschel Evans, Buck Clayton, Harry "Sweets" Edison, Dickie Wells, Jimmy Rushing, and that remarkable rhythm section. The highlights include "Honeysuckle Rose," "Boogie-Woogie," the original version of "One O'Clock Jump," "Topsy," "Sent for You Yesterday and Here You Come Today," "Swingin' the Blues," "Blue and Sentimental," "Jumpin' at the Woodside," and "Jive at Five."

9 *1947: Brand New Wagon / Jan. 3, 1947–Dec. 12, 1947 / Bluebird 2292*

9 *1949: Shouting Blues / Apr. 11, 1949–Feb. 6, 1950 / Bluebird 66158*

These two CDs are a strong sampling of Count Basie's work during the Bebop era. *Brand New Wagon* has 21 of the 40 selections cut by Basie in 1947, including seven numbers performed with a small group that includes trumpeter Emmett Berry and Paul Gonsalves. The big band titles include "Your Red Wagon," "One O'Clock Boogie," "South," and

"Robbins' Nest." *Shouting Blues* has 17 of the 19 tunes that Count Basie's big band recorded in 1949, shortly before its breakup. The arrangements (many by C. O. Price) are quite Boppish, and such players as trumpeters Harry Edison, Emmett Berry, and Clark Terry, Dickie Wells, and Paul Gonsalves are heard from, along with Jimmy Rushing. *Shouting Blues* also has three of the four numbers made on February 6, 1950, during Basie's first session with his new octet, which includes Edison, Wells, and both Georgie Auld and Gene Ammons on tenors.

10 *Count Basie Swings, Joe Williams Sings / July 17–26, 1955 / Verve 314 519 852*

10 *April in Paris / July 26, 1955-Jan. 5, 1956 / Verve 314 521 407*

10 *Count Basie at Newport / Sept. 7, 1957 / Verve 833 776*

The second Count Basie Orchestra got off to a promising start in 1952, and by 1955–56 its success had surpassed that of his first big band. Touched by Bop and based in swing, the 1950s Basie band really was in its own category. *Count Basie Swings, Joe Williams Sings* (which has such famous Williams vocals as "Everyday I Have the Blues," "Alright, Okay, You Win," "The Comeback," and "In the Evening") and *April in Paris* (highlighted by the title cut, Frank Foster's "Shiny Stockings," and Freddie Greene's "Corner Pocket") are both essential for any jazz collection. *Count Basie at Newport* is a reunion that teams a few significant alumni from the first band (Lester Young, Jimmy Rushing, Jo Jones, and Illinois Jacquet) with Roy Eldridge plus the second Basie Orchestra; Joe Williams also has a few vocals. Young's playing behind Rushing's vocals on "Boogie Woogie" and "Evenin' " are some of the great moments in jazz history.

* *The Complete Roulette Studio Count Basie / Oct. 21, 1957-July 26, 1962 / Mosaic 10-149*

8 *Sing Along with Basie / May 26, 1958-Sept. 3, 1958 / Roulette 7953322*

9 *Basie and Eckstine, Inc. / May 22, 1959-July 28, 1959 / Roulette 52029*

4 *The Gifted Ones / Feb. 3, 1977 / Original Jazz Classics 886*

7 *The Golden Years / Apr. 17, 1972-Dec. 14, 1983 / Pablo 4PACD-4419*

Although the later Count Basie Orchestra is beyond the confines of this Bebop book, a few of its many recordings should be mentioned. The band's Roulette period (1957–62) is reissued in full on the limited-edition ten-CD Mosaic box set, including such major albums as *The Atomic Mr. Basie, Basie Plays Hefti, One More Time,* and *Kansas City Suite* (many of them are also available individually). *Sing Along with Basie* mostly features Lambert, Hendricks, and Ross. That pacesetting vocal group had debuted with a very successful album (*Sing a Song of Basie*) in which they overdubbed their voices to recreate the Basie band. *Sing Along with Basie* actually matches the vocalists with Basie's men, including a unique version of "Goin' to Chicago," in which Joe Williams takes the lead vocal while Lambert, Hendricks, and Ross sing around him. *Basie and Eckstine* (which is not part of the Mosaic box) has one of Billy Eckstine's finest dates of his post-Bop years. The influential baritone performs a jazz-oriented program that includes "Jelly, Jelly," "Lonesome Lover Blues," "I Want a Little Girl," and "Stormy Monday Blues," clearly inspired by the swinging Basie Orchestra.

After Count Basie's period with the Roulette label ended, a decade of erratic recordings followed, although the big band never declined. In 1972 producer Norman Granz (who had documented Count for his Clef and Verve labels during the first half of the 1950s) had a reunion with Basie; he recorded him quite frequently during his final dozen years. *The Gifted Ones* probably seemed like a good idea at the time, teaming Basie with Dizzy Gillespie, but unfortunately it was done backwards. Instead of having Gillespie sit in with the Count Basie Orchestra, Dizzy and Basie were matched in a quartet. The trumpeter sounds merely OK while Basie is quite predictable; no magic occurs.

While with the Pablo label, Basie was recorded in three basic settings: with his big band, in all-star groups, and as a pianist (sometimes teaming up with Oscar Peterson for two-piano duets or in a quartet). No less than 33 Count Basie CDs are currently in the Fantasy/Pablo catalog (not counting a "Best of" sampler). The four-CD retrospective *The Golden Years* does an excellent job of summing up Basie's Pablo years, with the music divided into live concerts, small-group outings, dates with vocalists, and big band showcases.

FRED BECKETT

b. Jan. 23, 1917, Nellerton, MS, d. Jan. 30, 1946, St. Louis, MO

Fred Beckett, who never became well known and died tragically young, is included in this section because J. J. Johnson always mentioned Beckett as his main early influence. Beckett took up the trombone while in high school in his native Mississippi. After moving to Kansas City, he played with Eddie Johnson's Crackerjacks (1934) and the bands of Duke Wright, Buster Smith, Tommy Douglas, Andy Kirk (1937), Dee Stewart, and Nat Towles. Most notable was his association with Harlan Leonard's orchestra (1939–40), during which he recorded, taking solos on such numbers as "Skee," "Rockin' with the Rockets," "'400' Swing," and "Please Don't Squabble" with particularly strong (if brief) spots on "A La Bridges" and "My Gal Sal." Beckett did not actually sound like J. J. Johnson would (often coming closer in style to Dickie Wells and Benny Morton), but his technical ability was impressive. Fred Beckett spent time with Lionel Hampton's orchestra (1940–44) during which he appeared on a few more records (though rarely soloing), served in the Army, contracted tuberculosis, and died just a week after his 29th birthday.

10 *Harlan Leonard—1940 / Jan. 11, 1940–Nov. 13, 1940 / Classics 670*

All of Fred Beckett's recordings with Harlan Leonard's orchestra (other than three alternate takes) and, in fact, the complete output of Leonard as a leader is on this single CD, 23 strong examples of solid swing. Tenor saxophonist Henry Bridges is actually the main solo star, and of great interest is that Tadd Dameron contributed seven of the arrangements (including "A La Bridges" and "Dameron Stomp"). Fred Beckett never did have a chance to lead any of his own sessions, so this CD is practically his entire legacy.

JIMMY BLANTON

b. Oct. 5, 1918, Chattanooga, TN, d. July 30, 1942, Los Angeles, CA

The evolution of the string bass can be divided easily into two periods: pre-Blanton and post-Blanton. Prior to the rise of Jimmy Blanton, the bass had been used as strictly a four-to-the-bar accompaniment instrument. It had risen in significance as pianists' left-hand touch had become lighter during the 1930s, but bass solos were still very rare and quite basic before 1939. In contrast, Blanton played his solos with the fluidity of a guitarist or a saxophonist, and his backing of soloists challenged the lead voice rather just being subservient. So advanced was Blanton's playing that, when he first appeared on the national scene in 1939 at the age of 21, he was a decade ahead of virtually everyone else. In fact, most of the bassists of the Bop era (such as Tommy Potter and Curly Russell) still stuck to playing four-to-the-bar patterns during their solos, with the exception of Oscar Pettiford and (by the late 1940s) Charles Mingus. It would not be until the late 1950s that the mainstream of jazz caught up with (and eventually surpassed) Jimmy Blanton.

Blanton's life was tragically brief. He started off playing violin, switching to bass while at Tennessee State College in 1936. After playing with Fate Marable's band on a riverboat, Blanton dropped out of college, moved to St. Louis, and worked with the Jeter-Pillars Orchestra (1937–39). When he joined the Duke Ellington Orchestra in the fall of 1939, Blanton originally was one of two bassists, with Billy Taylor, but Taylor quickly recognized Blanton's superiority and left in January 1940. During his two-year period with Ellington, Blanton was remarkably well featured, and his playing was considered so significant that, years later, the early 1940s Ellington group would be nicknamed the Blanton/Webster band after the bassist and Ben Webster. Duke backed him on six recorded duets, gave Blanton short prominent solos on such orchestra numbers as "Jack the Bear," "Sepia Panorama," and "Ko Ko," and included him on small-group dates headed by Ellington's sidemen. Had he lived, Blanton would certainly have taken part in many Bebop sessions, for he participated in the after-hours scene in New York, jamming with the young modernists at Minton's Playhouse and Monroe's Uptown House. But in late 1941 Blanton contracted tuberculosis; he passed away in mid-1942 when he was just 23. There is no film footage of Jimmy Blanton and he never led his own record session, but he can be heard on many Duke Ellington recordings from 1939–41.

10 *The Blanton-Webster Band / Mar. 6, 1940–July 28, 1942 / Bluebird 5659*
10 *Fargo, ND, November 7, 1940 / Nov. 7, 1940 / Vintage Jazz Classics 1019/20*
8 *Solos, Duets and Trios / Feb. 9, 1932–Aug. 30, 1967 / Bluebird 2178*

These three Duke Ellington sets include the bulk of Jimmy Blanton's recordings. The bassist's earliest sessions with Duke (recorded for Columbia, including two of the duets) have not yet been reissued on CD. The three-disc Blanton-Webster Bluebird reissue has the master takes of all 66 of the Ellington's big band's recordings for RCA during 1940–42. Blanton is on all but the final sessions, and his most famous

He may have lived to be only 23, but Jimmy Blanton's fluid and creative bass playing was 20 years ahead of its time.

solos (including "Jack the Bear," "Sepia Panorama," and "Ko Ko") plus his strong contributions to such numbers as "Cottontail," "Harlem Air Shaft," and "In a Mellotone" are all here. *Fargo, ND,* a two-CD set, is a well-recorded dance date that was fortunately documented by Jack Towers. The Ellington Orchestra sounds quite inspired, cornetist Ray Nance was making his very first appearance with the band (he would stay over 20 years), and fortunately Jimmy Blanton can be heard quite prominently throughout the night's performance. *Solos, Duets and Trios* has a variety of intimate performances by Duke Ellington from a 35-year period, including solo piano numbers from 1932, 1941, and 1967, a meeting with Earl Hines in 1965, two trio selections from 1945, and a pair of piano duets with Billy Strayhorn in 1946 (including the adventurous "Tonk"). In addition, Duke's four duets with Jimmy Blanton in 1940 are here, as are five alternate takes. Blanton is in the lead throughout the nine

performances, playing solos that would influence bassists for the next 20 years.

DON BYAS

b. Oct. 21, 1912, Muskogee, OK, d. Aug. 24, 1972, Amsterdam, Holland

Don Byas might very well have been a major participant in the Bebop movement had he not permanently moved to Europe in 1946. He had already extended the innovations of Coleman Hawkins and, although falling stylistically between swing and Bop, he was one of the most advanced tenor-saxophonists of the mid-1940s. Byas gained early experience as an altoist with Bennie Moten, Terrence Holder, and Walter Page's Blue Devils (1929). During 1931–32 Byas had a band (under the name of Don Carlos and His Collegiate Ramblers) back home in Oklahoma. After switching to tenor, he toured with Bert Johnson's Sharps and Flats in 1933 and for several years lived in California, where he played with a variety of groups, including those led by Lionel Hampton, Eddie Barefield, and Buck Clayton. After touring with Ethel Waters (1936–38), Byas settled in New York and worked with the big bands of Don Redman, Lucky Millinder, Andy Kirk (1939–40), Edgar Hayes, and Benny Carter. He was Lester Young's replacement with Count Basie (1941–43), recording with Basie and gaining some recognition. During 1944–46, Byas was a regular on 52nd Street (including playing with one of Dizzy Gillespie's early groups), and he recorded frequently as a leader and as a sideman. His two tenor-bass duets with Slam Stewart at a 1945 Town Hall concert became famous. But in September 1946, while on a European tour with Don Redman's orchestra, Byas decided to stay abroad. He lived at different times in France, the Netherlands, and Denmark, working steadily throughout the Continent and recording occasionally, visiting the United States briefly in 1970. But it was a much larger world at the time than it would become, and Don Byas was largely forgotten at home, where his influence on modern saxophonists largely ended with his 1946 departure.

7 *Midnight at Minton's / 1941 / High Note 7044*
9 *1944–1945 / July 28, 1944–Mar. 1945 / Classics 882*
10 *Don Byas on Blue Star / Jan. 13, 1947–Mar. 7, 1952 / Emarcy 833 406*
8 *A Night in Tunisia / Jan. 13–14, 1963 / Black Lion 760136*
8 *Walkin' / Jan. 13–14, 1963 / Black Lion 760167*

Midnight at Minton's is from the Jerry Newman collection, private acetate discs recorded live at Minton's Playhouse in 1941. This set has some brilliant playing by Byas (especially on "Stardust"), a couple of excellent vocals from Helen Humes, and spots for the young (and unknown) Thelonious Monk and trumpeter Joe Guy. *1944–1945* is the first in a series of Classics CDs (including ones titled *1945, 1945 Vol. 2, 1946,* and *1947*) that have all of Byas's mid-'40s sessions as a leader. Eight songs on *1944–1945* (including "1944 Stomp" and the two-part "Savoy Jam Party") feature Byas in a combo with Charlie Shavers; he heads a group that includes trumpeter Joe Thomas; and he is heard in a quintet with blues guitarist-singer Big Bill Broonzy; everything works quite well.

After moving to Europe, Byas kept busy, even if most American jazz fans forgot about him. *Don Byas on Blue Star*

shows how strong a player the tenorman was in 1947 and 1950–52. The earlier performances find Byas and several other members of the Don Redman band (trumpeter Peanuts Holland, trombonist Tyree Glenn, and pianist Billy Taylor) interacting with some fine French musicians, including altoist Hubert Rostaing. Byas is featured on the later dates with local rhythm sections, playing advanced swing that hints at Bebop. *A Night in Tunisia* and *Walkin'*, which are from the same sessions, have Byas assisted by pianist Bent Axen, bassist Niels Pedersen, and drummer Williams Schiopffe. The two CDs are equally rewarding, with Byas (heard in prime form) stretching out on such Bop standards as "Anthropology," "Billie's Bounce," and "All the Things You Are."

CHARLIE CHRISTIAN
b. July 29, 1916, Dallas, TX, d. Mar. 2, 1942, New York, NY

Charlie Christian was to the electric guitar what Jimmy Blanton was to the bass, and he led a similar life. As with Blanton, Christian spent his brief career connected with one famous bandleader, he was recorded for about two years, and he died from tuberculosis. And, as with Blanton, Christian became the main influence on his instrument for decades (no one during the Bop era surpassed him), he was an advanced swing player who participated in the New York after-hours sessions that led to Bop, and he died before Bebop even had its name.

Although not the first electric guitarist, Christian was the first master of that instrument. He grew up in Oklahoma City, had brief flirtations with the trumpet and piano, and began playing guitar when he was 12. Christian played in a family band with four of his brothers and his father (also a guitarist) and he picked up experience working with (among others) Anna Mae Winburn, Nat Towles, Alphonso Trent (for whom he played bass), Lloyd Hunter, and the Jeter-Pillars Band. In 1937 Christian switched from acoustic to electric guitar. Rather than being influenced by other guitarists (though he was very familiar with Django Reinhardt), Christian was most inspired by Lester Young and the top swing-era horn soloists. He quickly created a horn-like style filled with catchy riffs and melodic ideas, developing the ability to play many choruses without repeating himself. Mary Lou Williams and Teddy Wilson were among the mu-

**Charlie Christian's improvised ideas and riffs became the
main influence on most jazz guitarists prior to the fusion era.**

sicians passing through the South who were impressed by the young guitarist.

In 1939, while working with Leslie Sheffield, Christian was heard by producer John Hammond, who flew him to Los Angeles in August for a tryout with Benny Goodman. The clarinetist was not impressed by Christian's flashy clothes. But he called out "Rose Room" and 45 minutes later they were still playing the song! Christian immediately became a regular member of BG's sextet/septet. Very soon Charlie Christian was the talk of jazz, a sensation among musicians, who made all of the other guitarists (except Django Reinhardt) sound quite dated. Christian was mostly featured with the Benny Goodman Sextet (which included at various times Lionel Hampton, Count Basie, Georgie Auld, and Cootie Williams). He was showcased on two numbers with the Goodman big band ("Honeysuckle Rose" and "Solo Flight"), sat in with Count Basie's Kansas City Six at the 1939 Spirituals to Swing concert (next to Lester Young and Buck Clayton), and made some freelance recordings. In 1941 Christian jammed regularly at Minton's Playhouse with Thelonious Monk and Dizzy Gillespie after his regular gig with Goodman. But in June (a couple of months before Blanton), he was stricken with tuberculosis. After a long period in a sanitarium, Christian passed away at the age of 25. Although other guitarists would emerge who displayed a bit of their own personality in their playing (Bill DeArango, Barney Kessel, Tal Farlow, Wes Montgomery, Grant Green, and George Benson, among others), it would not be until the rise of fusion in the late 1960s, 25 years after his death, that the evolution of the jazz guitar finally moved beyond Charlie Christian.

10 *The Genius of the Electric Guitar / Oct. 2, 1939–
    Mar. 13, 1941 / Columbia 40846*
10 *Benny Goodman Sextet, Featuring Charlie
    Christian / Oct. 2, 1939–Mar. 13, 1941 / Columbia
    45144*
9 *Solo Flight / Aug. 19, 1939–June 1941 / Vintage Jazz
    Classics 1021*

Although Charlie Christian's studio and radio appearances

have been reissued in a few overlapping European CD programs, the two most easily available sets came out on Columbia. *The Genius of the Electric Guitar* is highlighted by classic Benny Goodman Sextet versions of "Seven Come Eleven," "Wholly Cats," "Royal Garden Blues," "Breakfast Feud," and "Air Mail Special." In addition, Christian's showcase with Goodman's orchestra ("Solo Flight") and a couple of very interesting excerpts from a practice session when Goodman was late ("Blues in B" and "Waitin' for Benny") are included. Drawn from the same sessions, *Featuring Charlie Christian* (which was released under Goodman's name and is of equally high quality) includes the original versions of "Flying Home," "Stardust," "Gilly," "On the Alamo" and "A Smo-o-o-oth One." *Solo Flight* has some of the best radio performances of Goodman's sextet, plus a few real rarities, including five numbers from an all-star group consisting of Goodman, Buck Clayton, Lester Young, Count Basie, Christian, and the Basie rhythm section.

FILMS

No actual film exists of Charlie Christian. However, a half-hour documentary, *Solo Flight* (View Video 1353), does an excellent job of reconstructing the guitarist's story through interviews with his friends and associates.

NAT KING COLE

b. Mar. 17, 1917, Montgomery, AL, d. Feb. 15, 1965, Santa Monica, CA

By the early 1950s, Nat King Cole was much better known as a crooning middle-of-the-road pop vocalist than as a swing pianist, but it is as the latter that he made his biggest mark on jazz. Influenced by Earl Hines, Cole developed his own distinctive way of playing. And in the King Cole Trio (with guitarist Oscar Moore and bassist Wesley Prince), he performed music that looked towards Bop without really crossing the line. The piano-guitar-bass trio was so successful that Art Tatum (and, in the 1950s, Oscar Peterson and Ahmad Jamal) would form groups with the same instrumentation.

Born Nathaniel Coles, the pianist was raised in Chicago, led the Royal Dukes in 1934, and in 1936 made his first records with his brother Eddie Coles's group. Nat left Chicago to tour with a revival of "Shuffle Along," a show that broke up in Los Angeles. Cole lived for several years in Los Angeles, formed his trio, picked up the nickname of Nat "King"

Cole, played locally, and (at the urging of a club owner) began to sing now and then. In the late 1930s, Cole and his trio were recording radio transcriptions, and in December 1940 they made their first commercial record; "Sweet Lorraine" was a minor hit. It was not long before the Nat King Cole Trio became one of the most popular groups in jazz, appearing frequently on radio and, starting in 1943, recording scores of hot numbers for the Capitol label. Throughout the decade, the King Cole Trio worked steadily, even as the leader's vocal style gradually caught on, having best-selling records in "Straighten Up and Fly Right," "Nature Boy," "The Christmas Song," and "Lush Life." The King Cole Trio (which by then had guitarist Irving Ashby and bassist Johnny Miller) was at its most Boppish in 1949, when it added Jack Costanzo on bongos. However, the 1950 recording of "Mona Lisa" (featuring Nat's voice backed by a string orchestra) was a #1 hit and resulted in his becoming famous as a singer who once in a while showed audiences that he could play piano, too. The trio became merely his rhythm section, and, although Cole would have occasional jazz projects (most notably the After Midnight sessions of 1956) and he featured some jazz on his groundbreaking television series of 1956–57, these were merely departures from his pop singing career. Nat King Cole remained quite busy until lung cancer ended his life.

9 *The Complete Early Transcriptions / Oct. 1938–Feb. 1941 / Vintage Jazz Classics 1026/27/28*
8 *Birth of the Cole: 1938–1939 / Jan. 14, 1939–July 22, 1940 / Savoy ZDS 1205*
8 *The Trio Recordings / 1940–1956 / Laserlight 15 915*
9 *The MacGregor Years 1941–45 / Feb. 25, 1941–Jan. 1945 / Music & Arts 911*
8 *WWII Transcriptions / 1941–1944 / Music & Arts 808*

There are many collections available featuring the still-popular Nat King Cole Trio. All five of these sets feature radio transcriptions of the trio, mostly from its earliest years. Prior to 1941, Cole's solo vocals were rare, with most of the performances being either instrumentals, group vocals, or a guest singer with backup by the trio. The four-CD *Complete Early Transcriptions* (Standard Transcriptions) has 102 selections by the Cole trio, with some vocals by Bonnie Lake, Juanelda Carter, Pauline Byrns, and a unit from Six Hits and a Miss. *Birth of the Cole,* a single CD, includes Cole's other early transcription work (a dozen additional numbers) plus eight nearly unknown studio recordings for the Davis & Schwegler and Ammor labels, including "I Like to Riff," "On the Sunny Side of the Street," and "There's No Anesthetic for Love." The five-CD set *The Trio Recordings* (the music could have fit on three CDs) and *The MacGregor Years* (four CDs) partly overlap, both covering Cole's transcriptions for MacGregor. The Music & Arts box is a bit more complete, although the Laserlight release is less expensive. The Laserlight set has four discs that are mostly from 1944–45 and a fifth CD that jumps around from six numbers in 1940 to a few songs performed on the Dorsey Brothers TV show in 1956. *The MacGregor Years* has the King Cole Trio (with Oscar Moore and either Johnny Miller or Wesley Prince on bass) in 1941 and 1944–45, including 58 of the 120 numbers in a backup role with singers Anita Boyer, Ida James, Anita O'Day, and the Barrie Sisters. *WWII Transcriptions,* which does not duplicate the larger Music & Arts set but partly overlaps with some of the Laserlight music, is mostly from 1944, except for a few Anita Boyer vocals from 1941. There are also vocals from Anita O'Day and Ida James, but the emphasis is on the trio during the 30 swinging selections.

- **8**   *Hit That Jive Jack: The Earliest Recordings / Dec. 6, 1940–Oct. 22, 1941 / MCA/Decca 42350*
- *****   *The Complete Capitol Recordings of the Nat King Cole Trio / Oct. 11, 1942–Mar. 2, 1961 / Mosaic 138*
- **9**   *Jumpin' at Capitol / Nov. 30, 1943–Jan. 5, 1950 / Rhino 71009*
- **10**   *Jazz Encounters / Mar. 30, 1945–Jan. 5, 1950 / Capitol 96693*
- **7**   *Straighten Up and Fly Right / Dec. 1942–Jan. 28, 1948 / Vintage Jazz Classics 1044*
- **7**   *The King Cole Trios: Live 1947–48 / Mar. 1, 1947–Mar. 13, 1948 / Vintage Jazz Classics 1011*
- **8**   *Complete After Midnight Sessions / Aug. 15, 1956–Sept. 2, 1956 / Capitol 48328*

Hit That Jive Jack has the King Cole Trio's 16 recordings for the Decca label, including "Sweet Lorraine," "Honeysuckle Rose," and "Hit That Jive Jack." The huge 18-CD Mosaic box set contains every single recording made by the Nat King Cole Trio for Capitol during their very busy 1943–49 period, all of the radio transcriptions that are owned by Capitol, plus Cole's later recordings that feature his piano and at least the feel of the trio (including the complete After Midnight sessions). This limited-edition box (which has

349 performances!) is quite remarkable but will be difficult to find. *Jumpin' at Capitol* is a fine single-disc sampler drawn from the same sessions and features many of the King Cole Trio's most famous selections, including "Straighten Up and Fly Right," a remake of "Sweet Lorraine," "For Sentimental Reasons," "Come to Baby, Do," and "Route 66." *Jazz Encounters* has Nat King Cole as a featured soloist in a variety of jazz settings, including with the Metronome All-Stars, Stan Kenton's orchestra, the Capitol International Jazzmen, Jo Stafford, Nellie Lutcher, Woody Herman, and Johnny Mercer. The two Vintage Jazz Classic CDs are taken from the King Cole Trio's radio appearances. *Straighten Up and Fly Right* has guest appearances by the trio, while *Live 1947–48* is taken from the King Cole Trio's own radio shows of 1947–48. Six years after "Mona Lisa," Nat King Cole and his regular rhythm section (guitarist John Collins, bassist Charlie Harris, and drummer Lee Young) were joined by either Harry "Sweets" Edison, altoist Willie Smith, valve trombonist Juan Tizol, or violinist Stuff Smith for an excellent jazz project that is mostly swing-oriented, showing that Cole was still a top-notch pianist that late in his career.

LPS TO SEARCH FOR

Nat King Cole Meets the Master Saxes (Spotlite 136) features the pianist leading a 1942 quintet that includes Illinois Jacquet and trumpeter Shad Collins, interacting with Harry Edison and Dexter Gordon (in his debut recording) in 1943, and playing four numbers with Lester Young and bassist Red Callender. Cole hints at Bop in places while remaining true to his swing roots.

FILMS

The King Cole Trio pops up in many films, including *Here Comes Elmer* (1943), *Swing in the Saddle* (1944), *Stars on Parade* (1944), *See My Lawyer* (1945), *Breakfast in Hollywood* (1946), *Killer Diller* (1948), and *Make Believe Ballroom* (1949). *The Snader Telescriptions* (Storyville 6010) is a video that contains 17 performances by the Nat King Cole Quartet (with Jack Costanzo on conga) during 1950–51, shortly before the group became merely Cole's backup rhythm section. Some of the 17 selections (made originally as fill-ins for live television) have an unseen string section added and there is an emphasis on ballads on the later tracks; highlights include "Route 66," "Little Girl," "The Trouble with Me Is You," and "Mona Lisa." Two other videos, *The Incomparable Nat King Cole Vols. 1–2* (Warner Reprise Video 38266 and

38292), feature selections from Cole's 1956–57 television series, including a few numbers with the Jazz at the Philharmonic All-Stars and a memorable version of "Perdido" by Ella Fitzgerald.

HARRY "SWEETS" EDISON

b. Oct. 10, 1915, Columbus, OH, d. July 27, 1999, Columbus, OH

Harry "Sweets" Edison could be considered the Count Basie of the trumpet, because he was able to create a complete message with a minimum of notes. Sweets (who was given his lifelong nickname by Lester Young) was not really an influence on the Bebop musicians, but he had his own style and was touched by Dizzy Gillespie's, borrowing some of Dizzy's phrases despite their very different approaches. With Count Basie's orchestra during the Bebop era, Edison was able to adjust his playing a bit to fit in with the more modern arrangements while still improvising in his own classic swing style.

Harry Edison started on trumpet when he was 12, and he worked in the 1930s with many different territory groups, including Alphonso Trent, Eddie Johnson's Crackerjacks, and the Jeter-Pillars Band. After playing and recording with the Mills Blue Rhythm Band in 1937, he joined Basie for an 11½ year run (June 1938 until February 1950) that included the first few months of Count's small group after the Basie Orchestra was forced to break up in late 1949. Edison shared the trumpet solo space in the early years with Buck Clayton and was always one of Count's stars. After the Basie years ended, Edison played with Jimmy Rushing, Jazz at the Philharmonic, Buddy Rich, and his own groups, and in the studios. His background solos on many Frank Sinatra records were notable, and through the decades Edison worked constantly. He was a fixture in mainstream swing settings, was part of quite a few Basie alumni groups, and often teamed up with the equally distinctive tenor saxophonist Eddie "Lockjaw" Davis. Edison was active until a couple of months before his death, always saying the most with the least.

9 *Jawbreakers / Apr. 18, 1962 / Original Jazz Classics 487*
9 *Edison's Lights / May 5, 1976 / Original Jazz Classics 804*
10 *Harry "Sweets" Edison and Eddie "Lockjaw" Davis, Vol. 1 / July 6, 1976 / Storyville 4004*
10 *Harry "Sweets" Edison and Eddie "Lockjaw" Davis, Vol. 2 / July 6, 1976 / Storyville 4025*
6 *Simply Sweets / Sept. 22, 1977 / Original Jazz Classics 903*

Each of these five CDs matches Harry Edison with Eddie "Lockjaw" Davis. The music falls between swing and Bop and is full of friendly competitiveness between the co-leaders. *Jawbreakers*, which also includes pianist Hugh Lawson, bassist Ike Isaacs, and drummer Clarence Johnston, was the first meeting on records between Sweets and Lockjaw; "Broadway," "Four," and "A Gal in Calico" are highlights. *Edison's Lights* has Count Basie as the pianist on half of the tracks, with Dolo Coker on the other selections plus bassist John Heard and drummer Jimmy Smith. The program alternates between basic Edison originals and four standards. The two Storyville sets are particularly exciting. Trombonist John Darville is on two of the six cuts on each disc, and the repertoire includes "Lester Leaps In," Coleman Hawkins's "Spotlite," and "Blues Walk" on the first CD, with Vol. 2 featuring "Robbin's Nest," "Candy," and "There Is No Greater Love." Unfortunately, *Simply Sweets* (which has Coker, bassist Harvey Newmark, and drummer Smith in the quintet) has a disappointing program (including five similar blues and "Feelings"), so the results are merely OK despite some fiery moments.

FILMS

Harry Edison is well featured in the Lester Young short *Jammin' the Blues* (1944).

ROY ELDRIDGE

b. Jan. 30, 1911, Pittsburgh, PA, d. Feb. 26, 1989, Valley Stream, NY

Roy Eldridge was the most influential of all the swing trumpeters on the Bop brassmen, touching particularly the styles of Dizzy Gillespie, Howard McGhee, and Fats Navarro. His exciting solos were harmonically adventurous (hinting at Bop by 1939), and his combative style and wild chance-taking approach were perfect for jam sessions of the era. But, although he has been typecast a bit as the transition between Louis Armstrong and Dizzy Gillespie, Eldridge was a major stylist in his own right.

Known as "Little Jazz" (a nickname given him by Duke Ellington altoist Otto Hardwicke), David "Roy" Eldridge started on drums and occasionally fooled around on the piano but was a trumpeter ever since his youth. A professional starting in 1927, Eldridge led his own band (Roy Elliott and his Palais Royal Orchestra) and worked with Horace Henderson's Dixie Stompers, Zach Whyte, Speed Webb (1929–30), Cecil Scott, Elmer Snowden, Charlie Johnson, Teddy Hill, and McKinney's Cotton Pickers. Eldridge's style came partly from Coleman Hawkins (he used to play Hawk's 1925 solo on "Stampede" note for note) and Jabbo Smith, with touches of Louis Armstrong, particularly in the way Eldridge built up his solos. In 1935 Eldridge had a second stint with Teddy Hill, and it was his recordings with Hill during this era that originally inspired Dizzy Gillespie, who would play with Hill two years later. During the next few years Eldridge also recorded with Gene Krupa (an all-star group with Benny Goodman and Chu Berry), Teddy Wilson, and Billie Holiday and as a member of Fletcher Henderson's orchestra in 1936. He led his own band later in the decade, recording several startling sessions as a leader. Eldridge was well featured with Gene Krupa's orchestra during 1941–43 (on such numbers as "After You've Gone," "Rockin' Chair," and "Let Me Off Uptown," the last with Anita O'Day) and with Artie Shaw's big band during 1944–45.

Roy Eldridge led groups of his own during the Bop era (including a short-lived orchestra in 1946), toured with Jazz at the Philharmonic, and had a second stint with Gene Krupa in 1949. But despite being an inspiration to the Beboppers, Eldridge soon suffered from a slight identity crisis. Always proud of how modern and advanced a player he was, the competitive trumpeter found himself occasionally being defeated at trumpet battles in jam sessions (including by Gillespie). Dizzy Gillespie and Fats Navarro were playing solos that were ahead of Eldridge's, and Little Jazz was not sure if he should change his whole style (which he had spent years developing) to keep up with the modernists.

The trumpeter traveled to Europe with Benny Goodman in 1950 and decided to stay after the tour. After thinking it over and being greeted by enthusiastic crowds, Eldridge realized that it was more important to be himself than to try to keep up with the latest musical trends. Some fans might consider him old-fashioned, but others would think of him as classic. And that way he would have to satisfy only his own standards.

Roy Eldridge would never lack self-confidence again. In the 1950s he recorded regularly for Norman Granz's labels (most notably Verve), battled Dizzy Gillespie successfully on Jazz at the Philharmonic tours, often co-led a quintet with Coleman Hawkins, and was in prime form. Although the 1960s were relatively lean (with few recordings), Eldridge kept on working. In the 1970s he was featured nightly at Jimmy Ryan's club in New York and recorded for Granz again, this time on the Pablo label.

Bad health in 1980 forced his retirement and, other than rare appearances as a vocalist, Roy Eldridge spent his last nine years outside of music. But as an original improviser and one of the father figures of Bebop, Roy Eldridge made his mark on jazz.

10 *Little Jazz / Feb. 26, 1935-Apr. 2, 1940 / Columbia 45275*

9 *After You've Gone / Feb. 5, 1936–Sept. 24, 1946 / GRP/Decca 605*

8 *Roy Eldridge in Paris / June 9, 1950–June 14, 1950 / Vogue 68209*

Little Jazz has some of the recordings that originally inspired the up-and-coming Beboppers. The CD features Eldridge on a song apiece with Teddy Hill and Putney Dandridge, four selections (including the hit "Christopher Columbus") with Fletcher Henderson, and numbers with Teddy Wilson, Billie Holiday ("Falling in Love Again"), and Mildred Bailey ("I'm Nobody's Baby," which finds Eldridge sounding remarkably advanced). Most significant are the six songs (plus one alternate take) that resulted from his first two dates as a leader, including classic renditions of "Wabash Stomp," "Heckler's Hop," and "After You've Gone." Of the 30 performances (counting alternate takes) that the trumpeter recorded with his big band for Decca during 1944–46, 22 are on *After You've Gone* in addition to a rare version of "Christopher Columbus" from 1936. Even though the missing selections are unfortunate, Eldridge's exciting trumpet solos (particularly on "The Gasser," "I Can't Get Started," "Twilight Time," "Rockin' Chair," and two versions of "After You've Gone") make the Decca CD well worth picking up, showing what the major swing stylist was playing at the beginning of the Bebop era. *Roy Eldridge in Paris* is split between a quintet set with tenor saxophonist Zoot Sims and a quartet outing with pianist Gerald Wiggins. Eldridge rediscovered himself during this period, with his wonderful version of "Wrap Your Troubles in Dreams" serving as evidence.

8 *Just You, Just Me / 1959 / Stash 531*

4 *Jazz Maturity . . Where It's Coming From / June 3, 1975 / Original Jazz Classics 807*

Roy Eldridge and Coleman Hawkins always made a mutually inspired team, as they show on *Just You, Just Me;* highlights include "Blue Lou," "Just You, Just Me," "Rifftide," and "Honeysuckle Rose." Eldridge and Dizzy Gillespie teamed up for a few exciting sessions in the 1950s, but 1975's *Jazz Maturity* is a misfire. The two trumpeters sound very much like they were having an off day, and the material (blues and warhorses) does not cut it; Oscar Peterson is easily the main star. Eldridge plays with much more fire on *What It's All About,* and he is assisted by altoist Norris Turney, Budd Johnson, and (on half of the tunes) Milt Jackson for a fairly freewheeling outing. One of Roy Eldridge's greatest recordings was his next-to-last session (preceding a final studio album for Storyville), his appearance at the 1977 Montreux Jazz Festival. Eldridge was extremely inspired. With hard swinging contributed by Oscar Peterson, Niels Pedersen, and drummer Bobby Durham, Little Jazz is frequently explosive. He may have been 66, but he plays such numbers as "Between the Devil and the Deep Blue Sea," "Perdido," and "Bye Bye Blackbird" as if he were ready to take on all competitors, and he probably would have won any trumpet battle that day. A great recording!

LPS TO SEARCH FOR

Some of Roy Eldridge's radio appearances from the early days can be heard on *At the Three Deuces, Chicago* (Jazz Archives 24), which has his 1937 octet, and *At the Arcadia Ballroom* (Jazz Archives 14), featuring his 1939 tentet. The recording quality may be streaky, but Eldridge's exciting playing definitely communicates. *I Remember Harlem* (Inner City 7012) is from the trumpeter's stay in Paris (1950–51), and it contains more than its share of gems. Eldridge jams with a French septet, joins forces with Don Byas, has three rare piano solos, and (best of all) plays "Wild Man Blues" and "Fireworks" in duets with pianist Claude Bolling that recall Louis Armstrong and Earl Hines.

FILMS

Roy Eldridge has a few hot solos in *The Sound of Jazz* (1957) and is matched with Coleman Hawkins in 1961's *After Hours* (Rhapsody Films).

ELLA FITZGERALD

b. Apr. 25, 1917, Newport News, VA, d. June 15, 1996, Beverly Hills, CA

Ella Fitzgerald, like Harry "Sweets" Edison, was not so much an influence on Bop musicians as she was influenced by their music. Already a major name by 1944, Ella's ears were really opened up a couple years later during a tour with the Dizzy Gillespie big band, and it was during that period that she really started understanding Bebop. Although her ballad interpretations would remain rooted in the Swing era, her scatting was strongly influenced by that of Bop-era instrumentalists, and she could trade fours with anyone. Ella helped to bring the innovations of Bebop into the mainstream of popular singing.

Known as "The First Lady of Song," Ella Fitzgerald escaped from her depressing early years and a rather mundane private life into the joy of music. She was part of a very poor family, was homeless for much of a year, and hoped to become a dancer. However, Ella was a better singer than dancer and, after winning an amateur contest at the Apollo Theater, she was with Tiny Bradshaw's orchestra for a brief time. Fletcher Henderson was not impressed (the impoverished singer's appearance was a bit shabby at the time), but Chick Webb was persuaded by several people (including Benny Carter) to give the teenager a chance. Ella was an instant hit with audiences, and she became a permanent member of the Chick Webb Orchestra, as well as its biggest attraction. She first recorded in 1935, had a giant hit three years later in "A-Tisket, A-Tasket," and was such a big name that, when Webb died in 1939, she was picked to front his orchestra.

During the early days, Ella sounded much more comfortable on ballads than on medium-tempo tunes (which is the opposite for most young singers); it did not help that she was given many juvenile novelties to sing. After heading the Chick Webb Orchestra for two years, she went out on her own in 1941. Ella had several hits for Decca during the war years, and she continually grew as a singer. She became an expert improviser, performing Boppish solos that ranked with the finest instrumental solos of the time. A few of her classics from the Bop era include "Flying Home," "Lady Be Good," "How High the Moon," and "Robbins' Nest"; she even recorded a song called "My Baby Likes to Re-Bop."

In 1946, Ella Fitzgerald began touring with Jazz at the Philharmonic (which, in addition to her usual set, matched her with top Bop and swing all-stars in jam session settings) and Norman Granz became her manager. She was married to Ray Brown during 1948–52, recorded intimate duets with pianist Ellis Larkins in 1950 and 1954, was impressive in the movie *Pete Kelly's Blues* in 1955, and the following year left Decca to sign with Norman Granz's Verve company, a label that he formed specifically to record her.

The Ella Fitzgerald story would not make a very interesting documentary, for her professional life was continually successful while her private life was uneventful. After recording a series of composer songbooks (extensive sets of the songs of Cole Porter, George and Ira Gershwin, Rodgers and Hart, Duke Ellington, Harold Arlen, Jerome Kern, and lyricist Johnny Mercer), she was considered an American institution and worked steadily until the end of her career. Ella's recordings of the 1960s, after Granz sold Verve, tended to be streaky (occasionally finding her trying to add current pop songs to her repertoire), but her albums greatly improved after Granz formed the Pablo label in 1972. Ella Fitzgerald's health and voice gradually declined during the 1980s, and she retired in 1994. No other singer was ever able to out-swing her; during her prime, her voice could compete favorably with anyone's, including Sarah Vaughan's. There are scores of rewarding Ella Fitzgerald recordings available, covering all periods of her career.

10 *75th Birthday Celebration / May 2, 1938–Aug. 5, 1955 / GRP/Decca 2-619*

8 *The War Years / Oct. 6, 1941–Dec. 20, 1947 / GRP/ Decca 628*

9 *Pure Ella / Sept. 11, 1950–Mar. 30, 1954 / Decca 636*

10 *First Lady of Song / Sept. 18, 1949–July 29, 1966 / Verve 314 517 889*

* *The Complete Ella Fitzgerald Song Books / Feb. 7, 1956–Oct. 21, 1964 / Verve 314 519 832–848*

7 *Ella at the Opera House / Sept. 29, 1957–Oct. 7, 1957 / Verve 831 269*

10 *The Complete Ella in Berlin / Feb. 13, 1960 / Verve 314 519 584*

8 *Clap Hands, Here Comes Charlie! / June 22–23, 1961 / Verve 835 646*

Ella Fitzgerald's earliest recordings (including her dates with Chick Webb) have been reissued in full by the European Classics label, which is covered (along with many other recordings) in the swing book. The attractive two-CD set *75th Birthday Celebration* does a fine job of summing up El-

la's Decca years, covering most of her hits and her Bebop explorations, including "A-Tisket, A-Tasket," "Undecided," "Cow Cow Boogie," "Flying Home," "Lady Be Good," "How High the Moon," "Smooth Sailing," "Air Mail Special," "and "Hard Hearted Hannah." *The War Years* (also a two-CD set) traces Ella's career from just before the Bebop era right up to 1947. There are meetings with the Delta Rhythm Boys, Louis Jordan ("Stone Cold Dead in the Market"), Louis Armstrong ("You Won't Be Satisfied" and "The Frim Fram Sauce"), and pianist Eddie Heywood plus an alternate version of "Flying Home," her classic "Lady Be Good" and two new takes of "How High the Moon." In 1950 the singer performed duets with pianist Ellis Larkins, eight George Gershwin songs that predated her extensive series of songbooks. *Pure Ella* has those eight plus a dozen more duets with Larkins from 1954; the emphasis is on slower tempos, and the music is often exquisite, showing that when she was inspired, Fitzgerald could dig into the heart of lyrics and display emotions other than pure joy.

The three-CD *First Lady of Song* is a superior sampler of Ella Fitzgerald's years on the Verve label, a period when her voice was consistently at the peak of its powers. In addition to her Jazz at the Philharmonic appearance in 1949, *First Lady of Song* has most of the high points of Ella's career during the 1956–66 period, ballads and scatfests alike. *The Complete Ella Fitzgerald Song Books* is a 16-CD set packaged in an attractive red cube. The music (seven different songbooks in all) is also available individually. Ella mostly sticks to the lyrics (there is almost no scatting), and the orchestra arrangements are sometimes a bit straight, but these renditions do justice to the composers' original hopes; Cole Porter and Ira Gershwin were reportedly among those who thought highly of Ella's versions. The most jazz-oriented dates are the two that form the Duke Ellington Song Book. One of those outings has the full Ellington Orchestra, while the other is a combo date with violinist Stuff Smith and Ben Webster.

Ella at the Opera House features Ella swinging with the Oscar Peterson Trio during a Jazz at the Philharmonic tour. This single CD has the same nine songs repeated during two consecutive nights, with the exception of one substitution, allowing listeners to hear how the singer varied her interpretations, although the repetition may not be for everyone! Absolutely essential is *The Complete Ella in Berlin*. This version of "Mack the Knife" is quite famous, for Ella totally forgot the words and made up hilarious lyrics as she went along. Other highlights of this definitive outing include "Gone With the Wind," "The Lady Is a Tramp," and "Too Darn Hot." *Clap Hands, Here Comes Charlie!* is a superior studio date with the Lou Levy Quartet that is more jazz-oriented than many of Ella's orchestra sessions of the period. Among the songs that she swings are "Jersey Bounce," "Night in Tunisia," and "'Round Midnight."

Ella Fitzgerald's last period found her gradually declining but still providing some musical magic, particularly during the first half of the 1970s. The four-CD *The Concert Years* features Ella live in 1953, with Duke Ellington in 1966 and 1967, and in concerts with her regular combo in 1971, 1972, 1974, 1975, 1977, 1979, and 1983. Although available elsewhere in other sets, the music does include most of the high points of Ella's live dates owned by Pablo, including a remarkable version of "C Jam Blues" from 1972 that has the singer trading off in humorous fashion with Al Grey, Lockjaw Davis, Harry Edison, tenor saxophonist Stan Getz, and Roy Eldridge. *Ella á Nice,* which has a few surprising medleys, is a fine live set with the Tommy Flanagan Trio, Ella's backup band of the time. *Fine and Mellow* teams Ella with four major horn players (trumpeters Clark Terry and Harry Edison and tenors Zoot Sims and Eddie "Lockjaw" Davis) and finds everyone quite inspired by each other's presence. On *Ella & Oscar* the singer works well with Oscar Peterson both in duets and in trios that include bassist Ray Brown. She sounds pretty strong on *At the Montreux Jazz Festival,* another outing with the Tommy Flanagan Trio, which is highlighted by "Caravan," "Let's Do It," and "How High the Moon." Although Ella Fitzgerald's voice would soon fade and her range would shrink, she never lost her ability to swing, and she stayed joyful in her singing up until the end.

LPS TO SEARCH FOR

Ella in Hollywood (Verve 4052), from 1961, is one of Ella Fitzgerald's greatest jazz recordings, but it is practically unknown. Ella takes her longest scat vocal on record, a remarkable 9½-minute version of "Take the 'A' Train" that is filled with Bebop riffs and creative ideas. The full set finds her really stretching herself. This is a classic that is long overdue to be put out on CD.

FILMS

Ella Fitzgerald sings "A-Tisket, A-Tasket" in the Abbott & Costello movie *Ride 'Em Cowboy* (1941) and is in *Pete Kelly's Blues* (singing "Hard Hearted Hannah" in 1955), *St. Louis Blues* (1958), and *Let No Man Write My Epitaph* (1960), having a real acting role in the last. She also sings a wondrous version of "Perdido" as her feature on *The Incomparable Nat King Cole* (Warner Reprise Video 38266) from 1956.

SLIM GAILLARD

b. Jan. 1, 1916, Detroit, MI, d. Feb. 26, 1991, London, England

Although not a Bop musician, Bulee "Slim" Gaillard was a prominent figure in the mid-1940s and sometimes shared the bill with Bop players. Gaillard was much better known for his comedy routines and humorous jive talk than for his guitar playing, even though he was a good musician who was influenced by Charlie Christian and could also play decent, if basic, piano and vibes. Gaillard was an eccentric who started out in vaudeville in the 1930s, featuring an act in which he played guitar and tap-danced simultaneously! He hit it big in 1937, when he began teaming up with bassist Slam Stewart as Slim and Slam. Their recording of "Flat Foot Floogie" was a huge hit, and such songs as "Tutti Frutti," "Laughin' in Rhythm," "Chicken Rhythm," and "Matzoh Balls," among others, also included crazy vocals that hinted at the future scatting and wordplay of Dizzy Gillespie and Joe "Bebop" Carroll.

Slim and Slam broke up in 1942 when Gaillard began serving in the military. After he was discharged, Gaillard formed a musical partnership with bassist Bam Brown, and the singing and jive talk got even nuttier. For a couple of years, Gaillard was based in Los Angeles, often playing at Billy Berg's, where his absurd ad-lib routines (and extended renditions of "Cement Picker" and "Flat Foot Floogie") bordered on the hilarious. At the height of his fame, in 1945, Gaillard used Charlie Parker and Dizzy Gillespie on one of his record dates, which included the classic "Slim's Jam." However, his popularity began to fade later in the decade as jive singers went out of style and were either stereotyped as "dangerous" or completely ignored by the media. Also, Slim Gaillard failed to advance or develop beyond where he was in 1945, and he was not very flexible as a musician, usually sticking to blues or songs with "Flying Home" chord changes. Other than albums in 1958 and 1982, Gaillard was off records altogether after 1953 and just worked part-time in music, running a motel in San Diego for a period in the 1960s, and occasionally acting. However, Slim Gaillard was rediscovered and proclaimed a living legend later in his life, and he was always happy to perform an enthusiastic version of "Flat Foot Floogie."

- **10** *Complete Recordings 1938–1942 / Feb. 17, 1938–Apr. 4, 1942 / Affinity 1034-3*
- **6** *The Groove Juice Special / Jan. 19, 1938–Apr. 4, 1942 / Columbia/Legacy 64898*
- **9** *1945 / Sept. 1945–Dec. 1945 / Classics 864*
- **7** *In Birdland 1951 / Feb. 24, 1951–Sept. 29, 1951 / Hep 21*
- **8** *Laughing in Rhythm / Apr. 22, 1946–Dec. 1953 / Verve 314 521 651*
- **5** *Anytime, Anyplace, Anywhere! / Oct. 30, 1982 / Hep 2020*

Every recording by Slim and Slam is on the three-CD *Complete Recordings,* including 19 alternate takes, music that swings yet is often quite crazy. In addition to the co-leaders, such players as tenors Kenneth Hollon and Ben Webster, trumpeter Al Killian, pianist Jimmy Rowles, and drummer Chico Hamilton are among the guest sidemen. *The Groove Juice Special,* a single CD drawn from the same period, does not work that well as a sampler. Eight of the 20 selections are alternate takes (including "Flat Foot Floogie"), so this does not work as a "greatest hits" collection. In addition, the three numbers that were supposedly previously unissued are all included in *Complete Recordings.* The Classics CD *1945* picks up Gaillard's career after he got out of the military, and it's mostly a collection of rare studio sides. Slim is featured with a trio, a quartet, and a ten-piece group; among his sidemen are Bam Brown, Dodo Marmarosa, Howard McGhee, trombonist Vic Dickenson, and the three tenors of Lucky Thompson, Teddy Edwards, and Wild Bill Moore. Highlights include "Voot Orenee," "Tutti Frutti," "Laguna," "Dunkin' Bagel," "Ya Ha Ha," and "Buck Dance Rhythm." On *In Birdland 1951,* Gaillard has a reunion with Slam Stewart (for "Flat Foot Floogie" and "Cement Mixer") and is at the head of all-star groups that include tenors Eddie

"Lockjaw" Davis and Brew Moore, pianist Billy Taylor, and Terry Gibbs. *Laughing in Rhythm* has quite a few of the highlights of Gaillard's period with the Verve label, including an appearance at a Jazz at the Philharmonic concert in 1946 (the four-part "Opera in Vout") and tracks from 1951–53, including "The Bartender's Just Like a Mother," "Serenade to a Poodle," "Soony Roony," "Yo Yo Yo," "Potato Chips," and "Mishugana Mambo." The modestly titled "Genius" has Gaillard (via overdubbing) on vocals, trumpet, trombone, tenor, vibes, piano, organ, bass, drums, and tap dancing; it is quite hilarious! Gaillard's final album, *Anytime, Anyplace, Anywhere!,* has solos from tenors Buddy Tate and Jay Thomas plus pianist Jay McShann. The music is streaky, but there is a happily esoteric version of "How High the Moon" that serves as a perfect closer to Slim Gaillard's rather unusual career.

LPS TO SEARCH FOR

As wild as Slim Gaillard's studio recordings could be, he really stretched out when performing live. *McVouty Slim & Bam* (Hep 6), *Son of McVouty* (Hep 11), and *The Voutest* (Hep 28) date from 1945–47. Each contains its share of crazy moments and swing-oriented music.

FILMS

Slim Gaillard is in *Hellzapoppin'* (1941), *Almost Married* (1942), *Ovoutie O'Rooney* (1946), *Go, Man, Go* (1954), and *Too Late Blues* (1961). He also has an acting role in *Roots: The Next Generation* (1978).

TINY GRIMES

b. July 7, 1916, Newport News, VA, d. Mar. 4, 1989, New York, NY

After Charlie Christian's death in 1942, it seemed for a time as if Tiny Grimes would be his logical successor. He had a similar sound and style and, for a little while, was associating with the young modernists. But, as it turned out, Grimes chose to emphasize the blues and R&B over Bebop, and he was not the genius that Christian had been, although he was a talented player.

Lloyd "Tiny" Grimes started out as a drummer and occasional pianist, gigging in Washington, D.C., and New York. When he switched instruments in 1938, Grimes started playing the new electric guitar. After working with the Cats and a Fiddle (1939–41), he made a strong impression as the guitarist with the Art Tatum Trio (1943–44), a group that also included Slam Stewart. Somehow Grimes was able to keep up with Tatum, and his guitar offered a solo voice that was both complementary and a bit competitive.

After leaving Tatum, Grimes began leading his own groups. A record date in 1944 found him using Charlie Parker as a sideman, introducing the boppish "Red Cross," and singing "Romance Without Finance Is a Nuisance." However, Grimes did not continue in the Bebop movement. Dates during 1946–47 for Blue Note and Atlantic were more swing-oriented, and by 1948 he was leading his Rocking Highlanders, an R&B band that featured the extroverted tenor of Red Prysock. Among the other musicians who passed through his group were tenors Benny Golson and John Hardee, and pianists Freddie Redd and Sir Charles Thompson. After the Rocking Highlanders broke up in the mid-1950s, Tiny Grimes returned to the blues-oriented swing music that he loved best, staying active most of the time until his death in 1989.

7   *Blues Groove / Feb. 28, 1958 / Original Jazz Classics 817*

7   *Callin' the Blues / July 18, 1958 / Original Jazz Classics 191*

9   *Tiny in Swingville / Aug. 13, 1959 / Original Jazz Classics 1796*

Tiny Grimes's three albums for Prestige and Storyville (his first LPs as a leader) have all been reissued in the Original Jazz Classics series. Each of the swing-oriented sets is of interest. On *Blues Groove,* the great Coleman Hawkins really stretches out on "Marchin' Along," showing that late in life he had finally learned how to play the blues. Grimes and Hawkins are well showcased in a sextet with flutist Musa Kaleem, pianist Ray Bryant, bassist Earl Wormack, and drummer Teagle Fleming, Jr. *Callin' the Blues* teams Grimes and Eddie "Lockjaw" Davis with the past-his-prime-but-still-spirited trombonist J. C. Higginbotham plus Bryant, bassist Wendell Marshall, and drummer Osie Johnson. The group performs three blues and "Air Mail Special" with plenty of power. *Tiny in Swingville,* a quintet date with Jerome Richardson on flute, tenor, and baritone, Bryant, Marshall, and drummer Art Taylor, is a particularly strong example of the guitarist's playing. Grimes sounds in prime form on "Annie Laurie," "Frankie and Johnnie," "Ain't Misbehavin'," and three originals.

LPS TO SEARCH FOR

Tiny Grimes and His Rockin' Highlanders (Swingtime 1016) has some of the best recordings from Grimes's rhythm and blues period (1947–53). *Profoundly Blue* (Muse 5012), from 1974, is one of Grimes's finest late-period recordings (he would record for several European labels as late as 1977) and co-stars Houston Person on tenor.

COLEMAN HAWKINS
b. Nov. 21, 1904, St. Joseph, MI, d. May 19, 1969, New York, NY

Of all the swing greats portrayed in this section, Coleman Hawkins made the greatest contribution to Bebop. The first major tenor saxophonist and a top soloist and influence since 1925, Hawkins was always advanced harmonically, knowing his chords backwards and forwards. When Bebop began to form, he cheered it on, especially since he was more advanced than his contemporaries. Hawkins not only approved of the music, he hired many of the top young players to perform in his bands and for recordings. His support meant a great deal to the struggling music in its early days. And his distinguished nature and refusal to play the clown on stage, letting the music speak for itself, earned him respect from the Boppers, who sought to separate jazz from mere entertainment.

Coleman Hawkins played piano and cello early on but had switched to tenor by the time he was 9. A professional at 16, Hawkins worked a bit in Kansas City, was a member of Mamie Smith's Jazz Hounds during 1921–23 (with whom he made his earliest recordings), and joined Fletcher Henderson's orchestra in 1924, having cut some records for the bandleader the year before. At the time there were virtually no significant tenor saxophonists, not only in jazz but in any style of music! Hawkins's playing was actually a bit primitive during the era, using some slap-tonguing and staccato runs. But after Louis Armstrong joined Henderson and taught New Yorkers how to swing, Hawkins developed very quickly. His 1926 solo on "The Stampede" assured not only his place in jazz history but the place of the tenor in jazz. Another important early solo was "One Hour" with the Mound City Blue Blowers in 1929, one of the first mature ballad statements. By 1930, virtually every tenor saxophonist in jazz (other than Bud Freeman) sounded quite a bit like Hawk.

Hawkins remained with Henderson for ten years, leaving in 1934 when it was clear that the Fletcher Henderson band was struggling despite its all-star lineup. He spent the next five years in Europe, where he was treated as a major artist and was a popular attraction all over the Continent. When World War II looked like a strong possibility in 1939, he returned to the United States. Although Lester Young had emerged with an alternative way of playing tenor (with a softer tone and a simpler, floating style), Hawkins soon reasserted his supremacy in jam sessions. His 1939 recording of "Body and Soul," which became a hit despite his barely hinting at the melody, showed how advanced an improviser Hawkins was. It clearly looked toward Bebop, with its emphasis on using the chord structure rather than the melody as a basis for building up a solo. Hawkins had a short-lived big band in 1940 and then during 1941–46 was at the peak of his powers, although his musical prime actually lasted 40 years. He worked steadily on 52nd Street, recorded regularly, and used both swing veterans and Bop modernists in his groups.

Virtually every top Bop player worked with Hawkins at one time or another (except for Charlie Parker, who failed to show up for a possible record date). In late 1943 Max Roach made his recording debut with the tenor, and Oscar Pettiford was on several sessions, including a famous version of "The Man I Love" in a quartet with pianist Eddie Heywood and drummer Shelly Manne. On February 16 and 22, 1944, Hawkins led what is considered the first Bebop recording sessions. With Budd Johnson playing baritone and helping to organize the proceedings, the line-up included Dizzy Gillespie, Leo Parker, Don Byas, Clyde Hart, Pettiford, and Roach, introducing Gillespie's "Woody 'n You" and Hawkins's "Disorder at the Border." In addition to many swing dates during the year, Hawkins featured his regular quartet on four numbers on October 19, 1944, which served as the recording debut of Thelonious Monk. The year 1945 found Hawkins going to Los Angeles with a sextet that featured Howard McGhee, Pettiford, and Denzil Best, recording "Stuffy" and "Rifftide." Back in New York during 1946–47, Hawkins led dates that featured fellow tenor Allen Eager, Fats Navarro, J. J. Johnson, Hank Jones, Milt Jackson, Miles Davis, Kai Winding, and Max Roach, among others. He also toured with Jazz at the Philharmonic and in 1948 recorded the first unaccompanied tenor sax solo, "Picasso."

Although Coleman Hawkins's harmonic explorations were as advanced as anyone's, his hard sound and simpler rhythmic nature resulted in him being considered out of style by the early 1950s. Recordings and lucrative gigs became less common for a few years, but he survived and in 1957 had one of his most fulfilling years. Hawkins recorded a Bop-oriented set with J. J. Johnson and Idrees Sulieman, teamed up with Roy Eldridge in spectacular fashion at the Newport Jazz Festival, recorded an album with the Oscar Peterson Quartet, met up with Ben Webster on records, and recorded as a sideman with Thelonious Monk (in a band that included John Coltrane) and trumpeter Henry "Red" Allen; in addition he starred on the *Sound of Jazz* television special. A major influence on Sonny Rollins, Hawkins would be quite busy through 1965, playing regularly with either a quartet or a quintet co-led by Roy Eldridge. In addition to his own records, he was a sideman with Max Roach (playing alongside altoist Eric Dolphy and trumpeter Booker Little) and Abbey Lincoln, was on a Duke Ellington small-group date in 1962, and had a recorded meeting with Sonny Rollins, who tried unsuccessfully to confuse his idol with particularly eccentric free playing. Even in 1965, Coleman Hawkins still sounded fairly modern.

Unfortunately that would be his last good year. For reasons never fully explained, Hawkins quickly declined during his final four years, both physically and mentally, losing interest in food and his appearance, drinking excessively, and getting quite weak. He passed away in 1969 at the age of 64.

In addition to his many other accomplishments, the Bebop world owes Coleman Hawkins a great deal for lending his prestige to the music when it was new and struggling for recognition.

8 *A Retrospective: 1929–1963 / Nov. 7, 1929–July 15, 1963 / Bluebird 66617*

10 *In Europe 1934/39 / Nov. 18, 1934–May 26, 1939 / Jazz Up 317/18/19*

The two-CD *A Retrospective* covers Coleman Hawkins's career during 34 years, through his recordings for Victor-associated labels. Hawkins is featured on various selections with the Mound City Blue Blowers, McKinney's Cotton Pickers, Fletcher Henderson, Lionel Hampton, the 1941 Metronome All-Stars, the 1946 Esquire All-American Award Winners, singer Leslie Scott, Red Allen, Lambert, Hendricks & Bavan, and Sonny Rollins. In addition, the great tenor is heard on his own dates from 1939 (including "Body and Soul"), 1940, 1946–47, and 1956. The three-CD *In Europe* has all of Hawkins's overseas recordings of the 1930s, including each of the alternate takes. Best are the tenor's collaborations with the Ramblers (an excellent Dutch

A harmonically advanced soloist since the mid-1920s,
Coleman Hawkins not only supported the Bebop revolution but
also did all he could to hire younger Bop musicians for his bands.

band), duets with pianist Freddie Johnson, and a famous session with Benny Carter, tenor saxophonist Alix Combelle, and Django Reinhardt that resulted in classic versions of "Honeysuckle Rose" and "Crazy Rhythm."

9 *Rainbow Mist / Feb. 16, 1944–May 22, 1944 / Delmark 459*

9 *Bean and the Boys / Oct. 11, 1944–Dec. 1946 / Prestige 24124*

9 *Hollywood Stampede / Feb. 23, 1945–June 1947 / Capitol 92596*

Coleman Hawkins's most important Bop recordings are on these three CDs. *Rainbow Mist* has the six numbers that were recorded at Hawk's historic initial Bop date: three ballad features (including the title cut, which is based on "Body and Soul"), "Woody 'n You," "Disorder at the Border," and "Bu Dee Daht"; Dizzy Gillespie has a few early solos. *Rainbow Mist* also includes a date with Ben Webster, Georgie

Auld, and Charlie Shavers (highlighted by the first recording of Dizzy's "Salt Peanuts") and four numbers from Auld's 1944 big band. *Bean and the Boys* shows just how adventurous Hawkins could be. It has several advanced dates, including the quartet session that introduced Thelonious Monk and an octet date with Fats Navarro, J.J. Johnson, Hank Jones, Milt Jackson, and Max Roach, playing such complex numbers as "I Mean You" and "Bean and the Boys." *Hollywood Stampede* showcases the Hawkins Quintet with Howard McGhee on a dozen catchy numbers, including "Rifftide" and "Stuffy." Also on the CD is an obscure Hawkins septet session from 1947 that has a couple of short solos from Miles Davis.

6 *Body and Soul Revisited / Oct. 19, 1951–Oct. 13, 1958 / GRP/Decca 627*

7 *The Hawk in Paris / July 9–13, 1956 / Bluebird 51059*

9 *The Hawk Flies High / Mar. 12–15, 1957 / Original Jazz Classics 027*

7 *The Genius of Coleman Hawkins / Oct. 16, 1957 / Verve 825–673*

8 *Hawk Eyes / Apr. 3, 1959 / Original Jazz Classics 294*

8 *Bean Stalkin' / Oct. 1960–Nov. 1960 / Pablo 2310–933*

8 *Night Hawk / Dec. 30, 1960 / Original Jazz Classics 420*

7 *Alive! at the Village Gate / Aug. 13–15, 1962 / Verve 829 260*

7 *Hawkins! Eldridge! Hodges! Alive! at the Village Gate / Aug. 13–15, 1962 / Verve 314 513 755*

7 *Desafinado / Sept. 12 + 17, 1962 / GRP/Impulse 227*

8 *Wrapped Tight / Feb. 22, 1965–Mar. 1, 1965 / GRP/Impulse 109*

1 *Sirius / Dec. 20, 1966 / Original Jazz Classics 861*

Body and Soul Revisited has the majority of Coleman Hawkins's 1950s recordings for Decca, including some melodic mood music, the unaccompanied (if brief) "Foolin' Around," and tunes from albums led by drummer Cozy Cole and Tony Scott. A bit of a surprise is *The Hawk in Paris*, a set with a string section that comes off pretty well. Manny Albam's arrangements are not too inspiring, but Hawkins's strong sound and ability to create romantic music that is creative and witty makes this a success. *The Hawk Flies High* is a Bop date with J. J. Johnson and Idrees Sulieman that is full of joyful moments, particularly "Sanctity." *The Genius of Coleman Hawkins,* a set of mostly relaxed standards with the Oscar Peterson Trio and drummer Alvin Stoller, is also quite worthwhile. Many of Hawkins's Prestige/Moodsville sessions of the late 1950s/early 60s are not too exciting and feature slow tempos and sleepy playing. However, *Hawk Eyes* is a definite exception, a meeting with Charlie Shavers and Tiny Grimes that is full of spirit, including swinging versions of "Through for the Night," "La Rosita," "Hawk Eyes," and the slow blues "C'mon In." On *Bean Stalkin',* Hawkins jams with Roy Eldridge, Benny Carter, and Don Byas, and the competitiveness often makes the music quite stimulating. Hawkins battles the fiery Eddie "Lockjaw" Davis (who was influenced by the older tenor) to a draw on *Night Hawk*; lots of sparks fly. Pianist Tommy Flanagan, bassist Major Holley, and drummer Ed Locke form Hawkins's rhythm section on his two Village Gate CDs. *Alive!* has six selections, including lengthy versions of

"Joshua Fought the Battle of Jericho" and "Mack the Knife." The other set includes three exciting jams with Roy Eldridge and Johnny Hodges along with four previously unreleased quartet numbers. Hawkins still sounded good on his three Impulse projects, two of which have been reissued on CD. *Desafinado* is an easily enjoyable bossa nova session that has memorable versions of "O Pato," "One Note Samba," and "I'm Looking Over a Four Leaf Clover." *Wrapped Tight,* the last great Hawkins album, finds him keeping his style open to the influence of the avant-garde and making some powerful statements. Unfortunately his decline afterwards would be steep, and his final studio album, *Sirius,* is quite sad, with meandering solos, labored breathing, and plenty of painful moments. But there is no shortage of recommended Coleman Hawkins releases currently available.

LPS TO SEARCH FOR

Dating from 1945–57, *Hawk Variations* (Swingtime 1004) has many obscure items, including an unaccompanied two-part "Hawk Variation" (which predates "Picasso" by three years), dates as a leader from 1947 and 1949–50, and an appearance with the Elliot Lawrence Orchestra. *Disorder at the Border* (Spotlite 121) teams Hawkins with either Roy Eldridge or Howard McGhee on trumpet in 1952 plus Horace Silver a couple a couple years before the pianist became famous. The team of Coleman Hawkins and Roy Eldridge is heard in top form on *At the Opera House* (Verve 8266), *At the Bayou Club* (Honeysuckle Rose 5002), and *The Bayou Club, Vol. 2* (Honeysuckle Rose 5006). *The High and Mighty Hawk* (Affinity 163), a 1958 session with trumpeter Buck Clayton, is highlighted by the powerful "Bird of Prey Blues." *Today and Now* (Impulse 34), from 1963, finds Coleman Hawkins digging into some unusual material (such as "Go Lil Liza," "Put on Your Old Grey Bonnet," "Swingin' Scotch," and "Don't Sit Under the Apple Tree") and shows that, nearly 40 years after joining Fletcher Henderson's orchestra, he was still a creative and modern improviser.

FILMS

Coleman Hawkins appeared in several notable videos. He joins in with the Red Allen All-Stars and also with Billie Holiday in *The Sound of Jazz* (1957) and is in prime form with Roy Eldridge on *After Hours* (1961), a pilot for a television series that never made it. *Tenor Legends* (Shanachie 6308) has a superb perfomance by Hawkins in 1962 that includes the unaccompanied "Blowing for Adolphe Sax" and a lengthy "Disorder at the Border"; an unrelated Dexter Gordon date is also on the tape. The great tenor also appears in 1965, looking old but still sounding strong, on *Earl Hines and Coleman Hawkins* (Rhapsody Films).

MILT HINTON

b. June 23, 1910, Vicksburg, MS

Milt Hinton was among the most advanced bassists in jazz prior to the rise of Jimmy Blanton. He was a part of the Cab Calloway rhythm section at the same time that Dizzy Gillespie was a sideman, and he learned from the trumpeter's harmonic ideas, becoming a much more modern and flexible bassist. Probably the most recorded jazz musician of all time, Milt Hinton appeared on a remarkable number of record dates, studio sessions, and live performances during his long career. Hinton, who began playing bass and tuba in high school, was based in Chicago in his early days. He worked with Boyd Atkins, Tiny Parham (making his recording debut in 1930), Jabbo Smith, Cassino Simpson, Eddie South, and Fate Marable prior to becoming a fixture with Calloway (1936–51). In 1939, "Pluckin' the Bass" was an important showcase with Calloway for Hinton's bass. He stayed with the singer until Cab finally broke up his last combo, and then Hinton became an extremely busy studio musician, often recording several sessions a day. He spent a couple of months with the Count Basie Orchestra and was with Louis Armstrong's All-Stars for two brief stints during 1953–54. Otherwise Hinton was a very active studio musician, playing jazz at night. Milt Hinton kept the old swing style alive into the late 1990s (often slapping his bass rhythmically), yet was quite capable of playing with Branford Marsalis and with the surviving Beboppers, too.

10 *Old Man Time / Mar. 28, 1989–Mar. 27, 1990 / Chiaroscuro 310*

Milt Hinton was heard mostly as a sideman throughout his career, but he led occasional record dates starting in 1945. This two-CD set does a perfect job of summing up his career. Hinton has reunions with many of his musical associates from the 1930s, including Dizzy Gillespie, trumpeter Doc Cheatham, guitarist Danny Barker, saxophonists Eddie Barefield and Buddy Tate, pianist Red Richards, guitarist Al Casey, Cab Calloway (on "Good Time Charlie"), and Lionel Hampton. He sings the delightful "Old Man Time,"

jams with Clark Terry, Al Grey, Flip Phillips, and pianist Ralph Sutton, does a humorous rap, and is heard verbally on a pair of "Jazzspeaks," recalling his life in colorful fashion for 43 minutes and reminiscing with Calloway, Cheatham, and Barefield.

FILMS

Milt Hinton, who backs Cab Calloway in many of his film appearances, is also in *The Sound of Jazz* (1957) and *After Hours* (1961).

ILLINOIS JACQUET

b. Oct. 31, 1922, Broussard, LA

Illinois Jacquet combines elements of both Coleman Hawkins and Lester Young to form his own tenor sound. In the early 1940s his style (which was emotional and often used repetition and screams) led the way toward rhythm and blues. Although not really considered part of the Bebop movement, Jacquet was among the leading tenors of the mid-1940s (preceding Dexter Gordon), and his occasional solos on alto later in his career found him sounding surprisingly close to Charlie Parker.

Jean Baptiste "Illinois" Jacquet is the younger brother of the late swing/Bop trumpeter Russell Jacquet. Growing up in Houston, Jacquet played drums, soprano, and alto sax before switching to tenor. He worked locally, moved to Los Angeles in 1941 (touring with Floyd Ray's orchestra), and joined Lionel Hampton's band. His famous solo on "Flying Home" made him a star and served as the inspiration for most other R&B tenors, who recorded endless variations of that one record during the next decade. Jacquet was with Cab Calloway's orchestra during a barely documented period (1943–44), was a sensation at the first Jazz at the Philharmonic concert (biting his reed during a screeching solo on "Blues"), and was in the final number in the Lester Young film short *Jammin' the Blues*. Jacquet began the Bebop era as a solo star with Count Basie (1945–46), taking notable solos on such driving numbers as "Rambo," "The King," and "Mutton Leg."

After leaving Basie, Illinois Jacquet formed his own medium-size group and was a very popular attraction for many years. He has remained a big name in jazz up to the present time. He toured with Jazz at the Philharmonic, recorded for Norman Granz's labels in the 1950s, took up the bassoon the following decade (which he played on an occasional atmospheric ballad), led a variety of combos (including with organist Milt Buckner), toured Europe frequently, and has led a part-time big band since the late 1980s.

- ✳ *The Complete Illinois Jacquet Sessions 1945-50 / July 1945–May 22, 1950 / Mosaic 4-165*
- 8 *1945–1946 / July 1945–Jan. 8, 1946 / Classics 948*
- 8 *1946–1947 / Aug. 1946–Dec. 18, 1947 / Classics 1019*
- 9 *The Black Velvet Band / Dec. 18, 1947–July 3, 1967 / Bluebird 6571*
- 8 *The Kid and the Brute / Dec. 11, 1951–Dec. 13, 1954 / Verve 314 557 096*
- 9 *Bottoms Up / Mar. 26, 1968 / Original Jazz Classics 417*
- 7 *The King! / Aug. 20, 1968 / Original Jazz Classics 849*
- 8 *The Soul Explosion / May 25, 1969 / Original Jazz Classics 674*
- 9 *The Blues: That's Me! / Sept. 16, 1969 / Original Jazz Classics 614*

The Mosaic set (a four-CD, limited-edition box) has all of the dates that Illinois Jacquet led during his most influential years, sides originally cut for the Aladdin, Apollo, ARA, Savoy, and Victor labels. Jacquet's jump band of 1945-50 included such fine players as Russell Jacquet, Emmett Berry and/or Joe Newman on trumpets, Henry Coker, Trummy Young or J. J. Johnson on trombones, and sometimes baritonist Leo Parker and Sir Charles Thompson or Bill Doggett on piano; in addition, there is a rare big band date with Fats Navarro and Miles Davis in the trumpet section—lots of exciting music that falls between swing, Bebop and jump. Those not able to acquire the Mosaic box can get many of the recordings (although no alternates) by purchasing the two Classics CDs and *The Black Velvet Band*. The latter has Jacquet's top Victor recordings of 1947-50 plus a guest appearance with the Lionel Hampton Orchestra in 1967 for a remake of "Flying Home." *The Kid and the Brute* includes Illinois's one album with Ben Webster (the two tenors inspire each other) plus a former ten-inch release from 1953 by Jacquet's regular septet (which includes Cecil Payne).

Among Illinois Jacquet's later recordings, his four albums for Prestige (1968–69 dates reissued in the Original Jazz Classics series) are each easily recommended. *Bottoms Up,* which has hot versions of the title cut and "Jivin' with Jack the Bellboy" plus ballads, also features the Barry Harris

Trio. *The King!* is most notable for Jacquet's bassoon playing on "Caravan"; his group includes Joe Newman and Milt Buckner. *The Soul Explosion,* featuring a ten-piece group that also includes Newman and Buckner, mostly puts the focus on the leader's forceful tenor on such numbers as "The Soul Explosion," "After Hours," and "Still King." Best of the quartet of sets is *The Blues: That's Me!* The quintet (which has pianist Wynton Kelly and Tiny Grimes) performs (among others) the 10½-minute title cut, "Still King," "Everyday I Have the Blues," and a Jacquet bassoon feature on " 'Round Midnight."

LPS TO SEARCH FOR

Got It (Atlantic 81816) is still the only recording by Illinois Jacquet's big band of the 1980s and '90s. The 1987 set, long overdue to be made available on CD, includes "Tickletoe," "Stompin' at the Savoy," and "Three Buckets of Jive," and such soloists as trumpeters Irv Stokes and Jon Faddis, trombonist Frank Lacy, and pianist Richard Wyands.

FILMS

Illinois Jacquet steals the show during the final song of *Swingin' the Blues* (1944). He is also well portrayed in *Texas Tenor* (Rhapsody 9021).

BUDD JOHNSON

b. Dec. 14, 1910, Dallas, TX, d. Oct. 20, 1984, Kansas City, MO

Budd Johnson, a distinctive and talented swing tenor saxophonist and arranger, was a very important participant behind the scenes in the early days of Bebop. His older brother was trombonist Keg Johnson. Albert "Budd" Johnson worked on piano and drums before switching to tenor. Johnson played with Sammy Price (in Dallas), William Holloway's Blue Syncopators, Eugene Coy's Happy Black Aces, Terrence Holder, Jesse Stone, George E. Lee, Clarence Shaw, Eddie Mallory, the Louis Armstrong Big Band (1932–33), Jesse Stone's Cyclones (1934–35), and Earl Hines's orchestra for the first time (1935–36). Johnson would be associated with Hines off and on for 40 years. He spent a year as a staff arranger for Gus Arnheim, played alto with Hines (1937), had short stints in the bands of Fletcher Henderson and Horace Henderson, and then was featured on tenor with the Hines big band (1938–42), also contributing arrangements. He was one of the first tenormen whose tone was influenced by Lester Young.

While with Earl Hines, Johnson persuaded the pianist to modernize his band's sound and to hire such up-and-coming stars as Charlie Parker (who was used on tenor), Dizzy Gillespie, and Sarah Vaughan (singing and playing second piano). Although that particular orchestra (due to the recording strike) never recorded, Johnson deserves much credit for making the 1943 Earl Hines ensemble into the first Bebop big band. That year Johnson left Hines and worked with Don Redman and Al Sears, and as an arranger for Georgie Auld. He was a member of Dizzy Gillespie's early Bebop quintet on 52nd Street in early 1944, became the Billy Eckstine Orchestra's musical director for a time, and was a busy freelance arranger. Johnson helped to organize Coleman Hawkins's Bebop sessions of 1944, playing section baritone and tenor on the six numbers. He would also be a member of the Dizzy Gillespie big band in 1947.

Johnson was the musical director for Atlantic Records for a period in the 1950s, ran a publishing company, and played in many different situations, including with Benny Goodman (1956–57), the Quincy Jones Orchestra (1960), the Count Basie Big Band (1961–62), Earl Hines (1965–69 and off and on afterwards), and the JPJ Quartet (1969–75), which he led. Always an open-minded swing stylist, Budd Johnson (who began doubling on soprano sax in the 1960s) teamed up with Phil Woods for a strong Bop date just a short time before his death in 1984 at age 73.

10 ***Budd Johnson and the Four Brass Giants / Aug. 22, 1960 + Sept. 6, 1960 / Original Jazz Classics 209***

9 ***Let's Swing / Dec. 2, 1960 / Original Jazz Classics 1720***

8 ***The JPJ Quartet / 1969–June 20, 1971 / Storyville 8235***

Budd Johnson led record sessions as early as 1947, with two of his finest efforts being from 1960. *The Four Brass Giants* has him providing four of the eight numbers and all of the arrangements for a trumpet section made up of four very different stylists: Clark Terry, Harry "Sweets" Edison, Nat Adderley, and Ray Nance (who also plays violin on two songs). Johnson takes many fine tenor solos, and his inventive writing for the unusual group makes this CD reissue a classic. *Let's Swing* puts the focus on Budd Johnson's playing talents, featuring him in a quintet with his brother trombonist Keg Johnson, Tommy Flanagan, bassist George Duvivier, and drummer Charlie Persip. Johnson sounds fairly

modern on his originals and standards, and he is in peak form throughout. The JPJ Quartet recorded albums for Master Jazz and RCA during 1971–73. The Storyville CD has the quartet's 1971 Montreux Jazz Festival appearance (originally a Master Jazz LP) plus six previously unknown studio selections. The Mainstream swing group (which also consisted of pianist Dill Jones, bassist Bill Pemberton, and drummer Oliver Jackson) was an excellent outlet for Budd Johnson, who stretches out on both tenor and soprano in winning fashion.

LPS TO SEARCH FOR

In Memory of a Very Dear Friend (Dragon 94) and *The Ole Dude and the Fundance Kid* (Uptown 27.19) were Budd Johnson's last two albums as a leader, and both are impressive. The former (from 1978) is a quartet date with a trio that includes pianist Palle Thomsen, mostly playing swing standards other than "Now's The Time." The latter (recorded in 1984, eight months before Johnson's death) matches him with Phil Woods and shows that Budd Johnson was a fine modern improviser even at the end of his life.

JO JONES

b. Oct. 7, 1911, Chicago, IL, d. Sept. 3, 1985, New York, NY

As a member of Count Basie's orchestra, Jo Jones shifted the timekeeping function of the drums from the bass drum (which he used for occasional accents) to the hi-hat cymbal (Kenny Clarke would eventually move that function to the ride cymbal). Doing so gave Jones a much lighter touch than most of the drummers who came before him (including Gene Krupa) and he helped paved the way for the Bebop era.

Jo Jones, who started on trumpet, piano, and reeds, worked in carnival shows as a singer and dancer. He switched to drums in the late 1920s and worked with Ted Adams, Harold Jones's Brownskin Syncopators, Walter Page's Blue Devils, Bennie Moten, and Lloyd Hunter's Serenaders. After moving to Kansas City in 1934, Jones freelanced in the city's busy after-hours scene, playing with Count Basie on and off before officially joining Basie's orchestra in the fall of 1936. The drummer was with Count during all of his successes, traveling East from Kansas City. He was on virtually all of Basie's records (both with the big band and with the pianist's combos) until he went in the

Army in October 1944. After his discharge, Jones had a second period with Count (1946 to early 1948), worked with Illinois Jacquet's jump band (1948–50), toured with Jazz at the Philharmonic, and freelanced throughout the 1950s. Among his associations during that era were pianists Joe Bushkin (1951–53) and Teddy Wilson, plus other Basie alumni, including Lester Young. Known as "Papa" Jo Jones in his later years, Jones (who remained active into the late 1970s) was an inspiration for Max Roach, Art Blakey, Elvin Jones, and the other drummers who followed.

9   *The Essential Jo Jones / Aug. 11, 1955–Apr. 30, 1958 / Vanguard 101/2*

8   *The Main Man / Nov. 29, 1976–Nov. 30, 1976 / Original Jazz Classics 869*

Jo Jones did not lead many dates throughout his career, but most are quite rewarding. His two Vanguard sets are reissued in full (except for a second take of "Shoe Shine Boy") on the CD *The Essential Jo Jones*. Jones heads a septet that includes trumpeter Emmett Berry, Benny Green, and Lucky Thompson (Count Basie himself sits in on "Shoe Shine Boy"), while the later set is a trio with pianist Ray Bryant and bassist Tommy Bryant. Ray Bryant's "Little Susie" and "Cubano Chant" are heard in their earliest versions, and Jones takes a long drum solo on "Old Man River." *The Main Man*, recorded when Jones was 65, was one of his last records. The drummer joins in with a group of top veterans: Roy Eldridge, Harry Edison, trombonist Vic Dickenson, Eddie "Lockjaw" Davis, Tommy Flanagan, Freddie Green, and bassist Sam Jones. The octet performs a couple basic originals and four standards with swing and spirit.

FILMS

Jo Jones is in the award-winning *Jammin' the Blues* (1944), where he alternates on drums with Big Sid Catlett, is seen in a nightclub scene in *The Unsuspected* (1947), is one of the stars of *The Sound of Jazz* (1957), and is portrayed in *Born to Swing* (1973).

JOHN KIRBY

b. Dec. 31, 1908, Baltimore, MD, d. June 14, 1952, Hollywood, CA

The John Kirby Sextet was one of the most advanced bands of the Swing era. The group featured rapid unisons, unusual material, virtuoso horn players, and soft tones. Although it was a swing band, many of its musical qualities put it closer to Bebop and Cool Jazz. Its leader, bassist Kirby, originally played trombone and was a professional tuba player by the mid-1920s. He played tuba with Bill Brown's Brownies (1928–30) and then switched to bass while with Fletcher Henderson's Orchestra (1930–33). Kirby was a member of the big bands of Chick Webb (1933–35), Henderson again (1935–36), and Lucky Millinder (1936–37). While leading a combo at the Onyx Club for nearly a year during 1937–38, Kirby gradually formed the group he wanted, a sextet with trumpeter Charlie Shavers, altoist Russell Procope, clarinetist Buster Bailey, pianist Billy Kyle, and drummer O'Neil Spencer. During 1938–42, the John Kirby Sextet was at its prime, recording often, performing regularly, and sometimes accompanying Kirby's wife, singer Maxine Sullivan. No other group sounded like it, the sextet's interpretations of classical themes in particular were popular, and Shavers greatly impressed the up-and-coming modernists. But the draft, O'Neil Spencer's death in 1944, and a drop in the group's fortunes resulted in almost a complete turnover in its personnel during 1943–45; Dizzy Gillespie was one of many substitutes for a short time. Although most of the original members were back in 1946, that was only temporary, and the band broke up before it could make any impression during the Bebop era. Kirby was crushed, and he tried in vain to put together similar groups. A Carnegie Hall concert on December 20, 1950 that was supposed to be a comeback (with the original members plus Sid Catlett on drums) was poorly attended and served as a final attempt. During his last two years, John Kirby worked as a bored sideman with Red Allen, Buck Clayton, and Benny Carter, passing away at the age of 43 due to complications from diabetes.

10   *1938–1939 / Oct. 28, 1938–Oct. 12, 1939 / Classics 750*

10   *1939–1941 / Oct. 12, 1939–Jan. 15, 1941 / Classics 770*

9   *1941–1943 / Jan. 2, 1941–Dec .1943 / Classics 792*

8   *1945–1946 / Apr. 26, 1945–Sept. 3, 1946 / Classics 964*

These four Classics CDs contain every studio recording by the John Kirby Sextet (other than radio transcriptions), including their V-Discs. *1938–1939* is the most essential CD, with the original version of Charlie Shavers's "Undecided" among the highlights, along with "Rehearsin' for a Nervous Breakdown," "From a Flat to C," the haunting "Dawn on the Desert," "Anitra's Dance," "Royal Garden Blues," "Rose Room," and "Nocturne" among its 22 gems. *1939–*

1941 is equally satisfying, with the high points including "Humoresque," "Jumpin' in the Pump Room," "Sextet from Lucia," "Zooming at the Zombie," and "Beethoven Riffs On." *1941–1943* finds the personnel beginning to change, with an ailing O'Neil Spencer replaced by Specs Powell and eventually Bill Beason. The last five numbers, V-Discs from 1943, have Russell Procope and Billy Kyle's places taken by George Johnson and Clyde Hart. The performances include such notable numbers as "Coquette," "Close Shave," "Bugler's Dilemma," "Night Whispers," and "St. Louis Blues." *1945–1946* finds the sextet in its final days. Shavers had departed and his place was taken by Emmett Berry, Clarence Brereton, and finally George Taitt. Procope and Kyle returned for most of the selections but were eventually succeeded by Hilton Jefferson and Hank Jones. Budd Johnson makes the group a septet on one session, and Bill Beason is on drums throughout; Kirby and Bailey were the only original members still around at the end. Despite all of this, the group's sound did not really change, as can be heard on such fine performances as "K.C. Caboose," "Desert Sands," "Peanut Vendor Boogie," and "Schubert's Serenade." *1945–1946* also has four rare vocals by the young Sarah Vaughan with Kirby. It is a pity that the legendary group could not have survived into the 1950s, when the John Kirby Sextet would have been hailed as one of the first "Cool Jazz" bands.

FILMS

The John Kirby Sextet plays a couple spirited numbers in *Sepia Cinderella* (1947).

RED NORVO

b. Mar. 31, 1908, Beardstown, IL, d. Apr. 6, 1999, Santa Monica, CA

Red Norvo was one of the few swing stylists who easily adapted to Bebop. He had a crisp tone on the vibes and was an advanced player who had little difficulty fitting into several musical styles throughout his career without losing, watering down, or even slightly altering his musical personality. Born Kenneth Norville, his first instrument was piano, but he soon switched to xylophone and marimba. In 1925, Norvo toured with a marimba band (the Collegians); this was followed by stints with Paul Ash and Ben Bernie, work on radio, and appearances in vaudeville as a tap dancer. Norvo worked with Victor Young, was with Paul Whiteman's orchestra in the early 1930s (where he met and mar-

ried singer Mildred Bailey), and made his first recordings as a leader in 1933. Those sessions (including two numbers with an atmospheric chamber group that had Benny Goodman on bass clarinet) introduced the xylophone as a jazz instrument.

After leaving Whiteman, Norvo began leading his own groups in 1934. He played regularly on 52nd Street and in 1936 put together a small big band. Eddie Sauter's inventive arrangements made it possible for Norvo's xylophone to be heard over the horns. The group (with Mildred Bailey on vocals) had its own sound, and Norvo and Bailey were dubbed "Mr. And Mrs. Swing." During 1937–38, the Red Norvo Orchestra became a more conventional big band, and he led various-size groups until 1942, when Norvo cut back to a combo. The following year he switched permanently to the vibraphone. Norvo, whose marriage to Bailey ended with their 1945 divorce, was an important sideman with Benny Goodman during 1944–45 (including BG's sextet with Slam Stewart) and Woody Herman's First Herd in 1946. Bebop caused no problem for Norvo, as he showed on his record date of June 6, 1945, when he, Teddy Wilson, and Slam Stewart played alongside Charlie Parker and Dizzy Gillespie. He also recorded with Stan Hasselgard and used Dexter Gordon, Barney Kessel, and Dodo Marmarosa on a couple of his record dates.

Norvo settled in California for a time and then in 1949 emerged with a successful trio featuring guitarist Tal Farlow and bassist Charles Mingus. The vibes-guitar-bass combination worked very well, and Norvo worked in this format (with guitarist Jimmy Raney and bassist Red Mitchell being later members) for several years, helping to define Cool Jazz and mixing together swing and Bop standards. Red Norvo recorded frequently during the 1950s, had several reunions with Benny Goodman, made a comeback from a serious ear operation in 1961, and recorded as late as 1983. A stroke in the mid-1980s ended his career.

10 *Dance of the Octopus / Apr. 18, 1933–Mar. 16, 1936 / Hep 1044*

5 *Featuring Mildred Bailey / Aug. 26, 1936–Feb. 27, 1939 / Columbia/Legacy 53424*

7 *Volume One—The Legendary V-Disc Masters / Oct. 28, 1943–May 17, 1944 / Vintage Jazz Classics 1005*

8 *Red Norvo's Fabulous Jam Session / June 6, 1945 / Stash 2514*

Dance of the Octopus has many classic performances from Red Norvo's earliest period on records, before he put together his big band. Norvo's xylophone and marimba are heard on four numbers from 1933 (including Bix Beiderbecke's "In a Mist" and the eccentric "Dance of the Octopus"), with an octet in 1934 that includes clarinetist Artie Shaw, Charlie Barnet on tenor, trombonist Jack Jenney, and pianist Teddy Wilson, and on four songs (including "Honeysuckle Rose") in 1935 with a nonet that features Jenney, Wilson, tenorman Chu Berry, clarinetist Johnny Mince, trumpeter Bunny Berigan, and drummer Gene Krupa. The remainder of the disc showcases Norvo's regular octet of early 1936, with Eddie Sauter playing mellophone. In contrast, *Featuring Mildred Bailey* is a mess, jumping all over chronologically and mixing familiar numbers with two previously unissued cuts and two selections from a date actually led by Mildred Bailey (who appears on only six of the 18 numbers). The music is generally excellent with its Sauter arrangements, but hopefully someday it will receive more logical treatment.

Norvo had switched to vibes by the time he recorded the music on *Volume One,* which has most of his V-Discs from 1943-44. The music is essentially advanced swing, with the vibraphonist leading a young group that includes clarinetist Aaron Sachs, Flip Phillips on tenor, and pianist Ralph Burns, with vocals by Helen Ward and Carol Bruce. Highlights include "1-2-3-4 Jump," "Seven Come Eleven," "Flying Home," and "NBC Jump." The *Fabulous Jam Session* is the Norvo-Wilson-Dizzy-Bird set (plus Flip Phillips, Slam Stewart, and either Specs Powell or J. C. Heard on drums). The mixture of swing and Bop all-stars actually recorded only four numbers, but all of the music is here, including five full-length alternate takes and three incomplete versions. *Volume Two* has 30 concise radio transcriptions of the Norvo-Tal Farlow-Charles Mingus Trio during 1949-50 plus three leftover selections from Norvo's V-Disc dates. The Norvo Trio was often magical (their reactions to each other were almost instantaneous), as can also be heard on *Move* (which has a dozen of the group's 20 Savoy recordings

of 1950-51). *The Red Norvo Trios* has 19 of the 20 selections cut by the band for Fantasy, with Mitchell on bass and Raney the guitarist except for four numbers with Farlow.

Just a Mood, recorded 30 years before Red Norvo's career came to an end, is a perfect example of his versatility. Norvo performs four numbers with swing-era all-stars (including Harry "Sweets" Edison and Ben Webster), a quartet of "blue" songs with a Cool Jazz group that includes flutist Buddy Collette, Farlow, and drummer Chico Hamilton, and four "rose" tunes in a septet with trumpeter Shorty Rogers, clarinetist Jimmy Giuffre, and pianist Pete Jolly. Everything works!

LPS TO SEARCH FOR

Many Red Norvo dates have not been reissued on CD as of this writing. Obscure Norvo big band numbers from 1936-42 are on *Featuring Mildred Bailey* (Sounds of Swing 112). *Time in His Hands* (Xanadu 199) has three small-group sessions from 1945 (with appearances by Slam Stewart, pianist Johnny Guarnieri, Charlie Ventura, and some Ellington sidemen). *Norvo* (Pausa 9015) contains some of his largely Bop-oriented work for Capitol (sidemen include Benny Carter, Charlie Shavers, Jimmy Giuffre, Dexter Gordon, and tenor saxophonist Eddie Miller). All of Norvo's Savoy recordings (including alternate takes) with Farlow and Mingus arc on *The Red Norvo Trio* (Savoy 2212), a two-LP set that is easily superior to the single CD. Red Norvo's later recordings, including a 1979 quartet album with pianist Ross Tompkins (*Red & Ross*—Concord CJ-90) and a 1983 collaboration with the Bucky Pizzarelli Trio (*Just Friends*—Stash 230) are currently out of print.

FILMS

The original Red Norvo-Tal Farlow-Charles Mingus Trio is seen in *Texas Carnival* (1951); Norvo's late 50s group appears in *Screaming Mimi* (1957).

DJANGO REINHARDT
b. Jan. 23, 1910, Liverchies, Belgium, d. May 16,
1953, Fontainebleau, France

One of the top jazz guitarists in history, Jean Baptiste "Django" Reinhardt is best remembered for his work on acoustic guitar in the 1930s with violinist Stephane Grappelli and the Quintet of the Hot Club of France. However, during 1947-53, he was one of the top (maybe the very best)

Bebop guitarist in jazz, although this period has been greatly underpublicized.

Reinhardt was the first major European jazz musician and an extraordinary soloist by 1933. A gypsy who was barely literate and often quite unreliable, Django first played violin and worked primarily as a banjoist in the 1920s. A fire in his caravan in 1928 badly burned his left hand, rendering two of his fingers largely useless. However, he made a surprisingly quick comeback, switched to guitar, and altered his style a bit to make up for his disability. Inspired by Eddie Lang and Louis Armstrong, Reinhardt developed his own distinctive style and was a decade ahead of virtually all other guitarists by the early 1930s. After Django met Grappelli in early 1933, they formed the Quintet of the Hot Club of France (featuring the two soloists plus two rhythm guitars and a bass), began recording, and were soon the most popular jazz band in Europe. The Quintet worked steadily throughout the European Continent until they visited London in 1939. World War II broke out at that time, and Reinhardt spontaneously decided to return to France; Grappelli chose to stay in England. Back in occupied France, Django was able to work and record quite steadily during the war years, forming a new quintet with clarinetist Hubert Rostaing. When France was liberated in 1944, many fans were relieved to find that Reinhardt was not only alive and well but still playing in prime form.

In 1946, Django Reinhardt made two decisions that did not please everyone. He switched to electric guitar and he began exploring Bebop, not playing the works of Charlie Parker and Dizzy Gillespie but writing modern originals. It would take Reinhardt a couple years to be comfortable with both his new instrument and the newer style. In the interim, he made his only visit to the United States, touring with Duke Ellington. However, this trip was not a success. Reinhardt thought that he would be honored as a visiting celebrity, but the American press treated his visit with indifference, and Ellington did not write anything special for him to play. Django soon became homesick and missed some important engagements. Overall, it was a lost opportunity.

Django Reinhardt had several later reunions with Stephane Grappelli including a final marathon set of recording sessions in 1949. By then, he had successfully transferred his voice to the electric guitar and the awkwardness of his early Bebop playing was gone (as can be heard on his few recordings from this last period). In the early 1950s, Reinhardt was

playing Bop on the level of Tal Farlow and Barney Kessel. Unfortunately, Django Reinhardt was losing interest in music at the same time that his health had become erratic. He died from a stroke in 1953 when he was just 43, and plans for a second American tour (organized by Norman Granz) were never allowed to become reality.

7 *Djangology 49 / Jan. 1949–Feb. 1949 / Bluebird 9988*

9 *Peche à la Mouche / Apr. 16, 1947–Mar. 10, 1953 / Verve 8354 418*

9 *Brussels and Paris / Mar. 21, 1947–Apr. 8, 1953 / DRG 8473*

Most reissue programs overlook Django Reinhardt's later recordings despite their surprisingly high quality. Reinhardt and Stephane Grappelli had several reunions after World War II. Their last one was quite extensive, taking place in early 1949, with an Italian rhythm section. *Djangology 49* contains 20 of the better numbers with Django sounding comfortable at last on his electric guitar. The music falls between swing and Bop and, for what would be the last time, it displays the special musical magic that always existed between Reinhardt and Grappelli.

Peche à la Mouche, a two-CD set, has Reinhardt playing with his 1947 Quintet (featuring Hubert Rostaing mostly on clarinet), two numbers with cornetist Rex Stewart, and eight superior selections in 1953 with a modern rhythm section. The latter hint strongly at the type of Bop sessions that Django might have recorded in the 1950s with American all-stars had he lived. *Brussels and Paris* has a different date with Rostaing in 1947 and also showcases Django with a few combos during 1951–53, including a session cut less than six weeks before his passing. These valuable recordings show how modern a soloist Django Reinhardt had become in his later years, even while keeping his distinctive sound.

BUSTER SMITH
b. Aug. 26, 1904, Ellis County, TX, d. Aug. 10, 1991, Dallas, TX

Buster Smith, who composed "One O'Clock Jump," was one of the early inspirations for Charlie Parker, and it was said that Bird based his sound to an extent on Smith. Unfortunately Smith did not record all that much and spent much of his life in obscurity. He was self-taught on alto and started working professionally in local groups around Dallas.

Smith was a member of Walter Page's Blue Devils (1925–31), a group he took over when the bassist joined Benny Moten. The altoist became part of Moten's big band himself (1933–35) and then was a member of the Count Basie Orchestra in Kansas City (1935–36), writing some of the originals and contributing arrangements. Smith did not think that the Basie band would make it when it went East, so he chose to stay in Kansas City, a definite mistake! In 1937 he had his own group, which included the 17-year-old Charlie Parker, but the band never recorded. A couple of years later, Smith moved to New York, where he worked as a freelance arranger (contributing some charts for Basie, Benny Carter, and Harlan Leonard, among others) and played with a variety of combos, making sessions with Pete Johnson, Don Redman, Hot Lips Page, Eddie Durham, singer Bon Bon, and Chester Boone's Jumping Jacks; the last two on clarinet. In 1942 Smith moved back to Dallas, where he worked locally and taught for the remainder of his career. The only record he made after leaving New York was a fine 1959 album, but it was out-of-print for decades, until recently. By 1960 Buster Smith had given up playing alto, although he gigged occasionally on piano, guitar, and bass. The forgotten legend retired altogether in the late 1980s.

9 *The Legendary Buster Smith / June 7, 1959 / Koch 8523*

Other than six songs cut as obscure singles during 1951–55, this Atlantic album (reissued by Koch in 1999) was Buster Smith's only set as a leader. Listeners hoping to hear the missing link between Charlie Parker and swing will be disappointed, for Smith actually sounds closer to Benny Carter on this album than to Bird. However, the music, mostly rollicking blues plus "September Song," is quite enjoyable and swinging. In addition to Smith, the musicians in the Dallas octet include trumpeter Charles Gillum and baritonist Leroy Cooper (who a couple years later would record with Hank Crawford). Gunther Schuller's lengthy liner notes (which tell of the remarkably arduous task of making this recording happen) are quite fascinating.

SLAM STEWART

b. Sept. 21, 1914, Englewood, NJ, d. Dec. 10, 1987, Binghamton, NY

Slam Stewart, one of the top bassists of the Swing era, became famous for humming vocally an octave above his bowed bass during solos, in humorous fashion. His style was not too influential (Major Holley a generation later hummed and bowed in unison), but he had a strong technique and was one of the few bassists featured regularly on solos during the 1940s. Leroy "Slam" Stewart studied bass at the Boston Conservatory of Music and gained the idea for his style after seeing violinist Ray Perry singing along with his violin. Stewart worked with trumpeter Peanuts Holland (1936–37) and then was part of Slim and Slam (1938–42) with Slim Gaillard, waxing "Flat Foot Floogie" (a giant hit) and many other popular recordings. After Gaillard went in the military, Stewart was a member of the Art Tatum Trio (1943–44) with Tiny Grimes, recorded with Lester Young (including a famous rendition of "Sometimes I'm Happy"), dueted with Don Byas at a Town Hall concert, had a brief stint in Tiny Grimes's quartet, and in 1945 was a featured star with the Benny Goodman Orchestra and Sextet. That same year (on February 28) he appeared on classic recordings of "Groovin' High," "Dizzy Atmosphere," and "All the Things You Are" with the Dizzy Gillespie Sextet (which also featured Charlie Parker). Stewart was also part of the Red Norvo Jam Session that included Diz and Bird. For a few years, Stewart led his own trio, which for a period featured the young Erroll Garner. Having proved himself in Bop settings, Stewart largely returned to mainstream swing in his later years. He freelanced during the 1950s, playing with Tatum, Roy Eldridge, and pianists Billy Taylor, Beryl Booker (1955–57), and Rose Murphy, and kept busy during his next three decades. Among Slam Stewart's later associations were Benny Goodman (1973–75), Bucky Pizzarelli, and George Wein's Newport All-Stars. He remained unique up until the end, performing into the mid-1980s.

9 *1945–1946 / Jan. 30, 1945–Apr. 26, 1946 / Classics 939*

All of Slam Stewart's recordings as a leader prior to 1971 (other than two numbers in 1950) are on this single CD. The bassist is heard leading a trio and a quartet that features Errol Garner, interacting on a few cuts with Don Byas, heading a session with pianist Billy Taylor, and leading two dates in which Stewart's quintet features Red Norvo and Johnny Guarnieri. Overall this is obscure but highly enjoyable music that hints at Bop while generally being swing-oriented.

FILMS

Slam Stewart is in *Hellzapoppin'* with Slim Gaillard (1941) and appears in *Boy! What a Girl* (1947).

THE WAYNE KNIGHT COLLECTION

Art Tatum was such an advanced pianist when he arrived on the scene in the early 1930s that the innovations of Bud Powell, 15 years later, did not exactly scare him!

ART TATUM

b. Oct. 13, 1909, Toledo, OH, d. Nov. 5, 1956, Los Angeles, CA

Art Tatum was an inspiration to the Bebop movement even though his playing was based in Fats Waller and early swing and he never really explored Bebop songs. An incredible player who displayed blinding speed on the piano and a very advanced knowledge of chords, Tatum could suspend time à la Earl Hines and play hard-charging boogie-woogie but also was decades ahead of his time harmonically. Bud Powell loved Tatum's playing, and Art in time accepted Powell as a near equal.

Born with cataracts, Tatum was blind in one eye and had only partial vision in the other. Although he studied guitar and violin and played a bit of accordion, Tatum was a pianist from an early age. He worked in his native Toledo starting in

1926 and appeared regularly on local radio. It is not known how Tatum developed his phenomenal technique and who, besides Waller, was his inspiration. Musicians passing through town were amazed by his playing, which by the late 1920s surpassed that of even James P. Johnson, Waller, and Hines. In 1932 Tatum became part of a two-piano team that accompanied Adelaide Hall's vocals, although one might wonder what the other pianist did! Soon Tatum moved to New York, made his recording debut with Hall, and then in 1933 had his own first solo session. His version of "Tiger Rag" made it sound as if three or four pianists were playing at once.

Due to the forbidding nature of his music (many musicians were afraid to play with him), his blindness, being black during an age of segregation, and his quiet personality (there are very few interviews of the pianist), Art Tatum was barely known to the general public and never received the acclaim he deserved. However, the jazz world was quite aware of him and, whether it be Coleman Hawkins, Jon Hendricks, Charlie Parker (who in his early days got a job as a dishwasher at the same restaurant where Tatum played so he would have a nightly opportunity to see him play), or Bud Powell, he made an impact. During the 1930s Tatum was generally heard solo, both on records and in his club appearances. In 1943 he was inspired by the success of the Nat King Cole Trio to form a trio of his own, with guitarist Tiny Grimes and bassist Slam Stewart, which was quite popular. During the remainder of his life he alternated between solo engagements and trio dates, using Everett Barksdale on guitar in the later years. In the 1950s Art Tatum recorded an extensive series of all-star band sides for Norman Granz's Verve label (including with Lionel Hampton, Benny Carter, Buddy DeFranco, Ben Webster, Roy Eldridge, and Buddy Rich) plus a less significant solo series. A duet set with Charlie Parker never happened because the pianist (not Bird) forgot to show up!

Art Tatum died at the age of 46 from uremia. Over a half-century later, his best records still sound amazing.

10 *Piano Starts Here / Mar. 21, 1933–1949 / Legacy / Columbia 64690*

9 *Classic Early Solos / Aug. 22, 1934–Nov. 29, 1937 / GRP/Decca 607*

9 *Solos / Feb. 22, 1940–July 26, 1940 / MCA/Decca 42327*

9 *I Got Rhythm / Dec. 21, 1935–Jan. 5, 1944 / GRP/ Decca 630*

8 *The Standard Transcriptions / Dec. 1935–1943 / Music & Arts 673*

8 *God Is in the House / Nov. 11, 1940–Sept. 16, 1941 / High Note 7030*

7 *Tea for Two / 1944–July 1945 / Black Lion 760192*

7 *The V-Discs / Jan. 18, 1944–Jan. 21, 1946 / Black Lion 760114*

Piano Starts Here is the perfect place to start acquiring Art Tatum's recordings. His first date as a leader is here (including "Tiger Rag") along with a brilliant solo performance at a "Just Jazz" concert in 1949. Among the highlights of the latter are remarkable versions of "Yesterdays" (more advanced than any other Bebop solo), a rapid "I Know That You Know," and "Humoresque." All of Tatum's Decca recordings are on *Classic Early Solos*, *I Got Rhythm*, and *Solos*,

other than a few numbers with singer Joe Turner. Tatum's sessions of 1934 and 1937 are found on *Classic Early Solos,* including "Emaline," two versions of "After You've Gone," "The Shout," "Liza," and "The Sheik of Araby." *Solos* has 15 selections from 1940, such as "Humoresque," "Get Happy," "Indiana," a remake of "Tiger Rag," and a memorable reworking of "Begin the Beguine." *I Got Rhythm,* other than three solos from 1939, puts the emphasis on Tatum's rare work with other musicians during the era, including band dates from 1935, 1937, and 1940 and ten standards by the Tatum-Grimes-Stewart Trio in 1944. Tatum's radio transcriptions for the Standard company are reissued in full on the two-CD Music & Arts package, very concise (mostly two- to three-minute) solo performances that include a few songs he did not otherwise document. *God Is in the House* contains live cuts dating from 1940–41 that were part of the Jerry Newman Collection that also resulted in rare jam session dates by other musicians from Minton's and Monroe's Uptown House. Tatum is heard on piano solos, taking a couple of very rare vocals ("Knockin' Myself Out" and "Toledo Blues"), and stretching out on versions of "Lady Be Good" and "Sweet Georgia Brown" with trumpeter Frankie Newton and bassist Ebenezer Paul in a trio. *Tea for Two* finds Tatum playing in an unchanged style (unaffected by Bop) during lesser-known solo sessions from 1944–45 plus a trio version of "Tea for Two" and hot run-throughs of "Royal Garden Blues" and "I Got Rhythm" with an all-star nonet that includes Roy Eldridge, Charlie Shavers, Ben Webster, and clarinetist Edmond Hall. *The V-Discs* contains three trio numbers and a variety of solo pieces from 1945–46 that, although often quite relaxed, have their wondrous moments.

8 *The Complete Capitol Recordings, Volume One / July 13, 1949–Dec. 20, 1952 / Capitol 92866*

8 *The Complete Capitol Recordings, Volume Two / Sept. 29, 1949–Dec. 20, 1952 / Capitol 92867*

9 *20th Century Piano Genius / Apr. 16, 1950 + July 3, 1955 / Verve 314 531 763*

* *The Complete Pablo Solo Masterpieces / Dec. 28, 1953–Aug. 15, 1956 / Pablo 7PACD-4404*

* *The Complete Group Masterpieces / June 25, 1954– Sept. 11, 1956 / Pablo 6PACD-4401*

There was no reason for Art Tatum to alter his style in the 1950s for he was still as advanced as any pianist around and always had the ability to scare all potential competitors, even

Oscar Peterson! His 20 piano solos from 1949 and eight trio cuts with Everett Barksdale and Slam Stewart in 1952 for the Capitol label are split evenly on the two single discs titled *The Complete Capitol Recordings.* Even with the many remakes, this music is quite impressive. The two-CD *20th Century Piano Genius* gives listeners an idea of what Tatum sounded like at after-hours clubs, although it was actually recorded privately at a pair of Beverly Hills parties in 1950 and 1955. The 39 numbers find Tatum sounding similar to his studio recordings except that a few of the numbers feature him really stretching out. Most of the standards are taken at relaxed, medium tempos, but Tatum's double- and triple-time lines keep the results consistently exciting.

Pablo has released two box sets that reissue in full all of Art Tatum's work for Norman Granz; the music is also available as eight solo and eight combo CDs. The unaccompanied piano solos heard in the seven-CD box *The Complete Pablo Solo Masterpieces* were recorded in marathon sessions, but not much planning went into them and no real surprises occur, just one song after another (mostly swing standards) performed in workmanlike fashion. The band recordings, *The Complete Group Masterpieces,* a six-CD set, are more unique and they do frequently rank as masterpieces. The only Bop players who participated were Buddy DeFranco, Barney Kessel, and Red Callender; pity that Tatum was never teamed up on records with Dizzy Gillespie, Charlie Parker, or Coleman Hawkins. However, the pianist is heard in trios with Benny Carter and Louis Bellson, Lionel Hampton and Buddy Rich, and Red Callender and Jo Jones, and in quartets with Roy Eldridge, bassist John Simmons, and drummer Alvin Stoller, Ben Webster, Callender, and drummer Bill Douglass, and one with DeFranco in Webster's place. Essential music with many exciting moments.

FILMS

Other than a much-too-brief spot on a mid-1940s newsreel with his trio, Art Tatum's only film appearance is playing blues in a jam session scene in *The Fabulous Dorseys* (1947).

LEO WATSON

b. Feb. 27, 1898, Kansas City, MO, d. May 2, 1950, Los Angeles, CA

Leo Watson was a crazy singer who predated Babs Gonzales, Joe "Bebop" Carroll, Dizzy Gillespie, the Bop-oriented scat vocalists, and even Slim Gaillard. Watson made up words and sounds as he went along, and his often-bizarre vocals were usually quite humorous.

As early as 1929, Watson was in a vocal group that played shows and toured with the Whitman Sisters. When the unit went out on its own, it was named the Spirits of Rhythm. Guitarist Teddy Bunn was the solo star, and three of the singers (including Watson) also played tiples, small ukuleles. Watson would be with the Spirits off and on into 1941, the steadiest employment of his life. He also recorded with the Washboard Rhythm Kings, played drums and trombone with John Kirby during part of 1937, and spent a few months with the big bands of Artie Shaw and Gene Krupa, recording a few songs with each orchestra plus one date as a leader. Watson worked solo in Los Angeles during the first half of the 1940s, sometimes sharing the bill with Slim Gaillard (for whom he occasionally played drums) and Harry "the Hipster" Gibson in the mid-1940s. In 1946 he recorded four of his best titles, including impressionistic lyrics on "Jingle Bells," but his musical career was largely finished after that. Leo Watson only worked in music on a sporadic basis during his last period. When he died from pneumonia at the age of 52, he had been completely forgotten for several years. Although he was a natural to be in the Bebop movement, no one thought of bringing him to New York to perform with the Bebop giants.

10 *Spirits of Rhythm 1932–34 / Nov. 23, 1932–Sept. 4, 1941 / Retrieval 79004*

All of the recordings of the Spirits of Rhythm are on this single CD. Leo Watson is heard not only with the Spirits (in 1933–34 and 1941) but on dates backing singers Red McKenzie and Ella Logan plus sessions with the Washboard Rhythm Kings in 1932 and the Five Cousins (the Spirits under a different name). Despite the CD's title and its listing the final session as September 4, 1934, that was actually a reunion date from 1941. Watson's vocal contributions are often adventurous and eccentric, and the Spirits of Rhythm (on such songs as "I Got Rhythm," "I'll Be Ready When the Great Day Comes," "My Old Man," and "Shoutin' in That Amen Corner") lives up to its name. Fun music.

FILMS

Leo Watson is briefly in *Panama Hattie* (1942) and is in a scene with Bill "Bojangles" Robinson in *Stormy Weather* (1943).

BEN WEBSTER

b. Mar. 27, 1909, Kansas City, MO, d. Sept. 20, 1973, Amsterdam, Holland

Ben Webster was a supporter of Bebop and a fan of Charlie Parker's, being very impressed by the altoist from the start. The rise of Bop, just when Webster went out on his own (after his period with Duke Ellington), eventually cut into his work, but his recordings for Norman Granz in the 1950s remind listeners how viable a tenor saxophonist Webster always was.

Ben Webster ranks just below Coleman Hawkins and Lester Young among the major pre-Bop tenors. His huge and highly expressive sound (which could be alternately brutish and raspy on up-tempo material and very warm on romantic ballads) was influenced by Hawkins, but he stood out. His style was a lot simpler (he never knew chords the way Hawk did), making up in feeling for its lack of complexity. Early on he played violin (which he quickly gave up) and piano (which he always loved) before switching to tenor. Webster took lessons from Budd Johnson and toured for a short time with the Young Family Band (which was headed by Lester Young's father). Webster's early associations included Gene Coy, Jap Allen (1930), Blanche Calloway, the Bennie Moten Orchestra (1931–33), Andy Kirk, Fletcher Henderson (where he replaced Hawkins in 1934), Benny Carter, Willie Bryant, Cab Calloway, Henderson again, Stuff Smith, Roy Eldridge, and Teddy Wilson's Big Band (1939–40). A respected journeyman, Ben Webster became a star during his period with Duke Ellington (1940–43), particularly for his solos on "Cotton Tail" and "All Too Soon." He was Duke's first major tenor soloist and would forever be associated with Ellington, although his period with Duke was actually just a short part of his career.

Webster worked with Raymond Scott's radio orchestra and the John Kirby Sextet and, in the mid-1940s, when Bebop was coming to prominence, he was a fixture on 52nd Street, playing and recording with small advanced swing combos. He used modernists Oscar Pettiford, Al Haig, and Bill DeArango on some of his sessions, although his swing style remained unchanged. After the decline of 52nd Street, Webster struggled a bit. He rejoined Ellington (1948–49), worked with Jay McShann, and spent a period in Kansas City in the early 1950s. However, after hooking up with Norman Granz and signing to his Verve label, he recorded a series of several popular ballad albums and met up on record

(on separate dates) with Art Tatum, Coleman Hawkins, and baritonist Gerry Mulligan; he also went on several tours of Jazz at the Philharmonic. By the early 1960s, Webster's style was once again considered passé and, after the death of his mother in December 1964, he moved to Europe, eventually settling in Copenhagen. Ben Webster spent his final nine years overseas, playing the swing standards he loved and remaining in close-to prime form up until near the end.

7   *King of the Tenors* / May 21, 1953 + Dec. 8, 1953 / Verve 314 519 806
7   *Soulville* / Oct. 15, 1957 / Verve 833551
9   *Music for Loving* / May 28, 1954–Feb. 3, 1955 / Verve 314 527 774
9   *The Soul of Ben Webster* / Mar. 5, 1957–July 1958 / Verve 314 527475

Ben Webster first recorded as a leader for Savoy in 1944 and cut a fine session (using Benny Carter and trumpeter Maynard Ferguson) for Mercury in 1951. It was in 1953 that he began making albums on a regular basis for Norman Granz's Verve label. These four CDs contain the bulk of his high-quality Verve sessions. *King of the Tenors* matches Webster with the Oscar Peterson Quartet for five numbers and with Harry "Sweets" Edison and Benny Carter on the other six cuts. "Tenderly," "Danny Boy," two versions of "That's All," "Cotton Tail," and "Pennies From Heaven" are among the highlights. *Soulville* is in the same vein, with the Oscar Peterson Quartet accompanying Webster on a fine program of ballads and stomps. The double-CD *Music for Loving* has two full Webster albums with strings (*Music for Loving* and *Music with Feeling*), five alternate takes, five added numbers (four with pianist Teddy Wilson), plus the eight songs originally on the album *Harry Carney with Strings,* one of the great baritonist's very few dates as a leader. *The Soul of Ben Webster* (also a twofer) has three unrelated albums. Webster is the leader of a 1958 septet session with trumpeter Art Farmer and fellow tenor Harold Ashby and is a prominent sideman on the other former albums. Harry Edison is in prime form on his *Gee Baby Ain't I Good to You* (with Webster and the Oscar Peterson Quartet), while altoist Johnny Hodges's *Blues-a-Plenty* emphasizes blues, with solos from Hodges, Webster, Roy Eldridge, and trombonist Vic Dickenson.

9   *See You at the Fair* / Mar. 11, 1964–Nov. 10, 1964 / GRP/Impulse 121

8 *Stormy Weather* / *Jan. 30, 1965* / *Black Lion 760108*

8 *Gone with the Wind* / *Jan. 31, 1965* / *Black Lion 760125*

7 *There Is No Greater Love* / *Sept. 5, 1965* / *Black Lion 760151*

8 *The Jeep Is Jumping* / *Sept. 13-21, 1965* / *Black Lion 760147*

7 *Ben Webster Meets Bill Coleman* / *Apr. 27, 1967* / *Black Lion 760141*

7 *Ben & Buck* / *June 3, 1967* / *Sackville 2037*

Webster's final recording before permanently moving to Europe, *See You at the Fair*, was a perfect close to his American years. Joined by a trio with either Hank Jones or Roger Kellaway on piano, the lyrical tenor sounds quite beautiful on "Someone to Watch Over Me" and "Our Love Is Here to Stay"; the original set is augmented by two cuts with the Oliver Nelson Orchestra. Webster flourished in Europe, particularly during his first few years, recording six CDs worth of material in 1965 alone. Each of the four Black Lion sets from that year are easily recommended, with the first three all being recorded at the Club Montmartre in Copenhagen, teaming Webster with pianist Kenny Drew, bassist Niels Pederson, and drummer Alex Riel. Swing standards dominate, with romps on numbers such as "Mack the Knife" and "Sunday" alternating with ballads. *There Is No Greater Love* is from a slightly later Montmartre engagement and has an emphasis on slower tempos; among the songs are "Easy to Love," "Stardust," and "I Got It Bad." *The Jeep Is Jumping* is a bit different, for Webster is heard with a quintet led by trumpeter Arnved Meyer on a date that includes some offbeat material plus exciting versions of the two Duke Ellington–associated tunes "Stompy Jones" and "The Jeep Is Jumping." In fact, the band often sounds like an Ellington small group from the 1930s, an ideal setting for Webster. The 1967 Black Lion release teams Webster with trumpeter Bill Coleman, who was also an expatriate, having arrived in France 19 years before. With support from a British rhythm section, Webster and Coleman (who has two vocals) work together quite well on basic originals and standards such as "Sunday" and two versions of "But Not for Me." A Swiss concert five weeks later finds Webster joining forces with veteran swing trumpeter Buck Clayton and the Henri Chaix Quartet. The two classic horn players had rarely played together before, and Buck would fade quickly in 1968, so it is

lucky that this excellent swing concert (not released until 1994) was recorded.

LPS TO SEARCH FOR

Long overdue to be reissued on CD is the two-LP set *The Big Tenor* (Emarcy 824 836), which contains all of Ben Webster's output for the Emarcy label during 1951–53 (with many alternate takes). The twofer has the tenor's sessions with Jay McShann, Johnny Otis, Dinah Washington, Marshall Royal, and the Ravens in addition to two dates of his own, a sextet with Benny Carter and trumpeter Maynard Ferguson, plus Webster's first encounter with strings.

FILMS

Ben Webster is in *The Sound of Jazz* (1957) and is profiled in *The Brute and the Beautiful* (Shanachie 6302), a 1992 hour-long documentary.

MARY LOU WILLIAMS
b. May 8, 1910, Atlanta, GA, d. May 28, 1981, Durham, NC

Mary Lou Williams enthusiastically encouraged the young modernists of the mid-1940s, helping them to get work and supporting their efforts. A stride pianist when she started out, Williams managed to stay modern throughout her long career, and she easily adapted to Bop, both in her playing and in her arranging.

Mary Lou Scruggs was born in Atlanta, grew up in Pittsburgh, and played piano in public as a child. After dropping out of high school, she worked with Buzzin' Harris as part of John Williams's Syncopators and also after the group became known, independently, as the Synco Jazzers. The pianist married the leader (baritonist John Williams) and thereafter was known as Mary Lou Williams. The band worked in Memphis and Oklahoma City (1927–28) until John Williams joined Terence Holder's Clouds of Joy. In 1929 Andy Kirk took over the band and Mary Lou Williams was one of the group's main arrangers. She recorded with the orchestra from the start, although she was not actually an official member until 1931. Williams developed quickly into a major stride pianist, Kirk's top soloist, and his main arranger. "The Lady Who Swings the Band" was a tribute to her (a musical thank you), while her most famous originals were "Roll 'Em" (recorded by Benny Goodman) and "What's Your Story, Morning Glory?" She was largely responsible for the success of the band, although she was over-shadowed after 1936 by ballad singer Pha Terrell and Kirk's desire to feature more "sweet" music.

In 1942, after divorcing John Williams and becoming bored with big band work, Mary Lou Williams married trumpeter Harold "Shorty" Baker and went out on her own. When Baker joined Duke Ellington's orchestra, Williams traveled with Ellington for a time as one of his staff arrangers. "Trumpets No End" (based on "Blue Skies") was her most famous contribution to Duke's library. Her series of recordings for Asch and Folkways during 1944–45 looked both back to her stride roots and forward to the harmonic innovations of Bebop. Williams always advanced with the times and by the late 1940s could have passed for a swing-influenced Bop pianist, comping with her left hand à la Bud Powell. She wrote the Bebop fable "In the Land of Oo-Bla-Dee" for Dizzy Gillespie's big band, composed the 12-part "Zodiac Suite," and was a member of Benny Goodman's short-lived Bebop combo in 1948 with Stan Hasselgard and Wardell Gray.

After the Bebop era, Williams led trios in the 1950s, spent time overseas in Europe, and then retired from music for three years to concentrate on the Catholic religion. She struggled throughout the 1960s (when she barely recorded), wrote some religious works, and during her last few years, was active as an educator (at Duke University). Mary Lou Williams was one of the few pianists who could play in every style, from stride, swing, and Bop to hard Bop and free jazz (even performing an unsuccessful duet concert with Cecil Taylor), so she enjoyed performing "history of jazz" solo recitals. Her musical open-mindedness helped keep her style young and vital for over 50 years.

- **10** *1927–1940 / Jan. 1927–Nov. 18, 1940 / Classics 630*
- **7** *Zodiac Suite / June 29, 1945 / Smithsonian 40810*
- **7** *Town Hall: The Zodiac Suite / Dec. 31, 1945 / Vintage Jazz Classics 1035*
- **9** *Nite Life / May 1971–Oct. 22, 1971 / Chiaroscuro 103*
- **8** *Live at the Cookery / Nov. 1975 / Chiaroscuro 146*
- **8** *Solo Recital/Montreux Jazz Festival 1978 / July 16, 1978 / Original Jazz Classics 962*

Mary Lou Williams had a long career covering many different musical eras. *1927–1940* shows that, if she had retired in 1940, Williams would still be remembered today for her brilliant stride piano playing. All of her dates as a leader before 1944 are on this highly enjoyable Classics CD. There are three piano solos, ten trio/quartet numbers, and two combo dates with the short-lived tenor Dick Wilson plus six recordings with the Synco Jazzers in 1927. Her "Zodiac Suite" is a dozen selections that are sometimes introspective and at other times playful. The studio version (some cuts are solos while others are played by a trio with bassist Al Lucas and drummer Jack Parker) is on the Smithsonian CD plus five alternate takes. The Town Hall version features the Suite performed by a big band, a symphony orchestra, and guest tenor Ben Webster. That rendition plus a medley of Williams's compositions (including "Lonely Moments," "Roll 'Em" and an extended "Gjon Mill Jam Session") from the concert were released for the first time on the 1991 Vintage Jazz Classics CD.

Moving ahead more than 25 years, *Nite Life* (a double CD) has all of the music from the LP *From the Heart* plus 13 previously unreleased selections. Among the highlights are "Little Joe from Chicago," "What's Your Story, Morning Glory?" "For the Figs," a three-part "Nite Life Variations," and music from a ragtime concert that was improvised rather than written-out, a controversial way to interpret ragtime. Also quite valuable is a closing 32½-minute "Jazz-speak" that has Mary Lou Williams talking about her life. *Live at the Cookery* (duets with bassist Brian Torff) and *Solo Recital* are the type of history of jazz programs that Mary Lou Williams featured in her later years, going from spirituals and stride to swing, Bop, and a bit more modern (reaching up to the style of the late 1950s).

LPS TO SEARCH FOR

The Asch Recordings 1944–47 (Folkways 2966) is a wonderful two-LP box set featuring Williams in the mid-1940s in settings ranging from soloist to big band leader. *First Lady of the Piano* (Inner City 7006) reissues 1953 quartet selections that find Williams sounding very much like a Bebop pianist.

FILMS

Mary Lou Williams is seen with the Slam Stewart Trio in *Boy! What a Girl* (1947).

LESTER YOUNG

b. Aug. 27, 1909, Woodville, MI, d. Mar. 15, 1959, New York, NY

Lester Young was one of the father figures of the Bebop movement even though he actually preferred quiet and

**Lester Young's ability to float over bar lines inspired the Boppers,
while his cool tenor tone helped set the stage for 1950's West Coast Jazz.**

steady playing from his rhythm section. A nonconformist throughout his career, Young introduced a softer tone to the tenor saxophone, and was a subtle improviser whose solos often flowed over bar lines and were speechlike with a calm voice. Although he would be a bigger influence on the "Cool Jazz" saxophonists of the 1950s (including Stan Getz, Zoot Sims, Al Cohn, and Paul Quinichette) than on the Beboppers, Young's sound can be heard in the playing of Illinois Jacquet, Dexter Gordon, and Wardell Gray among others.

Lester Young was one of the giants of jazz history. His father ran a family band that included Lester's brother Lee Young (who became a professional drummer) and sister. Lester grew up in Minneapolis, had lessons on trumpet and violin, and originally played drums and later alto with the Young Family Band. He worked with Art Bronson's Bostonians (1928–29), where he switched permanently to tenor, spent a few years freelancing, and joined the Original Blue Devils (1932–33) when Buster Smith was its leader. Young

also played with Bennie Moten, Clarence Love, King Oliver, and Count Basie (1934), and was Coleman Hawkins's replacement with Fletcher Henderson's orchestra. Unfortunately his light tone and very different style (which was initially influenced by C-melody saxophonist Frankie Trumbauer) was met with opposition by the other sidemen and by Henderson's wife, resulting in a stay with the band of less than three months. After more freelancing and a short stint with Andy Kirk, Young rejoined Count Basie's orchestra in Kansas City.

Lester Young found a very comfortable home with Basie's big band, where his mellow sound and relaxed (yet often hard-swinging) solos fit in perfectly with the light rhythm section. He was a major part of Basie's success after the band went East in late 1936 and was Count's main soloist both in concerts and on records for a four-year period. Nicknamed "Pres" (short for president) by Billie Holiday (whom he called "Lady Day"), Young took many classic solos on records by Basie (including with the Kansas City Six) and Holiday, surprising listeners and musicians alike, who thought that the only way to play tenor was to sound like Coleman Hawkins. And his rare solos on clarinet were the ultimate in "cool."

After leaving Basie for unknown reasons in December 1940, Young led his own small band, co-led a group with his younger brother Lee Young, and worked with Al Sears's Big Band but made few recordings. In October 1943 Young returned to Basie's orchestra. Although the Musicians Union recording strike kept the big band from recording, Pres can be heard on air checks from the period and on some classic small-group titles, including "Sometimes I'm Happy" and "Afternoon of a Basie-ite" with pianist Johnny Guarnieri and Slam Stewart. Young also starred in the memorable film short *Jammin' the Blues*.

Unfortunately, Lester Young was soon drafted. He had a horrible time in the Army from October 1944 through the summer of 1945. He lived in very racist surroundings (which he had managed to largely avoid in his earlier years), was framed for drugs, and served time in a military prison. The experience permanently affected his state of mind. However, writers who have since used this dark chapter in his life to prove that Young's playing was not any good in his postwar years have simply not heard his recordings. In truth, Lester Young did some of his finest work during the second half of the 1940s, when he recorded for Aladdin and toured with Jazz at the Philharmonic. His playing now had a tinge of sadness. But when he was healthy enough, he was quite capable of playing one classic chorus after another. Usually leading a quartet or quintet, through the years Young utilized such young modern players as pianists Argonne Thornton, Junior Mance, Kenny Drew, and John Lewis, bassists Aaron Bell and Gene Ramey, drummers Roy Haynes and Connie Kay, and trumpeter Jesse Drakes. He recorded regularly for Verve and had a few reunions with Count Basie, including at the 1957 Newport Jazz Festival and on the television special *The Sound of Jazz*.

The 1950s should have been a golden age for Pres, since he was a major influence on younger tenors, was making decent money (thanks to Norman Granz), and was recognized as a giant by the jazz world. But unfortunately his state of mind was slipping and Young's will to live declined. He drank constantly while barely eating, invented a new spoken language of his own to discourage outsiders, and wasted away. When he was healthy, he played magnificently, but there were times when Young was too weak to play a coherent chorus. His health steadily declined after 1955 (although there were some great musical moments during the next two years). After an early-1959 visit to France, he returned home and drank himself to death. Lester Young was just 49.

9 *The "Kansas City" Sessions / Mar. 16, 1938–Mar. 27, 1944 / Commodore 402*
9 *1943–1946 / Dec. 28, 1943–Apr. 1946 / Classics 932*
10 *The Complete Aladdin Sessions / July 15, 1942–Dec. 29, 1947 / Blue Note 32787*

The Commodore disc has the three sessions by the Kansas City Five and Six, including all of the alternate takes. The Kansas City Five sides of March 16, 1938 (with trumpeter Buck Clayton, rhythm guitarist Freddie Green, bassist Walter Page, and drummer Jo Jones), feature Eddie Durham taking his first historic electric guitar solos, a year before Charlie Christian. The September 28, 1938, band is the same except that Lester Young is prominent on tenor and clarinet; his clarinet spot on "I Want a Little Girl" finds him sounding like altoist Paul Desmond from 20 years later! Also on this disc is a March 27, 1944, set that is more conventional, with Young, trumpeter Bill Coleman, and trombonist Dicky Wells (in top form) assisted by pianist Joe Bushkin, bassist John Simmons, and Jo Jones for driving versions of swing standards, including "Three Little Words" and three versions of "I Got Rhythm." *1943–1946* has Pres's first dates as a leader, including the famous "Afternoon of a Basie-ite/ Sometimes I'm Happy" session of 1943, a quintet set for Savoy with Count Basie, his first two Aladdin sessions, plus a historic trio outing with Nat King Cole and Buddy Rich. The two-CD *The Complete Aladdin Sessions* features some of the very best post-war Pres. The twofer begins with a 1942 date with Nat Cole in a trio with bassist Red Callender, and then there is Young's important 1945–46 recordings, including such gems as "D. B. Blues," "New Lester Leaps In," "Sunday," "Jumpin' with Symphony Sid" (which was a hit), "One O'Clock Jump," and "Tea for Two." The supporting cast includes trombonist Vic Dickenson, altoist Willie Smith, trumpeter Shorty McConnell, and pianists Dodo Marmarosa and Argonne Thornton. In addition, there is a rare set led by singer Helen Humes that has Pres as a sideman. Essential music.

* *The Complete Lester Young Studio Sessions on Verve / Mar. 1946–Mar. 4, 1959 / Verve 314 547 087*

8   *With the Oscar Peterson Trio / Nov. 28, 1952 / Verve 314 521 451*

9   *Jazz Giants '56 / Jan. 12, 1956 / Verve 825 672*

8   *Pres and Teddy / Jan. 13, 1956 / Verve 831 270*

Most of Lester Young's Verve recordings are quite worthwhile, and some rank with the best work of his career. The eight-CD *Complete on Verve* box has several classic sessions, including Pres's trio outing with Nat King Cole and Buddy Rich, superb encounters with the Oscar Peterson Trio and Teddy Wilson, and the Jazz Giants '56 date. There are also more erratic collaborations with Harry Edison, two albums with his regular working group (which has trumpeter Jesse Drakes), trio sets with John Lewis or Hank Jones on piano, a touching clarinet solo on "They Can't Take That Away From Me," his rather weak final recording, and Young's intriguing interviews with Chris Albertson and Francois Postif in 1958 and '59. More casual listeners are well advised to pick up any of the following three single-disc Verve reissues, which feature Young in his late prime: *With the Oscar Peterson Trio, Jazz Giants '56* (which matches Pres with Roy Eldridge and Vic Dickenson), and *Pres and Teddy*.

7   *In Washington, D.C., 1956, Vol. 1 / Dec. 3–9, 1956 / Original Jazz Classics 782*

7   *In Washington, D.C., 1956, Vol. 2 / Dec. 3–9, 1956 / Original Jazz Classics 881*

7   *In Washington, D.C., 1956, Vol. 3 / Dec. 3–9, 1956 / Original Jazz Classics 901*

7   *In Washington, D.C., 1956, Vol. 4 / Dec. 3–9, 1956 / Original Jazz Classics 963*

7   *In Washington, D.C., 1956, Vol. 5 / Dec. 3–9, 1956 / Original Jazz Classics 993*

In addition, these five CDs, recorded during a week's engagement at a Washington, D.C. jazz club, find Lester Young in surprisingly strong form, jamming standards with a local rhythm section (pianist Bill Potts, bassist Willie Williams, and drummer Jim Lucht) and on *Vol. 5* trombonist Earl Swope. Young's renditions are joyful, swinging, and creative. Among the last great recordings of Pres.

FILMS

Lester Young is the star of *Jammin' the Blues* (1944), takes the most memorable chorus of *The Sound of Jazz* (1957), and is definitively portrayed in the documentary *Song of the Spirit (Song of the Spirit)*. The last includes all of the footage from *Jammin' the Blues* plus many interviews with Young's contemporaries.

BEBOP FROM 1945 TO 1949

The year 1945 was when Bebop really emerged and began to cause a shock wave in the jazz world. During 1946–47, it consolidated its gains and helped drive a nail into the coffin of the big band era. A second Musicians Union strike kept most musicians off records in 1948, but that strike was not as tightly enforced as the first one; among the recordings that were made semilegally were Charlie Parker's "Parker's Mood." It was at that point that the major record labels (including Capitol and Victor) decided to latch onto Bop, hoping that it would be as big a moneymaker as swing had been. The mass media began to pay attention to Bop but unfortunately focused mostly on stereotypes such as Dizzy Gillespie and some of his followers' tastes in eyeglasses, berets, and goatees. By 1949 it seemed briefly as if Bop were everywhere and even many of the surviving swing big band leaders tried their best to play the new music, with varying results.

But then in 1950 the Bop fad collapsed. The larger labels deserted the music and stopped promoting Bop, the surviving swing bandleaders returned to their original styles, and the big bands of Dizzy Gillespie and Woody Herman broke up. The music survived and continued to evolve but no longer received all that much attention from the general public, being overshadowed by pop singers, novelties, rhythm and blues, Dixieland, and especially television. Within a couple years West Coast Cool Jazz was receiving the main headlines in the jazz press, but Bebop would continue both as an important influence and, in the hands of its more dedicated practitioners (such as Sonny Stitt), as an independent music form that nearly every young jazz musician explored before creating newer styles.

Here are a few highlights from the years of Classic Bebop:

1945: Charlie Parker and Dizzy Gillespie make their first joint recordings and amaze the jazz world. Gillespie leads a short-lived big band that quickly fails. Coleman Hawkins's Sextet with Howard McGhee visits Los Angeles and helps to introduce Bebop to the West Coast. Bird and Dizzy soon follow, teaming up for a Los Angeles engagement at Billy Berg's club opposite Slim Gaillard. Miles Davis, who had met Parker in New York, travels to the West Coast with Benny Carter's orchestra. Dave Lambert and Buddy Stewart record "What's This" (the first Bebop vocal) with Gene Krupa's orchestra. J. J. Johnson and Illinois Jacquet are the solo stars with Count Basie's orchestra. Artie Shaw's orchestra and his Gramercy Five feature Dodo Marmarosa and Barney Kessel. Oscar Pettiford joins the Duke Ellington Orchestra. Sarah Vaughan leaves the Billy Eckstine big band and begins her very successful solo career. Clyde Hart dies.

1946: The big band era collapses. Dizzy Gillespie leaves for New York while Charlie Parker cashes in his plane ticket and misses the flight. Parker tours with Jazz at the Philharmonic but struggles in Los Angeles, trying to combat his heroin withdrawals with alcohol. After a disastrous recording session and a few incidents, he is committed to Bellevue Hospital. Gillespie forms his successful Bebop big band, which lasts for three years. Erroll Garner begins to catch on as a popular attraction. Babs Gonzales leads his Three Bips and a Bop. Woody Herman's Herd with Flip Phillips, Bill Harris, and Sonny Berman is a sensation but breaks up before the end of the year. New York's 52nd Street begins to seriously decline while Los Angeles's Central Avenue district grows as a major jazz nightlife area. Red Rodney is Gene Krupa's main trumpet soloist. Kai Winding joins Stan Kenton's big band. Claude Thornhill forms his second orchestra, with Gil Evans as an important arranger.

1947: Released from Bellevue, Charlie Parker soon returns to New York, where he puts together his finest working group, a quintet with Miles Davis, Duke Jordan, Tommy Potter, and Max Roach. Bird and Diz have a reunion for a Carnegie Hall concert. Chano Pozo joins Gillespie's orchestra and Afro-Cuban (or Latin) jazz is born. Bud Powell and Thelonious Monk record their first sessions as leaders. Gillespie's big band is featured in the film *Jivin' in Bebop*. Billy Eckstine breaks up his orchestra. Chubby Jackson's Bebop group tours Scandinavia. Dexter Gordon records "The Chase" with Wardell Gray and "The Duel" with Teddy Edwards. Stan Hasselgard moves to New York from Sweden. With his Second Herd (featuring Stan Getz, Zoot Sims, Herbie Steward, and Serge Chaloff), Woody Herman records "Four Brothers." J. J. Johnson records with Charlie Parker and joins Illinois Jacquet's band. Freddie Webster and Sonny Berman die.

1948: Despite the recording strike, Bird records the classic "Parker's Mood." Later in the year he is heard in prime form broadcasting from the Royal Roost. In December, Miles Davis goes out on his own and is replaced in Parker's quintet by Kenny Dorham. The Dizzy Gillespie Orchestra visits Europe. Ray Brown marries Ella Fitzgerald. Tadd Dameron's sextet includes Fats Navarro. Terry Gibbs joins Woody Herman's Second Herd. The short-lived Benny Goodman Septet includes Wardell Gray, Stan Hasselgard, and Mary Lou Williams. Hasselgard dies in a car accident on November 18. Chano Pozo is killed in a bar brawl.

1949: Charlie Parker records with strings. Gene Ammons, Milt Jackson, and Oscar Pettiford join Woody Herman's Second Herd. Oscar Peterson makes his American debut at a Jazz at the Philharmonic concert. The big bands of Charlie Barnet, Artie Shaw, and even Benny Goodman are Bop-oriented, but all three break up by the end of the year. James Moody records a version of "I'm In the Mood for Love" that would be the basis for King Pleasure's "Moody's Mood for Love" vocalese classic three years later. Bud Powell records with a quintet that includes Fats Navarro and Sonny Rollins. Sonny Stitt makes his recording debut as a leader. The peak of the Bebop era is reached on Christmas Day during a Carnegie Hall concert featuring Charlie Parker's quintet (with Red Rodney), Bud Powell, Miles Davis, Serge Chaloff, Sonny Stitt, Stan Getz, Lennie Tristano, and Sarah Vaughan, among others. Miles Davis's "Birth of the Cool" Nonet signals the end of an era.

Why Bebop Did Not Become Popular

Swing overlapped with pop music constantly during 1935–46; in fact, swing could be considered the pop music of its day. In contrast, Bebop never caught on with the general public even though it influenced pop and virtually every style of nonclassical music. There were quite a few reasons that Bebop never made the Hit Parade:

1) Due to the first Musicians Union strike and World War II, the general public never had an opportunity to be introduced gradually to Bebop. It just seemed to spring from out of nowhere, and listeners accustomed to Glenn Miller were often quite startled by what they heard. When Benny Goodman launched the swing era in 1935, there had been similar swing bands at least as early as the Casa Loma Orchestra in 1930, and the music served as a logical push forward for the mainstream. When Bebop was heard in 1945, some listeners questioned not only whether it was good or whether it was considered jazz but whether it was music at all!

2) Because Bebop was a giant leap forward and the musicians did not give in to commercial pressures, its potential for sales was cut drastically. Few musicians employed female singers, played novelties (unless they were tied in with the esoteric nature of the music), or went out of their way to sell their music, other than Dizzy Gillespie, who was a natural showman.

3) A large reason for swing's popularity had been that it was considered dance music. Bebop was quite danceable (even at its most rapid tempos people could dance at half speed), and it employs a 4/4 rhythm that can be heard. But, due to the collapse of the big bands, countless dance halls closed during 1945–46. When people of the mid- to late 1940s danced, it was to singers of romantic ballads and to rhythm and blues combos. If the leaders of Bop had been more interested in selling the style as dance music (rather than as an art form that demanded that the audience sit down and listen quietly), they might have kept some of the audience. However, a 30% cabaret tax (which was reduced after a while to 20%) was a major incentive for jazz clubs to eliminate dance floors altogether.

4) Bebop was subject to the same problems that helped end the swing era. There was strong competition from other styles of music (including Dixieland, pop singers, rhythm and blues, and nostalgic dance bands, not to mention hillbilly music). Veterans from World War II were often more concerned with building a family and working at a good job than with going out to enjoy music. And the rise of television in the late 1940s severely cut into the potential audience, which was no longer used to visiting dance halls and clubs on a regular basis.

5) Bebop players and jazz musicians in general had a bad reputation by the mid-1940s. Because they played where alcohol flowed freely and they performed primarily at night (and slept by day), jazz players were thought of as bums by some of the more conservative Americans. Many musicians became alcoholics (the nighttime environment did not help), and quite a few smoked marijuana. Gene Krupa's marijuana bust in 1943 (which was blown out of proportion) made national headlines and inspired narcotics agents to try to top each other and nab bigger and bigger names. And

unfortunately the use of heroin (a much more serious drug than marijuana) began to become epidemic in jazz at that time. Charlie Parker (who somehow avoided prison) was a heroin addict from the time he was a young teenager and, despite his wishes, many other Beboppers followed his example. Dizzy Gillespie stayed clean, but quite a few of the most important young jazz musicians of the 1940s and '50s spent at least part of their careers as heroin addicts, and some (including Dexter Gordon, Gene Ammons, Tadd Dameron, Joe Albany, and Red Rodney, among others) served prison time that caused interruptions in their careers; Billie Holiday's troubles were particularly well publicized. Even more serious, Sonny Berman, Freddie Webster, and Wardell Gray died directly from their heroin use, and the drug helped lead to the premature deaths of Charlie Parker and Fats Navarro. It was a plague that did not lessen in jazz until the 1960s; fortunately it is a problem for only relatively few jazz musicians today.

The drug use led to unreliability, and that certainly did not help the image of jazz and Bebop. The mass media's depiction of modernists as nutty pill poppers who were amusing but could not be trusted made Bebop seem dangerous and forbidden, not suitable for the middle class.

6) In addition to these problems, in the mid-1940s younger jazz musicians wanted their music to be treated as an art form rather than as entertainment. Some performers barely acknowledged their audience and seemed to be playing only for themselves. Showmanship (other than Dizzy Gillespie's) was frowned upon along with any real attempt to widen the audience. The result is that many people permanently cut their ties to jazz, preferring to listen nostalgically to Benny Goodman and not bother with Charlie Parker. And because virtually all of the most important Bebop innovators were black (there was no Harry James or Tommy Dorsey to appeal to conservative white audiences), Bebop was thought of as an esoteric minority music.

And yet Bebop was one of the most lively and exciting musical styles ever created. But only when it was tamed a bit and transformed in the 1950s into both the softer, cooler West Coast jazz and the more soulful Hard Bop would jazz recapture some of the audience that had been lost.

The Giants of Bebop

As with any style of jazz, Bebop had many musicians who were responsible for the music's formation and development, including the ones listed in the Pacesetters section. However, I cannot imagine Bebop even being formed without the existence of Charlie Parker and Dizzy Gillespie.

The brilliance of Charlie Parker's quick mind, technique, and constant creativity both astounded and inspired the younger musicians who came up directly after him. Dizzy Gillespie's very adventurous solos were a match for Parker's, and both his showmanship and his desire to write everything down (and teach Bebop to anyone willing to listen) helped make Bop a permanent part of jazz. Bud Powell completely transformed the way that the piano is played in jazz, indirectly changing the function of each part of the rhythm section. Max Roach extended the innovations of Kenny Clarke and became the definitive Bop drummer in addition to being an important bandleader for decades. And Thelonious Monk (Tadd Dameron's significance notwithstanding) was the top jazz composer to emerge from the Bebop era in addition to being a pianist so original that his individuality epitomized the spirit of Bebop.

CHARLIE PARKER

b. Aug. 29, 1920, Kansas City, KS, d. Mar. 12, 1955, New York, NY

Charlie "Bird" Parker towers over the Bebop era and all of jazz that followed. Considered a genius due to his very original style, Parker had the ability to create remarkably coherent solos at ridiculously fast tempos; slow down his improvi-

sations to half speed; and in most cases, every note he played fits. As with Louis Armstrong and Lester Young before him and Miles Davis and John Coltrane in later years, Parker's ideas and phrases (even his throwaways) became a permanent part of jazz's vocabulary, emulated, copied, and studied by countless younger musicians.

Bird's rapid musical thoughts and knack for creating completely new melodies over chord changes was unprece-

Charlie Parker (seen in 1947 with Miles Davis) was such a dominant influence on jazz that even his throwaway ideas became part of the jazz vocabulary.

dented at the time, as was his advanced harmonic sense. He was also an underrated composer. Parker wrote "Yardbird Suite," "Confirmation," "Scrapple from the Apple," "Ko Ko" (a rapid improvisation played over the chord changes of "Cherokee"), and such blues lines as "Now's the Time," "Billie's Bounce," and "Parker's Mood."

Unfortunately Charlie Parker's lifestyle was far from stable and was also destructively influential. A heroin addict since he was a teenager, Parker never recommended heroin to anyone else, and he was distressed when it became epidemic in the jazz world, partly because some musicians mistakenly thought that it might have added to Bird's genius. In addition to heroin making his life quite difficult, Parker also drank excessively at times (often when he was trying to stay off heroin), ate huge amounts of food, and never took much care of his health. He lived to be only 34; a doctor examining his body after his death concluded that he was in his mid-50s!

Charlie Parker packed a lot of living into his brief life. Born in Kansas City, Kansas, he grew up in Kansas City, Missouri. He started on baritone horn, switching to alto when he was ten. Parker found the Kansas City jazz scene so appealing that he dropped out of school when he was 14 to try to make it as a musician, even though he was clearly not ready. He was humiliated at a few jam sessions but kept at it. Parker spent a summer woodshedding to Lester Young records, and by the fall he had his early style together. Local musicians were impressed. In 1937 Parker became a member of Jay McShann's Orchestra. His nickname of "Yardbird" or "Bird" came about during this period. Although its origins have been disputed, it seems that it had something to do with his love of eating chicken.

After playing with McShann and other musicians in Kansas City (including Lawrence Keyes, Harlan Leonard, and Buster Smith, who Parker said influenced his sound), in 1939 Bird visited New York for the first time. The highlight of the trip was probably when he worked for a time as a dishwasher at a restaurant, specifically so he could hear Art Tatum play there every night! Back in Kansas City, in 1940 he made his recording debut on some private recordings with a small group from Jay McShann's band. Parker's playing on "Lady Be Good" and "Honeysuckle Rose," while showing his debt to Lester Young, was already quite original and innovative. In 1941, the Jay McShann Orchestra signed with Decca and traveled to New York. Unfortunately the group was stereotyped by the label as a blues band, and its studio recordings were mostly all blues; they did not have an opportunity to document their more advanced arrangements. However, Parker's short solos on a few of the numbers were heard and admired by musicians of the era. He had more opportunities to stretch out on radio broadcasts with McShann (a couple of which were finally released on record in the 1990s) and in after-hours jam sessions at Monroe's Uptown House and Minton's Playhouse.

Charlie Parker was barely on records at all during 1942–44, although some private recordings came out decades later that help to trace his evolution. After leaving McShann in 1942, Parker worked with Noble Sissle, and in 1943 he became part of Earl Hines's Big Band. Since there was no opening on alto, Bird switched to tenor for that gig. Among the other sidemen in the orchestra were Dizzy Gillespie (whom Parker had first met and jammed with in 1940), Sarah Vaughan, and Billy Eckstine. Together they helped make the Earl Hines band into the first Bebop orchestra, but unfortunately that association went completely unrecorded. Bird had brief associations with the Cootie Williams Big Band and Andy Kirk and then spent a few months with the Billy Eckstine Big Band in 1944, but he departed before Eckstine had an opportunity to record. The first time that the mature Bird appears on record is on a 1944 four-song session led by Tiny Grimes that resulted in "Red Cross."

Parker started really making history during the first few months of 1945, when he teamed up regularly with Dizzy Gillespie on 52nd Street. Their music, featuring rapid unisons, crackling solos, and lots of fresh ideas, amazed listeners. "Bird and Diz" collaborated on a set of classic studio recordings (issued under Gillespie's name), including "Groovin' High," "Dizzy Atmosphere," "Hot House," and

"Shaw 'Nuff." Later in the year Parker led his first record date (which resulted in "Thriving From A Riff," "Now's the Time," "Billie's Bounce," and the monumental "Ko Ko") and then traveled to Los Angeles with Dizzy. Their group helped to introduce Bebop to the West Coast and impressed many young musicians, but their engagement at Billy Berg's attracted mostly disappointingly small audiences. After a couple months, Dizzy Gillespie bought plane tickets for the band to return to New York, but Bird cashed his in and bought drugs instead. It would be some time before he came back East.

While in Los Angeles, Parker performed locally, usually using either Miles Davis or Howard McGhee on trumpet along with top local musicians. He started an association with the Dial label even though he was signed to Savoy (his Savoy and Dial recordings during the next couple of years included many classics), and he played a few concerts with Jazz at the Philharmonic, constructing a very memorable two-chorus solo on "Lady Be Good" that would later be turned into vocalese by Eddie Jefferson. Unfortunately, though, there was a heroin shortage by the late spring and Parker tried to combat his withdrawal symptoms with alcohol. While his March 28, 1946, recording date with Miles Davis resulted in the debut of "Moose the Mooche," "Yardbird Suite," and "Ornithology," the July 29 session with Howard McGhee was a complete disaster. Parker was in terrible shape but recorded four songs anyway, a pair of overly fast romps plus "The Gypsy" and "Lover Man." His timing and tone were off, he was lost in spots, and he was unable to finish the session. Later in the day he had a complete mental breakdown. After accidentally setting his hotel room on fire, he was committed to the Camarillo State Hospital. During his six month confinement, the recordings from the "Lover Man" session were released, to his dismay.

Against the odds, in 1947 Charlie Parker was released, in the best health of his career. His next few years would be full of accomplishments. After recording two dates in Los Angeles (among them "Dark Shadows" with singer Earl Coleman and the Erroll Garner Trio plus an instrumental date with Howard McGhee, Wardell Gray, and Dodo Marmarosa that included "Relaxin' at Camarillo"), Parker returned to New York. Soon he had formed his finest working group, a quintet with Miles Davis, Duke Jordan, Tommy Potter, and Max Roach. Recognized as the most important modern musician in jazz by his contemporaries (although Dizzy Gillespie was much better known to the general public), Parker was soon at the height of his fame. His group recorded such notable numbers as "Donna Lee," "Chasin' the Bird," "Bongo Bop," "Embraceable You," "Scrapple from the Apple," "Crazeology," "Bird Gets the Worm," "Barbados," "Constellation," and "Parker's Mood," among others. Although there were some personnel changes in the quintet (John Lewis and Al Haig had their turns in the piano chair, Curly Russell was sometimes on bass and when Miles Davis departed in December 1948 he was replaced by Kenny Dorham), this was Bird's golden era. He visited Europe in 1949 and 1950, toured with Jazz at the Philharmonic (playing opposite Lester Young), signed with Verve in 1949, and soon realized his dream of recording with violins in the "Bird 'n' Strings" series, which resulted in one classic ("Just Friends") and some of the most accessible and popular music of his career. He had a reunion with Dizzy Gillespie at a 1947 Carnegie Hall concert and on Christmas Eve 1949 was part of an all-star Bebop concert (also at Carnegie Hall), playing a stunning set with his quintet, which by then consisted of Red Rodney, Al Haig, Tommy Potter, and Roy Haynes.

Even with the end of the classic Bebop era, Charlie Parker should have found the early 1950s to be a busy and potentially lucrative period. He was making good money and was recognized in the jazz world as one of the greats. But his heroin addiction and general unreliability cut greatly into his commercial potential. His erratic lifestyle resulted in lost opportunities and in his scuffling instead of flourishing. In 1951 Parker's cabaret license was revoked due to his drug use, making it more difficult for him to find club work in New York until it was reinstated in 1953. He was still capable of playing at his best, which can be heard on a 1951 radio broadcast with Dizzy Gillespie and Bud Powell and the 1953 Massey Hall concert with Diz, Bud, Charles Mingus, and Max Roach, but he was slipping. Moments of brilliance alternated with more indifferent performances, and Parker spoke of how he was becoming bored with Bop; he had played some of the same songs for seven or eight years by then. But whether he would have blazed new paths in the future or become part of the Hard Bop world, and how he would have handled the rise of John Coltrane, Ornette Coleman, and the avant-garde in the 1960s (when he would have still been just in his forties) will never be known. In 1954 Parker (greatly depressed by the death of his baby daughter) tried to commit suicide twice; he spent some time in Bellevue, and he made a few minor comebacks. He was not too pleased with King Pleasure's vocalese version of "Parker's

Mood," which predicted his death! Unfortunately the prediction was not far from the truth, and in 1955 Charlie Parker passed away, prematurely worn out when he should have been just entering his prime.

Bird's legend has grown since his death. During his life, several fanatics (most notably Dean Benedetti) recorded him constantly, and many of those erratic live recordings have since been released. Bird's studio recordings are all in print, there have been many tributes to Parker during the past 45 years, and Clint Eastwood made a well-intentioned movie (*Bird*) that only partly brought Charlie Parker back to life. However, his influence (which is still felt decades later) can be summed up best in the graffiti that appeared shortly after his death: Bird Lives!

9 *The Complete Birth of the Bebop / May 1940–Dec. 29, 1945 / Stash 535*
9 *Early Bird / Aug. 1940–1944 / Stash 542*
Until the mid-1970s, there was very little of Charlie Parker on record prior to the Tiny Grimes session of 1944, just his brief studio solos with Jay McShann's orchestra during 1941–42. However, the Onyx and Stash labels unearthed several very interesting sessions, which were reissued in full on these two CDs in 1991. *The Complete Birth of the Bebop* (the title is a takeoff on Miles Davis's "Birth of the Cool" sessions) starts off with Parker's very first recording, an unaccompanied alto solo from around May 1940 that features him playing "Honeysuckle Rose" and "Body and Soul." Next are four selections in which Parker in 1942 jams on standards (including "Cherokee") while backed by just guitar and drums. Bird is also heard in 1943 (on tenor) playing with a variety of small groups, including a remarkable version of "Sweet Georgia Brown" in a trio with Dizzy Gillespie and Oscar Pettiford and a few instances where he jams along with records by Benny Goodman and Hazel Scott! There are two numbers taken from a 1945 jam session with Gillespie and Don Byas, and the final three performances (extended versions of "Shaw 'Nuff," "Groovin' High," and "Dizzy Atmosphere") are taken from a *Jubilee* radio broadcast of December 29, 1945. During the last, Parker stretches out with a sextet in Los Angeles consisting of Dizzy Gillespie, Milt Jackson, Al Haig, Ray Brown, and drummer Stan Levey. *The Complete Birth of the Bebop* is a rather significant collection.

The same can be said for *Early Bird*. Parker is heard as a sideman with a Jay McShann nonet on November 30, 1940 for his first official recordings (only predated by the solo improv); this music was not released until the 1970s. Although the seven selections (six swing standards plus a blues) have some solid solos from the other musicians, it is the 20-year-old altoist's choruses, particularly his classic spots on "Lady Be Good" and "Honeysuckle Rose," that are most notable and are Bebop in its formative stage. This CD also features Bird jamming on "Cherokee" in 1942 and, most intriguingly, being well featured on a radio broadcast with McShann's big band on February 13, 1942. Unlike in his studio dates with McShann, on the radio Parker had several opportunities to really stretch out, most notably here on "I'm Forever Blowing Bubbles." The recording quality is just decent (the speed wavers a little), but this valuable air check shows today's listeners why musicians at the time were so impressed by Bird's playing in its early stage. Also on the CD are eight numbers by McShann's 1944 band (long after Parker had departed), with tenor-saxophonist Paul Quinichette being the most notable soloist, plus a poorly recorded live version of "I Got Rhythm" by McShann's band with Bird from August 1940. Parker's studio recordings with the Jay McShann big band are reviewed under the bandleader's name.

9   *Yardbird Suite: The Ultimate Charlie Parker Collection / Feb. 28, 1945–Sept. 26, 1952 / Rhino 72260*

10   *The Complete Savoy Studio Sessions / Sept. 15, 1944–Sept. 24, 1948 / Savoy 5500*

10   *The Complete Dial Sessions / Feb. 5, 1946–Dec. 17, 1947 / Stash 567–570*

Yardbird Suite is a 38-song sampler of Charlie Parker's prime years, drawing its material from the catalogs of Musicraft (sides originally released under Dizzy Gillespie's name), Savoy, Dial, and Verve plus live dates owned by Columbia and Jazz Classics. Many (but not all) of the high points of Bird's career are here, including his early collaborations with Gillespie, quite a few of the prime Savoy and Dial performances, and a live date with strings, making this an excellent introduction to Parker's career. More serious Bebop collectors will instead have to get the *Complete Savoy* and *Complete Dial* sets, which feature the genius on most of his finest studio recordings. Because Bird was so important and a constant improviser, all of his alternate takes have their moments of interest (his solos tended to be completely different each time), and happily both the three-CD Savoy and four-CD Dial/Stash sets contain all of his alternate takes

from those sessions. The Savoy reissue (which has unaccountably gone out of print and needs to be reissued again) starts with Parker's date with Tiny Grimes and then has five of his own sessions, outings that usually include Miles Davis and are highlighted by "Billie's Bounce," "Now's the Time," "Ko Ko," "Donna Lee," "Chasing the Bird," "Constellation," and "Parker's Mood." In addition, Parker is heard as a sideman with Davis, switching to tenor and helping to debut four songs, including "Milestones" and "Half Nelson." There are many overlapping and streaky Charlie Parker samplers that have been made available by the Japanese Denon label (which now owns Savoy), but hopefully this very significant music will return again in complete form.

The Dial sessions, which took place during the same period, started out in Hollywood with a truncated session with Gillespie that resulted only in "Diggin' Diz." A set with Miles Davis and top Bop musicians then based in Los Angeles (including Lucky Thompson and Dodo Marmarosa) has the first versions of "Moose the Mooche," "Yardbird Suite," and "Ornithology," but it was followed a few months later by the infamous and somewhat scary "Lover Man" date (which should never have been released). From shortly after his release from Camarillo, Bird is heard on a few poorly recorded jam session numbers and then on an excellent studio date with Earl Coleman and the Erroll Garner Trio. A superb session with Howard McGhee, Wardell Gray, and Marmarosa (highlighted by "Relaxin' at Camarillo") was his farewell to Los Angeles. Back in New York for the remainder of these dates, Parker's last three Dial sessions feature his regular quintet (with Miles Davis, Duke Jordan, Tommy Potter, and Max Roach) plus J. J. Johnson on the final date; highlights include "Dewey Square," "The Hymn," "Embraceable You," "Scrapple from the Apple", and "Crazeology." As with the Savoy set, the many alternate takes add to Bird's legacy.

*   *Bird: Complete on Verve / Jan. 28, 1946–Dec. 10, 1954 / Verve 837 141*

9   *Bird & Diz / June 6, 1950 / Verve 831 133*

5   *Charlie Parker Big Band / July 5, 1950–May 25, 1953 / Verve 314 559 835*

9   *Charlie Parker / Dec. 1947–July 30, 1953 / Verve 314 539 757*

In late 1948, Charlie Parker signed with producer Norman Granz. Granz's labels (Clef, Norgran, and later Verve) would be Bird's musical home for the remainder of his life. The ten-

CD set *Complete on Verve* starts out with Parker's 1946 appearances with Jazz at the Philharmonic, which are highlighted by his famous "Lady Be Good" solo. There is also an exciting 1949 JATP concert with Lester Young, Flip Phillips, and Roy Eldridge that has a brilliant Bird improvisation on "Embraceable You" (one that tops his more famous studio version) and a furious solo on "The Closer." Otherwise, Parker is heard in the studios in a wide variety of settings, including with Machito's orchestra, his *"Bird with Strings"* dates, an all-star outing in 1950 with Gillespie, Thelonious Monk, Curly Russell, and Buddy Rich, a few Latin-oriented dates, a Norman Granz jam session (which teams him with altoists Benny Carter and Johnny Hodges), a few odd orchestra and voices dates, and some small-group sessions. Among the highlights of this magnificent set are "The Bird," "Just Friends," "Star Eyes," the "Afro-Cuban Jazz Suite," "Au Privave," "K.C. Blues," "My Little Suede Shoes," "Blues for Alice," and "Confirmation."

As with the Savoy and Dial sessions, Bird's Verve recordings have also been reissued many times in smaller sets that generally stick to a certain theme or format. *Bird & Diz* has all of the complete takes (including four of "Leap Frog") from the June 6, 1950, all-star outing with Gillespie, Monk, Russell, and Rich. These concise performances include "Bloomdido," "Relaxin' with Lee," and two intriguing versions of "My Melancholy Baby"; this was the only time that Bird and Monk ever recorded together. Although Bird never led an orchestra of his own, *Charlie Parker Big Band* does include his eight titles (arranged by Joe Lippman) with a large group in 1952, plus two Bird-with-strings numbers. Unfortunately more is really less on this set for, not only does it add three not-so-hip titles from 1953 with the Dave Lambert Singers but it has five alternate takes of "In the Still of the Night" and six of "Old Folks," including five false starts!

The 14 selections (plus five full-length alternates and four unnecessary false starts) included on the Verve single-disc known simply as *Charlie Parker* were Bird's only quartet performances for the label, and they were taken from five sessions; also included are septet renditions of "Cardboard" and "Visa." Overall these recordings find Parker at his freest, stretching out on such numbers as "Now's the Time," "Confirmation," "Star Eyes," and "The Bird."

10 *The Complete Live Performances on Savoy / Sept. 29, 1947–Oct. 23, 1950 / Savoy Jazz 17021*

6 *Rara Avis (Rare Bird) / Feb. 21, 1949–1954 / Stash 21*

10 *Charlie Parker and the Stars of Modern Jazz at Carnegie Hall / Dec. 25, 1949 / Jass 16*

7 *The Complete Legendary Rockland Palace Concert 1952 / Sept. 26, 1952 / Jazz Classics 5014*

8 *Boston, 1952 / Dec. 14, 1952–Jan. 18, 1954 / Uptown 27.42*

8 *Montreal, 1953 / Feb. 5 + 7, 1953 / Uptown 27.36*

7 *Bird at the Hi-Hat / Dec. 18, 1953–Jan. 24, 1954 / Blue Note 99787*

7 *Bird / 1988 / Columbia 44299*

Because Charlie Parker was a legendary figure even during his lifetime, he was constantly recorded while performing in clubs and at concerts, often without his knowledge. The CDs covered in this section are among the finest examples of his live performances. In fact, one could argue that Bird never sounded better than on the *Royal Roost* broadcasts of 1948–49, which make up the bulk of the four-CD set *The Complete Live Performances on Savoy*. With Miles Davis or Kenny Dorham on trumpet, Al Haig, Tommy Potter, and Max Roach on most of these numbers (with occasional guests, such as Lucky Thompson, Milt Jackson, and the team of Dave Lambert and Buddy Stewart), Bird is heard as he normally sounded in clubs. He often plays five-minute (as opposed to three-minute) versions of his standards along with some offbeat material, including a classic Beboppish transformation of "White Christmas." In addition, this set has the five numbers that Parker performed with Dizzy Gillespie at their 1947 Carnegie Hall concert (including the most exciting version ever of "Confirmation") and a decent 1950 club date in Chicago with local musicians.

Rara Avis finds Bird featured on a television show in 1949 (including a blues dominated by Sidney Bechet), a 1952 program that is highlighted by a "Bop vs. Dixieland" blues number with Miles Davis, Kai Winding, and a Dixieland group, and some numbers from a 1954 radio broadcast with trumpeter Herb Pomeroy. There is some excessive talking in spots, but Bird fans will enjoy the frequently unusual and previously unissued music.

One of the high points of the entire Bebop era took place on Christmas in 1949. The Carnegie Hall concert that day (much of which is included on the Jass single CD) featured performances by the Bud Powell Trio, a septet with Miles Davis, Serge Chaloff, Sonny Stitt, and Benny Green, the Stan Getz-Kai Winding Quintet, Sarah Vaughan, and the Lennie Tristano Sextet. Good as those performances are, it is the five numbers by the Charlie Parker Quintet (with Red

Rodney, Al Haig, Tommy Potter, and Roy Haynes) that steal the show, particularly stunning versions of "Ko Ko" and "Now's the Time." Rodney rarely sounded better, and Bird is often quite miraculous.

Much of the music from Charlie Parker's 1952 appearance at Rockland Palace has been out in piecemeal fashion before, but usually with terrible recording quality. The two-CD Jazz Classics release greatly improved the sound (making it listenable), corrected the pitch, and expanded the number of tunes from 19 to 31. Parker is heard with a trumpetless quintet (which was very unusual for him), and on some numbers he is joined by a string section and an oboe player. Bird was trying to get beyond Bebop both in his repertoire (which includes Gerry Mulligan's "Gold Rush" and "Rocker," "Repetition," and "Sly Mongoose") and his adventurous solos. *Boston, 1952* has a pair of radio broadcasts (one apiece from 1952 and 1954) with pickup groups featuring either Joe Gordon or Herbie Williams on trumpet and Parker's usual songs, but happily Bird is inspired in both situations and even says a few words to disc jockey Symphony Sid. The recording quality on that set and on *Montreal, 1953* is excellent. The latter has Parker appearing both in concert and on a television special with Canadian musicians, including (on three numbers) the young pianist Paul Bley; tenor saxophonist Brew Moore pops up on two songs, too. *Bird at the Hi-Hat* is from late in Parker's career (an album of Cole Porter tunes for Verve would be his final recording) and features the great altoist in Boston with a local rhythm section and trumpeter Herbie Williams. Although the repertoire (which includes "Now's the Time," "Ornithology," and "My Little Suede Shoes") has no surprises, Charlie Parker showed that there was still life to be found in those familiar chord changes.

The 1988 film *Bird,* a well-intentioned biography of Charlie Parker, was particularly unusual in that some of the solos of Parker (from both studio sessions and rare club dates) were isolated and rerecorded with more current Bop players. Lennie Niehaus was the music supervisor and among the other players heard on the soundtrack album with Bird are pianists Monty Alexander, Barry Harris, and Walter Davis Jr., trumpeters Red Rodney (who played the solos for his own character) and Jon Faddis (who logically ghosted for Dizzy Gillespie), bassists Ray Brown and Ron Carter, and drummer John Guerin. This is a historical curiosity that finds Charlie Parker still sounding surprisingly contemporary.

1 *The Dean Benedetti Recordings of Charlie Parker / Mar. 1, 1947–July 1, 1948 / Mosaic 7-129*

2 *The Unheard Charlie Parker: Bird Seed / 1947–1950 / Stash 2500*

3 *Bird on 52nd Street / July 1948 / Original Jazz Classics 114*

3 *Bird at St. Nick's / Feb. 18, 1950 / Original Jazz Classics 041*

6 *The Bird You Never Heard / Aug. 28, 1950–Jan. 18, 1954 / Stash 10*

6 *Inglewood Jam / June 16, 1952 / Time Is 19801*

Throughout the last decade of his life, Charlie Parker was worshipped by some fanatical fans who tried their best to record every note he played. While some of their tapes are valuable, the fanatics often made the bad decision of turning off their machines when Bird was finished soloing, and the results are often quite difficult to listen to, a series of fragments that add little to one's understanding of Parker. Dean Benedetti was the most famous of the Bird worshippers, and his extensive collection of tapes was lost for decades. The Mosaic label was eventually able to obtain the rights to these legendary performances, and they released every bit of the music as a seven-CD set. But, although they did what they could, including making the sound decent and putting together a large and informative booklet, the incomplete music is very frustrating. Guests such as Thelonious Monk and Carmen McRae are introduced, play two notes, and then the recorder was turned off! It ultimately makes for an annoying listening experience.

The Unheard Charlie Parker looks like it might be significant, until one sees how brief many of the selections are. Parker is heard in a very rare appearance with the Dizzy Gillespie big band in 1948 along with dates with his quintet during 1947–48 and with Chicago musicians in 1950. But the recording quality is poor, and most of the numbers are mere excerpts; still, it is interesting to hear Parker on such unlikely material as "Things to Come," "Good Bait," and "Manteca." *Bird on 52nd Street* is a series of excerpts by Parker with his 1948 band (with Miles Davis, Duke Jordan, Tommy Potter, and Max Roach), while *Bird at St. Nick's* (with Red Rodney, Al Haig, Potter, and Roy Haynes), from 1950, has a remarkable Parker solo on "Confirmation." But once again the recording quality is lousy and little is heard of anyone but Bird. *The Bird You Never Heard* is on a higher level, with all of the performances (except three items with the Chet Baker Quartet in 1953) being complete. Parker is heard with Herb Pomeroy in Boston in 1954; with an unknown band from 1950; and with Bud Powell and percussionist Candido in 1953. The music is not essential but is worth picking up by Parker fans. The same can be said for *Inglewood Jam*, four selections in which Bird jams with Chet Baker (heard just prior to his joining the Gerry Mulligan Quartet), Sonny Criss, pianist Russ Freeman, bassist Harry Babison, and drummer Lawrence Marable; these are among Baker's earliest recordings, and they find Parker and Criss both in fine form, contrasting their very different sounds.

But when it comes to Charlie Parker live recordings, let the buyer beware!

LPS TO SEARCH FOR

The double-LP *Every Bit of It* (Spotlite 150) gathers together many of Charlie Parker's lesser-known sideman recordings of 1945, including dates with the Clyde Hart All-Stars, the Cootie Williams Orchestra, Sarah Vaughan, Sir Charles Thompson, and Slim Gaillard. Highlights include "Sorta Kinda," "Floogie Boo," "Mean to Me," "Takin' Off," and "Slim's Jam." *Yardbird In Lotus Land* (Spotlite 123) features Bird appearing on a January 1946 radio broadcast with Dizzy Gillespie (including extended versions of "Shaw 'Nuff," "Groovin' High," and "Dizzy Atmosphere"), with Miles Davis in an early quintet that includes Joe Albany, and on a medley with fellow altoists Benny Carter and Willie Smith.

A series of radio broadcasts in 1947 sought to have all-star bands of Bebop and Dixieland musicians challenging each other. *Lullaby in Rhythm* (Spotlite 107) has the modern half of the event, with Parker joined by Dizzy Gillespie, clarinetist John LaPorta, pianist Lennie Tristano, Billy Bauer, Ray Brown, and Max Roach on broadcasts from September 13 and 20. In addition to individual features, the most amusing selection is the Bebopper's transformation of "Tiger Rag." Also on this LP are a few fragments of early post-Camarillo live performances of Parker in Los Angeles. *Anthropology* (Spotlite 108) has a November 8, 1947, all-star broadcast (with Fats Navarro, LaPorta, Allen Eager, Tristano, Bauer, Tommy Potter, Buddy Rich, and Sarah Vaughan). Bird gets to romp on "Donna Lee" and "Ko Ko," while Vaughan sings "Everything I Have Is Yours" and Navarro is showcased on "Fats Flats." This album also has three numbers by Tadd Dameron's quintet (with Allen Eager and Wardell Gray on tenors) from September 1948.

Bird with Strings—Live at the Apollo, Carnegie Hall &

Birdland (Columbia 34832) finds Parker doing his best at several locations in 1951, despite the fact that his small string section is capable of playing only written-out music, forcing Bird's solos to be brief and a bit restricted. *Summit Meeting at Birdland* (Columbia 34831) is much more freewheeling, particularly four numbers (including explosive versions of "Blue 'n Boogie" and "Anthropology") performed with Dizzy Gillespie, Bud Powell, Tommy Potter, and Roy Haynes. Also on this exciting LP is a version of "Groovin' High" with the Milt Buckner Trio (probably the only time that Parker can be heard with an organist) and a few numbers with John Lewis, Curly Russell, Kenny Clarke, and (on "Broadway") the guest conga of Candido.

FILMS

Only two sound film clips have thus been found of Charlie Parker. He can be seen playing "Hot House" on a television show in 1952 in a quintet with Dizzy Gillespie and pianist Dick Hyman (which has sometimes been included in other documentaries), and performing "Ballade" in 1950 with Coleman Hawkins. Some additional silent footage exists. The fascinating 1966 Dick Gregory film *Sweet Love, Bitter* (Rhapsody 9019) depicts a saxophonist who has some similarities to Bird; pianist Mal Waldron wrote the score and Charles McPherson ghosted the alto solos. The Clint Eastwood film *Bird* (Warner Home Video), although far from flawless, has some fairly factual scenes and uses Charlie Parker's actual solos in the soundtrack.

DIZZY GILLESPIE

b. Oct. 21, 1917, Cheraw, SC, d. Jan. 6, 1993, Englewood, NJ

The contributions of Dizzy Gillespie, one of the all-time giants of jazz history, to jazz are so huge as to be very difficult to measure. His trumpet style, originally influenced by Roy Eldridge, was quite radical by 1944–45 and still sounds adventurous today. In fact, he could be considered the most advanced of all trumpeters (even over a half-century later), for Gillespie had the ability to hit notes that seemed completely wrong and hold on to them, making them somehow fit, as if putting a square inside a triangle. His technique was quite impressive and his sound distinctive, but it was his highly original phrases and deep knowledge of chord structures that made him one of the greatest trumpeters of all time. In fact, although Howard McGhee and Fats Navarro were

As trumpeter, bandleader, pioneer of Bebop and Afro-Cuban Jazz, goodwill ambassador and informal teacher (not to mention comedian and scat-singer), Dizzy Gillespie contributed to jazz in ways that are impossible to fully measure.

among those influenced by his style, by 1949 most young trumpeters were looking at Navarro and Miles Davis as role models; Dizzy was simply too difficult to copy! It would not be until Jon Faddis appeared in the 1970s that a Gillespie protégé emerged who could sound just like him.

Gillespie's accomplishments went far beyond just his remarkable trumpet playing. As a bandleader, Dizzy had one of the very few Bop-oriented orchestras of 1946–49 (particularly after Billy Eckstine broke up his band in 1947), and he demonstrated that Bebop did not have to be limited to smaller combos. While heading the big band, Dizzy helped to found Afro-Cuban (or Latin) jazz by using Chano Pozo on conga during 1947–48, the first Latin percussionist to be featured regularly with an American jazz orchestra. Gillespie would be a major proponent of Latin jazz throughout his career.

Despite the complexity of his trumpet playing, Gillespie did a great deal to make Bebop seem accessible. One of the

few Bop musicians who was a natural showman, the trumpeter loved to make wisecracks to his audiences, and he enjoyed performing comedy vocals and scatting. Gillespie saw no contradiction between playing creative music and putting on an entertaining show. Because of that fact, he was much better known to the general public during the Bop era than Charlie Parker or any of the other Bop musicians. Also, unlike Bird, whose innovations seemed to fly out of nowhere, Dizzy was quick to explain and demonstrate to other musicians what it was he was doing. Gillespie insisted that other musicians learn to play chords on the piano so they would understand how to improvise better, and he emerged as one of jazz's first important unofficial educators. It is partly due to his willingness to tutor younger players that Bebop became a major part of jazz's mainstream rather than merely being thought of as music for outcasts.

Born the last of nine children to a poor family, John Birks Gillespie (who was nicknamed Dizzy early on due to his wit and sly brilliance) started on trombone, switching to trumpet when he was 12. He won a scholarship to the Laurinburg Institute in North Carolina (an agriculture school), where he studied music, but in 1935 he dropped out of school to try to make it as a musician. Gillespie was particularly inspired by the dramatic playing of Roy Eldridge, whom he heard on records with Teddy Hill and on radio broadcasts. Dizzy gained early experience playing with Frankie Fairfax's orchestra in Philadelphia, and in 1937 he took over Eldridge's old spot with Hill's big band, making his recording debut on "King Porter Stomp," sounding very close to his idol. However, Gillespie, who always had a very strong musical curiosity, would not remain in Eldridge's shadow for long, and he was soon being criticized for stretching himself during solos and not playing it safe.

After his period with Hill ended (following a visit to Europe), Gillespie freelanced for a year and then joined Cab Calloway's orchestra (1939–41). His many short solos on Calloway's records are quite fascinating, for Gillespie can be heard gradually forming his style. "Pickin' the Cabbage" is considered the trumpeter's most famous recording with Cab, but he is also heard on many others. Calloway's criticism of Dizzy's playing during this era (calling it "Chinese music") in hindsight makes sense, for the trumpeter was improvising over more complex chords than the rhythm section was playing! After a fight broke out in 1941 (Gillespie was accused of throwing spitballs at the singer when Calloway was performing on stage, but decades later it was revealed that fellow trumpeter Jonah Jones was the culprit), Dizzy was fired.

In 1940 Gillespie met the man whom he called his "heartbeat," Charlie Parker, and they jammed together now and then, exchanging musical ideas. During 1941–42, Dizzy had short term associations with quite a few bands, including those headed by Ella Fitzgerald (the Chick Webb ghost orchestra), Coleman Hawkins, Benny Carter, Charlie Barnet, Fess Williams, Les Hite, Claude Hopkins, Lucky Millinder, Calvin Jackson, and Duke Ellington (with whom he subbed for four weeks). Dizzy's recorded solos with Hite ("Jersey Bounce") and Millinder ("Little John Special") point out how his style was progressing and the fact that he was musically almost mature by 1942. Gillespie also jammed at Monroe's Uptown House (where he was captured on a few private recordings) and Minton's Playhouse and wrote arrangements for the big bands of Woody Herman ("Down Under" and "Woody 'n You"), Benny Carter, and Jimmy Dorsey.

Near the end of 1942, Gillespie became a member of the Earl Hines big band, the first Bebop orchestra and one that also included Charlie Parker on tenor, Sarah Vaughan, and Billy Eckstine. Unfortunately the band never recorded, due to the Musicians Union strike, but it gave Dizzy an opportunity to play next to sympathetic modernists. And during his year with the band he wrote "A Night in Tunisia," his most famous composition. After his departure from Hines, he co-led (with Oscar Pettiford) the first Bebop combo to be heard on 52nd Street, and in early 1944, when Billy Eckstine formed his own orchestra, Bird and Diz went along with him. Parker was gone by the time Eckstine had an opportunity to record, but Gillespie was still there, taking solos on "Opus X" and "Blowing the Blues Away." He was also on the first full-fledged bop recording date, having solos on a few numbers with Coleman Hawkins, including "Woody 'n You" and "Disorder at the Border." At the end of the year, Gillespie was on a Sarah Vaughan record date, cutting Vaughan's vocal version of "A Night in Tunisia," which was renamed "Interlude" for the occasion. By then the Boyd Raeburn Orchestra and the Glenn Miller All-Stars overseas had already recorded the future standard.

In 1945 the 27-year-old trumpeter became famous in the jazz world. He recorded a series of classic Bebop combo records with Charlie Parker, including "Hot House," "Salt Peanuts," "Dizzy Atmosphere," "Shaw 'Nuff," and "Groovin' High"; all but Tadd Dameron's "Hot House" were Gillespie compositions. Other originals of his that eventually became well known include "Blue 'n Boogie," "Bebop," "Tour de Force," and (from a later era) "Con Alma." Dizzy's complex reharmonization of "I Can't Get Started" for his 1945 recording really defined Bebop, particularly if you compare it to Bunny Berigan's famous record of eight years earlier. Gillespie put together his first big band in 1945, but it soon failed, killed by a tour through the South where audiences complained that they could not dance to the music; no recordings exist of that group. Later in the year Gillespie led a combo with the increasingly unreliable Charlie Parker to visit the West Coast. They played at Billy Berg's in Hollywood for a time, but the music was considered too radical and Slim Gaillard's jive band (which played opposite Dizzy's) was much more popular. After a few recordings and appearances with Jazz at the Philharmonic, Gillespie and his sidemen (other than Parker) returned to New York.

In 1946 Dizzy Gillespie formed his second big band, and this one would be quite successful for the next three years, not only setting the standard among Bebop-oriented orchestras but easily outdistancing all competitors on an artistic basis. With Gil Fuller as his chief arranger and such sidemen as James Moody, Jimmy Heath, Cecil Payne, John Lewis, Milt Jackson, Ray Brown, Kenny Clarke, and later on J.J. Johnson, tenor saxophonist Yusef Lateef and the up-and-coming John Coltrane, Gillespie had a perfect forum for his music and for his trumpet. "Things to Come" was the band's futuristic masterpiece, "Manteca" helped to introduce Latin jazz, and Chano Pozo (who was with the big band from 1947 until his tragic death the following year) starred on "Cubana Be/Cubana Bop." Gillespie became the most famous of all Beboppers, and his glasses, beret, and goatee were much imitated if not the way his cheeks puffed out when he played. His trademark bent trumpet would come in 1953 when a dancer tripped over his horn. In trying out his damaged trumpet, Gillespie discovered that he could hear what he played a split-second sooner with his trumpet shaped in that eccentric way, so he had his future horns made in that fashion.

A 1947 Carnegie Hall concert in which Dizzy's big band had a set, backed Ella Fitzgerald, and Gillespie had a reunion with Charlie Parker was a high point of the period, as was his orchestra's visits to Europe. However, by 1949 the Dizzy Gillespie big band was struggling to exist, and at the end of the year, Gillespie reluctantly broke up the orchestra. He formed a sextet that included Milt Jackson and John Coltrane, cofounded the short-lived Dee Gee label, employed Joe "Bebop" Carroll as his vocalist for a time (although Dizzy was actually a better singer), and recorded some slightly commercial material that mixed aspects of R&B with humorous vocals and Bop solos. In 1953 he had his final recorded reunion with Charlie Parker at the famed Massey Hall concert; Bird's death two years later hit him hard. Gillespie worked with Jazz at the Philharmonic for a few tours (having trumpet battles with Roy Eldridge), and he recorded regularly and quite favorably for Verve throughout the remainder of the 1950s, including all-star meetings with Sonny Stitt, Sonny Rollins, and Stan Getz. In 1956 Dizzy put together a new big band, which, under the sponsorship of the State Department, toured Europe, the Near East and South America during the next two years. Among his sidemen were trumpeters Lee Morgan and Joe Gordon, trombonist-arranger Melba Liston, Al Grey, the tenors of

Billy Mitchell and Benny Golson, altoists Ernie Henry and Phil Woods, and pianist Wynton Kelly; Quincy Jones was one of his arrangers. This mighty orchestra can be heard at its best during its 1957 Newport Jazz Festival recording.

After the Dizzy Gillespie big band broke up in 1958, Dizzy mostly led quintets, although he would head a specially assembled orchestra on several occasions in later years (including a 1968 reunion tour). Pianist Junior Mance and altoist-flutist Leo Wright were early members of the quintet and were succeeded by James Moody (on tenor, alto, and flute) and pianists Lalo Schifrin and Kenny Barron as the 1960s progressed. Gillespie would remain a very popular attraction throughout his life, and he never lost his joy for the music. Later in the 1960s his music was often a bit funk-oriented, and he sometimes emphasized the Latin jazz side of his music, but his solos were pure Bebop. He toured with the Giants of Jazz during 1971–72 and in 1974 began recording for Norman Granz's Pablo label. At that point, Gillespie began his long and gradual slip as a trumpeter, a decline that lasted nearly 20 years. He always had his moments of brilliance, but by the early 1980s his greatest days as a trumpeter were behind him. However, as a scat singer, showman, bandleader, and teacher, and as an inspiration in general, Gillespie was very significant until the end. His final big band project, the *United Nation Orchestra* (1988–92), featured altoist Paquito D'Rivera, pianist Danilo Perez, and trumpeters Arturo Sandoval and Claudio Roditi. After a final burst of activity (and several recordings) in January 1992, Dizzy Gillespie was struck down by bad health. He was inactive during his last year, passing away at the age of 75, a much beloved figure.

8 *Vol. 4, 1943–1944 / Oct. 1941–Dec. 31, 1944 / Masters of Jazz 86*

10 *Shaw 'Nuff / Feb. 9, 1945–Nov. 12, 1946 / Musicraft 53*

10 *The Complete RCA Victor Recordings / May 17, 1937–July 6, 1949 / Bluebird 66528*

9 *Diz 'n Bird at Carnegie Hall / Sept. 29, 1947 / Roost 57061*

8 *Dizzy Gillespie/Max Roach in Paris / Feb. 28, 1948 + May 15, 1949 / Vogue 68213*

9 *Dizzy Gillespie and His Big Band / Jul. 26, 1948 / GNP/Crescendo 23*

All of Dizzy Gillespie's earliest recordings, including his many dates with Cab Calloway, have been made available by the French Masters of Jazz label; the Classics label also covers the Calloway dates (although under Cab's name). *Vol. 4* of the Masters of Jazz series is of particularly strong interest because it covers Gillespie's career just when his style was coming together. His jam session appearances at Monroe's Uptown House have been out before (and are included on an earlier volume in this series), but this CD has a newly discovered number ("The Dizzy Crawl"). Otherwise the performances are from 1944, with the exception of a remarkable version of "Sweet Georgia Brown" played in 1943 in a trio with Charlie Parker (on tenor) and Oscar Pettiford. Also on this CD is a valuable but very poorly recorded version of "A Night in Tunisia" from January 1944 with the otherwise-undocumented quintet that Dizzy co-led with Pettiford, the three Coleman Hawkins numbers, and five from the Billy Eckstine big band that include Gillespie solos, Jimmy Dorsey's "Grand Central Getaway" (no Dizzy here, but he wrote the arrangement), and the historic December 31, 1944, record date with Sarah Vaughan. And as if that were not enough, there are five numbers from a pair of radio broadcasts in which Gillespie is heard as a member of the John Kirby Sextet! Dizzy emerges from the tightly arranged cool-toned ensembles and creates radical and explosive solos in memorable fashion.

Shaw 'Nuff has many of the early Bebop recordings that permanently changed jazz and (indirectly) the entire music world. With the exception of "A Hand Fulla Gimme" (featuring an Alice Roberts vocal) that was left off, all of Gillespie's Musicraft recordings are on this disc. Gillespie plays "Blue 'n Boogie" in a sextet with Dexter Gordon, and then there are the seven classic performances by Diz and Bird that shocked their contemporaries: "Groovin' High," "Dizzy Atmosphere," "All the Things You Are," "Shaw 'Nuff," "Lover Man" (with guest Sarah Vaughan), "Salt Peanuts," and "Hot House." A 1946 small-group date that resulted in four titles (including "Oop Bop Sh'Bam") features Gillespie with Sonny Stitt and Milt Jackson. The remainder of this essential CD has the first nine selections cut by the Dizzy Gillespie Big Band, including "One Bass Hit," "Our Delight," two versions of "He Beeped When He Should Have Bopped," and the remarkable "Things to Come."

Although Gillespie also cut sessions for Manor (which resulted in "I Can't Get Started") and Dial (while in Los Angeles), his most notable association during the Bop era was with the Victor label. The two-CD *The Complete RCA Victor Recordings* has his three initial recorded solos (cut with

Teddy Hill's orchestra in 1937, including "King Porter Stomp"), a 1939 appearance on "Hot Mallets" with a Lionel Hampton all-star group in 1939, an exciting 1946 septet date (highlighted by "A Night in Tunisia" and "Anthropology") with Don Byas, Milt Jackson, and Al Haig, and a session by the 1949 Metronome All-Stars; a tradeoff among Gillespie, Miles Davis, and Fats Navarro on "Overtime" finds all three of the trumpeters sounding like Dizzy! However, the bulk of this twofer features the mighty Dizzy Gillespie big band during 1946–49. Everything is here, including such classics as "Manteca," "Two Bass Hit," "Cubana Be/Cubana Bop," "Good Bait," "Hey Pete! Le's Eat More Meat," "Jumpin' with Symphony Sid," and Mary Lou Williams's Bop lullaby "In the Land of Oo-Bla-Dee" plus the Johnny Hartman ballad vocals that tend to be left off reissues.

Fortunately the Dizzy Gillespie big band was also captured live on several occasions. *Diz 'n Bird at Carnegie Hall* (which actually gives Charlie Parker top billing) starts off with a 25-minute five-song set by Gillespie and Parker that is highlighted by "Confirmation" and "Ko-Ko." In addition, there are ten selections from the 1947 Dizzy Gillespie big band, including "One Bass Hit" (featuring Al McKibbon), "Cubano Be/Cubano Bop," John Lewis's "Toccata for Trumpet," and "Things to Come." The 1948 orchestra plays a similar repertoire on the Vogue CD (including "Two Bass Hit," the "Afro-Cuban Drum Suite," and "Things to Come"); there are also four selections from 1949 by the Max Roach Quintet with Kenny Dorham and James Moody. The GNP/Crescendo set gives a well-rounded picture of the big band at a Pasadena concert, featuring James Moody, Cecil Payne, Chano Pozo, and Gillespie on such numbers as "Emanon," "Good Bait," and "Manteca." What a classic band!

7 *Dee Gee Days / Mar. 1, 1951–July 18, 1952 / Savoy 4426*

8 *Dizzy Gillespie in Paris, Vol. 1 / Feb. 9, 1953 / Vogue 68360*

9 *Dizzy Gillespie in Paris, Vol. 2 / Mar. 27, 1952–Feb. 22, 1953 / Vogue 68361*

7 *On the Sunny Side of the Street / 1952–Feb. 1953 / Moon 077*

6 *Ooh-Shoo-Be-Doo! / Mar. 18, 1953–Apr. 16, 1953 / Natasha Imports 4018*

After a brief association with the Capitol label in 1949 (cutting erratic material that did not sell), the Dizzy Gillespie big band reluctantly broke up. The Bebop fad might have ended, but Gillespie was still a big name and throughout the 1950s he played at the peak of his powers. All of his 1951–52 recordings for the Dee Gee label are on the single-disc *Dee Gee Days* put out by Savoy (when it was owned by Muse) in 1985. The emphasis is on humorous Bop vocals, and there are some definite highlights along the way, including guest spots for violinist Stuff Smith and such numbers as "Birks' Works," "We Love to Boogie" (which has John Coltrane's first recorded studio solo for a nonprivate label), an explosive "The Champ," "School Days," and the hilarious "Umbrella Man" (a funny tribute to Louis Armstrong). But overall the generally fun music is purposely a bit commercial; the venture did not last.

"Fun" is also the keyword for the music on *Dizzy Gillespie in Paris, Vol. 1*. Featured at a concert are Gillespie, Bill Graham (who, despite what the liner says, sticks to baritone), pianist Wade Legge, bassist Lou Hackney, drummer Al Jones, and the enthusiastic singer Joe Carroll. Crazy scat singing by both Carroll and Gillespie (check out "The Champ") alternates with some superior trumpet playing; the crowd loves everything. *Vol. 2* has the same group in the studios, with trombonist Nat Peck in Graham's place, in 1953 and two studio sessions from 1952 with Don Byas. Gillespie is wonderful throughout, being particularly inventive on "I Cover the Waterfront," "Somebody Loves Me," "Wrap Your Troubles in Dreams," and "S' Wonderful." He would often reprise his vocal on the blues "Cripple Crapple Crutch" in later years. Other music from Gillespie's visits to Europe in 1952–53 is included on *On the Sunny Side of the Street*. There are four lengthy numbers (including a version of "Perdido" that exceeds 13 minutes) from a 1952 concert that has Don Byas sitting in with Dizzy's group, a Joe Carroll vocal feature on the title cut (which was actually cut in New York later in the year), and five selections from the Gillespie-Graham quintet of 1953 in Germany (including "Manteca"). The Natasha Imports CD has five radio appearances from 1953 by the Gillespie-Graham-Legge-Hackney-Jones quintet with Joe Carroll. There are some rewarding moments but lots of repetition ("Ooh-Shoo-Be-Doo-Be" pops up four times), and some of the Bop singing by Carroll and Gillespie gets a bit tired after a while.

6   *Dizzy's Diamonds: The Best of the Verve Years /
June 6, 1950–Nov. 6, 1964 / Verve 314 513 875*

8   *Diz and Getz / Dec. 9, 1953 / Verve 833 559*

8   *The Modern Jazz Sextet / Jan. 12, 1956 / Verve 314
559 834*

10   *Dizzy Gillespie with Roy Eldridge / Oct. 29, 1954 /
Verve 314 521 647*

Dizzy's Diamonds is a three-CD sampling of Dizzy Gillespie's many classic Verve recordings. Not programmed chronologically, the discs are divided into Big Band, Small Groups & Guests, and In An Afro-Cuban, Bossa Nova, Calypso Groove. The music is generally quite worthwhile but jumps around a lot and seems ultimately pointless, mixing together familiar performances with quite a few that have still not been reissued properly. For beginners only.

One advantage to being associated with Norman Granz's labels is that Gillespie had the opportunity to record a series of all-star combo dates. *Diz and Getz* is a 1953 sextet date with Getz, the Oscar Peterson Trio, and Max Roach. Although Getz was thought of as one of the founders of the "cool school," the great tenorman could play as heatedly as anyone, and he holds his own with Gillespie on the up-tempo material. *The Modern Jazz Sextet* (the title is a play on the Modern Jazz Quartet) teams Gillespie with Sonny Stitt, guitarist Skeeter Best, drummer Charlie Persip, and two members of the MJQ (John Lewis and Percy Heath). The music is pure Bebop, consisting of "Blues for Bird," the "I Got Rhythm"-based "Dizzy Meets Sonny," a three-song ballad medley, "Mean to Me," and a lengthy rendition of Gillespie's "Tour de Force" (a Bebop line played on the chords of "Jeepers Creepers"). Dizzy and Stitt are both quite competitive (to exciting effect) in their tradeoffs.

But the classic of Dizzy Gillespie's 1950s encounters is his meeting with his early influence, Roy Eldridge. Backed by the Oscar Peterson Trio and Louie Bellson, Diz and Roy battle it out on a variety of heated numbers, including "I've Found a New Baby" and "Limehouse Blues"; play a five-song ballad medley; and share the vocals on "Pretty Eyed Baby." The fireworks between the two trumpeters (Eldridge never lets up even if Gillespie is more advanced) makes this a very special set.

10   *Birks' Works—The Verve Big-Band Sessions / May
25, 1956–Apr. 8, 1957 / Verve 314 527 900*

8   *Live, 1957 / June 14, 1957 / Jazz Unlimited 2040*

7   *Dizzy Gillespie Big Band / June 14, 1957 / Jazz
Hour 1029*

10   *Dizzy Gillespie at Newport / July 6, 1957 / Verve 314
513 754*

8 *Duets / Dec. 11, 1957 / Verve 835 253*
10 *Sonny Side Up / Dec. 19, 1957 / Verve 825 674*

In 1956, Dizzy Gillespie became a goodwill ambassador by leading his new big band overseas for a series of State Department-sponsored tours. He managed to keep the band together for two years, and all of their studio recordings are on the two-CD set *Birks' Works,* including the music from the earlier LPs *Birks' Works, Dizzy in Greece,* and *World Statesman,* plus some unissued material (mostly alternate takes). The sidemen heard from include trumpeters Joe Gordon and Lee Morgan, trombonist Al Grey, altoists Phil Woods and Ernie Henry, tenors Billy Mitchell and Benny Golson, and pianists Walter Davis Jr. and Wynton Kelly. The arrangers (Quincy Jones, Ernie Wilkins, Melba Liston, and Benny Golson) were clearly inspired to write for this ensemble, and among the 42 performances are such numbers as "Dizzy's Business," "Jessica's Day," "Dizzy's Blues," "Cool Breeze," "Whisper Not," and "I Remember Clifford."

Both the Jazz Unlimited and Jazz Hour CDs are listed as having a live performance by the Gillespie big band from the same day. Five of the 11 selections on the Jazz Hour CD are among the 13 on the Jazz Unlimited set. Yet these do not seem to be the same performances, so they were probably performed during different sets. The Jazz Unlimited program is stronger overall, but completists will want both. However, the live Gillespie big band CD to get is their appearance at the 1957 Newport Jazz Festival. The versions of "Cool Breeze" and "Dizzy's Blues" are blazing and feature exciting solos by the leader, Al Grey, and Billy Mitchell. "Doodlin'" is given humorous treatment, "Manteca" is spirited, and "I Remember Clifford" is full of honest feeling. In addition, the CD reissue adds three numbers to the original program, including pianist Mary Lou Williams's guest appearances on her "Zodiac Suite" and "Carioca." Highly recommended.

During an eight-day period in December 1957, Gillespie recorded enough material for three albums: the modestly titled *The Greatest Trumpet of Them All* (an octet date not yet reissued on CD) and two sets that team Dizzy with Sonny Stitt, Sonny Rollins, pianist Ray Bryant, bassist Tommy Bryant, and Charlie Persip. The earlier date, *Duets,* actually has Stitt and Rollins on separate numbers with Gillespie, forming a quintet. Highlights include the debut of Dizzy's "Con Alma" and Rollins's playing overall. However, *Sonny Side Up* (which uses the full sextet) is more essential. Dizzy has a happy vocal on "On the Sunny Side of the Street," "Af-

ter Hours" works quite well, and "The Eternal Triangle" is heated Bebop. Sonny Rollins steals the show altogether with his explosive stop-time solo on "I Know That You Know."

8 *Copenhagen Concert / Sep. 17, 1959 / Steeplechase 36024*
9 *Gillespiana and Carnegie Hall Concert / Nov. 14, 1960–Mar. 4, 1961 / Verve 314 519 809*
8 *An Electrifying Evening with the Dizzy Gillespie Quintet / Feb. 9, 1961 / Verve 314 557 544*
7 *Perceptions / May 22, 1961 / Verve 314 537 748*
9 *Something Old, Something New / Apr. 23, 1963 / Verve 314 558 079*
8 *Dizzy Gillespie & the Double Six / July 8, 1963 / Philips 830 224*
7 *The Cool World—Dizzy Goes Hollywood / Sept. 11, 1963–Apr. 23, 1964 / Verve 314 531 230*
6 *Jambo Caribe / Nov. 4-6, 1964 / Verve 314 557 492*

After the breakup of his big band in 1958, Dizzy Gillespie cut back to a quintet and continued traveling the world. He is in excellent form on *Copenhagen Concert,* a performance released for only the first time in 1992. With altoist Leo Wright, pianist Junior Mance, bassist Art Davis, and drummer Teddy Stewart, Dizzy sings "Ooh-Shoo-Be-Doo-Bee," scats on "Lady Be Good," and stretches out on lengthy versions of "I Found a Million Dollar Baby," "Wheatleigh Hall," and "A Night in Tunisia."

The single-CD *Gillespiana and Carnegie Hall Concert* combines two related LPs. Pianist Lalo Schifrin (who had recently joined Dizzy's group) was encouraged to write new music, and he came up with the five-movement "Gillespiana," a work that uses a 21-piece group (including four French horns) and grows in interest with each listen. The studio version of the work makes up the first half of the rewarding CD, while the remainder was cut at Carnegie Hall (where the work was actually debuted) with a similar band. Gillespie performs "Manteca," a rather silly version of "Ool Ya Koo" (with Joe Carroll), "Tunisian Fantasy," "Kush," and "This Is the Way."

An Electrifying Evening is most notable for Gillespie's rather incredible trumpet break on "A Night in Tunisia." Otherwise he is in fine form playing "Kush," "Salt Peanuts," and a definitive version of "The Mooche" with his quintet, which at the time included Wright (doubling on alto and flute), Schifrin, bassist Bob Cunningham, and drummer

Chuck Lampkin. The CD is rounded off by an interesting and occasionally humorous 18-minute interview conducted by Charles Schwartz with Dizzy on stage the same night as the performance. *Perceptions* is a six-piece work by J.J. Johnson featuring Gillespie's trumpet with a 21-piece band comprising six trumpets, two trombones, two bass trombones, four French horns, two tubas, bass, drums, percussion, and two harps! The music is a bit dry and somber in spots during this Third Stream work, but Gillespie generally sounds quite inspired by the challenge.

By 1963, Dizzy's group consisted of James Moody (on tenor, alto, and flute), pianist Kenny Barron, bassist Chris White, and drummer Rudy Collins. *Something Old, Something New* has three "newer" works by Tom McIntosh (including "Cup Bearers") along with one other recent piece, but it is most notable for Gillespie's interpretations of the older material. "Bebop" is taken at a furious pace, as is "Dizzy Atmosphere," "Good Bait" has some classic playing, and the medley of "I Can't Get Started" and "'Round Midnight" is perfect. The reissue is rounded off by "Early Mornin' Blues," which was only previously out as a "45." Dizzy's collaboration with the Double Six of Paris (a French vocal group) mostly comes off well as the singers perform vocalese in French! Gillespie either wrote or was associated with each of the dozen songs, and he has plenty of solo space, as does Bud Powell. Pierre Michelot and Kenny Clarke complete the group, except on two numbers that have Dizzy's quintet with Moody. An intriguing effort.

The same quintet recorded a pair of relatively lightweight albums in 1963 and 1964 that are combined on *The Cool World—Dizzy Goes Hollywood.* The former set is comprised of themes from the forgotten film of the same name, while *Dizzy Goes Hollywood* has the trumpeter performing brief but swinging renditions of themes from 11 movies (including *Exodus, Days of Wine and Roses,* and *Never on Sunday*). *Jambo Caribe* finds the quintet joined by Kansas Fields on percussion for a set of music associated with or influenced by the Caribbean. There is not much stretching out here and nothing too essential occurs, but the results are fun and "And Then She Stopped" became part of Gillespie's repertoire.

6 *With Gil Fuller & the Monterey Jazz Festival Orchestra / Oct. 1965 / Blue Note 80370*

5 *Dizzy Gillespie and His Quintet / Nov. 24, 1965 / RTE 1008*

3 *Swing Low, Sweet Cadillac / May 25–26, 1967 / Impulse 178*

8 *Live at the Village Vanguard / Oct. 1, 1967 / Blue Note 80507*

7 *Things to Come / 1968 / Laserlight 17 107*

For the decade after Dizzy Gillespie ended his associations with Verve, Philips, and Limelight (all of which labels are now owned by Polygram), his recording career became streaky. However, he still played quite well. For the 1965 Monterey Jazz Festival, he had a reunion with arranger Gil Fuller, but the big band that was gathered functions mostly as a mere prop behind the trumpeter. Best are the versions of "Groovin' High" and "Things Are Here" (an answer to the earlier "Things to Come"), but overall the set is a slight disappointment. The concert that was released on an RTE CD also does not live up to expectations. Joined once again by Moody, Barron, White, and Collins, Gillespie never really cuts loose on the Latin- and Brazilian-oriented material. He sounds best on "Chega De Saudade" and has a good-natured vocal on the calypso "Oh Joe," but otherwise James Moody often takes solo honors; his flute is showcased on "Umh, Umh." *Swing Low, Sweet Cadillac* suffers from an excess of joking around and far too little music. There is less than 34 minutes of music on this rather weak CD, and that includes a so-so 16-minute version of "Kush" and a tired comedy routine on "Swing Low, Sweet Cadillac."

The double-CD *Live at the Village Vanguard* is much more interesting. Dizzy Gillespie is heard as part of an all-star group that includes baritonist Pepper Adams, either violinist Ray Nance or trombonist Garnett Brown, pianist Chick Corea, bassist Richard Davis, and either Elvin Jones or Mel Lewis on drums. The selections with Nance in particular are colorful (featuring an unusual trumpet-baritone-violin frontline), and it is intriguing to hear Gillespie playing with the rather modern rhythm section. The six standards and a blues are all given lengthy treatment (only "Blues for Max" is under 11 minutes long) and Dizzy pushes himself in this setting.

In 1968, Dizzy Gillespie led a big band for a European tour. The outstanding ensemble recorded a long-out-of-print album for MPS. *Things to Come* is from the tour, and there is some outstanding music to be heard on this budget release. But Laserlight's packaging is quite crummy. The chatty liner notes say nothing about the music, and the very incomplete personnel listing is full of errors (with Sahib Shihab changed to Sahib Jihal and Cecil Payne becoming

Cecil Pain!). Despite that, there are some hot moments, particularly on "Things to Come" and "Manteca." Hopefully this important music will be reissued someday much more coherently.

9 *Dizzy Gillespie Big Four / Sept. 19, 1974 / Original Jazz Classics 443*

6 *Afro-Cuban Jazz Moods / June 4-5, 1975 / Original Jazz Classics 447*

6 *The Dizzy Gillespie Big 7 / July 16, 1975 / Pablo 739*

8 *The Trumpet Kings at Montreux '75 / July 16, 1975 / Original Jazz Classics 445*

6 *Bahiana / Nov. 19-20, 1975 / Pablo 2625-708*

3 *Dizzy's Party / Sept. 15-16, 1976 / Original Jazz Classics 823*

4 *Free Ride / Feb. 1-2, 1977 / Original Jazz Classics 784*

7 *Montreux '77 / July 14, 1977 / Original Jazz Classics 381*

8 *Trumpet Summit Meets Oscar Peterson Big Four / Mar. 1980 / Original Jazz Classics 603*

4 *Digital at Montreux, 1980 / July 19, 1980 / Original Jazz Classics 882*

6 *Musician-Composer-Raconteur / July 17, 1981 / Pablo 2620*

9 *To a Finland Station / Sept. 9, 1982 / Original Jazz Classics 733*

With a few exceptions (including collaborations with the Mitchell-Ruff Duo and dates with his 1968 big band and with the Giants of Jazz), Dizzy Gillespie's recording career was quite erratic during 1965-73. In 1974 he signed with Norman Granz's Pablo label, where he would record on a regular basis for the next eight years. Dizzy was 57 at the time, and his trumpet playing was just starting to decline, not being as sharp or as accurate as it had been a few years earlier. That decline would be gradual at first, becoming much steeper during the 1980s.

Dizzy Gillespie Big Four, a meeting with Joe Pass, Ray Brown, and drummer Mickey Roker, was among the trumpeter's finest dates of the decade, with a stunning version of "Be Bop" and fine renditions of "Tanga," "Russian Lullaby," and "Birks' Works" being among the highlights. In contrast, *Afro-Cuban Jazz Moods* is a slight disappointment. Gillespie teams up with Machito's Afro-Cuban Orchestra and arranger Chico O'Farrill, but the use of synthesizers does not work too well, the influence of rock is a minus, and

Dizzy, despite some good moments, is not strong enough to uplift what should have been a classic album. *Dizzy Gillespie Big 7,* recorded at the 1975 Montreux Jazz Festival, is better, although it also does not live up to its potential. Dizzy is joined by Milt Jackson, Eddie "Lockjaw" Davis, Johnny Griffin, Tommy Flanagan, Niels Pedersen, and Mickey Roker for three standards, but there are some meandering moments, particularly on a 16-minute version of "Lover, Come Back to Me."

On an occasional basis in the mid-1970s, Dizzy Gillespie, Clark Terry, Roy Eldridge, and Harry "Sweets" Edison came together as "The Trumpet Kings." Their Montreux set, made the same day as the Gillespie *Big 7,* features plenty of fireworks from the competitive veterans, who are joined by Oscar Peterson, Niels Pedersen, and drummer Louie Bellson on two blues and four swing standards. *Bahiana* mostly showcases Gillespie's regular band of the mid-1970s (with Roger Glenn on flutes, Al Gafa and Mike Howell on guitars, bassist Earl May, Mickey Roker, and percussionist Paulinho Da Casto). But, despite some good moments, most of the material (other than "Olinga," "Barcelona," and "Carnival") is weak and just not worthy of the trumpeter. The same can certainly be said of *Dizzy's Party* (a forgettable sextet date with Ray Pizzi on reeds, and Rodney Jones) and the discoish *Free Ride,* which finds Gillespie joined by six horns and an oversized electric rhythm section arranged by Lalo Schifrin. With such songs as "Ozone Madness," "The Last Stroke of Midnight," and "Shim-Sham Shimmy on the St. Louis Blues," it is little wonder that those two sets are among Gillespie's artistic low points.

Montreux '77 is one of the few albums that matched Gillespie with his protégé Jon Faddis; they should have recorded together much more. Playing in a sextet with Milt Jackson, pianist Monty Alexander, Ray Brown, and drummer Jimmie Smith, the two trumpeters are complementary rather than competitive (Faddis never tries to blow Dizzy out), and the results are enjoyable if not explosive, without any trumpet tradeoffs. The *Trumpet Summit* date has Gillespie, Clark Terry, and Freddie Hubbard (a bit of a wild card) playing three standards and the blues "Chicken Wings" with the Oscar Peterson Quartet. This date does have its inspiring moments (Dizzy flew in specifically for the chance to play with Hubbard) and is worthy of some close listens to hear the three very different trumpet styles. A bit of an experiment and not too successful is *Digital at Montreux,* a live set at the 1980 Montreux Jazz Festival by the unusual trio of Gillespie, Toots Thielemans (who sticks to guitar), and drummer Bernard Purdie. The musicians try their best to fill in the gaps, but it sounds incomplete and a touch frivolous. The two-CD *Musician-Composer-Ranconteur* is subtitled, not too accurately, "Dizzy Gillespie plays and raps in his greatest concert." Gillespie's joking around is often left in and comes across well, but this was just a typical performance, although it includes Milt Jackson, James Moody, and guitarist Ed Cherry in the sextet. The lengthy versions of "A Night in Tunisia," "Olinga," and "Con Alma" have their moments.

Dizzy Gillespie was nearly 65 when he recorded *To a Finland Station,* and this was his last significant recording as a trumpeter. He shares the spotlight with the great Cuban trumpeter Arturo Sandoval, a wondrous player who was a decade away from defecting to the United States. With backing by a Finnish rhythm section, the trumpeters sound inspired by each other on five originals, including "Wheatleigh Hall" and "And Then She Stopped." Recommended.

6   *New Faces / 1984 / GRP 9512*
6   *Dizzy Gillespie Meets Phil Woods Quintet / Dec. 14, 1986 / Timeless 250*
8   *Live at the Royal Festival Hall / June 10, 1989 / Enja 79658*
5   *The Symphony Sessions / Aug. 26–27, 1989 / Projazz 698*
4   *The Winter in Lisbon / Aug. 1990 / Milan 35600*
5   *To Diz with Love / Jan. 29, 1992–Feb. 1, 1992 / Telarc 83307*
5   *To Bird with Love / Jan. 23–25, 1992 / Telarc 83316*
5   *Bird Songs / Jan. 23–25, 1992 / Telarc 83421*

Dizzy Gillespie probably should have stopped recording altogether after the early 1980s, since he was no longer on the same level as earlier, but he remained active and was documented until he was forced to stop playing. *New Faces* is of interest mostly because Dizzy is teamed up with such younger talents as tenor saxophonist Branford Marsalis, pianist Kenny Kirkland, and bassist Lonnie Plaxico. The music (which includes "Birks' Works" and "Tin Tin Deo") is decent but not memorable. For the Timeless set, Gillespie sits in with the Phil Woods Quintet of the time (which also includes trumpeter Tom Harrell, pianist Hal Galper, bassist Steve Gilmore, and drummer Bill Goodwin) for "'Round Midnight," "Love for Sale," and three recent pieces (two by

Gillespie). Dizzy tries his best, but Woods and Harrell easily have the best solos. *Live at the Royal Festival Hall* is the only recording released thus far by Gillespie's United Nation Orchestra. With such major players as James Moody, altoist Paquito D'Rivera, Slide Hampton, and Arturo Sandoval well featured (not to mention singer Flora Purim, percussionist Airto, trumpeter Claudio Roditi, and trombonist Steve Turre), Gillespie assumes more of a figurehead position, taking short solos and letting his sidemen stretch out. Highlights include "Tin Tin Deo," "Tanga," and an 18½-minute version of "A Night in Tunisia."

Unfortunately, 1989 was much too late in Dizzy Gillespie's career for him to be teamed with a symphony orchestra; his chops were no longer very strong. The Projazz date, which has Gillespie's quintet (with tenor saxophonist Ron Holloway, Ed Cherry, bassist John Lee, and drummer Ignacio Berroa) joined by the Rochester Philharmonic Orchestra on seven of the trumpeter's compositions, falls under the "nice try" category. Also too little too late was Dizzy's work in the film *The Winter in Lisbon,* a poorly distributed movie in which he had his only real acting role. The CD of the same name has Gillespie's score (with Slide Hampton arrangements) and is played by a faltering Dizzy, pianist Danilo Perez, bassist George Mraz, drummer Grady Tate, a string quartet, four French horns, and two other horn players; Leola Jiles sings "Magic Summer."

In January 1992, to launch what was supposed to be a year of celebration culminating in his 75th birthday, Dizzy Gillespie took up residence at New York's Blue Note and recorded with many of his admirers. These would be his final recordings, for he was permanently forced out of action a month later. The three Telarc CDs were all recorded at the Blue Note and, historic value aside, are of interest mostly because of the musicians Gillespie was playing with. *To Diz with Love* has Gillespie (plus pianist Junior Mance, bassist Peter Washington, and drummer Kenny Washington) jamming five songs with two guest trumpeters apiece on each number, chosen from Claudio Roditi, Wallace Roney, Wynton Marsalis, Red Rodney, Doc Cheatham, Jon Faddis, and Charlie Sepulveda. Cheatham, who was 86 at the time, tops both Dizzy and Faddis on "Mood Indigo"! *To Bird with Love* has Gillespie, pianist Danilo Perez, bassist George Mraz, and either Lewis Nash or Kenny Washington on drums assisted by two saxophonists apiece on five numbers, drawn from tenors Benny Golson, David Sanchez, and Clifford Jordan, and altoists Antonio Hart, Paquito D'Rivera, and

Jackie McLean. Bobby McFerrin literally came out of the audience to scat "Oo-Pop-A-Da" with Dizzy. *Bird Songs* has the exact same players as *To Bird with Love,* with McFerrin helping out on "Ornithology" and Gillespie showcased in a quartet during "Con Alma." This final version of "A Night in Tunisia" (a song that was now 49 years old) lasts over 21½ minutes and serves as a good closer to a remarkable career.

LPS TO SEARCH FOR

It Happened One Night (Natural Organic 7000), from September 29, 1947, repeats the five numbers that Dizzy Gillespie and Charlie Parker played at Carnegie Hall but adds Ella Fitzgerald's six selections with the Gillespie big band; she scats wildly on "Lady Be Good" and "How High the Moon." *Bebop Enters Sweden 1947–1949* (Dragon 34) has nine selections by the 1948 Gillespie orchestra from a performance in Stockholm (including "Our Delight," "Manteca," and "Oo-Pop-A-Da"), three songs from Chubby Jackson's Fifth Dimensional Jazz Group (a Bop sextet with Terry Gibbs and Conte Candoli) in 1947, and three numbers in which James Moody is featured with a group of Swedish allstars in 1949. *Good Bait* (Spotlite 122) features a couple of rare broadcasts from the Dizzy Gillespie big band during its final year (December 1948–July 1949), including solo spots for J.J. Johnson, Ernie Henry, Yusef Lateef, and singer Johnny Hartman.

Diz Big Band (Norgran 1090) from 1954 features Johnny Richards arrangements for a specially assembled orchestra. *One Night in Washington* (Elektra Musician 60300) showcases Gillespie with the Bill Potts Orchestra in 1955 on a variety of inspired material, including "The Afro Suite." *Big Band at Birdland* (Sandy Hook 2106) and *On Tour with Dizzy Gillespie and His Orchestra* (Artistry 111) add to the legacy of Gillespie's 1956 big band. Several of Dizzy's Verve albums have not yet been reissued, including *The Greatest Trumpet of Them All* (Verve 2304 382), which is a rather tame octet date from 1957 arranged by Benny Golson, and a pair of more stimulating 1959 quintet outings with Junior Mance and Les Spann (on flute and guitar): *Have Trumpet, Will Excite* (Verve 8313) and *The Ebullient Mr. Gillespie* (Verve 8328).

Dizzy on the French Riviera (Philips 600–048) and *New Wave* (Philips 200–070) are both long overdue to return, and they find Gillespie exploring a variety of rhythms, including bossa nova. The former date also features Leo Wright, Lalo Schifrin, and an expanded rhythm section on

spirited renditions of such numbers as "No More Blues," "Desafinado," and "Here 'Tis," while the last has a guest spot by Charlie Ventura (on bass sax) during "Chega De Saudade" and guitar work from Bola Sete; other highlights include "In a Shanty in Old Shanty Town," "Careless Love," and "One Note Samba." *The Dizzy Gillespie Reunion Big Band* (Verve/MPS 821 622) is a particularly exciting release from 1968. *Giants* (Perception 19) has Gillespie sharing the spotlight in a quintet with cornetist Bobby Hackett and Mary Lou Williams; their version of "My Man" is a classic. Dizzy's two teamings with the Mitchell-Ruff Duo (pianist Dwike Mitchell and Willie Ruff on bass and French horn) from 1971–80 are also quite rewarding: *In Concert* (Mainstream 325) and *Enduring Magic* (Blackhawk 51801). But avoid 1984's *Closer to the Source* (Atlantic 81646), an inferior commercial release that is a dud on all levels!

FILMS

Things to Come (Vintage Jazz Classics 2006), in addition to including the 1946 Billy Eckstine big band short *Rhythm on a Riff*, features the 1947 Dizzy Gillespie Orchestra in *Jivin' in Bebop,* a poorly recorded but rather remarkable film that documents Gillespie's repertoire of the period and features Milt Jackson, James Moody, John Lewis, Ray Brown, singer Helen Humes, and others. Dizzy Gillespie appears in the formerly very rare 1952 television performance of "Hot House" with Charlie Parker and much later in his career on the performance videos *A Night in Chicago* (View Video 1334) and as a guest on *Sarah Vaughan & Friends* (A Vision 50209). It is surprising that Dizzy Gillespie, an extroverted and humorous personality, was barely utilized at all in Hollywood films other than in 1990's *The Winter in Lisbon.*

BUD POWELL

b. Sept. 27, 1924, New York, NY, d. Aug. 1, 1966, New York, NY

While Charlie Parker added greatly to the vocabulary of jazz and Dizzy Gillespie was Bop's most important teacher (in addition to playing remarkably radical solos), Bud Powell was largely responsible for permanently changing the piano's role in jazz. It has been said that he transferred the lines of Bird to the piano, but his significance was much greater than merely adapting Parker's playing. Prior to the rise of Powell, pianists usually stated the beat steadily with their left hand (whether playing stride, a lighter swing style, or boogie-woogie) while creating melodic variations with their right. Powell instead put the emphasis on his right hand with powerful single-note lines, while his left stated the chords irregularly with rhythmic accents, almost in the same fashion that Bop drummers used their bass drum. Because the string bassists were playing four-to-the-bar anyway, there was no reason for pianists to duplicate their function. By 1950, nearly every young pianist started out sounding highly influenced by Powell before eventually gaining his or her own sound. Powell would dominate the field until the rise of McCoy Tyner and Bill Evans in the early 1960s.

If there was justice in the world, Bud Powell would have been rich and famous, since he revolutionized his instrument, but it was not to be. Not only did he have the "inconvenience" of being black in a segregated society where even Art Tatum was not that well known, but he suffered from mental illness caused by a brutal beating from racist police in 1945.

Early on, Powell was encouraged by his lifelong friend Thelonious Monk. Bud left school when he was 15 to play music, and he freelanced, including sitting in at Minton's Playhouse. His first major job was with the Cootie Williams Orchestra (1943–44), with whom he made his recording debut. After the beating, Powell seemed to recover. But he suffered from headaches throughout his life, and his increasingly erratic behavior resulted in his being institutionalized several times. Despite all of this, he was a brilliant pianist during his prime. During the second half of the 1940s, Powell played with most of the major jazz musicians, including Charlie Parker (though he was never a regular member of his group), Dizzy Gillespie, Fats Navarro, Sonny Stitt, J.J. Johnson, Allan Eager, and Dexter Gordon, and with his own trios. During 1947–51, the pianist recorded a series of classic dates for Roost, Verve, and Blue Note, and wrote such songs as "Bouncing with Bud," "Dance of the Infidels," "Tempus Fugit," "Parisian Thoroughfare," "Celia," "I'll Keep Loving You," "Budo," and "Un Poco Loco." Powell was out of action during part of 1951–53 when he was hospitalized but was released in time to appear at the famous Massey Hall concert in Toronto with Bird, Dizzy, Charles Mingus, and Max Roach. His playing ranged from incredible to indifferent during the remainder of the 1950s (sometimes interpreting ballads with a very scary intensity), with his best dates being for Blue Note, while his output for Verve was up and down in quality.

In 1959 Powell moved to Paris, and for a few years (despite a bout with tuberculosis) he had a bit of a renaissance, playing in a trio with Kenny Clarke and Oscar Pettiford (and later Pierre Michelot). He stayed with photographer Francis Paudras, who befriended and helped him (as portrayed in disguised form in the Hollywood film 'Round Midnight). But in 1964 Bud Powell returned to New York and, after playing at Birdland, he largely disappeared, making few appearances before his death two years later. Bud Powell's life was quite tragic, but few pianists have ever played at the high level of nonstop creativity that Powell displayed when at his best.

* **The Complete Blue Note and Roost Recordings / Jan. 10, 1947–Dec. 29, 1958 / Blue Note 30083**

9 **The Bud Powell Trio Plays / Jan. 10, 1947 + Sept. 1953 / Roulette 93902**

10 **The Amazing Bud Powell, Vol. 1 / Aug. 8, 1949–May 1, 1951 / Blue Note 81503**

10 **The Amazing Bud Powell, Vol. 2 / May 1, 1951–Aug. 14, 1953 / Blue Note 81504**

9 **Bud! / Aug. 3, 1957 / Blue Note 93902**

8 **Time Waits / May 25, 1958 / Blue Note 46820**

8 **The Scene Changes / Dec. 29, 1958 / Blue Note 46529**

Although he made some classic recordings elsewhere (including his early Verve dates), in general Bud Powell's greatest recordings were made for Blue Note. The four-CD *The Complete Blue Note and Roost Recordings* has all of the music on the six Roulette and Blue Note CDs covered in this section, plus some alternate takes. It is the best way to acquire this classic music, although that set will probably become difficult to find after a year or two. *The Bud Powell Trio Plays* has the pianist's two dates that were originally cut for Roost. The first eight numbers from 1947 were Powell's debut as a leader, and they are full of classic solos as Bud (backed by Curly Russell and Max Roach) uplifts six standards, Thelonious Monk's "Off Minor," and his own "Bud's Bubble." The second half of the CD, a 1953 session with bassist George Duvivier and drummer Art Taylor, is not quite on the same level but has its strong moments, particularly "Burt Covers Bud" (which is really Coleman Hawkins's "Bean and the Boys") and "Woody 'n You."

The two *Amazing* volumes live up to their billing. *Vol. 1* has a very exciting quintet date with Fats Navarro, Sonny Rollins, Tommy Potter, and Roy Haynes (highlighted by "Bouncing with Bud," "52nd Street Theme," and "Dance of the Infidels") plus a May 1951 trio outing with Curly Rus-

The piano would never be the same after Bud Powell replaced striding with comping.

sell and Max Roach; the latter session has "Parisian Thoroughfare" plus three stunning versions of "Un Poco Loco." *Vol. 2* finishes off the trio outing and then includes a Powell-Duvivier-Taylor trio date in 1953 that finds the pianist digging into such numbers as "The Glass Enclosure," "Reets and I," and "I Want to Be Happy."

By the time that Bud Powell recorded his last three Blue Note albums in 1957–58, his health was much more erratic, and yet he rose to the occasion for each of these sets, easily outshining his later Verve and RCA albums. The *Bud!* album, also known as *The Amazing Bud Powell, Vol. 3*, has Powell's unique solo version of "Bud on Bach," four trio numbers with bassist Paul Chambers and Art Taylor, and three Bop standards on which the trio is joined by Curtis Fuller's trombone. *Time Waits* (with bassist Sam Jones and drummer Philly Joe Jones) has Powell performing seven of his originals, including "Time Waits," "John's Abbey," and "Monopoly," while *The Scene Changes* (with Chambers and

Taylor again) features nine other Powell compositions, all obscure but most quite worthy of being revived. If only Bud Powell had been healthy enough to play at this level all of the time!

⊛   *The Complete Bud Powell on Verve* / *Jan. 1949– Sept. 13, 1956* / *Verve 314 521 669*

[7]   *Jazz at Massey Hall, Vol. 2* / *1953* / *Original Jazz Classics 111*

[7]   *Strictly Powell* / *Oct. 5, 1956* / *RCA 51423*

[8]   *Swingin' with Bud* / *Feb. 11, 1957* / *RCA 51507*

[7]   *Time Was* / *Oct. 5, 1956 + Feb. 11, 1957* / *Bluebird 636*

[8]   *Bud Plays Bird* / *Oct. 14, 1957–Jan. 30, 1958* / *Roulette 37137*

After a brilliant start, Bud Powell's Verve recordings (which overlap with the period that he was recording for Blue Note) became quite erratic. Sometimes he was just not in the right mental shape to record, but he was obligated to make enough music to complete the records that he had started. Often, indifferent choruses would be followed by moments of genius. The five-CD set *The Complete Bud Powell on Verve* (which has a 150-page booklet) has an exciting opening disc (three trio dates and a set of unaccompanied solos) that includes such classic performances as "Tempus Fugit," "Celia," "I'll Keep Loving You," "Parisian Thoroughfare," and "Hallucinations"; these are also available on two single CDs titled *The Genius of Bud Powell* (Verve 827 901) and *Jazz Giant* (Verve 829 937). But the other four discs on the large Verve set (trio outings from 1954–56) are quite streaky and augmented by many so-so alternate takes. The completeness of this package cannot be faulted, but some of the material (particularly the many instances where Powell is clearly lost) did not need to be released. Still, Bud Powell collectors will find much of the music quite intriguing.

The famous 1953 Massey Hall concert had two sets, one featuring a quintet with Charlie Parker and Dizzy Gillespie and *Vol. 2*, which is played by the rhythm trio of Powell, Charles Mingus, and Max Roach. In addition to the six selections actually taken from the concert, there are a few other trio numbers from the time period (with George Duvivier and Art Taylor) plus Roach's solo piece "Drum Conversation" and "Bass-ically Speaking" which actually has Billy Taylor in Powell's place. During 1956–57, Powell (along with Duvivier and Art Taylor) recorded 22 selections on two albums for RCA. These have been reissued in full on *Strictly Powell* and *Swingin' with Bud*, while the single-disc *Time Was* has 18 of the 22 numbers. Powell's RCA dates, while not on the level of the Blue Notes, are superior to his later Verves. *Swingin' with Bud*, which has "Like Someone in Love," "Oblivion," and "Swedish Pastry," gets the edge.

The Powell-Duvivier-Taylor trio was reunited for *Bud Plays Bird*, a previously unreleased set put out for the first time in 1996. With the exception of "Salt Peanuts," all 15 performances (which include "Yardbird Suite," "Relaxin' at Camarillo," "Confirmation," and two versions of "Big Foot") are Charlie Parker compositions. Even with a few minor errors, this is one of Bud Powell's most swinging and exciting dates from this troubled period.

9 *The Complete Essen Jazz Festival Concert / Apr. 2, 1960 / Black Lion 760105*
8 *A Tribute to Cannonball / Dec. 15, 1961 / Columbia/Legacy 65186*
9 *A Portrait of Thelonious / Dec. 17, 1961 / Columbia/Legacy 65187*
6 *Blue Note Cafe Paris 1961 / 1961 / ESP 1066*
7 *'Round About Midnight at the Blue Note / 1962 / Dreyfus 36500*
8 *Bouncing with Bud / Apr. 26, 1962 / Delmark 406*
7 *Bud Powell in Paris / Feb. 1963 / Reprise 45817*

Moving to Paris in 1959 probably extended Bud Powell's life by a few years. In Europe he worked regularly and his health improved for a time. The Black Lion disc finds Powell sounding exuberant in a trio with Oscar Pettiford and Kenny Clarke on five numbers (including "Shaw 'Nuff" and "Salt Peanuts") and being joined by Coleman Hawkins for four others (highlighted by "All the Things You Are" and "Stuffy").

A Tribute to Cannonball was always inaccurately titled, for this is actually a quartet/quintet session co-led by Powell and Don Byas that also includes Pierre Michelot, Kenny Clarke, and (on four numbers) trumpeter Idrees Sulieman. It is particularly valuable in showing how strongly Byas (who was forgotten in the United States by then) could still play. The CD reissue adds an alternate take plus a second version of "Cherokee" that finds producer Cannonball Adderley joining the group so he could jam with Byas and Powell.

The Three Bosses was originally made up of Powell, Pettiford, and Clarke. After the bassist's premature death in 1960, Pierre Michelot filled his spot. *A Portrait of Thelonious* was one of the trio's finest recordings, featuring four Thelonious Monk tunes plus Beboppish romps on "I Ain't Foolin'" and "Squatty." The ESP and Dreyfus discs have the same group and a similar repertoire (although not the latter two songs), but the renditions are a bit less inspired if still worthwhile.

Bouncing with Bud finds bassist Niels Pedersen (a month shy of his 16th birthday!) and drummer William Schiopffe joining Powell for exhilarating versions of such songs as "Rifftide," "Move," "52nd Street Theme," and the title cut. *Bud Powell in Paris*, which was produced by Duke Ellington for the Reprise label, has Powell, drummer Kansas Fields, and bassist Gilbert Rovere digging inventively into nine selections (including "How High the Moon," "Jordu," and "Satin Doll") plus previously unreleased versions of "Indiana" and "B-Flat Blues."

9 *Vol. 1 / Jan. 1944–Dec. 19, 1948 / Mythic Sound 6001*

These two interesting series, although not essential, add greatly to the discography of Bud Powell. Photographer Francis Paudras, who did his best to rehabilitate the pianist during his stay in Paris, put out ten LPs (later CDs) of previously unreleased material posthumously. Volumes 7 and 9 were not available at the time this book went to press, and all of the Mythic Sound releases have become scarce. *Vol. 1* is the most historic, featuring Powell as a member of the Cootie Williams Orchestra in 1944, including on a version of "West End Blues" that is a duet with the leader-trumpeter. At the time, although tied a bit to swing, Powell was already sounding innovative. Also heard prominently with Cootie Williams's band during this set are altoist-singer Eddie "Cleanhead" Vinson and Sam "the Man" Taylor on tenor; Ella Fitzgerald sits in for two vocals. This intriguing release concludes with versions of "Perdido" and "Indiana" from a *Royal Roost* broadcast in 1948 with an all-star group that includes Benny Harris, J.J. Johnson, and Buddy De-Franco.

Vol. 2 has mostly trio renditions from 1953 and 1955 but is most notable for two numbers with Charles Mingus, Max Roach, and Dizzy Gillespie in a quartet (the recording date is wrong, since this was not recorded at the Massey Hall concert) plus a rare showcase with a big band ("Big Band Blues"). *Vol. 3* was recorded at the Saint-Germain in France during a 1957 visit and in 1959 when Bud settled in Paris. Powell is heard throughout with Pierre Michelot and Kenny Clarke, including on seven numbers in which the trio is joined by tenor saxophonist Barney Wilen and/or trumpeter Clark Terry.

Vol. 4 is much weaker, home recordings of Powell playing unaccompanied solos over a three-year period. There are some strong moments and Bud is heard singing "The Christmas Song" (!) but the recording quality is erratic and there are too many throwaways. *Vol. 5* is better, with Powell showcased at Paris's Blue Note with a couple trios, jamming three lengthy numbers with Zoot Sims, Pierre Michelot, and Kenny Clarke, and on a brief "How High the Moon" in a quintet that includes Dizzy Gillespie. *Vol. 6* has outtakes and previously unreleased material from the *Bud Powell in Paris* trio date with Kansas Fields and Gilbert Rovere, including seven otherwise unknown (but often superior) Powell originals. *Vol. 8*, recorded shortly before Bud Powell decided to return to the United States, was recorded informally during a vacation in France and finds Bud mostly in a trio with bassist Guy Hayat and drummer Jacques Gervais. Best are two numbers ("Body and Soul" and a long version of "Hot House") in which the excitable Johnny Griffin makes the group a quartet. However, the recording quality overall is a bit streaky. *Vol. 10* is taken from Bud Powell's final important club gig of his career, a stay at Birdland after his return home in 1964. He is heard accepting an award and then playing a dozen numbers (standards plus his original "Monopoly") in a trio with bassist John Ore and drummer J.C. Moses. The music is decent and shows that Powell still had something left at that late date although he would soon be disappearing.

Back in 1962, Bud Powell and local players (bassist Torbjorn Hultcrantz and drummer Sune Spangberg) recorded 3¼-hours worth of music during an engagement in Stockholm. The five CDs that resulted are generally excellent. Here are a few highlights: *Vol. 1* has "Move" and an emotional version of "I Remember Clifford" (which could have been subtitled "I Remember Richie Powell," for Bud's younger brother, who died in the same car accident with Clifford Brown), *Vol. 2* includes Monk's "Hackensack" and a lengthy "Blues in the Closet," *Vol. 3* is highlighted by an 18-minute version of "Swedish Pastry," *Vol. 4* features six concise numbers, including "Star Eyes" and "John's Abbey," and *Vol. 5* is most notable for a 20-minute version of "Straight No Chaser" and a rare Powell vocal on "This Is No Laughin' Matter." Fine music overall, even if all of the performances could have been released on three rather than five CDs.

3 *Strictly Confidential / 1963-1964 / Black Lion 760196*

6 *Blues for Bouffement / July 31, 1964 / Black Lion 760135*

7 *Salt Peanuts / Aug. 1964 / Black Lion 760121*

4 *Ups 'n Downs / 1964-1965 / Mainstream 724*

The music on *Strictly Confidential* should probably have remained confidential! A series of solos recorded by Powell at Francois Paudras's apartment, the music has its moments (including a bit of striding by Bud), but the erratic recording quality and some missteps keep it from being recommended to anyone but completists. *Blues for Bouffement* (which has also been released as *The Invisible Cage*) is a better-than-expected trio date by Powell with bassist Michel Gaudry and drummer Art Taylor. The faster material (such as "Little Willie Leaps," "Moose the Mooche," and "Relaxin' at Camarillo") fares much better than the pianist's intense and sometimes lost interpretations of ballads. *Salt Peanuts* is taken from the same period that resulted in *Vol. 8* of the Mythic Sound releases. Four numbers are by Powell with bassist Guy Hayat and drummer Jacques Gervais, but the reason to acquire this CD is the three Bebop standards ("Hot House," "Wee," and "Straight No Chaser") in which Johnny Griffin romps with the group, clearly inspiring Powell.

After returning to the United States in September 1964, Bud Powell recorded two trio albums and then disappeared. *Ups 'n Downs,* although the weak liner notes hint that the music is from the 1950s, was actually the pianist's final recording. He is joined by an unidentified bassist and drummer less than two years before his death, and the music has, uh, its ups and downs. Although it is sometimes better than expected, this was an anticlimactic final act in the career of a truly great pianist.

LPS TO SEARCH FOR

New York All Star Sessions (Bandstand 1507) has a variety of odds and ends, including two selections with an all-star group from the Royal Roost in 1948, Powell's numbers at the Stars of Jazz Carnegie Hall concert from Christmas 1949, three trio numbers from 1957, and, of greatest interest, versions of "Dance of the Infidels" (with guest Charlie Parker) and "Woody 'n You" (with Dizzy Gillespie). *Inner Fires* (Elektra Musician 60030) features high-quality and generally exciting trio performances by Powell, Charles Mingus, and Roy Haynes from 1953. The music was released for the

first time in 1982, and the album concludes with a couple of interviews with Powell from 1963. *Bud in Paris* (Xanadu 102) has live performances by Powell from 1959-60 with Pierre Michelot, Kenny Clarke, and, on four numbers, tenorman Barney Wilen. Best is a pair of piano-tenor duets with Johnny Griffin.

MAX ROACH

b. Jan. 10, 1924, New Land, NC

Unlike the other Bebop giants included in this section, Max Roach continued to evolve after the early 1950s, in later years becoming an important part of Hard Bop, Free Jazz, and Post-Bop. This biography and the recording reviews therefore largely cut off after 1956.

Kenny Clarke was the first drummer to shift the timekeeping role from the bass drum and the hi-hat cymbal to the ride cymbal. Max Roach emulated that innovation and then built and improved upon it. A fiery player, Roach always recognized the value of space and knew how to methodically build up a solo. This approach allowed him as early as the 1953 Massey Hall concert to play occasional unaccompanied pieces that held onto the audience's attention. Always curious about new styles and forms of music, Max Roach not only outlived the other Bebop giants but was one of the few to outgrow the music while remaining justifiably proud of his contributions to the idiom.

Max Roach, who grew up in Brooklyn, began playing drums when he was ten, and studied at the Manhattan School of Music. Never really a part of the swing era, Roach was part of the house band at Monroe's Uptown House by 1942 and was already acquainted with Charlie Parker and Dizzy Gillespie. In 1943 he made his recording debut with Coleman Hawkins. Among his activities prior to the explosion of Bebop in 1945 were playing with Benny Carter's orchestra, sitting in with Duke Ellington in 1944, participating in Hawkins's historic first Bebop recording dates, and working with Dizzy Gillespie on 52nd Street.

By 1945, Roach was the most in-demand of all drummers for Bebop-oriented dates; Kenny Clarke's stay in the military allowed the younger drummer to overshadow him. He was on Charlie Parker's famous "Ko Ko" date, worked with Stan Getz, Allen Eager, and Hawkins in 1946, and was a key part of Bird's 1947-49 quintet. Roach also participated in Miles Davis's *Birth of the Cool* recordings (1949-50) and

THE WAYNE KNIGHT COLLECTION

A musical architect, Max Roach showed that the drums can do much more than merely keep time.

played with Parker off and on during 1951–53, including at the famous Massey Hall concert of 1953.

In the early 1950s, Roach was involved in a wide variety of activities. He cofounded the Debut label with Charles Mingus in 1952, although Mingus ended up doing most of the work. The drummer freelanced, including playing with Louis Jordan and Red Allen, touring with Jazz at the Philharmonic in 1952, leading his first studio record date (1953), and working with the Lighthouse All-Stars in 1954.

In 1954 he formed a quintet with Clifford Brown that would be one of the leading groups in jazz during the next two years. With Richie Powell (Bud's younger brother) on piano, bassist George Morrow, and (after a short period with Teddy Edwards) Harold Land on tenor, this was a brilliant band that bridged the gap between classic Bebop and Hard Bop. By 1956, Sonny Rollins was on tenor and it was a remarkable all-star band, but tragically it would not last long. On June 26, a car accident ended the lives of Clifford Brown and Richie Powell. Max Roach would not be able to talk about the tragedy for years.

Eventually the drummer hired Kenny Dorham and Ray Bryant in Brown's and Powell's places. Roach has continued leading significant groups up to the present time. Through the years, his sidemen have included trumpeters Booker Little, Tommy Turrentine, Freddie Hubbard, Charles Tolliver, and Cecil Bridgewater, tenors Hank Mobley, George Coleman, Stanley Turrentine, Clifford Jordan, Billy Harper, and Odean Pope, trombonist Julian Priester, and bassists Art Davis, Calvin Hill, and Tyrone Brown. In addition, there were special projects with his wife, singer Abbey Lincoln, in the late 1950s and '60s, Roach's all-percussion group M'Boom, the Uptown String Quartet, and duet dates with Cecil Taylor, Anthony Braxton, and Archie Shepp. Through it all, Max Roach displayed the lessons that he had learned from Charlie Parker, Coleman Hawkins, and the earlier giants: to be himself and to be enthusiastic about new musical challenges.

7 *Featuring Hank Mobley / Apr. 10–21, 1953 / Original Jazz Classics 202*

8 *Max Roach Plus Four / Oct. 12, 1956–Mar. 21, 1957 / Emarcy 822 673*

Other than a 1949 concert date that was reissued under James Moody's name, *Featuring Hank Mobley* was Max Roach's debut as a leader. Four selections feature Roach with a septet that includes Idrees Sulieman, trombonist Leon Comegys, altoist Gigi Gryce, tenor saxophonist Hank Mobley (his recording debut), Walter Davis Jr., and bassist Franklin Skeete, while five other cuts have the same rhythm section but with Mobley as the only horn. In addition, there is the two-part "Drums Conversation," Roach's first recorded unaccompanied drum solo. Roach and Mobley contributed three originals apiece, and the band also interprets "Just One of Those Things," "Glow Worm," Charlie Parker's "Chi-Chi," and "I'm a Fool to Want You." The music is well played, though not essential, and falls between Bop and Hard Bop.

Max Roach Plus Four, the drummer's first recording after the tragic deaths of Clifford Brown and Richie Powell, features the other surviving members of his quintet (Sonny Rollins and bassist George Morrow) joined by Kenny Dorham and Ray Bryant. In addition to the original six-song program, there are three "bonus cuts" from the following year, with Billy Wallace in Bryant's place. Rollins was a mighty force by this time and his solos are a highlight, as are the many explosive outbursts by Roach. Among the other highlights are George Russell's "Ezz-thetic," "Just One of Those Things," and "Woody 'n You."

LPS TO SEARCH FOR

The recordings of the Clifford Brown-Max Roach Quintet are discussed under Brownie's name, with one exception. *Live at Basin Street, April 1956* (Ingo Two), an Italian LP, gives Roach top billing and is the last recording by the co-leaders. With Rollins, Powell, and Morrow completing the group, these rare club recordings consist of five numbers (including Rollins's "Valse Hot," and Brown's "Daahoud") plus Roach's solo "Drum Conversation." The 32½-minute

LP is much more valuable than its brief length might lead listeners to believe, giving fans a few more solos from the short-lived Clifford Brown.

FILMS

Max Roach appears briefly in *Carmen Jones* (1954).

THELONIOUS MONK

b. Oct. 10, 1917, Rocky Mount, NC, d. Feb. 17, 1982, Weehawken, NJ

It is a bit ironic that Thelonious Monk is today considered one of the most famous of all jazz musicians and one whose influence continues to grow, for during the Bebop era he was largely neglected, even by other modernists. Although thought of as one of the founders of Bebop, Monk's music actually stood apart in its own category, and most of his songs were considered too difficult to play by the typical jazzman of 1947 (although not by Dizzy Gillespie and Charlie Parker). Bop was originally considered a nonconformist's music, yet Monk was made fun of and underrated precisely because he did not sound like Bud Powell (a close friend). But Thelonious was able to wait out his detractors and in 1957 was celebrated for his genius, even though he sounded virtually the same as he had in 1947!

Thelonious Sphere Monk moved to New York as a child and started playing piano when he was six. His first work was accompanying an evangelist, and early on he was influenced by the great stride pianist James P. Johnson (who was a neighbor in Harlem) and to a lesser extent by Teddy Wilson. As a member of the house band at Minton's Playhouse during 1940–43, Monk was an integral part of the late-night jam sessions, and during that period he developed his unique style. He came up with his own fresh chord voicings, learned the value of space and dynamics, and began to compose pieces, including "Epistrophy" (his unofficial theme song), which was recorded by the Cootie Williams Orchestra in 1942; in 1944 Williams would also be the first to record "'Round Midnight." Monk worked with Lucky Millinder's big band (1942) and for a few months in 1944 was the pianist with Coleman Hawkins's quartet, with whom he made his recording debut (other than some private recordings from Minton's).

By 1944, Monk's style was mostly fully formed but, because he did not fit the Bebop mold (sounding futuristic and old-fashioned at the same time), he would find the next

THE WAYNE KNIGHT COLLECTION

So far ahead of his contemporaries that most Beboppers found his music too difficult, Thelonious Monk had to wait for the jazz world to catch up to him.

dozen years quite difficult. Thelonious's introverted personality and unwillingness to compromise at all would keep him in obscurity, known mostly to the jazz public as an eccentric. Even most of those who were Bebop followers tended to think of Monk as a limited pianist (when in fact he had purposely pared his style down to the essentials) and as a composer whose works (other than "'Round Midnight," "Straight No Chaser," and "Blue Monk") were simply too complex. Monk did record extensively for Blue Note during 1947–48 and 1951–52, worked on a 1950 Verve date with Charlie Parker and Dizzy Gillespie, played on sessions for Prestige during 1952–54, and on a Vogue solo set in 1954, and as a sideman with Miles Davis, but he did not work all that often during the Bebop era or the first five years afterwards.

Things began to change in 1955. Monk began a longtime association with Riverside and worked with the sympathetic young producer Orrin Keepnews, recording a trio exploration of Duke Ellington tunes and a full album of standards. Those two relatively accessible projects helped set the stage for *Brilliant Corners,* the pianist's classic set with Sonny Rollins in 1956. The breakthrough came the following year, as Monk was booked into the Five Spot for several months; his quartet included tenor saxophonist John Coltrane. The jazz press, and soon the public, finally discovered Monk during this period, and he became a major celebrity. In 1958 Monk's quartet featured Johnny Griffin on tenor (who was perfect for the group). Thelonious had special big band concerts in 1959 and 1963 (featuring some of his piano solos transcribed and orchestrated for a larger group), and he signed with Columbia in 1962. His highly unlikely rise to fame climaxed in February 1964 when Thelonious Monk was on the cover of *Time* magazine!

Although Monk continued writing new compositions

now and then, his playing and composing styles were virtually unchanged in the 1960s from how they had been in the 1940s, when he was ridiculed for his individuality. A partial list of his compositions that are now considered timeless include "52nd Street Theme," "Ruby My Dear," "Well You Needn't," "In Walked Bud," "I Mean You," "Bemsha Swing," "Hackensack," "Nutty," "Little Rootie Tootie," "Think of One," "Evidence," "Rhythm-a-Ning," "Monk's Dream," "Off Minor," "Misterioso," "Criss Cross," "Four in One," and "Ask Me Now."

Monk was at the peak of his fame during the 1960s, traveling the world and appearing at quite a few jazz festivals with his quartet, which during the years 1959–70 featured Charlie Rouse's tenor. But then, after touring with the Giants of Jazz during 1971–72 and recording some final trio and solo sides (for Black Lion), he abruptly retired. Monk suffered from mental illness during his final decade, and he made just a few special appearances after 1972. He was not seen at all in public during the five years that preceded his death in 1982 at the age of 64.

As so often happens after such a death, Thelonious Monk's passing resulted in countless tributes (" 'Round Midnight" was recorded so often that it was practically a pop hit!), and he became much more famous than he had been at his height. His son, drummer T. S. Monk, led a Hard Bop group in the 1990s that often played his father's compositions and founded the Thelonious Monk Institute of Jazz, an organization that hosts an annual competition in Monk's name.

As the 20th century ended, Thelonious Monk, who had to withstand some pretty harsh criticism and ridicule during the Bebop era, was unanimously considered one of the jazz giants.

- *   *The Complete Blue Note Recordings / Oct. 15, 1947– Apr. 14, 1957 / Blue Note 30363*
- 10 *Genius of Modern Music, Volume 1 / Oct. 15, 1947– Nov. 21, 1947 / Blue Note 81510*
- 10 *Genius of Modern Music, Volume 2 / July 23, 1951– May 30, 1952 / Blue Note 81511*
- 9   *Featuring John Coltrane—Live at the Five Spot / Sept. 11, 1958 / Blue Note 99786*

In 1947, when Alfred Lion and Francis Wolff of Blue Note decided to start recording more modern musicians, Thelonious Monk was one of the first artists whom they began documenting. It is fortunate that they did, for Monk had a great deal of pent-up creativity and many fascinating compositions that had never been recorded before. There would be three sessions in 1947, one in 1948, and one apiece in 1951 and 1952. All of the music plus two selections cut as a sideman with Sonny Rollins in 1957 and a live set with John Coltrane in a quartet is included in the four-CD *Complete Blue Note Recordings*. Fortunately the often-classic performances, other than the 1948 session (a six-song quartet date with Milt Jackson that includes "Evidence," "Misterioso," and "I Mean You") and the two Rollins cuts ("Reflections" and a version of "Misterioso" that has Horace Silver splitting the piano duties with Monk) are also available on the other three Blue Note single discs.

Genius of Modern Music, Volume 1 has the 1947 dates (Monk's debut as a leader), sextet, trio and quintet sessions that include among the sidemen Idrees Sulieman, Art Blakey, and bassist Gene Ramey. In addition to the first example of the composer playing his " 'Round Midnight," the highlights include the debuts of "Thelonious," "Ruby My Dear," "Well You Needn't," "Off Minor," "In Walked Bud," and "Monk's Mood." *Volume 2* has a pair of extensive sessions: Monk, altoist Sahib Shihab, Milt Jackson, Al McKibbon, and Art Blakey as a 1951 quintet plus a 1952 sextet with Kenny Dorham, Lou Donaldson, Lucky Thompson, Nelson Boyd, and Blakey. Among the classic performances are "Four in One," "Criss Cross," "Straight No Chaser," "Ask Me Now," and "Let's Cool One."

Thelonious Monk's 1957 quartet with John Coltrane recorded only three songs in the studio. Decades later, a tape was discovered of Monk and 'Trane playing live at the Five Spot. Although originally thought to have been from the summer of 1957, it was actually recorded a year later when the tenor saxophonist sat in one night with Thelonious's band, which at the time included bassist Ahmed Abdul-Malik and Roy Haynes. The five songs (including lengthy versions of "Trinkle Tinkle," "In Walked Bud," and "I Mean You") are given exciting treatment by the unique unit, making this CD an obvious must for fans of Thelonious Monk and John Coltrane who do not already own the four-CD *Complete Blue Note* box.

- 9   *Thelonious Monk Trio / Oct. 15, 1952–Sept. 22, 1954 / Original Jazz Classics 010*
- 9   *Monk / Nov. 13, 1953–May 11, 1954 / Original Jazz Classics 016*
- 8   *Thelonious Monk/Sonny Rollins / Nov. 13, 1953– Oct. 25, 1954 / Original Jazz Classics 059*

8 *Thelonious Monk/Joe Turner in Paris / Mar. 1952 + June 7, 1954 / Vogue 68210*

In mid-1952, Thelonious Monk signed with the Prestige label, making five sessions during the next two years. Unfortunately the label had little idea what to do as far as promoting the pianist-composer, and he did not work all that often during the period. However, the resulting music, reissued in full on three Original Jazz Classics CDs, is quite rewarding. *Thelonious Monk Trio* teams him with either Gary Mapp or Percy Heath on bass and Art Blakey or Max Roach on drums on ten numbers from 1952 and two from 1954. Highlights include "Blue Monk," "Bemsha Swing," "Little Rootie Tootie," and "Trinkle Tinkle." The CD titled simply *Monk* has two songs (plus an alternate take) from a quintet date with Sonny Rollins, Percy Heath, drummer Willie Jones, and the great French horn player Julius Watkins, plus four numbers from a different date with trumpeter Ray Copeland, tenor saxophonist Frank Foster, Curly Russell, and Art Blakey. The selections include "Let's Call This," "We See," and "Hackensack." The program that is under both Monk's and Rollins's names is a mixture of items. "Friday the 13th" is from the date with Julius Watkins; there are two leftover trio numbers plus lengthy versions of "The Way You Look Tonight" and "I Want to Be Happy" that were originally issued under the tenor's name.

The Vogue CD has all of the music from two unrelated solo piano dates. Thelonious Monk's nine selections, which were cut in Paris in 1954, have been reissued many times in different ways. "'Round Midnight," "Evidence," and "Hackensack" are among the tunes (all but one being Monk originals). The remainder of the CD features stride pianist Joe Turner (no relation to singer Big Joe Turner) in 1952, who romps through a varied and exciting program that includes "Between the Devil and the Deep Blue Sea," "You're the Cream in My Coffee," "Wedding Boogie," and three versions of "Tea for Two."

* *The Complete Riverside Recordings / July 21, 1955–Apr. 21, 1961 / Riverside 022*

8 *Plays Duke Ellington / July 21-27, 1955 / Original Jazz Classics 024*

7 *The Unique Thelonious Monk / Mar. 17, 1956 + Apr,. 3, 1956 / Original Jazz Classics 064*

10 *Brilliant Corners / Dec. 17-23, 1956 / Original Jazz Classics 026*

7 *Thelonious Himself / Apr. 5-16, 1957 / Original Jazz Classics 254*

9 *Thelonious Monk with John Coltrane / June 25, 1957-July 1957 / Original Jazz Classics 039*

9 *Monk's Music / June 26, 1957 / Original Jazz Classics 084*

Arguably the most interesting body of work of Thelonious Monk's career are his Riverside recordings, which feature his piano in a variety of stimulating settings. The 15-CD *Complete Riverside* box has every bit of it, including music released on the following 14 Original Jazz Classics CDs plus some previously unreleased tracks (including a date made with Shelly Manne). This box is an essential purchase for listeners who have the money.

Fortunately most of the music is also available individually. *Plays Duke Ellington,* which was Orrin Keepnews's way of introducing the forbidding Monk to the general public, finds Thelonious in a trio (with Oscar Pettiford and Kenny Clarke) inventively exploring a set of Ellington tunes. The more memorable interpretations include "It Don't Mean a Thing," "Mood Indigo," "Caravan," and especially "Black and Tan Fantasy." *The Unique Thelonious Monk* was his second Riverside project, featuring the pianist (with Oscar Pettiford and Art Blakey) creating fresh interpretations of seven standards (including "Liza," "Honeysuckle Rose," and "Just You, Just Me"), some of which would remain in his repertoire. *Brilliant Corners* finds Thelonious performing four of his originals (including the classic title cut and "Pannonica") plus "I Surrender Dear" with such all-stars as Sonny Rollins, Ernie Henry, and (on "Bemsha Swing") Clark Terry. The music on this set is quite innovative and still sounds advanced today.

Thelonious Himself is (not too surprisingly) a set of unaccompanied solos, mixing together standards with originals and including Monk rehearsing his rendition of "'Round Midnight" at great length. The one exception to the solos is a version of "Monk's Mood" that has John Coltrane and bassist Wilbur Ware forming a trio. *Thelonious Monk with John Coltrane* is particularly valuable, because it contains the only three studio recordings by the legendary Monk Quartet of 1957 (with Coltrane, Ware, and drummer Shadow Wilson): "Nutty," "Trinkle Tinkle," and "Ruby My Dear." The chemistry between Monk and Coltrane is quite apparent. In addition, there is an alternate solo version of "Functional" and two lesser band pieces, but get this set for the quartets. *Monk's Music* has all of the performances (including alternate takes) from a very interesting group comprising both John Coltrane and Coleman Hawkins on tenors (the only time that the two tenor titans recorded together), altoist Gigi Gryce, trumpeter Ray Copeland, Ware, Blakey, and Monk. Their version of "Well You Needn't" is a definite high point.

10 *Misterioso / Aug. 7, 1958 / Original Jazz Classics 206*

10 *Thelonious in Action / Aug. 7, 1958 / Original Jazz Classics 103*

10 *At Town Hall / Feb. 28, 1959 / Original Jazz Classics 135*

8 *Five by Monk by Five / June 1–2, 1959 / Original Jazz Classics 362*

8 *Thelonious Alone in San Francisco / Oct. 21–22, 1959 / Original Jazz Classics 231*

8 *At the Blackhawk / Apr. 29, 1960 / Original Jazz Classics 305*

7 *Monk in France / Apr. 18, 1961 / Original Jazz Classics 670*

7 *Monk in Italy / Apr. 21, 1961 / Original Jazz Classics 488*

Although Thelonious Monk finally came to fame in 1957 when John Coltrane was his tenor saxophonist, it can be argued that his finest regular combo was the 1958 group with the fiery Johnny Griffin. With bassist Ahmed Abdul-Malik and Roy Haynes completing the group, this exciting unit is well featured on both *Misterioso* and *Thelonious in Action*; Griffin really knew Monk's music and frequently tears into the pieces.

Thelonious Monk's 1959 Town Hall concert was a special event, the first time that his music was presented by a larger group. Hall Overton arranged Monk's pieces (and in a few cases his transcribed piano solos) for a ten-piece band that includes the leader, trumpeter Donald Byrd, Phil Woods, Charlie Rouse, and baritonist Pepper Adams. Their playing on "Little Rootie Tootie" in particular is remarkable.

In 1959, Charlie Rouse started working regularly with Thelonious. *Five by Monk by Five* has Rouse joined in the frontline by trumpeter Thad Jones (who is in top form) in a quintet including bassist Sam Jones and Art Taylor. The repertoire is highlighted by "Ask Me Now," "Straight No Chaser," and three versions of "Played Twice." *Thelonious Alone in San Francisco,* Monk's second set of unaccompanied solos for Riverside, mostly sticks to moody ballads and in some cases offbeat material, including "There's Danger in Your Eyes, Cherie," "You Took the Words Out of My Heart," and "Remember." *At the Blackhawk* has Monk's 1960 quartet (with Rouse, bassist John Ore, and drummer

Billy Higgins) uplifted by the additions of trumpeter Joe Gordon and tenorman Harold Land; highlights include "Four in One," "I'm Getting Sentimental Over You," and "Evidence."

Thelonious Monk's final Riverside recordings were made during a 1961 tour of Europe with Rouse, Ore, and drummer Frankie Dunlop. As would often be true in Monk's performances of the 1960s, the bass and drum solos by his sidemen are mostly run-of-the-mill, but Thelonious and Rouse both sound spirited and stretch out before the enthusiastic audiences, who rightfully enjoyed what they were hearing.

7 *The Thelonious Monk Quartet in Copenhagen / May 15, 1961 / Storyville 8283*

7 *Monterey Jazz Festival '63 / Sept. 21–22, 1963 / Storyville 8255/6*

7 *Solo Monk / Oct. 31, 1964–Mar. 2, 1965 / Columbia/Legacy 47854*

9 *The Complete Columbia Solo Studio Recordings of Thelonious Monk / Nov. 1, 1962–Nov. 19, 1968 / Columbia/Legacy 65495*

8 *Criss-Cross / Nov. 6, 1962–Mar. 29, 1963 / Columbia/Legacy 48823*

7 *Live at the It Club / Oct. 31, 1964–Nov. 1, 1964 / Columbia/Legacy 65288*

8 *Straight No Chaser / Nov. 14, 1966–Jan. 10, 1967 / Columbia/Legacy 64886*

10 *Big Band and Quartet in Concert / Dec. 30, 1963 / Columbia/Legacy 57636*

The Monk-Rouse-Ore-Dunlop Quartet is heard playing typically fine on *In Copenhagen,* from 1961, and the double disc from the 1963 Monterey Jazz Festival. Both of these Storyville imports consist of music that was not originally released until the mid-1990s. Few surprises occur, but Rouse and Monk were able to come up with continually fresh variations in their solos.

Solo Monk originally consisted of a dozen charming piano solos (including a striding version of "Dinah," "I'm Confessin'," "Everything Happens to Me," and "Ask Me Now"). The CD reissue adds a previously unissued version of "Introspection" to the program. The two-CD *Complete Columbia Solo Studio Recordings* has all of these 13 cuts plus ten solo numbers from other dates and (best of all) 14 previously unreleased alternate takes. Since Monk was always spontaneous in his improvisations, the double CD is full of revelations that add to Thelonious's recorded legacy.

Thelonious Monk spent most of the 1960s touring the

world with his quartet and recording fairly regularly for the prestigious Columbia label. Not all of his Columbia albums have been reissued on CD yet, but they do seem to be returning on a gradual basis. *Criss-Cross* (with Rouse, Ore, and Dunlap) has an additional number ("Pannonica") added to the original program, with the more memorable performances including "Hackensack," "Tea for Two," and a lengthy "Don't Blame Me." The two-CD *Live at the It Club* originally appeared as a double LP with three fewer numbers and most selections edited a bit for length; usually with a bass and/or drum solo being shortened or eliminated. Other than the inclusion of "Teo" and "Gallop's Gallop," most of the material is typical of a Monk set of the period, but the quartet (with Rouse, bassist Larry Gales, and drummer Ben Riley) sounds quite consistent and occasionally inspired, making this a good example of their live show. *Straight No Chaser,* by the same musicians during 1966–67, has 25 minutes (including two unissued performances) added to the original 50-minute program. Best are "Locomotive," "Japanese Folk Song," "We See," and "Green Chimneys."

Of all of Thelonious Monk's projects for Columbia, his big band concert of December 30, 1963, is his most rewarding. As with the 1959 special event, Monk's regular group was greatly expanded, and Hall Overton contributed arrangements. The two-CD set *Big Band and Quartet in Concert* has all of the music that exists from the concert (including three "new" performances), and the six band numbers feature cornetist Thad Jones, trumpeter Nick Travis, Steve Lacy on soprano (surprisingly he does not have any solos, although he makes his presence felt in the ensembles), Rouse, Phil Woods, baritonist Gene Allen, Eddie Bert, Monk, bassist Butch Warren, and Dunlop. While Thelonious's quartet plays "Misterioso" and "Played Twice" and Monk takes "Darkness on the Delta" as a solo, it is the group selections that are of greatest interest. On those, Jones and Woods have plenty of solo space, with the ensembles on "Four in One" (which has Monk's original solo transcribed to startling effect) being miraculous. Essential music.

7   *The Nonet-Live! / Nov. 3, 1967 / Le Jazz 7*
5   *Monk's Blues / Nov. 19-20, 1968 / Columbia/Legacy 53581*
10 *The Complete London Collection / Nov. 15, 1971 / Black Lion 7601*
6   *Straight No Chaser: Thelonious Monk / Sept. 1956–1968 / Columbia 45358*

In 1967 Thelonious Monk went on a European tour with the largest regular band of his career, a nine-piece unit in which Monk, Rouse, Gales, and Riley were joined by trumpeters Ray Copeland and Clark Terry, Jimmy Cleveland, Phil Woods, and Johnny Griffin. The tour was just a mixed success and there were few arrangements (and almost no rehearsal) for the band. The group did not record commercially, but the Le Jazz CD has some live performances. The regular quartet plays "Ruby My Dear," Copeland makes the band a quintet on "We See," and the versions of "Epistrophy," "Oska-T," and "Evidence" feature an octet, with Clark Terry being heard only on his feature on "Blue Monk." A historically interesting release of a project that should have gone much further.

In contrast, *Monk's Blues* was a bit of a misfire. Monk was teamed with a big band arranged by Oliver Nelson, and the mixture does not work all that well. However, the reissue does give listeners an opportunity to hear Monk playing (in addition to his originals) a couple of obscure Teo Macero compositions along with a previously unreleased solo version of "'Round Midnight." Much more essential is the three-CD set *The Complete London Collection.* The 29 selections (Monk's final recordings except for a couple of dates with the Giants of Jazz) find the pianist in brilliant form. The music is split between unaccompanied solos and trio numbers with Al McKibbon and Art Blakey. For some unexplained reason, Monk is quite inspired, and he is heard at the peak of his powers throughout even though he would soon retire. Highlights include "Little Rootie Tootie," "Meet Me Tonight in Dreamland," "My Melancholy Baby," "Blue Sphere," "Trinkle Tinkle," and "Nutty," but everything works during this final and definitive effort.

Also quite interesting is *Straight No Chaser,* which contains music used in the documentary film of the same name. While three of the performances were released on other albums, there are also some previously unreleased piano solos (versions of "Pannonica," "Lulu's Back in Town," "Don't Blame Me," and "Sweetheart of All My Dreams"), a couple of rehearsal fragments, Monk's 1967 octet performing "Evidence," and part of a quartet rendition of "'Round Midnight." Nothing too essential, but completists will want this.

LPS TO SEARCH FOR

The bootleg album *Monk/Tatum—The Vibes Are On* (Chazzer 2002) is valuable for releasing three numbers from a 1948 radio broadcast. Monk, Idrees Sulieman, Curly Russell, and Art Blakey perform "Just You, Just Me," "All the Things

You Are," and "Suburban Eyes"; virtually the only live Monk club date ever documented from the classic Bebop era. Also on the obscure LP are 1951 piano solos from Art Tatum plus Charlie Parker and Dizzy Gillespie in 1952 performing "A Night in Tunisia."

Thelonious Monk/Herbie Nichols (Savoy 1166) has four numbers ("Brake's Sake," "Gallop's Gallop," "Shuffle Boil," and "Nica's Tempo") of Monk as a sideman with altoist Gigi Gryce's quartet plus a lesser-known 1952 date by pianist Herbie Nichols. Performed a day after Storyville's *Monk in Copenhagen* CD, the two-LP *Live in Stockholm 1961* (Dragon 151/152) has a fine performance by the Monk-Rouse-Ore-Dunlop quartet.

From the Thelonious Monk Quartet's Columbia period, *Monk's Dream* (Columbia 40786), the two-LP *Tokyo Concerts* (Columbia 38510), *Misterioso* (Columbia 2416), *It's Monk's Time* (Columbia 8984), *Monk* (Columbia 9091), the two-LP *Live at the Jazz Workshop* (Columbia 38269), and *Underground* (Columbia 9632) have not been reissued yet. Also worth getting is *Live at the Village Gate* (Xanadu 202), *The Great Canadian Concert* (Can Am 1100), *Sphere* (Yes to Jazz 10051), and *Epistrophy* (Yes to Jazz 20058). None of these quartet outings are essential, but all are excellent and add to the legacy of the unique Thelonious Monk.

FILMS

Thelonious Monk can be seen playing "Blue Monk" in both 1957's *The Sound of Jazz* (Vintage Jazz Classics 2001) and at the 1958 Newport Jazz Festival in *Jazz on a Summer's Day* (New Yorker Video 16590). *Thelonious Monk in Oslo* (Rhapsody 9024) has three selections by the pianist's quartet in 1966. *American Composer* (BMG Video 80065) is a decent documentary on Monk but is easily topped by the utterly fascinating *Straight No Chaser* (Warner Video 11896), which does a superb job of showing what the legendary Thelonious Monk was really like; he is even seen in bed ordering room service!

The Pacesetters of the Bebop Era

While Charlie Parker, Dizzy Gillespie, Bud Powell, Max Roach, and Thelonious Monk tower over the classic Bebop era with their innovations, there were quite a few other significant contributors to the music. Any list of major Bebop pioneers would be lacking if it did not include Fats Navarro, J. J. Johnson, Dexter Gordon, Sonny Stitt, Oscar Pettiford, Kenny Clarke, and Tadd Dameron plus the others discussed in this "Pacesetters" section.

Trumpeters

The main influence on the trumpeters of the Bebop era was Roy Eldridge, whose advanced harmonic flights in the late 1930s/early '40s particularly inspired Dizzy Gillespie. Others who were thought of very highly by the young modernists included Charlie Shavers, Hot Lips Page, Louis Armstrong (whose influence was indirect), Bobby Hackett, and, surprisingly, Harry James, who was (along with Satch) the best-known trumpeter of the 1940s.

Dizzy Gillespie was the leading trumpeter not only of the Bebop era but arguably of post-1940 jazz, although the complexity of his improvisations discouraged most trumpeters from trying to copy him too closely. Howard McGhee was considered a close competitor during 1945–48, even if he was surpassed by Fats Navarro. Navarro's influence (through Clifford Brown by the mid-1950s) would be enormous long after his early death. Miles Davis offered an alternative, "cooler" approach to playing Bebop, but his influence would be felt much more by later generations of trumpeters. Most of the other trumpeters in this section mixed together aspects of Eldridge, Gillespie, and Navarro to form their own styles.

SONNY BERMAN

b. Apr. 21, 1925, New Haven, CT, d. Jan. 16, 1947, New York, NY

One of the early casualties from drugs, Sonny Berman had great potential. With Woody Herman's First Herd, Berman's Boppish playing, which sometimes found him alternating between two keys, was becoming increasingly distinctive in 1946, and his future seemed limitless.

The shortage of talented musicians during the World War II years (due to the draft) made it possible for Berman to start working regularly as a dance band musician when he was just 15. He passed through many orchestras, including those of Louis Prima, Sonny Dunham, Tommy Dorsey, Georgie Auld, Harry James, and Benny Goodman. Most significant was Berman's association with Woody Herman's Herd (1945–46). He took notable solos on quite a few recordings with Herman, including "Sidewalks of Cuba," "Let It Snow, Let It Snow, Let It Snow," and a crazy bitonal flurry on "Your Father's Mustache." Berman was also featured on a couple sessions with the Woodchoppers (a small band out of the Herman Orchestra), a record date for Dial co-led with Bill Harris, and a jam session released decades later by Esoteric and reissued by Onyx. After Herman broke up the Herd, Sonny Berman briefly freelanced but then died from a heart attack that was caused by drugs when he was just 21. He had barely gotten started with what most likely would have been a significant career.

LPS TO SEARCH FOR

Most of Sonny Berman's most important solos were made with Woody Herman's Herd and Woodchoppers. *Beautiful Jewish Music* (Onyx 211), four lengthy live selections from January 24, 1946, features Berman with a nonet of players who were then or would be in the future associated with Woody Herman, including tenor saxophonist Al Cohn, Serge Chaloff, and pianist Ralph Burns. The occasionally loose music has Berman's longest surviving trumpet solos. *The Tempo Jazzmen/The Hermanites* (Spotlite 132), in addition to a Dizzy Gillespie date with the Tempo Jazzmen, includes Berman's Dial session, highlighted by his haunting solo on "Nocturne."

MILES DAVIS

b. May 25, 1926, Alton, IL, d. Sept. 28, 1991, Santa Monica, CA

One of the true giants of jazz history, Miles Davis was one of the rare jazz innovators whose style constantly evolved with time, going through many different eras, some of which he helped found. His contributions to Cool Jazz, Hard Bop, modal music, the avant-garde, fusion, and crossover through the decades sometimes confounded fans who wished he would quit changing, but they resulted in his creating an enormous body of musical accomplishments and changing jazz history on a few occasions. He played a mostly Bebop-oriented repertoire through 1956 (up until the time his first classic quintet broke up), so that will be the cutoff

point in this biography and discussion of his recordings; the trumpeter's later periods will be covered in other books in this series.

During the Bebop Era, Miles Davis's mellow tone and simpler approach was to Dizzy Gillespie what Bix Beiderbecke had been to Louis Armstrong in the 1920s, offering a "cool" alternative to the "hot" virtuoso. While few trumpeters could copy Gillespie (whose style and technical abilities were just too wondrous), Davis and Fats Navarro would in the long run be more closely emulated; at least it was possible to sound like them!

Miles Davis grew up in a middle-class family in East St. Louis, Illinois. He was given his first trumpet by his father for his 13th birthday, and early on he admired Bobby Hackett's lyricism (Hackett's 1938 recording of "Embraceable You" made an impression on him), Harry James (although Miles sounded nothing like him), and local hero Clark Terry. Davis played with Eddie Randall's Blue Devils during 1941–43 and had a musical thrill sitting in with the Billy Eckstine Orchestra in 1944 when it passed through town; Dizzy Gillespie and Charlie Parker were in the band at the time.

A promising young trumpeter with a small range and a developing sound, Davis went to New York in September 1944, supposedly to study at Juilliard. However, he spent more time in 52nd Street clubs, sitting in now and then with bands in addition to seeing Bird and Diz whenever he could. After a short time, he dropped out of school and was playing nightly with Coleman Hawkins's combo. Davis made his recording debut on April 24, 1945, on a date with dancer-singer Rubberlegs Williams but sounded quite nervous. However, he fared a bit better the next time, playing on a Charlie Parker session in the fall that resulted in the original versions of "Now's the Time" and "Billie's Bounce." Dizzy Gillespie had to fill in for him on "Ko Ko" since Miles (who was still just 19) could not yet negotiate the rapid tempo.

Charlie Parker and Dizzy Gillespie went to Los Angeles in late 1945, and a few months later Davis joined Benny Carter's orchestra so as to follow his idols West. Gillespie soon left for New York, but Bird stayed in Los Angeles. Davis was on a record date with Bird (March 28, 1946) that included famous versions of "Moose the Mooche," "Yardbird Suite," and "Ornithology." Parker's mental collapse a few months later resulted in his being committed for a time and Davis returned East. But when the altoist was released in early 1947, he formed his finest working group, a quintet with Miles, Duke Jordan, Tommy Potter, and Max Roach. Miles

Davis was improving month by month as a trumpeter during this time and, realizing that he would never be a virtuoso on the level of Gillespie, he became comfortable with his own lyrical and thoughtful style, sounding relaxed even on the faster pieces and being a particularly strong asset on ballads.

Other than an odd session with Gene Ammons in which they backed two singers on four songs (an October 18, 1946, outing that was not released initially for over four decades), Miles Davis's first date as a leader took place on October 14, 1947, when he fronted the Charlie Parker Quintet (with Bird switching to tenor) for his four compositions "Milestones," "Little Willie Leaps," "Half Nelson," and "Sippin' at Bells." Although he remained a member of Parker's group into December 1948, Davis made an attempt to lead his own band a few months earlier. Becoming acquainted with arranger Gil Evans (who would remain his lifelong best friend) and often hanging out with Gerry Mulligan and other like-minded modernists, Miles conceived of forming a band that had the tonal qualities of Claude Thornhill's orchestra (which utilized French horns and a tuba) along with the innovations of Bebop. He put together a nonet consisting of baritonist Mulligan, altoist Lee Konitz, John Lewis, Al McKibbon, Max Roach, French horn, tuba, and trombonist Mike Zwerin that in September 1948 played for two weeks at the Royal Roost as the intermission band for Count Basie's orchestra. With arrangements by Miles, Evans, Mulligan, John Lewis, and Johnny Carisi ("Israel"), the cool-toned nonet introduced a new sound to jazz.

Unfortunately that would be its only gig. However, after Davis left Parker's quintet, he led three recording sessions by the group during 1949–50 (with Jay Johnson or Kai Winding on trombone) that resulted in a dozen titles that would be quite influential during the 1950s, when it was dubbed "The Birth of the Cool Nonet." Typically, by then the trumpeter had moved on.

He never forgot his roots in Bebop. On a live recording from the 1949 Paris Jazz Festival with Tadd Dameron, Davis sounds surprisingly extroverted and quite boppish. After returning from Europe in 1949, the trumpeter entered into a dark period in which he became addicted to heroin, struggled from day to day, and scuffled, mostly playing in pickup groups that at times included Sonny Rollins and altoist Jackie McLean. However Davis's 1952–54 recordings can be considered some of the very first Hard Bop sessions, often featuring such players as J. J. Johnson, Jimmy Heath, Art Blakey, and Horace Silver; a date in 1953 had a final reunion with Charlie Parker (heard again on tenor).

In 1954 Davis finally kicked heroin and made such major recordings as a meeting with Thelonious Monk and Milt Jackson, the first versions of "Four" and "Solar," and the classic "Walkin'/Blue 'n Boogie" jam session-flavored set with J. J. Johnson and Lucky Thompson. In 1955 he had a full comeback. Davis's appearance at the Newport Jazz Festival, which was climaxed by playing "'Round Midnight" with Monk, alerted the jazz press and public that he was back. Later in the year he formed his first classic quintet, a group also including tenor saxophonist John Coltrane, pianist Red Garland, bassist Paul Chambers, and drummer Philly Joe Jones. Their recordings for Prestige and Columbia during 1955–56 are still famous. Davis's signing with Columbia resulted in a longtime association that gave him fame and would result in the recording of many influential gems.

After his quintet temporarily broke up in early 1957, Miles Davis began to move further from his Bebop roots. During the next few years he would be showcased on recordings with the Gil Evans Orchestra, lead a super sextet (with Coltrane and altoist Cannonball Adderley) that explored modal music, and become one of the most famous of all jazz musicians. Miles Davis became so well known that his wardrobe, stage manner (often leaving the stand during his sidemen's solos), and public behavior would make headlines. But that is another story.

⏹ 10 *The Complete Birth of the Cool / Sept. 4, 1948–Mar. 9, 1950 / Capitol 94550*

Other than an obscure set from 1946 not released until the 1980s (*Bopping the Blues*) and a date in which he fronted the Charlie Parker Quintet, Miles Davis's first recordings as a leader were with his legendary "Birth of the Cool" nonet. This deluxe CD has not only the original dozen studio sides but all of the music that exists from two radio broadcasts that took place during the nonet's only actual gig, a two-week period at the Royal Roost. The music, although based in Bebop, is notable for the cool tones of the principals (which include the leader-trumpeter, Kai Winding, J. J. Johnson or Mike Zwerin on trombone, altoist Lee Konitz, and baritonist Gerry Mulligan plus French horn and tuba), the creative and tightly-arranged charts (by Mulligan, Davis, John Lewis, Gil Evans, and Johnny Carisi), and the short but effective solos. Highlights include "Move," "Moon Dreams," "Boplicity," and "Israel," while the live sessions (which are mostly alternate versions of the same songs) include two numbers ("Why Do I Love You" and "S'il Vous Plait") not recorded in the studios by the band. Classic and highly influential music.

5 *Bopping the Blues / Oct. 18, 1946 / Black Lion 760102*

6 *Birdland Days / Feb. 18, 1950–Sept. 29, 1951 / Fresh Sound 124*

Bopping the Blues surprised collectors when it came out since no one had ever heard of this music before. Consisting of four songs that, with eight alternate takes, total a dozen performances, none of the performances had been out prior to the release of this 1987 CD. Actually the music is of lesser interest with all of the selections featuring vocals by either Earl Coleman or Ann Baker, but there are short spots for Miles Davis and Gene Ammons, who are joined by a four-piece rhythm section that includes Art Blakey and pianist Linton Garner. It may not be essential, but it gives listeners some additional glimpses of Davis's playing at an early period in his career. *Birdland Days* has three radio broadcasts from Birdland during 1950–51 that feature Davis with young all-star Bop groups. The recording quality is a bit erratic, but the solos (from the likes of J.J. Johnson and tenors Stan Getz, Sonny Rollins, Eddie "Lockjaw" Davis, and Big Nick Nicholas) are enthusiastic and freewheeling.

* *Chronicle—The Complete Prestige Recordings / Jan. 17, 1951–Oct. 26, 1956 / Prestige 012*

6 *And Horns / Jan. 17, 1951 + Feb. 19, 1953 / Original Jazz Classics 053*

7 *Dig / Oct. 5, 1951 / Original Jazz Classics 005*

5 *Our Delight / 1952 / Prestige 24117*

8 *Collectors' Items / Jan. 30, 1953–Mar. 16, 1956 / Original Jazz Classics 071*

During 1951–56, Miles Davis recorded primarily for Prestige (other than a few important sessions for Blue Note and his first Columbia album). All of the Prestige studio recordings are on the eight-CD box *Chronicle*; not included is the live music that makes up *Our Delight*. All of the music is also available individually in the Original Jazz Classics single-disc reissues. Together they trace an important period in Miles Davis's life, from his scuffling years to his first classic quintet. *And Horns* has two of the trumpeter's more obscure sets, his first recordings with Sonny Rollins (a slightly subpar effort from Davis in 1951) and four titles with tenors Al Cohn (who contributed the arrangements) and Zoot Sims; nice music, but not that substantial. *Dig* is more consistent, an early date with Sonny Rollins and Jackie McLean that consists of two standards (including "My Old Flame"), four lesser-known originals, and "Dig." Miles Davis was scuffling at the time he recorded *Our Delight* (which was formerly two LPs), a live performance from St. Louis with tenor saxophonist Jimmy Forrest and a local rhythm section. The trumpeter plays reasonably well, but the recording quality is on and off. *Collectors' Items* is much better, living up to its name. It consists of Davis's last recording with Charlie Parker (a sextet date from 1953 that has both Parker and Sonny Rollins on tenors) and a 1956 quintet outing with Rollins, Tommy Flanagan, Paul Chambers, and drummer Art Taylor. The latter is highlighted by Davis's version of Dave Brubeck's "In Your Own Sweet Way."

9 *Volume One / May 9, 1952 + Mar. 6, 1954 / Blue Note 81501*

9 *Volume Two / Apr. 20, 1953 / Blue Note 81502*

The music on these two CDs has never been crowned "The Birth of the Hard Bop," but the three sessions are among the earliest recordings in that idiom. *Volume One* has a 1952 sextet date with J.J. Johnson, Jackie McLean, pianist Gil Coggins, Oscar Pettiford, and Kenny Clarke that includes "Dear Old Stockholm" and "Woody 'n You" among its more memorable selections. The other session on the disc is a quartet outing from 1954 with pianist Horace Silver, Percy Heath, and Art Blakey that has some particularly strong playing from Davis and Silver, with the trumpeter's muted feature on "It Never Entered My Mind" looking ahead toward his quintet period. *Volume Two* consists of six songs (plus five alternate takes) from a strong 1953 date with J.J. Johnson, Jimmy Heath, Coggins, Percy Heath, and Blakey that includes "Ray's Idea," "Tempus Fugit," and "C. T. A." Despite the trumpeter's personal problems during this era, he is heard in top form on all three of his Blue Note dates.

9 *Blue Haze / May 19, 1953–Apr. 3, 1954 / Original Jazz Classics 093*

9 *Walkin' / Apr. 3 + 29, 1954 / Original Jazz Classics 213*

9 *Bags' Groove / June 29, 1954 + Dec. 24, 1954 / Original Jazz Classics 245*

8 *Miles Davis and the Modern Jazz Giants / Dec. 24, 1954 + Oct. 26, 1956 / Original Jazz Classics 347*

8 *The Musings of Miles / June 7, 1955 / Original Jazz Classics 004*

6 *Blue Moods / July 9, 1955 / Original Jazz Classics 043*

6 *Quintet/Sextet / Aug. 5, 1955 / Original Jazz Classics 012*

During 1953–55, Miles Davis recorded quite a few albums for Prestige with a variety of pickup groups. *Blue Haze,* which includes such sidemen as John Lewis, Percy Heath, Max Roach, Horace Silver, and Art Blakey, is notable for containing classic versions of "Tune Up," "When Lights Are Low," "Four," and "Old Devil Moon." Miles Davis's comeback after several years of struggling officially began with the *Walkin'* set. There are three titles (including "Solar") with a quintet that includes Horace Silver and altoist Dave Schildkraut plus versions of "Walkin'" and "Blue 'n Boogie" with a superb sextet also featuring Silver, J. J. Johnson, and Lucky Thompson; the title cut is considered a classic. The June 29, 1954, session that is heard on *Bags' Groove* (which has a quintet made up of Davis, Rollins, Silver, Percy Heath, and Kenny Clarke) introduced three of Rollins's best-known originals: "Airegin," "Oleo," and "Doxy." Also included are two long versions of "Bags' Groove," with the issued rendition having a classic Thelonious Monk piano solo; that quintet date also includes Milt Jackson, Heath, and Clarke. *Miles Davis and the Modern Jazz Giants* has the remainder of the latter session ("Swing Spring" and "Bemsha Swing" and two versions of "The Man I Love") along with a 1956 rendition of "'Round Midnight" that pales next to the Columbia version. The Miles-Monk-Jackson combination was magical, so it is a pity that this was a one-time encounter.

The Musings of Miles was recorded as Davis was in the early stages of forming his quintet. Future band members Red Garland and Philly Joe Jones are heard on this quartet set with Davis and Oscar Pettiford. The focus throughout is mostly on the trumpeter, who sounds quite lyrical on such numbers as "Will You Still Be Mine?" "A Gal in Calico," and the blues "Green Haze." *Blue Moods* is a bit unusual, since the instrumentation is trumpet, trombone (Britt Woodman), vibes (Teddy Charles), bass (Charles Mingus), and drums (a young Elvin Jones). The four selections (which include "Nature Boy" and "There's No You") are melancholy and introspective, with the emphasis being on the ensemble's tone colors rather than on individual solos. Both *Blue Moods* and *Quintet/Sextet* are quite brief (being straight reissues of skimpy LPs). *Quintet/Sextet* is a lesser-known set in which Davis, Milt Jackson, pianist Ray Bryant, Percy Heath,

and Art Taylor perform four numbers (including "Dr. Jackle"); altoist Jackie McLean is on two of the songs.

10 *Miscellaneous Miles Davis 1955–1957 / July 17, 1955–Dec. 18, 1957 / Jazz Unlimited 2050*

7 *The New Miles Davis Quintet / Nov. 16, 1955 / Original Jazz Classics 006*

8 *Cookin' with the Miles Davis Quintet / May 11, 1956 + Oct. 26, 1956 / Original Jazz Classics 128*

8 *Workin' with the Miles Davis Quintet / May 11, 1956 + Oct. 26, 1956 / Original Jazz Classics 296*

8 *Relaxin' with the Miles Davis Quintet / May 11, 1956 + Oct. 26, 1956 / Original Jazz Classics 190*

8 *Steamin' with the Miles Davis Quintet / May 11, 1956 + Oct. 26, 1956 / Original Jazz Classics 391*

10 *'Round About Midnight / Oct. 27, 1955–Sept. 10, 1956 / Columbia 40610*

Miscellaneous Miles Davis in 1993 for the first time released Davis's legendary set from the 1955 Newport Jazz Festival, a 22-minute performance that made the jazz critics aware that the trumpeter had returned as a giant. On the bandstand with Zoot Sims, Gerry Mulligan, Thelonious Monk, Percy Heath, and drummer Connie Kay (and introduced in humorous fashion by Duke Ellington), Miles performs "Hackensack," "Now's the Time," and a classic version of "'Round Midnight," the last in a quartet with its composer on piano. Also on this CD is a 1957 Birdland miniset with tenor saxophonist Bobby Jaspar, three songs with a European orchestra, and a trio of numbers from Davis's 1956 tour of Europe, including a version of "Lady Be Good" in which he shares the bandstand with Lester Young.

By the fall of 1955, Miles Davis had his new band together, a unit that included the unknown tenorman John Coltrane, Red Garland, bassist Paul Chambers, and Philly Joe Jones. Their first recording, *The New Miles Davis Quintet,* is generally rewarding, although Coltrane's part is quite minor; he sounds a little nervous, and his solos are brief. Best among Davis's performances are "How Am I to Know" and "Stablemates." In 1956, Columbia was very interested in signing Miles Davis, but he still owed four records to Prestige. So, to quickly fulfill his obligations, on May 11 and October 26, Davis and his quintet went through their usual nightclub repertoire, playing one song after another without repeating any of the numbers. Although recorded a bit like a jam session, the four resulting albums (*Cookin', Workin', Relaxin',* and *Steamin'*) are consistently excellent and largely interchangeable. *Cookin'* includes Davis's first recording of "My Funny Valentine," *Relaxin'* has "If I Were a Bell" and "Oleo," *Workin'* is notable for "It Never Entered My Mind" and "Four," and *Steamin'* includes "Surrey with the Fringe on Top," "Diane," and "When I Fall in Love."

But the best recording by the original Miles Davis Quintet is its debut on Columbia. Each of the six selections is given definitive treatment, particularly "'Round Midnight," "Ah Leu Cha," "Dear Old Stockholm," and "Bye Bye Blackbird." Miles Davis sounds quite mature, John Coltrane is distinctive, and both Miles and 'Trane sound ready to stretch jazz beyond Bebop. A classic.

LPS TO SEARCH FOR

First Miles (Savoy 1196) has all of the music recorded at Miles Davis's very first recording (the April 24, 1945 date by singer Rubberlegs Williams with tenorman Herbie Field's group) plus the 1947 session in which Davis fronted the Charlie Parker Quintet (with Bird on tenor) and introduced four originals (including "Milestones"). *The Paris Festival International* (Columbia 34804) is a real surprise, for not only does it feature Davis playing extroverted Bebop in Paris with Tadd Dameron, James Moody, Kenny Clarke, and bassist Barney Spieler (the trumpeter even hits some high notes), but Miles also verbally introduces some of the songs, years before his speaking voice was reduced to a whisper.

FILMS

Miles Davis's earliest appearance on film is in the half-hour special *Theater for a Story* (1959) that finds him playing "So What" with his quintet (which includes John Coltrane) and several numbers with the Gil Evans Orchestra. His trumpet is featured throughout the soundtrack of the 1958 French film *Elevator to the Gallows*.

KENNY DORHAM

b. Aug. 30, 1924, Fairfield, TX, d. Dec. 5, 1972, New York, NY

A very good trumpeter and an underrated composer, Kenny Dorham was overshadowed throughout his career by more flamboyant players. He was one of the early Bebop soloists and evolved into becoming one of the key Hard Bop musicians of the 1960s, helping to introduce tenor saxophonist Joe Henderson.

Dorham played piano first, switching to trumpet while in high school. He served in the army in 1942–43, worked with Russell Jacquet in Houston, and in New York really launched his career by playing with the first short-lived Dizzy Gillespie big band and with Billy Eckstine's orchestra, both in 1945. Dorham recorded two sessions with the Bebop Boys in 1946 (which also included Sonny Stitt, Bud Powell and, on one occasion, Fats Navarro), gigged with Mercer Ellington and Lionel Hampton, and in December 1948 became Miles Davis's replacement with the Charlie Parker Quintet, staying a year. Dorham freelanced in the early 1950s, was a member of the first edition of the Jazz Messengers in 1954, and led the Jazz Prophets. After Clifford Brown's tragic death, Dorham took his place with Max Roach's quintet (1956–58) and then was primarily a bandleader. He recorded for Riverside (including a 1958 date on which he sang), New Jazz, Time, and most notably Blue Note (several classics during 1961–64). Among his compositions were "Blue Bossa" (which became a standard), "Minor Holiday," "Lotus Blossom," "Prince Albert," and "Una Mas."

Surprisingly, after 1964 Dorham (who was just 40) deemphasized his playing, did not lead any more full record dates, and instead often contributed witty jazz reviews to *Downbeat,* including some that tore apart free jazz. He only played on a part-time basis, working in the post office, and his health faded in the late 1960s. Kenny Dorham died from kidney disease in 1972 at the age of 48, underrated to the end.

7 ***Blues in Bebop / Jan. 3, 1946–May 22, 1956 / Savoy 17028***

7 ***Kenny Dorham Quintet / Dec. 15, 1953 / Original Jazz Classics 113***

Kenny Dorham did not lead his first record date until 1953. *Blues in Bebop* is a sampling of some of his sideman sessions for Savoy, mostly from the classic Bebop era. Dorham takes a short solo with the Billy Eckstine Orchestra on "The Jitney Man" and is featured on one of the Bebop Boys dates (eight songs plus two alternates with Sonny Stitt and Bud Powell), with a Milt Jackson sextet in 1949, on three broadcast titles with Charlie Parker, and for four songs from a 1956 LP by Cecil Payne. The music is fine, but, since the sessions are not complete, it is a pity that this valuable music was not released in a more comprehensive form. Dorham's actual debut as a leader, a quintet outing with Jimmy Heath (on tenor and baritone), Walter Bishop, Percy Heath, and Kenny Clarke, has been expanded in the Original Jazz Classics CD reissue with two extra blues and an additional alternate take. The playing on such songs as "An Oscar for Oscar," "I Love You," and even "Be My Love" is fine and, although nothing unusual happens, this is a solid showcase for the trumpeter.

9 *Afro-Cuban / Jan. 30, 1955 + Mar. 29, 1955 / Blue Note 46815*

8 *'Round About Midnight at the Café Bohemia / May 31, 1956 / Blue Note 33576*

Kenny Dorham was one of the few major Bop trumpeters to become an important force in Hard Bop, since Dizzy Gillespie and Miles Davis (who helped found the idiom) had other musical interests, drugs short-circuited the careers of Howard McGhee and Red Rodney, and an early death kept Fats Navarro from making any direct contributions. *Afro-Cuban* can easily be divided into two. The first five performances (which include the original recorded versions of Dorham's "Lotus Flower" and "Minor's Holiday") match the trumpeter on a Latin jazz-flavored set with J. J. Johnson, tenor saxophonist Hank Mobley, Cecil Payne, Horace Silver, Oscar Pettiford, Art Blakey, and Potato Valdes on congas. The remaining four selections (four of Dorham's originals, including "La Villa") is by a sextet with Dorham, Mobley, Payne, Silver, Percy Heath, and Blakey and is much more straight-ahead in nature. The double-CD *'Round About Midnight* expands the original 42 minutes heard on the earlier single LP to over two hours. Dorham's regular sextet of that period, a group also including J. R. Monterose on tenor, guitarist Kenny Burrell, pianist Bobby Timmons, bassist Sam Jones, and drummer Arthur Edgehill, was not destined for longevity. However, the swinging music that the band created is quite enjoyable, and the 14 numbers (plus three alternate takes) include eight Dorham originals.

9 *Jazz Contrasts / May 21 + 27, 1957 / Original Jazz Classics 028*

8 *2 Horns, 2 Rhythm / Nov. 13, 1957–Dec. 1957 / Original Jazz Classics 463*

6 *This Is the Moment / July 1958–Aug. 1958 / Original Jazz Classics 812*

8 *Blue Spring / Feb. 18, 1959 / Original Jazz Classics 134*

7 *Quiet Kenny / Nov. 13, 1959 / Original Jazz Classics 250*

During 1957–59, Kenny Dorham recorded four albums for the Riverside label and one for New Jazz; all have been reissued on Original Jazz Classics CDs. The projects are diverse but generally quite rewarding, predating most of Dorham's famous Blue Note dates. *Jazz Contrasts* has some particularly wonderful music. Dorham teams up with Sonny Rollins, Hank Jones, Oscar Pettiford, and Max Roach for memorable versions of "Falling in Love with Love," "I'll Remember April," and the trumpeter's "La Villa." At the time Dorham, Rollins, and Roach were playing regularly in Roach's quintet. In addition, there are three numbers (all but "My Old Flame" without the tenor saxophonist) that add the fluent harp of Betty Glamman and put the emphasis on the trumpeter's melodic skills. *2 Horns, 2 Rhythm* has Dorham and altoist Ernie Henry (on his final recording) performing in a quartet with either Eddie Mathias or Wilbur Ware on bass plus drummer G. T. Hogan; Dorham makes a rare appearance on piano during "Soon." Dorham and Henry blend quite well on three of the trumpeter's originals (including "Lotus Blossom") and five standards, highlighted by "Is It True What They Say About Dixie?"

This Is the Moment is a particularly unusual entry in Kenny Dorham's discography, for it is his only vocal album. Dorham sings on all ten standards (he was probably trying to go after Chet Baker's audience) and, although his voice is pleasant, there is nothing all that special about it. More significant is Curtis Fuller's muted trombone in the ensembles and the fact that this was pianist Cedar Walton's recording debut. A historical curiosity. *Blue Spring* is also unusual but on a higher level. All six selections have the word "spring" in their title ("It Might As Well Be Spring," "Spring Is Here," and four of the trumpeter's originals). Dorham's creative arrangements feature a septet that includes altoist Cannonball Adderley (in typically jubilant form), Cecil Payne, David Amram on French horn, Cedar Walton, bassist Paul Chambers, and either Jimmy Cobb or Philly Joe Jones on drums. High-quality straight-ahead jazz. *Quiet Kenny*, as can be guessed from the title, puts the emphasis on ballads. Dorham is showcased with a quartet that includes Tommy Flanagan, Paul Chambers, and drummer Art Taylor on such numbers as his "Lotus Blossom," "Alone Together," "I Had the Craziest Dream," and a brief "Mack the Knife." Tasty music.

9 *Whistle Stop / Jan. 15, 1961 / Blue Note 28978*

10 *Matador/Inta Somethin' / Nov. 1961–Apr. 15, 1962 / Blue Note 84460*

10 *Una Mas / Apr. 1, 1963 / Blue Note 46515*

8 *Trompeta Toccata / Sept. 14, 1964 / Blue Note 84181*

Whistle Stop is a high-quality Hard Bop date that is particularly noteworthy for featuring seven forgotten but superior Kenny Dorham compositions, tunes that today's Hard Boppers should be inspired to revive. Dorham is heard in prime form in a quintet with Hank Mobley, pianist Kenny Drew, Paul Chambers, and Philly Joe Jones. *Matador/Inta Somethin'* is a single CD that has all of the music originally released on two separate but complementary LPs. In both cases Dorham and altoist Jackie McLean (a forward thinking Hard Bopper) share the frontline, with either Bobby Timmons or Walter Bishop on piano, Teddy Smith or Leroy Vinnegar on bass, and J. C. Moses or Art Taylor on drums. Everyone plays quite well, and among the more memorable selections are "El Matador," "Smile," Dorham's "Una Mas," and "It Could Happen to You." While *Matador* originally came out on United Artists and *Inta Something* was a Pacific Jazz release, *Una Mas* (which has a remake of the title cut that at 15 minutes is twice as long as the earlier version) was always on Blue Note. In addition to bassist Butch Warren, Dorham presents three of the most enduring "young lions" of the period: tenor saxophonist Joe Henderson, pianist Herbie Hancock, and drummer Tony Williams. Henderson is heard in his recording debut, while Hancock and Williams had yet to join the Miles Davis Quintet. In addition to the catchy "Una Mas," the repertoire includes two other Dorham originals ("Straight Ahead" and "Sao Paulo") plus a previously unreleased version of "If Ever I Would Leave You." A classic. *Trompeta Toccata* was Dorham's last full album as a leader, and there is certainly no sign of decline. He teams up with Henderson, Flanagan, bassist Richard Davis, and drummer Albert "Tootie" Heath for three originals plus the tenor's "Mamacita" and sounds quite modern. It is difficult to believe that his career largely stopped after this recording.

LPS TO SEARCH FOR

The Kenny Dorham Memorial Album (Xanadu 125) is an obscure outing from 1960 in a quintet with baritonist Charles Davis, Tommy Flanagan, Butch Warren, and drummer Buddy Enlow. "Stage West," "I'm An Old Cowhand," "Stella By Starlight," and "Lazy Afternoon" are among its best selections. Also in 1960, Dorham recorded two albums for the Time label, both reissued by Bainbridge. *Kenny Dorham* (Bainbridge 1048) is a fine quintet date with Davis, pianist Steve Kuhn, Enlow, and either Jimmy Garrison or Warren on bass. The repertoire has three Dorham originals

(including "Horn Salute") and a trio of jazz standards. Even better is *Showboat* (Bainbridge 1043), six songs from the Kern-Hammerstein show performed by Dorham, Jimmy Heath, Kenny Drew, Jimmy Garrison, and Art Taylor. Their versions of "Why Do I Love You," "Make Believe," and "Ol' Man River" are standouts.

JOE GUY

b. Sept. 20, 1920, Birmingham, AL, d. ca. 1962, New York, NY or Birmingham, AL

A promising if overly enthusiastic trumpeter in the early 1940s, Joe Guy had a career that was ruined by drug abuse, and he never fulfilled his potential. After short stints with the big bands of Fats Waller and Teddy Hill in the late 1930s, Guy was a member of the Coleman Hawkins Orchestra (1939–40), where he took occasional solos. He was with Charlie Barnet briefly in 1941 and then became a regular at Minton's Playhouse, working as a member of the after-hours house band that also included Thelonious Monk, bassist Nick Fenton, and Kenny Clarke. Guy pops up on quite a few of the live recordings captured by Jerry Newman during 1941–42 (including dates with Charlie Christian, Hot Lips Page, Don Byas, and Roy Eldridge). Unfortunately he sounds musically immature and consistently overextends himself, coming across as a Roy Eldridge disciple who was trying (not always successfully) to incorporate some of Dizzy Gillespie's ideas into his playing. Perhaps if he had had a longer career, he would have straightened his style out.

Guy was with the Cootie Williams Orchestra in 1942 (soloing on the debut recording of Thelonious Monk's "Epistrophy"). He became Billie Holiday's boyfriend, and both became heroin addicts. Guy played with Jazz at the Philharmonic on a few occasions during 1945–46 (including on a very good Lady Day session), but in 1947 he was busted for drug use. After a short time in jail and some freelancing, Joe Guy permanently dropped out of music in 1950. He never led his own record date and died in obscurity in 1962.

BENNY HARRIS

b. Apr. 23, 1919, New York, NY, d. Feb. 11, 1975, San Francisco, CA

Benny Harris made some important contributions to classic Bebop but dropped out of music early. He started out on French horn, switching to trumpet when he was 18. Harris played with the Tiny Bradshaw Orchestra in 1939 and was with Earl Hines's big band twice, in 1941 and with the legendary unrecorded unit of 1943. He worked on 52nd Street in a variety of small groups, including with Benny Carter, Pete Brown, the John Kirby Sextet, Herbie Fields, Coleman Hawkins, Don Byas, and Thelonious Monk. Bailey recorded with Clyde Hart (December 1944) and Byas (1945), and was with Boyd Raeburn's orchestra during 1944–45. However, after 1945 he played less often, his most notable later associations being with the 1949 Dizzy Gillespie big band and on a record date with Charlie Parker in 1952. Harris, a decent if limited trumpeter, is most notable for having composed "Ornithology," "Crazeology," "Reets and I," and "Wahoo" (which is based on "Perdido"). After moving to California in 1952, Benny Harris (who never led his own record date) retired from music.

HOWARD McGHEE

b. Mar. 6, 1918, Tulsa, OK, d. July 17, 1987, New York, NY

One of the most exciting trumpeters of the classic Bebop era and an early influence on Fats Navarro (who influenced Clifford Brown, who in turn influenced practically every trumpeter that followed), Howard McGhee had a prime that was unfortunately brief. He originally played clarinet and tenor and did not actually start on the trumpet until he was 17. McGhee worked in territory bands in the Midwest, was with Lionel Hampton in 1941, and was fairly well featured with Andy Kirk's orchestra (1941–42), including on "McGhee Special." At that time, McGhee was influenced mostly by Roy Eldridge, but he already had his own clipped sound and was playing nightly at the jam sessions at Minton's and Monroe's Uptown House.

McGhee worked with the orchestras of Charlie Barnet (1942–43), Andy Kirk again (Fats Navarro was also in the trumpet section), Georgie Auld, and Count Basie. By 1945 he had learned from Dizzy Gillespie's innovations and ranked almost at the top with Dizzy. He made a strong impression as a member of Coleman Hawkins's Quintet, traveled to Los Angeles with Hawk (where he helped to introduce Bebop to the West Coast), and stayed for a couple years. McGhee performed with Jazz at the Philharmonic, was on a couple sessions with Charlie Parker (including the disastrous "Lover Man" date), and played in Central Avenue clubs, recording for Dial. After returning to New York, he participated on an exciting date with Navarro in 1948 and worked steadily for a time.

Unfortunately heroin largely fouled up McGhee's career for many years, and he lost his best opportunity for fame in the jazz world. McGhee was on a USO tour during the Korean War and recorded for Bethlehem during 1955–56. But in general the 1950s were a wasted period, and the trumpeter seemed to largely fade away after 1952. He did make a comeback during 1960–62, recording several strong dates. But other than a big band session in 1966, he was barely on records again until 1976. Although he had a burst of recording activity during 1976–79 and there were some good moments, McGhee by then had been forgotten for decades and was doomed to be underrated if not completely overlooked in the jazz history books. But a listen to some of his records from the 1945–49 period shows that, at his peak, Howard McGhee was one of the masters of Bebop.

10 *Trumpet at Tempo / Sept. 4, 1945–Dec. 3, 1947 / Jazz Classics 6009*
9 *1948 / Feb. 1948–Oct. 11, 1948 / Classics 1058*

Howard McGhee is heard at the peak of his powers on these two exciting CDs. *Trumpet at Tempo* has a date for Aladdin from 1945, two numbers from the same day as Charlie Parker's "Lover Man" date (ridiculously fast versions of "Trumpet at Tempo" and "Thermodynamics") that were recorded after Bird's departure, and 15 selections from Dial sessions in 1946–47 that are made up entirely of the trumpeter's originals. Among McGhee's sidemen are Teddy Edwards, James Moody, Dodo Marmarosa, Hank Jones, Milt Jackson, Ray Brown, J. C. Heard, and Roy Porter. Whether reinventing "Stardust" or jamming on "Midnight at Minton's," "Sleepwalker Boogie," and the haunting "Night Mist," Maggie never sounded better. *1948,* a chronological reissue that covers most of McGhee's activity for that year, draws its material from the Savoy, Vogue, Blue Star, and Blue Note catalogs. The first seven numbers (from Savoy dates) feature McGhee in a pair of sextets with Jimmy Heath (on alto and baritone), Milt Jackson, and (on the second date) Billy Eckstine, who sounds quite effective on valve trombone. Much rarer are McGhee's Vogue and Blue Star selections, cut in Paris in May 1948 with Jimmy Heath, tenor saxophonist Jesse Powell, and pianist Vernon Biddle. Wrapping up the CD are McGhee's three numbers from a classic Blue Note encounter with Fats Navarro. Highly recommended.

The "missing link" between Roy Eldridge and Fats Navarro, Howard McGhee was one of the finest trumpeters of the classic Bebop era.

THE WAYNE KNIGHT COLLECTION

7 *Maggie: The Savoy Sessions / Feb. 1948–1952 / Savoy 2219*

8 *Howard McGhee—Introducing the Kenny Drew Trio / Jan. 23, 1950–Apr. 16, 1953 / Blue Note 95747*

8 *Howard McGhee Volume 2—Tal Farlow Quartet / May 20, 1953 + Apr. 11, 1954 / Blue Note 95748*

Originally a two-LP set, *The Savoy Sessions* has been reissued by Japanese Denon as a single CD, bringing back the first 23 of the 27 selections. Unfortunately, in its desire to put out "reproductions," Denon reissued the CD with the earlier liner notes, which are now quite microscopic (they cannot be read without a magnifying glass), and they mention the four missing selections as if they are on the CD! The best music on the set is during the two sessions from 1948, which have McGhee sharing the frontline with altoist Jimmy Heath and vibraphonist Milt Jackson on one date and Billy

Eckstine (on valve trombone) and the obscure tenor Kenny Mann for the later session. Much of this music is also on the Classics CD *1948*, but this set also has a few alternate takes. The other part of the Savoy reissue is from McGhee's 1952 tour of the Pacific and was recorded in Guam. Despite the presence of J. J. Johnson, the pianoless sextet sounds a bit weak, and the "history of jazz" format of some of the music is a bit slapdash. Also, the former swing altoist Rudy Williams sounds quite awkward playing Bebop on tenor.

The two *Howard McGhee* Blue Note CDs actually both reissue a pair of former ten-inch LPs, with McGhee's session being paired with unrelated dates. The first disc has McGhee's all-star sextet (with J. J. Johnson, Brew Moore on tenor, Kenny Drew, Curly Russell, and Max Roach) performing six concise numbers (plus an alternate take), with four of the numbers being originals by Drew. The second half of the CD has Drew, Russell, and Art Blakey showcased on eight trio selections (plus two alternates) from 1953, playing their brand of classic Bebop. *Howard McGhee Volume 2* finds McGhee in a Hard Bop setting in 1953 with such modernists as altoist Gigi Gryce, Tal Farlow, Horace Silver, Percy Heath, and drummer Walter Bolden. McGhee sounds excellent, but this would be a last hurrah for his vintage style, because he would record only two further albums (both for Bethlehem) during the next seven years. The remainder of the disc is also significant, for it has Tal Farlow's first session as a leader, a quartet date with rhythm guitarist Don Arnone, bassist Clyde Lombardi, and drummer Joe Morello.

7 *Dusty Blue / June 13, 1960 / Bethlehem/Avenue Jazz 75818*
10 *Maggie's Back in Town / June 26, 1961 / Original Jazz Classics 693*
8 *Sharp Edge / Dec. 8, 1961 / Black Lion 60110*
7 *Jazzbrothers / Oct. 19, 1977 / Storyville 8266*

During 1960–66, Howard McGhee recorded six albums as a leader, one apiece for Felsted, Bethlehem, Contemporary, Black Lion, Winley, and United Artists. *Dusty Blue* features McGhee with a septet that includes Bennie Green, baritonist Pepper Adams, Roland Alexander on tenor, Tommy Flanagan, bassist Ron Carter, and Walter Bolden. The septet performs a few Boppish romps (including "Groovin' High"), and McGhee (who contributed three originals) is in fine form on the ballads, even bringing life to "The Sound of Music." The most rewarding of McGhee's middle-period recordings is *Maggie's Back in Town* (formerly on Contemporary), which features him in a quartet with the brilliant pianist Phineas Newborn, bassist Leroy Vinnegar, and drummer Shelly Manne. The 43-year-old trumpeter is heard regaining his earlier form, really digging into a pair of Teddy Edwards tunes ("Sunset Eyes" and a lengthy version of the title cut), three standards, and "Brownie Speaks." Also quite worthwhile is *Sharp Edge,* a quintet set with tenor saxophonist George Coleman, pianist Junior Mance, bassist George Tucker, and drummer Jimmy Cobb. The swinging music (eight songs, including four McGhee originals plus four alternate takes) falls between Bop and Hard Bop and is well played, showing that Howard McGhee still was a potentially mighty force. Unfortunately he led only one record date during 1963–75 (a big band date for Hep in 1966). By 1976, when McGhee was back on records, he was 58 and still sounding reasonably strong, even if he was largely forgotten.

Jazzbrothers is one of McGhee's better albums from his final period, a sextet outing with tenor saxophonist Charlie Rouse, Barry Harris, bassist Lisle Atkinson, drummer Grady Tate, and Jual Curtis on conga. Seven of the eight songs (all but "When Sunny Gets Blue") are McGhee's originals, and they are joined by a pair of alternate takes. The playing is excellent, and several of these compositions deserve to be revived.

LPS TO SEARCH FOR

That Bop Thing (Bethlehem 6039) finds Howard McGhee in 1955 still sounding in prime form despite the fact that he was playing only part-time during the period. Assisted by baritonist Sahib Shihab, Duke Jordan, Percy Heath, and Philly Joe Jones, McGhee performs six jazz standards (including "Get Happy" and "Rifftide") plus five of his worthy if obscure originals. The trumpeter recorded many records during the 1976–79 period, and most of the dates are worth picking up, including *Just Be There* (Steeplechase 1204), which is a quintet set with baritonist Per Goldschmidt, pianist Horace Parlan, bassist Mads Vinding, and Kenny Clarke, *Live at Emerson's* (Zim 2006), which costars Charlie Rouse in 1978, and *Home Run* (Storyville 4082), with Benny Bailey on second trumpet and Sonny Redd on tenor. Howard McGhee's final recordings were an extensive quintet project with Teddy Edwards (his old friend from the mid-1940s), pianist Art Hillery, bassist Leroy Vinnegar, and Billy Higgins. *Young in Heart* (Storyville 4080) is a well-balanced program of mostly Bop standards, while *Wise in Time* (Storyville 4081), from the same dates, is a set of leftovers (far too many dreary renditions of ballads) and can be passed by. But in any case, first get Howard McGhee's classic recordings from the 1940s.

FILMS

In the 1945 film *The Crimson Canary,* Howard McGhee is featured on one Boppish number with the Coleman Hawkins Sextet.

DOUG METTOME

b. Mar. 19, 1925, Salt Lake City, UT, d. Feb. 17, 1964, Salt Lake City, UT

Doug Mettome was a talented Bebop trumpeter who made a strong impression for a brief period of time but never became famous. He started out leading his own band in Salt

Lake City, spent three years in the military, and then was with the Billy Eckstine big band (1946–47). Mettome freelanced in New York (including with Herbie Fields), recorded with Allen Eager, and was the Bebop trumpet soloist with Benny Goodman's orchestra and sextet in 1949, including on the notable record "Undercurrent Blues." His early influence was Roy Eldridge, but by the late '40s he was closer in style to Dizzy Gillespie and Fats Navarro. After Goodman switched back to swing, Mettome had associations with Woody Herman's Third Herd (1951–52), Tommy Dorsey, Pete Rugolo, and Johnny Richards. In New York in the early '60s, he led a swing-oriented quartet. Mettome recorded with all of the previously mentioned names plus Sam Most and Urbie Green but never led his own record date. Unfortunately Doug Mettome passed away a month before his 39th birthday.

FATS NAVARRO

b. Sept. 24 1923, Key West, FL, d. July 7, 1950, New York, NY

Theodore "Fats" Navarro was a very powerful Bebop trumpeter with an advanced yet logical style and a warm sound, one that through Clifford Brown has remained a major influence on jazz trumpeters to this day. During 1946–50 Navarro was second to Dizzy Gillespie among modern jazz trumpeters, but his heroin addiction weakened his health and eventually helped end his life prematurely, a major loss.

Navarro played a little bit of piano and tenor before switching to trumpet, where he developed quickly. He was with Snookum Russell's big band (1941–42) and the Andy Kirk Orchestra during 1943–44, playing next to Howard McGhee who, along with Roy Eldridge and Dizzy Gillespie, became a major influence. Navarro was with the Billy Eckstine big band (1945–46) where he replaced Gillespie (who had recommended him). During 1946–49 Fats appeared on many important Bebop recording sessions, including with the Bebop Boys, Coleman Hawkins, Eddie "Lockjaw" Davis, Don Lanphere, Illinois Jacquet, Tadd Dameron, Bud Powell, and the 1949 Metronome All-Stars in addition to his own dates for Savoy. Navarro spent a couple periods working with Dameron, was with Jacquet during 1947–48, and in '48 was a member of both the Lionel Hampton big band and Benny Goodman's small group (recording a Boppish version of "Stealin' Apples" with BG).

Although there was a recorded Birdland session with

Charlie Parker in 1950 that found Navarro in surprisingly strong form (which has led some to speculate that the date must be wrong), by that year Fats was suffering from tuberculosis that was exasperated by his longtime heroin use. The combination led to his wasting away and living to be only 26. Most of Fats Navarro's recordings are currently available, but listeners can only speculate as to what he would have accomplished in the 1950s had he been much more concerned with his health.

10 *Goin' to Minton's / Sept. 6, 1946–Dec. 5, 1947 / Savoy 92861*
10 *Fats Navarro and Tadd Dameron / Sept. 26, 1947– Aug. 8, 1949 / Blue Note 33373*
8 *Fats Navarro Featured with the Tadd Dameron Band / 1948 / Milestone 47041*

The only recording dates that Fats Navarro ever led were two explosive sessions for Savoy and a lesser-known outing partly made for Dial and later released in full on a Xanadu Bebop sampler LP. *Goin' to Minton's* has all of Navarro's Savoy recordings (both as a leader and as a sideman) with the exception of two vocal numbers and the alternate takes (which will hopefully resurface eventually). Included are four two-part jams with the Bebop Boys (which also has Kenny Dorham, Sonny Stitt, and Bud Powell) and quintet/sextet dates with either Eddie "Lockjaw" Davis, Leo Parker, Ernie Henry, or tenorman Charlie Rouse as Navarro's frontline partner. The encounters with Parker and Lockjaw (including an accurate number called "Hollerin' and Screamin'") are quite passionate, and many of the selections are quite memorable, including "Webb City," "Calling Dr. Jazz," "Stealing Trash," "Eb Pop," "Goin' to Minton's," "A Bebop Carol," and "Nostalgia" (Navarro's melody line on "Out Of Nowhere"). An essential acquisition.

The same is true of the Blue Note double CD, which has the complete output of Navarro and Tadd Dameron for the label. The trumpeter is heard as a sideman with Dameron's combos on ten selections plus seven alternate takes, including "The Chase," "Our Delight," and "Lady Bird." Other sidemen include Kai Winding, Ernie Henry, Charlie Rouse, Wardell Gray, and Dexter Gordon. There are also four songs by Dameron's band with Miles Davis in Navarro's spot, Fats' version of "Stealin' Apples" with the Benny Goodman Septet, and two particularly classic dates. In one case, Navarro is teamed with Howard McGhee (his early influence) on four numbers, plus two alternate takes that are not included on McGhee's *1948* Classics CD. The other session is led by Bud Powell, also includes Navarro, the young Sonny Rollins, Tommy Potter, and Roy Haynes, and introduces three famous Powell compositions ("Bouncing with Bud," "Dance of the Infidels," and "Wail") in addition to including a definitive version of "52nd Street Theme." A particularly exciting session (also currently available under Powell's name) which is uplifted by the inclusion of four intriguing alternate takes.

The Milestone CD has all of the music formerly on a double LP, live performances of the Tadd Dameron sextet/septet from the Royal Roost in the summer and fall of 1948. Navarro is the key soloist on the first ten of the 13 numbers, with Kai Winding taking his place on the last three songs. Also in the band are Allan Eager on tenor, altoist Rudy Williams (on the first six tunes), Curly Russell, and Kenny Clarke. The recording quality is decent, and this set is an important addition to Fats Navarro's relatively slim but consistently exciting discography. Highlights include "Our Delight," "Tadd Walk," "The Squirrel," and "Good Bait."

RED RODNEY

b. Sept. 27, 1927, Philadelphia, PA, d. May 27, 1994, Boynton Beach, FL

Subject to some of the same problems that beset Fats Navarro, Red Rodney was much more fortunate in that life gave him a second chance. Born Robert Chudnick, he played at the age of 15 with Jerry Wald's orchestra. Jobs were plentiful for talented teenagers during the World War II years, so Rodney also had short-term associations with Jimmy Dorsey, Elliot Lawrence, Georgie Auld, Benny Goodman, and Les Brown, among others. His early idol was Harry James, but by 1945 Rodney was listening closely to Dizzy Gillespie and learning how to play Bebop. He was well featured with Gene Krupa's underrated Bop orchestra in 1946, worked with Buddy Rich, Claude Thornhill, and Woody Herman's Second Herd (1948–49), and was a member of the Charlie Parker Quintet (replacing Kenny Dorham) during 1949–51 (sounding brilliant during Bird's Christmas Eve 1949 Carnegie Hall set) in addition to working with Charlie Ventura. During his period with Parker, Rodney became a heroin addict, to Bird's dismay. He was busted in 1951 and spent most of the next decade in and out of prison, although he did play on an occasional basis and recorded his first sessions as a leader during 1955–59.

Ironically, what hurt Rodney's career even more than his heroin use (he would eventually totally give up drugs) was a long period (virtually all of the 1960s) spent playing for Las Vegas shows, which made his jazz chops rusty. In 1972, when he moved to New York, Rodney began a long and gradual comeback; it took several years for him to get back to his former level. Unlike most veteran Beboppers, Rodney (who lived in Europe during 1974–78) was playing at the peak of his powers by the late 1970s and looking ahead musically. He formed a quintet with Ira Sullivan (who played various saxophones, flute, and very good trumpet) that, far from being just a Bebop revival band, performed post-Bop music that was influenced to an extent by the innovations of Ornette Coleman. With new tunes from pianist Garry Dial and stimulating playing by Sullivan, Rodney was consistently challenged to stretch himself, and his career was revitalized. By the mid-1980s Sullivan had returned to Florida, but Rodney came up with a very viable permanent replacement when he discovered a promising (and eventually brilliant) tenor saxophonist named Chris Potter, who toured with him for a few years. Rodney received additional publicity during his last few years when he was portrayed sympathetically in the Clint Eastwood film *Bird*, playing his own solos. Beating the odds, Red Rodney was as famous at the time of his death as he had ever been, ending his life on top.

8   *Live At The Village Vanguard / May 8, 1980–July 5, 1980 / 32 Jazz 32167*
7   *No Turn on Red / Aug. 10–11, 1986 / Denon 73149*
5   *Red Alert! / Oct. 1990–Nov. 1990 / Continuum 19101*
7   *Then and Now / May 13 + 15, 1992 / Chesky 79*

Most Red Rodney albums have yet to be reissued on CD, including his valuable sets for Fantasy, Xanadu, and most of the Rodney-Sullivan Quintet albums for Muse. *Live At The Village Vanguard* is an exception. The six selections (performed by Rodney; Sullivan who is on soprano, tenor, flute and flugelhorn; pianist Garry Dial; bassist Paul Berner; and drummer Tom Whaley) swing but are generally pretty advanced. Rodney, who was still just 52, plays with a great deal of power yet blends in well with Sullivan on two obscurities, three originals by trumpeter Jack Walrath, and Johnny Mandel's "A Time For Love."

The other three CDs are among Rodney's last recordings. *No Turn on Red*, recorded after Ira Sullivan had gone home to Florida, has Dick Oatts (on soprano, alto, and tenor) in

Sullivan's place along with Garry Dial (who contributed five of the nine numbers), bassist Jay Anderson, and drummer Joey Baron. As was true of the Rodney/Sullivan band, the music here is primarily post-Bop rather than Bebop, with the trumpeter challenged by the complex tunes ("Young and Foolish" and "Greensleeves" are the only standards) and his young sidemen. *Red Alert!* and *Then and Now* are notable for featuring Chris Potter (19 at the time of *Red Alert!* and at the beginning of his career) on tenor, alto, and soprano. *Red Alert!*, which also has pianist David Kikoski, bassist Chip Jackson, and drummer Jimmy Madison plus Bob Belden on synthesizer and drum machine, and Charles Telerant (who does a rap on "Moose the Mooche"!), is an attempt to "update" Bebop that mostly falls flat. Such songs as "Little Willie Leaps" and "Moose the Mooche" did not need the "contemporary" treatment, and none of the originals caught on, for good reason. Instead of playing creative modern jazz, this is a misguided attempt at commercialism. *Then and Now,* Rodney's final recording, finds the 64-year-old trumpeter reuniting with Garry Dial in a group also including Chris Potter, Jay Anderson, and Jimmy Madison. The repertoire comprises ten Bebop standards plus Rodney's "Yard's Pad." Although the songs are old, the harmonies are often more complex, and the solos sound quite modern. This rewarding final effort is rounded off by a ten-minute interview with Rodney that finds the trumpeter summing up his life, less than two years before his death.

LPS TO SEARCH FOR

Red Rodney's most significant recordings as a leader have yet to be reissued on CD. He led a pair of four-song sessions during 1946–47 for Mercury and Emarcy. *New Music from Chicago* (Original Jazz Classics 048), from 1955, for the first time teamed Rodney with Ira Sullivan (heard on trumpet, tenor, and alto). The quintet date (with Roy Haynes) is mostly straightahead Bop, with Rodney taking a surprise vocal on "Rhythm in a Riff." Rodney and Sullivan (mostly on tenor) are also teamed on *The Red Arrow* (Onyx 204) with Tommy Flanagan, Oscar Pettiford, and either Philly Joe Jones or Elvin Jones in 1957. The Bop and blues date is most memorable for "Red Arrow," which has both Rodney and Sullivan on trumpets, trading off in exciting fashion.

After an obscure Argo album in 1959, Rodney did not lead any more sessions until he began his comeback in 1973. Starting with *Bird Lives* (Muse 5371), a Bop revival date with Charles McPherson and Barry Harris, Rodney improved

from year to year, getting stronger as the 1970s progressed. *Superbop* (Muse 5046) finds him trading off with fellow trumpeter Sam Noto (the title cut has them harmonized on Clifford Brown's solo from "Daahoud"). Also quite worthwhile in the modern Bop vein are *The Red Tornado* with trombonist Bill Watrous (Muse 5088), *Red, White, and Blues* (Muse 5111), *Home Free* (Muse 5135), and *The 3 R's* (Muse 5290); the last three albums also feature Richie Cole.

However, as the 1970s ended, Red Rodney was in danger of being stuck spending the remainder of his career playing revival Bebop. Fortunately he had a reunion with his old friend Ira Sullivan, and the resulting quintet (which featured the piano solos and compositions of Garry Dial) put Rodney in a much more modern setting. All of the unit's recordings are rewarding: *Hi Jinx at the Vanguard* (Muse 5267), *Alive in New York* (Muse 5307), *Night and Day* (Muse 5274), and *Spirit Within* (Elektra Musician 60020). Best of all is *Sprint* (Elektra Musician 60261), which in spots finds the quintet (with Jay Anderson and drummer Jeff Hirschfield) playing as free as Ornette Coleman! Red Rodney rose to the challenge, and his career and style were revitalized as a result.

FILMS

Red Rodney is in several shorts with the 1946–47 Gene Krupa Orchestra plus the full-length film *Beat the Band* (1947). He can also be seen playing a set with a quintet in 1990 on *A Tribute to Charlie Parker* (Storyville 6048). In the Hollywood film *Bird* (Warner Home Video), Rodney plays all the trumpet solos for the character who is depicting him during his period with Charlie Parker.

FREDDIE WEBSTER

b. 1917, Cleveland, OH, d. Apr. 1, 1947, Chicago, IL

Because he recorded relatively little (never leading his own record date), and died young, Freddie Webster is a mystery figure in jazz history. He was cited by Miles Davis (a close friend) as an important early inspiration (Dizzy Gillespie said that he had the greatest tone he had ever heard on the trumpet).

Webster's contributions to Bebop are difficult to evaluate. He mostly played first trumpet (with few solos) for a variety of swing big bands, including Earl Hines (1938), Erskine Tate, Benny Carter, Eddie Durham, Lucky Millinder, Jimmie Lunceford (1942–43), Sabby Lewis, and Cab Calloway.

Webster's best solos on record were on dates from 1945–46 led by Miss Rhapsody, Frankie Socolow, and Sarah Vaughan. Although his spot on "If You Could See Me Now" with Vaughan has been greatly praised, he is actually barely heard on that record (just eight bars); "You're Not the Kind" is a better showcase. Freddie Webster had short stints with the John Kirby Sextet and the Dizzy Gillespie big band. Webster died from a drug overdose when he was 30. His importance in the development of Miles Davis's sound and to early Bebop remains very difficult to assess.

Trombonists

The trombone, which before the mid-1920s was thought of as primarily a supportive percussive instrument, came a long way over the next 20 years. Jack Teagarden liberated it from being a gruff rhythmic horn (á la Kid Ory) and showed that it was possible to play the potentially clumsy slide trombone with the fluency of a trumpet. Other approaches, such as the smooth ballad playing of Tommy Dorsey and the eccentric emotional outbursts of Dickie Wells, helped to expand the options available to trombonists. But none really prepared the instrument for its necessary adjustment to Bebop.

The clarinet was eclipsed by Bebop, and the same thing could have happened to the trombone were it not for J. J. Johnson. The new music's rapid tempos and complex chord structures meant that Bebop trombonists had to have very strong control of the horn and be able to use alternate positions with great speed while relying less on emotional sounds and slurs. J. J. Johnson played so effortlessly (essentially transferring the language of Charlie Parker and Dizzy Gillespie to the trombone) that at first some listeners thought that he must have been utilizing a valve trombone rather than one with a slide. After a few years, other players emerged who sounded like close relatives of J. J.'s, although it would not be until the 1960s and the rise of the avant-garde before newer trombone styles began to emerge. In the meantime, Kai Winding was a close competitor of Johnson's and brought the Bebop trombone sound into the Stan Kenton Orchestra. In contrast, Bill Harris had more of a swing style, but his flexibility, open ears, and sense of humor made him an important trombonist during the Bebop era too.

BILL HARRIS

b. Oct. 28, 1916, Philadelphia, PA, d. Aug. 21, 1973, Hallandale, FL

Bill Harris, a major star with Woody Herman, was one of the very few "new" trombonists during the Bebop era who did not sound like J. J. Johnson. While Johnson could shoot out an impressive series of notes, Harris had a more emotional sound, one that included both humor and sentiment. J. J. would be a very powerful influence on Beboppers, while in contrast Harris seemed to have strongly affected the sound of only one other trombonist: Les Brown's Ray Sims (Zoot's brother).

Harris had brief periods playing piano, tenor, and trumpet before he switched permanently to the trombone. After working locally in Philadelphia, he served with the Merchant Marines for two years. During 1942–44, Harris had mostly unnoticed stints with many big bands, including those of Buddy Williams, Gene Krupa, Ray McKinley, Bob Chester, Benny Goodman, Charlie Barnet, and Freddie Slack.

However, things changed when Bill Harris became one of the most important players with Woody Herman's Herd, staying from August 1944 until its breakup in late 1946. His dramatic feature on "Bijou" was famous, and his solos on many uptempo tunes bordered on the riotous, which fit in well with the highly emotional band. Harris was considered second to Flip Phillips in importance among Herman's soloists. After Herman disbanded the Herd, Harris led his own group for a time and worked with Charlie Ventura. He was one of the few members of the First Herd to rejoin Herman as part of his Second Herd (1948–50), where he continued being showcased.

Bill Harris's post-Herman years were brief but colorful. He went on several tours with Jazz at the Philharmonic, where his extroverted solos helped to inspire Flip Phillips and the trumpeters. Harris worked with Oscar Pettiford (1952) and the Sauter-Finegan Orchestra (1953), was back with Woody Herman (1956–58) and co-led bands with Flip Phillips; their group served as the nucleus for Benny Goodman's 1959 unit. Although only 43 in 1960, Harris decided to leave the big time to settle in Las Vegas, where he worked with trumpeter Charlie Teagarden (1962–64) and Red Norvo (1965–66). Bill Harris spent his last years playing locally in Florida, passing away at the age of 56 in 1973.

9 *Bill Harris and Friends / Sept. 23, 1957 / Original Jazz Classics 083*

Bill Harris led sessions for Keynote (1945–46), Dial (1946), Capitol (1948–49),and Clef (1952) but only headed two full-length albums in his career. For his Fantasy record (reissued in the OJC series), he works well with his frequent JATP partner, tenor saxophonist Ben Webster. The quintet (with pianist Jimmy Rowles, bassist Red Mitchell, and drummer Stan Levey) performs a variety of swing standards, Rowles is showcased on "I'm Getting Sentimental Over You," Harris is featured on "It Might As Well Be Spring," and a very humorous version of "Just One More Chance" (which has Harris and Webster joking around verbally) is certainly unique.

LPS TO SEARCH FOR

The trombonist's other record as a leader, *The Bill Harris Memorial Album* (Xanadu 191), was made a week after the Fantasy date in 1957. This frequently exuberant set revives eight songs from the Woody Herman First Herd songbook. Harris is assisted enthusiastically by Terry Gibbs, Lou Levy, Red Mitchell, and Stan Levey.

FILMS

Sweet and Low Down (1944), which has an acting part for Benny Goodman, features Bill Harris playing the trombone solos for actor James Cardwell. The trombonist also pops up as part of Woody Herman's Orchestra in *Earl Carroll Vanities* (1945) and *Hit Parade of 1947* (1947).

J. J. JOHNSON

b. Jan. 22, 1924, Indianapolis, IN

The Charlie Parker of the trombone, J. J. Johnson has dominated his instrument ever since his emergence in 1945. So closely is he associated with the trombone that, even during a period when he was not actively playing (the late '60s/early '70s), J. J. still won popularity polls on his ax!

Born James Louis Johnson but nicknamed J. J. from an early age, Johnson picked up early experience playing with the territory orchestras of Clarence Love and Snookum Russell during 1941–42. While with the Benny Carter Orchestra (1942–45), Johnson had his first recorded solo (on 1943's "Love for Sale") and appeared at the initial Jazz at the Philharmonic concert (in 1944). He also began to gain attention from his peers, particularly when he was a key soloist with Count Basie's big band (1945–46). Johnson played his instrument with the fluidity of a trumpet and showed that even the rapid tempos and complex lines of Bebop caused him no problem. He recorded with Charlie Parker in 1947 (when he made Bird's quintet briefly into a sextet), toured with Illinois Jacquet's popular band (1947–49), was with the Dizzy Gillespie Orchestra, and was Miles Davis's main choice to play trombone with the Birth of the Cool Nonet. In addition to recording with all of those groups plus as a member of the Metronome All-Stars, J. J. Johnson led five record dates of his own during 1946–49; among his sidemen were Cecil Payne, Bud Powell, Max Roach, Leo Parker, Hank Jones, Sonny Rollins, John Lewis, Kenny Dorham, and Sonny Stitt.

Despite the fact that J. J. was at the top of his field, the trombone had declined greatly in popularity since the glory days of Tommy Dorsey, and Johnson struggled for work in the early 1950s. J. J. played a bit with Oscar Pettiford in 1951 and Miles Davis the following year but then dropped out of music, working as a blueprint inspector for two years (although he did lead one record date in 1953 that featured Clifford Brown). However, in August 1954 his fortunes changed with the formation of a two-trombone quintet with Kai Winding that was informally known as J. J. and Kai. For the next two years their group was one of the most popular in jazz, playing melodic middle-of-the-road music filled with Bop solos and witty arrangements. After appearing successfully at the 1956 Newport Jazz Festival, the two trombonists went their separate ways, but they would have occasional reunions through the years.

During this era, J. J. Johnson began to really develop as a writer, not just in jazz but in Third Stream classical music. Most notable among his works were "Poem for Brass," "El Camino Real," an album for Dizzy Gillespie that consisted of a six-movement suite (*Perceptions*), and one song that became a standard, "Lament." The trombonist led small Hard Bop-oriented groups that at various times featured Bobby Jaspar on tenor and flute, cornetist Nat Adderley, and trumpeter Freddie Hubbard. He recorded steadily as a leader both with combos and larger bands and was part of the unrecorded Miles Davis Sextet during part of 1961–62. As the 1960s progressed J. J. became very busy in the studios as a composer and arranger for films and television. After a few dates with Kai Winding for A&M during 1968–69, Johnson was off records altogether until 1977, working as a full-time writer.

Fortunately J. J. Johnson did return to playing jazz more regularly again, and his abilities were still very much in their prime. A 1977 concert record with Nat Adderley launched his "comeback," and during the 1980s and '90s he recorded regularly, including a successful meeting with fellow trombonist Al Grey, sessions with his regular quintet (featuring tenor saxophonist Ralph Moore), and a few projects with larger groups. J. J. Johnson, one of the last major survivors of the Bebop era, continued winning popularity polls, although after the mid-1990s his erratic health forced him to greatly cut back on his playing.

8 *J. J. Johnson Jazz Quintet / June 26, 1946–May 11, 1949 / Savoy 0151*

7 *Jay and Kai / Dec. 24, 1947–Aug. 26, 1954 / Savoy 0163*

7 *Trombone by Three / May 26, 1949–Oct. 5, 1951 / Original Jazz Classics 091*

9 *The Eminent Jay Jay Johnson, Volume 1 / June 22, 1953 / Blue Note 81505*

9 *The Eminent Jay Jay Johnson, Volume 2 / Sept. 24, 1954 + June 6, 1955 / Blue Note 81506*

J. J. Johnson's first three recording sessions as a leader were made for Savoy during 1946–49. The dozen selections are all included on *J. J. Johnson Jazz Quintet,* although the 11 existing alternate takes are skipped over and the total playing time is just around 32 minutes. Johnson is featured with three different quintets with either Cecil Payne (playing alto), Leo Parker, or Sonny Rollins in the frontline and Bud Powell, Hank Jones, or John Lewis on piano. The other Savoy CD, *Jay and Kai,* has the first eight selections that J. J. Johnson and Kai Winding recorded together, with the exception of a four-trombone set from 1953 that was actually led by bassist Charles Mingus. Mingus is present for the two dates from 1954, which include "Blues for Trombones" and "Lament"; this can be considered the official birth of the popular quintet. Also on the CD is a repeat of J. J.'s version of "Yesterdays" from 1947 and three numbers from a Kai Winding date with an enlarged rhythm section from 1952.

Trombone by Three has a session apiece led by J. J. (a sextet that includes Kenny Dorham, Sonny Rollins, and John Lewis), Kai Winding (his sextet has Brew Moore and baritonist Gerry Mulligan), and Bennie Green (a heated septet with both Eddie "Lockjaw" Davis," and Big Nick Nicholas on tenors). Of greatest interest are the opportunities to hear Rollins and Mulligan this early in their careers and the contrasting differences between Green's swing-oriented style and that of Johnson and Winding.

The pair of Eminent *Jay Jay Johnson* CDs reshuffle the music from the two original LPs, making the release more logical and adding alternate takes. *Volume 1* has Johnson featuring Clifford Brown (on one of his first important sessions), Jimmy Heath (doubling on tenor and baritone), John Lewis, Percy Heath, and Kenny Clarke performing three originals (including J. J.'s "Turnpike") plus a trio of standards that are highlighted by a burning rendition of "Get Happy." *Volume 2* is lengthier than the first volume and consists of two complete quintet sessions: one with Wynton Kelly, Charles Mingus, Kenny Clarke, and Sabu on congas and a date with Hank Mobley, pianist Horace Silver, Paul Chambers, and Kenny Clarke. Johnson contributes five numbers and digs into such songs as "Old Devil Moon," "Pennies from Heaven," and "Portrait of Jennie."

* *The Complete Columbia J. J. Johnson Small Group Sessions / July 24, 1956–Jan. 12, 1961 / Mosaic 7-169*

7 *J. J. Inc. / Aug. 1–3, 1960 / Columbia/Legacy 65296*

8 *The Great Kai & J. J. / Nov. 4–9, 1960 / MCA/Impulse 42012*

8 *Proof Positive / May 1, 1964 / GRP/Impulse 145*

8 *Say When / Dec. 7, 1964–Dec. 5, 1966 / Bluebird 6277*

Although the J. J. Johnson-Kai Winding Quintet was one of the most popular jazz groups of 1954–56, few of their prime recordings (other than their Savoy and Prestige dates) are currently in print, including their work for RCA, Bethlehem, and especially Columbia. The limited-edition seven-CD Mosaic box documents Johnson's career during the 4½ years after the quintet's breakup, and includes nine LPs of material plus 21 previously unreleased selections. J. J. Johnson shows why he was considered the pacesetting trombonist of Bebop and Hard Bop as he leads quartets, quintets, and sextets featuring such notable sidemen as tenors Bobby Jaspar and Clifford Jordan, cornetist Nat Adderley, and trumpeter Freddie Hubbard plus top-notch rhythm sec-

THE WAYNE KNIGHT COLLECTION

Even 55 years after he began to have an impact, J. J. Johnson is still considered jazz's best trombonist.

tions. The straight-ahead but rarely predictable music mixes standards with many J. J. Johnson originals. *J. J. Inc.* is a single disc consisting of the next-to-last album on the Mosaic set, a sextet with Freddie Hubbard and Clifford Jordan, and may be seen as a decent sampler of Johnson's playing during this prime period (although even here the Mosaic box has two extra selections from the dates).

J. J. Johnson and Kai Winding had several recorded reunions through the years. Their Impulse CD, which finds the two trombonists joined by pianist Bill Evans, Paul Chambers or Tommy Williams on bass, and Roy Haynes or Art Taylor on drums, is one of their best. There is plenty of wit in the arrangements and short solos during such numbers as "This Could Be the Start of Something Big," "Blue Monk," and "Side by Side." But why were the liner notes reproduced so microscopically?

Proof Positive and *Say When* unintentionally celebrated the first 20 years of J. J. Johnson's musical mastery. *Proof Pos-*

itive (on all but one selection J. J. is joined by pianist Harold Mabern, bassist Arthur Harper, and drummer Frank Gant) puts the emphasis on his playing. There is a definite Miles Davis influence, both in the repertoire (which includes Miles's "Neo," "Stella By Starlight," and "My Funny Valentine") and in the melancholy feel of the music. Johnson had been with an unrecorded version of Davis's band the year before. *Say When*, which reissues all but three selections from a pair of albums, features J. J. not only as a soloist but as a big band arranger-composer, contributing nine of the 15 numbers and arranging everything but "Stolen Moments." Hank Jones also has plenty of solo space, and the music overall is high-quality modern Mainstream Jazz of the period.

7 *Yokohama Concert / Apr. 20, 1977 / Pablo 2620–109*
7 *Concepts in Blue / Sept. 23–26, 1980 / Original Jazz Classics 735*

9 *Things Are Getting Better All the Time / Nov. 28–29, 1983 / Original Jazz Classics 745*

9 *Quintergy / July 1988 / Antilles 422 848 214*

9 *Standards / July 1988 / Antilles 314 510 059*

Other than three out-of-print reunion dates for A&M with Kai Winding during 1968–69, J.J. Johnson did not record as a leader or as a trombonist during 1967–76. When he came back as a player in 1977, he was still just 53 and there was no decline in his sound or in his improvising abilities. The two-CD *Yokohama Concert,* an outing with Nat Adderley, keyboardist Billy Childs, bassist Tony Dumas, and drummer Kevin Johnson, features mostly originals by band members, and the music (which includes "Work Song") is decent if not all that memorable; the electric piano seems out of place. *Concepts in Blue* has a blues-oriented repertoire and lots of colorful solos from J.J., tenor saxophonist Ernie Watts, and Clark Terry. However, *Things Are Getting Better All the Time* is on a higher level. J.J. Johnson teams up with fellow trombonist Al Grey, and the contrast between the cool-toned Bopper and the often-exuberant wa-wa mute specialist is quite striking. Influenced by Grey, J.J. has rarely sounded happier on record. The trombonists make for a very potent team on such numbers as "Soft Winds," "Things Ain't What They Used to Be," and the title track.

Quintergy and *Standards* are both from the same Village Vanguard sessions in 1988, with J.J. Johnson featuring his regular quintet of the period, a group with tenor saxophonist Ralph Moore, pianist Stanley Cowell, bassist Rufus Reid, and drummer Victor Lewis. *Quintergy* alternates between J.J. originals (including "Lament") and such tunes as "Blue Bossa," an unaccompanied "It's All Right with Me" (a high point), "Nefertiti," and even "When the Saints Go Marching In." *Standards sticks* mostly to familiar tunes, although Johnson does toss in one of his vintage originals, "Shortcake"; highlights include "My Funny Valentine," "Just Friends," and "Autumn Leaves." These two CDs might have been just a typical gig in the productive life of J.J. Johnson, but the trombonist is heard throughout at the peak of his powers.

7 *Vivian / June 2–3, 1992 / Concord 4523*

8 *Let's Hang Out / Dec. 7–9, 1992 / Verve 314 5514 454*

7 *Tangence / July 13–15, 1994 / Verve 314 526 588*

8 *The Brass Orchestra / Sept. 24–27, 1996 / Verve 314 537 321*

9 *Heroes / Oct. 1–4, 1996 / Verve 314 528 864*

Vivian, dedicated to his late wife, is a ballad set, with J.J. Johnson accompanied by pianist Rob Schneiderman, guitarist Ted Dunbar, bassist Rufus Reid, and drummer Akira Tana. The mood is quiet and the tempos generally fairly slow, but Johnson's warm tone and creative ideas keep his renditions of the veteran ballads from getting sleepy. *Let's Hang Out* is a bit of a grab bag, with Johnson joined by Stanley Cowell or Renee Rosnes on piano, Rufus Reid, Lewis Nash or Victor Lewis on drums, and occasionally trumpeter Terence Blanchard or Ralph Moore. In addition, Jimmy Heath has a couple of guest appearances and Johnson takes "It Never Entered My Mind" as an unaccompanied solo. Other highlights include the lengthy "Kenya," "Beautiful Love," and "I Got It Bad." *Tangence* puts J.J. Johnson's trombone in the spotlight most of the time while backed by a large string orchestra conducted by Robert Farnon. Surprisingly Farnon (not Johnson) is responsible for the arrangements. The set is uplifted by a few surprises, with trumpeter Wynton Marsalis making three guest appearances and J.J. taking "For Dancers Only" as a duet with Marsalis and being backed by just bassist Chris Laurence on the blues "Opus De Focus." Farnon's charts have the potential of being overblown, but Johnson's swinging and witty playing greatly uplifts the music.

J.J. Johnson's final recordings to date are a pair of Verve sets made when he was 72. *The Brass Orchestra,* recorded with a large trumpet section, other trombonists, French horns, euphonium, tuba, harp, a rhythm section, percussionists, and just one reed, was arranged mostly by Johnson. The music ranges from classical and Third Stream to straight-ahead jazz and Bebop. The diverse set has solos from J.J., tenor saxophonist Dan Faulk, trumpeters Eddie Henderson and Jon Faddis, pianist Renee Rosnes, and trombonist Robin Eubanks. It does a fine job of summing up J.J. Johnson's career, even bringing back two movements from Johnson's suite for Dizzy Gillespie, *Perceptions.* In contrast, *Heroes,* a sextet date with Faulk, Rosnes, Rufus Reid, and Victor Lewis, mostly looks ahead. There are tributes to Thelonious Monk, Miles Davis, John Coltrane, and Wayne Shorter (who plays tenor on "In Walked Wayne"), but the arrangements and compositions (only "Blue in Green" and "Blue Train" were not written by Johnson) are advanced and adventurous. *Heroes* shows that, even a half-century after he emerged as the top Bebop trombonist, J.J. Johnson still had something very original and fresh to contribute to jazz.

LPS TO SEARCH FOR

The double-LP *Mad Be Bop* (Savoy 2232) has all of the music from J.J. Johnson's Savoy dates of 1946–49 and 1954, including the alternate takes thus far bypassed by the CD reissues. The J.J. Johnson/Kai Winding Quintet has been poorly represented on CD, so you will want to look for *The Finest of Kai Winding and J.J. Johnson* (Bethlehem 6001), *Trombone for Two* (Columbia 742), *Jay & Kai + 6* (Columbia 892), which actually has eight trombonists (!), and *Jay and Kai* (Columbia 973). *J.J.'s Broadway* (Verve 8530) features Johnson playing show tunes both with a quartet and with a five-trombone octet. *Pinnacles* (Milestone 9093), from 1979, will probably be reissued eventually in the Original Jazz Classics series, for it matches J.J. Johnson with trumpeter Oscar Brashear and tenor saxophonist Joe Henderson in inspired groups ranging from a quintet to a septet.

KAI WINDING

b. May 18, 1922, Aarhus, Denmark, d. May 6, 1983, Yonkers, NY

Kai Winding, one of the top Bebop trombonists, helped to bring the instrument to prominence in Stan Kenton's orchestra. He had a productive career despite being overshadowed by J.J. Johnson and making surprisingly few recordings as a leader in stimulating settings. Winding moved from his native Denmark to the United States with his family when he was 12. He began his professional career playing with the big bands of Shorty Allen, Bobby Say, Alvino Rey, and Sonny Dunham in the early 1940s, and he was part of a service band in the Coast Guard for three years during World War II. After a stint with Benny Goodman (1945–46), Winding came to fame with Stan Kenton (1946–47), during which time his brilliant playing resulted in the trombone's becoming a major part of the Kenton sound.

Winding, who led his first two record sessions in 1945 and showed that he was one of the first trombonists to adapt to the new Bop style, played with Tadd Dameron during 1948–49 and recorded with Miles Davis's Birth of the Cool Nonet. He had brief periods in the big bands of Charlie Ventura and Benny Goodman, led some record sessions during 1949–53 (with Brew Moore, Gerry Mulligan, George Wallington, Red Rodney, and Kai Winding being a few of his sidemen), and then in 1954 collaborated with J.J. Johnson in co-leading a popular quintet that worked steadily for two years.

After the band broke up in mid-1956, Winding (who loved the sound of multiple trombones) formed a four-trombone septet that worked and recorded steadily for the next decade. Many of its performances were closer to middle-of-the-road pop music than to jazz, and the recordings tended to be concise and a bit commercial. Among the fellow bonemeisters who were with the group at one time or another were Carl Fontana, Frank Rehak, Jimmy Knepper, Urbie Green, and Bill Watrous. The band cut many dates for Verve during the 1960s, all of which are long out of print.

Kai Winding had a few recorded reunions with J.J. Johnson during 1967–69, toured with the Giants of Jazz during 1971–72 (which found him holding his own with Dizzy Gillespie, Sonny Stitt, Thelonious Monk, Al McKibbon, and Art Blakey), and freelanced during his final decade. In his later years he continued the J.J. and Kai tradition by recording in quintets with Curtis Fuller and the Italian trombonist Dino Piana, and sharing a "Trombone Summit" in 1980 with Albert Mangelsdorff, Bill Watrous, and Jiggs Whigham.

8 *Kai and Jay—Bennie Green with Strings / May 13, 1952 + Dec. 3, 1954 / Original Jazz Classics 1727*

Kai Winding's earliest recordings (a date released by Xanadu and sessions for Savoy, Prestige, and Roost) either have been reissued as samplers under other musicians' names (particularly J.J. Johnson's) or have stayed out of print. This particular CD starts off with four ballads featuring the swing trombonist Bennie Green with a rhythm section and six strings; pleasant mood music. The other eight selections, however, are of greater historic value, for they feature the J.J. Johnson-Kai Winding Quintet in one of their earlier dates; this time around Winding receives top billing. The group performs such numbers as "Dinner for One Please James," "We'll Be Together Again," and "Bags' Groove" in winning fashion.

LPS TO SEARCH FOR

Kai Winding's trombone band records are usually only of minor interest, pleasant the first time around but not music that sticks in the mind afterwards. Among the better ones are *The Swingin' States* (Columbia 8062), which has a dozen songs with state names in their titles, and 1960's *The Incredible Kai Winding Trombones* (Impulse A-3). *Solo* (Verve 8525), from 1963, was a temporary departure, giving Winding an opportunity to be the only horn with a quartet/quintet, although even here the 11 selections all clock in at around three minutes apiece. From later in his life comes the loose but decent quartet outing *Danish Blue* (Glendale 6003), *Lionel Hampton Presents Kai Winding* (Who's Who 21001), which is a quartet set with pianist Frank Strazzeri, and a collaboration with trombonist Dino Piana called *Duo Bones* (Red 143).

Alto Saxophonists

Prior to the rise of Charlie Parker in 1944–45, the alto sax was dominated by the styles of Johnny Hodges and Benny Carter. Every big band had at least one altoist and often two, with the lead altoist being the most important voice in the saxophone section during ensembles. While most orchestras had a tenor soloist, many of the altoists rarely had a chance to be heard. However, the emergence of Tab Smith with Count Basie's band in the early 1940s and Louis Jordan with his Tympany Five gave the alto a strong role in jump (and early R&B) bands, culminating in Earl Bostic's string of hit records in the 1950s.

In jazz, the blues/ballad/stomp style of Johnny Hodges was quite influential, as was Benny Carter's thoughtful and flawless improvisations. In the early 1940s, Charlie Parker began to really excite young saxophonists. His vocabulary was quite fresh, he could play very coherent and adventurous solos at ridiculous speeds, and his phrases became the foundation for Bebop. Soon it was nearly impossible for any up-and-coming player to escape Bird's influence. And while musicians on other instruments at least were able to develop their own sounds, young alto players of the time tended to sound very close to Parker during their formative periods. Jimmy Heath, who was tagged "Little Bird," was one of several altoists who felt compelled to switch to tenor to lessen Bird's dominant influence, and James Moody also changed his emphasis to the tenor. Sonny Stitt, who in 1949 began doubling on tenor but never gave up the alto, managed to develop his own approach to Charlie Parker's musical language while never completely emerging from Bird's shadow.

It would not be until the late 1940s/early '50s that altoists such as Lee Konitz, Paul Desmond, and Art Pepper came up with alternative, "cooler" sounds that allowed them to express their musical individualities beyond Bird.

SONNY CRISS

b. Oct. 23, 1927, Memphis, TN, d. Nov. 19, 1977, Los Angeles, CA

One of the most promising alto saxophonists to emerge during the Bebop era, Sonny Criss had an episodic career, one in which he seemed to be rediscovered every five years or so. Because he had a heavier sound than Charlie Parker, Criss was not plagued with the "little Bird" or "member of the Bird school" tags that hurt other Bebop-oriented altoists from the era.

Born William Criss, the young saxophonist moved to Los Angeles with his family in 1942. He was an important part of the emerging "modern jazz" scene of the mid-1940s, working with Howard McGhee (including playing alongside Charlie Parker) and Teddy Edwards, and in many groups on L.A.'s legendary Central Avenue. Criss played with Johnny Otis, Gerald Wilson's orchestra, Jazz at the Philharmonic, Flip Phillips, the Lighthouse All-Stars, Billy Eckstine, Stan Kenton's orchestra (1955), and Buddy Rich (on and off during 1955–59). Criss, who led his first record session in 1947, made three albums for Imperial in 1956, all of which are quite obscure.

Criss spent a few years in Europe (1962–65) and then returned to Los Angeles, where work (unlike during the 1950s) was just sporadic. He did record some of his finest work for Prestige (1966–69) and Muse (1975) but never became that well known or prosperous, partly due to living in L.A. He seemed set for greater recognition and more work in the mid-1970s but, due to the pain of cancer, Sonny Criss committed suicide less than four weeks after his 50th birthday.

- **7** *Intermission Riff / Oct. 12, 1951 / Original Jazz Classics 961*
- **9** *This Is Criss! / Oct. 21, 1966 / Original Jazz Classics 430*
- **8** *Portrait of Sonny Criss / Mar. 12, 1967 / Original Jazz Classics 655*
- **8** *Up, Up and Away / Aug. 18, 1967 / Original Jazz Classics 982*
- **9** *Sonny's Dream / May 8, 1968 / Original Jazz Classics 707*

8 *Rockin' in Rhythm / Mar. 23, 1967 + July 2, 1968 / Original Jazz Classics 1022*

7 *I'll Catch the Sun / Jan. 20, 1969 / Original Jazz Classics 811*

Sonny Criss first recorded as a leader in 1947 (music later released on Crown and Xanadu) and on four numbers in 1949. Although not documented very well, Criss worked with Jazz at the Philharmonic on and off during 1948–51. *Intermission Riff* has one of the JATP concerts, four standards (including "How High the Moon" and "Perdido") plus the original "High Jump" performed by Criss, trumpeter Joe Newman, Bennie Green, Eddie "Lockjaw" Davis, pianist Bobby Tucker, Tommy Potter, and Kenny Clarke. This CD has a very different JATP lineup than usual, but the music (decently but not impeccably recorded) is up to the usual standards, with plenty of spirited moments.

Criss led three scarce dates for Imperial in 1956 and sessions for Peacock (1959) and Polydor (1962–63). However, it was his seven Prestige dates of 1966–69 (all but *The Beat Goes On* have been reissued on CD in the Original Jazz Classics series) that really find Criss at the peak of his powers. *This Is Criss* features the distinctive altoist in a quartet with Walter Davis, bassist Paul Chambers, and drummer Alan Dawson, romping through standards and blue ballads, with the highlights including "Black Coffee," "When Sunny Gets Blue," and a previously unreleased "Love for Sale." *Portrait of Sonny Criss* has the same quartet and fine reinterpretations of "Wee," "On a Clear Day," and "Blues in the Closet"; the only minus is the brief (32-minute) playing time. *Up, Up and Away* (with pianist Cedar Walton, Tal Farlow, bassist Bob Cranshaw, and drummer Lenny McBrowne) features Criss uplifting a pair of current pop tunes (the title cut and "Sunny") and digging into "Scrapple from the Apple," "Paris Blues," "Willow Weep for Me," and Horace Tapscott's "This Is for Benny." Tapscott is a major force on *Sonny's Dream,* for he wrote all six selections (which are augmented by a pair of alternate takes) and arranged the music for a ten-piece band. Criss is the main soloist, with the other key sidemen including Teddy Edwards, Conte Candoli, and Tommy Flanagan. Colorful music.

Rockin' in Rhythm (a quartet album with pianist Eddie Green, Bob Cranshaw, and Alan Dawson) starts off with Criss doing what he can with "Eleanor Rigby" but really excelling on "Sonnymoon for Two," "Rockin' in Rhythm," and "I'm Afraid the Masquerade Is Over." A previously unreleased "All the Things You Are" from 1967 matches Criss with Davis, Chambers, and Dawson. The final Prestige date, *I'll Catch the Sun,* has two blues, two standards (including an emotional "Cry Me a River"), and a pair of pop tunes performed by Criss, Hampton Hawes, bassist Monty Budwig, and Shelly Manne.

10 *Criss Craft / Feb. 24, 1975 + Oct. 20, 1975 / Muse 6015*

9 *Out of Nowhere / Oct. 20, 1975 / 32 Jazz 32028*

Other than an Italian live session in 1974, Sonny Criss did not record as a leader during 1970–74. However, when he came back, he created *Criss Craft,* a classic. Criss's style was unchanged from the Prestige days, but he sounds very inspired and creative throughout this quintet outing with Dolo Coker, guitarist Ray Crawford, bassist Larry Gales, and drummer Jimmy Smith, particularly on the lengthy "The Isle of Celia"; two additional selections augment this definitive reissue. *Out of Nowhere* (with Dolo Coker, Larry Gales, and Jimmie Smith) is almost on the same level, with Criss coming up with many creative choruses on four standards, two originals, and one song by the pianist. It is difficult to believe, listening to this lively and spirited music, that Sonny Criss had only two years left.

LPS TO SEARCH FOR

The Sonny Criss Memorial Album (Xanadu 200) has five boppish pieces from 1947 by a Criss-led sextet with trumpeter Al Killian and Wardell Gray, a live number apiece from 1950 (with singer Damita Jo) and 1952, and five cuts from 1965 (with Hampton Hawes) that were cut as a demo and not released before this LP. *Saturday Morning* (Xanadu 105), recorded a week after much of *Criss Craft* in 1975, is nearly on the same level, a superb Bop date with Barry Harris, bassist Leroy Vinnegar, and Lenny McBrowne. Sonny Criss's final two recordings, *Warm & Sonny* (ABC 9312) and *The Joy of Sax* (ABC 9326), are not without interest but are rather commercial efforts from 1976.

FILMS

Sonny Criss appears briefly in the French film *Two Are Guilty* (1962) and plays in the early 1970s on the video *The L.A. All Stars* (Rhapsody Films).

CHARLIE KENNEDY

b. July 2, 1927, Staten Island, NY

Charlie Kennedy, who is mostly forgotten today, was important in bringing the Charlie Parker sound and his boppish style into Gene Krupa's orchestra. He began playing clarinet when he was 12, soon switching to alto and tenor. Kennedy played with Louis Prima's orchestra in 1943 and then became an important soloist with the Krupa big band of 1945–48. At the time he was virtually the first Bop-oriented alto soloist to be heard in a swing orchestra (if one discounts Charlie Parker's association with Jay McShann).

Kennedy, who led his only record date in 1945 (five numbers for Savoy on which he played tenor), also recorded with Charlie Ventura, Chubby Jackson, and Chico O'Farrill. In the 1950s he moved to Los Angeles, where he was part of the West Coast scene, playing in the studios and working with Bill Holman's orchestra, Terry Gibbs's Dream Band (1959–62), Jimmy Witherspoon, and Shelly Manne (1964). Charlie Kennedy retired from playing music in the 1970s.

FILMS

Kennedy can be seen with the Gene Krupa Orchestra in *Beat the Band* (1947).

SONNY STITT

b. Feb. 2, 1924, Boston, MA, d. July 22, 1982, Washington, DC

Sonny Stitt was one of the all-time great jazz saxophonists, but there has to be an asterisk attached to his name. In jazz, one of the main goals is to achieve one's own sound, but Stitt's alto playing was often identical to Charlie Parker's, although without the genius. Unlike other Parker imitators, who faded away or switched instruments, Stitt continued playing alto in a very Birdlike style throughout his career, even while he also doubled on tenor, where his ideas were similar but his tone was closer to Lester Young's.

A master of the Bebop vocabulary, Stitt (unlike his close friend Gene Ammons) was not all that flexible; he always sounded like a Bebopper, even when he was in an R&B or blues-oriented setting. Born Edward Stitt, he worked early on in Detroit and Saginaw, Michigan, and in Newark, New Jersey. His first notable job was with Tiny Bradshaw's big band in 1943, about the time that he originally met Charlie Parker. Stitt gained early recognition for playing in Billy Eckstine's orchestra in 1945. He already sounded like a near-clone of Charlie Parker's by that time and, although he claimed that he had developed his style independently, that seems a bit doubtful! In 1946 Stitt worked with the Dizzy Gillespie big band and was quite effective on a Gillespie small-group recording; he also recorded with the Bebop

Boys. Drug problems caused Stitt to cut back on his activities during 1947–48, but he returned with renewed energy in 1949. By then he was doubling on tenor and occasionally playing baritone (which in the mid-1950s he unfortunately chose to give up totally). Stitt made records with Bud Powell and J. J. Johnson, and during 1950–52 he co-led a two-tenor quintet with Gene Ammons that had a minor hit in "Blues Up and Down."

After the band with Ammons broke up, Sonny Stitt's life fell into a pattern. He spent much of his career touring the United States (and later Europe) as a single, picking up local rhythm sections along the way. Stitt, who recorded an enormous number of records as a leader (some of which are classic), enjoyed defeating local up-and-coming horn players in jam sessions, acting as a gladiator or warrior in slaying all competitors. Few could match his mastery of the Bebop vocabulary; he could play "Cherokee" effortlessly at a rapid pace in any of the twelve keys. Other than a short stint with the Miles Davis Quintet in 1960 (where his Bebop style really did not fit in as a replacement for John Coltrane), reunions with Gene Ammons, tours with the Giants of Jazz (1971–72), and participation in occasional all-star groups, Stitt worked mostly as a loner throughout his life, playing and recording steadily. Despite some ups and downs (including some frivolous late-'60s recordings using the electronic Varitone attachment on his horns), Sonny Stitt was still in prime form in the early 1980s, before passing away from cancer in 1982 at the age of 58.

10 *Sonny Stitt/Bud Powell/J. J. Johnson / Oct 17, 1949–Jan. 26, 1950 / Original Jazz Classics 009*

9 *Prestige First Sessions Vol. 2 / Feb. 17, 1950–Aug. 14, 1951 / Prestige 24115*

9 *Kaleidoscope / Oct. 8, 1950–Feb. 25, 1952 / Original Jazz Classics 060*

8 *At the Hi-Hat / Feb. 11, 1954 / Roulette 98582*

8 *Live at the Hi-Hat Volume Two / Feb. 11, 1954 / Roulette 37200*

Sonny Stitt's first dates as a leader were with the Bebop Boys in 1946 and for Galaxy in 1948 (the latter has been reissued under Milt Jackson's name). He recorded a steady stream of gems for Prestige during 1949–52 (not counting his sides with the band he co-led with Gene Ammons), and these have been reissued in the first three CDs listed in this section. *Sonny Stitt/Bud Powell/J. J. Johnson* contains classic Bebop, with two sessions featuring Stitt in a quartet with Bud Powell, Curly Russell, and Max Roach while the third

The Wayne Knight Collection

Stuck in Charlie Parker's shadow on alto, the highly competitive Sonny Stitt wisely started doubling on tenor in the late 1940s.

is a quintet outing under J. J. Johnson's leadership that also includes John Lewis, Nelson Boyd, and Max Roach. All of the music from these dates is here (including five alternate takes), and Stitt (who sticks exclusively to tenor) is quite brilliant on such tunes as "All God's Chillun Got Rhythm," "Fine and Dandy," "Strike Up the Band," and Lewis's "Afternoon in Paris." *Prestige First Sessions Vol. 2* has Stitt (playing tenor except for two alto numbers) on seven different sessions dating from 1950–55. The 24 Boppish selections (transformations of such tunes as "Avalon," "Mean to Me," "There Will Never Be Another You," "Jeepers Creepers," and "Cherokee") include such players as pianists Kenny Drew, Duke Jordan, and Junior Mance and drummer Art Blakey. *Kaleidoscope* has Stitt in three different trios (with Drew and Mance again) and two sextet/septets from 1950–52, jamming basic originals (including "Stitt's It" and "Sonny Sounds") and standards. Highlights are the two numbers ("P. S. I Love You" and "This Can't Be Love") that Stitt takes on baritone, jamming away quite effectively.

On February 11, 1954, Stitt appeared at Boston's Hi-Hat club with a local rhythm section (pianist Dean Earl, bassist Bernie Griggs, and drummer Marquis Foster). Two CDs of material have come out from this day's engagement and, although the backup group is pretty anonymous, Stitt sounds quite inspired on a variety of standards and basic originals. Most unusual is that, in addition to tenor and alto, he plays baritone on "Tri-Horn Blues" from the first set and a 12-minute version of "One O'Clock Jump" from *Volume Two*, about the last time that he was ever heard on the large instrument. It might have just been a typical night for Stitt, but the music still sounds exciting over 45 years later.

7 *Only the Blues / Oct. 11, 1957 / Verve 314 537 753*

9 *Sits In with the Oscar Peterson Trio / Oct. 11, 1957 + May 18, 1959 / Verve 849 396*

7 *Sonny Stitt / 1958 / MCA/Chess 9317*

5 *How High the Moon / Aug. 1, 1958–Jan. 25, 1965 / GRP/Chess 817*

7 *Stitt Meets Brother Jack / Feb. 16, 1962 / Original Jazz Classics 703*

7 *Low Flame / Apr. 4, 1962 + Mar. 19, 1964 / Prestige 24236*

6 *Autumn in New York / 1962–Oct. 1, 1967 / Black Lion 760130*

10 *Stitt Plays Bird / Jan. 29, 1963 / Atlantic 1418*

Despite its title, *Only the Blues* was originally four lengthy jams with Stitt on alto, trumpeter Roy Eldridge, the Oscar Peterson Trio, and drummer Stan Levey that consisted of three blues and "The String" (an "I Got Rhythm"-based piece that is identical to Stitt's "The Eternal Triangle"). Stitt and Eldridge made for an explosive combination, since they were among the most competitive of jazzmen. This CD also has some previously unreleased material: two standards without Eldridge and a rather tedious 22-minute stretch in which Stitt plays "I Know That You Know" over and over again, including three complete versions and lots of breakdowns, incomplete versions, and attempts at playing a coda to splice in. Why was this included on what had been an excellent CD?

Sits In with the Oscar Peterson Trio is taken mostly from 1959, when Stitt performed seven standards and a themeless blues with Peterson, Ray Brown, and Ed Thigpen. Stitt cannot help but sound inspired when backed by such a strong rhythm section as he shows on "Au Privave," "I'll Remember April," and "Moten Swing." In addition, this CD has two standards ("I Didn't Know What Time It Was" and "I Remember You") plus one of the complete versions of "I Know That You Know" that was tacked on to the *Only the Blues* CD, which makes me wonder why *Only the Blues* was also saddled with the same performances! The Chess CD, called simply *Sonny Stitt,* is a live set that the saxophonist had apparently forgotten about when asked about it years later. Backed by an unidentified rhythm section that might have Barry Harris on piano in 1958, Stitt plays mostly "originals" based on the chord changes of standards plus "This Is Always," "Just You, Just Me," "Cool Blues," and "Dancing on the Ceiling." An above-average and rather spontaneous session.

The music on *How High the Moon* is fine, but this CD is only a sampler of three of Stitt's Chess albums (1958's *Burnin'*, *Inter-action,* from 1965, and 1964's *Sonny Stitt and Benny Green*), reissuing just 13 of the 22 selections. Stitt

sounds fine in a quartet with Barry Harris and sharing a pair of groups with tenor saxophonist Zoot Sims and trombonist Bennie Green, but this CD is an obvious frivolity and should have been used to reissue two complete albums instead. *Stitt Meets Brother Jack* is a fine Bop/soul jazz date with organist Jack McDuff, guitarist Eddie Diehl, drummer Art Taylor, and Ray Barretto on conga. Stitt (on tenor) jams happily on such tunes as "All of Me," "Time After Time," and his original "When Sonny Gets Blue" (which is not the same song as the standard). Several of Stitt's collaborations with organists have been reissued (usually two complete LPs on one CD) as part of Prestige's *Legends of Acid Jazz* series. *Low Flame* has the 1962 Jazzland album of the same name plus the music (from 1964) originally put out as *Shangri-La.* Stitt is joined by organist Don Patterson, drummer Billy James, and (just on the first date) guitarist Paul Weeden, mostly playing alto and taking a surprise vocal on "Mama Don't Allow." Basic originals dominate the repertoire, and Stitt clearly enjoyed working with Patterson, with whom he would make quite a few albums. *Autumn in New York* combines a four-song quartet/quintet date from 1967 with Walter Bishop Jr., Tommy Potter, Kenny Clarke, and (on three of the numbers) Howard McGhee, with a live set from 1962 that has Stitt backed by an unknown rhythm section. Each of the McGhee selections is blues and, although Stitt plays with his usual spirit on the other date (particularly on "Stardust," "Cherokee," and "Autumn in New York"), there are many Sonny Stitt recordings currently available that are on at least the same level.

In contrast, *Stitt Plays Bird* is an obvious classic. Sticking to alto and joined by John Lewis, guitarist Jim Hall, bassist Richard Davis, and drummer Connie Kay, Stitt performs ten songs composed by Parker (two of these performances were unreleased until the CD reissue) plus Jay McShann's "Hootie Blues." Stitt was so familiar with this material that the saxophonist could play these songs in his sleep or backwards. He was definitely up for the project, as can be heard on such numbers as "My Little Suede Shoes," "Constellation," "Confirmation," and "Ko-Ko."

9 *Salt and Pepper / Sept. 5, 1963 / GRP/Impulse 210*

7 *Night Letter / Sept. 17, 1963 + Oct. 27, 1969 / Prestige 24165*

8 *Soul People / Aug. 25, 1964–1966 / Prestige 24127*

6 *Made for Each Other / July 13, 1968 / Delmark 426*

7 *Legends of Acid Jazz Vol. 2 / Sept. 23–24, 1968 /*
    Prestige 24210

4 *Legends of Acid Jazz / Jan. 4, 1971 + July 9, 1971 /*
    Prestige 24169

Salt and Pepper reissues both that LP and Stitt's *Now.* The former set is particularly special, matching Stitt and fellow tenor Paul Gonsalves on jam session versions of the blues "Salt and Pepper," "S'posin'," and "Perdido." Actually, the high point is "Stardust," which has beautiful statements by (and a remarkable blend between) Gonsalves and Stitt's alto. The music on the quartet date *Now* also has Stitt pushing himself, and his solos on such numbers as "Lester Leaps In," "Estralita," "Please Don't Talk About Me When I'm Gone," and "I'm Getting Sentimental Over You" rank with some of the best of his career. *Night Letter* has the complete contents of two former LPs (the other one was *Soul Shack*), teaming Stitt with organist Jack McDuff's trio in 1963 (best are "Sunday" and "Love Nest") and with organist Gene Ludwig, guitarist Pat Martino, and drummer Randy Gelispie in 1969. The last date finds Stitt playing well on songs such as "Stringin' the Jug" and "You'll Never Know" but, since he utilizes a Varitone sax (which he experimented with in the late '60s before giving it up), he does not sound as distinctive as usual.

Soul People matches Stitt with tenor saxophonist Booker Ervin on five performances with organist Don Patterson and drummer Billy James. Ervin always had his own sound, and his intense playing lights a bit of fire under Stitt; their trade-offs often border on the explosive. In addition to their numbers (which include "C-Jam Blues," a two-song ballad medley, and "Flyin' Home"), there is a trio feature for Don Patterson ("There Will Never Be Another You") and a rare meeting between Stitt and guitarist Grant Green on "Tune-Up." *Made for Each Other,* a trio outing with Patterson and drummer Billy James, has good material and lots of potential, but unfortunately Stitt mostly uses the Varitone attachment on his horns, weighing down the music. There are some strong moments ("Samba de Orfeo," "The Glory of Love," and two versions of "The Night Has a Thousand Eyes") but the results are not essential.

Legends of Acid Jazz, Vol. 2 (which predates the first volume) reissues the music from *Funk You* and *Soul Electricity.* *Funk You* (despite its dumb title) is noteworthy because it has Stitt interacting with altoist Charles McPherson plus guitarist Pat Martino, Patterson, and drummer James. The material is mostly strong, including "Airegin," "It's You or

No One," and even "Funk in 3/4." The second set has Stitt, Patterson, James, and guitarist Billy Butler playing some fine standards, but unfortunately the Varitone is used in spots; still, the music is better than expected. In contrast, *Legends of Acid Jazz* reissues two of Sonny Stitt's weaker sessions (*Turn It On* and *Black Vibrations*). The first date has Stitt using the Varitone and being overshadowed by the chugging rhythm section (organist Leon Spencer, guitarist Melvin Sparks, and drummer Idris Muhammad) on generally weak material, sounding like a guest on his own record; trumpeter Virgil Jones often takes solo honors. *Black Vibrations* is a little better, since Stitt plays acoustically and Don Patterson replaces Spencer on three tracks, but the overall results are still rather sluggish.

10 *Endgame Brilliance / Feb. 8, 1972 + June 27, 1972 /*
    32 Jazz 32009

6 *The Champ / Apr. 18, 1973 / Muse 5429*

5 *Best of the Rest / Apr. 18, 1973–June 9, 1982 / 32*
    Jazz 32076

6 *Moonlight in Vermont / Nov. 23, 1977 / Denon 8566*

5 *Duty Free / 1979 / Laserlight 17129*

8 *In Style / Mar. 18, 1981 / Muse 5228*

6 *Just in Case You Forgot How Bad He Really Was /*
    Sept. 1981 / 32 Jazz 32051

7 *Battle of the Saxes / Dec. 1981 / AIM 1010*

9 *The Last Stitt Sessions, Vols. 1 & 2 / June 8–9,*
    1982 / 32 Jazz 32127

By 1972, Sonny Stitt had given up using the Varitone, and at age 48 he was at the peak of his powers. His two classic quartet albums for Muse, *Tune-Up!* and *Constellation,* with Barry Harris, bassist Sam Jones, and either Roy Brooks or Alan Dawson on drums, have been reissued on the single-CD *Endgame Brilliance* by 32 Jazz. It can be said without exaggeration that Stitt never played better than he sounds on such numbers as "Constellation," "Webb City," "It's Magic," "Tune Up," "Groovin' High," and a lengthy "I Got Rhythm." Switching between alto and tenor, he is full of exuberance on these dates and sounds remarkably inspired, showing that Bebop really does live when played by the very best. Every respectable jazz collection has to include *Endgame Brilliance.*

Although Stitt is also in great form on *The Champ,* this date is hurt by the inclusion of trumpeter Joe Newman, who was having an off day. Stitt and the rhythm section (Duke Jordan, Sam Jones, and Roy Brooks) do their best on the title cut, "The Eternal Triangle," and "Walkin'," but the leader cuts his solos a bit short so Newman can take his choruses, and the set is a slight disappointment. In 1998 producer Joel Dorn of 32 Jazz announced that he was reissuing only some of Sonny Stitt's Muse albums because he felt that particular ones were much than others. *Best of the Rest,* a sampler drawn from *In Style, Blues for Duke, The Champ,* and *The Last Stitt Sessions Volume Two,* was supposed to contain all of the remaining Stitt recordings that Dorn was willing to reissue, but fortunately he has since reconsidered. This sampler is therefore a bit useless except as an introduction to the saxophonist's playing since, in time, all of the cuts will be duplicated in more complete collections.

Moonlight in Vermont is a swinging, if mostly uneventful, meeting with Barry Harris or Walter Davis, bassist Reggie Workman, and drummer Tony Williams that includes a remake of "Constellation," three originals, and a trio of standards. The same can be said for *Duty Free* from the budget label Laserlight. Stitt is backed by a quiet rhythm section (pianist Gerald Price, bassist Don Mosley, and drummer Bobby Durham) for a rather brief (33-minute) program of familiar standards and blues-based tunes. *In Style* is a reunion with Barry Harris that took place nine years after *Tune-Up.* Stitt proves to still be in inspired form whenever he plays with the Boppish pianist, as he shows on "Just You, Just Me," "Is You Is or Is You Ain't My Baby?" and "Yesterdays"; bassist George Duvivier and drummer Jimmy Cobb complete the quartet. *Just in Case* is a club appearance from September 1981 that was not released until 1998. Stitt is the main star (with assistance from pianist Cedar Walton, bassist Herbie Lewis, and drummer Billy Higgins), but there are also guest appearances from vibraphonist Bobby Hutcherson, altoist Richie Cole, and John Handy on tenor and alto. Some of the music is overly loose and the notes do not bother saying which saxophonists play on which track (though they all participate on a ballad medley), but listeners should be able to identify the soloists after a few listens. An interesting if not-too-essential date. Also quite intriguing is *Battle of the Saxes,* an obscure release from the Australian AM label that teams Stitt with the hyper altoist Richie Cole. Backed by pianist Jack Wilson, bassist Ed Gaston, and drummer Allan Turnbull, the two Boppish saxophonists play their best on such songs as "I Hear a Rhapsody," "The Night Has a Thousand Eyes," and "Cherokee."

Six weeks before his death, and just a few days before he was diagnosed with cancer, Sonny Stitt unwittingly recorded his final sessions on two consecutive days. With either Junior Mance or Walter Davis on piano, bassist George Duvivier, drummer Jimmy Cobb, and (during the second session) trumpeter Bill Hardman, Stitt showed that he was still at the top of his game, playing creatively in the Bebop language that he had long ago mastered. This single CD has 14 of the 15 selections on the albums, and Stitt once again sounds wonderful on such tunes as "I'll Be Seeing You," "Bouncin' with Bud," and "Bye, Bye Blackbird." A particularly strong ending to a rather busy career.

LPS TO SEARCH FOR

Symphony Hall Swing (Savoy 1165) has music from Sonny Stitt's two Savoy dates. He plays tenor on a complete session from 1952 while joined by pianist Fletcher Peck, bassist John Simmons, and drummer Jo Jones. And he plays alto in 1956 for a few alternate takes from a Roost LP with the Dolo Coker Trio. *Sonny Stitt & the Top Brass* (Atlantic 90139) features Stitt (on alto) in 1962 accompanied by three trumpets (including Blue Mitchell, who has a few solos), two trombones, Willie Ruff on French horn, and a rhythm section. The arrangements (by Tadd Dameron and Jimmy Mundy) uplift the set and make it particularly special. *Pow!* features the potent team of altoist Stitt and trombonist Benny Green in a 1965 quintet on mostly obscure but viable material.

Recorded in 1972 after the classic *Tune-Up* session and before *Constellation, Goin' Down Slow* (Prestige 10048) is on a pretty high level, particularly the 14-minute "Miss Ann, Lisa, Sue and Sadie," which has Stitt, trumpeter Thad Jones, Hank Jones, and guitarist Billy Butler playing over a string section arranged by Billy Ver Planck. Also from 1972, *So Doggone Good* (Prestige 10074) is not quite on the same level but does have Stitt in good form on four originals, an R&B tune, and "The More I See You" with the assistance of Hampton Hawes, bassist Reggie Johnson, and drummer Lenny McBrowne. *12!* (Muse 5006), from later that year, is almost on the same level as *Tune-Up,* using a similar rhythm section (Barry Harris, Sam Jones, and Louis Hayes) for two basic originals and superior versions of such standards as "I Never Knew," "The Night Has a Thousand Eyes," and Tadd Dameron's "Our Delight." The music on 1975's *Mellow* (Muse 5067) is relaxed but not exclusively ballads. In fact, this meeting between Stitt and Jimmy Heath (heard on tenor, soprano, and flute), along with Barry Harris, bassist Richard Davis, and Roy Haynes, has some heated moments; highlights include "A Sailboat in the Moonlight," "Soon," and "How High the Moon."

Long overdue to be reissued is *In Walked Sonny* (Sonet 691), an exciting encounter between Stitt and the 1975 version of Art Blakey's Jazz Messengers, which includes trumpeter Bill Hardman, Dave Schnitter on tenor, and Walter Davis, Jr. *My Buddy* (Muse 5091) is Stitt's heartfelt tribute to his recently deceased friend Gene Ammons, a high-quality quartet date with Barry Harris, Sam Jones, and drummer Leroy Williams that includes "Red Top," "Confirmation," and the title cut. Stitt and Red Holloway (on alto and tenor) battle it out on *Forecast: Sonny and Red* (Catalyst 7608), a hot but now rare quintet date from 1975 that features intense interplay on "The Way You Look Tonight," "Lester Leaps In," and "All God's Chillun Got Rhythm." *Blues for Duke* (Muse 5129) and *Sonny Stitt with Strings* (Catalyst 7620) are both tribute albums to Duke Ellington. The title of *I Remember Bird* (Catalyst 7616), which also features trombonist Frank Rosolino, has more to do with Leonard Feather's original composition than the repertoire. Although Stitt plays just average on *Stomp Off, Let's Go* (Flying Dutchman 1538), the four standards on his 1976 date are notable for including plenty of solos from the two high-note trumpeters Jon Faddis and Lew Soloff. Other worthwhile LPs from the 1978–81 period that have not been reissued yet include *Sonny Stitt Meets Sadik Hakim* (Progressive 7034), a collaboration with tenor saxophonist Ricky Ford called *Sonny's Back* (Muse 5204), and two albums from a 1981 concert that has guest appearances by trumpeter Harry "Sweets" Edison and tenor saxophonist Eddie "Lockjaw" Davis: *Sonny, Sweets & Jaws* (Who's Who 21022) and *Sonny* (Who's Who 21025).

FILMS
Sonny Stitt is in *Jazz on a Summer's Day* (New Yorker Video 16590) from the 1958 Newport Jazz Festival.

Tenor Saxophonists

Prior to the Bebop era, there were two major ways for jazz musicians to play the tenor. Coleman Hawkins created harmonically complex solos that thoroughly investigated chords, and he played with a large, thick tone. His most important follower, Ben Webster, played much simpler solos, but his tone was just as powerful. In contrast, Lester Young had a soft sound that seemed to float lazily over bar lines, swinging hard but with great subtlety and making each note (along with silence) count. There were a few other approaches (including those of Bud Freeman and Eddie Miller), but basically Hawk and Pres were the pacesetters before 1940.

With the rise of Illinois Jacquet (whose "Flying Home" solo with Lionel Hampton in 1942 essentially launched rhythm and blues, a bonanza for tenor players who enjoyed repetition and were colorfully exhibitionistic), some tenor saxophonists began to combine aspects of the two main influences. Some would have a hard sound but a more relaxed style, while others emulated Young's sound but played many more notes.

As Bebop began to develop, Dexter Gordon (who briefly played next to Jacquet with Hampton) became the pacesetter. He had a unique sound, was able to hold his own in jam sessions with Wardell Gray and Teddy Edwards, and understood the innovations of Charlie Parker, taking from the altoist whatever he felt suited his style. Wardell Gray had a style similar to Gordon's except that his tone was lighter, and Allen Eager became one of the first important "cool school" tenors. Flip Phillips and Lucky Thompson built their sounds out of the swing era but kept their ideas fresh and modern. Gene Ammons showed that it was possible to play both bebop and R&B, while Jimmy Heath and James Moody helped their careers greatly by concentrating on tenor rather than alto and not being shy to gradually modernize their styles through the years.

GENE AMMONS
b. Apr. 14, 1925, Chicago, IL, d. July 23, 1974, Chicago, IL

Gene Ammons was part of several different musical idioms at the same time. His huge sound was a throwback to the swing era and his ability to soulfully state ideas (sometimes with just a few notes) fit in perfectly in R&B settings, where he was probably the most influential. And yet Ammons could also play Bebop with the best of them, holding his own against his pal Sonny Stitt and anyone else in saxophone battles. All he had to play was two or three notes in his distinctive and emotional sound, and both audiences and fellow saxophonists knew that "Jug" was a force to be reckoned with.

The son of boogie-woogie pianist Albert Ammons (they recorded one happy session together in 1947), Gene Ammons started playing tenor early on in his native Chicago. In 1943 he toured with King Kolax's big band and then became well known for his playing with Billy Eckstine's orchestra (1944–47). Ammons traded off with Dexter Gordon on Eckstine's hit record of "Blowin' the Blues Away" and was an important soloist with the singer's influential Bebop orchestra. Ammons was featured with Woody Herman's Third Herd in 1949 (including on "More Moon") and co-led a two-tenor quintet with Sonny Stitt during 1950–52; "Blues Up and Down" and "Walkin'" were among their most popular records.

After the group broke up, Ammons worked as a single during 1952–58, recording a superior series of jam session records for Prestige. Unfortunately drug problems resulted in Jug's being jailed during part of 1958–60. After an outburst of activity (resulting in many recordings), Ammons had the book thrown at him when he was busted again and this time spent seven long years (1962–69) in prison. Upon his release, Ammons was 44 and still in peak playing form. He had listened to the avant-garde in the interim and opened up his style to include many highly expressive sounds. Although some of Gene Ammons's later sessions are rather commercial (with pop songs featured on some of his records plus electronic and funky rhythm sections), he still had the ability to hold his own with Sonny Stitt, and they had several reunions in the early 1970s. Gene Ammons remained a potent force until the end, and his final recording (before he was diagnosed with cancer) was, ironically, the Gordon Jenkins ballad "Goodbye."

8 *Young Jug / Oct. 12, 1948–Mar. 24, 1952 / GRP/ Chess 801*

8 *All Star Sessions with Sonny Stitt / Mar. 5, 1950– June 16, 1955 / Original Jazz Classics 014*

8 *The Gene Ammons Story: The 78 Era / Mar. 5, 1950–Nov. 4, 1955 / Prestige 24058*

Young Jug is an excellent CD that, if made into a double set, could have been definitive. Gene Ammons recorded 24 titles for the Chess and Aristocrat labels during 1948–52. All were reissued on the two-LP set *Early Visions. Young Jug* has 16 of those titles plus a very rare four-song Decca date from

1952, but leaves out eight songs. The music that is here is excellent, including "Swingin' for Xmas," "Once in a While," a remake of "More Moon," and "My Foolish Heart." The sidemen on various cuts include Sonny Stitt (on baritone), J.J. Johnson, pianist Junior Mance, and bassist Eugene Wright, but Ammons is the star throughout.

From 1953 until his death in 1974, Gene Ammons recorded almost exclusively for the Prestige label (and its subsidiaries), which means that much of the music has been reissued on CDs in the Original Jazz Classics series or as a Prestige set. *All-Star Sessions with Sonny Stitt* skips around a bit, but it contains quite a bit of valuable music. The best selections from the Ammons-Stitt quintet are here, including "Stringin' The Jug," three takes of "Blues Up and Down," and two versions of "You Can Depend On Me." In addition, there are two lengthy jam session numbers from 1955 with trumpeter Art Farmer, Lou Donaldson, pianist Freddie Reed, bassist Addison Farmer, and Kenny Clarke that would be the first in a notable series of Ammons-led jams. *The 78 Era* has 26 of the 30 titles previously put out on a two-LP set of the same name. With the exception of the last five numbers (which are from 1955), all of the music dates from 1950–51, and the performances are quite concise, clocking in around three minutes apiece. The music alternates heated romps with warm ballads, and features Ammons and his jump band (which sometimes has Sonny Stitt on baritone and such sidemen as Duke Jordan, Junior Mance, Tommy Potter, Eugene Wright, and drummers Jo Jones and Art Blakey) on such songs as the original version of "Walkin'" (made famous by Miles Davis in 1954), "Back in Your Own Backyard," "Wow," "Blue and Sentimental," and (in a nod to Gene's late father) "Ammons Boogie."

10 *The Happy Blues / Apr. 23, 1956 / Original Jazz Classics 013*

8 *Jammin' with Gene / July 13, 1956 / Original Jazz Classics 211*

8 *Funky / Jan. 11, 1957 / Original Jazz Classics 244*

8 *Jammin' in Hi-Fi with Gene Ammons / Apr. 12, 1957 / Original Jazz Classics 129*

8 *The Big Sound / Jan. 3, 1958 / Original Jazz Classics 651*

8 *Groove Blues / Jan. 3, 1958 / Original Jazz Classics 723*

7 *Blue Gene / May 3, 1958 / Original Jazz Classics 192*

In contrast to his three-minute recordings of the early 1950s, by 1956 Gene Ammons's Prestige recordings were emphasizing much longer jam-session-flavored performances. Ammons proved to be an excellent leader in this format (as was trumpeter Buck Clayton in his more swing-oriented jams for Columbia), setting riffs behind soloists and allowing his sidemen to stretch out. On the title cut of *The Happy Blues*, everything works and the solos are classic; the other three selections are also excellent. Ammons interacts joyfully with Art Farmer, altoist Jackie McLean, Duke Jordan, Addison Farmer, drummer Art Taylor, and Candido on conga. *Jammin' with Gene* has just three selections ("Not Really the Blues," "Jammin' with Gene," and "We'll Be Together Again") that total over 40 minutes. Ammons shares the solo space with McLean, Farmer, trumpeter Donald Byrd, pianist Mal Waldron, bassist Doug Watkins, and Art Taylor this time around, and the results are quite fun and swinging; even "We'll Be Together Again" is taken medium tempo after a ballad chorus. *Funky* has a pair of compositions by arranger Jimmy Mundy, a Kenny Burrell blues, and "Stella By Starlight." Ammons, Farmer, McLean, guitarist Burrell, Waldron, Watkins, and Taylor make for a particularly strong band, full of energy, original voices, and swinging ideas. *Jammin' in Hi-Fi with Gene Ammons* continues the series, with a similar band (Ammons, Idrees Sulieman, McLean, Waldron, bassist Paul Chambers, and Taylor) stretching out on "Four," "Pennies from Heaven," and two Waldron originals.

The Gene Ammons jam session of January 3, 1958, resulted in two albums worth of material that were released as *The Big Sound* and *Groove Blues*. Ammons, joined by Waldron, bassist Jamil Nasser, and drummer Taylor, on *The Big Sound* has "Cheek to Cheek" and "Blue Hymn" as his own features (with Jerome Richardson on flute), baritonist Pepper Adams helps out on "That's All," and, on Waldron's "The Real McCoy," Jug shares the frontline with Richardson, Adams, fellow tenor Paul Quinichette, and John Coltrane (making a very rare appearance on alto). *Groove Blues* has the full group on the title cut and "Groove Blues," features Ammons and Coltrane as the only horns on "It Might As Well Be Spring," and finds Jug and Richardson being showcased on "Jug Handle." The two CDs are of equal interest and, even though some of the ballads are quite long ("That's All" lasts 14 minutes), the music is of a consistently high quality. The final entry in the jam session series, *Blue Gene,* matches Ammons with Sulieman, Adams, Waldron,

Watkins, Taylor, and Ray Barretto on conga. The so-so material (three blues of various tempos plus Waldron's ballad "Hip Tip") is uplifted by the generally enthusiastic solos. It is a pity that this series had to end, but Ammons's trouble with the law meant that his next recording would not take place for two years.

9 **Boss Tenor / June 16, 1960 / Original Jazz Classics 297**

6 **Angel Eyes / June 17, 1960 + Sept. 5, 1962 / Original Jazz Classics 980**

8 **The Gene Ammons Story: Organ Combos / June 17, 1960–Nov. 28, 1961 / Prestige 24071**

7 **The Gene Ammons Story: Gentle Jug / Jan. 26, 1961 + Apr. 14, 1962 / Prestige 24079**

7 **Jug / Jan. 27, 1961 / Original Jazz Classics 701**

6 **Late Hour Special / June 13, 1961–Apr. 13, 1962 / Original Jazz Classics 943**

During 1960–62 Gene Ammons recorded quite a bit for Prestige and its subsidiaries. Even after Ammons was convicted of drug possession and was awaiting sentencing, he continued making records. During his long prison term, Prestige was able to gradually release Jug's stockpile of performances, keeping his name alive even while he was totally off the scene.

Boss Tenor is an excellent all-round effort, with Ammons joined by Tommy Flanagan, Doug Watkins, Art Taylor, and Ray Barretto. This warm version of the ballad "Canadian Sunset" was quite popular, "Hittin' the Jug" is a swinger, and all of the numbers on this date (which also includes "Close Your Eyes," "My Romance," "Blue Ammons," Charlie Parker's "Confirmation," and "Savoy") feature Jug at the top of his game. *Angel Eyes* draws its material from separate sessions in 1960 and 1962, with the former date also including Frank Wess (on tenor and flute), organist Johnny Hammond Smith, and Art Taylor. The 1962 set is by a quartet with Waldron, bassist Wendell Marshall, and Ed Thigpen. The title cut is the most notable of the six selections, which also include "Water Jug" and "You Go to My Head." Oddly enough, the four-song 1960 session (including "Angel Eyes") is repeated in the rather generous (over 77 minutes) *Organ Combos* CD. Also included are two other numbers from the same session (but originally released on the *Velvet Soul* LP) plus all the music from the LP *Twistin' the Jug*, on which Ammons is joined by trumpeter Joe Newman, organist Jack McDuff, Wendell Marshall, drummer

Walter Perkins, and Ray Barretto. The versatile Ammons sounds quite at home playing standards, blues, and ballads as a soul jazz soloist in this setting.

Unlike *Gentle Jug, Vol. 2* (Prestige 24155), which is merely a sampler of Gene Ammons's ballad performances, *The Gene Ammons Story: Gentle Jug* has two complete sessions (originally released as *Nice an' Cool* and *The Soulful Mood of Gene Ammons*) that the tenor cut for Prestige's Moodsville label. With backing by two quiet rhythm sections (Richard Wyands or Patti Bown on piano, Doug Watkins or George Duvivier on bass, and J. C. Heard or Ed Shaughnessy on drums), Ammons caresses 16 ballads with his warm tone and distinctive sound, making every note count. Among the songs that Ammons makes love to on this mood music set are "Till There Was You," "Little Girl Blue," "I Remember You," "But Beautiful," and "Skylark."

Jug is a fairly typical set, with Ammons performing six standards and two originals (including "Easy to Love," "Exactly Like You," and "Tangerine") with the assistance of Richard Wyands (replaced by Sleepy Anderson on two songs), Doug Watkins, drummer J. C. Heard, and Ray Barretto. *Late Hour Special*, originally released in 1964 while Ammons was serving his sentence, features the tenor on three numbers in a quartet/quintet and on four selections as part of a ten-piece group arranged by Oliver Nelson. Nothing unusual happens, but these renditions of "I Want to Be Loved," "Things Ain't What They Used to Be" (which has a solo by Clark Terry), and "Soft Winds" are strong enough to compensate for the brief (35 minutes) playing time.

7 *Soul Summit / June 13, 1961–Apr. 13, 1962 / Prestige 24118*

8 *We'll Be Together Again / Aug. 26, 1961 / Original Jazz Classics 708*

9 *Boss Tenors / Aug. 27, 1961 / Verve 837 440*

9 *Boss Tenors in Orbit / Feb. 1962 / Verve 8468*

7 *Live! In Chicago / Aug. 29, 1961 / Original Jazz Classics 395*

8 *Up Tight! / Oct. 17-18, 1961 / Prestige 24140*

7 *Preachin' / May 3, 1962 / Original Jazz Classics 792*

7 *Jug & Dodo / May 1962 / Prestige 24021*

7 *Bad! Bossa Nova / Sept. 9, 1962 / Original Jazz Classics 351*

Gene Ammons always played some of his best Bebop when teamed up with Sonny Stitt. *Soul Summit* has the complete contents of *Soul Summit* (a quartet date with Stitt, organist

Jack McDuff, and drummer Charlie Persip) and *Soul Summit Vol. 2*. The latter features Ammons on two additional tracks from the date with Oliver Nelson, backing singer Etta Jones on three songs, and sharing a quintet with fellow tenor Harold Vick on "Ballad for Baby"; "Scram" is Vick's feature. Although the variety is welcome, the Stitt date (which includes a variety of riff tunes and a medium-tempo "When You Wish Upon a Star") is the main reason to acquire this disc. Since Stitt was signed to Verve at the time that Ammons was at Prestige, they collaborated for four albums during 1961–62, two apiece for each label. *We'll Be Together Again,* with the backing of pianist John Houston, bassist Buster Williams, and drummer George Brown, is highlighted by the two tenors (Stitt plays alto on two of the ten numbers) inspiring each other on "Red Sails in the Sunset," "New Blues Up and Down," and "Autumn Leaves." However, Verve got the better of the deal, for the following day Ammons and Stitt are heard at their most competitive on the five songs that comprise *Boss Tenors*, most notably "Blues Up and Down," "There Is No Greater Love" (Stitt's only appearance on alto), and another version of "Autumn Leaves." *Boss Tenors in Orbit,* which was only in print as a CD for a brief time (the catalog number listed above is for the original LP) was Verve's answer to *Soul Summit,* using organist Don Patterson, guitarist Paul Weeden, and drummer William James in this version of the Ammons-Stitt Quintet. The two tenors play so well on "Walkin'," "John Brown's Body," and "Bye, Bye Blackbird" that this ranks with their very best work.

Live! In Chicago, a set on which Jug is joined just by organist Eddie Buster and drummer Gerald Donovan, is stronger than expected and a good example of how Ammons sounded in clubs during this era. It was a typical night for the tenor, yet his emotional rendition of "Please Send Me Someone to Love" and his swinging on "Sweet Georgia Brown" and "Fast Track" (based on "I Got Rhythm") shows at how high a level he played even on a routine gig. *Up Tight!* has two albums' worth of material (*Up Tight!* and *Boss Soul*) recorded during a two-day period with Walter Bishop, Jr. or Patti Bown on piano, Art Davis or George Duvivier on bass, Art Taylor, and Ray Barretto. Ammons is in the spotlight throughout the 14 selections, and the 36-year-old sounds in prime form on such numbers as "The Breeze and I," "I'm Afraid the Masquerade Is Over," "Jug's Blue Blues," "Lester Leaps In," and "Don't Go to Strangers." One of the least known of all of Gene Ammons's recordings is *Preachin',* an unusual date in which the tenor plays 11 religious themes, mostly obscure other than "Abide with Me" and "You'll Never Walk Alone." Backed by a trio that includes Sleepy Anderson's organ, Ammons takes the melodies straight but gives them a great deal of soul and honest feeling during the rather emotional set.

Jug & Dodo, which has all of the music from a former two-LP set, is of particular interest for the playing of the legendary pianist Dodo Marmarosa. Only occasionally active in the 1950s, Marmarosa made an album for Argo in 1961, and in May 1962 cut six trio numbers (with bassist Sam Jones and drummer Marshall Thompson) plus six selections with Ammons, making the group a quartet. These last dozen tunes (plus two alternate takes) were the troubled pianist's final recordings, even though he is still alive at this writing, residing in Pittsburgh. Ammons sounds fine on such numbers as "Georgia on My Mind," "You're Driving Me Crazy," and "Falling in Love with Love," but this CD is recommended primarily because of Dodo Marmarosa's playing.

Gene Ammons's final record before going to prison was his exploration of Brazilian rhythms on *Bad! Bossa Nova*. Actually, the Latin-flavored jazz does not really use bossa nova rhythms, so this recording was an attempt to cash in on a fad. Ammons plays well throughout, anyway. The music is surprisingly upbeat considering the tenor's situation at the time. He is joined by an expanded rhythm section that includes both Bucky Pizzarelli and Kenny Burrell on guitars, and two percussionists.

7	*The Boss Is Back!* / Nov. 10–11, 1969 / Prestige 24129
7	*The Chase!* / July 26, 1970 / Prestige 24166
5	*Legends of Acid Jazz* / May 1962–Feb. 8, 1971 / Prestige 24188
8	*Gene Ammons and Friends at Montreux* / July 7, 1973 / Original Jazz Classics 1023

Finally released from prison after seven years, in 1969, Gene Ammons (just 44 years old) emerged with his playing unimpaired. His tone was still recognizable, but Ammons had opened up his style to an extent (as Art Pepper would), incorporating a wider range of emotional sounds. *The Boss Is Back!* reissues the first two LPs that Ammons recorded after his release (*The Boss Is Back* and *Brother Jug*). One date has Ammons as part of a straight-ahead quintet (with pianist Junior Mance and Candido), with guest appearances by tenors Houston Person and Prince James. The second set is with a funky rhythm section (organist Sonny Phillips, elec-

tric bassist Bob Bushnell, drummer Bernard Purdie, and two appearances by guitarist Billy Butler) that plays boogaloo rhythms and shows that Ammons was familiar with the current scene. Highlights include "Here's That Rainy Day," "Didn't We?" and "He's a Real Gone Guy."

The Chase is a fun, if loose, jam session with fellow tenor Dexter Gordon performed live in Chicago. Jug and Dexter had traded off while with Billy Eckstine's orchestra on "Blowin' the Blues Away" 26 years earlier, in 1944, so this was a long-overdue reunion. Actually Gordon has a lengthy "Wee Dot" and "Polka Dots and Moonbeams" as his features, while "The Happy Blues" features Ammons as the only horn. The two tenors do share the bandstand for "Lonesome Lover Blues" (which has a spirited vocal by Vi Redd), a four-song ballad medley, and a fiery tradeoff on "The Chase." *Legends of Acid Jazz* (which actually has nothing to do with acid jazz other than that it features a couple of organists) reissues all of the music on the Ammons-Stitt album *You Talk That Talk*, plus Jug's *The Black Cat* and two leftover selections from 1962 that were out previously only on a sampler. The Stitt-Ammons rematch is flawed by Stitt's using an electrified Varitone sax that distorts his playing and makes him sound like a cross between an electric piano and a guitar! *The Black Cat* is also an erratic date, for some of the songs (including "Something" and "Long Long Time") are unsuitable to Ammons's style. So overall, this CD is a bit of a mixed bag, although it does have some good moments from Jug along the way.

Wrapping up Gene Ammons's career on CD (although he still had three more Prestige albums to go) is his performance at the 1973 Montreux Jazz Festival. A strictly straight-ahead outing (with electric pianist Hampton Hawes, electric bassist Bob Cranshaw, Kenny Clarke, and Kenneth Nash on conga), Ammons really digs into "Yardbird Suite," "Since I Fell for You," "Sophisticated Lady," and Stitt's "New Sonny's Blues." To close off the set, a 17-minute blues ("'Treux Bleu") adds three major guests: Dexter Gordon, cornetist Nat Adderley, and altoist Cannonball Adderley. Nearly 30 years after he first starred with Billy Eckstine's orchestra, Gene Ammons shows that he could still play with the very best.

LPS TO SEARCH FOR

Gene Ammons's early non-Prestige recordings tend to be scarce. The two-LP *"Jug" Sessions* (Emarcy 2–400) has all of the tenor's recordings for the Mercury and Emarcy labels, valuable sessions from 1947 and 1949 that include his one meeting on records with his father, Albert Ammons, two versions of "Red Top," lots of jumping originals, and contributions from such sidemen as trumpeter Gail Brockman, pianist Junior Mance, and bassist Eugene Wright; Earl Coleman has two vocals. *Red Top* (Savoy 1103) has Ammons as a sideman on a sextet date led by Leo Parker (and featuring Howard McGhee) plus Jug's dates as a leader for United and Savoy with a jumping octet during 1952–53. Highlights include "Stairway to the Stars" and a remake of "Red Top." The two-LP *Early Visions* (Cadet 60038) has all 24 of Ammons's Chess recordings of 1948–51, 16 of which have been reissued on the CD *Young Jug*. Among the titles not put out on CD yet are a couple of tenor battles with Tom Archia ("The Battle" and "Jam for Beboppers") and "Cha Bootie."

Just a few of Ammons's Prestige albums have not yet been reissued on CD. *Blue Groove* (Prestige 2514), a 1962 date that was not initially released until 1982, has Jug leading a quintet that includes Sleepy Anderson on piano and organ, primarily playing blues and ballads in spirited fashion. From Ammons's later years, *Night Lights* (Prestige 7862) is a rare set from 1970 (not put out until 1985) that features the tenor playing six songs (mostly ballads) associated with Nat King Cole, assisted by the Wynton Kelly Trio. *My Way* (Prestige 10022) is a rather commercial effort as Ammons does his best to find meaningful things to play on "What's Going On," "A House Is Not a Home," and other R&B-ish vamps; his tone largely overcomes the unimaginative funk backgrounds. *Chicago Concert* (Prestige 10065) was an attempt at an old-time tenor battle featuring Ammons and James Moody (with pianist Jodie Christian, bassist Cleveland Eaton, and drummer Marshall Thompson). But for whatever reason, few sparks fly and the chemistry is not present on their four shared numbers. The best cuts are actually Ammons's features on "Work Song" and "I'll Close My Eyes." *Big Bad Jug* (Prestige 10070) and *Got My Own* (Prestige 10058) were both recorded at the same sessions in 1972, featuring some indifferent material (including "Papa Was a Rolling Stone" on the former and the theme from the movie "Ben" on the latter), but *Got My Own* does find Ammons putting lots of feeling into four Billie Holiday-associated songs. The dated arrangements of David Axelrod for a 12-piece band (which includes keyboardist George Duke) weigh down *Brasswind* (Prestige 10080) a bit, but Ammons generally comes through, particularly on Wes Montgomery's "Cariba," Jo-

bim's "Once I Loved," and " 'Round Midnight." *Together Again for the Last Time* (Prestige 10100) was the last meeting on records between Ammons and Sonny Stitt. Fortunately it is an excellent encounter. Assisted by the Junior Mance Trio, the two tenors battle it out on three of Ammons's basic originals; Stitt is featured on "For All We Know," while Ammons is showcased on "The More I See You" and "I'll Close My Eyes." The final Gene Ammons session, *Goodbye* (Prestige 10093), is a septet outing with Nat Adderley, altoist Gary Bartz, Kenny Drew, Sam Jones, drummer Louis Hayes, and Ray Barretto on conga, in the freewheeling spirit of the Ammons jam sessions of the 1950s. Jug sounds quite happy on tunes such as "It Don't Mean a Thing" and "Jeannine," and quite fittingly, the final song he played at his last recording session was an emotional rendition of "Goodbye."

FILMS

Gene Ammons is featured prominently with Billy Eckstine's orchestra throughout *Rhythm on a Riff* (1946), a very musical film short that is included on the video *Things to Come* (Vintage Jazz Classics 2006).

ALLEN EAGER

b. Jan. 10, 1927, New York, NY

Of the many tenor saxophonists who are closely identified with the "cool school," Lester Young-influenced tenors who smoothed down the rough edges of Bebop (including Stan Getz, Zoot Sims, Al Cohn, Brew Moore, and Paul Quinichette), Allen Eager was the first one to make a strong impression. Because his main contributions to jazz were made during the second half of the 1940s rather than later on, he is covered in the Bebop book; the other tenors will be more fully discussed in a future book dealing with 1950s West Coast Cool Jazz.

It is ironic that out of the six tenors mentioned, Allen Eager is the only one still alive, for he retired from the music business quite early. Eager gained experience playing music professionally as a teenager during World War II, working in the big bands of Bobby Sherwood, Sonny Dunham, Shorty Sherock, Hal McIntyre, Woody Herman (1943–44), Tommy Dorsey, and Johnny Bothwell. Eager was a fixture on 52nd Street during 1945–47, and he recorded with Kai Winding and Coleman Hawkins. He was with Tadd Dameron's band during 1948, playing opposite Fats Navarro, but after that association he gradually became less active. Eager recorded with Gerry Mulligan (1951), Terry Gibbs, and Tony Fruscella, worked with Buddy Rich, and had his own group off and on during 1953–55. But after making an album with Mulligan in 1957, Eager (then only 30) dropped out of music altogether. Instead he worked as a race car driver, as a ski instructor, and at various odd jobs. In 1982 he returned to the jazz scene to record a so-so set for Uptown. But, other than occasional gigs during the next few years in Florida, little has been heard from Allen Eager in the music world since.

LPS TO SEARCH FOR

Allen Eager led three record dates for Savoy during 1946–47 that generally have been reissued on samplers. Other than a few scattered numbers from live dates during 1948 and 1953, his only other session as a leader was *Renaissance* (Uptown 27.09), an OK quartet date from 1982 with pianist Hod O'Brien, bassist Teddy Kotick, and drummer Jimmy Wormworth. Eager sounds a bit rusty and his tone was harder than earlier, but there are some good moments. Unfortunately he has since slipped back into complete obscurity.

TEDDY EDWARDS

b. Apr. 26, 1924, Jackson, MS

One of the big three of Bebop tenors in the mid- to late 1940s, Teddy Edwards was frequently featured in tenor battles in Los Angeles with Dexter Gordon and Wardell Gray. Due to his decision to live in Los Angeles throughout his career, he never achieved the recognition of Gordon and Gray, but he has always been on their high level and, at 76, is one of the last survivors of the classic Bebop era.

Edwards began working in public in 1936, when he was only 12, playing clarinet and alto with Doc Parmlee. He had other local jobs, played in Detroit in 1942, led his own band in the South, and toured with Ernie Fields's big band. After moving to Los Angeles in 1945, Edwards first worked as an altoist with Roy Milton. He switched to tenor when he joined Howard McGhee's influential Bebop band, and Edwards began to gain a reputation as one of L.A.'s top young players. He jammed often on Central Avenue, recorded "The Duel" with Dexter Gordon in 1947, and led his own groups.

Among Edwards's relatively few sideman jobs through the years were those with the early Lighthouse All-Stars, the Clifford Brown/Max Roach Quintet in 1954 (where he was the original tenor saxophonist, before Harold Land), Benny Carter in 1955, Gerald Wilson's Big Band, Terry Gibbs, and Benny Goodman in 1964. Edwards also recorded with Milt Jackson in the 1960s, Jimmy Smith the following decade, and on other occasional projects. Otherwise Edwards has headed quartets and occasionally larger groups, for which he provided the arrangements and compositions, since the late 1940s; his best-known song is "Sunset Eyes." East Coast jazz fans rediscover the veteran tenor now and then, but Teddy Edwards has long been very active and a major part of the Los Angeles jazz scene.

8 *Sunset Eyes / Aug. 16, 1959–Aug. 16, 1960 / Pacific Jazz 94848*

9 *Teddy's Ready / Aug. 17, 1960 / Original Jazz Classics 748*

6 *Back to Avalon / Dec. 7–13, 1960 / Contemporary 14074*

9 *Together Again / May 15 + 17, 1961 / Contemporary 424*

9 *Good Gravy! / Aug. 23–25, 1961 / Original Jazz Classics 661*

6 *Heart & Soul / Apr. 24, 1962 / Original Jazz Classics 177*

Teddy Edwards first recorded as a leader for the Rex label during 1947–48 (music later released on an Onyx LP). He recorded a few isolated titles in the 1950s and had his first album as a leader for Pacific Jazz (the out-of-print *It's About Time*) in 1959. The second record, *Sunset Eyes,* has fortunately been reissued, featuring Edwards with quartets that have either Amos Trice, Joe Castro, or Ronnie Ball on piano. Three previously unreleased performances augment the original program on the CD reissue, and among six Edwards originals is the earliest recording of "Sunset Eyes." Edwards lives up to the title of *Teddy's Ready* on what was his debut recording for the Contemporary label (reissued by OJC), teaming up with Castro, bassist Leroy Vinnegar, and drummer Billy Higgins for three standards, three originals, and Hampton Hawes's "The Sermon." He plays brilliantly throughout. The music on *Back to Avalon,* which features Edwards's 1960 octet, was not released for the first time until 1995, due to some slip-ups in the ensembles. Edwards plays fairly well with the group (which also includes altoist Jimmy Woods and baritonist Modesto Brisenio) and is the main soloist, although the music is not flawless. The tenor also wrote five of the nine songs (including "Steppin' Lightly" and "Good Gravy!") and contributed the colorful if some-times overly complex arrangements.

Together Again reunites Edwards with Howard McGhee, and the rhythm section (pianist Phineas Newborn, Ray Brown, and Ed Thigpen) is rather impressive, too! This Boppish outing (which has three standards and three originals) is quite strong, finding McGhee, in particular, in excellent shape. *Good Gravy!* features Edwards back in a quartet setting with either Newborn (on two songs) or Danny Horton on piano, Vinnegar, and drummer Milt Turner. Edwards alternates his newer songs with such standards as "On Green Dolphin Street," "Stairway to the Stars," and "Laura." *Heart and Soul* is a bit unusual, for pianist Gerald Wiggins plays organ exclusively, where his personality is not as strong as on his main ax. Edwards, Vinnegar, and drummer Turner swing away as usual and the music is not without interest, but it is not as essential as the other OJCs.

7   *Nothin' but the Truth! / Dec. 13, 1966 / Original Jazz Classics 813*

8   *It's All Right! / May 24 + 27, 1967 / Original Jazz Classics 944*

8   *Out of This World / Dec. 5, 1980 / Steeple Chase 1147*

7   *Good Gravy! / Dec. 26, 1981 / Timeless 139*

Nothin' but the Truth has Edwards joined by Walter Davis Jr., the obscure guitarist Phil Orlando, bassist Paul Chambers, Billy Higgins, and percussionist Montego Joe for six songs split between originals and vintage tunes (including "On the Street Where You Live" and "But Beautiful"). Unfortunately the set, at 32 minutes, is rather brief. *It's All Right,* from 1967, is of particular interest because Edwards shows in subtle ways that he was well aware of the avant-garde of the period, even though he essentially plays hard bop; some of the harmonies for the sextet are pretty advanced. Edwards is joined by trumpeter Jimmy Owens, trombonist Garnett Brown, pianist Cedar Walton, bassist Ben Tucker, and drummer Lenny McBrowne for what would be his last session as a leader for seven years.

Skipping ahead to 1980: Edwards's sound was basically unchanged from the 1950s, as he shows during the four standards and two originals (including "April Love") featured on *Out of This World,* a quartet date with Kenny Drew, bassist Jesper Lundgard, and drummer Billy Hart. *Good Gravy!,* from the following year, is a live outing in which the tenor stretches out on three standards (including a 14½ minute

version of "Lady Be Good") and his title cut with a Dutch rhythm section that includes pianist Rein De Graaff.

7   *Mississippi Lad / Mar. 13–14, 1991 / Antilles 314 511 411*

9   *Blue Saxophone / June 8–10, 1992 / Antilles 314 517 527*

8   *Horn to Horn / Dec. 27, 1994 / Muse 5540*

8   *Close Encounters / Nov. 6, 1996 / High Note 7002*

9   *Midnight Creeper / Mar. 7, 1997 / High Note 7011*

After another nine years off records (at least as a leader), Edwards finally had an opportunity to be heard again in 1991, heading a septet date that included a variety of L.A.-based musicians (trumpeter Nolan Smith, Jimmy Cleveland, pianist Art Hillery, Leroy Vinnegar, Billy Higgins, and percussionist Ray Armando). What is most unusual about *Mississippi Lad* is that singer Tom Waits guests on two numbers ("Little Man" and "I'm Not Your Fool Anymore"); the very raspy singer's participation helped get this CD a lot of publicity, although his own vocals are not too good. Edwards contributed all nine songs (including "The Blue Sombrero," "Three Base Hit" and "Symphony on Central"), wrote the lyrics for the two Waits features, and plays well throughout. The ambitious *Blue Saxophone* is a gem, a date in which Edwards is joined by five brass, five strings, a harp, a rhythm section, and (on three songs) the up-and-coming singer Lisa Nobumoto. Edwards wrote ten of the twelve songs, arranged all dozen pieces (all well worth hearing), and takes the opening "Prelude" as a solo piece.

Horn to Horn and *Close Encounters* are both excellent collaborations with fellow tenor Houston Person that are a throwback to the Sonny Stitt-Gene Ammons tenor battles or to Edwards's encounters in the 1940s with Dexter Gordon and Wardell Gray. Edwards and Person battle it out on eight numbers on *Horn to Horn,* each dedicated to a different tenorman (John Coltrane, Ben Webster, Lester Young, Stan Getz, Coleman Hawkins, Eddie "Lockjaw" Davis, Ammons, or Gordon). With the assistance of pianist Richard Wyands, bassist Peter Washington, and drummer Kenny Washington, the two tenors share a few warm ballads and engage in heated playing on such numbers as "Lester Leaps In," "Red Top," and even "The Girl from Ipanema." *Close Encounters* utilizes the rhythm section of pianist Stan Hope, bassist Ray Drummond, and Kenny Washington, with the two tenors on such songs as "Twisted," "Pennies from Heaven," and "The Breeze and I." Overall, the two matchups are of equal quality and more complementary than competitive, although some sparks fly.

1997's *Midnight Creeper,* which has Edwards joined by Wyands, bassist Buster Williams, drummer Chip White, and (on four of the eight numbers) trumpeter Virgil Jones, starts off with three originals by the tenor and concludes with five standards, including "Sunday" and a superb slower-than-usual 10½-minute version of "Lady Be Good." He might have been a major tenor saxophonist for over 50 years at that point, but there was no sign of slowing down or decline in the playing and ideas of Teddy Edwards.

LPS TO SEARCH FOR

The Inimitable Teddy Edwards (Xanadu 134) is a superior quartet date in which Edwards performs four standards, "Sunset Eyes," and his "One On One" with Duke Jordan, bassist Larry Ridley, and drummer Freddie Waits. "That Old Black Magic" really moves, and "Stella By Starlight" is given a memorable opening tenor cadenza.

FILMS

Teddy Edwards is featured with his 1962 band as half of the hour-long video *Jazz Scene USA—Cannonball Adderley/Teddy Edwards* (Shanachie) and is a featured guest with *The L.A. All Stars* (Rhapsody Films) in the early 70s.

DEXTER GORDON

b. Feb. 27, 1923, Los Angeles, CA, d. Apr. 25, 1990, Philadelphia, PA

Dexter Gordon, a major tenor saxophonist throughout his career, had a life full of ups and downs, including three major comebacks. Nicknamed "Long Tall Dexter" due to his height and distinguished nature, Gordon was among the first tenors to master the Bebop vocabulary. Gordon started playing clarinet when he was 13, switched to alto at 15, and settled on tenor two years later. After playing locally with the Harlem Collegians, he worked with the Lionel Hampton big band during 1940–43, sitting next to Illinois Jacquet (who, like Dexter, mixed together the Coleman Hawkins and Lester Young styles) for much of the time. Due to Jacquet's presence, Gordon did not receive any significant solo space, but the experience had an influence on him, as did the rise of Charlie Parker. He recorded in a quintet with Nat King Cole in 1943 and played briefly with Lee Young, Jesse Price, the Fletcher Henderson big band, and the Louis Armstrong Orchestra. After moving to New York in 1944, Gordon was with the Billy Eckstine big band, where he traded off with Gene Ammons on "Blowin' the Blues Away" and began to make a name for himself. He recorded "Blue 'n Boogie" with Dizzy Gillespie, led important record dates for Savoy, and then moved back to Los Angeles in the summer of 1946. For the next few years he was an important part of the Central Avenue scene, where he often participated in saxophone battles with Wardell Gray and Teddy Edwards. His recordings of "The Chase" with Gray (a jazz hit) and "The Duel" with Edwards documented some of the excitement of those days.

A major name in jazz throughout the Bebop era, Gordon suffered from some of the same drug problems as his contemporaries. The 1953–59 period was largely a waste (although he recorded two good albums in 1955), with some time spent in jail and recovering at Synanon. However, by 1960 Gordon was clean and he began recording a series of classic Hard Bop albums for Blue Note, acting in the West Coast production of *The Connection.* As he was regaining his popularity and beginning to show the influence of John Coltrane (staying modern without losing his musical personality), Gordon moved to Europe in 1962. He would spend 14 years overseas, playing at the peak of his powers (his recordings for Steeple Chase, particularly the many from 1974–76, rank with the finest of his career), returning to the United States on an occasional basis (recording domestically in 1965, 1969–70, and 1972). But by 1975, it seemed as if Dexter Gordon was largely forgotten in his native country.

With the creative decline of fusion and the rise of interest in acoustic jazz, Gordon took a chance and came home in 1976. To his surprise, and that of the jazz world, he was treated as a conquering hero. At clubs, there were literally lines around the block, of fans anxious to see the living legend play. Gordon was signed to Columbia, and his popularity remained high during a busy few years until ill health made him semiretired by the early 1980s. There would be one more comeback when he was picked to play the lead in the 1985 film *'Round Midnight.* Dexter Gordon was a little past his prime, but his acting was realistic and touching, and he topped off his career by receiving an Academy Award nomination for best actor. Quite a life!

9 *Settin' the Pace / Oct. 30, 1945–Dec. 22, 1947 / Savoy 17027*

10 *The Chase! / June 5, 1947–Dec. 4, 1947 / Stash 2513*

8 *Daddy Plays the Horn / Sept. 1955 / Bethlehem 20-30132*

7 *The Resurgence of Dexter Gordon / Oct. 13, 1960 / Original Jazz Classics 929*

Settin' the Pace is full of Dexter Gordon's classic Savoy recordings, which, other than four titles cut in 1943 with Nat King Cole and Harry "Sweets" Edison, are the first four sessions that the tenor ever led. This single CD will frustrate completists, for it adds five previously unissued alternate takes to Dexter's discography but (due to lack of space) leaves off three alternates that were issued on the double-LP *Long Tall Dexter* in 1976. That fault aside, the music is wonderful and shows how mature a soloist Gordon already was when he was 22. He is heard heading a quartet with Argonne Thornton, a quintet with Bud Powell and trumpeter Leonard Hawkins, and a group with Leo Parker and Tadd Dameron, and teaming up with Fats Navarro on the final session. Many of the titles of his originals take advantage of his name, including "Blow Mr. Dexter," "Dexter's Deck," "Dexter's Cuttin' Out," "Dexter's Minor Mad," "Long Tall Dexter," "Dexter Rides Again," "Dexter Digs In," "Dextrose," and "Dextivity"!

All of Dexter Gordon's recordings for the Dial label (including alternate takes) are on *The Chase!* The title cut was his famous "battle" with Wardell Gray and both "The Duel" and "Hornin' In" (the alternate for "The Duel") have Gordon trading off with Teddy Edwards. In addition, there is a quintet date with trombonist Melba Liston, a few quartet numbers, and a feature for Edwards on "Blues in Teddy's Flat." Classic straight-ahead Bop.

After the Savoy and Dial recordings of 1945–47, Gordon did not record as a leader until 1952, when he was captured on an obscure date with Wardell Gray and on two live jam session numbers with Gray; the latter was put out by Decca. Otherwise, the 1950s had just three recording dates for the scuffling tenor: a sideman appearance on drummer Stan Levey's album, an out-of-print Dootone session, and *Daddy Plays the Horn.* Joined by Kenny Drew, bassist Leroy Vinnegar, and drummer Lawrence Marable, Gordon is in fine form on the last, playing in a style very similar to how he would sound in the 1960s on such tunes as "Autumn in New York," "Confirmation," and "Darn That Dream."

In 1960 Dexter Gordon began his first comeback with a date for Jazzland later reissued in the OJC series. This fine sextet outing with trumpeter Martin Banks, trombonist Richard Boone, Dolo Coker, bassist Charles Green, and drummer Lawrence Marable served as a prelude to one of the golden periods of Gordon's career; it includes four obscure Coker originals and two by the tenor.

* *The Complete Blue Note Sixties Sessions / May 6, 1961–May 29, 1965 / Blue Note 34200*

9 *Doin' Alright / May 6, 1961 / Blue Note 84077*

8 *Dexter Calling. . . / May 9, 1961 / Blue Note 46544*

9 *Go / Aug. 27, 1962 / Blue Note 46094*

9 *A Swingin' Affair / Aug. 29, 1962 / Blue Note 84133*

8 *Our Man in Paris / May 23, 1963 / Blue Note 46394*

7 *One Flight Up / June 2, 1964 / Blue Note 84176*

7 *Clubhouse / May 27, 1965 / Blue Note 84445*

8 *Gettin' Around / May 28, 1965 / Blue Note 46681*

7 *The Squirrel / June 29, 1967 / Blue Note 57302*

Dexter Gordon recorded a remarkable number of sessions during 1961–76, particularly when you count the many radio broadcasts that have since been issued. During this era, Gordon made his first comeback, signed with Blue Note, moved to Europe, was largely forgotten in the United States, and in 1976 made a triumphant return to the States that could count as his second comeback (although he had been playing at the peak of his powers in Europe). His style, emphasizing a distinctive hard sound, a relaxed approach, lots of song quotes, and straightforward chordal improvising on his favorite standards, remained unchanged and consistent.

After signing with Blue Note, Gordon recorded nine albums for the label during 1961–65. *The Complete Blue Note Sixties Sessions* has all of the music from those records plus the "bonus cuts" that were added to the CD reissues, a previously unreleased saxophone battle with Sonny Stitt on "Lady Be Good," and four excerpts from an interview that took place in 1973. For those with tighter budgets, fortunately eight of the nine albums (all but *Landslide*) are also available individually, and all are easily recommended. *Doin' Alright* teams Gordon with trumpeter Freddie Hubbard, pianist Horace Parlan, bassist George Tucker, and drummer Al Harewood for six numbers plus an alternate take, including "You've Changed," "Society Red" (which would pop up again in the *Round Midnight* movie 15 years later), and "It's You or No One." *Dexter Calling* is an all-star quintet album with Kenny Drew, Paul Chambers, and Philly Joe Jones. Excellent playing, although none of these songs (mostly Gordon and Drew originals plus "Smile") became permanent parts of Dexter's repertoire.

Go and *A Swingin' Affair* were recorded within two days of each other and have Gordon joined by the identical trio of Sonny Clark, bassist Butch Warren, and Billy Higgins. *Go* is most notable for "I Guess I'll Hang My Tears Out to Dry" and "Three O'Clock in the Morning," while *A Swingin' Affair* has "You Stepped Out of a Dream," "Until the Real Thing Comes Along," and an emotional "Don't Explain" as the high points. Later in 1962, the tenor moved to Europe, where he recorded *Our Man in Paris,* a meeting with "The Three Bosses": Bud Powell, Pierre Michelot, and Kenny Clarke. Because Powell was not in the best mental shape, it was decided to simply jam through standards rather than attempt any new material. Fortunately Bud played quite well, so these renditions of tunes such as "Scrapple from the Apple," "Broadway," and "A Night in Tunisia" are quite successful and hard-swinging. *One Flight Up,* from 1964, has Gordon stretching out on four songs with trumpeter Donald Byrd, Kenny Drew, Niels Pedersen, and drummer Art Taylor, including a lengthy rendition of Byrd's "Tanya" and Dexter's ballad showcase on "Darn That Dream."

In 1965, Dexter Gordon briefly returned to the United States to record two further albums for Blue Note. *Clubhouse,* a quintet date with Freddie Hubbard, Barry Harris, bassist Bob Cranshaw, and Billy Higgins, was not released until the 1980s, despite its excellent quality. The repertoire is mostly originals, other than the high point, a moving version of "I'm a Fool to Want You." Gordon's last official Blue Note recording from this era, *Gettin' Around,* teams him with vibraphonist Bobby Hutcherson, Harris, Cranshaw, and Higgins on a particularly strong repertoire, including "Manha De Carnaval," "Heartaches," and "Shiny Stockings." In 1998, *The Squirrel,* a live set from 1967, was released for the first time. Gordon, Kenny Drew, bassist Bo Stief, and Art Taylor stretch out on long versions of Tadd Dameron's "The Squirrel," Gordon's "Cheesecake" (over 20 minutes), "You've Changed," and "Sonnymoon for Two." To the tenor's great credit, he never seems to run out of ideas.

7   *Cry Me a River / Nov. 28, 1962 + June 3, 1964 / Steeplechase 36004*

8   *Cheesecake / June 11, 1964 / Steeplechase 31008*

8   *King Neptune / June 24, 1964 / Steeplechase 36012*

8   *I Want More / July 9, 1964 / Steeplechase 36015*

8   *Love for Sale / July 23, 1964 / Steeplechase 36018*

8   *It's You or No One / Aug. 6, 1964 / Steeplechase 36022*

8   *Billie's Bounce / Aug. 20, 1964 / Steeplechase 36028*

6   *After Hours / 1964–1965 / Steeplechase 31224*

6   *After Midnight / 1964–1965 / Steeplechase 31226*

Cry Me a River has two unrelated live performances, only one of which involves Dexter Gordon. The great tenor is heard at the Montmartre in Copenhagen in 1962, shortly after he moved overseas. He performs "I'll Remember April" and "Cry Me a River" with backing by a trio led by the talented Danish pianist Atli Bjorn. The Boppish Bjorn is also showcased on two trio numbers without Gordon from 1964: "The Thrill Is Gone" and his "Suite."

The next six CDs all feature radio broadcasts of Gordon playing at the Montmartre (they aired every other Thursday) during a three-month period in 1964 with pianist Tete Montoliu, Niels Pedersen (then barely 18), and drummer Alex Riel. Dexter is in prime form throughout and was clearly pleased to be playing with such a high-quality rhythm section before an appreciative audience. Each of these sets definitely has its moments, and the well-recorded music is quite consistent and swinging. *Cheesecake,* in addition to the title cut, has fine versions of "Manha De Carnaval" and "Second Balcony Jump." *King Neptune* is highlighted by "Body and Soul" and the jump piece "I Want to Blow Now," which includes a spirited vocal by Gordon. *I Want More* repeats that number and is highlighted by "Come Rain or Come Shine" and "Where Are You?" *Love for Sale* has a remake of "I Guess I'll Hang My Tears Out to Dry" and a hard-cooking "Cherokee." *It's You or No One* features a lengthy version of the title cut and "Three O'Clock in the Morning" among its four pieces. The last in the series, *Billie's Bounce,* features a 17-minute version of the title cut (a Charlie Parker blues) plus "Satin Doll," Gordon's "Soul Sister," and "A Night in Tunisia."

From later in the year, *After Hours* and *After Midnight,* recorded live at Gamlingen, Stockholm, team Gordon with a Swedish rhythm section and trumpeter Rolf Ericson. However, the recording quality is not as good as it could be, although Gordon plays up to his usual level. *After Hours* consists of long versions of "I Remember You," "All the Things You Are," "Darn That Dream," and "Straight No Chaser," while *After Midnight* contains a 20-minute version of "Three O'Clock in the Morning" and a rendition of Miles Davis's "No Blues" that tops 26 minutes! The music is good but not essential.

- * *Live at the Montmartre Jazzhus* / July 20–21, 1967 / Black Lion 7606
- 9 *Both Sides of Midnight* / July 20, 1967 / Black Lion 760103
- 9 *Body and Soul* / July 20, 1967 / Black Lion 760118
- 9 *Take the 'A' Train* / July 21, 1967 / Black Lion 760133

During two days at the Montmartre in Copenhagen, Dexter Gordon recorded enough material to fill up three CDs. *Live at the Montmartre Jazzhus* is a box that simply holds the three CDs that resulted, all of which are also available individually. Gordon is joined throughout by Kenny Drew, Neils Pederson, and drummer Albert "Tootie" Heath. The playing is quite consistent, so any preference from among this trio of discs will probably be due to the repertoire. *Both Sides of Midnight* includes "Doxy" and "Sonnymoon for Two" among its four songs, *Body and Soul* is highlighted by "There Will Never Be Another You" and "Blues Walk," and *Take the 'A' Train* includes "But Not for Me," a second version of "Blues Walk," and a 15-minute version of "Love for Sale." All three discs find Gordon in inspired form.

- 6 *The Tower of Power* / Apr. 2 + 4, 1969 / Original Jazz Classics 299
- 6 *More Power!* / Apr. 2 + 4, 1969 / Original Jazz Classics 815
- 8 *At Montreux, with Junior Mance* / June 18, 1970 / Prestige 7861
- 8 *The Panther!* / July 7, 1970 / Original Jazz Classics 770
- 7 *The Jumpin' Blues* / Aug. 27, 1970 / Original Jazz Classics 899
- 7 *Ca'Purange* / June 28, 1972 / Original Jazz Classics 1005
- 8 *Generation* / July 22, 1972 / Original Jazz Classics 836

Though still living in Europe, Dexter returned to the United States in 1969, 1970, and 1972 to make records for the Prestige label, music that has been reissued in most cases as part of the Original Jazz Classics series. *The Tower of Power* and *More Power* sessions team Gordon with Barry Harris, bassist Buster Williams, Albert "Tootie" Heath, and guest tenor James Moody. The Gordon-Moody matchup (which occurs on two of the four numbers on the former set and on "Sticky Wicket" from *More Power*) really does not come off that memorably. However, Gordon's version of "Those

Were the Days" from *The Tower of Power* is haunting, and he introduces "Fried Bananas" (his line on "It Could Happen to You") on *More Power*. The Montreux meeting with pianist Junior Mance, bassist Martin Rivera, and drummer Oliver Jackson is full of spirit and swing as Gordon enthusiastically stretches out on "Fried Bananas," "Sophisticated Lady," "Rhythm-A-Ning," "Body and Soul," "Blue Monk," and his "The Panther." The last is the title track for a studio date with Tommy Flanagan, bassist Larry Ridley, and drummer Alan Dawson that has a heated version of "The Blues Walk" and near-classic renditions of "Body and Soul" and "The Christmas Song." *The Jumpin' Blues* finds Gordon joined by pianist Wynton Kelly (in one of his final dates), bassist Sam Jones, and drummer Roy Brooks on a fine six-song program that includes "Star Eyes," "Rhythm-A-Ning," and "If You Could See Me Now."

The 1972 United States trip resulted in two collaborations with major trumpeters. *Ca'Purange* shows that Gordon and trumpeter Thad Jones were a highly compatible team (along with Hank Jones, bassist Stanley Clarke, and drummer Louis Hayes). The four songs include "The First Time Ever I Saw Your Face" and two versions of Sonny Rollins's "Airegin." *Generation* is a touch hotter as Freddie Hubbard has a reunion with Gordon. With pianist Cedar Walton, bassist Buster Williams, and Billy Higgins, the horns perform the obscure "Scared to Be Alone," Dexter's "The Group," Thelonious Monk's "We See," and two versions of "Milestones."

- 7 *The Shadow of Your Smile* / Apr. 21, 1971 / Steeplechase 31206
- 7 *Revelation* / 1974 / Steeplechase 31373
- 9 *The Apartment* / May 24, 1974–Sept. 8, 1974 / Steeplechase 31025
- 7 *More Than You Know* / Feb. 21, 1975–Mar. 27, 1975 / Steeplechase 31030
- 9 *Stable Mable* / Mar. 10, 1975 / Steeplechase 31040
- 8 *Swiss Nights, Vol. 1* / Aug. 23, 1975 / Steeplechase 31050
- 8 *Swiss Nights, Vol. 2* / Aug. 23–24, 1975 / Steeplechase 31090
- 8 *Swiss Nights, Vol. 3* / Aug. 23–24, 1975 / Steeplechase 31110
- 9 *Something Different* / Sept. 13, 1975 / Steeplechase 31136

9 *Bouncin' with Dex* / Sept. 14, 1975 / Steeplechase 31060

5 *Strings & Things* / Feb. 1975–May 19, 1976 / Steeplechase 31145

9 *Lullaby for a Monster* / June 15, 1976 / Steeplechase 31156

9 *Biting the Apple* / Nov. 9, 1976 / Steeplechase 31080

Dexter Gordon recorded some of the finest albums of his life for the Danish Steeplechase label during 1974–76. *The Shadow of Your Smile* is a slightly earlier effort, four long versions of songs (including "Secret Love" and "Summertime") performed in Sweden with pianist Lars Sjosten, bassist Sture Nordin, and drummer Fredrik Noren. *Revelations* has Gordon joined again by Sjosten in a trio plus guest trumpeter Benny Bailey (who is exciting on his "At Ronnie's"). Dexter steals the show on "Polka Dots and Moonbeams" and "Days of Wine and Roses."

Dexter Gordon was consistently inspired during his Steeplechase recordings, at the top of his game and at the peak of his powers. Age 51 at the time of *The Apartment,* Gordon (assisted by Drew, Pedersen, and Heath) uplifts such songs as J.J. Johnson's "Wee-Dot," "Old Folks," and "Stablemates." *More Than You Know* has the tenor as the featured soloist, backed by a large orchestra conducted and arranged by Palle Mikkelborg. Gordon plays quite well (particularly on "Naima" and "More Than You Know"), but there is not much interplay between Dexter and the orchestra, and this date falls a little short of its potential. *Stable Mable* has Gordon joined by pianist Horace Parlan, Pedersen, and drummer Tony Inzalaco for such tunes as "Just Friends," Charlie Parker's "Red Cross," and Miles Davis's "So What"; Dexter is heard on soprano sax for the first time on "In a Sentimental Mood."

The three CDs in the *Swiss Nights* series feature Gordon performing with Drew, Pedersen, and drummer Alex Riel at the 1975 Zurich Jazz Festival. Few surprises occur, but Dexter is heard stretching out on some of his favorite songs during the two-day period. *Vol. 1* is highlighted by "Tenor Madness" and "You've Changed," *Vol. 2* has "Wave" and "Rhythm-A-Ning," and *Vol. 3* includes Gordon singing Billy Eckstine's old blues hit "Jelly Jelly" and trumpeter Joe Newman sitting in on "Days of Wine and Roses." *Something Different* has Gordon with a piano-less quartet that includes guitarist Philip Catherine, Niels Pedersen, and Billy Higgins; these versions of "Freddie Freeloader," "Invitation," and "Polka Dots and Moonbeams" are memorable.

Bouncin' with Dex reunites Gordon with Tete Montoliu, Pedersen, and Higgins, and has hard-charging renditions of "Billie's Bounce" and "Four" plus two relaxed runthroughs on "Easy Living." *Strings and Things* was a real rarity for a Dexter Gordon Steeplechase recording, a misfire! The arrangements for a large unidentified orchestra are intrusive, sometimes have dated electronic effects, and distract from rather than enhance Gordon's playing. And Dexter should have been talked out of singing Jobim's "This Happy Madness"! Only "More Than You Know" and Thad Jones's "A Good Time Was Had by All" (which has some solos from the Scandinavian sidemen) partly save this disc.

Returning to much more successful projects, *Lullaby for a Monster* really puts the focus on Dexter's sound, since he is accompanied by just Pedersen and Riel. His playing on such songs as "On Green Dolphin Street," "Good Bait," and Donald Byrd's "Tanya" is inspired. The last of the Steeplechase sessions, *Biting the Apple,* was recorded in New York just when Gordon was finally being rediscovered by American audiences. Gordon digs into four standards (including "I'll Remember April" and "Skylark") plus two of his originals with the assistance of Barry Harris, Sam Jones, and drummer Al Foster. A brilliant ending to an important period in his career.

9 *Homecoming: Live at the Village Vanguard* / Dec. 11–12, 1976 / Columbia 46824

8 *Sophisticated Giant* / June 21, 1977–Jan. 26, 1979 / Columbia/Legacy 65295

7 *Nights at the Keystone, Vol. 1* / May 13, 1978–Mar. 24, 1979 / Blue Note 94848

7 *Nights at the Keystone, Vol. 2* / May 16, 1978–Mar. 27, 1979 / Blue Note 94849

7 *Nights at the Keystone, Vol. 3* / Sept. 16, 1978–Mar. 24, 1979 / Blue Note 94850

9 *Live at Carnegie Hall* / Sept. 23, 1978 / Columbia/Legacy 65312

In late 1976, Dexter Gordon's triumphant return to the United States made headlines. The double-CD *Homecoming* gives listeners an excellent idea of what he sounded like at the time, as Gordon performs such numbers as "Little Red's Fantasy," "It's You or No One," "Fried Bananas," and "Body and Soul" with trumpeter Woody Shaw, pianist Ronnie Mathews, bassist Stafford James, and drummer Louis Hayes. Although his style was virtually unchanged from 15 years earlier, it was perfect timing for him to be rediscovered, and he sounds quite happy to be playing for such an enthusiastic crowd; Shaw is in top form, too. *Sophisticated Giant* builds on the success with six numbers (including "Red Top," "Fried Bananas," and "Laura") from a studio date in 1977 that has Gordon heading an all-star 11-piece group that includes Shaw, Benny Bailey, Slide Hampton, and Bobby Hutcherson in the personnel. This CD reissue adds two vocal numbers by Eddie Jefferson ("Diggin' In" and "It's Only a Paper Moon") from 1979 that also feature the frontline of Gordon, Shaw, and trombonist Curtis Fuller.

The three Blue Note CDs all put the spotlight on the Dexter Gordon Quartet (with George Cables, Rufus Reid, and drummer Eddie Gladden) during their three engagements at San Francisco's legendary club Keystone Korner. Considering all he had accomplished, it is hard to believe that Gordon was still only 55–56 at the time. Each CD is worth acquiring, even though no new revelations are heard. *Vol. 1* includes "It's You or No One" and "Easy Living," *Vol. 2* has "Tangerine" and "More Than You Know," and the final volume includes "You've Changed" and "Body and Soul."

Although not his final record, *Live at Carnegie Hall* serves as a fine close to Dexter Gordon's career, 33 years after his debut as a leader. Joined again by Cables, Reid, and Gladden, Gordon stretches out on "Secret Love," "The End of a Love Affair," and "More Than You Know." Those three numbers serve as warm-ups to a couple of explosive tenor battles ("Blues Up and Down" and "Cheesecake") that he has with Johnny Griffin that look back toward the earlier prime of his career and show that, in 1978, he was still a mighty saxophonist.

LPS TO SEARCH FOR

Completists may want to get the two-LP set *Long Tall Dexter,* (Savoy 2211) which has all of the tenor's work for the Savoy label: his four dates as a leader, one with an all-star group headed by baritonist Leo Parker and a jam session number ("After Hours Bebop") with Howard McGhee and Sonny Criss. The five new alternate takes put out on the CD *Settin' the Pace* are absent, but this album has the three alternates that the CD bypassed. The two-LP *The Hunt* (Savoy 2222) has four lengthy live jam session performances from a Central Avenue club. Though the recording quality is only decent, the playing by Gordon, Wardell Gray, Sonny Criss, Howard McGhee, trombonist Trummy Young, Hampton Hawes, Barney Kessel, and a pair of bassists and drummers

is frequently exciting and competitive. *Dexter Blows Hot and Cool* (Dootone 207), one of only two dates that he led during 1953–59, is a fine straight-ahead quintet outing with trumpeter Jimmy Robinson, pianist Carl Perkins, Leroy Vinnegar, and drummer Chuck Thompson in Los Angeles.

Landslide (Blue Note 1051), music from 1961–62 that was not originally released until the 1980 LP, has selections from three sessions, including the title cut (which has now been included as part of *Dexter Calling*), and quintet performances with Tommy Turrentine or Dave Burns on trumpet and Sir Charles Thompson or Sonny Clark on piano. Most of the selections would be recorded again for other projects; highlights include "Serenade In Blue" and "Second Balcony Jump." *Live at the Amsterdam Paradiso* (Affinity 27) is a two-LP set featuring Gordon in 1969 stretching out on seven songs (including "Fried Bananas," "Good Bait," and Thelonious Monk's "Rhythm-A-Ning") with a Dutch rhythm section made up of pianist Cees Slinger, bassist Jacques Schols, and drummer Han Bennink. Also from that year, *A Day in Copenhagen* has Gordon and Slide Hampton co-leading a sextet that includes trumpeter Dizzy Reece, Kenny Drew, Niels Pedersen, and Art Taylor. While Gordon is the main soloist, the arrangements and three of the six compositions were contributed by Hampton. *Blues á La Suisse* (Prestige 10079) consists of Gordon's appearance at the 1973 Montreux Jazz Festival with keyboardist Hampton Hawes, bassist Bob Cranshaw, and Kenny Clarke, highlighted by Jimmy Heath's "Gingerbread Boy" and "Secret Love." *Dexter Gordon-Sonny Grey* (Spotlite 10) is taken from a Paris concert in which Gordon and trumpeter Sonny Grew co-lead a quintet for four numbers, all originals by bandmembers (including "Fried Bananas" and "Dexter Leaps Out").

Lionel Hampton with Dexter Gordon (Who's Who 21011), from 1977, is a slightly odd date, because Gordon plays half of the music on soprano rather than tenor, and the music overall is swing rather than Bop-oriented. Gordon is assisted by vibraphonist Hampton, Hank Jones, and an expanded rhythm section. *Manhattan Symphonie* (Columbia 35608) is Dexter Gordon's last great studio album, a quartet outing with George Cables, Rufus Reid, and Eddie Gladden from 1978 that is highlighted by "Moment's Notice" and touching ballad versions of "As Time Goes By" and "Body and Soul"; the last shows the influence of John Coltrane on Dexter's playing, which is only right, since Gordon was the main early influence of 'Trane! *Gotham City* (Columbia

36853) has four songs (three standards plus Dexter's own "Gotham City"); it was recorded in 1980 with Cedar Walton, Percy Heath, Art Blakey, guitarist George Benson, and (for "The Blues Walk") trumpeter Woody Shaw. *Jive Fernando* (Chiaroscuro 2029) finds Gordon overcoming weak recording quality and a less-than-ideal rhythm section (keyboardist George Duke, bassist Ralph Garrett, and drummer Oliver Johnson) on a 1981 performance by still playing in near-prime form. *American Classic* (Elektra Musician 60126), from 1982, was Dexter Gordon's final official recording other than his work for the film *'Round Midnight* (which was released as two sampler albums) a few years later. The classic tenor is OK, if just a touch past his prime, on five numbers (best are "Besame Mucho" and "Skylark") with a sextet that includes guest Grover Washington, Jr., adding his soprano to a few songs.

FILMS

Dexter Gordon appears as part of Louis Armstrong's Orchestra in *Atlantic City* (1944) and *Pillow to Post* (1945) but does not get any solos. He has a small acting role in *Unchained* (1955) and can be seen in performances from 1979 on *The Dexter Gordon Quartet* (Rhapsody 9035) and on *Tenor Legends* (Shanachie 6308); he shares the last video with Coleman Hawkins. In addition, he is the star of *'Round Midnight* (1985) and has a nonmusical acting role in the Robin Williams drama *Awakenings*.

WARDELL GRAY

b. Feb. 13, 1921, Oklahoma City, OK, d. May 25, 1955, Las Vegas, NV

Wardell Gray was a perfect complement to Dexter Gordon in tenor sax battles during the late 1940s. While Gordon had a hard tone, Gray's was softer, his style influenced by both Charlie Parker and Lester Young. Gray appealed to a particularly wide audience, equally admired by Benny Goodman and Annie Ross, who wrote famous vocalese lyrics to his solos on "Twisted," "Farmer's Market," and "Jackie."

Gray grew up in Detroit, played locally, and then was with Earl Hines's big band during 1943–45. While the 1943 edition (which included Dizzy Gillespie and Charlie Parker on tenor) did not record, the 1945 band did and Gray was well featured. After moving to Los Angeles later that year, Gray was an important force in the L.A. Bebop scene, playing nightly in the Central Avenue area and, by 1946, engaging in

jam sessions that often included Dexter Gordon; their recording of "The Chase" was a hit. Gray worked with Benny Carter and Billy Eckstine, recorded with Charlie Parker (including "Relaxin' at Camarillo") and Dodo Marmarosa, and led sessions of his own. He was part of the Benny Goodman Septet (the 1948 group that also included Stan Hasselgard), Goodman's bebop-oriented big band, Tadd Dameron's group, and the Count Basie Septet (1950–51), being featured with the Basie big band in 1951 on a session that included a classic feature on "Little Pony."

Wardell Gray participated on some of Norman Granz's studio jam sessions (including "Apple Jam") and recorded with Dexter Gordon (1952) and Louie Bellson (1952–53). His premature death was ironic, because he was considered at one time to be a role model to younger musicians due to his clean lifestyle. But by the mid-1950s, he had become involved with heroin. Wardell Gray died of a drug overdose when he was 34, found under mysterious circumstances in the desert near Las Vegas—another Bebop tragedy.

6 *One for Prez / Nov. 23, 1946 / Black Lion 60106*

8 *Wardell Gray Memorial, Vol. 1 / Nov. 11, 1949 + Feb. 20, 1953 / Original Jazz Classics 050*

9 *Wardell Gray Memorial, Vol. 2 / Aug. 27, 1950–Jan. 21, 1952 / Original Jazz Classics 051*

7 *Live in Hollywood / Sept. 9, 1952 / Fresh Sound 157*

Wardell Gray's first session as a leader resulted in five titles. *One for Prez* (which matches Gray with Dodo Marmarosa, Red Callender, and either Doc West or Chuck Thompson on drums) has those performances plus no less than 11 alternate takes! The music is excellent, but the repetition in this very complete set makes the CD of interest mostly to collectors. The two *Wardell Gray Memorial* CDs also contain many alternates. *Vol. 1* has a quartet date with Al Haig, Tommy Potter, and Roy Haynes from 1949 that is most notable for including "Twisted" (four versions!). Also on the CD is a set that Gray recorded in 1953 with Frank Morgan, Sonny Clark, vibraphonist Teddy Charles, bassist Dick Nivison, and drummer Lawrence Marable. *Vol. 2* has all of the music from three dates. Gray jams lengthy versions of "Scrapple from the Apple" and "Move" with an all-star group that includes Clark Terry, Sonny Criss, and (on "Move") Dexter Gordon. He is also showcased on a quartet date and on a sextet session that includes trumpeter Art Farmer and is highlighted by famous versions of "Jackie" and "Farmer's Market."

Live in Hollywood includes seven ten-minute versions of eight Bebop standards performed in a club by Gray, Farmer, Hampton Hawes, bassist Joe Mondragon, and Shelly Manne. The recording quality is decent and the playing is swinging and competitive. Every recording made by Wardell Gray during his short life is valuable.

LPS TO SEARCH FOR

Wardell Gray and the Big Bands (Official 3029) puts the spotlight on the great tenor as a featured sideman with the Earl Hines big band, Billy Eckstine, Benny Goodman, Count Basie, and Louie Bellson; some of these selections remain quite rare. *Wardell Gray/Stan Hasselgard* (Spotlite 134) has live performances of Gray with Howard McGhee, Sonny Criss, and Dodo Marmarosa in a sextet, with the 1948 Count Basie Orchestra, and on two jam sessions with Stan Hasselgard.

FILMS

Wardell Gray appears with the Count Basie Septet on some *Snader Telescriptions* from 1950 that were made for television.

JIMMY HEATH

b. Oct. 25, 1926, Philadelphia, PA

Throughout much of his career, Jimmy Heath has been valuable not just on tenor saxophone but also on soprano and flute (he took up the latter two instruments in the 1960s) and as an arranger-composer. He actually started out on alto, but the Charlie Parker influence was so strong that Heath wisely switched instruments.

The middle brother of the three Heath Brothers (Percy is three years older and drummer Albert "Tootie" Heath is nine years his junior), the son of a clarinetist, and the father of percussionist Mtume, Jimmy Heath's long career covers several different eras. He began playing alto when he was 14 and worked with the Calvin Todd-Mel Melvin group in 1944, Nat Towles (1945–46), and with his own band in Omaha (1946–47). Heath spent the classic Bebop years playing with Howard McGhee (1947–48) and the Dizzy Gillespie big band and sextet (1949–50) as an altoist. After he was dubbed "Little Bird," Heath switched to tenor (where he has long been distinctive) and has rarely played alto since.

Heath wrote "C.T.A." and recorded with Miles Davis, but spent much of the 1950s scuffling, due to drug problems. He

wrote music for Chet Baker and Art Blakey during 1956–57 and then in 1959 returned to full-time playing, recording a particularly strong series for the Riverside label. Heath was briefly with Miles Davis's band, worked with Kenny Dorham and Gil Evans, and in the 1960s teamed up with Art Farmer (1965–67) and now and then with Milt Jackson. Heath also worked as a freelance arranger (his "Gingerbread Boy" was recorded by Miles Davis) and as an educator. During 1975–83 he was part of the Heath Brothers (a band that recorded seven albums) with his two siblings. In the years since, Jimmy Heath has appeared in countless straight-ahead-oriented settings on his various reeds, continued his writing, and played with the reunited Heath Brothers on a part-time basis since 1997.

7 *The Thumper / Nov. 27, 1959–Dec. 7, 1959 / Original Jazz Classics 1828*

8 *Really Big / June 24 + 28, 1960 / Original Jazz Classics 1799*

8 *The Quota / Apr. 14 + 20, 1961 / Original Jazz Classics 1871*

8 *Triple Threat / Jan. 4 + 17, 1962 / Original Jazz Classics 1909*

8 *Swamp Seed / Mar. 11, 1963 + May 28, 1963 / Original Jazz Classics 1904*

9 *On the Trail / 1964 / Original Jazz Classics 1854*

Jimmy Heath's first opportunities to lead his own record dates resulted in six superior projects for the Riverside label during 1959–64, on all of which he exclusively played tenor; each set has been reissued in the Original Jazz Classics series. Although the music often falls into the Hard Bop (rather than Bebop) genre, the fact that Heath was a Bebop pioneer gives these sessions great relevance even within the limited confines of Bop. His later recordings and work with the Heath Brothers will be covered in the Hard Bop book in this series.

The Thumper finds Heath playing in a sextet that includes cornetist Nat Adderley, trombonist Curtis Fuller, pianist Wynton Kelly, bassist Paul Chambers, and younger brother Tootie Heath on drums. The leader contributed five originals to the nine-song set (best known is "For Minors Only") and has two ballads as his solid features with the rhythm section. *Really Big*, a tentette set, gives Heath an opportunity not only to solo but to arrange for the ensemble, which includes both of his brothers, Clark Terry, altoist Cannonball Adderley, and Nat Adderley. "Big P" and "A Picture of

Heath" are his most significant originals for the date, and his versions of "Dat Dere" and "On Green Dolphin Street" make those songs sound fresh. *The Quota,* even with four Heath originals among the seven tunes plus his arrangements for each song, is essentially a blowing date. Heath is matched with his brothers, pianist Cedar Walton, trumpeter Freddie Hubbard, and Julius Watkins on French horn for music that is at various times fiery or exquisite. *Triple Threat,* from the following year, uses the same personnel for four of Heath's tunes (including "Gemini") and the ballad "Goodbye." In addition, Heath is showcased on "Make Someone Happy" and "The More I See You," playing quite well throughout.

Swamp Seed has Heath, a rhythm section, trumpeter Donald Byrd joined by two French horns (including Watkins), and the tuba of Don Butterfield; Heath's charts make the octet sound like a big band. Although none of the three originals that Heath brought to this project became standards, the music is quite colorful, including transformations of Thelonious Monk's "Nutty" and "Just in Time." Heath's tenor is showcased on "More Than You Know." His final Riverside set, *On the Trail,* is one of the best showcases ever for Heath's tenor playing. Joined by just a rhythm section (Wynton Kelly, Kenny Burrell, Paul Chambers, and Albert "Tootie" Heath), Heath introduces his "Gingerbread Boy" and "Project S," and stretches out on "All the Things You Are" and "On the Trail." All of Jimmy Heath's Riverside sets are easily recommended.

LPS TO SEARCH FOR

Perhaps the most Boppish of all of Jimmy Heath's post-Riverside dates as a leader is *Picture of Heath* (Xanadu 118), from 1975. Inspired by Barry Harris, Sam Jones, and Billy Higgins, Heath plays five of his best originals (including "For Minors Only" and "C.T.A.") and "Body and Soul," doubling on tenor and soprano.

DON LANPHERE

b. June 26, 1928, Wenatchee, WA

Don Lanphere made a strong impression for a short time during the classic Bebop era, but his career was really reborn in the 1980s. Lanphere played locally in Washington from the time he was 12. After studying at Northwestern University, Lanphere worked with Johnny Bothwell's band. In 1947, at the age of 19, he moved to New York and proved to be quite adept at playing Bebop, leading two record sessions in 1949 (including one with Fats Navarro) and playing with Woody Herman's Second Herd and Artie Shaw's Bebop Orchestra. Lanphere also worked with the big bands of Jerry Wald, Claude Thornhill, Charlie Barnet, and Billy May.

Unfortunately drug problems hurt his career, and after 1951 Don Lanphere stayed mostly in Washington, where he helped run the family music store. He did play well while with Woody Herman's orchestra during 1959–61, but otherwise little was heard from him on the national jazz scene until he began a longtime association with the Hep label in 1982. Since that time, Don Lanphere (who had become sober and a born-again Christian) has played at the peak of his powers, not only on tenor but on soprano, recorded regularly, and been active as both an adventurous post-Bop musician and as an important educator.

7	*Don Loves Midge / Oct. 21-24, 1984 / Hep 2027*
8	*Stop / Aug. 22, 1983–Jan. 4, 1986 / Hep 2034*
8	*Don Lanphere/Larry Coryell / Apr. 11-12, 1990 / Hep 2048*
9	*Lopin' / Dec. 1992 / Hep 2058*
8	*Get Happy / Apr. 25, 1996 / Origin 82363*
7	*Don Still Loves Midge / June 10-11, 1997 / Hep 2072*

Other than two sessions that he led in 1949, Don Lanphere made his recording debut as a leader in 1982, recording nine albums for the Hep label during the next decade. *Don Loves Midge,* dedicated to his wife of many decades, is a relaxed outing, with Lanphere playing standards at medium to slow tempos in a very melodic fashion. "And the Angels Sing" starts things off with a "heavenly" soprano-harp duet, and along the way there are some quintet numbers with trumpeter Jon Pugh and a few performances played in more intimate settings. Frequently exquisite music.

Stop is a particularly strong outing, with Lanphere heard in a variety of instrumentations ranging from a duet with bassist Chuck Deardorf on "Laura" to a couple of different quartet/quintets. His sidemen include trumpeter Pugh and either Marc Seals or Don Friedman on piano. Four Lanphere originals (including a remake of "Stop," which he had originally recorded in 1949 with Fats Navarro) alternate with a quartet of standards, all creatively played. Lanphere's collaboration with guitarist Larry Coryell works surprisingly well, since both musicians are more flexible than one might think. Lanphere (heard on tenor, soprano, and alto) and Coryell play with top Seattle-based musicians in settings ranging from a quartet to an octet. The guitarist is showcased with the synthesizer of Marc Seales on "Spring Can Really Hang You Up the Most," Horace Silver's "Peace" is taken as a soprano-guitar duet, and the co-leaders plus Seales contributed six of the 11 selections. *Lopin'* is a particularly rewarding set that finds Lanphere (on tenor and soprano) heading a sextet that also includes the great Bud Shank on alto, and the underrated but talented baritonist Denney Goodhew. This time around Lanphere performed six group originals (including four by Seales) and three standards; everyone sounds inspired.

Get Happy has more of a jam session feel to it, with Lanphere (on tenor, alto, and soprano) matching wits and ideas with the hard-driving Pete Christlieb (who doubles on alto). Originals and obscurities dominate the program, although "Old Folks," Silver's "Peace," and the romping title cut are among the highlights. As with the original, *Don Loves Midge, Don Still Loves Midge* features an assortment of standards played with taste and sensitivity by Lanphere, including "Deep in a Dream," "Just the Way You Are," "My Buddy," and "Early Autumn" plus two of the leader's originals. Although not strictly associated these days with the classic Bebop era, Don Lanphere has proven to be one of that period's most enduring survivors.

JAMES MOODY

b. Mar. 26, 1925, Savannah, GA

One of the most productive saxophonists to emerge from the Bebop era, James Moody has been a major soloist for over a half-century, on tenor, flute, and occasionally alto. Moody was in the Air Force during 1943–46 and then joined Dizzy Gillespie's big band; he would be associated with Dizzy on and off for the next 46 years, playing mostly tenor with Gillespie. In 1948, Moody entered a three-year period of living and working in Europe. His recording of "I'm in the Mood for Love" on alto in 1949 was a surprise hit. It was turned into the classic vocalese piece "Moody's Mood for Love" in 1952, when it became a best-seller for King Pleasure and a jazz standard. Moody performed it himself in later years, taking a hilarious vocal that included yodeling while feeling free to improvise his original ideas; every one else's version of this song is a note-for-note recreation.

Moody led a spirited septet for five years in the 1950s (one that often included singer Eddie Jefferson) and began doubling on flute; during 1963–68 he was a member of a particu-larly strong version of the Dizzy Gillespie Quintet. Moody's only period off the jazz scene was during 1975–79, when he worked in Las Vegas show bands. However, he was back in jazz full-time by the 1980s, sometimes playing with Gillespie but mostly working as a leader. In the 1990s Moody continued leading his own groups, and he also recorded with Lionel Hampton's Golden Men of Jazz. James Moody (who, like Dizzy Gillespie, enjoys putting on a show that includes humor and showmanship) has had a distinctive tone since the late 1940s. Although remaining essentially a Bop player throughout his career, his solos have never been predictable and are always quite modern.

9 *Greatest Hits! / Oct. 6, 1949–Jan. 24, 1951 / Prestige 24228*

8 *James Moody/Frank Foster in Paris / July 13, 1951– July 13, 1954 / Vogue 68208*

8 *Moody's Mood for Blues / Jan. 8, 1954–Jan. 28, 1955 / Original Jazz Classics 1837*

9 *Hi Fi Party / Aug. 23–24, 1955 / Original Jazz Classics 1780*

8 *Wail, Moody, Wail / Dec. 12, 1955 / Original Jazz Classics 1791*

8 *Return from Overbrook / Nov. 1956–Sept. 16, 1958 / GRP/Chess 810*

8 *At the Jazz Workshop / 1961 / GRP/Chess 815*

James Moody's first dates as a leader were for Blue Note in 1948. While in Europe, he recorded quite a bit during 1949–51, including two albums of material that were issued by Prestige as *James Moody's Greatest Hits* and *More of James Moody's Greatest Hits;* all 24 selections have been reissued on the single-CD *Greatest Hits!*. The title is somewhat ironic since, other than the instrumental version of "I'm In the Mood for Love" (which became the basis for "Moody's Mood for Love"), none of these selections were exactly best-sellers. Recorded in Stockholm, the performances match Moody (on tenor and alto) with some of Sweden's best musicians of the period, including baritonist Lars Gullin and altoist Arne Domnerus on a variety of three-minute classics (mostly standards). Two other Moody sessions in Europe are included on the Vogue CD. He jams eight selections (mostly ballads) in France with a quintet that includes trumpeter Roger Guerin and pianist Raymond Fol, and is showcased on six lyrical selections with string and woodwind sections. In addition, this CD features tenor saxophonist Frank Foster in 1954 with the Henri Renaud Trio on six generally hard-driving numbers split between standards and obscurities.

Returning to the United States in 1951, Moody formed a four-horn septet that worked steadily for several years, recording regularly for Prestige; all of the material has been reissued on three CDs in the Original Jazz Classics series. With trumpeter Dave Burns, trombonist William Shepherd, baritonist Pee Wee Moore, pianist Jimmy Boyd, bassist John Lathan, and drummer Clarence Johnson (Sadik Hakim and drummer Joe Harris are on some of the earliest tracks), this was one of the better Bop-oriented bands of the mid-1950s, one that had fun, included hot riffing, and sometimes hinted at R&B. *Moody's Mood for Blues* has two guest appearances by Eddie Jefferson (who performs "Workshop" and "I Got the Blues"), and Iona Wade sings "That Man o' Mine" á la Dinah Washington. Otherwise the 16 selections are all instrumentals. Of the three CDs, *Hi Fi Party* gets the edge due to the length of some of the selections (which includes an 11 1/2-minute "Jammin' with James") and Eddie Jefferson's one appearance, singing alternate lyrics to Charlie Parker's famous solo on "Lady Be Good," which here is renamed "Disappointed." *Wail, Moody, Wail* is strictly instrumental, including a nearly 14-minute version of the title cut, "Moody's Blue Again," and "A Sinner Kissed an Angel."

Moody recorded regularly for the Argo label during 1956–63, but only a small portion of the music has thus far been reissued. *Return from Overbrook* is a particularly good buy, for it has the complete contents of two former LPs: *Flute 'n the Blues* and *Last Train from Overbrook*. *Last Train* has Moody (on tenor, alto, and flute) joined by a 14-piece band, including ten horns, for such numbers as "Don't Worry About Me," "Tico-Tico," and "All the Things You Are," while *Flute 'n the Blues* features Moody's septet in 1956 playing "Parker's Mood," "It Could Happen to You," and "Body and Soul" among others; Eddie Jefferson helps out on "Birdland Story" and "I Cover the Waterfront" (the latter based on a Lester Young solo). *At the Jazz Workshop* adds four numbers to the original LP and has Moody featured with a completely different septet (one that includes Howard McGhee), with three vocals by Jefferson (including "Moody's Mood for Love") and such instrumentals as "It Might As Well Be Spring," "Bloozey," and "The Jazz Twist."

6   *The Blues and Other Colors / Aug. 14, 1968–Feb. 11, 1969 / Original Jazz Classics 954*

7   *Don't Look Away Now / Feb. 14, 1969 / Original Jazz Classics 925*

8   *Feelin' It Together / Jan. 15, 1973 / Muse 5020*

The Blues and Other Colors is a rather unusual James Moody set, for he does not play tenor or alto at all, sticking to soprano (on the first four selections) and flute. The eight numbers (recorded with two very different nonets) have inventive arrangements by Tom McIntosh, with some tunes utilizing three strings and the voice of Linda November. However, Moody was never a great soprano player, so it is a pity that he did not utilize alto or tenor a bit instead, although overall this is a successful date. His final Prestige set, *Don't Look Away Now,* is more conventional, being a quartet outing with Barry Harris, electric bassist Bob Cranshaw, and drummer Alan Dawson that includes some standards and one colorful vocal by Eddie Jefferson ("Hey Herb! Where's Alpert?").

Moody plays tenor, alto, and flute on *Feelin' It Together,* a set that finds Kenny Barron showing a strong personality not only on piano but on electric piano and even electric harpsichord! With the assistance of bassist Larry Ridley and drummer Freddie Waits, Moody stretches out on three standards (including "Anthropology" and "Autumn Leaves"), the unusual "Kriss Kross," and some adventurous ballads.

8   *Something Special / July 1–2, 1986 / Novus 3004*

9   *Moving Forward / Sept. 10, 1987–Nov. 18, 1987 / Novus 3026*

8   *Sweet and Lovely / Mar. 11–13, 1989 / Novus 3063*

8   *Honey / Oct. 1–3, 1990 / Novus 3111*

7   *Moody's Party / Mar. 23–26, 1995 / Telarc 83382*

5   *Moody Plays Mancini / Feb. 4–5, 1997 / Warner Bros. 46626*

After his Las Vegas years, Moody had reunions with Dizzy Gillespie but mostly led his own quartet. He was largely off records in the 1980s until signing with Novus, which resulted in four CDs. *Something Special* features Moody (with pianist Kirk Lightsey, bassist Todd Coolman, and drummer Idris Muhammad) playing four of producer Tom McIntosh's originals plus the warm ballad "More Than You Know" and a remake of "Moody's Mood for Love." Despite its title, *Moving Forward* consists mostly of veteran songs (other than Moody's "What Do You Do," on which he takes a good-natured vocal). Joined by Kenny Barron (whose name is misspelled Darron!), bassist Coolman, drummer

Akira Tana, and (on three of the six numbers) Onaje Allan Gumbs on synthesizer, Moody (heard on tenor, alto, and flute) is in top form. He really digs into "Autumn Leaves," "Giant Steps," and a nearly 11-minute version of "The Night Has a Thousand Eyes," certainly not sounding like he was 62! *Sweet and Lovely* (with Coolman, Tana, and pianist Marc Cohen) is nearly on the same level, finding Moody in often-exuberant form on four standards, and originals by Cohen and Dizzy Gillespie. Dizzy guests on his "Con Alma," while "Get the Booty" has Moody joining Gillespie on the humorous vocal.

Honey features Moody at 65 adding soprano to his tenor and alto, alternating standards (including "It Might As Well Be Spring," and a beautiful rendition of "When You Wish Upon a Star"), and originals by Cohen and the saxophonist's new wife, Linda Moody, with the assistance of Barron, Coolman, and Tana. *Moody's Party,* a live-at-the-Blue-Note CD that celebrates Moody's 70th birthday, has guest appearances by tenor saxophonist Chris Potter (who holds his own with the birthday boy on "Bebop"), Grover Washington Jr. (playing soprano on "It Might As Well Be Spring"), and trumpeter Arturo Sandoval (battling Moody on a rather ragged "Groovin' High"). Moody takes the vocal on "Benny's from Heaven," is backed by pianist Mulgrew Miller, bassist Coolman, and drummer Terri Lyne Carrington, and is heard in prime form on "The Eternal Triangle" and a lengthy "Polka Dots and Moonbeams."

The well-meaning *Moody Plays Mancini* is a bit of a misfire. On this tribute to Henry Mancini, Moody makes the mistake of singing two songs (the repetitive "Don't You Forget It" and a not-so-exciting rendition of "Moon River") in his limited voice, and playing soprano (which is mostly out of tune) on a couple of numbers. The other selections (with keyboardist Gil Goldstein, Coolman, and Carrington) are better, but there are many stronger James Moody recordings currently available.

LPS TO SEARCH FOR

The Moody Story (Emarcy 36031), from 1951–52, features the saxophonist (heard on tenor and alto) right after he returned from Europe and before he formed his septet. These are mostly titles with six- to seven-piece groups (including "Until the Real Things Comes Along," "Margie," "Wiggle Wag," and "Moody's Home"). "The James Moody Story" is sung by Babs Gonzales and Moody, telling the saxophonist's life history up to 1952. *Moody and the Brass Figures* (Mile-stone 9005) features the saxophonist (sticking to tenor except for a workout on flute during "Cherokee") with a quartet including Kenny Barron on four numbers and with five added brass arranged by Tom McIntosh on five other cuts. Charlie Parker's "Au Privave," Monk's "Ruby, My Dear," and "Smack-a-Mac" are among the highlights of this 1967 album. *Never Again* (Muse 5001) is a particularly strong quartet outing from 1972 (with organist Mickey Tucker, electric bassist Roland Wilson, and drummer Eddie Gladden) that showcases Moody's tenor on such numbers as "Secret Love," "St. Thomas," and "Freedom Jazz Dance."

FILMS

James Moody is featured with Dizzy Gillespie's orchestra in *Jivin' in Bebop* (1947), which is available on the video *Things to Come* (Vintage Jazz Classics 2006).

FLIP PHILLIPS

b. Mar. 26, 1915, Brooklyn, NY

Flip Phillips is a swing player influenced by Ben Webster, but he reached his greatest fame during the Bebop era due to his solos with Woody Herman's First Herd and Jazz at the Philharmonic. Born Joseph Filipelli, the future Flip Phillips began playing the clarinet when he was 12. He played music during much of 1934–39 at Schneider's Lobster House in Brooklyn. After working on clarinet with Frankie Newton (mostly at Kelly's Stable) during 1940–41, Flip switched to the tenor sax. He worked with Larry Bennett, Benny Goodman, Wingy Manone, and Red Norvo before hitting it big with Woody Herman (1944–46). A booting tenor player with a warm sound, Phillips was (with Bill Harris) the most popular star of Herman's most popular band. After the orchestra broke up, Phillips became a regular with Jazz at the Philharmonic, playing alongside Lester Young, Charlie Parker, Coleman Hawkins, and Ben Webster plus many trumpet players. Flip's solo on "Perdido" made him famous.

Flip Phillips worked on and off as a leader in the 1950s, appearing as a member of the Gene Krupa Trio in 1952 and sometimes teaming up with Bill Harris. Phillips worked with Benny Goodman in 1959 and then moved to Florida, where he played locally during the 1960s, adding the bass clarinet as a double. Unlike Bill Harris, who went into semi-retirement at the same time as Phillips, the tenor saxophonist survived to become a full-time player again in the 1970s. Flip Phillips had several reunions with Woody Herman, played at jazz festivals and parties, began recording again, and has remained a strong player up to the present time, retaining the same style that excited JATP audiences in the late 1940s.

9   *A Melody from the Sky / Sept. 1944–Nov. 1945 / Sony 39419*

*   *The Complete Verve/Clef Charlie Ventura & Flip Phillips Studio Sessions / Sept. 1947–May 1957 / Mosaic 6-182*

A Melody from the Sky has four sessions led by Flip Phillips during his period with Woody Herman. Phillips mostly uses other Herman sidemen (such as Bill Harris and Ralph Burns) in a variety of settings. He is mellow on the ballads and romping on the more torrid numbers, showing why he was one of the most popular saxophonists of the era; this version of "Sweet and Lovely" was well known. On the limited-edition Mosaic box set, Phillips is featured on four of the six CDs (the other two showcase Charlie Ventura's sessions of 1951–54), and there is a remarkable amount of rewarding music to be heard. All of Phillips's studio sides for the Norman Granz labels during 1947–57 are here, including performances with groups ranging from a trio to a nonet. Among Flip's many sidemen are Howard McGhee, Harry Edison, Charlie Shavers, Kai Winding, Bill Harris, Sonny Criss, Charlie Kennedy, Hank Jones, Lou Levy, Oscar Peterson, Ray Brown, Jo Jones, Buddy Rich, and J.C. Heard, plus many others. In addition to his dates as a leader, Phillips is heard as a sideman with Buddy Rich, guitarist Nick Esposito, and trombonist Tommy Turk. An essential acquisition, but this box (which came out in 1999) will certainly go out of print fast.

8   *The Claw / Oct. 20, 1986 / Chiaroscuro 314*

8   *A Sound Investment / Mar. 1987 / Concord Jazz 4334*

9   *A Real Swinger / May 1988–June 1988 / Concord Jazz 4358*

6   *Try a Little Tenderness / June 30, 1992–July 1, 1992 / Chiaroscuro 321*

8   *Live at the 1993 Floating Jazz Festival / Nov. 1–3, 1993 / Chiaroscuro 327*

9   *Swing Is the Thing / Oct. 12–13, 1999 / Verve 314 543 477*

Since returning to performing jazz full-time in the 1970s, Flip Phillips has been remarkably consistent and still plays in the timeless style that he had developed by the mid-1940s.

The Claw, performed live at the 1986 Floating Jazz Festival, is a jam session in which Flip interacts with three major tenors (Buddy Tate, Al Cohn, and Scott Hamilton) plus Clark Terry on three of the five numbers, all of which are at least ten minutes long. Although it concludes with a disappointingly dull nine-minute "Jazzspeak" during which Phillips mostly rambles on about the music, the performances are full of explosive moments and easily recommended. *A Sound Investment* teams Phillips with Scott Hamilton and pianist John Bunch in a swinging sextet; the two tenors clearly inspire each other and consistently swing hard.

A Real Swinger is one of Phillips's finest recordings. Backed by a five-piece rhythm section that has both Howard Alden and Wayne Wright on guitars, and Dick Hyman on piano, Flip digs into ten numbers. Highlights include Oscar Pettiford's "Tricotism," "Cotton Tail," "I Got a Right to Sing the Blues" (which features Phillips on his atmospheric bass clarinet), and "I Want to Be Happy." *Try a Little Tenderness* was a nice idea, with Flip (switching between tenor and bass clarinet) backed by a string section, but the lack of mood variation makes it a rather sleepy affair; too many ballads and too little adventure. Better to pick up Flip Phillips's recording from the 1993 Floating Jazz Festival. Phillips is joined by pianist Derek Smith, guitarist Bucky Pizzarelli, Milt Hinton, and drummer Ray Mosca on such numbers as a lengthy workout on "Poor Butterfly," "Jumpin' at the Woodside," and "How High the Moon." A typically exciting effort by a classic tenor saxophonist.

In 1999, Flip Phillips was still in excellent form at age 84. In ways, much of *Swing Is the Thing* is a throwback to his past, with pianist Benny Green, guitarist Howard Alden, bassist Christian McBride, and drummer Kenny Washington filling in for Oscar Peterson, Herb Ellis, Ray Brown, and Louie Bellson! Phillips romps on medium-tempo standards, basic originals and ballads. Highlights include "I Hadn't Anyone Till You," a duet version of "In a Mellow Tone" with McBride, a duet with Alden on "This Is All I Ask," "Swing Is the Thing" (based on "Pennies from Heaven"), and a charming version of "Music, Maestro, Please," played in a trio with Green and Alden. Guest tenors James Carter and Joe Lovano make potent appearances on "The Mark of Zorro—Intro" and "The Mark Of Zorro—Outro" (a couple of uptempo blues); Carter interacts with Phillips on "Where or When"; and "Flip the Whip" (a romp based on "Cottontail") has a tradeoff by Lovano and Flip. Highly recommended.

LPS TO SEARCH FOR

Flip Phillips's only recording of the 1960s, *Flip in Florida* (Onyx 214), a quartet date with a Florida rhythm section from 1963, found him making his recording debut on bass clarinet for three of the ten numbers. 1981's *Flipenstein* (Progressive 7063) has Flip often sounding explosive on eight songs having titles that refer to ghosts and Halloween themes (such as "Satan Takes a Holiday," "Ghoul of My Dreams," and "Hangman's Noose").

FILMS

Flip Phillips appears with Woody Herman's orchestra in *Earl Carroll Vanities* (1945) and *Hit Parade of 1947* (1947). *80th Birthday Party* (Arbors 2) is a 1995 all-star concert in which the veteran tenor is heard and seen in prime form.

FRANKIE SOCOLOW

b. Sept. 18, 1923, Brooklyn, NY, d. Apr. 29, 1981, New York, NY

A fine musician who never became too famous, Frankie Socolow played with many of the who's who of Bebop. He started on clarinet when he was 13 before switching to tenor and doubling on alto. Socolow worked with the big bands of Jack Melvin (1941), Georgie Auld (1942), Ted Fio Rito, Roy Stevens, Van Alexander, Shep Fields, and, most importantly, the Boyd Raeburn Orchestra (1944). On May 2, 1945, Socolow led a record date for the Duke label that featured a quintet that included Freddy Webster (in top form) and Bud Powell (on one of his earliest recordings). He also recorded as a sideman with clarinetist Edmond Hall and drummer Sid Catlett. During the Bebop era, Socolow worked with Buddy Rich, Chubby Jackson (including touring Scandinavia in 1947–48), and the short-lived Artie Shaw Bebop Orchestra (1949). But Socolow's solo career never really took off. He freelanced in New York in the 1950s, led his only full album for Bethlehem in 1956 (a long-out-of-print sextet date), worked with Terry Gibbs, Charlie Ventura, Buddy DeFranco, Gene Krupa, and the Johnny Richards Orchestra, and recorded with Joe Morello, Maynard Ferguson, Hal McKusick, and Phil Woods. Frankie Socolow faded from the scene in the 1960s and few jazz history books now mention his name. Three of the four songs from his important Duke session were reissued on an LP from the 1980s, *Bebop Revisited, Vol. 6* (Xanadu 208).

LUCKY THOMPSON

b. June 16, 1924, Columbia, SC

Eli "Lucky" Thompson's lifelong nickname was always a bit ironic, for his luck was never all that good and he quit music prematurely. He grew up in Detroit, where he started out playing with local musicians. After moving to New York in 1943, Thompson had stints with Lionel Hampton, Don Redman, Sid Catlett, and Hot Lips Page. Thompson was with the Billy Eckstine Orchestra and Lucky Millinder for brief periods in 1944, really coming into his own while with Count Basie's band during 1944–45, where he succeeded his main influence, Don Byas, as Basie's tenor sax soloist, sitting next to Buddy Tate.

Thompson had the sound of a swing player but was open to the harmonic innovations of Bebop. Moving to the West Coast, he was part of Dizzy Gillespie's band in late 1945, hired as "insurance" in case Charlie Parker did not show up! Thompson recorded with both Parker and Gillespie, played and recorded with Boyd Raeburn's orchestra, and was with the last Louis Armstrong Orchestra (including when Armstrong was working on the film *New Orleans*). He made many records during this period, including a classic ballad statement on "Just One More Chance." After spending part of 1947 in Detroit, he moved back to New York, where he freelanced for a few years. Thompson led the house band at the Savoy during 1951–53, was on Miles Davis's classic *Walkin'* album in 1954, and in 1956 toured with Stan Kenton's orchestra (on baritone!), which included visiting Europe. During 1956 Thompson recorded enough material as a leader (mostly in Europe) to fill 11 albums. The 1957–62 period was spent living in France, where Thompson made many recordings, worked steadily, and took up the soprano sax, becoming one of the first Bop-oriented soloists on the instrument. After a few years back in the United States, where his swing-to-Bop style was considered out of fashion, Thompson returned to France for three years (1968–71). Back in the United States, he made a few records during 1972–73, taught at Dartmouth during 1973–74, and then completely disappeared from the jazz world. Only 50 at the time, Thompson never played again.

He has since been seen in the Seattle area, and has spent periods of time as a homeless person. If Thompson had returned to jazz at any time in the 1980s or '90s, he would have been celebrated as a living legend and probably have made a lucrative living. But apparently Lucky Thompson lost the desire and let his frustrations over the music business end his career much too early.

- **8** *The Beginning Years / Nov. 1945–July 7, 1947 / IAJRC 1001*
- **8** *Lucky Thompson/Gigi Gryce in Paris / Sept. 28, 1953–Apr. 17, 1956 / Vogue 68216*
- **10** *Tricotism / Jan. 24, 1956–Dec. 12, 1956 / GRP/ Impulse 135*
- **8** *Lucky in Paris / Jan. 14-15, 1959 / High Note 7045*

Lucky Thompson recorded many sessions while in Los Angeles during 1945–47. A few of the rarer dates are on *The Beginning Years,* including outings with Bob Mosley's All-Stars, Estelle Edson, Karl George's Dukes and Duchess, David Allyn, Lyle Griffin, the Basin Street Boys, Ike Carpenter, Ernie Andrews, and Mills Blue Rhythm Band that generally feature a solo from the tenor. In addition, two songs from Lucky's first session as a leader (which resulted in six titles in 1945) is included on this collector's item.

Another very busy period for Thompson in the recording studios was 1956, a year filled with many recordings and optimism. On the CD that Thompson shares with altoist Gigi Gryce, Lucky performs a dozen numbers (ten are his own originals) that were last available as the Xanadu LP *Brown Rose.* Thompson is showcased with drummer-arranger Dave Pochonet's nonet; best known among the mostly obscure sidemen is pianist Martial Solal. Also on this CD are six selections featuring Gryce in 1953 when he was in Paris with Lionel Hampton's big band (these titles are rarely reissued, unlike the numbers that Gryce recorded with Clifford Brown during the same trip) and two selections headed by Art Farmer from the same period.

Tricotism features Lucky Thompson at the peak of his powers. Eight selections have Thompson featured with a quintet also including Jimmy Cleveland, either Hank Jones or Don Abney on piano, Oscar Pettiford, and drummer Osie Johnson, but it is the eight trio numbers with guitarist Skeeter Best and Pettiford that are most memorable. Thompson just rips through the chord changes (as his earlier influence Don Byas had done in 1944 in duets with Slam Stewart) and comes up with one stunning chorus after another. Essential music.

Lucky in Paris is also on a high level. Thompson is mostly heard with a quintet, again led by Gerard Pochonet and including Martial Solal. These sessions are most notable for including Thompson's debut on soprano sax and for two

duets ("Soul Food" and "Brother Bob") that he had with percussionist Gana M'Bow. Otherwise the music is fairly conventional but of strong quality.

- **7** *Lord, Lord, Am I Ever Gonna Know? / 1961 / Candid 79035*
- **7** *Happy Days / Mar. 8, 1963 + Feb. 16, 1965 / Prestige 24144*
- **8** *Lucky Strikes / Sept. 15, 1964 / Original Jazz Classics 194*
- **7** *Tea Time / 1972–1973 / Laserlight 17132*

Lord, Lord, Am I Ever Gonna Know? was unissued prior to the release of the 1997 Candid CD, with the exception of the title cut, which was out on an earlier sampler. Thompson splits his time between tenor and soprano and is assisted by Martial Solal, bassist Peter Trunk, and Kenny Clarke. On "Choose Your Own" (one of his eight originals on the formerly long-lost date) Thompson plays unaccompanied solos on tenor and soprano. The other selections, essentially melodic Bop, are performed by the full group. The CD opens with an interesting spoken introduction by Thompson from 1968 in which he is philosophical and tells members of the public to ignore hype and depend on their own ears to determine what is best.

After returning to the United States in 1963, Lucky Thompson recorded two albums for Prestige and one for Prestige's subsidiary, Moodsville. *Happy Days* reissues one of the former dates plus the Moodsville session on a single CD. The Moodsville project has Thompson interpreting eight Jerome Kern ballads (such as "Long Ago and Far Away," "Look for the Silver Lining," and "They Didn't Believe Me") plus his own "No More" with a rhythm section that includes Hank Jones. The other set is a tribute to a new singer, Barbra Streisand (!), and has five songs that she was singing during the era (including "Happy Days Are Here Again" and "People") plus Thompson's own "Safari." During both outings, Thompson uplifts the material. The playing time of *Lucky Strikes* is briefer, but the material has more variety than *Happy Days* and serves as a strong introduction to Lucky Thompson's playing of the 1960s. He plays four songs apiece on tenor and soprano while joined by Hank Jones, bassist Richard Davis, and Connie Kay. The two standards and six originals are all well worth hearing, with Thompson's concise solos not wasting a note.

During 1972–73, Lucky Thompson made his final recordings, two and a half albums' worth of material for the Groove

Merchant label. *Tea Time* is a sampler, with five of the seven songs from 1972's *Goodbye Yesterday* and three of the seven numbers from 1973's *I Offer You*. It is a pity that all of the Groove Merchant sessions were not reissued complete on two CDs. What is here (quartet numbers with Cedar Walton on keyboards, Larry Ridley or Sam Jones on bass, and Billy Higgins or Louis Hayes on drums) is fine, for Thompson plays well on his eight originals, although this CD is obviously not for completists. It was a major loss when Lucky Thompson decided to give up his struggle against the commercial music world shortly after these dates.

LPS TO SEARCH FOR

Test Pilot (Swingtime 1005) has more of Lucky Thompson's early and generally obscure sessions from 1944–50. Included is the two-part title cut (played by the odd quartet of Thompson, violinist Stuff Smith, pianist Erroll Garner, and drummer George Wettling!) and titles with Estelle Edson, Freddie Green, Dinah Washington, and Fletcher Henderson plus some selections from Lucky's own dates in 1945 and 1950. *Paris 1956, Volume One* (Swing 8404) features Thompson in a quintet that includes former Count Basie trumpeter Emmett Berry (Berry has "Blues for Frank" as his feature, while Thompson takes "Thin Ice" backed by just bass and drums) and with a quartet/quintet with Martial Solal and (on three cuts) fellow tenor Guy Lafitte. Also from that busy year of 1956 is *Lucky Thompson* (Inner City 7016), a dozen swing standards that showcase the tenor with a five-piece rhythm section that includes Solal and Pochonet. *Body & Soul* (Nessa 13) is an underrated classic cut in 1970. Thompson alternates between tenor and soprano while joined by the Tete Montoliu Trio on five standards and five originals, including "Blue 'n Boogie," "When Sunny Gets Blue," and "I Got It Bad." Thompson was still in prime form during his final sessions, which resulted in *Goodbye Yesterday* (Groove Merchant 508), *I Offer You* (Groove Merchant 517), and *Friday the 13th Cook County Jail* (Groove Merchant 515). The last has the two-part "Freedom Suite" played by organist Jimmy McGriff's group and three numbers (including a burning "Cherokee") performed by Thompson with Cedar Walton (on electric piano), Sam Jones, and Louis Hayes.

FILMS

Lucky Thompson can be seen in the distance with Louis Armstrong's orchestra in *New Orleans* (1947).

CHARLIE VENTURA

b. Dec. 2, 1916, Philadelphia, PA, d. Jan. 17, 1992, Pleasantville, NJ

Charlie Ventura was a rambunctious tenor saxophonist, technically skilled but often so emotional in his playing as to go over the top. Essentially a big-toned swing player, Ventura for a time had a group that he billed as "Bop for the People." He started playing C melody sax at 15, switching to tenor two years later. Ventura's first major job was with the 1942–43 Gene Krupa Orchestra. After a stint with Teddy Powell (1943–44), the tenor became famous during his second period with Krupa (1944–46). Ventura was a key soloist with Krupa's big band and was showcased with the Gene Krupa Trio (which also included pianist Teddy Napoleon); "Dark Eyes" was a hit for the trio. Ventura, who began recording as a leader in 1945, went out on his own in 1946, putting together a short-lived big band. His 1947 quintet (with Kai Winding, pianist Lou Stein, bassist Bob Carter, Shelly Manne, and Buddy Stewart) fell between swing and Bop, and had the humorous "Bop for the People" title. Ventura's group evolved during the next couple of years, and in 1949 he had a memorable outfit that consisted of Conte Candoli, Benny Green, Boots Mussulli on alto and baritone, bassist Kenny O'Brien, drummer Ed Shaughnessy, and the vocal duo of Roy Kral (who also played piano) and Jackie Cain. Their Pasadena Civic Auditorium concert of May 9, 1949, was a high point for the band and for Ventura's career.

Charlie Ventura had another short-term big band during 1949–50, recorded for a variety of labels during 1951–57 (playing alto, baritone, and bass saxophones in addition to his tenor), had occasional reunions with Gene Krupa, and then largely faded away, playing just now and then in obscurity during his final 30 years, recording only once after 1957. He is still remembered for his often-tasteless but always-colorful playing with Krupa's trio.

9 *1945–1946 / Mar. 1, 1945–Mar. 1946 / Classics 1044*
8 *A Charlie Ventura Concert / May 9, 1949 / MCA 42230*

* *The Complete Verve/Clef Charlie Ventura & Flip Phillips Studio Sessions / Sept. 1947–May 1957 / Mosaic 6–182*
7 *Runnin' Wild / July 16 + 19, 1956 / Similar 56122*
Charlie Ventura began recording as a leader while still with

Gene Krupa. The Classics disc features Ventura with a sextet that costars Howard McGhee, on three live numbers with the Krupa Trio, heading a swing sextet with trumpeter Buck Clayton, showcased during a quartet date for Savoy, in a septet with clarinetist Barney Bigard, and sharing the frontline with Red Rodney and altoist Willie Smith. Unfortunately, Ventura's other sessions from 1946–48 are mostly out of print. The famous 1949 Pasadena Civic Auditorium concert (probably the high point of his career) was released in two halves, one set apiece by Decca and GNP. The Decca part was reissued by MCA and has Ventura's notable septet playing such numbers as "Euphoria," "East of Suez," "How High the Moon," and a bizarre version of "I'm Forever Blowing Bubbles" that features Jackie & Roy's vocals.

While four of the CDs on the six-CD, limited-edition Mosaic box set showcase Flip Phillips, the first two discs have Ventura's sessions for Clef and Norgran, dating from 1951–54. Ventura (heard on tenor, alto, baritone, and bass saxes) was still in prime form, whether heard with a nonet, with five different quartets, or with Conte Candoli in a quintet; singers Betty Bennett and Mary Ann McCall make a few appearances. During 1956–57 Ventura recorded three quintet dates, one apiece for Baton, King, and Tops. The Tops set has been reissued by Simitar and features Ventura (on all four of his axes) along with pianist Dave McKenna, guitarist Billy Bean, bassist Richard Davis, and drummer Mousey Alexander playing mostly vintage material, some of it Dixieland standards. Ventura (who was still just 39) displays plenty of spirit on such numbers as "Honeysuckle Rose," "Dark Eyes," "Exactly Like You," and even "The Saints" and "Bill Bailey." The only post-1957 Charlie Ventura record, *Chazz '77* (Famous Door 115), from 1977, has long been out of print.

LPS TO SEARCH FOR

Charlie Ventura's Savoy recordings of 1945 and 1947–48 are among the most significant of his career, but many titles remain quite scarce. The double-LP *Euphoria* (Savoy 2243), which has his complete Savoy output, deserves to be brought back. The same can be said for *In Concert* (GNP Crescendo 1), the second half of Ventura's 1949 performance at the Pasadena Civic Auditorium concert; highlights include "Lullaby in Rhythm," "Boptura," and "High on an Open Mike."

FILMS

Charlie Ventura is featured with Gene Krupa in *George White's Scandals* (1945).

BUDDY WISE

b. Feb. 20, 1928, Topeka, KS, d. July 15, 1955, Las Vegas, NV

A solid tenor saxophonist who was the soloist with Gene Krupa's big band after Charlie Ventura left, Buddy Wise was a reliable player who unfortunately died rather young. He played with the big bands of Hal Wasson (1943) and Mal Hallett before joining Krupa (1945–50). Wise soloed on most of Krupa's dates from 1946 on, up until the time the drummer broke up his band. Wise spent nine months with Woody Herman's Third Herd (a period when his tone became cooler) and 18 months with Ray Anthony's big band. Buddy Wise never led his own record, but he can be heard on many of the Gene Krupa big band sessions.

FILMS

Buddy Wise appears with the Gene Krupa Orchestra in *Beat the Band* (1947).

Baritone Saxophonists

The baritone sax was a latecomer to jazz. Although Harry Carney was playing baritone with Duke Ellington's orchestra as early as 1927 and would be the dominant voice on the instrument for the next two decades, the baritone was not a regular part of many big band's saxophone sections during the swing era. In fact, the orchestras of Benny Goodman and Artie Shaw did not include a baritonist. Jack Washington with Count Basie, and Jimmy Lunceford's Haywood Henry were well respected, and Ernie Caceres made a name for himself playing with Eddie Condon (where he was virtually the only Dixieland baritone saxophonist) and with Glenn Miller. But the baritone was not considered an essential component of big bands until the mid-1940s, and Carney, Washington, Henry, and Caceres did not lead any recording sessions of their own during the swing era.

As a solo instrument, the baritone would not become widely accepted until the rise of Gerry Mulligan in the early

1950s, but there were a few pioneer soloists during the classic Bebop era, most notably Serge Chaloff (whose cool tone preceded Mulligan's), Cecil Payne, and Leo Parker. Not only did they add to the ensemble sound of big bands, but all were strong soloists who were potentially on the level of the best tenormen.

SERGE CHALOFF

b. Nov. 24, 1923, Boston, MA, d. July 16, 1957, Boston, MA

The most important baritone saxophonist to emerge during the classic Bebop era, Serge Chaloff had a much lighter sound on his instrument than Harry Carney. Chaloff played his instrument with the fluidity of a tenor, and he became most famous as one of the "Four Brothers" with Woody Herman's Second Herd. But unlike his fellow "Brothers," Stan Getz, Zoot Sims, and Al Cohn (who replaced Herbie Steward with Herman), Chaloff did not have a long career or life, and in the 1950s he was overshadowed by Gerry Mulligan. His heroin addiction led to unreliability and an irresponsible lifestyle. In addition, Chaloff did not have a subtle personality! He tended to ridicule Herman's playing abilities behind his back (even while Woody was paying his salary and putting up with his drug habit), and he was not too kind in his criticisms of other musicians.

The son of the noted music teacher Madame Chaloff, Serge started off playing in the big bands of Tommy Reynolds (1939), Stinky Rogers (1941–42), Shep Fields, and Ina Ray Hutton. He made a strong impression during his stints with the orchestras of Boyd Raeburn (1944–45), Georgie Auld (1945–46), and Jimmy Dorsey (1946–47). While with Woody Herman (1947–49), Chaloff was one of the few baritone saxophonists with a big band to receive a fair amount of solo space. After the Second Herd broke up, he worked a bit with Count Basie's octet in 1950. Chaloff returned to his native Boston and endured several years of scuffling and working mostly locally, eventually kicking his dangerous drug habit. But ironically, just when Serge Chaloff finally became clean, he contracted spinal paralysis, which soon caused his death at age 33; he appeared at his last record date (a 1957 reunion of the Four Brothers) in a wheelchair.

*   *The Complete Serge Chaloff Sessions / Sept. 21, 1946–Mar. 14, 1956 / Mosaic 4-147*
9   *The Fable of Mable / June 9, 1954 + Sept. 3, 1954 / Black Lion 60923*

8   *Boston 1950 / Nov. 17, 1946–Oct. 15, 1950 / Uptown 27.38*

The four-CD Mosaic box has every session that Serge Chaloff led during his career, dates originally cut for Dial, Savoy, Futurama, Motif, Storyville, and Capitol, including the complete sets titled *The Fable of Mable, Boston Blow-Up*, and *Blue Serge* (the last a superb quartet date with Sonny Clark). Obviously, this is the definitive Chaloff acquisition! The material consists of sessions from 1946–47, 1949, and 1954–56 with such sidemen as Ralph Burns, Red Rodney, George Wallington, Al Cohn, Terry Gibbs, altoists Charlie Mariano and Boots Mussulli, and trumpeter Herb Pomeroy. All 17 selections from *The Fable of Mable* sessions (Boston dates with Mussulli, Mariano, Pomeroy, and pianist Russ Freeman), including all of the alternate takes, are also on the single CD of the same name. Recommended for listeners unable to acquire the Mosaic box. Chaloff sounds quite healthy during this brief period after his heroin addiction and before he became seriously ill.

The music on *Boston 1950* is not on the Mosaic box, since it was released for the first time by Uptown in 1994. The performances (all taken from radio appearances in Boston) are often quite intriguing, particularly four duets with pianist Rollins Griffith in 1946. Chaloff is also heard in quartets and quintets that include among the key musicians pianist Nat Pierce, bassist Joe Shulman, and Sonny Truitt or Milt Gold on trombone. The recording quality is decent, and the fine CD adds to the legacy of the short-lived Serge Chaloff.

LEO PARKER

b. Apr. 18, 1925, Washington DC, d. Feb. 11, 1962, New York, NY

Leo Parker had great potential early in his career. A baritonist with a thick, deep, and guttural sound, Leo Parker extended the legacy of Harry Carney and excelled in both Bebop and R&B settings. Parker actually began on alto, starting on the lighter horn in high school and playing it on Coleman Hawkins's debut Bebop records in 1944. He switched to baritone when he joined the Billy Eckstine Orchestra (1944–45). Parker worked with Dizzy Gillespie's or-

One of Woody Herman's "Four Brothers," Serge Chaloff was the finest Bebop baritonist before the rise of Gerry Mulligan.

chestra in 1946 and toured with the Illinois Jacquet band during 1947–48, two stints that gave him strong recognition in the Bop world. He also recorded with Fats Navarro, J. J. Johnson, Dexter Gordon, and Sir Charles Thompson, and as a leader with three dates for Savoy (1947–48), one released years later for Misterioso (1950), and on lesser-known titles put out by Onyx (1950), United (1952), and Chess (1951 and 1953).

With his sound, Parker could have been a hit in rhythm and blues, but by the early 1950s drugs were ruining his life. He was active only on a part-time basis during the entire decade, not recording at all during 1954–60. Parker eventually cleaned up his act and in 1961 started a comeback that resulted in two fine albums for the Blue Note label. But, as in Chaloff's case, Parker's second period was quite brief. It all ended when Leo Parker died of a heart attack in early 1962 at the age of 36.

8 *Let Me Tell You 'Bout It / Blue Note / Sept. 9, 1961 / Blue Note 4087*

8 *Rollin' with Leo / Oct. 12 + 20, 1961 / Blue Note 4095*

Leo Parker is in excellent form during his "comeback" record *Let Me Tell You 'Bout It,* playing a variety of basic straight-ahead originals (including the gospel-oriented title cut) plus two performances not on the earlier LP. He is heard with a talented but obscure group of sidemen that include trumpeter John Burks, tenor saxophonist Bill Swindell, and pianist Yusef Salim. *Rollin' with Leo,* not released until 1980, is just as exciting, with Parker again in a sextet (best known among his players are trumpeter Dave Burns and pianist Johnny Acea). The group's jump style and mixture of romps and ballads recall the late '40s Illinois Jacquet band that Parker had played with. Such a pity that the baritonist did not stick around longer!

Leo Parker can be seen in the video *Things to Come* (Vintage Jazz Classics 2006), playing with the Dizzy Gillespie big band in 1947's *Jivin' in Bebop*.

CECIL PAYNE

b. Dec. 14, 1922, Brooklyn, NY

A fine baritonist who adapted easily to the Bebop style, Cecil Payne is a survivor who has not had much recognition through the years, despite his talents. Early on he played guitar, clarinet, and alto sax, studying on the last with Pete Brown. After serving in the military during 1943-46, Payne debuted on records as an altoist with J. J. Johnson but soon switched to baritone. A short stint with Clarence Briggs and a gig with Roy Eldridge were followed by three years (1946-49) as a key member of the Dizzy Gillespie Orchestra, where he was showcased most notably on "Ow" and "Stay on It." Payne started the 1950s playing with Tadd Dameron, James Moody, and Illinois Jacquet (1952-54) but then spent two years working at a day job. After returning to music in 1956, he was with Randy Weston on and off for a decade, and recorded fairly regularly as a sideman and occasionally as a leader. Payne was a part of the 1961 version of the play *The Connection* and worked with many groups as a sideman, including those of Machito (1963-64), Lionel Hampton, the Woody Herman Orchestra (1966-68), Slide Hampton, Dizzy Gillespie, Count Basie (1969-71), Benny Carter, and Dameronia (the early '80s). Cecil Payne, who started doubling on flute in the 1970s, has freelanced up to the present time, including leading an album as recently as 1998 for Delmark.

9   *Cerupa / June 1-2, 1993 / Delmark 478*
8   *Scotch and Milk / Sept. 2-3, 1996 / Delmark 494*
7   *Payne's Window / Aug. 17-18, 1998 / Delmark 509*

Cerupa is a particularly strong outing by Cecil Payne. The baritonist (who also makes a couple of fine appearances on flute) is inspired and was clearly pushed by his sidemen (the exciting tenor saxophonist Eric Alexander, pianist Harold Mabern, who here sounds quite influenced by McCoy Tyner, bassist John Ore, and drummer Joe Farnsworth). The resulting music is often intense yet tied to the Bop tradition. Trumpeter Dr. Odies Williams III sits in on "Brookfield Andante," while the great trumpeter Freddie Hubbard, in one of his last appearances on record before being forced to retire, is OK on his original "Be Wee."

Scotch and Milk is on nearly the same level, although Payne is often overshadowed by the battling tenors of Eric Alexander and Lin Halliday. The septet (which also includes trumpeter Marcus Belgrave and the Mabern-Ore-Farnsworth rhythm section) performs "If I Should Lose You" and seven of Payne's straightahead originals with creativity and often hard-driving swing. Alexander returns to help the baritonist out on *Payne's Window,* a sextet set with trombonist Steve Davis, Harold Mabern, bassist John Webber, and drummer Joe Farnsworth. Although at this point, Payne's tone on baritone was not quite as strong as it had been earlier (he was 75), he still comes up with consistently inventive solos. Highlights include the title cut, "Delilah," and "Hold Tight."

LPS TO SEARCH FOR

Other than eight numbers made for Decca in 1949, *Patterns* (Savoy 1167) has Cecil Payne's first dates as a leader. The quartet and quintet selections from 1956 are with Duke Jordan (a longtime friend), Tommy Potter, Art Taylor, and (on four of the eight songs) Kenny Dorham. The music is excellent, falling between Bop and Hard Bop. *Performing Charlie Parker Music* (Charlie Parker 801), from 1961, has six Bird numbers plus Payne's "Communion" played by a quintet that also includes Clark Terry, Duke Jordan, the young bassist Ron Carter, and Charlie Persip; "Shaw 'Nuff," "Relaxin' at Camarillo," and "The Hymn" are among the highlights of this little-known album. *Brookfield Andante,* from 1966, finds Payne stretching out enthusiastically on four of his originals in a British club with an English rhythm section. Skipping a decade to 1976, *Bird Gets the Worm* (Muse 5061) is another rewarding Charlie Parker tribute set. This time the quintet consists of trumpeter Tom Harrell, Duke Jordan, bassist Buster Williams, and drummer Al Foster playing a variety of tunes associated with Bird (including "Repetition," "Ko Ko," and "Constellation") plus Payne's "Ninny Melina." *Casbah* (Empathy 1005), from 1985, has Payne supported quite tastefully by guitarist Joe Carter, pianist Richard Wyands, and bassist Stafford James. The intimate and well-rounded set is highlighted by Tadd Dameron's "Casbah," "Carney," "Wave," and Benny Carter's "A Walking Thing."

Pianists

Much more than the other instruments in the rhythm section (guitar, bass, and drums), the piano went through some revolutionary changes during the Bebop era, in large part due to the innovative Bud Powell. In the 1920s, the piano was considered a self-sufficient, miniature orchestra. With the stride pianist's powerful left hand keeping the rhythm and stating the chords while the right played melodic variations, jazz pianists often functioned as a one-man band. Gradually during the 1930s, the touch of pianists became lighter (as can be heard in the playing of Teddy Wilson), and Count Basie went out of his way to leave space for the rhythm guitar and string bass. Nat King Cole in his trio took jazz piano about as far as it could go while still staying within the swing idiom.

Although Earl Hines played a bit with time (as early as the late '20s), suspending the rhythm to dramatic effect before catching it again, it was Bud Powell who largely changed everything. Powell's left hand was no longer bound to the timekeeping function. His left hand instead stated chords irregularly, punctuating rather than stating the rhythm and giving a kick to the music rather than serving as a metronome. His right hand emphasized long single-note lines (á la Charlie Parker) when not stating complex chords, and his style overall became the way that jazz piano was played by most keyboardists during the 1945–65 period.

There were exceptions as new voices with their own personalities rose to prominence. Erroll Garner was uncategorizable, George Shearing made Bebop accessible to the masses (stripping his piano style of Bud Powell's danger), and, in the 1950s, Lennie Tristano, Oscar Peterson, Dave Brubeck, Ahmad Jamal, and of course Thelonious Monk did not sound much like Powell. But it would be difficult to imagine the rise of such Bop pianists as Joe Albany, Al Haig, Duke Jordan, Lou Levy, Dodo Marmarosa, Claude Williamson, and, later on, Barry Harris without the arrival of Bud Powell on the scene first to show the way.

JOE ALBANY

b. Jan. 24, 1924, Atlantic City, NJ, d. Jan. 12, 1988, New York, NY

One of the first pianists to adapt his style to Bebop, Joe Albany had great promise which, after a 24-year "interruption," he was able to partly realize. Born Joseph Albani, he originally played accordion, switching to piano as a teenager. Albany worked with Leo Watson, Benny Carter, Georgie Auld, and Boyd Raeburn during 1942–45, and he had a brief association with Charlie Parker when Bird was on the West Coast. His 1946 studio recordings with Lester Young were among the high points of his career, and he seemed to have a great future as a Bud Powell-influenced pianist with a sound of his own.

But major problems with drugs and alcohol kept Albany entirely off records (with one exception) during 1947–70, and his private life was a complete mess, with his second wife committing suicide and his third almost dying from a drug overdose. Other than a rehearsal session with Warne Marsh from 1957 that was released and a short stint with Charles Mingus in 1963, Albany struggled in obscurity for decades. Finally, in 1971 he began to gradually straighten out his life. Albany made a record for the British Spotlite label that year, started to appear more often in public, cut an al-

bum with violinist Joe Venuti, and led sessions for a variety of labels during 1972–82. The 1980 documentary *Joe Albany . . . A Jazz Life* finds him honestly discussing his personal problems and his difficult life. Until bad health slowed him down in the mid-1980s, Joe Albany had a reasonably busy decade, although he never really made up for all of the lost years.

7 *The Right Combination / Sept. 1957 / Original Jazz Classics 1749*

9 *Bird Lives! / Jan. 4, 1979 / Storyville 4164*

Joe Albany's only recording date as a leader before 1971 was actually a rehearsal from 1957 that was released years later. Albany performs seven jazz standards in a trio with tenor saxophonist Warne Marsh and bassist Bob Whitlock, and, despite the informal nature of the performance (which contains a few slips), the music (which includes Clifford Brown's "Daahoud," "Body and Soul," and "All the Things You Are") is quite worthwhile.

During 1971–82, Albany recorded for Spotlite, Steeplechase, Horo, EMI, Musica, Fresh Sound, Interplay, and Elektra Musician. Most of his recordings have not yet been reissued on CD, but *Bird Lives!* (his next-to-last date) has. Teamed with bassist Art Davis and Roy Haynes, Albany is heard throughout in prime form, playing seven Charlie Parker tunes, "They Can't Take That Away from Me," and the ad-lib "Charlie Parker Blues." Joe Albany shows how strong a classic Bebop pianist he could be, and the results are swinging and quite enjoyable; highly recommended.

LPS TO SEARCH FOR

Joe Albany at Home (Spotlite JA1) was Albany's comeback record. It features him in 1971 playing 11 standards plus his "Birdtown Birds" solo on his own piano. The recording quality is decent, and it is obvious that Albany still had a lot to contribute to jazz. *Proto-Bopper* (Spotlite JA3) finds Albany overcoming an out-of-tune piano on solo and trio numbers (with bassist Bob Whitlock and Jerry McKenzie or Nick Martinis on drums) to create some fine Bop. *The Albany Touch* (Sea Breeze 1004) is an excellent solo album from 1977 that is relaxed and mostly at slower tempos, with a few exceptions; "A.B. (After Bird) Blues II," "Autumn Leaves," and "A Night in Tunisia" are highlights. One of Joe Albany's finest recordings was his last one, *Portrait of an Artist* (Elektra Musician 60161), from 1982. The emphasis is again mostly on ballads, with guitarist Al Gafa, bassist George Duvivier, and drummer Charlie Persip helping out. Some of the better selections are "Autumn in New York," "They Say It's Wonderful," and "Confirmation." His final recording concludes with a short interview in which Joe Albany discusses a few aspects of his colorful, if erratic, life.

FILMS

Joe Albany . . . A Jazz Life (1980) is an hour-long documentary that does a fine job of portraying the classic but troubled pianist.

WALTER BISHOP, JR.

b. Apr. 10, 1927, New York, NY, d. Jan. 24, 1998, New York, NY

Walter Bishop, Jr., was an excellent pianist from the classic Bebop era who, although never too famous, had a long and productive career. His father, Walter Bishop, Sr., was a songwriter in the 1930s. After working with trumpeter Louis Metcalf in 1945 and spending a period in the military (1945–47), Walter Bishop, Jr., became part of the New York jazz scene, playing with several groups at Minton's Playhouse and working with Art Blakey, Oscar Pettiford, Terry Gibbs, Kai Winding, Miles Davis, Andy Kirk (1950), and, most importantly, Charlie Parker (off and on during 1951–54).

After a few years off the scene, Bishop made a comeback in 1959, playing regularly on Monday nights at Birdland. He worked with Curtis Fuller in 1960, had a short stint with the Cannonball Adderley Quintet, was featured with Clark Terry in 1977 and was with the Bill Hardman–Junior Cook Quintet in 1980 but spent most of his career leading trios or quartets. In Los Angeles during 1969–75, Bishop headed the group 4th Cycle and also worked with Supersax, Terry Gibbs, trumpeter Blue Mitchell, tenor saxophonist Stanley Turrentine, and Art Farmer. As a leader, Bishop made his debut for Black Lion in 1961, had a few sessions from 1962–64 released by Prestige, Cotillion, and Xanadu, recorded fairly extensively in the 1970s, and led a CD as late as 1991. Although flexible enough to appear in Hard Bop and even avant-garde settings (including with Archie Shepp and Ken McIntyre), Walter Bishop played primarily in a Bebop-oriented style where his enthusiastic solos and accompaniment were always a major asset.

7 *Milestones / Mar. 14, 1961 / Black Lion 60109*
9 *The Walter Bishop, Jr., Trio / 1962–Oct. 1963 / Original Jazz Classics 1896*
8 *What's New / Oct. 25, 1990 / DIW 605*
9 *Midnight Blue / Dec. 12, 1991 / Red 123251*

The debut of Walter Bishop, Jr., as a leader resulted in six songs plus three alternate takes, all of which are reissued on the Black Lion CD. He is assisted by bassist Jimmy Garrison (shortly before he joined John Coltrane), whose bowed solos sometimes recall Paul Chambers, and the supportive drummer G. T. Hogan. The music, which includes "Sometimes I'm Happy," Oscar Pettiford's "Blues in the Closet," and "Alone Together," is excellent and very much in the Bebop tradition. The Original Jazz Classics reissue (with bassist Butch Warren and Hogan or Jimmy Cobb on drums) includes 16 concise numbers, all under four minutes apiece (12 are under three minutes). Bishop gets his message across in a short period of time, introducing five originals, reviving six real obscurities and giving new life to five standards. An often-overlooked classic.

Twenty-eight years and countless experiences later, Walter Bishop, Jr., in 1990 was still playing in a recognizable style falling between Bebop and Hard Bop. *What's New* teams him with bassist Peter Washington and drummer Kenny Washington for his original "Waltz Zweetie" and seven jazz standards, including "I'll Remember April," "Crazy She Calls Me," and Kenny Dorham's "Una Mas." All of the musicians play up to par, and this is a very tight trio, with both Washingtons reacting quickly to Bishop's every idea. *Midnight Blue,* another trio date (this time with bassist Reggie Johnson and drummer Doug Sides), is most notable for the definitive version of "Sweet and Lovely" (the arrangement is perfect for the song) and high-quality interpretations of "Never Let Me Go," "The More I See You," "Up Jumped Spring," and "What Is This Thing Called Love?" One of the best all-around recordings of Walter Bishop's career.

LPS TO SEARCH FOR

Bish Bash (Xanadu 114) has a pair of sessions not released until 1977. Bishop's only dates as a leader from this period, he is heard in 1964 on long versions of "Days of Wine and Roses" and "Willow Weep for Me" with tenor saxophonist Frank Haynes (who did not record much), bassist Eddie Khan, and drummer Dick Berk, on a trio version of "Summertime" from the same date, plus five songs from 1968 with bassist Reggie Johnson and drummer Idris Muhammed. This album is particularly valuable for Haynes's solos, although Bishop is also in excellent form.

GENE DiNOVI

b. May 26, 1928, Brooklyn, NY

A fine Bop pianist who also learned from the swing players, Gene DiNovi was influenced early on by Bud Powell but was flexible enough to also be featured in swing and Mainstream settings throughout his career. He began playing piano when he was six and, as a teenager, started out playing with Henry Jerome (1943), Joe Marsala (with whom he made his recording debut in 1945), and the Boyd Raeburn Big Band. During the Bop years, DiNovi had stints with Buddy Rich, Chuck Wayne, Stan Hasselgard, Benny Goodman, Anita O'Day, the Chubby Jackson Big Band (1949), and Artie Shaw, also recording with Lester Young. A fine accompanist, DiNovi worked behind singers Peggy Lee, Tony Bennett, Carmen McRae, and Lena Horne (1955–59) in addition to playing with Benny Goodman. He spent the 1960s mostly as a writer in the studios and, after moving to Toronto, Canada, he played mostly locally in the 1970s and '80s, although he recorded with cornetist Ruby Braff (1984 and 1987) and made a solo piano album in 1977 (all three were for the Canadian Pedi Mega label). DiNovi, who has performed and recorded with Benny Carter in more recent

times, re-emerged, after decades out of the jazz spotlight, in the 1990s to play concerts and record for the Japanese Century and British Candid labels.

8 *Live at the Montreal Bistro / Oct. 20–22, 1993 / Candid 79726*

7 *Gene DiNovi Plays the Music of Benny Carter / June 1, 1999 / Hep 2076*

An excellent example of Gene DiNovi's playing, *Live at the Montreal Bistro* is a trio set with bassist Dave Young and drummer Terry Clarke that displays his gentle yet swinging style. Bop-oriented while hinting at melodic swing, DiNovi is in excellent form on such numbers as Tiny Kahn's "T.N.T." (he dedicated the release to the late drummer-composer), "Terry's Little Tune," "It Happened in Monterey," and "Tiny's Blues." DiNovi's solo piano tribute to Benny Carter features mostly slow- to medium-tempo explorations of ten Carter songs (including "Souvenir," "When Lights Are Low," "Only Trust Your Heart," and "Blues in My Heart") plus his own "Conversation." Very tasteful.

ERROLL GARNER

b. June 15, 1921, Pittsburgh, PA, d. Jan. 2, 1977, Los Angeles, CA

A distinctive stylist and a brilliant pianist, Erroll Garner is in his own category. He initially became famous during the classic Bebop era, and he recorded with Charlie Parker in 1947. But his orchestral style owes at least as much to swing as to Bop. Garner was unique in several respects. It was not unusual for him to sit down at the piano and emerge three hours later with enough music to fill up two or more albums, all impeccably played first takes. His jubilant style (which often found his left hand strumming chords like a rhythm guitar while his right played a tiny bit behind the beat) was so accessible that he was a popular attraction throughout his entire career without having to alter his natural approach in the slightest. And Garner, whose happy grunting in live performances sometimes came close to drowning out his playing, always seemed to be having so much fun!

The younger brother of pianist Linton Garner, Erroll was completely self-taught. He began playing piano when he was three and at seven started appearing on the radio with the Kan-D Kids. A professional since 1937, he worked locally in Pittsburgh (including with Leroy Brown's orchestra during 1938–41), moved to New York in 1944, was part of Slam

Stewart's trio (1944–45), and then went out on his own, gaining a loyal audience from the start. From 1945 until illness forced his retirement in 1975, Garner worked steadily, led trios, recorded prolifically, toured Europe often, was a frequent guest on television variety shows, and was one of the most popular of all jazz musicians. His style was easy to copy (George Shearing and Steve Allen delighted in emulating him) but impossible to top. And Erroll Garner's inability to read music did not stop him from composing several numbers, of which "Misty" became a standard.

6 *1944 / Nov. 16, 1944–Dec. 14, 1944 / Classics 802*
6 *1944, Vol. 2 / Dec. 14–20, 1944 / Classics 818*
6 *1944, Vol. 3 / Nov. 3, 1944–Dec. 25, 1944 / Classics 850*
7 *1944–1945 / Dec. 22, 1944–Mar. 9, 1945 / Classics 873*
8 *1945–1946 / Sept. 25, 1945–Feb. 1946 / Classics 924*

These five CDs consist of the earliest Erroll Garner recordings—all of his work as a leader during his first 15 months as a soloist. A lot of the music is quite unusual, for during November–December 1944, Baron Timme Rosenkrantz documented the pianist on his tape recorder while Garner practiced and stretched out at the baron's apartment. The music was not supposed to be put out, but in the 1950s it was released due to its historic value and Garner's great popularity (along with Rosenkrantz's need for money!). The pianist did not have his style together yet, and many of his improvisations (which are sometimes ten minutes long) are quite impressionistic, particularly on the slower and more introspective pieces. *1944* includes lengthy versions of "The Clock Stood Still," "Floating on a Cloud," "Cloudburst," and "Overture to Dawn." *1944, Vol. 2* has two more of these spontaneous sessions (including an eight-minute rendition of "I Hear a Rhapsody") along with Garner's first official studio sides. Those ten numbers, originally cut as piano solos, have John Simmons's bass and Doc West's drums overdubbed from a few years later, and the sidemen tend to be better recorded than the pianist! *1944, Vol. 3* continues with more private performances, including a nearly ten-minute "Variations on a Nursery Rhyme" (a medley of four tunes), "White Christmas," "I Got Rhythm," and a November 3 rendition of "Somebody Loves Me" with Inez Cavanaugh's vocal that actually predates all of the other material on these three CDs.

1944–1945 starts out with six songs from a December 22, 1944, jam session on which Garner is joined by trumpeter Charlie Shavers, trombonist Vic Dickenson, altoist Lem Davis, bassist Slam Stewart, drummer Cliff Leeman, and (on one song) clarinetist Hank D'Amico. The playing is loose and sometimes humorous, with Shavers in good form. The last eight selections on this disc are the beginning of the "real" Erroll Garner sound. He is heard on four trio numbers (with bassist Eddie Brown and Doc West) and four piano solos; this music was originally released by the Black and White and Signature labels. *1945–1946* has 21 selections, all but the final two being cut in the studios within a ten-week period. There are four trio numbers (with bassist John Levy and drummer George DeHart) that were made for Savoy ("Laura" was a hit) and piano solos cut for Disc, Mercury, and (in the last two cases) V-Discs. Garner is quite recognizable, and his work on the medium-tempo pieces in particular is a joy.

10 *The Complete Savoy Master Takes / Jan. 30, 1945–June 20, 1949 / Savoy 17025–26*
8 *Long Ago and Far Away / June 28, 1950–Jan. 11, 1951 / Columbia 40863*
8 *Body and Soul / Jan. 11, 1951–Jan. 3, 1952 / Columbia 47035*

Although the double-CD *The Complete Savoy Master Takes* makes it sound as if something is being left out, no Erroll Garner alternate takes have yet been released by Savoy, so everything is here. The pianist is heard on the four selections that he recorded as part of Slam Stewart's trio in 1945 (including "Play, Fiddle, Play" and "Laff, Slam, Laff") and his four trio numbers from 1945 (with John Levy and George DeHart) plus his 33 selections from 1949 with bassist John Simmons and drummer Alvin Stoller. A perfect introduction to Garner's music, this set (highlighted by "Laura," "Penthouse Serenade," "Love Walked In," "All of Me," and "A Cottage for Sale") is full of rhapsodic ballads and exuberant romps. This music is impossible not to enjoy.

Garner's steadily rising popularity led to his being signed by Columbia in 1950, spending four years with the label. *Long Ago and Far Away* has 16 trio numbers from 1950–51 with John Simmons and drummer Shadow Wilson. "When Johnny Comes Marching Home," "When You're Smiling," "Poor Butterfly," "The Petite Waltz," "The Petite Waltz Bounce," and a remake of "Laura" are in the repertoire. The

Always in his own category, Erroll Garner, who was able to emulate a swinging big band on the piano, never seemed to play an uninspired chorus.

same trio is featured on 20 selections on *Body and Soul*, playing mostly swing standards plus "Robbins' Nest" and a few songs (such as "Indiana" and "Please Don't Talk About Me When I'm Gone") that are more closely associated with Dixieland. No matter, Garner turns every tune into his own personal and happy statement.

8   *Too Marvelous for Words / May 26, 1954 / Emarcy 842 419*

9   *Solo Time! / July 7, 1954 / Emarcy 314 511 821*

8   *Mambo Moves Garner / July 27, 1954 / Mercury 834 909*

8   *Contrasts / July 27, 1954 / Emarcy 314 558 077*

8   *Solitaire / Mar. 14, 1955 / Mercury 314 518 279*

8   *Afternoon of an Elf / Mar. 14, 1955 / Emarcy 826 457*

10   *Concert by the Sea / Sept. 19, 1955 / Columbia 40859*

8   *Dancing on the Ceiling / June 1, 1961–Aug. 19, 1965 / Emarcy 834 935*

8   *Easy to Love / July 14, 1961–Aug. 19, 1965 / Emarcy 832 994*

Erroll Garner recorded prolifically for Mercury (and its subsidiary Emarcy) during 1954–55 before switching back to Columbia. Mercury/Emarcy has wisely reissued pretty much all of its Garner recordings on CD, including five discs of music that were not out at all until released as "The Erroll Garner Collection": *Too Marvelous for Words*, the double *Solo Time!*, *Dancing on the Ceiling*, and *Easy to Love*. The pianist was so consistent that he never seems to have played an uninspired chorus; one can always tell that he just loved playing. On May 26, 1954, Garner sat down at the piano and performed 24 selections, one after the other, with no second takes. Fourteen are on *Too Marvelous for Words*, and nearly all of the song titles contain either women's names (including "Margie," "Louise," and "Dinah") or places ("Idaho," "Stars Fell on Alabama," and "California, Here I Come"). On July 7 of that year Garner topped himself, recording 35 songs in three hours! Twenty-four are on the double-CD *Solo Time,* including such numbers as "It Might As Well Be Spring," "In a Little Spanish Town," "Slow Boat to China," "Cottage for Sale," and "Coquette." *Mambo Moves Garner* has 11 tunes (including two added to the original program for the reissue), with Garner joined by bassist Wyatt Ruther, drummer Eugene Heard, and Candido on conga. The pianist loved Latin rhythms, and he clearly enjoyed playing off Candido's ideas on tunes such as "Mambo Garner," "Mambo Blues," "Mambo Nights," and "Cherokee."

Contrasts (which has Garner joined again by Ruther and Heard plus Candido on one number) is most notable for including the original version of "Misty" plus "You Are My Sunshine," "My Heart Sings," and "I've Got to Be a Rugcutter." *Solitaire* and *Afternoon of an Elf* are equally rewarding solo programs recorded the same day by Garner, who is typically spontaneous, witty, and swinging throughout. *Afternoon of an Elf* includes "Don't Be That Way," "A Smooth One," and "Is You Is or Is You Ain't My Baby?" among its highlights, while *Solitaire* has a 10½-minute version of "Over the Rainbow," "I'll Never Smile Again," and "When a Gypsy Makes His Violin Cry."

Concert by the Sea is Erroll Garner's most famous album, a live set recorded by Will Thornbury and released by Columbia upon the pianist's return to the label. Garner (joined by bassist Eddie Calhoun and Denzil Best) was even more inspired than usual. Everything works during this definitive and well-rounded program, including "I'll Remember April," "It's All Right with Me," "Red Top," and "Where or When." Moving to the 1960s, *Dancing on the Ceiling* is mostly from 1961, and Garner (with Eddie Calhoun and drummer Kelly Martin) uplifts such standards as "It Had to Be You," "Crazy Rhythm," "There Will Never Be Another You," and "Ain't Misbehavin'." *Easy to Love* has the same unit reinvigorating veteran tunes, including "Somebody Stole My Gal," "My Blue Heaven," and even "As Time Goes By"; once again the music is mostly from 1961 plus, in this case, three performances from 1964–65.

* **Erroll Garner / Dec. 18, 1959–Oct. 30, 1973 / Telarc Archive 83475**

9 **Dreamstreet & One World Concert / Dec. 18, 1959– Aug. 25, 1962 / Telarc 83350**

8 **Close-up in Swing & A New Kind of Love / July 7, 1961–July 1963 / Telarc 83383**

7 **Campus Concert & Feeling Is Believing / Mar. 13, 1962–Dec. 2, 1969 / Telarc 83390**

7 **Now Playing: A Night at the Movies & Up in Erroll's Room / July 24, 1964 + Mar. 19, 1968 / Telarc 83378**

7 **That's My Kick & Gemini / Apr. 1966–Dec. 2, 1971 / Telarchive 83332**

8 **Magician/Gershwin and Kern / Aug. 5, 1964–Oct. 30, 1973 / Telarchive 83337**

Under the direction of his manager, Martha Glaser, the Telarc label has been reissuing many Erroll Garner records in recent times, with each CD containing two former LPs. The box *Erroll Garner* simply packages together the six Telarc (or Telarchive) releases, containing all dozen albums, a convenient way to acquire this music. The only fault to this reissue series is that the recording dates are not included (kind of an odd omission). But taken as a whole, Telarc has now reissued the majority of Garner's authorized recordings of 1959–73, the last work of his career. *Dreamstreet,* a 1959 trio set with Eddie Calhoun and Kelly Martin, consists of six swing-era standards plus the pianist's "Dreamstreet" and "Mambo Gotham." The *One World Concert* half of the CD is a solo recital recorded live at the 1963 Seattle World's Fair that includes a medley from "Oklahoma," "Mack the Knife," and "The Way You Look Tonight" plus a pair of brief encores. *Close-up in Swing* has another outing by the Calhoun–Martin trio (including "My Silent Love," "St. Louis Blues," and "The Best Things in Life Are Free"). *A New Kind of Love* is a bit unusual, for Garner is heard with a big band conducted by Leith Stevens, performing his score (which mixes together originals and standards) for the Paul Newman film of the same name. *Campus Concert* (with Calhoun and Martin) has Garner playing some of his favorite standards (including "Indiana," "Almost Like Being in Love," and "Lulu's Back in Town") plus his "Mambo Erroll." *Feeling Is Believing* finds Garner doing his best to uplift five then-current pop tunes (including "For Once in My Life," "Strangers in the Night," and "The Look of Love"), although his five originals are on a much higher level.

A Night at the Movies has Garner (with bassist Ike Isaacs, drummer Jimmie Smith, and percussionist Jose Mangual) performing a dozen songs that found their birth in movies. These renditions are surprisingly brief, most clocking in between two and three minutes apiece. *Up in Erroll's Room* finds the Garner-Calhoun-Martin trio joined by a seven-piece horn section arranged by Don Sebesky for a diverse set of standards (ranging from "A Lot of Living to Do" and "The Girl from Ipanema" to "Groovin' High" and "Watermelon Man") plus the pianist's title cut. *That's My Kick* has Garner assisted by an expanded rhythm section in 1966 for six originals (including "Nervous Waltz") and five standards, while *Gemini* (from 1971) features the Garner quartet (with bassist Ernest McCarty, Jimmie Smith, and Jose Mangual on conga) swinging on everything from "Tea for Two" and "How High the Moon" to George Harrison's "Something." *Gershwin and Kern* is a trio set that obviously contains superior material (highlighted by "Strike Up the Band," "A Foggy Day," "Can't Help Lovin' That Man," and "Ol' Man River"), while *Magician,* Garner's final recording, has the pianist, bassist Bob Cranshaw, drummer Grady Tate, and Jose Mangual introducing four Garner originals plus fresh renditions of four vintage songs and "Close to You."

Suffice it to say, there is no shortage of worthy Erroll Garner records!

LPS TO SEARCH FOR

Play, Piano Play (Spotlite 129) has all of Erroll Garner's recordings for the Dial label in 1947, including "Fantasy on Frankie & Johnny," "Pastel," and "Trio." Obscurities from 1949–50 are on *The Greatest Garner* (Atlantic 1227) and *Garnering* (Emarcy 36026). Other than the CDs *Long Ago and Far Away* and *Body and Soul,* few of Garner's Columbia recordings of 1950–54 have been reissued in recent times. Garner fans will want to pick up the two-LP *Play It Again, Erroll!* (Columbia 33424), *Erroll Garner* (Columbia 535), *Gone Garner Gonest* (Columbia 617), and *Plays for Dancing* (Columbia 667); someone should alert the label as to the treasures in their vaults! And, other than *Concert by the Sea,* later Columbia gems have been neglected too, including *The Most Happy Piano* (Columbia 939), the orchestral *Other Voices* (Columbia 9820), 1957's *Soliloquy* (Columbia 1060), and the two-LP *Paris Impressions* (Columbia 5100), which can also be found as two individual albums.

FILMS

Erroll Garner pops up briefly in the West German movie *My Bed Is Not for Sleeping* (1967). He wrote the score for *A New Kind of Love* (1963), and his piano playing can be heard throughout the soundtrack.

AL HAIG

b. July 22, 1924, Newark, NJ, d. Nov. 16, 1982, New York, NY

One of the first great Bop pianists, Al Haig made a strong impression in the 1940s, went through a long period of neglect, and was rediscovered during his final decade. Haig had opportunities to play music while in the Coast Guard (1942–44) and then worked around Boston and had a short stint with Jerry Wald's orchestra. He caught on quickly to Bud Powell's innovations and by 1945 was a strong enough player to work with Dizzy Gillespie. Haig was with Dizzy on and off during 1945–46 (including traveling to Los Angeles with Bird and Diz) and also worked with Charlie Barnet, Jimmy Dorsey, Ben Webster, Fats Navarro, Eddie "Lockjaw" Davis, and Coleman Hawkins, among others. He replaced Duke Jordan in the Charlie Parker Quintet (1948–50) and also played often with Stan Getz during 1949–51. Haig appeared on many records during the classic Bebop era (including with Parker and Gillespie) and led sessions of his own during 1948–50.

But then Al Haig slipped away from the spotlight. He was mostly out of music during 1951–54. Haig recorded a few sessions in 1954, but otherwise led only one album (in 1965) until 1974. He was with Chet Baker in 1954 and for a short time played with Dizzy Gillespie's big band (1956–57) but worked mostly as a single in obscurity on the East Coast and was largely forgotten. Haig's fortunes began to change in 1973, when he was noticed again and rightfully recognized as a Bebop giant; his style had not changed much through the years. Al Haig made several visits overseas and appeared on record often during his final nine years, keeping the legacy of Bebop piano alive into the 1980s.

8   *Jazz Will o' the Wisp / Mar. 13, 1954 / Fresh Sound 38*
8   *Al Haig Trio / Mar. 13, 1954 / Fresh Sound 45*
8   *Al Haig Quartet / Sept. 1954 / Fresh Sound 12*

Al Haig recorded as a leader as early as 1948, including titles that have been reissued on LPs by Spotlite, Dawn, Misterioso, and Xanadu. Other than a 1965 album, the music featured on three Fresh Sound CDs were the pianist's only opportunities to lead his own sessions during 1953–73. The trio of discs from 1954 are equally rewarding, with the first two matching Haig with bassist Bill Crow and drummer Lee Abrams, while the quartet date has guitarist Benny Weeks, bassist Teddy Kotick, and drummer Phil Brown giving the pianist support. Sticking to standards (including several from the Bebop era), Haig shows that there was no logical reason for his neglect during this era. Certainly his playing was still full of fire and creativity. Unfortunately nearly all of his later recordings (he recorded for Spotlite, Choice, East Wind, Sea Breeze, Musica, and Interplay during 1974–82) have yet to be reissued on CD.

LPS TO SEARCH FOR

Al Haig Meets the Master Saxes Vols. One-Three (Spotlite 139, 140, and 143) mostly brings together the pianist's live sideman recordings of the 1940s, and each album has its rewarding moments. *Volume One* features Haig on dates led by tenors John Hardee, Coleman Hawkins, and Wardell Gray plus one song featuring singer Buddy Stewart and two numbers from a date that Haig led in late 1948. *Volume Two* has collaborations with Stan Getz, Buddy Stewart, and Allen Eager in addition to two selections with the team of Stewart and Dave Lambert. *Volume Three* has further titles with Getz, a 1948 quartet set led by Haig (with singer Terry Swope), and dates with Kai Winding and Herbie Steward. *Live in Hollywood* (Xanadu 206) is a loose jam session from 1952 with Chet Baker and sometimes Ted Ottison on trumpets, Sonny Criss, Jack Montrose on tenor, bassist Dave Bryant, and drummer Larry Bunker that consists of seven familiar standards. Les Thompson sits in on harmonica during "Avalon." Moving to Haig's later years, 1974's *Special Brew* (Spotlite 8) is a meeting with guitarist Jimmy Raney in a quartet that is hurt a little by Haig's playing electric piano on half of the eight tunes. *Manhattan Memories* (Sea Breeze 1008), from 1977, is purely acoustic, with Haig in a trio/ quartet, showing on Bud Powell's "I'll Keep Loving You" and Cedar Walton's "Voices Within Me" that he had not lost a thing through the years. *Plays the Music of Jerome Kern* (Inner City 1073) has four piano solos, four duets with Jamil Nasser, and a vocal by Helen Merrill on "They Didn't Believe Me." Another successful "theme" album is *Expressly Ellington* (Spotlite 20), which in 1978 matched Haig and Nasser in London with tenor saxophonist Art Themen and drummer Tony Mann. All eight of the songs (except "Body and Soul") were associated with Duke Ellington even though he actually only composed four of them. Al Haig's final recording, *Bebop Lives* (Spotlite 23), is a jam session on six standards (including "Bags' Groove," "A Night in Tunisia," and "Birks' Works") with Themen, altoist Peter King,

bassist Kenny Baldock, and drummer Allan Ganley that was cut when Haig (in excellent form) was still only 57.

SADIK HAKIM (Argonne Thornton)

b. July 15, 1921, Duluth, MN, d. June 20, 1983, New York, NY

During the Bebop era, Sadik Hakim had one of the oddest piano styles of all, full of eccentric and jagged lines that were quite personal. Born Argonne Thornton (he changed his name to Sadik Hakim after converting to Islam in 1947), he was self-taught on piano. Among his early jobs was working with Fats Dudley (1940) and Jesse Miller. Hakim was with Ben Webster (who enjoyed his style) during 1944–46 and played piano on part of Charlie Parker's famous "Ko Ko" session in 1945. Hakim, who also recorded with Dexter Gordon, was a member of Lester Young's band during 1946–48 and gigged with Slam Stewart and trumpeter Louis Metcalf (in Canada).

By the 1950s, Hakim's style had become more conventional and smoother. He spent periods with James Moody's combo (1951–54) and Buddy Tate's orchestra (1956–59), freelancing in the 1960s and playing briefly with Sonny Rollins in 1964. In later years (1973–80), Sadik Hakim recorded fairly steadily, visited Europe several times, and toured Japan during 1979–80.

8 *Lazy Bird / Apr. 4, 1980 / Storyville 4156*
Other than a half-album for the Charlie Parker label in 1962, all of Sadik Hakim's recordings as a leader were made for Canadian, European, and Japanese labels, including CBC, Progressive, and Steeplechase. This European release, his final recording, was originally cut for the Japanese Full House label before being reissued by Storyville. Hakim, with the assistance of bassist Errol Waters and drummer Clifford Barbaro, performs two originals ("48th Street" and "I'd Ling") plus seven standards, mostly from the Bebop era. His renditions of "Now's the Time," "Yardbird Suite," and "My Little Suede Shoes," although not as eccentric as his earlier work, are still fairly distinctive.

LPS TO SEARCH FOR

Sadik Plays Ellington Plus Hakim (Can-Am 1800), dating from 1974, features the pianist with obscure but reasonably talented players in a sextet. Hakim performs five familiar Duke Ellington-associated tunes (including "Things Ain't What They Used to Be" and "Cotton Tail") plus his own "Ging Gang Gong Song."

CLYDE HART

b. 1910, Baltimore, MD, d. Mar. 19, 1945, New York, NY

Clyde Hart's early death cut short a very promising career. An important transitional pianist who comped with his left hand like a Bebopper but still played essentially advanced swing piano, Hart was on many recording dates during his final year. His early jobs included associations with Gene Coy (1929), Jap Allen (1930–31), Blanche Calloway (1931–35), and the declining McKinney's Cotton Pickers (1935). He contributed arrangements to Andy Kirk's orchestra, was part of Stuff Smith's popular band with Jonah Jones (1936–38), and had stints with Lucky Millinder, Roy Eldridge, Lester Young, Frankie Newton, John Kirby's Sextet (1942), Oscar Pettiford, Wilbur DeParis, and Tiny Grimes (1944). Hart was in the process of converting his style from swing to Bop during 1944, as can be heard in his work with Don Byas.

The pianist's playing is heard on quite a few recordings late in his life, including three sessions that he led during 1944–45 (his sidemen included Budd Johnson, singer Rubberlegs Williams, trombonist Trummy Young, and Bird and Diz), plus dates with Coleman Hawkins, Ben Webster, Don Byas, Lester Young, and the February 28, 1945, session with Dizzy Gillespie and Charlie Parker that resulted in "Groovin' High" and "Dizzy Atmosphere." But tuberculosis struck and Clyde Hart died just 19 days later, ending what would probably have been a very significant career.

HANK JONES

b. July 31, 1918, Vicksburg, MS

The oldest of the three famous Jones brothers (which included cornetist-arranger Thad and drummer Elvin), Hank Jones has long had a flexible style (influenced by Art Tatum and Teddy Wilson) that ranges from swing to Bop and Hard Bop. He was the first in a series of notable pianists to emerge from Detroit; the string would also include Tommy Flanagan, Barry Harris, and Roland Hanna, among others. Jones has had such a long career that it is surprising to note that he was already in his mid-20s before he left his hometown. He

had been playing professionally since he was 13, often in territory bands. After joining Hot Lips Page in New York in 1944, Jones was soon gigging with many top musicians, including John Kirby, Howard McGhee, and Coleman Hawkins, and the big bands of Andy Kirk and Billy Eckstine. Jones appeared at Jazz at the Philharmonic concerts starting in 1947 (he was Oscar Peterson's predecessor), and he was Ella Fitzgerald's accompanist during 1948–53. Throughout the 1950s, Jones played with the who's who of jazz, including recording with Charlie Parker, Lester Young, Artie Shaw (he was in the clarinetist's Gramercy Five), Billie Holiday, Benny Goodman (1956–58), and Cannonball Adderley, among countless others.

Jones was on the staff of CBS for a long time (1959–76) but continued playing jazz in his unchanged style, usually leading a trio and also as part of the Thad Jones–Mel Lewis Orchestra in 1966. In the late 1970s he played piano in the Broadway musical *Ain't Misbehavin'* (which led him to add some Fats Waller songs to his regular repertoire), and for a time Jones led an all-star group dubbed the Great Jazz Trio. Jones, who has recorded prolifically as a leader since 1947 and remains a flawless and tasteful pianist, has been quite active up to the present time, adding class and dignity to every session in which he appears. His solos are so consistently logical and flawless that he can be accurately dubbed the Teddy Wilson of Bop!

8   *Urbanity / Sept. 1947 + Sept. 4, 1953 / Verve 314 537 749*

7   *Bluebird / Nov. 11, 1955–Dec. 20, 1955 / Savoy 1193*

6   *Hank / Jan. 24, 1976 / All Art Jazz 11003*

9   *Master Class / Jan. 18, 1977–Jan. 25, 1978 / 32 Jazz 32022*

Hank Jones's first dates as a leader are included on *Urbanity*. The six piano solos from 1947 and four trio numbers (with guitarist Johnny Smith and Ray Brown) from 1953 are augmented by multiple alternate takes of "Thad's Pad" and "Things Are So Pretty in the Spring" from the later date. Although his roots are clearly in swing (as is much of the repertoire), Jones's solos are quite Boppish. The pianist recorded five albums' worth of material for Savoy during 1955–56, but little has thus far appeared on CD. *Bluebird*, a 1989 disc, features Jones in many settings, ranging from a trio to a quintet and with appearances by Kenny Clarke, flutist Herbie Mann, trumpeters Joe Wilder and Donald Byrd, and Jerome Richardson on tenor and flute, among others.

Although Hank Jones also recorded for Epic (1956), Golden Crest, Capitol, Argo, ABC-Paramount, and Impulse, very few of his recordings prior to 1976 have been reissued on CD yet. *Hank,* from the Concord subsidiary All Art Jazz, is a relaxed solo piano date cut in Tokyo (where Jones has made many records). His versions of 14 standards are melodic and lightly swinging if somewhat predictable; the seven Duke Ellington songs that open up this recital have all been done to death! In contrast, *Master Class* combines all of the music from two of Jones's finest dates of the 1970s, the former LPs *Bop Redux* and *Groovin' High.* The former, a trio outing with bassist George Duvivier and drummer Ben Riley, has four songs apiece composed by Charlie Parker and Thelonious Monk, including "Yardbird Suite," "Relaxin' with Lee," "Bloomdido," and "'Round Midnight." *Groovin' High* is more of a jam session with cornetist Thad Jones, tenor saxophonist Charlie Rouse, bassist Sam Jones, and drummer Mickey Roker. Thad's abilities as an arranger are utilized here, with different combinations of musicians being used on some of the songs (which were composed by Charlie Parker, Dizzy Gillespie, Miles Davis, and Monk); four have the full quintet, but two are by the trio, and "Groovin' High" has an unusual cornet-piano-drums trio. Highly recommended.

- **7** *Just for Fun / June 27-28, 1977 / Original Jazz Classics 471*
- **6** *Tiptoe Tapdance / June 29, 1977-Jan. 21, 1978 / Original Jazz Classics 719*
- **6** *Rockin' in Rhythm / 1977 / Concord Jazz 4032*
- **7** *Ain't Misbehavin' / Aug. 5-6, 1978 / Original Jazz Classics 1027*
- **8** *In Japan / Mar. 2, 1979 / All Art Jazz 11001*
- **5** *Moods Unlimited / Oct. 28 + 30, 1982 / Evidence 22072*

Just for Fun mostly features Hank Jones in a trio with Ray Brown and Shelly Manne; guitarist Howard Roberts helps out on three of the seven selections. This set has compositions by Jones, Brown, Thad Jones, Pepper Adams, Sara Cassey, and J. J. Johnson, none of which caught on and became standards. The playing, however, is typically excellent. *Tiptoe Tapdance* is a mellow solo piano set with the emphasis on thoughtful ballads, including three songs that are religious themes plus "Emily," "I'll Be Around," and "Memories of You." *Rockin' in Rhythm* finds Jones alternating between acoustic and electric pianos, sounding reasonably fluent on the latter even if his personality is not as strong.

Highlights include "My Ship," the title cut, "Bags' Groove," and the Fats Waller-associated "Your Feet's Too Big" (done in a rare instrumental version). Because Jones was the pianist for the Broadway show *Ain't Misbehavin',* he was inspired to record a full set of Fats Waller tunes for an album of the same name. Joined by bassist Richard Davis, Roy Haynes, and (on three of the six numbers) trumpeter Bob Ojeda, Teddy Edwards, and guitarist Kenny Burrell, Jones brings back to life some of Waller's joy, even if his own swing-to-bop style does not sounds like Fats. Among the numbers explored are "Mean to Me," "Honeysuckle Rose," and "The Joint Is Jumpin'."

In Japan is a particularly strong trio outing by Jones, bassist George Duvivier, and Shelly Manne. The live set, in addition to a Duvivier blues, finds the trio digging into a lot of strong standards and ballads, including "Cotton Tail," "Crazy Rhythm," and "Yardbird Suite"; Jones sounds inspired throughout this date. In contrast, *Moods Unlimited* does not live up to its potential. Jones and bassist Red Mitchell are joined by saxophonist Bill Evans (heard on tenor and soprano), who at the time was best known for having played with Miles Davis. Evans has rarely been heard in a straight-ahead setting, and the trio performs five veteran standards, but unfortunately the tempos tend to be slow, the playing is lazy, and no real sparks fly. Overall, the moods are just too limited on this date!

- **9** *The Oracle / Mar. 1989 / Emarcy 846 376*
- **8** *Lazy Afternoon / July 1989 / Concord Jazz 4391*
- **8** *With the Meridian String Quartet / Nov. 15-16, 1990 / Laserlight 17 122*
- **8** *With Mads Vinding & Al Foster / Mar. 19, 1991 / Storyville 4180*
- **7** *Flowers for Lady Day / Sept. 24-25, 1991 / Evidence 21240*
- **9** *Live at Maybeck Recital Hall, Vol. 16 / Nov. 11, 1991 / Concord Jazz 4502*
- **7** *Handful of Keys / Apr. 28-29, 1992 / Verve 314 514 216*

In the 1980s and '90s Hank Jones recorded extensively for Japanese labels and less often for American companies. *The Oracle* was cut for Japanese Emarcy but made available domestically by its American counterpart. On this trio outing with bassist Dave Holland and drummer Billy Higgins, Hank Jones sounds surprisingly modern, closer to McCoy Tyner than to Bud Powell. He seems quite inspired by his sidemen and the material, which includes three originals by

Dave Holland and superior obscurities in addition to "Beautiful Love," "Yesterdays," and "Blood Count." On *Lazy Afternoon,* Jones is joined again by Holland plus drummer Keith Copeland and (on half of the songs) Ken Peplowski, who plays mostly alto, with just a touch of clarinet. The repertoire is a little more conventional (including "Work Song," "Speak Low," and "Comin' Home, Baby") but does include four fine Jones originals and his effective use of celeste on "Lazy Afternoon."

The Laserlight CD (which is available at a budget price) does not give the recording dates, but it does contain some exquisite music as Jones, bassist Rufus Reid, and drummer Dennis Mackrel are joined by a string quartet on ten standards. The emphasis is on ballads, but Jones does not coast and the results are quite enjoyable and full of subtle surprises. The set with bassist Mads Vinding and drummer Al Foster features jazz originals that caught on, including "Pent Up House," "Midnight Sun," "Bemsha Swing," and "Four." The 72-year-old pianist shows plenty of spirit as he stretches himself and consistently comes up with fresh ideas. Jones, bassist George Mraz, and Roy Haynes perform an excellent tribute to Billie Holiday on *Flowers for Lady Day,* even if not all of the ten songs (including "Sometimes I'm Happy," "Baby Won't You Please Come Home," and Jones's own "Time Warp") are actually associated with the singer. Although Hank Jones tends to sound best in trios, his unaccompanied solo concert at Maybeck Recital Hall in 1991 exceeded expectations. His background in swing came in handy, for he strides lightly in spots, and listeners will not miss the bass and drums. Among the high points of this excellent set are "I Guess I'll Have to Change My Plans," "Bluesette," "A Child Is Born," "Blue Monk," and "Oh, Look at Me Now." Jones, who can sound comfortable in modern settings (he shared the bandstand in 1999 with the fiery altoist Kenny Garrett), returns to Fats Waller on *Handful of Keys.* He performs ten Waller compositions, three other songs that Fats recorded, plus three additional tunes from the era. Although Hank Jones is really a more modern player, he sounds quite happy to be playing this joyous vintage material, doing a fine job striding lightly on such tunes as "Handful of Keys," "Honeysuckle Rose," "I've Got a Feeling I'm Falling," and "Believe It, Beloved."

LPS TO SEARCH FOR

A pair of Savoy records from the 1950s contain material not yet reissued: *Solo Piano* (Savoy 1124) and *Relaxin' at Camarillo* (Savoy 1138), the latter a quartet date from 1956 with

Bobby Jaspar on flute. In the 1970s, Jones frequently worked with combos under the title of "The Great Jazz Trio." *Love for Sale* (Inner City 6003) matches him with bassist Buster Williams and drummer Tony Williams, while three albums utilize bassist Ron Carter and Williams: *The Great Jazz Trio at the Village Vanguard* (Inner City 6013), *Kindness, Joy, Love & Happiness* (Inner City 6023), and *Milestones* (Inner City 6030).

DUKE JORDAN
b. Apr. 1, 1922, New York, NY

A classic Bebop pianist whose gentle yet swinging style is still largely unchanged, Duke Jordan remains best known for being a member of the 1947 Charlie Parker Quintet. He studied classical music from the time he was eight. His early experiences included associations with Coleman Hawkins, the Savoy Sultans, and the 1946 Roy Eldridge big band. While with Bird, Jordan became particularly renowned for his introductions to songs, especially "Embraceable You." His smooth and logical yet explorative Bop solos perfectly fit the group's music.

After leaving Parker in 1948 (he would rejoin him occasionally during the next two years), Jordan worked with Stan Getz (1949), the Sonny Stitt-Gene Ammons band (1950–51), and then Getz again (1952–53). He made his recording debut as a leader in 1954, introducing his most famous composition, "Jordu." Although never garnering many headlines, Jordan worked fairly steadily in the 1950s and '60s (other than the 1967–71 period, which he largely spent outside of music); he was married for a time to singer Sheila Jordan and in 1959 wrote most of the soundtrack for the French film *Les Liaisons Dangéreuses.* Duke Jordan began recording regularly for the Steeplechase label in 1973 (very extensively in the late '70s) and has made quite a few records for the label since moving in 1978 to Denmark, where he remained active throughout the 1980s and '90s.

8 *Duke Jordan/Bud Powell—New York—Paris / Jan. 28, 1954 + Oct. 14, 1960 / RCA/Vogue 45727*

9 *Flight to Jordan / Aug. 4, 1960 / Blue Note 46824*

The Vogue CD has Duke Jordan's first session as a leader, a trio date with bassist Gene Ramey and drummer Lee Abrams that consists of eight songs plus three alternate takes. Among the standards is a remake of "Embraceable You," while Jordan's three originals include "Minor Escamp," which would soon be renamed "Jordu." This excellent CD is rounded off by four selections from "The Three Bosses," a 1960 trio comprised of Bud Powell, bassist Pierre Michelot, and Kenny Clarke. The best-known Duke Jordan set, and his only one as a leader for Blue Note, is *Flight to Jordan*. For this project, he performs six of his originals in a quintet with trumpeter Dizzy Reece, tenor saxophonist Stanley Turrentine, bassist Reggie Workman, and drummer Art Taylor. None of the originals became a standard like "Jordu," but the songs offer viable chord changes and worthwhile themes; several are worth reviving. The CD reissue adds a seventh original plus a trio rendition of "I Should Care" to the program.

8   *Flight to Denmark / Nov. 25, 1973 / Steeplechase 31011*
8   *Duke's Delight / Nov. 18, 1975 / Steeplechase 31046*
8   *Tivoli One / Nov. 16–17, 1978 / Steeplechase 31189*
8   *Tivoli Two / Nov. 16–17, 1978 / Steeplechase 31193*
8   *Wait and See / Nov. 16–17, 1978 / Steeplechase 31211*
7   *One for the Library / Oct. 6, 1993 / Storyville 4194*

Other than an album and a half for the Charlie Parker label in 1962, Duke Jordan did not record as a leader again after his Blue Note album until 1973, when he cut a set for Spotlite and began a long-term association with Steeplechase. He cut many albums for Steeplechase (at least 32), starting with *Flight to Denmark,* a trio outing with bassist Mads Vinding and Ed Thigpen. The six originals (highlighted by "No Problem," the title cut, and "Jordu") are joined by four standards, including "How Deep Is the Ocean." Most of Jordan's Steeplechase dates are trios or unaccompanied solos. *Duke's Delight* was an exception, a quintet outing with trumpeter Richard Williams (an underrated but very talented player), tenor saxophonist Charlie Rouse, bassist Sam Jones, and drummer Al Foster. Jordan and his sidemen perform his originals and he takes Duke Ellington's "Solitude" as a solo piano feature.

The music on *Tivoli One, Tivoli Two,* and *Wait and See* was recorded during two nights at the Tivoli Gardens in Copenhagen, and it is pretty typical of Jordan's Steeplechase output. Assisted by bassist Wilbur Little and drummer Dannie Richmond, Jordan plays essentially classic Bebop. His style had not changed much at all during the previous 30 years and he was so consistent that his many Steeplechase recordings are mostly all of equal quality and value. *Tivoli One* includes "Embraceable You," "Four," and "I Remember April," *Tivoli Two* is highlighted by "No Problem," "How Deep Is the Ocean," and a lengthy "A Night in Tuni-

sia," and *Wait and See* contains several Jordan originals plus "Misty" and "Out of Nowhere."

One for the Library, Duke Jordan's most recent recording to date, is a set of unaccompanied piano solos cut in Copenhagen. Jordan performs six of his best-known originals (including "No Problem," "Flight to Jordan," and "Jordu") plus a dozen of his favorite standards, most from the swing era. Although he plays well and strides lightly in spots, it is obvious that Duke Jordan is best heard in a trio format. Still, this relaxed outing has its strong moments.

LPS TO SEARCH FOR

East and West of Jazz (Charlie Parker 805) from 1962 has a quintet date by Jordan (with Cecil Payne and trumpeter Johnny Coles) and a particularly rare quartet outing from Sadik Hakim (featuring five of his originals). Both halves of this LP work quite well. *The Murray Hill Caper* (Spotlite 5) includes eight Duke Jordan originals and Cole Porter's "Night and Day" played by a trio (with bassist Lloyd Buchanon and drummer Brian Brake) or a notable quartet that includes Cecil Payne, bassist David Williams, and drummer Al Foster.

LOU LEVY
b. Mar. 5, 1928, Chicago, IL

A classic Bebop pianist who has long been closely associated with the West Coast jazz scene, Lou Levy has worked with virtually every important jazz musician in the Los Angeles area through the decades. He began playing piano when he was 12 and started playing major jobs seven years later. Levy worked with Georgie Auld (1947), Sarah Vaughan, Chubby Jackson (1947–48, including a tour of Scandinavia), the Boyd Raeburn Orchestra, Woody Herman's Second Herd (1949–50), Tommy Dorsey's orchestra, and Flip Phillips. He had a day job during 1952–54 (working as an advertising salesman in Minneapolis) and then returned to the scene, gaining a strong reputation as a sympathetic accompanist to singers. Levy had a longtime association with Peggy Lee (starting in 1955) and toured with Ella Fitzgerald (1957–62), June Christy, Anita O'Day, Nancy Wilson, Lena Horne, Tony Bennett, and Frank Sinatra (1986). Levy has also played (and in most cases recorded) with Stan Getz, Shorty Rogers, Conte Candoli, Terry Gibbs, Benny Goodman, Supersax, Bud Shank, Al Cohn, and Herb Geller, among many others. In more recent times, Lou Levy has worked closely with singer Pinky Winters and appeared at several major

West Coast jazz festivals, still playing in prime form as the 20th century ended.

Lou Levy's earlier recordings as a leader, for Nocturne (1954), RCA (1956–57), Jubilee (1958), Philips (1962), Interplay (1977), Dobre (1978), and Jazzizz (1982), are either long out of print or widely available only in Europe. In 1992 Levy had an opportunity to record his first date as a leader in a decade and the result was *Lunarcy*, a superior quartet set with three fellow Angelenos (Pete Christlieb on tenor and alto flute, bassist Eric Von Essen, and drummer Ralph Penland). Christlieb is an underrated giant, Levy sounds inspired, and the repertoire includes a pair of originals by the leader, several standards, Johnny Mandel's "Zoot," and Al Cohn's "Ah Moore." *Ya Know* is a bit unusual, with six of the ten numbers featuring both Eric Von Essen (who plays cello on two other songs) and Pierre Michelot on bass, along with drummer Alvin Queen. Not surprisingly there are a lot of bass solos, but the music (which is highlighted by "This Heart of Mine," "Dancing in the Dark," and "The Hymn" plus a pair of Levy tunes) is enjoyable and swinging. Chances are that both of these Verve CDs will be difficult to find.

LPS TO SEARCH FOR

Of Lou Levy's earlier LPs, *A Most Musical Fellow* (RCA 45136), trios with bassist Max Bennett and drummer Stan Levey from 1956–57, might still be found in used-record stores. Another excellent trio date, *The Kid's Got Ears* (Jazzizz 4002), features Levy in 1982 with bassist John Heard and drummer Shelly Manne performing standards, Al Cohn's "High On You" and a joyous romp on "Ding, Dong the Witch Is Dead."

FILMS

Lou Levy can be seen with Shorty Rogers's quintet in a half-hour television show from 1962 that is available on the video *Jazz Scene USA: Shelly Manne/Shorty Rogers* (Shanachie).

JOHN LEWIS

b. May 3, 1920, La Grange, IL

John Lewis is world famous for having been the musical director of the Modern Jazz Quartet, but some people may forget that the pianist's roots were not in Cool Jazz or Third Stream classical-oriented music but in Bebop. In fact Lewis, who early on was strongly influenced by Bud Powell, is also a brilliant blues player, and his tasteful solos and use of space make him "the Count Basie of Bebop!"

Lewis grew up in New Mexico, started taking piano lessons when he was seven, and attended the University of New Mexico before he was drafted into the Army. After his discharge, he gained notice as the pianist with the Dizzy Gillespie Orchestra (1946–48). He wrote "Toccata for Trumpet" for the band and also arranged several songs, including "Two Bass Hit" and "Emanon." Lewis recorded with Charlie Parker on a few occasions during 1947–48 (including "Parker's Mood") and then became involved in the Cool Jazz movement as pianist and one of the arrangers with Miles Davis's Birth of the Cool Nonet. He showed his versatility by working regularly with Illinois Jacquet (1948–49) and Lester Young (1950–51) and in 1951 recorded with the Milt Jackson Quartet, a unit that also included Ray Brown and Kenny Clarke.

In 1952, with Percy Heath taking Brown's spot, the Modern Jazz Quartet was formed. The legacy of that band and of Lewis's Third Stream projects will be covered in future books, but it was always related to its members' beginnings in Bebop, particularly when they jammed such tunes as "Bags' Groove" and John Lewis's most famous composition, "Django." The MJQ, with Connie Kay succeeding Clarke in 1954, became an institution, combating the negative image of Bebop musicians by dressing well, being reliable, playing concert halls, and sometimes fusing their playing with classical music. John Lewis toured the world with the MJQ during 1952–74 in addition to working on occasional side projects, including film scores (*Odds Against Tomorrow, No Sun in Venice,* and *A Milanese Story*) and some small-group dates.

When Milt Jackson tired of the group and the MJQ broke up in 1974, Lewis worked as an educator and recorded additional dates on his own. The MJQ came back together successfully during 1981–95. But after Connie Kay's death in 1994 and a final tour with Albert "Tootie" Heath on drums, the group permanently disbanded. John Lewis has remained semiactive up to the present time.

8 *Delaunay's Dilemma / Oct. 2, 1987 / Emarcy 834 478*

8 *Evolution / Jan. 12–15, 1999 / Atlantic 83211*

Two Degrees East—Three Degrees West (also known as *The Grand Encounter*) is a "Cool Jazz" classic. Tenor saxophonist Bill Perkins's very mellow tone (which would change in later years) perfectly fit the quintet, which also includes guitarist Jim Hall, Percy Heath, and drummer Chico Hamilton. The title cut and such numbers as "Almost Like Being in Love," "Love Me or Leave Me," and Lewis's trio feature on "I Can't Get Started" are laid-back Cool Jazz at its finest.

Most of Lewis's many Atlantic dates are long overdue to be reissued on CD. One that was briefly back in print was the underrated *The Wonderful World of Jazz*. While three numbers (including a remake of "Two Degrees East—Three Degrees West") features Lewis in a quartet with Jim Hall, George Duvivier, and Connie Kay, "Body and Soul" has a brilliant tenor solo by Paul Gonsalves, while "Afternoon in Paris" has spots for several major horn players, including the explosive altoist Eric Dolphy and Benny Golson on tenor.

Delaunay's Dilemma (also known as *The Garden of Delight*) is an excellent example of John Lewis's more recent playing. This 1987 effort features him in a drumless trio with guitarist Howard Collins and bassist Marc Johnson, often sounding quite playful on six of his originals (including a few blues and "Django"), "Billie's Bounce," and "I'll Remember April."

John Lewis had not recorded as a leader in a while when he recorded *Evolution*. This consistently delightful solo set is a happy surprise. Lewis is heard in a light-hearted mood on "Sweet Georgia Brown" (which he almost turns into a classical piece) and "At the Horse Show." He revisits some of the high points of his career (including "Afternoon in Paris," "Two Degrees East—Three Degrees West," and "Django"), strides lightly, and sounds quite relaxed, as if he were telling his life story through music. John Lewis, 78 at the time, still had plenty of spirited music left to express.

LPS TO SEARCH FOR

The John Lewis Piano (Atlantic 1272), from 1956–57, features the more lyrical side of Lewis's piano playing in duets with Connie Kay and guitarists Barry Galbraith and Jim Hall plus two trio numbers with Kay and Percy Heath. *Improvised Meditations & Excursions* (Atlantic 1313) is a relatively straight-ahead trio set from 1959 (with Connie Kay and either George Duvivier or Percy Heath on bass) while *European Encounter* (Atlantic 90533) is a successful 1962

quartet recording that co-stars veteran violinist Svend Asmussen. Lewis made quite a few recordings during the MJQ's "retirement" years. *P.O.V.* (Columbia 33534) is an unusual but worthwhile sextet outing with flute, violin, and cello. A frequently joyous collaboration with fellow pianist Hank Jones, *An Evening with Two Grand Pianos* (Little David 1079) includes romps on "Stompin' at the Savoy," "Confirmation," and "Billie's Bounce." *Kansas City Breaks* (Finesse 38187), a 1982 outing with flutist Frank Wess, violinist Joe Kennedy, and guitarist Howard Collins in a sextet, has a variety of old and new Lewis originals, including colorful versions of "Django," "Valeria," and "Milano." And a real obscurity is 1982's *Genes of Jazz* (Sounds of Soul 0970), a blues-oriented date released in 1987 that matches Lewis with Ray Brown, guitarist Rodney Jones, and drummer Mickey Roker.

FILMS

John Lewis is seen with Dizzy Gillespie's Orchestra in *Jivin' in Bebop* (1947), which has been released as part of the video *Things to Come* (Vintage Jazz Classics 2006). In addition, Lewis wrote the score and can be heard on the soundtracks (with the Modern Jazz Quartet in the first two films) of *No Sun in Venice* (1957), *Odds Against Tomorrow,* (1959) and *A Milanese Story* (1962).

DODO MARMAROSA
b. Dec. 12, 1925, Pittsburgh, PA

Michael "Dodo" Marmarosa was a brilliant pianist during the Bop era, but, due to weak willpower and mental problems, he did not stick on the jazz scene very long. After gigging locally in Pittsburgh, Marmarosa made very strong impressions playing with the big bands of Gene Krupa (1942–43), Tommy Dorsey (1944), and particularly Charlie Barnet (he takes the piano solo on "Skyliner") and Artie Shaw (including recordings with the Gramercy Five in 1945). After moving to Los Angeles in 1946, Marmarosa became the house pianist for the Atomic label and also recorded with Boyd Raeburn's orchestra, Lester Young, Lucky Thompson, Howard McGhee, Slim Gaillard, Tom Talbert's orchestra, Stan Hasselgard, and Charlie Parker (including "Relaxin' at Camarillo"). His own dates as a leader are among the best Bop piano records of the period. He was part of Artie Shaw's Bebop big band of 1949, although quit after Shaw was compelled to play "Frenesi" one time too many!

After 1950, Marmarosa slipped into obscurity. The

breakup of his marriage and a bad experience in the military caused inner damage. He returned to the scene briefly in Chicago during 1961–62, made a couple of trio dates and a session with Gene Ammons, but then he dropped out again, never to really return. Dodo Marmarosa lives in Pittsburgh, where he reportedly still practices piano but never appears in public.

10 *Up in Dodo's Room* / 1946–Dec. 3, 1947 / *Jazz Classics 6008*
8 *Pittsburgh 1958* / Mar. 1956–1962 / *Uptown 27.44*

With the exception of some radio transcriptions cut in 1946 (released on a Phoenix LP), quartet numbers with Lucky Thompson (put out on an Onyx sampler LP), and four trio tunes for Savoy from 1950, *Up in Dodo's Room* has all of the pianist's early dates as a leader, sides originally cut for Dial. Marmarosa is heard in brilliant form on four unaccompanied piano solos (including the impressionistic "Tone Paintings I" and "Tone Paintings II") and five trio numbers plus six alternate takes from a 1947 set with pioneer jazz cellist Harry Babasin and drummer Jackie Mills. In addition, there are a couple alternate takes from a Howard McGhee date and "Bird Lore" with Charlie Parker. During this period of time, Marmarosa ranked at the top with Bud Powell and Al Haig among Bop pianists, and there is plenty of excitement in these performances.

Marmarosa's later recordings as a leader are a pair of trio sets, an obscure outing for Argo (from 1961), and a set for Prestige the following year. *Pittsburgh 1958* consists of music not released until the 1997 CD, which added to Dodo's rather slim discography. The bulk of the performances are taken from a live date in Pittsburgh with a trio that includes bassist Danny Mastri and drummer Henry Sculler. Marmarosa is also heard on one cut from a concert in 1956 with a trio, on two songs from 1957 with a local quintet, and for three numbers taken from a television show in 1962. In addition Marmarosa was persuaded to say a few brief words about the music after hearing it in 1995, and the liner notes include an in-depth interview with the brilliant, if troubled, pianist.

GEORGE SHEARING

b. Aug. 13, 1919, London, England

Bebop may have separated itself from entertainment, but George Shearing, through his charm, emphasis on strong melodies, roots in classical music, and the catchy sound of his longtime quintet, managed to be remarkably popular for decades. His music, which ranged from Bop to easy listening, caught on with the masses in a way that Bud Powell's never did.

One of the few household names to emerge from the Bebop era, Shearing's professional career began in his native England at the height of the swing era. Born blind, he started playing piano when he was three. Shearing was musically trained at the Linden Lodge School for the blind and was inspired by Teddy Wilson and Fats Waller. He picked up experience playing with Ambrose's orchestra for two years and in 1937 made his recording debut. He began recording as a leader in 1939 (sounding influenced most by Wilson). When violinist Stephane Grappelli spent World War II in London, Shearing was his pianist. Shearing became a star in England, winning seven straight Melody Maker polls and working steadily, occasionally doubling on accordion. As late as 1949 (on "Cherokee," "Four Bars Short," and "Good to the Last Bop"), Shearing recorded on accordion, being one of the first Bop accordionists, although it is not something that he pursued.

In 1947, George Shearing (urged on by lifelong friend Leonard Feather) visited the United States, where he would move permanently two years later. He recorded some trio sides for Savoy, became a member of the Oscar Pettiford Trio, and quickly learned Bebop. In 1949 Shearing, who had mastered the block chord style of Milt Buckner, put together a quintet consisting of his piano, guitar, vibes, bass, and drums. The piano, guitar, and vibes all played the melody in unison, and the result was a very distinctive group sound, one that made Bop accessible to the average listener; they had a quick hit with "September in the Rain." During the next 30 years, the George Shearing Quintet (which was also associated with West Coast jazz even though Shearing lived on the East Coast) would be the pianist's main vehicle, although the group was de-emphasized after 1968. Among Shearing's sidemen through the years were vibraphonists Marjorie Hyams, Don Elliott, Joe Roland, Cal Tjader, Johnny Rae, Emil Richards, and Gary Burton, guitarists Chuck Wayne, Toots Thielemans, Dick Garcia, and Ron Anthony, bassists John Levy and Al McKibbon, and drummer Denzil Best, among others.

In addition to playing his easy-listening version of Bebop and introducing to the jazz world a standard in "Lullaby of Birdland," Shearing helped to popularize Afro-Cuban jazz, regularly featuring guest Armanda Peraza on conga. He also recorded a series of "mood records" that found the quintet augmented by brass, strings, and/or voices and collaborated on albums with Nancy Wilson, Peggy Lee, Nat King Cole, and Wes Montgomery. After leaving the Capitol label in 1968 (his home since 1955), Shearing played less often with his quintet, working more in a trio context, often with bassist Andy Simpkins. He had his own label (Sheba) for a time in the 1970s, and then in 1979 signed with Concord. Since that time, Shearing has recorded many gems, including classic meetings with Mel Torme, solo piano albums, and duet dates with his bassists Brian Torff, Don Thompson, and most recently Neil Swainson. Switching to Telarc in 1992, George Shearing put together a new quintet for a recording and a tour, and has otherwise continued working steadily with Swainson, keeping up a very busy schedule as he entered his eighties.

9 *The London Years / Mar. 2, 1939–Dec. 21, 1943 / Hep 1042*
8 *Jazz Masters 57 / Feb. 17, 1949–Mar. 26, 1954 / Verve 314 529 900*

During 1939–43, George Shearing recorded 31 selections as a leader. Twenty-five are on *The London Years,* which features Shearing as a piano soloist along with two duets with drummer Carlo Krahmer and one number ("Squeezin' the Blues") in which he switches to accordion and is backed by Krahmer and Leonard Feather's piano. It is intriguing to hear Shearing's style prior to the rise of Bebop, bringing together Teddy Wilson, Art Tatum, and Earl Hines as he worked on developing his own voice.

Shearing would record eight selections in London during 1944, make an album's worth of material for Savoy in 1947, cut eight trio sides in 1948, and then move permanently to the United States the following year. It is surprising that most of his popular quintet records (an album for Discovery in 1949 and then a series for MGM during 1949–54) are not easily available; the opposite is true. *Jazz Masters 57* is a single-CD sampler covering that period and is just about the only CD available by the early George Shearing Quintet. The 16 selections jump around chronologically and feature four different versions of the group but do hit some of the high spots, including "September in the Rain," "Lullaby of Birdland," "East of the Sun," "Mambo Inn," "Jumpin' with Symphony Sid," and "I'll Remember April." But since the George Shearing Quintet made 102 recordings for MGM, a much more extensive reissue series is long overdue.

* *The Complete Capitol Live Recordings of George Shearing / Mar. 8, 1958–July 6, 1963 / Mosaic 5-157*
8 *The Swingin's Mutual / June 29, 1960–Jan. 7, 1961 / Capitol 99190*
7 *George Shearing and the Montgomery Brothers / Oct. 9, 1961 / Original Jazz Classics 040*
8 *Jazz Moments / June 20–21, 1962 / Capitol 32085*
7 *My Ship / June 25, 1974 / MPS 821664*

During his Capitol years (1955–68), Shearing recorded extensively with his quintet, which was often augmented on their studio records by orchestras, strings, singers, and/or Latin percussion. The limited-edition five-CD Mosaic box set puts the spotlight on the quintet, with regular "guest" Armanda Peraza on conga appearing on some numbers. The five live performances (two apiece from 1958 and 1963, and one from 1960) not only include the original five records but double in length the two concerts from 1963. The sidemen include vibraphonist Emil Richards, Warren Chiasson, and Gary Burton, guitarists Toots Thielemans (who switches to harmonica on "Caravan"), Dick Garcia, John Gray, and Ron Anthony, bassists Al McKibbon, Wyatt Ruther, Bill Yancey, and Gene Cherico, and drummers Percy Brice, Lawrence Marable, and Vernel Fournier. Shearing sounds in top form throughout, swinging away with his usual charm and showing that he is a strong Bop-based improviser.

The Swingin's Mutual originally split the dozen songs between instrumentals by Shearing's 1960–61 quintet/sextet and vocal features for Nancy Wilson. However, the CD issue has six additional tracks, five of which are instrumentals, so now Wilson sings on only seven of the 17 tracks. On this set and her classic album with Cannonball Adderley, Nancy Wilson proved how strong a jazz singer she could have been if she had stuck to that course. "The Nearness of You" and "The Things We Did Last Summer" are highlights. Shearing's group has fine features on "Evansville," "Blue Lou," and "Lullaby of Birdland"; vibraphonist Warren Chiasson and guitarist Dick Garcia were in the band at the time.

George Shearing and the Montgomery Brothers matches Shearing, drummer Walter Perkins, and Peraza with guitarist Wes, vibraphonist Buddy, and bassist Monk Montgomery. The music is pleasing and the combination works, but many of the selections are overly concise; no one stretches himself much. As with MGM, most of the Capitol recordings by George Shearing's quintet (along with their many augmented sets) are long out of print. *Jazz Moments* is a rare trio date in which Shearing is joined by Ahmad Jamal's former sidemen, bassist Israel Crosby (in his final recording) and drummer Vernel Fournier. Shearing rises to the occasion, particularly on "Makin' Whoopee," "What Is This Thing Called Love," "Symphony," and "It Could Happen to You."

After leaving Capitol, Shearing ran the Sheba label for a time (recording seven albums, none of which have yet appeared on CD). *My Ship* comes from his association with the European MPS label. A solo piano date from 1974, this freewheeling effort has Shearing digging into such unusual songs as "Happy Days Are Here Again," "Londonderry Air," "The Entertainer," and "Send In the Clowns" (which he sings, unfortunately) plus more conventional jazz standards.

10 *Blues Alley Jazz / Oct. 1979 / Concord Jazz 4110*
8 *Two for the Road / June 1980 / Concord Jazz 4128*
9 *On a Clear Day / Aug. 1980 / Concord Jazz 4132*
7 *Alone Together / Mar. 1981 / Concord Jazz 4171*
8 *First Edition / Sept. 1981 / Concord Jazz 4177*
10 *An Evening with George Shearing & Mel Torme / Apr. 15, 1982 / Concord Jazz 4190*
9 *Top Drawer / Mar. 1983 / Concord Jazz 4219*
8 *Live at the Café Carlyle / Jan. 1984 / Concord Jazz 4246*
6 *An Elegant Evening / May 1985 / Concord Jazz 4294*

During 1979–89, George Shearing recorded some of the finest work of his career, making many memorable records for Concord, most of which are currently available on CD. The virtuosic Brian Torff was Shearing's regular bassist through 1982, and they often performed as a duo. *Blues Alley Jazz* is full of intuitive playing, sly wit, and both light and hard swinging. The highlights of this classic duo date include Billy Taylor's "One for the Woofer," "The Masquerade Is Over," a lighthearted "Up the Lazy River," and even Shearing's effective vocal on "This Couldn't Be the Real Thing." *Two for the Road* has Shearing accompanying singer Carmen McRae on an appealing set of ballads, including "Ghost of a Chance," "More Than You Know," and "What Is There to Say," although the date would have benefited from the inclusion of a cooker or two. The Shearing-

Torff duo performs some more magic during *On a Clear Day,* a live set highlighted by a lengthy "Love for Sale," "Have You Met Miss Jones," and their inevitable encore, "Lullaby of Birdland."

Alone Together is a different type of duo as the pianos of Shearing and Marian McPartland prove quite compatible (if not terribly competitive or fiery) on seven sophisticated standards and three originals, including Shearing's "To Bill Evans." Shearing and guitarist Jim Hall also form a tasteful duo for their meeting on *First Edition,* but there are some subtle surprises here on five originals and obscurities plus three standards. Hall's advanced chords are no problem for Shearing, and they consistently inspire each other.

One of the happiest partnerships of the 1980s resulted in the occasional joint concerts of George Shearing and Mel Torme, most of which were issued under Torme's name. *An Evening* is a classic for Torme, Shearing, and Torff (who is featured on "Manhattan Hoe-down") were clearly quite inspired. Their renditions of "All God's Chillun Got Rhythm," "Give Me the Simple Life," "A Nightingale Sang in Berkeley Square," and "Lullaby of Birdland" are quite memorable, with each of the participants stretching himself. By the time Shearing and Torme teamed up for *Top Drawer* a year later, Don Thompson was the pianist's new bassist. No matter, this date is nearly the equal of the previous one, with exciting versions of "Shine on Your Shoes," "Oleo" (one of two instrumentals), "Hi Fly," and the early Bop vocal classic "What's This?" being among the better tracks, not to mention a beautiful rendition of "Stardust"; what a voice Torme had at this point in time!

Live at the Café Carlyle features the Shearing-Thompson duo on such numbers as "Pent Up House," the Charlie Parker blues "Cheryl," and the bassist's "Stratford Stomp." In addition, Thompson switches to second piano on "Tell Me a Bedtime Story," and Shearing takes an expressive "I Cover the Waterfront" as a solo piece. Exquisite music that holds its own with the earlier Shearing-Torff duo. *An Elegant Evening* differs from the other Shearing-Torme collaborations in that this is a duo set without any bassist. The problem is that the music sticks to a slow ballad tempo (with the exception of the closing "You're Driving Me Crazy"), and the mood is sometimes a bit sleepy. However, Torme's occasional long notes are always beautiful, so this set has its moments, particularly during a "Moon Medley" and "I'll Be Seeing You."

6 *Grand Piano / May 1985 / Concord Jazz 4281*

6 *Plays the Music of Cole Porter / Jan. 1986 / Concord Concerto 42010*

7 *More Grand Piano / Oct. 1986 / Concord Jazz 4318*

8 *Breakin' Out / May 1987 / Concord Jazz 4335*

8 *Dexterity / Nov. 1987 / Concord Jazz 4346*

8 *A Perfect Match / May 1988 / Concord Jazz 4357*

8 *The Spirit of 176 / Mar. 1988 / Concord Jazz 4371*

4 *George Shearing in Dixieland / Feb. 1989 / Concord Jazz 4388*

5 *Piano / May 1989 / Concord Jazz 4400*

George Shearing again sticks mostly to ballads on his solo *Grand Piano,* other than on "Nobody Else But Me" and "Easy to Love," singing on his original "Imitations." He even takes "Mack the Knife" and "Taking a Chance on Love" at a slow pace, so *Grand Piano* is mostly introspective. The easy-listening *Plays the Music of Cole Porter* has Shearing sharing the spotlight with the classical French horn player Barry Tuckwell. They are backed by a string section, two bassists, and drummer Grady Tate on five pieces and perform two numbers with a quartet plus four duets. Since Tuckwell hardly improvises, the emphasis is on the melody and Shearing's rhapsodic piano on such numbers as "I Concentrate On You," "I've Got You Under My Skin," "Every Time We Say Goodbye," and "So in Love." *More Grand Piano* is on a higher level than *Grand Piano* due to more variety in Shearing's repertoire and much more tempo variation. He spontaneously picked out ten songs to record as solo piano pieces while he was in the studio, and these include "My Silent Love," "Ramona," "East of the Sun," "Dream," and "People."

Unlike his previous few recordings, on *Breakin' Out,* Shearing plays as if a fire were lit under him. His matchup with Ray Brown and drummer Marvin "Smitty" Smith includes four Duke Ellington songs, Bud Powell's "Hallucinations," Leonard Feather's "Twelve Tone Blues," two other standards, and Shearing's "Break Out the Blues." A surprisingly hard-swinging date. On *Dexterity,* a live set from Tokyo, Shearing performs duets with his new bassist, Neil Swainson, who has continued touring with the pianist to this day. Shearing seems inspired by his sideman and pushes himself on "Dexterity," "Can't We Be Friends," and a fine five-song Duke Ellington medley. In addition, singer Ernestine Anderson fares quite well on "As Long As I Live" and an emotional "Please Send Me Someone to Love." In fact, the combination worked so well that Shearing and An-

derson (along with Swainson and drummer Jeff Hamilton) recorded a full album six months later. Highlights include "Body and Soul" (taken as a vocal-piano duet), "The Best Thing for You" (the lone instrumental), "Falling in Love with Love," "I Won't Dance," and "Some Other Time."

The Spirit of 176 (which has a witty title since 176 is the total number of keys on two pianos!) is a duet set with fellow pianist Hank Jones. Shearing and Jones stay out of each other's way, challenge each other a bit, and perform an inspired repertoire that includes "Oh, Look at Me Now," Thelonious Monk's "I Mean You," Mary Lou Williams's "Lonely Moments," "Confirmation," and an original apiece. In contrast, *George Shearing in Dixieland* falls far short of its potential. Although teamed up with four top mainstream/Dixieland players (cornetist Warren Vache, clarinetist Kenny Davern, Ken Peplowski on tenor, and trombonist George Masso), Shearing wrote out far too many of the ensembles, eliminating most of the potential excitement. Even a Dixiefied "Lullaby of Birdland" has few sparks, and the interesting repertoire (which includes "Truckin'," "Destination Moon," "Take Five," and "Jazz Me Blues") receives consistently dull and cliched treatment. *Piano,* Shearing's third and final solo piano date for Concord (and the last in his long string of Concord recordings) is relaxed, melodic, lyrical, and unexciting. The pianist plays well on such songs as "It Had to Be You," "It's You or No One," "Happiness Is a Thing Called Joe" and quite a few obscurities, but no surprises occur.

9 *I Hear a Rhapsody / Feb. 27–29, 1992 / Telarc 83310*

9 *Walkin' / Feb. 27–29, 1992 / Telarc 83333*

3 *How Beautiful Is Night / Sept. 1992 / Telarc 83325*

8 *The Shearing Sound / Feb. 14–16, 1994 / Telarc 83347*

7 *Paper Moon / Mar. 1–3, 1995 / Telarc 833675*

6 *Favorite Things / Mar. 26–27, 1996 / Telarc 83398*

In 1992, George Shearing switched to the Telarc label, where he continued documenting his brand of accessible Bebop. *I Hear a Rhapsody* and *Walkin',* taken from the same live dates recorded at New York's Blue Note, find the pianist swinging away with Neil Swainson and drummer Grady Tate. The repertoire is fairly fresh, the Boppish numbers often cook, and the ballads are melancholy and emotional. *I Hear a Rhapsody* includes "Bird Feathers," "The Masquerade Is Over," and Bud Powell's "Wail," while *Walkin'* has such Bop-era favorites as "That's Earl, Brother," "Celia," and "Bags' Groove." *How Beautiful Is Night* is reminiscent of Shearing's mood albums of the 1950s, with Robert Farnon's 29-piece string orchestra playing so prettily in spots (check out the waltz treatment of "Lady Be Good") as to be absolutely sickening. The music overall is overblown and way too dramatic. The saving grace of this project is the revival of the Shearing Quintet sound on "Dancing in the Dark," "Put On a Happy Face," and "The Surrey with the Fringe on Top." Better to skip this CD and instead get *The Shearing Sound,* which is a full CD by Shearing's new but short-lived quintet, a unit with Swainson, drummer Dennis Mackrell, vibraphonist Steve Nelson, and guitarist Louis Stewart. The classic arrangements of "East of the Sun," "I'll Never Smile Again," and "Lullaby of Birdland" are brought back, Shearing's band plays his originals "Conception" and "Consternation," and a variety of high-quality standards are performed in vintage fashion.

Paper Moon finds Shearing (with guitarist Stewart and Swainson) paying tribute to Nat King Cole and his famous trio, performing songs usually associated with the pianist-singer. In spots, Shearing closely emulates the older pianist's introductions, but overall he mostly plays in his own relaxed style on tunes such as "Straighten Up and Fly Right," "Sweet Lorraine," "Lost April," and a very impressionistic and moody "Nature Boy." *Favorite Things,* as with most Shearing solo piano albums, is relaxed and introspective in easy-listening fashion, with the tension existing just beneath the surface. Among the tunes are "Angel Eyes," "Taking a Chance On Love," "Moonray" (which has a bit of Artie Shaw's other song "Nightmare" appearing now and then), and a heartfelt vocal on "It Amazes Me." Although not his finest recording, George Shearing (except for his vocal) certainly does not sound 76 during this solo recital. He remains a vital force in jazz.

LPS TO SEARCH FOR

So Rare (Savoy 1117) unfortunately lives up to its name. This historically significant but now-rare LP has Shearing's eight trio sides of 1947 (his first American recordings) plus the debut date (originally cut for Discovery) of his quintet in 1949. Highlights include "Buccaneer's Bounce," "Bop's Your Uncle," "Cozy's Bop" (with drummer Cozy Cole), "Sorry, Wrong Rhumba," "Bebop's Fables," and "Four Bars Short." The two-LP set *Lullaby of Birdland* (Verve 827 977) gives an excellent sampling of Shearing's 1949–54 recordings for MGM. Additional titles from that era are on *An Evening*

with the George Shearing Quintet (MGM 3122), which, despite its title, actually covers a three-year period, and *George Shearing Goes Hollywood* (Lion 70117), which was recorded almost entirely in New York! Among the many Capitol records that have not reappeared yet are *The Shearing Spell* (Capitol 648), the rare solo date *The Shearing Piano* (Capitol 909), a collaboration with singer Dakota Staton called *In the Night* (Capitol 1003), and a series of Latin-oriented records that add percussionists: *Latin Escapade* (Capitol 11454), *Latin Lace* (Capitol 1082), *Latin Affair* (Capitol 1275), and *Mood Latino* (Capitol 1567). *As Requested* (Sheba 105), from 1972, was one of the last recordings by the George Shearing Quintet (which at the time included vibraphonist Charles Shoemake and guitarist Ron Anthony) before he broke it up. Shearing's MPS recordings of 1974–79 include the trio sets *Light, Airy & Swinging* (MPS 21960), *500 Miles High* (MPS 21968), and *Getting in the Swing of Things* (last made available on Pausa 7088); the latter two dates are with guitarist Louis Stewart and bassist Niels Pedersen.

FILMS

George Shearing appears in the little-known British film *Theatre Royal* (1943). His quintet is seen in *Disc Jockey* (1951), *The Big Beat* (1957), and 1959's *Jazz on a Summer's Day* (New Yorker Video 16590). The hour-long video *Lullaby of Birdland* (View Video 1332) features the pianist with Neil Swainson at a live performance in 1991.

GEORGE WALLINGTON

b. Oct. 27, 1924, Palmero, Sicily, Italy, d. Feb. 15, 1993, New York, NY

One of the earliest and finest of the Bop pianists, George Wallington was one of the brightest players on the modern jazz scene of the 1940s and '50s. Born in Sicily (his original name was Giacinto Figilia), Wallington moved with his family to the United States in 1925. He played piano from the age of eight, started working in New York in 1940, and was such an advanced player that he was part of the first Bop group to play on 52nd Street: Dizzy Gillespie's quintet of 1943–44 (which also included Don Byas, Oscar Pettiford, and Max Roach). Wallington spent a year working with clarinetist Joe Marsala's group and then freelanced during 1946–52, playing with many top musicians, including Charlie Parker, Serge Chaloff, Allan Eager, Kai Winding, Terry Gibbs, Brew Moore, Al Cohn, Gerry Mulligan, Zoot Sims, and Red

Rodney, among others. He was part of the Lionel Hampton big band that toured Europe in 1953 and then spent much of 1954–60 leading his own bands in New York. Trumpeter Donald Byrd and altoist Jackie McLean (by 1956, Phil Woods) were part of his quintet, and Wallington recorded fairly steadily as a leader during 1949–57.

In 1960 George Wallington surprised the jazz world by retiring from music to work in his family's air conditioning business. After years of rumors about his whereabouts, in 1984 he returned to music on a part-time basis, recording three albums of original but swinging material during 1984–85 before going back into semi-retirement. In addition to his fine playing, George Wallington is noteworthy for composing the two Bop standards "Lemon Drop" and "Godchild."

- **10** *The George Wallington Trios / Sept. 4, 1952–May 25, 1953 / Original Jazz Classics 1754*
- **8** *Live! at Café Bohemia / Sept. 9, 1955 / Original Jazz Classics 1813*
- **7** *Jazz for the Carriage Trade / Jan. 20, 1956 / Original Jazz Classics 1704*
- **8** *The New York Scene / Mar. 1, 1957 / Original Jazz Classics 1805*
- **7** *Jazz at Hotchkiss / Nov. 14, 1957 / Savoy 78994*

The 15 brief selections on *Trios* (all but one number is under three minutes) often qualify as classic miniatures and serve as one of George Wallington's finest showcases. The pianist, who is joined by Charles Mingus, Oscar Pettiford or Curly Russell on bass, drummer Max Roach, and (on "Love Beat") Chuck Wayne on mandola, contributed ten of the 15 selections, several of which are well worth reviving, and his playing is frequently brilliant.

The other four CDs covered in this section feature Wallington's regular quintet of 1955–57. *Live! at Café Bohemia* is notable for giving listeners early glimpses of trumpeter Donald Byrd and altoist Jackie McLean; bassist Paul Chambers and drummer Art Taylor complete the group, which is very Bebop-oriented. By the following year, Phil Woods was on alto and Teddy Kotick on bass, but the band's sound was similar. They play three standards (including Tadd Dameron's "Our Delight"), Frank Foster's "Foster Dulles," and a couple Woods originals on *Jazz for the Carriage Trade*. Nick Stabulas took over on drums by early 1957. *The New York Scene* has obscure originals by Byrd, Woods, and Mose Allison plus the lone standard "Indian Summer," but the Byrd-Woods combination results in plenty of fireworks. The final

George Wallington recording before his retirement, *Jazz at Hotchkiss*, has the Byrd-Woods-Stabulas band, with Knobby Totah on bass. Two group originals, the obscure "Strange Music," Dizzy Gillespie's "'Ow," and Bud Powell's "Dance of the Infidels" are all given hard-swinging treatment. This was an underrated group!

- **8** *Virtuoso / July 5, 1984 / Denon 35C38-7248*
- **8** *The Symphony of a Jazz Piano / 1985 / Denon / Interface 33C38-7825*
- **8** *The Pleasure of a Jazz Inspiration / Aug. 19, 1985 / V.S.O.P. 84*

During 1984–85, George Wallington returned to the jazz scene and recorded three solo albums. Although all 30 selections on this trio of CDs are Wallington originals, many are based on the chord changes of familiar standards. The pianist's style was virtually unchanged from the 1950s (still very Boppish), so, despite the unfamiliarity of the material, his long-time fans will find much to enjoy here. It is a pity that Wallington did not also record with a trio or a group at this point in his career, and it is surprising that latter-day Boppers have not explored this music yet.

CLAUDE WILLIAMSON
b. Nov. 18, 1926, Brattleboro, VT

A classic Bebop pianist who was still quite active in the late 1990s, Claude Williamson early on mastered the Bud Powell-inspired approach and has played in that style ever since. The older brother of trumpeter Stu Williamson, Claude had ten years of classical piano lessons (starting when he was seven) and studied at the New England Conservatory. He played with the Charlie Barnet big band in 1947, Red Norvo the following year, and then in 1949 was an important member of Barnet's Bebop Orchestra, taking a well-known solo on "Claude Reigns."

After working with June Christy (1950–51), Williamson was in the military (1952–53), settled on the West Coast, and was a regular member of the Lighthouse All-Stars (1953–56), the Bud Shank Quartet (1956–58), and Red Norvo's group (1959–60). Williamson recorded eight albums as a leader of trios and quartets during 1954–62 and also recorded with various West Coast players, including Chet Baker, Barney Kessel, Art Pepper, and Gerry Mulligan. He worked mostly in the studios during the 1960s and '70s but appeared more often in Los Angeles-area clubs with his trio from the late '70s on. In 1995 Claude Williamson recorded a superb CD of Bud Powell tunes for the V.S.O.P. label.

7 *'Round Midnight / Dec. 1956 / Bethlehem 20-3021*
10 *Hallucinations / Feb. 28, 1995 + Mar. 1, 1995 / V.S.O.P. 95*
9 *Live! At the Jazz Bakery / Mar. 22. 1995 / Fresh Sound 5014*

Claude Williamson's earlier recordings are mostly unavailable, and even *'Round Midnight,* which was reissued in 1996 when Evidence was handling the Bethlehem catalog, might be difficult to find. The 1956 set has the pianist joined by bassist Red Mitchell and drummer Mel Lewis for Boppish versions of 11 standards plus Horace Silver's "Hippy."

Pleasing as that music is, Claude Williamson grew as a pianist in the years since. *Hallucinations,* a tribute to Bud Powell (which has fine support from bassist Dave Carpenter and drummer Paul Kreibich), is an exciting set that consists of a dozen songs associated with Powell, including six of Bud's originals. On tunes such as "Parisian Thoroughfare," "Reets and I," and "Bouncing with Bud," Williamson brings back the style of Bud Powell, often sounding very close to the immortal pianist while creating within his style. A classic. *Live! At the Jazz Bakery,* from a month later, is in the same style with the same sidemen. In fact, four songs (including "Hallucinations") are repeated, and there are also two additional Bud Powell compositions performed that did not make it onto the studio date. Bebop Piano Lives!

LPS TO SEARCH FOR

Keys West (Affinity 62), one of the "Stan Kenton Presents" albums for Capitol that has not yet appeared on CD, has eight trio numbers (with Max Bennett or Buddy Clark on bass and Stan Levey or Larry Bunker on drums) and two solo piano performances from 1955. It is up to the level of Claude Williamson's usual fine work from the period.

Guitarists

The guitar was in an odd transitional period during the Bebop era. Up until the early 1940s, the acoustic guitar was used as a purely rhythmic instrument in big bands. There had been a few major soloists, particularly in blues and in the hands of such talented jazz artists as Eddie Lang, Carl Kress, Dick McDonough, and most notably Django Reinhardt, but the guitar was thought of as mostly a minor instrument in jazz. It was barely audible in conventional jazz groups except when being strummed to produce chords, and even then (when played expertly by Freddie Green with Count Basie's orchestra and Allan Reuss with Benny Goodman) it was more felt than heard.

That began to change with the emergence of Charlie Christian in 1939. The electric guitar was just beginning to be played (Eddie Durham the previous year had pioneered its use on records with Count Basie's Kansas City Five and Six) and Christian was its first virtuoso. But more than just a major technician, Christian was a brilliant improviser who played his guitar as if it were a horn, with the fluidity and riff-filled ideas of a Lester Young. With the Benny Goodman Sextet (and on rare occasions BG's big band), Christian sounded years ahead of his time, hinting at Bebop while revitalizing swing. He even played regularly at Minton's Playhouse in 1941 with Thelonious Monk, Kenny Clarke, and occasionally Dizzy Gillespie. Tragically, tuberculosis soon ended his career and, in 1942, his life. He never had an opportunity to really play Bebop.

Christian's death left a huge hole that would not be filled for many years. His influence was felt by virtually all jazz guitarists for the next 25 years (and indirectly up to the present time). Other than the still-active Django Reinhardt, no guitarist was on Christian's level during the classic Bebop era. From the swing world, Tiny Grimes, Al Casey, Oscar Moore, and Slim Gaillard all switched to electric guitar and sounded like relatives of Christian's. Barney Kessel, who was the closest thing that the Bop world had to Christian, would develop his own style over time and be a major force by the 1950s. Remo Palmieri, Chuck Wayne, Billy Bauer, and Mary Osborne all had great potential but spent much of their careers in the studios, and none succeeded in growing much beyond Christian (though Bauer came the closest). And Bill DeArango, the most advanced guitarist in the era, largely dropped out in 1948. It would not be until the 1950s and the rise of Tal Farlow, Jimmy Raney, Kenny Burrell, and Herb Ellis that the guitar would really begin to be taken seriously as a solo instrument in jazz, and it would not be until the rise of fusion in the late 1960s that the guitar would move significantly beyond Charlie Christian.

BILLY BAUER

b. Nov. 14, 1915, New York, NY

Billy Bauer made his biggest impact playing adventurous "Cool Jazz" with Lennie Tristano, but he was a part of the classic Bebop era too. Bauer started on banjo (playing in public as early as 1928), switched to guitar in the early 1930s, and played with Jerry Wald's orchestra, Carl Hoff (with whom he recorded in 1941), Dick Stabile, and Abe Lyman. As a member of Woody Herman's First Herd during 1942–46, he had occasional solos but mostly played rhythm guitar. After leaving Herman, Bauer worked with Chubby Jackson (1947), Benny Goodman, and most importantly Lennie Tristano (1946–49). Bauer's cool-toned guitar fit in very well with Tristano's music (including on the first recorded free improvisations), and during 1949–53 he won the *Downbeat* and *Metronome* polls as best jazz guitarist.

At that point, Bauer began working mostly in the studios. He did record in jazz settings now and then (including with the J.J. Johnson-Kai Winding Quintet, cornetist Bobby Hackett, altoist Lee Konitz, and trumpeter Cootie Williams), and he led albums for Ad Lib (1953) and Verve (1956) plus some private dates from 1959–69 that were later released by Interplay. Bauer ran his own jazz club on Long Island for a few years in the early '60s, played locally, and in 1970 opened up a guitar school. Although he has played a lot less after suffering from a serious ear infection in 1975, Billy Bauer has stayed active as a jazz educator to the present time.

LPS TO SEARCH FOR

Billy Bauer's three albums have yet to be reissued on CD. The most recent one (and the most common) is *Anthology* (Interplay 8603). Included on the record is a trio outing from 1969 and solo guitar performances from 1959, 1960, and 1969. Much of the music is laid-back and melodic (particularly the solo numbers), but Bauer does include a heated trio version of "I'll Remember April."

FILMS

Billy Bauer can be seen with Woody Herman's orchestra in *Earl Carroll Vanities* (1945) and appears in one scene in *The Hustler* (1961).

BILL DeARANGO

b. Sept. 20, 1921, Cleveland, OH

A remarkably advanced improviser during the Bebop era, Bill DeArango on a small-group date with Dizzy Gillespie in 1946 almost sounded as if he were playing his guitar backwards! He was one of the first guitarists to move his instrument beyond Charlie Christian, but unfortunately he chose to retire from the major league jazz scene very early, so his impact on jazz history was minimal despite his abilities.

DeArango started his career playing Dixieland and swing locally in his native Cleveland. After attending Ohio State University, he was in the Army during 1942–44, moving to New York after his discharge. Very quickly he became a fixture on 52nd Street and a member of Ben Webster's group. During 1945–47 DeArango was on many record dates, including with Webster, Gillespie (highlighted by "Anthropology" and "A Night in Tunisia"), Sarah Vaughan, Slam Stewart, Charlie Kennedy, Ike Quebec, Eddie "Lockjaw" Davis, and Charlie Ventura along with two of his own sessions in 1946 (both using Webster, Idrees Sulieman, and Tony Scott in his septet). He also led a group that included Terry Gibbs.

In 1948, Bill DeArango (who was just 26) chose to move back to Cleveland, where he has lived ever since, running a music store, teaching, and playing locally. He returned to New York to lead a record date for Emarcy but otherwise was not heard from nationally until he made a CD for GM in 1993. The latter set finds the 71-year-old guitarist sounding very modern, indulging in free improvisations, and interacting quite colorfully with tenor saxophonist Joe Lovano. It does make one wonder, though, what Bill DeArango could have accomplished in jazz had he chosen to pursue it on a full-time basis.

9 *Anything Went / Apr. 1–2, 1993 / GM 3027*

There are two particularly surprising aspects to this CD. Most Bebop fans probably thought that Bill DeArango was long dead by the early 1990s, because nothing much had been heard from him since his 1954 Emarcy recording. And others might have believed that if DeArango ever emerged again, he would be playing classic Bebop. Wrong on both counts! With the assistance of tenor saxophonist Joe Lovano, bassist Ed Schuller, and drummer George Schuller, DeArango plays quite freely on four guitar-tenor duets, four hornless trio pieces, and three quartet numbers. Other than

The best of the Charlie Christian–inspired guitarists to emerge during the classic Bebop era, Barney Kessel was a major soloist for 48 years.

a trio of standards and an original by Ed Schuller, all of the music is freely improvised explorations, and DeArango's tonal distortions sometimes recall Bill Frisell, showing that he was very aware of current musical events. Most of the selections are quite successful (although a few are overly brief), and there are plenty of explosive moments. A remarkable "comeback" record from a long-forgotten legend.

BARNEY KESSEL

b. Oct. 17, 1923, Muskogee, OK

Of the jazz guitarists who were active in the mid-1940s, Barney Kessel went the furthest in taking Charlie Christian's style and adapting it to Bebop. In time, Kessel developed a sound and style of his own that was flexible enough to fit into Cool Jazz and Hard Bop settings in later years.

Kessel's career started out strong. Self-taught on guitar

(other than three months of lessons when he was 12), Kessel played locally in Oklahoma as a teenager until moving to Los Angeles in 1942. He was with a big band organized by drummer Ben Pollack that was fronted by Chico Marx (1942–43) and had an early break by appearing in the Lester Young short film *Jammin' the Blues.* Kessel was a featured soloist with the big bands of Charlie Barnet (1944–45) and Artie Shaw (1945) and also recorded with Shaw's Gramercy Five opposite Roy Eldridge and Dodo Marmarosa.

With the end of the big band era, Barney Kessel became a busy studio musician while always playing jazz, including with Charlie Parker in 1947. He took time off from the studios to tour as a member of the Oscar Peterson Trio (1952–53) and occasionally with Jazz at the Philharmonic. During 1953–61, Kessel made some of the finest records of his career for the Contemporary label, performing Boppish music that looked toward both West Coast jazz and swing. He was teamed in a trio with Ray Brown and Shelly Manne for other recordings under the title of The Poll Winners and also had opportunities to record with Art Tatum and Sonny Rollins. Kessel worked steadily in the 1960s, toured with George Wein's Newport All-Stars in 1968, lived in London during 1969–70 (where he recorded with violinist Stephane Grappelli), and during 1973–92 was a member (with Herb Ellis and Charlie Byrd) of the Great Guitars in addition to recording regularly for Concord and finally back at Contemporary. A major stroke in 1992 put Barney Kessel permanently out of action.

8 *Vol. 1: Easy Like / Nov. 14, 1953–Dec. 19, 1953 / Original Jazz Classics 153*

9 *Kessel Plays Standards / June 4, 1954–Sept. 12, 1955 / Original Jazz Classics 238*

10 *Vol. 3: To Swing or Not To Swing / Mar. 28, 1955 / Original Jazz Classics 317*

9 *Music to Listen to Barney Kessel By / Aug. 6, 1956– Dec. 4, 1956 / Original Jazz Classics 746*

As a leader, Barney Kessel recorded four titles for Atomic in 1945 (reissued on an Onyx sampler LP) and four songs on Verve in 1953. His first full album was for Contemporary, and he would be a fixture at that label for eight years. *Easy Like* features Kessel with two separate quintets: in 1953 with Bud Shank (on flute and alto) and pianist Arnold Ross and in 1956 with Buddy Collette (also on flute and alto) and Claude Williamson. Kessel's bright sound and quick ideas on such tunes as "Easy Like," "Lullaby of Birdland," "Salute to Charlie Christian," and "North of the Border" show why he was considered one of the top guitarists of the 1950s. For *Kessel Plays Standards,* he is matched with Bob Cooper (mostly on oboe but also playing some tenor), either Claude Williamson or Hampton Hawes on piano, Monty Budwig or Red Mitchell on bass, and Shelly Manne or Chuck Thompson on drums. Other than "Barney's Blues" and the leader's "64 Bars on Wilshire," all dozen selections are standards that are uplifted by colorful frameworks and consistently strong solos.

To Swing or Not To Swing is a classic, ranging from Bop to Cool Jazz and modern swing. Kessel heads a septet that includes trumpeter Harry "Sweets" Edison, Georgie Auld or Bill Perkins on tenor, pianist Jimmy Rowles, the rhythm guitar of Al Hendrickson, bassist Red Mitchell, and Irv Cottler or Shelly Manne on drums. The standards are given inventive treatment (including "Louisiana," "Indiana," and even "12th Street Rag"), and the four Kessel originals (highlighted by "Begin the Blues" and "Wail Street") swing hard. *Music to Listen to Barney Kessel By* (what a title!) is particularly unusual, for Kessel not only plays guitar but contributed the arrangements for five woodwinds and the rhythm section (which has either Andre Previn, Jimmy Rowles, or Claude Williamson on piano). On 11 standards and Kessel's "Blues for a Playboy," the woodwinds (which include Buddy Collette and Ted Nash) mostly stick to their parts, and such instruments as alto flute, oboe, English horn, bassoon, and bass clarinet are utilized on fresh versions of a variety of numbers including "Makin' Whoopee," "Carioca," "Mountain Greenery," and "Fascinatin' Rhythm." Fascinating music!

7 *Kessel Plays Carmen / Dec. 19 + 23, 1958 / Original Jazz Classics 269*

9 *Some Like It Hot / Mar. 30, 1959–Apr. 3, 1959 / Original Jazz Classics 168*

7 *Workin' Out / Sept. 9–10, 1961 / Original Jazz Classics 970*

In the late 1950s, many jazz albums came out featuring music from recent Broadway shows. *Kessel Plays Carmen* is more unusual, for the guitarist is heard turning nine themes from Bizet's opera *Carmen* into jazz. Some of the melodies will be quite familiar, and in general Kessel is quite successful, whether utilizing five woodwinds in a nonet, several horns (including trumpeter Ray Linn and altoist Herb Geller) on other pieces, or jamming two songs with the rhythm section. After the movie *Some Like It Hot* came out, Kessel used that event as an excuse to play nine songs from the 1920s (plus the movie's theme) with an all-star group (Art Pepper on alto, clarinet, and tenor, trumpeter Joe Gordon, Jimmy Rowles, rhythm guitarist Jack Marshall, Monty Budwig, and Shelly Manne). The arrangements are updated to 1950s Cool Jazz but retain the flavor of earlier versions. It is quite intriguing to hear these "modern" musicians play such songs as "I Wanna Be Loved by You," "Runnin' Wild," and "Sweet Georgia Brown." *Workin' Out* has Kessel leading a quartet with little-known sidemen (Marvin Jenkins on piano and flute, bassist Jerry Good, and drummer Stan Popper), performing five standards and three originals, including "When Johnny Comes Marching Home" and "My Funny Valentine." This set, the final of his original string of recordings for Contemporary, signaled the end of Kessel's classic period.

8 *The Poll Winners / Mar. 18–19, 1957 / Original Jazz Classics 156*

7 *The Poll Winners Ride Again! / Aug. 19 + 21, 1958 / Original Jazz Classics 607*

7 *Poll Winners Three! / Nov. 1959 / Original Jazz Classics 692*

8 *The Poll Winners/Exploring the Scene! / Aug. 1960–Sept. 1960 / Original Jazz Classics 969*

7 *The Poll Winners/Straight Ahead / July 12, 1975 / Original Jazz Classics 409*

Because Barney Kessel, Ray Brown, and Shelly Manne seemed to win so many jazz polls in the mid-to-late 1950s on guitar, bass, and drums for *Downbeat, Metronome,* and *Playboy,* the Contemporary label teamed them as "The Poll Winners." Since their first release sold well, there would be five recordings in all. The pianoless trio format, although allegedly featuring all three musicians, was mostly a showcase for Kessel. The first *Poll Winners* CD is highlighted by "Jordu," "It Could Happen to You," and "On Green Dolphin Street." Its follow-up set, *The Poll Winners Ride Again!,* is most notable for some offbeat material, including Kessel's "Be Deedle Dee Do," "Volare," "When the Red, Red Robin Comes Bob, Bob Bobbin' Along," and "The Merry-Go-Round Broke Down." *Poll Winners Three!* returns to more conventional songs, including swinging versions of "Soft Winds," "It's All Right with Me," and "Mack the Knife." *Exploring the Scene!* has nine then-recent jazz tunes (including "Little Susie," "So What," "Doodlin'," "This Here," and Ornette Coleman's "The Blessing") and finds the trio challenged by the material. Fifteen years later, The Poll Winners reunited for *Straight Ahead,* and each of the players shows how much he had grown through the years on three originals and a trio of standards (including "Caravan").

6 *Autumn Leaves / Oct. 29, 1968–Sept. 19, 1969 / Black Lion 760112*

9 *Limehouse Blues / June 23–24, 1969 / Black Lion 760158*

7 *Yesterday / July 1973 / Black Lion 760183*

6 *Barney Kessel & Friends / Apr. 1975 / Concord 6009*

7 *Soaring / Aug. 25, 1976 / Concord Jazz 6033*

5 *Poor Butterfly / 1976 / Concord Jazz 4034*

4 *Live at Sometime / Feb. 23, 1977 / Storyville 4157*

6 *Jellybeans / Apr. 1981 / Concord Jazz 4164*

5 *Solo / Apr. 1981 / Concord Jazz 4221*

7 *Spontaneous Combustion / Feb. 20–22, 1987 / Contemporary 14033*

7 *Red Hot and Blues / Mar. 15–17, 1988 / Contemporary 14044*

In general, Barney Kessel's later recordings are much less interesting than those in the 1950s, often being sleepy and too laid-back. *Autumn Leaves* has a rather routine trio date with bassist Kenny Nepper and drummer John Marshall plus three slightly more interesting big band numbers, with Teddy Edwards making a guest appearance. *Limehouse Blues* is on a higher level because it teams Kessel in a pianoless quintet with the great violinist Stephane Grappelli on seven swing standards (including hot versions of "It Don't Mean a Thing," "How High the Moon," and "Undecided") plus one original. *Yesterday,* from the 1973 Montreux Jazz Festival, has its moments. Kessel takes two ballads (including the title cut) as unaccompanied solos, plays "Laura" with a trio, performs three numbers with a quartet that includes pianist Brian Lemon, and adds tenor saxophonist Danny Moss for his "Bridging the Blues"; the encore is a guitar-violin duet with Grappelli on "Tea for Two."

Barney Kessel began his association with Concord with a date that is slightly unusual. *Barney Kessel & Friends* has the guitarist leading a group through nine of his obscure originals (no standards at all this time), and Herbie Steward (one of the original Woody Herman Four Brothers) is heard, not on tenor but on alto, soprano, and flute. Also in the band is Jimmy Rowles on keyboards, vibraphonist Victor Feldman, bassist Chuck Domanico, drummer Jake Hanna, and percussionist Milt Holland. But despite some good solos, nothing unusual occurs. *Soaring* has Kessel (in a trio with bassist Monty Budwig and Jake Hanna) playing six ballads, but mostly at faster-than usual tempos, and cooking on such numbers as "You Go to My Head," "Like Someone in Love," and "Beautiful Love." In addition, he contributes two of his strongest originals: "Seagull" and "You're the One for Me." *Poor Butterfly* was the first meeting on records by Kessel and Herb Ellis. The music (standards, a couple of obscurities, and two songs by Ellis) by the quartet (with Budwig and Hanna) is relaxed, swinging, tasteful, and largely forgettable. However, it is exciting compared to *Live at Sometime,* a trio outing in Tokyo with bassist Kunimitsu Inaba and drummer Tetsujiroh Obara in which Kessel mostly runs through warhorses (including "Georgia on My Mind," "Bye Bye Blackbird," and even "Feelings") with taste but no real adventure or chance-taking moments.

Jellybeans finds Kessel mostly coasting with the support of bassist Bob Maize and drummer Jimmie Smith. He plays with fire on a few numbers (particularly on "St. Thomas" and "Stella by Starlight"), but little that is memorable occurs and there are too many slower pieces. The words "relaxed," "melodic," and "tasteful" also fit his unaccompanied guitar recital on *Solo*. Although pleasant, Kessel's solo playing lacks the excitement and innovations of Joe Pass's similar efforts from the period. Nice background music.

After six years passed since his last recording as a leader, Barney Kessel returned to Contemporary in 1987, where he cut his final two albums. *Spontaneous Combustion* is a big improvement on most of his Concord releases due to the strong rhythm section (pianist Monty Alexander, bassist John Clayton, and drummer Jeff Hamilton), which really pushes and inspires the guitarist; "Bluesy," "Ah, Sweet Mystery of Life," and "Get Me to the Church on Time" are among the highlights. Though Kessel would record again with The Great Guitars, his last date as a leader is *Red Hot and Blues*, a modern Bop session with vibraphonist Bobby Hutcherson, pianist Kenny Barron, bassist Rufus Reid, and drummer Ben Riley that contains three Kessel tunes (including "Blues for Bird") plus such numbers as "It's You or No One," "I'm Glad There Is You," and "By Myself."

LPS TO SEARCH FOR

Thus far overlooked by the Original Jazz Classics series, *Let's Cook* (Contemporary 7603), from 1957, has three numbers by Kessel in a quintet with vibraphonist Victor Feldman and Hampton Hawes, and memorable versions of "Tiger Rag" and "Jersey Bounce" by a sextet featuring tenor great Ben Webster and trombonist Frank Rosolino. Also thus far overlooked is *Feeling Free* (Original Jazz Classics 179), a 1969 meeting with vibraphonist Bobby Hutcherson, bassist Chuck Domanico, and drummer Elvin Jones that has four fairly free originals (slightly influenced by the avant-garde) plus jazz versions of a pair of pop tunes. *Two Way Conversation* (Gazell 1003) is a fine (if often overly relaxed) set of duets with bassist Red Mitchell in 1973. *Just Friends* puts the spotlight on Kessel (also in 1973) in a trio for a standards-oriented date with bassist Sture Nordin and drummer Pelle Hultin.

FILMS

Barney Kessel is in *Jammin' the Blues* (1944) with Lester Young. He is also in quite a few videos (not counting his appearances with Great Guitars), including *Barney Kessel—Rare Performances 1962–1991* (Vestapol 13013), three songs on *Legends of Jazz Guitar Vol. 1* (Vestapol 13009), two on *Vol. 2* (Vestapol 13033), and four on *Vol. 3* (Vestapol 13047).

MARY OSBORNE

b. July 17, 1921, Minot, ND, Mar. 4, 1992, Bakersfield, CA

A superior Bop guitarist, Mary Osborne started out strong in her career. But because she chose to settle in Bakersfield, she failed to live up to her great potential and was not as well documented as she could have been. When she was 15, Osborne played guitar, violin, and bass, sang, and danced in a trio. After hearing Charlie Christian play in North Dakota with Alphonse Trent's band, she switched to electric guitar. During the 1940s Osborne played with many bands, including those led by Buddy Rogers, Dick Stabile, Terry Shand, Joe Venuti, and Russ Morgan. She was able to make the transition from swing to Bop with little difficulty and recorded with a variety of combos, including some specially assembled all-female groups and with Mary Lou Williams, the Beryl Booker Trio, Coleman Hawkins, and Wynonie Harris, among others. She also made 16 little-known selections under her own name during 1945–52. Osborne was featured on Jack Sterling's daily radio program on CBS (1952–63), did studio work, and appeared on several jazz television shows in the 1950s. In 1959 she recorded an album for Warwick.

In 1968 Mary Osborne settled in Bakersfield, California, with her husband and went into semiretirement, playing just now and then locally. However, in the decade before her death she became a bit more active, appearing at a few festivals, mostly in California, recording six titles as a leader in 1981, and showing that, despite the lack of much recognition, she was one of the best of the surviving Bop guitarists.

9 *A Memorial / 1959–1981 / Stash 550*
Mary Osborne recorded remarkably little in her career as a leader. Other than the 16 early selections, this CD has all of her dates: a 1959 set originally cut for the Warwick label (in a quintet with Tommy Flanagan, rhythm guitarist Danny Barker, Tommy Potter, and Jo Jones) and six titles from 1981 in a trio with bassist Steve Laspina and drummer Charlie Persip. Listening to her solid Bop playing on a variety of standards (including "Soft Winds," "Just Friends," "Body and Soul," and "How High the Moon"), it seems bizarre that

she recorded so little else during her half-century as a professional guitarist. Highly recommended.

REMO PALMIERI

b. Mar. 29, 1923, New York, NY

Remo Palmieri (who later changed his name to Remo Palmier) showed a great deal of potential during the 1944–46 period, when he was an important player on the New York Bebop scene. But Palmieri chose the life of a studio musician and was rarely heard in jazz settings for decades, a major loss.

Palmieri, who had originally planned to be an artist, started playing music professionally (originally to raise money to pay for art studies) in 1942 with pianist Nat Jaffe. He worked with Coleman Hawkins (1943), Red Norvo, Billie Holiday, and Mildred Bailey, recording with Dizzy Gillespie and Charlie Parker in 1945 on their famous "Groovin' High/Dizzy Atmosphere" date. He also recorded with the Esquire All-Stars in 1946 and with Teddy Wilson and Sarah Vaughan. But in 1945 Palmieri joined the staff of CBS, and he was featured on the Arthur Godfrey show during the next 27 years, which largely removed him from the jazz world.

In the early 1970s, Palmieri returned to jazz on a part-time basis, working with Hank Jones, Bobby Hackett, Benny Goodman, Dick Hyman, the Swing Reunion band, Benny Carter, and Louie Bellson, among others. He also led his only record date for Concord in 1978 (which has not yet been reissued on CD). But Remo Palmieri's many years off the jazz scene kept him from accomplishing all that much in creative music.

CHUCK WAYNE

b. Feb. 27, 1923, New York, NY

As with the other guitarists in this section, Chuck Wayne's early influence was Charlie Christian, although he considered Charlie Parker and Lester Young to be just as important in shaping his style. Early on, the self-taught Wayne played mandolin with a Russian balalaika group. After switching to guitar and immersing himself in jazz, Wayne worked on 52nd Street with the Clarence Profit and Nat Jaffe trios. He served in the Army (1942–44), had a regular job with clarinetist Joe Marsala (1944–46), and played with Dizzy Gillespie, Red Norvo, Woody Herman's First Herd (1946), Jack Teagarden, Coleman Hawkins, Phil Moore, Bud Powell, Lester Young, and the Barbara Carroll Trio, showing that he was quite capable of playing practically any style of jazz. Wayne was a member of the original George Shearing Quintet (1949–52) and was in Tony Bennett's backup band (1954–57), also working with George Wallington, Brew Moore, Zoot Sims, and the Gil Evans Orchestra (1958–59). He spent the 1960s as a member of the staff of CBS, performed duos with Joe Puma (1972–76), and freelanced around the New York area, including playing for Broadway shows and backing singers. He has also long been active as a jazz educator. Although he never became famous, Chuck Wayne was one of the finest guitarists to emerge from the Bebop era. He has led albums for Progressive (1953), ABC/Paramount (1956), Vik (1957), Focus (1963), Prestige (1964), Choice (1973), and a different Progressive label (1976), none of which have been reissued on CD yet.

LPS TO SEARCH FOR

Tasty Pudding (Savoy 1144) brings back the eight songs from Chuck Wayne's 1953 Progressive quintet date plus four numbers that he cut as a sideman with pianist John Mehegan's quartet in 1954. The earlier set also includes Brew Moore or Zoot Sims on tenor, and throughout these concise numbers (all clocking in around three minutes apiece), Wayne shows how masterful a Bop guitarist he was in his early days. *Traveling* (Progressive 7008), from 1976, is still Wayne's most recent set, featuring the swinging guitarist in a trio/quartet with electric bassist Jay Leonhart, drummer Ronnie Bedford, and sometimes Warren Chiasson on vibes.

Bassists

The string bass was in a similar situation as the guitar at the beginning of the Bebop era. Used strictly as an accompanying four-to-the-bar instrument in the 1930s and made much more necessary by the lighter touch that pianists later in the decade had developed (as opposed to the heavier orchestral stride style of the 1920s), the bass was considered a background instrument, until Jimmy Blanton joined Duke Ellington in 1939. Blanton, during his two years before being struck down by tuberculosis, showed that the bass had unlimited potential as a solo instrument (it did not have to be used like a metronome) and that it could be played with the fluidity of a guitar or a saxophone.

With the development of Bud Powell's dominant style in the mid-1940s (which put the emphasis on pianist's right hands), the string bass became quite essential in most jazz settings. But it would take until the 1950s before many bassists began to catch up with Blanton. There were a few exceptions. Oscar Pettiford and Ed Safranski built on the Blanton legacy and became major soloists (although Safranski defected to the studios by the early '50s), and Ray Brown showed a great deal of potential that he would realize in later years. But most other bassists of the classic Bebop era followed the examples of Tommy Potter and Curly Russell, rarely soloing but proving their worth by being able to play advanced chords and keep the rhythm steady with four-to-the-bar bass lines, even on endless songs at rapid tempos.

NELSON BOYD

b. Feb. 6, 1928, Camden, NJ

A fine journeyman bassist, Nelson Boyd popped up on a lot of recording sessions with top Bebop players, although he himself rarely ever soloed. Boyd played locally in Philadelphia in the mid-1940s, moved to New York in 1947, and worked with Coleman Hawkins, Tadd Dameron, Sarah Vaughan, Dexter Gordon, and the big bands of Charlie Barnet and Dizzy Gillespie (1948). He stayed busy during the 1950s and early '60s (including with the Dizzy Gillespie Orchestra in 1956), recording an album (*Bebop Revisited*) with Charles McPherson as late as 1964 but dropping out of the music scene a few years later. Among the musicians with whom Nelson Boyd recorded (he did not lead any sessions of his own) are Charlie Parker (the "Milestones" session, actually led by Miles Davis), Thelonious Monk, Fats Navarro, Miles Davis (he was on one of The Birth of the Cool Nonet sessions), Milt Jackson, Dexter Gordon, Sonny Stitt, and Dizzy Gillespie.

RAY BROWN

b. Oct. 15, 1926, Pittsburgh, PA

Considered by many to be the definitive Bebop bassist, Ray Brown has a huge tone, impeccable technical skills, and the ability to swing at any tempo, consistently inspiring every musician with whom he performs. Brown remains as vital a bassist in 2000 as he was in 1950.

It would not be an exaggeration to say that Brown started at the top. After he played locally in Pittsburgh with Jimmy Hinsley and Snookum Russell, he arrived in New York in 1945. On his very first day in town he jammed with Dizzy Gillespie, Charlie Parker, and Bud Powell! Brown was closely associated with Gillespie for a few years, playing with his big band and occasional small groups, and being well-featured on "One Bass Hit" and "Two Bass Hit." While with Gillespie, Brown helped form an unbeatable rhythm section for a time with Kenny Clarke, John Lewis, and Milt Jackson, which would form the nucleus of the Modern Jazz Quartet (although Brown was never actually a member). In 1947 he played with Jazz at the Philharmonic and met Ella Fitzgerald. They were married for four years (1948–52). For a period, he led the trio that backed Ella.

Ray Brown's most significant musical association was with Oscar Peterson, whom he also met at JATP. Brown toured the world with Peterson during 1951–66, starting as a duo and then more famously as a trio with Barney Kessel, Herb Ellis, and later Ed Thigpen in the third spot. Brown also appeared with many other top jazz stars, helped out by his association with Norman Granz, JATP, Peterson, and the Verve label, and was one of the "Poll Winners," recording a series of albums with Barney Kessel and Shelly Manne for Contemporary. When he finally tired of the road and left OP, Brown settled in Los Angeles and became a studio musician but also continued as a freelance jazz bassist. He spent a period managing a few artists (including the Modern Jazz Quartet and Quincy Jones), was very important as a talent scout (advancing the careers of Ernestine Anderson and Gene Harris), played with the L. A. Four, and led exciting trios in the 1980s and '90s. Among the musicians who were members of the popular Ray Brown Trio were pianists Monty Alexander (including a group called Triple Treat), Gene Harris, Bennie Green, and Geoff Keezer and drummers Mickey Roker, Jeff Hamilton, and Gregory Hutchinson. Ray Brown has recorded prolifically, both as a sideman and as a leader, through the years, starting in 1946 and making albums for Verve (1956–65, including doubling a bit on cello), Impulse (1969), Concord, (1975–91), Contemporary (1977), Capri (1989–91), and most recently Telarc.

7 *Bass Hit / Nov. 21–23, 1956 / Verve 314 559 829*

The still-active Ray Brown has always had a glorious tone, along with the ability to sound relaxed at any tempo.

8 *Much in Common/All-Star Big Band / Jan. 22, 1962–Jan. 5, 1965 / Verve 314 533 259*

5 *Brown's Bag / Dec. 1975 / Concord Jazz 6019*

7 *As Good As It Gets / Dec. 22, 1977 / Concord Jazz 4066*

7 *Tasty! / Oct. 22, 1979 / Concord Jazz 4122*

7 *Something for Lester / June 22–24, 1979 / Original Jazz Classics 412*

7 *Live at the Concord Jazz Festival / Aug. 1979 / Concord Jazz 4102*

Ray Brown first led his own record date back in 1945. But, other than two trio titles in 1950, his next opportunity to head a session was not until 1956, resulting in *Bass Hit*. For this project, Brown was joined by a big band that included Harry "Sweets" Edison, Herb Geller, Jimmy Giuffre on clarinet and tenor, and pianist Jimmy Rowles, among others, playing arrangements by Marty Paich. The original set had nine songs, including "All of You," "Alone Together," and "Solo for Unaccompanied Bass." In the interest of being complete, "After You've Gone" (which was not among the issued selections) from the same dates is heard in four complete takes plus three false starts and three breakdowns; a bit excessive! Brown led other Verve sessions (one apiece in 1958 and 1960) and then the three albums (plus seven new alternate takes) that have been reissued as the double CD *Much in Common./All-Star Big Band*. Milt Jackson is co-leader on two of the sessions and a participant on the third. Two are big band dates, with arrangements by Ernie Wilkins and Oliver Nelson, and the soloists on the first set include altoist Cannonball Adderley and cornetist Nat Adderley, playing one of the earliest versions of "Work Song." Brown switches to cello on three numbers, and Milt Jackson is well featured throughout. The third date is an unusual small-group effort due to its featuring quite successfully the gospel vocals of Marion Williams on a few numbers.

Other than a big band date in 1969, Ray Brown's next opportunity to lead his own session was in 1975, and he would be prolific as a leader from then on. *Brown's Bag* has Brown heading two separate groups: a quintet with trumpeter Blue Mitchell, tenor saxophonist Richie Kamuca, pianist Art Hillery, and drummer John Guerin (best on "Blues for Eddie Lee" and "Surrey with the Fringe on Top") and a quartet with keyboardist Dave Grusin, guitarist John Collins, and drummer Jimmie Smith that plays three ballads. The brief playing time of this CD (less than 35 minutes) and the non-occurrence of anything special makes this a lesser effort. *As Good As It Gets* and *Tasty!* both feature the duo of Brown and pianist Jimmy Rowles. The music is quite subtle, the pianist shows off his sly wit and bits of striding, and some of the songs receive surprising treatment, including "Honey" (with its bass lead) and "Love" on the former and "Smile" and the obscure "The Night Is Young and You're So Beautiful" on the latter.

Ray Brown's lone Contemporary album as a leader, *Something for Lester,* was named after producer Lester Koenig rather than Lester Young. The interplay between Brown and pianist Cedar Walton and drummer Elvin Jones, along with the tight arrangements, is the direct predecessor of the series of trios that the bassist would soon be leading. Highlights include "Love Walked In," "Little Girl Blue," and "Sister Sadie"; Brown contributed "Slippery." The early Ray Brown Trio (with pianist Monty Alexander and drummer Jeff Hamilton) is featured on four mostly Brazilian tunes on *Live at the Concord Jazz Festival* but primarily plays in support of singer Ernestine Anderson on five other spirited numbers, including "Honeysuckle Rose" and "Please Send Me Someone to Love."

7   *A Ray Brown 3 / Feb. 1982 / Concord Jazz 4213*
8   *Soular Energy / Aug. 1984 / Concord Jazz 4268*
8   *Don't Forget the Blues / May 1985 / Concord Jazz 4293*
8   *The Red Hot Ray Brown Trio / Nov. 1985–Dec. 1985 / Concord Jazz 4315*
8   *Summer Wind / July 1988 / Concord Jazz 4426*
8   *Bam Bam Bam / Dec. 1988 / Concord Jazz 4375*
9   *Black Orpheus / May 23, 1989 + Feb. 7, 1991 / Evidence 22076*
8   *Moore Makes 4 / May 22, 1990 / Concord Jazz 4477*

8   *Three Dimensional / Aug. 4, 1991 / Concord Jazz 4520*
7   *Super Bass / 1989 / Capri 74018*
7   *New Two Bass Hits / Apr. 29, 1991 / Capri 74034*

On *A Ray Brown 3,* the bassist uses a different type of trio then expected, a unit with Monty Alexander and flutist Sam Most. Most, one of the great flutists, works well in this group, while Alexander stretches from Oscar Peterson to Caribbean rhythms. Among the songs explored are "I Wish You Love," "Blue Monk," and "You're My Everything."

The Ray Brown Trio really debuted on *Soular Energy,* which features Brown with pianist Gene Harris (whose comeback from obscurity was due largely to Brown) and drummer Gerryck King. Seven of the eight songs on the set (including "Exactly Like You," "Teach Me Tonight," and "Sweet Georgia Brown") showcase the trio on soulful swinging. The other selection, "Mistreated but Undefeated Blues," adds guitarist Emily Remler and Red Holloway on tenor. *Don't Forget the Blues* is a change of pace, with Brown and Harris joined by guitarist Ron Eschete, Al Grey, and drummer Grady Tate. The majority of the songs are blues (including the bassist's "Blues'd Out," "Night Train," and "Jumpin' the Blues"), with "If I Could Be with You" being an exception. There are plenty of fine, concise solos from the lead voices.

Although the personnel would occasionally change, by 1985 the Ray Brown Trio had developed its basic sound. Mixing together blues-based originals, ballads, blues, and standards, Brown and his sidemen added funkiness, soul, and swing to each song they interpreted, often having arranged (or worked-out) interludes between the solos and ensembles. Their recordings would be consistent and large in number; fans of one set will have little difficulty enjoying all of the others. *The Red Hot Ray Brown Trio* (which includes "Have You Met Miss Jones?" "Lady Be Good," and Tyree Glenn's "How Could You Do a Thing Like This to Me?") has Mickey Roker playing drums with Brown and Harris. By 1988, when *Summer Wind* was recorded, Jeff Hamilton was on drums; this date is highlighted by "The Real Blues," "Li'l Darlin'," and "Bluesology." The live *Bam Bam Bam* finds the group stretching out on "Put Your Little Foot Right Out," "Days of Wine and Roses," and "A Night in Tunisia." *Black Orpheus* was recorded in Japan in 1989 for the King label and added two numbers from two years later, when it was made available domestically by Evidence. Although several of the songs had been recorded previously by the Brown-Harris-Hamilton group, these versions are a bit lengthier and more fully developed, including "The Days of Wine and Roses," "Ain't Misbehavin'," and "Things Ain't What They Used to Be."

Ralph Moore had become associated with the Ray Brown Trio when they all played as part of Gene Harris's touring big band. *Moore Makes 4* is largely a showcase for the tenor saxophonist (whose tone is influenced by John Coltrane, although he is essentially a Hard Bop player). Moore rises to the occasion on a standards-oriented date that includes "Bye Bye Blackbird," "Like Someone in Love," and "Polka Dots and Moonbeams." *Three Dimensional* was the final recording by this version of the Ray Brown Trio, and it holds its own with the others, particularly on "Ja-Da," "My Romance," and a four-song Duke Ellington medley.

In 1988, for an obscure European label, Ray Brown recorded *Two Bass Hits,* a project with Pierre Boussaguet on second bass and pianist Dodo Moroni. In 1989, for Capri, he teamed up with fellow bassist John Clayton, with the number of basses on a song ranging from two to (via overdubbing) as many as ten. The wit and swing of Brown and Clayton keep the music continually interesting; they are assisted by rhythm guitarist Freddie Green, drummer Hamilton, and altoist Jeff Clayton on some numbers. *New Two Bass Hits* reunited Brown and Boussaguet with Jacky Terrasson, this time on piano. Despite the emphasis on bass solos, this music (which includes "How High the Moon," Duke Ellington and bossa nova medleys, and "Bye Bye Blackbird") never gets too predictable.

8 | *Bass Face* / *Apr. 1993* / *Telarc 83340*
8 | *Don't Get Sassy* / *Apr. 21-22, 1994* / *Telarc 83368*
9 | *Seven Steps to Heaven* / *May 22-23, 1995* / *Telarc 83384*
8 | *Live at Scullers* / *Oct. 17-18, 1996* / *1996* / *Telarc 83405*
7 | *Super Bass* / *Oct. 17-18, 1996* / *Telarc 83393*
8 | *Summertime* / *Aug. 26-28, 1997* / *Telarc 83430*

By 1993, Brown and Hamilton were joined by pianist Benny Green in their trio. Green was a perfect choice to take Gene Harris's place, because, although he could emulate Harris closely, he could also stretch to Bobby Timmons, Oscar Peterson, and McCoy Tyner while displaying a gradually developing musical personality of his own. *Bass Face* has such numbers as "Milestones," "Tin Tin Deo," "Taking a Chance on Love," and "Makin' Whoopee." The musicians

pay close attention to dynamics, and there are plenty of subtle surprises throughout each of their recordings. *Don't Get Sassy* includes "Everything I Love," "Brown's New Blues," Dizzy Gillespie's "Con Alma," and yet another Ellington medley (although the songs in the medley had been slightly changed). *Seven Steps to Heaven* finds Gregory Hutchinson taking over the drum slot, with guitarist Ulf Wakenius making the group temporarily into a quartet. The arrangements are tight and witty, and the overall music is reminiscent of the Oscar Peterson Trio during Brown's period with the great pianist. *Live at Scullers* was the last official CD by this particular trio (without Wakenius), and there can be little doubt, listening to this stirring music, that Benny Green had developed into a giant. Highlights include "Freddie Freeloader," "But Not for Me," and "Bye Bye Blackbird."

From the same engagement, *Super Bass* teams Brown with fellow bassists John Clayton and Christian McBride, with support from Green and Hutchinson. Due to the strong personalities of the three bassists, plus their mutual love and respect, the music is swinging and witty. *Summertime* matches Brown with guitarist Wakenius and Hutchinson again, although this time with Green's replacement, Geoff Keezer, on piano. Keezer's soulful Hard Bop style is not that much different than Benny Green's, and there is a definite continuity between this group and the previous one. "West Coast Blues," "Topsy," "It's Only a Paper Moon," and "Honeysuckle Rose" are among the more rewarding selections.

7 | *Some of My Best Friends Are . . . The Piano Players* / *Nov. 18 + 21, 1994* / *Telarc 83373*
8 | *Some of My Best Friends Are . . . The Sax Players* / *Nov. 20, 1995-Feb. 13, 1996* / *Telarc 83388*
8 | *Some of My Best Friends Are . . . Singers* / *Dec. 15, 1997-Apr. 29, 1998* / *Telarc 83441*
4 | *Christmas Songs With The Ray Brown Trio* / *Dec. 15, 1997-Apr. 29, 1998* / *Telarc 83437*

Everyone wants to play with Ray Brown, and many of his favorite musicians had opportunities in his "Some of My Best Friends Are" series. The pianist date has Brown and drummer Lewis Nash being joined on three songs apiece by Ahmad Jamal and Benny Green, by Dado Moroni and Oscar Peterson on a pair each, and by future trio member Geoff Keezer on "Close Your Eyes." The music is nice, but, other than Jamal, all of the pianists sound a lot like Oscar Peterson! The Brown-Green-Hutchinson Trio on the saxophone project is joined on two songs apiece by altoists Benny Carter and

Jesse Davis and tenors Joe Lovano, Ralph Moore, Joshua Redman, and Stanley Turrentine. Everyone plays very well (Carter's "Love Walked In" and Turrentine's "Port of Rico" take honors) and, at the close, Brown has a brief verbal conversation with each of the saxophonists; pity that this section was not much longer (the conversations clock in mostly at less than a minute apiece). The singers' set, which has the Brown-Keezer-Hutchinson trio assisted by three guests (Ralph Moore, altoist Antonio Hart, and guitarist Russell Malone), features two vocals apiece by Diana Krall (including "I Thought About You"), Etta Jones, Dee Dee Bridgewater (cooking hard on "Cherokee"), Nancy King, Marlena Shaw, and Kevin Mahogany. The music is often quite heartwarming and is quite successful. The same singers plus Vanessa Rubin take one vocal apiece on the Christmas set (which was recorded at the same sessions), but this program (which also includes four instrumentals and a dumb rap by Hutchinson) falls flat although Krall (on "Santa Claus Is Coming To Town") does her best; no fresh ideas!

FILMS

Ray Brown is featured with Dizzy Gillespie's Orchestra in *Jivin' in Bebop* (1947), which is included in the video *Things to Come* (Vintage Jazz Classics 2006).

RED CALLENDER

b. Mar. 6, 1916, Haynesville, VA, d. Mar. 8, 1992, Saugus, CA

One of the busiest of all the bassists, Red Callender appeared in countless settings through the years, performing quite credibly with musicians from virtually all eras of jazz while also being a greatly in-demand studio musician. Callender grew up in Atlantic City. He played briefly in New York and freelanced in the Midwest before moving to Los Angeles in 1936. Callender worked with Buck Clayton's orchestra, debuted on records in 1937 (filling in for Pops Foster with Louis Armstrong's big band), and taught bass to the young Charles Mingus. He worked and recorded with Nat King Cole's early trio (1938–39), did movie work, and was with the Lee and Lester Young band in the early '40s. Callender made his most notable contribution to the Bebop era when he appeared with Louis Armstrong in the movie *New Orleans*. Although it was supposed to be 1915, Callender took a bass break on one song that was pure Bop!

In addition to gigging with Armstrong, Callender worked with the Erroll Garner Trio and made records with (among

many others) Charlie Parker, Dexter Gordon, Lester Young, and Benny Goodman. He spent 1947–50 living in Honolulu, where he led a trio and played with the Honolulu Symphony. However, Callender returned to Los Angeles as the 1950s began, and he became very busy in the studios, so busy in fact that he turned down job offers to join both the Louis Armstrong All-Stars and the Duke Ellington Orchestra! He began doubling on tuba, and in 1954 recorded a record (*Callender Speaks Low*) which was the first "modern jazz" album to feature the tuba as a lead solo instrument; it was followed by another tuba showcase, 1958's *The Lowest*. Through the years, Callender kept working, recording with Art Tatum (1955–56), and playing Bop, Dixieland, Kansas City swing (with the Cheathams), and even avant-garde jazz as a founder of the Wind College (with clarinetist John Carter, flutist James Newton, and multireedist Charles Owens). Red Callender's excellent autobiography, *Unfinished Dream,* came out in 1985, and he remained an active musician up until his death in 1992, two days after his 76th birthday.

LPS TO SEARCH FOR

Red Callender led a record date as early as 1944 (for Exclusive) and headed sessions for Swing (1945–46), Black & White (1946), Victor (1951–52), RIH (1952), and Cash (1955) plus full albums for Crown (1954 and 1956), Metrojazz (1958), and Legend (1973); good luck finding any of them! His final album as a leader, *Night Mist Blues* (Hemisphere 1002), is a fine all-round trio set from 1984 with pianist Gerry Wiggins and drummer Sherman Ferguson. Callender mostly plays bass (including on a cooking version of "The Way You Look Tonight") but also is quite effective on tuba for "Lush Life" and sings his "Baby I'm Gone."

FILMS

Films: Red Callendar appears with the Hazel Scott Trio in *I Dood It* (1943) and with Louis Armstrong in *New Orleans* (1947).

PERCY HEATH

b. Apr. 30, 1923, Wilmington, NC

A reliable bassist with a strong and frequently joyful personality in his playing, Percy Heath is one of the three famous Heath brothers, three years older than saxophonist Jimmy and a dozen years older than drummer Albert "Tootie" Heath. All of the Heaths grew up in Philadelphia, where

Percy was a violinist from the time he was eight, not switching to bass until 1946, when he was already 23. He picked up important experience as the house bassist at Philadelphia's Down Beat Club and developed quickly. In 1947, both Percy and Jimmy moved to New York to join Howard McGhee's group. Percy Heath played with all of the top Bop musicians during the next few years, including Charlie Parker, Thelonious Monk, Fats Navarro, J. J. Johnson, Dizzy Gillespie (his 1950–52 sextet), and Miles Davis, appearing on many records during 1947–52.

In 1951 Heath joined the Milt Jackson Quartet, which the following year became the Modern Jazz Quartet. The bassist was with the MJQ during its entire existence, touring the world during its first 23 years before its temporary breakup in 1975. He was not out of work long, for he got together with his two siblings and formed the Heath Brothers Band, working steadily for the next seven years (1975–82). When the MJQ was reformed in 1982, Heath rejoined the group, staying until it finally ended its remarkable run in 1996. Soon afterwards the Heath Brothers came back together on a part-time basis, recording for Concord and playing some dates. By 1999 Percy was largely retired except for occasional appearances. Strangely enough, Percy Heath never led his own record date, although the bassist was well featured as a sideman with the MJQ and with others, occasionally doubling on cello or on his "baby bass."

CHUBBY JACKSON

b. Oct. 25, 1918, New York, NY

A solid bassist, Chubby Jackson (who was born Greig Jackson) was perhaps most important as a cheerleader for Woody Herman and Bebop in general, often letting loose vocal shouts during other players' heated solos. He started on clarinet when he was 16, switching to bass soon afterwards, and played professionally by the time he was 19. Jackson had stints with the big bands of Raymond Scott, Jan Savitt, Henry Busse, and Charlie Barnet (1941–43). With Barnet for a time he was one of two bassists, playing alongside Oscar Pettiford. Jackson first joined Herman's big band in 1943, and he helped encourage the transition of the orchestra from a swing band and one influenced by Duke Ellington into a Bop-oriented outfit. Jackson was an important force behind the scene, helping to persuade Herman to hire many spirited modernists, players who were not only quite individual and adventurous in their playing but, like Jackson, enjoyed having fun with music.

Chubby Jackson was with Woody Herman's Herd until its breakup in 1946. He played with Charlie Ventura in 1947, put together his own band, and during an important tour helped to introduce Bebop to Scandinavia. Jackson was back with Herman during part of 1948, playing with the Second Herd, and he had several short-term reunions with Herman through the years. Jackson led a big band during 1948–49 (it did not stand much of a chance), played with Ventura again in 1951, had an on-and-off group with Bill Harris, and spent the 1950s as a studio musician. He also hosted his own children's television show. Since the early '60s, Jackson has spent periods playing and living in Chicago, Las Vegas, Miami, and Los Angeles, performing mostly locally, although he was with Lionel Hampton during 1978–79. Chubby's son Duffy Jackson has long been an impressive drummer. As a leader, Chubby Jackson (who retired from playing in the mid-1990s) recorded for King, Keynote, MGM, Century, Columbia, and the Swedish Cupol label in the 1940s and for New Jazz, Norgran, Argo, Everest, and Crown in the '50s.

LPS TO SEARCH FOR

Chubby Jackson Sextet and Big Band (Prestige 7641) has a combo session with Conte Candoli and tenor saxophonist Emmett Carls from 1947 and an all-star big band session from 1950. The latter does not feature Jackson's short-lived orchestra (which had broken up the year before) but does have such major soloists as Charlie Kennedy, Zoot Sims, Georgie Auld, J. J. Johnson, Kai Winding, Gerry Mulligan, and Howard McGhee. The charts of Tiny Kahn, Al Cohn, and Mulligan are quite colorful. *Bebop Enters Sweden 1947–1949* (Dragon 34) includes sessions by the Dizzy Gillespie Big Band and James Moody along with three numbers by Chubby Jackson's "Fifth Dimensional Jazz Group," a 1947 sextet with Conte Candoli, Frank Socolow, Lou Levy, Terry Gibbs, and Denzil Best.

FILMS

Chubby Jackson is seen with Woody Herman's Orchestra in *Earl Carroll Vanities* (1945).

AL McKIBBON

b. Jan. 1, 1919, Chicago, IL

A valuable if underrated bassist for over a half-century, Al McKibbon tends to be overlooked, but he is an asset on every session on which he appears. He grew up in Detroit, studied bass and piano at Cass Technical High School, and played early on in Detroit with Kelly Martin and Teddy Buckner. After moving to New York he worked with many groups, including those led by Lucky Millinder (1943), Tab Smith (1945–46), Coleman Hawkins, J. C. Heard, Bud Powell, Thelonious Monk, and, most importantly, the Dizzy Gillespie Big Band (1948–49). McKibbon performed with the Miles Davis Nonet at their Royal Roost engagement in 1948 and was on one of the group's three recording sessions (1950). After playing with Count Basie's small group in 1950, McKibbon was a longtime member of the George Shearing Quintet (1951–58). Long interested in Latin jazz, the bassist was in Cal Tjader's group during 1958–59. He settled in Los Angeles and became a studio musician in the 1960s. McKibbon toured with the Giants of Jazz during 1971–72 and recorded with the all-star sextet (Dizzy Gillespie, Sonny Stitt, Kai Winding, Thelonious Monk, and Art Blakey) and with Monk and Blakey in a trio. Since that time Al McKibbon (who moved back to New York in the early '90s to play with Broadway shows) has continued freelancing, in both straightahead jazz and Latin jazz settings. He finally led his first record date in 1999, when he was 80.

9 *Tumbao Para Los Congueros Di Mi Vida / 1999 / Blue Lady/Chartmaker 1080*
In 1999, bassist Al McKibbon at last had his first opportunity to lead his own record date. He performs Bop-oriented Afro-Cuban jazz in a small combo with flutist Charles Owens (who also has a couple of saxophone solos), pianist Phil Wright, both Jose "Papo" Rodriguez and Ramon Banda on Latin percussion, and (on two songs) Justo Almario on saxophones. These versions of Thelonious Monk's "Off Minor," "Tin Tin Deo," Ray Bryant's "Cubano Chant," and "I Mean You" are both danceable and creative, and the band frequently sounds a lot larger than just five or six pieces. Recommended.

OSCAR PETTIFORD

b. Sept. 30, 1922, Okmulgee, OK, d. Sept. 8, 1960, Copenhagen, Denmark
Arguably the most talented jazz bassist of the classic Bebop era and one of the finest of all time, Oscar Pettiford was the first bassist to build upon and extend the innovations of Jimmy Blanton. While most other bassists of the 1940s played merely a supportive role and took very basic solos,

Pettiford was a virtuoso whose improvisations were as complex as any taken by the best saxophonists. An underrated songwriter, among his compositions are "Tricotism," "Swingin' Till the Girls Come Home," "Blues in the Closet," and "Bohemia After Dark." In addition, along with Harry Babasin, he was the first jazz cellist. Although Pettiford's occasional excessive drinking (which tended to put him in a fighting mood) cost him a few jobs along the way, he had a productive, if relatively brief, career.

After a short period on piano, Pettiford (one of 11 children) switched to bass and played in a family band led by his father, Doc Pettiford. In 1942 he joined Charlie Barnet's orchestra as half of a two-bass team with Chubby Jackson. In 1943 Pettiford began to be noticed as he played with Coleman Hawkins (including Hawk's famous "The Man I Love" record session) and Ben Webster, also recording with Earl Hines. Pettiford worked with Roy Eldridge, co-led the first Bebop group on 52nd Street with Dizzy Gillespie, and went to the West Coast with Coleman Hawkins in 1945. The bassist, who appeared on quite a few records during the Bebop era (leading a session of his own in 1945), spent much of the 1945–48 period as a member of Duke Ellington's orchestra, where he was well featured in Jimmy Blanton's former role. He was also part of Woody Herman's Second Herd in 1949.

In the 1950s, Pettiford led several short-term bands (including a 13-piece orchestra), recorded as both a leader and as a sideman (including with Miles Davis, Thelonious Monk, John Coltrane, and Lucky Thompson), and was, along with Charles Mingus, the top jazz bassist of the decade. He was showcased on cello on a record date with a Duke Ellington quartet in 1950 and led sessions for Mercer (1951), Savoy (1952), Debut (1953), Swing (1954), Bethlehem (three albums during 1954–55), and ABC/Paramount (1956–57). In 1958 Pettiford went to Europe and soon settled in Copenhagen, where he worked with Stan Getz and in a group with Bud Powell and Kenny Clarke that was called "The Three Bosses." He also played with many top European musicians. Very active in 1960 (recording a few titles as late as August 30, 1960), Oscar Pettiford's death from a virus 22 days before his 38th birthday was a major loss to the jazz world.

7 *The New Oscar Pettiford Sextet / Mar. 10, 1949–Aug. 22, 1959 / Original Jazz Classics 1926*
9 *First Bass / June 1953–July 5, 1960 / IAJRC 1010*

The first bassist to build upon the innovations of Jimmy Blanton, Oscar Pettiford was also a major soloist on cello and an underrated songwriter.

8   *Sextet / Mar. 21, 1954 / RCA/Vogue 40945*

7   *Another One / Aug. 12, 1955 / Bethlehem/Avenue Jazz 75910*

9   *Deep Passion / June 11, 1956–Sept. 6, 1957 / GRP/ Impulse 143*

Oscar Pettiford led ensembles and record dates on an occasional basis in the 1950s. *The New Oscar Pettiford Sextet* has five selections from a very interesting 1953 sextet that is made up of the leader on cello, tenor saxophonist Phil Urso, Julius Watkins on French horn, pianist Walter Bishop, bassist Charles Mingus, and drummer Percy Brice. The tenor-French horn-cello frontline gives a unique sound to the cool Bop date. Two other songs on the CD date from August 22, 1959, and match Pettiford (on bass) in Copenhagen with vibraphonist Louis Hjulmand and pianist Jan Johansson. Wrapping up the expanded disc is a 1949 session that actu-

ally finds the bassist as a sideman on a Serge Chaloff date filled with interesting Bop players, including Red Rodney, Terry Gibbs, Denzil Best, pianist Barbara Carroll, trombonist Earl Swope, and Al Cohn on tenor; Shorty Rogers provided the arrangements.

First Bass is full of rarities, starting off with an extraordinary four-song date from 1953 that features both Pettiford and Harry Babasin on soloing and dueling cellos while backed by a rhythm section; the tunes include "Monti Cello" and "In a Cello Mood!" In addition, Pettiford jams with a Lionel Hampton septet, is heard on a German television show with guitarist Atilla Zoller and Kenny Clarke, performs at a concert with altoist Lee Konitz and tenor saxophonist Zoot Sims, has three trio numbers with pianist Phineas Newborn and Kenny Clarke, and is featured in Europe on two numbers from 1960. A must for Bebop collectors and

Oscar Pettiford fans, since none of this material is currently available elsewhere.

Sextet features Pettiford on bass and occasional overdubbed cello in an all-star group with Al Cohn, Kai Winding, Tal Farlow, pianist Henri Renaud, and Max Roach; the original six songs (which include "Stardust" and the lengthy "Burt's Pad") are augmented by two alternate takes. *Another One*, the only one of Pettiford's three Bethlehem albums currently available on CD, has four Pettiford originals (including "Bohemia After Dark" and "Oscalypso") along with five other songs performed by an octet also including trumpeter Donald Byrd, valve trombonist Bob Brookmeyer, and altoist Gigi Gryce. The arrangements (by Quincy Jones, Gryce, Tom Talbert, Ernie Wilkins, Pettiford, and others) fit very well into the 1950s jazz mainstream and the concise solos (including quite a few from the leader) uplift the often-challenging music. *Deep Passion* could also be titled "The Complete Oscar Pettiford Big Band Studio Sides" for the single disc has all of the music from the two albums recorded by the bassist's short-lived orchestra. Gigi Gryce, Lucky Thompson, and Benny Golson provided the arrangements, a harpist (either Janet Putnam or Betty Glamann) is an important part of the ensembles, and the soloists include trumpeter Art Farmer, trombonists Jimmy Cleveland and Al Grey, Julius Watkins on French horn, and the tenors of Lucky Thompson and Benny Golson in addition to Pettiford. Boppish, swinging, and highly recommended.

8 *Vienna Blues: The Complete Session / Jan. 9 + 12, 1959 / Black Lion 760104*
8 *Montmartre Blues / Aug. 22, 1959–July 6, 1960 / Black Lion 760124*

Vienna Blues is a European quartet date with tenor saxophonist Hans Koller, guitarist Attila Zoller, and drummer Jimmy Pratt. On some tracks, Pettiford switches to cello while Zoller plays bass. Pettiford and Koller contributed three songs apiece and also perform the standards "All the Things You Are," "Stardust," and "There Will Never Be Another You." This is fine music that falls between Bop and Hard Bop. Pettiford's final recordings (other than six selections) are on *Montmartre Blues,* and there is no sign of any decline. Pettiford interacts with a group of young Europeans (including trumpeter Allan Botschinsky and pianist Jan Johansson), is showcased on "Willow Weep for Me," and brought in five of the ten songs, including "Laverne Walk" and his answer to Miles Davis's "So What," which he called "Why Not? That's What!"

LPS TO SEARCH FOR

Discoveries (Savoy 1172) has some very rare performances featuring Oscar Pettiford. Seven of the 14 selections are alternate takes from a 1952 date that Pettiford (on cello) had with pianist Billy Taylor, bassist Charles Mingus, and drummer Charlie Smith; ironically the master takes have not been made available in recent times. It is particularly interesting hearing Pettiford and Mingus playing together. Also on this LP is a long-lost session by Charlie Smith (in a trio with Pettiford's bass and Hank Jones) and leftover tracks with accordionist Mat Mathews, pianist Eddie Costa, and tenorman Paul Quinichette. *Oscar Pettiford and His Birdland Band* (Spotlite 153) gives listeners a rare opportunity to hear Pettiford's short-lived big band of 1957 playing live. Among the many impressive names in the orchestra are such featured soloists as Donald Byrd, Al Grey, and altoist Gene Quill.

FILMS

Oscar Pettiford is featured with the Coleman Hawkins-Howard McGhee Quintet on one number in *The Crimson Canary* (1945)

TOMMY POTTER

b. Sept. 21, 1918, Philadelphia, PA, d. Mar. 3, 1988, Philadelphia, PA

Tommy Potter is best known for his playing with the Charlie Parker Quintet during 1947–49. Somewhat typical of the bassists of the era, Potter rarely ever soloed, and he stuck to accompanying other players. But his advanced choice of notes and endurance at rapid tempos were, if taken for granted, certainly appreciated by other musicians.

Potter grew up in New Jersey and studied piano and guitar before switching to bass when he was in his early twenties. He worked with pianist John Malachi, trombonist Trummy Young, Billy Eckstine's orchestra (1944–45), tenor saxophonist John Hardee, and Max Roach. As a member of the classic Parker quintet, Potter played alongside Miles Davis (later Kenny Dorham), Duke Jordan, and Roach, appearing on most of Bird's recordings of the era.

His post-Parker years were anticlimactic, if relatively busy. Potter worked with Stan Getz, the Count Basie small group in 1950, Billy Eckstine again (1950–51), Earl Hines (1952–53), Artie Shaw's Gramercy Five, Eddie Heywood, the Bud Powell Trio (including a 1956 tour of Scandinavia), Tyree Glenn, Harry "Sweets" Edison (1959–61), Buck Clayton, and the Al Cohn-Zoot Sims Quintet, touring Europe in

1965 with a Charlie Parker tribute band. Potter, who led his only two record sessions in 1956 while in Stockholm, mostly faded out of the jazz scene after the mid-1960s, working a day job but still gigging now and then up until 1980.

CURLY RUSSELL

b. Mar. 19, 1920, New York, NY, d. July 3, 1986, New York, NY

Curly Russell performed a similar role in his playing as Tommy Potter, and their careers often overlapped. Russell started out playing trombone before switching to bass. He gigged with the big bands of Don Redman (1941) and Benny Carter (1943). Starting in 1944, Russell played with most of the top Bop players, and he appeared on many records during the next decade, including with Dizzy Gillespie (1945) and Charlie Parker (1945, 1948, and 1950). He worked regularly with Parker, Dexter Gordon, Sarah Vaughan, Bud Powell, Tadd Dameron (1947–49), Coleman Hawkins, Fats Navarro, Miles Davis, Sonny Stitt, Stan Getz, and Buddy DeFranco (1952–53), among many others. Russell, who recorded with Horace Silver, Thelonious Monk, Clifford Brown, and Art Blakey in the mid-1950s, played in R&B groups later in the decade and then dropped out of music. Although considered a valuable and reliable player during the Bop era, Curly Russell never led any record dates of his own and was quite obscure during his final 30 years.

EDDIE SAFRANSKI

b. Dec. 25, 1918, Pittsburgh, PA, d. Jan. 10, 1979, Los Angeles, CA

One of the first important bass soloists to emerge after Jimmy Blanton, Eddie Safranski might have been one of the pacesetters of the 1950s had he not chosen to become a studio musician. He studied violin as a youth, switching to bass in high school. Safranski was the most impressive player in Hal McIntyre's orchestra during 1941–45, taking occasional solos and being a strong force in the ensembles. After gigging with trombonist Miff Mole, he became famous for his work with Stan Kenton's orchestra (1945–48), where he was well showcased frequently and updated the Jimmy Blanton tradition. Among his better features were "Safranski (Artistry in Bass)," "Concerto to End All Concertos," "Artistry in Bolero," and "Painted Rhythm." After Kenton broke up the band, Safranski was with Charlie Barnet's Bop orchestra

(1948–49) and then became a fixture in the studios as a staff musician with NBC. Other than a stint with Benny Goodman in 1951–52 and five songs recorded as a leader during 1952–53 (he had headed a pair of four-song sessions during 1946–47 for Savoy and Atlantic), the bassist was rarely heard in a jazz setting again. Eddie Safranski spent his later years (from the late 1960s on) as a jazz educator, working for a bass manufacturer and playing now and then in the Los Angeles area.

JOHN SIMMONS

b. June 14, 1918, Haskell, OK. D. Sept. 19, 1979, Los Angeles, CA

John Simmons was a swing bassist who was flexible enough to fit into Bop settings without much difficulty. He started his career working in San Diego and Los Angeles, including with the early Nat King Cole Trio, making his recording debut with Teddy Wilson in 1937. Simmons spent a period playing in Chicago, including with trumpeter Johnny Letman and Roy Eldridge (1940). He was with the big bands of Benny Goodman (1941), Cootie Williams, and Louis Armstrong and appeared in the classic Lester Young short film *Jammin' the Blues*. During 1944–49, Simmons played with a wide variety of top jazz artists who covered virtually every style. His resumé was quite impressive, since it included work with Louis Armstrong, the Eddie Heywood Sextet, Illinois Jacquet, stride pianist James P. Johnson, trumpeter Hot Lips Page, drummer Big Sid Catlett, Ben Webster, Billie Holiday, Coleman Hawkins, Thelonious Monk, and the Erroll Garner Trio (1949–52)! Simmons was also quite active during the 1950s, recording with Art Tatum, Milt Jackson and as part of a Tadd Dameron quartet with John Coltrane, visiting Scandinavia with Rolf Ericson in 1955, playing with Harry "Sweets" Edison, and working with Phineas Newborn (1959–60). Unfortunately illness led to the bassist's retirement in the early 1960s, and he is largely forgotten today. But John Simmons was a superior accompanist and, although he led no record dates of his own, he can be heard on many sessions as a sideman.

FILMS

John Simmons is with the Louis Armstrong Orchestra in *Jam Session* (1944) and appears briefly in *Boy! What a Girl* (1947).

Drummers

Prior to the Bebop era, drummers were relegated to a mostly supportive position behind soloists and ensembles. There were occasional drum features, and Gene Krupa, Buddy Rich, and Chick Webb were major names, but those were exceptions. Drummers were expected primarily to keep time and add a bit of color and drive to ensembles.

That began to change in the mid-1940s. The Bebop era found drummers taking their first steps toward becoming equal partners with the horn soloists. Jo Jones had introduced a lighter sound in his swinging style, and Kenny Clarke extended his ideas, putting the timekeeping function of the drum on the ride cymbal and often "commenting" on the proceedings by "dropping bombs" with his bass drum and playing unusual accents. While Clarke was in the military, Max Roach emerged and became the pacesetter among modern drummers. His solos were unpredictable statements that had the logic of a superior horn solo, using dynamics, contrast, and space rather than just being displays of technique. Most other drummers were inspired by Roach and came up with their personal approaches. Art Blakey was among the most fiery of all drummers, Don Lamond developed into one of the best modern big band players, Denzil Best and Tiny Kahn both showed strong talent as writers, and Shelly Manne became a top studio drummer who never abandoned jazz. Chano Pozo was in a different category altogether, jazz's first conga player and one who helped to develop Afro-Cuban jazz.

DENZIL BEST

b. Apr. 27, 1917, New York, NY, d. May 24, 1965, New York, NY

Denzil Best was one of the finest drummers of the classic Bebop era, but erratic health and two accidents hurt his career and eventually cut short his life. Early on, Best had lessons on both piano and trumpet. He played trumpet with Chris Columbus in 1940 and jammed at Minton's Playhouse, but a serious lung disease during 1940–41 forced him to give up the horn. Best took jobs on piano and bass for a few years until permanently switching to drums in 1943. Although he was already 26, within a few months he was ready to play with major musicians, starting with nine months as Ben Webster's drummer.

Best worked with Coleman Hawkins (1944–45), Illinois Jacquet (1946), and Chubby Jackson (including the bassist's tour of Sweden in 1947–48). He was an original member of the George Shearing Quintet (1949–52), staying until injuries from a car accident put him out of action for most of two years. Best came back in 1954, playing with Artie Shaw's Gramercy Five. The drummer was with Erroll Garner's trio (1956–57) and freelanced in New York, including with Nina Simone and Tyree Glenn. Best was less active in his later years due to calcium deposits in his wrists. He died at the age of 48 from a skull fracture caused when he fell down a flight of stairs at a subway. Unlike most drummers of the 1940s, Denzil Best (who never led his own recording date) was also a skilled composer, writing "Bemsha Swing" (with

Thelonious Monk), "Move," "Allen's Alley," and "Nothing But D. Best."

FILMS

Denzil Best plays one number with Coleman Hawkins and Howard McGhee in *The Crimson Canary* (1945).

ART BLAKEY

b. Oct. 11, 1919, Pittsburgh, PA, d. Oct. 16, 1990, New York, NY

One of the most explosive drummers in jazz history (his ferocious drum rolls had to be seen to be believed), Art Blakey was one of the most important percussionists to emerge during the Bebop era. In addition, his importance to jazz as the leader of the Jazz Messengers (the definitive Hard Bop group) and as a masterful talent scout who seemed to employ just about every top young straight-ahead player of the 1950s, '60s, '70s, and '80s is impossible to measure. Since his huge contributions will be dealt with in great detail in the Hard Bop book in this series, this entry deals with just his career prior to 1956.

Art Blakey took piano lessons early on, and he even played professionally on piano for a little while, until he was replaced on one job with Erroll Garner! He soon switched to drums, playing swing in his early days. After working with Mary Lou Williams (1942) and the Fletcher Henderson Orchestra (1943–44), Blakey became the drummer with Billy Eckstine's big band (1944–47). Inspired by Dizzy Gillespie, he greatly modernized his style, became a master at dropping "bombs," and was the driving force behind that innovative orchestra.

After Eckstine broke up his big band, Blakey had a rehearsal group called the Seventeen Messengers, and in 1947 he recorded four titles at the head of an octet. He traveled to Africa and studied the local music and Islam (1948–49), played with Lucky Millinder (1949), and was part of the Buddy DeFranco Quartet (1951–53). In 1954 he led a band at Birdland consisting of Clifford Brown, Lou Donaldson, pianist Horace Silver, and Curly Russell that recorded three albums' worth of material. The following year Blakey and Silver co-led the Jazz Messengers, using Kenny Dorham, tenor saxophonist Hank Mobley, and bassist Doug Watkins in the quintet. When Silver went out on his own in 1956, Blakey became the group's sole leader, and he would make the Jazz Messengers a jazz institution. The Hard Bop quintet (which was sometimes expanded to a sextet or a septet) continued under the drummer's leadership until his death in 1990 and featured a remarkable series of top up-and-coming players, including trumpeters Lee Morgan, Freddie Hubbard, Wynton Marsalis, and Terence Blanchard, saxophonists Johnny Griffin, Benny Golson, and Wayne Shorter, and pianists Bobby Timmons, Cedar Walton, Keith Jarrett, and Benny Green, among many others. Art Blakey, through his intense playing and inspiring leadership of the many editions of the Jazz Messengers, helped solidify Bebop and Hard Bop's takeover of the jazz modern mainstream, and he was the unofficial godfather of the 1990s "Young Lions" movement.

8 *New Sounds / Dec. 27, 1947 -Oct. 25, 1948 / Blue Note 84436*

9 *A Night at Birdland, Vol. 1 / Feb. 21, 1954 / Blue Note 46519*

9 *A Night at Birdland, Vol. 2 / Feb. 21, 1954 / Blue Note 46520*

10 *Horace Silver and the Jazz Messengers / Nov. 13, 1954 + Feb. 6, 1955 / Blue Note 46140*

9 *At the Café Bohemia, Vol. 1 / Nov. 11, 1955 / Blue Note 46521*

9 *At the Café Bohemia, Vol. 2 / Nov. 11, 1955 / Blue Note 46522*

New Sounds is listed as being co-led by Art Blakey and James Moody. Included are the five 1947 titles by Blakey's Messengers (an octet with Kenny Dorham and Walter Bishop), plus two sessions headed by James Moody (including one on which Blakey plays drums). The latter dates have arrangements by Gil Fuller (one of his few important projects outside of the Dizzy Gillespie big band), and most of Moody's sidemen (which include trumpeter Dave Burns, Ernie Henry, Cecil Payne, and on one date Chano Pozo) are taken from Dizzy's orchestra. Such titles as "The Fuller Bop Man," "Moody's All Frantic," "Cu-Ba," and "Tin Tin Deo" are classic Bebop.

Moving up to 1954, Art Blakey led a band at Birdland that was the direct predecessor of the Jazz Messengers. In addition to his future co-leader, Horace Silver, the unit features the great trumpeter Clifford Brown, Lou Donaldson, and Curly Russell. The two volumes that are available from Blue Note (which leave out "Lullaby of Birdland" and two alternate takes available only in Japan) are of equal quality, with the musicians sounding inspired on such numbers as "Split Kick" and "A Night in Tunisia" on *Vol. 1* and "Wee Dot" and "Confirmation" on the second set.

The official debut of the Jazz Messengers was released under Horace Silver's name because he wrote the majority of the songs, including two ("The Preacher" and "Doodlin' ") that would quickly become standards. The Café Bohemia titles from up to a year later use the same personnel, which, in addition to Blakey and Silver, consists of Kenny Dorham, Hank Mobley, and Doug Watkins. Two domestic CDs have been released that contain most but not all of the valuable music (six cuts have been released only on a Japanese Vol. 3), and the performances are as hard-swinging as one would expect. In certain ways these three CDs as a whole contain the unofficial beginning of Hard Bop (although Miles Davis had recorded in a Hard Bop style as early as 1951), for this band features the funky piano of Silver, very active drumming for Blakey, and advanced solos from Dorham and Mobley that are a little distant from Dizzy Gillespie and Charlie Parker. The music looks beyond Bop to future versions of the Jazz Messengers.

FILMS

Art Blakey can be seen in 1946 with Billy Eckstine's orchestra in *Rhythm on a Riff*, which is included in the video *Things to Come* (Vintage Jazz Classics 2006).

KENNY CLARKE

b. Jan. 2, 1914, Pittsburgh, PA, d. Jan. 26, 1985, Montreuil-sous-Bois, France

Considered the first Bebop drummer, Kenny Clarke shifted the timekeeping function of the drums from the bass drum

(Gene Krupa) and the hi-hat cymbal (Jo Jones) to the ride cymbal. His use of the bass drum to "drop bombs" as irregular accents changed the way that drums "accompany" soloists, leading to much more interaction and setting a standard for the drummers who followed.

As a child, Clarke played vibes, piano, and trombone in addition to drums. He worked with Leroy Bradley (1930–35), Roy Eldridge (1935), the Jeter-Pillars Band, and Edgar Hayes's orchestra (1937–38), sounding very impressive as an accompanist on his records with Hayes. During a European tour with Hayes, Clarke led his first record date, although his doubling on xylophone makes one grateful that he settled on drums!

After playing with Claude Hopkins's big band, Clarke worked with Teddy Hill's orchestra (1939–40), where his adventurous playing was sometimes seen as disruptive. However, when Hill broke up the ensemble and became the manager at Minton's Playhouse, he wisely hired Clarke for the house band, which soon also included Thelonious Monk, bassist Nick Fenton, and Joe Guy. While at Minton's, Clarke fully formed his Bebop style and gained the nickname of "Klook-Mop" from his rhythmic accents. A versatile musician who cowrote "Epistrophy" with Thelonious Monk and "Salt Peanuts" with Dizzy Gillespie, Clarke was able to play fairly conventionally with the bands of Louis Armstrong, Ella Fitzgerald, Benny Carter, Henry "Red" Allen, and Coleman Hawkins, and he recorded with Sidney Bechet. A stint in the military (1943–46) kept Clarke off the scene during some key years. By the time he was discharged, Max Roach was the pacesetter among drummers. However, Clarke was soon a major part of the Bebop scene. He led a notable record session that included Fats Navarro, Kenny Dorham, Sonny Stitt, and Bud Powell and worked with Tadd Dameron and the Dizzy Gillespie big band, visiting Europe with Gillespie in 1948. After playing with Billy Eckstine's backup band in 1951, Clarke became an original member of the Modern Jazz Quartet in 1952. However, he was soon dissatisfied with the musical restrictions of the MJQ (he preferred to play more freewheeling music), and he left the band in 1955. During 1955–56 the drummer freelanced and appeared on many recordings.

In 1956 Clarke moved to France, where he chose to spend the remainder of his life (other than rare and brief visits back to the United States). The drummer worked with Miles Davis (1957), Bud Powell and Oscar Pettiford (later Pierre Michelot) as the Three Bosses (1959–62), did studio work, freelanced in many situations, and during 1960–73 co-led the Kenny Clarke-Francy Boland Orchestra, an all-star big band filled with both Europeans and expatriate Americans. Strangely enough, the orchestra had two drummers, with Kenny Clarke playing next to Kenny Clare! Kenny Clarke worked steadily to the end of his life (including with Dexter Gordon and Gene Ammons), recorded a percussion album in 1983 with avant-garde drummers Milford Graves, Don Moye, and Andrew Cyrille, and played with an early version of the Paris Reunion Band before his death at age 71.

7   *Telefunken Blues / Nov. 1, 1954–Feb. 7, 1955 / Savoy 106*

7   *Bohemia After Dark / June 28, 1955–July 14, 1955 / Savoy 107*

8   *Meets the Detroit Jazzmen / Apr. 30, 1956–May 9, 1956 / Savoy 243*

9   *Clarke Boland Big Band / Oct. 29, 1969 / RTE 1501*

Kenny Clarke CDs tend to be difficult to find. The three Savoy CDs, put out by Japanese Denon, all contain excellent music, but the packaging is not always the best, being attempts at recreating LPs from the 1950s. *Telefunken Blues* has a pair of sextet dates arranged by either Eddie Beal or Ernie Wilkins. Half of the music has Frank Morgan, tenor saxophonist Walter Benton, and Milt Jackson in the frontline, while the other selections (which have Jackson doubling on piano) feature trombonist Henry Coker, Frank Wess on tenor and flute, and baritonist Charlie Fowlkes. The music overlaps between 1950s swing, Bebop, and early Hard Bop. *Bohemia After Dark* is historically quite significant (being the first recordings of altoist Cannonball Adderley), but the hard-swinging music is available in more complete form on the two-CD set by the Adderley Brothers called *The Summer of '55* (Savoy 92860). *Meets the Detroit Jazzmen* features Clarke in his last American date as a leader, heading a quintet that includes four major musicians who had just "emigrated" to New York from Detroit: baritonist Pepper Adams, Tommy Flanagan, guitarist Kenny Burrell, and bassist Paul Chambers, all of whom play quite well on the straight-ahead material.

Recordings by the Kenny Clarke-Francy Boland big band have always been difficult to find in the United States, and many go for very high prices on auction lists. The two-CD RTE release was fortunately put out in 1992 and gives a strong idea of the band's power and solo power. Among the musicians heard from are trumpeters Benny Bailey, Art

Farmer, and Idrees Sulieman, trombonist Ake Persson, Johnny Griffin, and Tony Coe on tenors, and the co-leaders. Until Mosaic or some other label is persuaded to put together a "complete" series on this classic band, this twofer is the best current example of the legendary orchestra.

LPS TO SEARCH FOR

The Paris Bebop Sessions (Prestige 7605) puts together three European dates that have been reissued elsewhere. Clarke is heard with a 1948 octet that features Howard McGhee, Jimmy Heath (on alto), and John Lewis, with a sextet from that year with Benny Bailey and Cecil Payne, and in a supportive role with a 1950 James Moody quartet. The latter two dates also include pianist Ralph Schecroun, who years later would emerge as a highly original avant-gardist named Errol Parker.

Kenny Clarke in Paris Vol. One (Swing 8411) features Clarke with a variety of bands during 1957–60 with such sidemen as Lucky Thompson, Don Byas, and Pierre Michelot. Among the Clarke/Boland Orchestra's LPs that have been briefly available in the United States are *Open Door* (Muse 5056), *Sax No End* (Pausa 7097), *All Smiles* (MPS 15214), and *At Her Majesty's Pleasure* (Black Lion 131).

FILMS

Kenny Clarke is on the soundtrack of *Elevator to the Gallows* (1958) with Miles Davis. He also appears briefly in the French films *Two Are Guilty* (1962) and *The Only Game in Town* (1969).

JOE HARRIS

b. Dec. 23, 1926, Pittsburgh, PA

A fine drummer, Joe Harris is best known for his association with Dizzy Gillespie. After playing locally starting from the age of 15, he was with the Dizzy Gillespie Big Band on and off during 1946–48 (with whom he recorded) and was part of a quintet with Diz and Bird at their 1947 Carnegie Hall concert. Freelancing in New York, Harris played with many top musicians and singers, including Arnett Cobb (1948), Billy Eckstine (1950), Erroll Garner's trio (1952), and James Moody (1954) plus working in the house band at the Apollo Theatre. After touring Sweden with Rolf Ericson, Harris settled in Stockholm in 1956, moving to Germany in 1961, where he worked with the Kenny Clarke-Francy Boland Orchestra for five years. He returned to the United States in

1967, working with Benny Carter and touring with Ella Fitzgerald in 1968. After spending much of 1970–72 in Germany, Harris resettled back in his native Pittsburgh, where he was active as both a drummer and an educator at the University of Pittsburgh into the late 1980s. Although he appeared on many Bop-oriented records (including with Howard McGhee, Milt Jackson, James Moody, King Pleasure, and the Clarke-Boland big band), Joe Harris never led his own record date.

J. C. HEARD

b. Oct. 8, 1917, Dayton, OH, d. Sept. 30, 1988, Royal Oak, MI

The versatile J. C. Heard was able to fit into Bebop, swing, Mainstream, big bands, and combo settings with equal confidence and skill throughout his career. Born James Charles Heard, he started out performing as a dancer in vaudeville. After playing locally in Detroit, Heard worked with the Teddy Wilson Big Band (1939–40), Wilson's sextet, Coleman Hawkins, Benny Carter, and the Cab Calloway Orchestra (1942–45). During the classic Bebop era, Heard recorded with many of the top modernists in addition to leading his own group at Café Society (1946–47). He spent time as a member of Erroll Garner's trio, toured with Jazz at the Philharmonic, and spent much of 1953–57 playing in Japan (including using pianist Toshiko Akiyoshi as a sideman), Australia, China, and the Philippines. During 1957–66, Heard freelanced in the New York area, playing mostly with swing-oriented groups, including gigging with the Coleman Hawkins-Roy Eldridge Quintet, touring Europe with Sammy Price (1960), and working with Teddy Wilson's trio (1961) and Dorothy Donegan. In 1966 he moved to Detroit, where he lived for the remainder of his life, leading a local big band and inspiring many younger players. In addition to the musicians mentioned, Heard recorded with Pete Johnson, Sir Charles Thompson, Sidney Bechet, Red Norvo, Count Basie, Charlie Parker, Lester Young, Doc Cheatham, Billie Holiday, Illinois Jacquet, Oscar Peterson, Howard McGhee, Ben Webster, Gene Ammons, and many others; he was obviously quite valuable! J. C. Heard also led record dates for Keynote (1945), Continental (1946), Apollo (1948), Epic (1956), Argo (1958), Parkwood (1983), and with his big band for Hiroko (1986).

The Detroit Jazz Tradition (Parkwood 102), from 1983, was Heard's first date as a leader in 25 years. In addition to Canadian bassist Dave Young, the quartet features a pair of Detroit musicians: pianist Claude Black and George Benson (no relation to the guitarist) on tenor and alto. They perform five standards and three group originals, with Heard taking a rare vocal on "J. C.'s Blues"; fine straight-ahead music. *Some of This, Some of That* (Hiroko 0187) is the only album that has come out thus far from the J. C. Heard Orchestra. The 13-piece big band (heard in 1986) does not include any major names but plays high-quality Hard Bop, including four of Heard's songs, "Nica's Dream," and Woody Shaw's "Sweet Love of Mine"; trumpeter Walter Szymanski (who also contributed the arrangements) stars among the sidemen.

FILMS

J. C. Heard appears with Teddy Wilson's orchestra in the film short *Boogie Woogie Dream* (1941).

TINY KAHN

b. May, 1924, New York, NY, d. Aug. 19, 1953,
Martha's Vineyard, MA

A solid timekeeper, Tiny Kahn, had he lived past the age of 29, would probably have been most significant as an arranger-composer. Born Norman Kahn, he started playing drums when he was 15 and during the Bebop era worked with Georgie Auld (1947), Boyd Raeburn, the Chubby Jackson Big Band (1949) (for whom he also contributed arrangements), and Charlie Barnet's Bebop Orchestra. Kahn, who also recorded with Lester Young and Red Rodney, worked with the Stan Getz Quartet (1951), played vibes with Elliott Lawrence on a daily radio show, and freelanced. Among his compositions were "Tiny's Blues," "Father Knickerbopper," and "Leo the Lion." Tiny Kahn, who was far from small, died of a heart attack, cutting short his life and an increasingly significant career. He never led his own record date.

DON LAMOND

b. Aug. 18, 1921, Oklahoma City, OK

Famous for his contributions to Woody Herman's first two Herds, Don Lamond has long been a solid big band drummer who could also play quite effectively in small combos. He grew up in Washington D. C., attended the Peabody Institute, and started his career working with the big bands of Sunny Dunham (1943) and Boyd Raeburn (1944). Lamond gained fame after he replaced an ailing Dave Tough with Woody Herman in 1945, appearing on many records with the popular band until its breakup in 1946. Following a period of freelancing, he was a major part of Herman's Second Herd (1947–49), where his drumming was definitive.

Later on Lamond displayed his versatility through such associations as Marian McPartland's trio (1951), Johnny Smith, Stan Getz, Bud Powell, Charlie Parker, Dick Hyman, Johnny Guarnieri, Jack Teagarden, Willie "The Lion" Smith, Ruby Braff (1958–59), George Wein's Newport All-Stars, Stephane Grappelli, Joe Venuti, Red Norvo, and Maxine Sullivan (1971), among many others. Don Lamond also worked steadily in the studios, and on an occasional basis from the mid-1970s on he has led his own big band in Florida, where he eventually settled.

7 *Extraordinary / 1977–Sept. 4, 1982 / Circle 148*
Other than a drum demonstration record for Command in 1962, Don Lamond's only album as a leader was a big band program cut for Progressive in 1977 and 1982. That entire project plus one in which he and his quartet (with trumpeter Ben Clement) back his wife, singer Terry Lamond, in 1981 are reissued in full on this consistently swinging CD. As with the J. C. Heard big band album, there are no big names to be heard from in this local band, but the music (which ranges from swing to middle-of-the-road) is quite pleasing. Best is a "Woody Herman Medley," consisting of "Early Autumn," "Four Brothers," and Apple Honey."

FILMS

Don Lamond can be seen with Woody Herman's Orchestra in *Hit Parade of 1947* (1947).

SHELLY MANNE

b. June 11, 1920, New York, NY, d. Sept. 26, 1984,
Los Angeles, CA

One of the most important drummers of the West Coast jazz movement of the 1950s, Shelly Manne owes his inclusion in this book to his early work with Stan Kenton and the classic Bebop era. This entry deals with his career prior to his settling in Los Angeles in 1952; Manne's later work and his recordings (his first date as a leader was in November 1951) will be covered in detail in the West Coast Jazz book in this series.

Shelly Manne began as an alto saxophonist but switched to drums when he was 18. He played with Bobby Byrne and clarinetist Joe Marsala (with whom he recorded in 1941), had stints with the big bands of Bob Astor, Raymond Scott, Will Bradley, and Les Brown, and was on Coleman Hawkins's famous "The Man I Love" recording session of 1943, despite being in the Coast Guard during 1942–45! By 1945, Manne was increasingly in demand as a freelancer, and he had developed into a subtle but consistently creative modern drummer. He recorded "Blue 'n Boogie" with Dizzy Gillespie and in 1946 joined the Stan Kenton Orchestra for the first time, staying with Kenton until he broke up the band in 1948. During this time Manne showed that he could swing the potentially pompous Stan Kenton ensemble while being virtuosic enough to expertly play the more ambitious concert pieces written by Kenton and Pete Rugolo. After the orchestra disbanded, Manne worked with Jazz at the Philharmonic and Woody Herman's Second Herd (1949). Manne was back with Kenton when the huge Innovations Orchestra was formed, and his versatility made him one of the few drummers who could flourish in that setting.

In 1952, after permanently leaving Kenton, the drummer went out on his own and moved to Los Angeles. He would work with the Lighthouse All-Stars and Shorty Rogers, form his group Shelly Manne and His Men, and lead a long string of important and enjoyable recordings for the Contemporary label during 1953–62 while also being a busy studio musician. He ran the club Shelly's Manne-Hole (1960–74), was a member of the L. A. Four in the mid-1970s, and retained his popularity as an important fixture on the Los Angeles jazz scene up until his death in 1984.

ROY PORTER

b. July 30, 1923, Walsenburg, CO, d. Jan. 25, 1998, Los Angeles, CA

Roy Porter was very significant for a remarkably brief period of time before he disappeared into history. After playing with Milt Larkin's band (1943) and serving in the military, the drummer settled in Los Angeles. He quickly became a major part of the modern jazz scene, playing regularly with Howard McGhee during 1945–46 (with whom he made his recording debut), recording with Charlie Parker in 1946 (in-

cluding "Moose the Mooche," "Yardbird Suite," "Ornithology," and the infamous "Lover Man" session), and working regularly on Central Avenue. Porter appeared on many records during the Bebop era (particularly for the Dial label), including dates headed by Dexter Gordon, Wardell Gray and Teddy Edwards. In 1949 he formed an adventurous big band that included among its sidemen trumpeter Art Farmer, altoist Eric Dolphy, and trombonist Jimmy Knepper. They recorded two sessions for Savoy, last reissued on the two-LP set *Black California* (Savoy 2215), and one long-lost session for the soon-defunct Knockout label. In 1950, Porter moved to San Francisco, where for a little while he worked regularly at Bop City.

And then it all came to an end. Busted for drugs, Roy Porter was soon off the scene. When he came back, he pretty much had to start from the bottom, and he did not have the will power or the initiative to make much of a comeback. Porter mostly did session work in the 1950s (including appearing on dates with Earl Bostic and Louis Jordan) and '60s, playing anonymously on many commercial dates. He recorded obscure albums for the Chelan (1971) and Bel-Ad (1975) labels that went nowhere, and he retired altogether in 1978. In 1991 Roy Porter completed his memoirs (*There and Back*) with the assistance of David Keller, helping to set the record straight about his often-overlooked but important place in Bebop history.

CHANO POZO

b. Jan. 7, 1915, Havana, Cuba, d. Dec. 12, 1948, New York, NY

The first major percussionist in jazz history and one who introduced the conga to jazz, Chano Pozo was one of the early innovators (along with Dizzy Gillespie, Machito, and Mario Bauza) who helped to form the fusion of Cuban folk music and Bebop that resulted in Latin (or Afro-Cuban) Jazz.

Pozo's background was playing drums and percussion instruments with Cuban and Nigerian religious cults in his native Havana. He moved to New York in 1947 and was introduced to Gillespie by Bauza; soon Dizzy eagerly invited Pozo to join his band. The use of a percussionist was unprecedented in a jazz big band at the time. Pozo was featured on a variety of special numbers, including George Russell's "Cubana Be/Cubana Bop" and two songs that he cowrote with Gillespie: "Manteca" and "Tin Tin Deo." After touring Europe and becoming a major influence on Latin music,

Chano Pozo (who always had a bad temper) was killed in a fight in a Harlem bar when he was a month short of his 34th birthday. His cousin Chino Pozo would be a valuable percussionist in the 1950s, but Chano Pozo (who in his short period in New York had also recorded with James Moody, Charlie Parker, Illinois Jacquet, Chico O'Farrill, and Milt Jackson) was irreplaceable.

Vocalists

Although there were vocalists in jazz from the very beginning, it would not be an exaggeration to say that jazz singing began with Louis Armstrong. His relaxed phrasing, his dramatic ability to contrast sound with silence, and his way of subtly altering melody lines became hugely influential by the late 1920s. Bing Crosby learned from Satch, and Crosby's style ended up permanently affecting pop music.

During the swing era, most big bands featured a female and a male vocalist. Generally one singer was employed primarily for straight renditions of ballads, while the other was more of a "rhythm singer," someone who swung tunes and sometimes sang blues. Although there were countless vocalists during this time period who were at least slightly associated with jazz, the most significant ones to emerge were Ella Fitzgerald (whose style would become strongly influenced by Bebop), Jimmy Rushing, Billie Holiday, Nat King Cole, Big Joe Turner, Cab Calloway, Mildred Bailey, Lee Wiley, Maxine Sullivan, Helen Humes, Dinah Washington, and Leo Watson. The adventurous and somewhat-crazy Watson could be considered the direct predecessor of Bebop singing. Of the singers listed, all but Cole, Turner, and Sullivan had important experience with big bands. In addition there were other singers, such as Frank Sinatra, Doris Day, Jo Stafford, and Dick Haymes, who would emerge from the orchestras to have important solo careers in middle-of-the-road pop music, leaving jazz altogether by the classic Bebop era.

Three singers who sang with big bands just as the swing era was ending had very important careers in Bop and beyond: Sarah Vaughan, Billy Eckstine, and Anita O'Day. But otherwise the singers who were most active with Bop groups during the 1945–49 period, such performers as Joe "Bebop" Carroll, Earl Coleman, Babs Gonzales, Pancho Hagood, Jackie and Roy, Dave Lambert, Jackie Paris, and Buddy Stewart, were destined to become mostly cult figures, although Jackie and Roy kept working for a half-century, and Lambert would find fame a decade later with Lambert, Hendricks and Ross. Singing Bebop was not the best way to achieve hit records and fame with the general public!

Many of the modern musicians of the period thought of vocalists as a frivolity (although Dizzy Gillespie enjoyed their presence), while most singers preferred to interpret standards rather than tackle the more difficult Bop lines. Vocalese, which involved assigning words to the recorded instrumental solos of Bop and swing players (and resulted in a few hits), would not be documented until the early 1950s, while the cooler-toned vocalists who were just starting to emerge (such as June Christy, Helen Merrill, and Chris Connor) really fit into a later era. Most classic Bebop singers were as obscure as the musicians, and this was one of the very few periods when up-and-coming male jazz vocalists outnumbered the females.

JOE "BEBOP" CARROLL

b. Nov. 25, 1919, Philadelphia, PA, Feb. 1, 1981, Brooklyn, NY

A limited but enthusiastic scat singer, Joe "Bebop" Carroll came to fame due to his association with Dizzy Gillespie. He sang early on with Paul Bascomb's orchestra and had a very small part in the film *Stormy Weather* (1943). In 1949 Carroll joined the Dizzy Gillespie big band (replacing Poncho Hagood), singing such numbers as "Hey Pete! Let's Eat Mo' Meat" and "In the Land of Oo-Bla-Dee." He remained with Dizzy after the orchestra broke up, being featured on humorous Bebop novelties such as "Oo-Shoo-Be-Do-Be" and "School Days." After touring Europe with Gillespie's quintet in 1953, Carroll went out on his own and, although he worked fairly steadily, he soon faded away. Other than touring with Woody Herman during 1963–64, the singer worked as a single throughout the remainder of his career, never achieving much fame on his own. As a leader, Joe Carroll recorded for Prestige (1952), Vogue (1953), Epic (1956), the

Charlie Parker label (1962's *Man with a Happy Sound*), and Jazzmania (1978); in addition two selections from 1950 were later released by Spotlite. Only the four Prestige numbers are currently available on CD as part of a sampler.

EARL COLEMAN

b. Aug. 12, 1925, Port Huron, MI, d. July 12, 1995, New York, NY

An excellent ballad singer whose voice was strongly influenced by Billy Eckstine's, Earl Coleman is best known for recording "This Is Always" and "Dark Shadows" with Charlie Parker and the Erroll Garner Trio in 1947; Bird had insisted that Coleman be on the session, over producer Ross Russell's wishes. Coleman began his career singing with Ernie Fields, Jay McShann (1943), Earl Hines (1944, replacing the departing Eckstine), King Kolax, and back with McShann. "This Is Always" was a minor hit, but Coleman never became famous, probably due to the similarity of his approach to Eckstine's. He recorded 11 songs in 1948 (including five with Fats Navarro) but then was off records altogether during 1949–76 other than an album apiece for Prestige (1956) and Atlantic (1967) plus a few titles on Sonny Rollins and Elmo Hope records. Coleman did work through the years with such major names as Gene Ammons, the Gerald Wilson Orchestra, Don Byas (in Paris), and Billy Taylor. Later in his career he made two records for Xanadu (1977 and 1979) and one for Stash (1984), but, although he sounded strong even at that late stage, Earl Coleman never really caught on.

9 *Earl Coleman Returns / Mar. 2, 1956–June 8, 1956 / Original Jazz Classics 187*

This Earl Coleman reissue is so strong that it seems remarkable that this was his only full album of the 1950s. Coleman is joined by Art Farmer, Gigi Gryce, and Hank Jones on most of the six original selections, including "Say It Isn't So," "Reminiscing," and a definitive version of Gryce's "Social Call." Four other "bonus" numbers are included on the CD reissue by a septet/octet with Gene Ammons, including a fine remake of "This Is Always."

LPS TO SEARCH FOR

Love Songs (Atlantic 8172), from 1967, has Coleman joined by a quintet and sometimes a larger band led by pianist Billy Taylor. Despite a couple of throwaways (particularly "Peo-

ple" and "Charade"), the hits outnumber the misses, especially "There's No You," "I Wish I Knew," and "When Did You Leave Heaven?" *A Song for You* (Xanadu 147), from 1977, is a superior effort with the Hank Jones Trio and guest tenor Al Cohn, 1979's *There Something About an Old Love* (Xanadu 175) has mostly veteran ballads interpreted with the assistance of a rhythm quartet, and Coleman's final recording, 1984's *Stardust* (Stash 243), features a quintet arranged by pianist Michael Abene and including trumpeter Tom Harrell. Earl Coleman never made a bad record (he stopped recording a decade before his death), so all of these lyrical LPs are well worth acquiring.

BILLY ECKSTINE

b. July 8, 1914, Pittsburgh, PA, d. Mar. 8, 1993, Pittsburgh, PA

Billy Eckstine was one of the great heroes of the Bebop era. Although already a very popular vocalist by 1944, rather than go out as a single, he formed a Bebop orchestra simply because he loved the music. And despite the economic difficulties of heading an innovative big band (and one that conservative listeners often complained they could not dance to), Eckstine kept the orchestra together for three years.

Eckstine started singing professionally in 1937, becoming a member of the Earl Hines Orchestra in 1939. Possessor of a deep baritone voice, in a more enlightened time Eckstine probably would have played romantic leads in Hollywood movies; however no such opportunities existed for black singers of the 1940s. He did have a few hits while with Hines, including "Jelly, Jelly." Eckstine encouraged Hines to hire some of the up-and-coming Beboppers, resulting in the 1943 Earl Hines Orchestra, featuring Charlie Parker (on tenor), Dizzy Gillespie, and Sarah Vaughan (on vocals and second piano). Tragically, the recording strike kept that big band from ever recording.

In 1944 Billy Eckstine (then known as "Mr. B") formed his own orchestra, which ranks as the second Bebop big band after Hines's. Charlie Parker was with his unit for a few months (on alto) but was gone before the Eckstine Orchestra made its first recordings. However, Dizzy Gillespie and Sarah Vaughan were still aboard, along with tenors Gene Ammons and Dexter Gordon, who traded off in memorable fashion on "Blowin' the Blues Away." During its three-year existence, the Billy Eckstine big band featured nearly all of

The definitive baritone singer of the Bop era, Billy Eckstine also led the second Bebop big band (after Earl Hines).

the most significant young Bebop musicians, including trumpeters Gillespie, Fats Navarro, Freddie Webster, Miles Davis, Kenny Dorham, and Doug Mettome, altoists Parker, Budd Johnson (doubling on tenor), Norris Turney, and Sonny Stitt, tenors Ammons, Gordon, Wardell Gray, and Frank Wess, baritonist Leo Parker, bassist Tommy Potter, drummer Art Blakey, and Eckstine himself on valve trombone.

Although he did his best to keep his band economically viable by alternating the Bop instrumentals with his warm vocal ballads, the collapse of the big band era and a certain hostility toward Bebop eventually forced Billy Eckstine to face the inevitable and break up his orchestra in 1947. From

then on, Eckstine was primarily a middle-of-the-road pop singer, one who had quite a few hits (including "Everything I Have Is Yours," "I Apologize," and "My Foolish Heart"). Every once in a while, he was heard in a jazz setting, such as his guest appearances with the 1953 Metronome All-Stars (which find him scatting quite effectively), a superb 1959 album with Count Basie, and 1960's *No Cover, No Minimum*, which features him taking a few short trumpet solos. In later years, "Mr. B" looked back at his Bebop Orchestra with great nostalgia and not undeserved pride.

8 *Airmail Special / Feb. 1945–Mar. 4, 1945 / Drive Archive 42415*

9 *Everything I Have Is Yours / May 20, 1947–Apr. 26, 1957 / Verve 819 442*

8 *No Cover, No Minimum / Aug. 30, 1960 / Roulette 98583*

6 *Billy Eckstine Sings with Benny Carter / Nov. 17–18, 1986 / Verve 832 011*

The Billy Eckstine Orchestra's earliest recordings (from 1944, when Dizzy Gillespie was in the band) are available on Gillespie's *1943–44* (Masters of Jazz 86). Unfortunately his Savoy recordings from 1945–47 are currently out of print. The Drive Archive CD has a couple of broadcasts from 1945 that were formerly available as an Alamac LP. Eckstine has four vocals and the young Sarah Vaughan takes two, but it is the instrumentals that are of greatest interest. Such musicians as Fats Navarro, Gene Ammons, Budd Johnson, and Art Blakey are heard from, with "Airmail Special" and "Opus X" being the high points.

By the time he recorded the 42 selections included on the double-CD *Everything I Have Is Yours,* Billy Eckstine's Bebop Orchestra was history. Most of the music falls into pop, with Eckstine's warm baritone voice backed by strings and an orchestra, including hit versions of the title cut, "Blue Moon," "Caravan," "My Foolish Heart," and "I Apologize." There are some jazz numbers, including Eckstine's valve trombone playing on "Mr. B's Blues," collaborations with Woody Herman and George Shearing, eight selections with the Bobby Tucker Quartet, five ballad duets with Sarah Vaughan, and especially a couple of classic performances with the 1953 Metronome All Stars that show that he had not lost his jazz chops.

No Cover, No Minimum has 24 songs recorded during a Las Vegas performance. Eckstine, who surprisingly also takes a few short trumpet solos, is joined by an orchestra arranged by pianist Bobby Tucker. His voice is heard throughout in prime form, including on such numbers as "I've Grown Accustomed to Your Face," "Without a Song," "I Want a Little Girl," "'Deed I Do," and "I Apologize," making this an excellent example of his singing. By 1986, when he recorded his final album at age 72, Mr. B's voice was a bit weaker, but he still had his trademark phrasing and enthusiasm. The 79-year-old Benny Carter (on alto other than a trumpet solo on "September Song") is a major asset, the Bobby Tucker Trio provides a cushion for Eckstine, and singer Helen Merrill assists on two songs, helping make this final effort quite worthwhile.

LPS TO SEARCH FOR

I Want to Talk About You (Xanadu 207) has 13 of Billy Eckstine's 1940–41 vocals with the Earl Hines Orchestra (including "Jelly, Jelly," "I Got It Bad," "The Jitney Man," and "Stormy Monday Blues") plus three numbers from the Eckstine Orchestra's broadcast of March 4, 1945. *Blowing the Blues Away* (Contact 1015), released by a Danish label, has the elusive 1944 Eckstine big band sessions (including his ballad vocals that are left off of the Dizzy Gillespie Master of Jazz CD) plus his two 1953 Metronome All-Stars appearances. And well deserving of being reissued is *Mister B and the Band* (Savoy 2214), a two-LP set that contains the cream of the Eckstine Orchestra's 1945–47 studio recordings, including "I Love the Rhythm in a Riff," "Prisoner of Love," "The Jitney Man," "Cool Breeze," and "Oo Bop Sh'Bam."

FILMS

The Billy Eckstine Orchestra's short film *Rhythm on a Riff* (1946), which has solos by Gene Ammons and Frank Wess, is included in the video *Things to Come* (Vintage Jazz Classics 2006) along with Dizzy Gillespie's *Jivin' in Bebop.* In addition, Billy Eckstine (without his orchestra) appears in the film *Flicker Up* (1946), and he has an acting role in *Let's Do It Again* (1975).

BABS GONZALES

b. Oct. 27, 1919, Newark, NJ, d. Jan. 23, 1980, Newark, NJ

If enthusiasm and self-confidence counted for everything, Babs Gonzales (who knew how to put up a great front) would be considered one of the greatest jazz singers of them all. Despite having a limited voice and imagination, he loved to sing Bebop, developing an odd scatting style that emphasized vowels over consonants.

Gonzales (who was born Lee Brown!) studied piano and drums early on. After brief periods with the big bands of Charlie Barnet and Lionel Hampton, Babs put together the Three Bips and a Bop in 1946, a vehicle for his vocals that also often featured such top sidemen as Tadd Dameron, James Moody, J. J. Johnson, and Sonny Rollins (who made his recording debut with Babs). During 1947–49 Gonzales recorded 24 numbers (including the debut of "Oop-Pop-A-Da," "Weird Lullaby," "A Lesson in Bopology," "Professor Bop," and "Prelude to a Nightmare"), but the end of the classic Bebop era resulted in his becoming a cult figure.

Gonzales sang with and managed James Moody (1951–54), had periods working as a disc jockey and a promoter, recorded with organist Jimmy Smith and Johnny Griffin, had his own label (Expubidence, which included a couple of his spoken word jive records), worked as a single, and wrote two colorful (if semifictional) autobiographies: *I Paid My Dues* and *Movin' On Down de Line*.

9 *Weird Lullaby / Feb. 24, 1947–Nov. 23, 1958 / Blue Note 84464*

Other than a date apiece that have been released on sampler sets by Delmark and Xanadu, this single CD has all of Babs Gonzales's recordings from the Bebop era. The list of sidemen on the four sessions from 1947–49 is certainly quite impressive if eclectic, including Tadd Dameron, Sonny Rollins (on his recording debut), Bennie Green, J. J. Johnson, French horn master Julius Watkins, pianist Linton Garner, Art Pepper, pianist Wynton Kelly, pioneer flutist Alberto Socarras, Don Redman on soprano, and violinist Ray Nance. Babs is quite enthusiastic on such selections as "Oop-Pop-A-Da," "Stompin' at the Savoy," "Babs' Dream," "Weird Lullaby," "Professor Bop," "Prelude to a Nightmare," and "Real Crazy." In addition, this CD has a pair of selections with organist Jimmy Smith from 1956 and two versions of "Encore" from a very obscure 1958 date. The definitive Babs Gonzales reissue.

PANCHO HAGOOD

b. 1926, Detroit, MI, d. Nov. 9, 1989, Farmington, MI

Kenny "Pancho" Hagood, whose heavy voice seemed a bit unsuited to the speedy Bebop vocals that he usually sang, was a minor figure in jazz who had some major associations. He started out in 1943 singing with Benny Carter's orchestra and is best remembered for his vocalizing with Dizzy Gillespie's big band during 1946–48, mostly ballads (such as "I Waited for You") but also some duet scat vocals with Gillespie ("Oop-Pop-A-Da" and "Ool-Ya-Koo"). Hagood recorded three songs as a leader for Savoy in 1947, cut "I Should Care" with Thelonious Monk (1948), was with the Miles Davis Nonet during its one gig in 1948 (singing "Why Do I Love You" and "Darn That Dream"), and recorded "Darn That Dream" with the Davis Nonet in 1950. Hagood, who also worked with Tadd Dameron, faded away in the 1950s, living, and occasionally performing, in Chicago,

Paris, and (by the 1980s) Detroit. A Spotlite sampler album features him on a few live numbers from 1948 and 1967, and Pancho Hagood can also be heard on an obscure Montreux-Detroit Festival record in 1982 singing "Ooh-Pop-A-Da" and "'Round Midnight."

FILMS

Kenny Hagood is with Dizzy Gillespie's Orchestra in *Jivin' in Bebop* (1947), which is included in *Things to Come* (Vintage Jazz Classics 2006).

JACKIE AND ROY

In 1999, Jackie and Roy celebrated their 50th wedding anniversary and their 52nd year working as a vocal duo. They have always been Bop-based, although through the years they have often performed music that bordered on cabaret and middle-of-the-road pop.

Singer-pianist Roy Kral (born October 10, 1921, in Chicago) studied classical piano for eight years but switched to jazz in the mid-1930s after being inspired by Earl Hines. He had his own group during 1939-40, worked with Charlie Agnew (1940–41), played in Army bands while in the military (1942–46), and made his recording debut with Georgie Auld in 1947. His younger sister was singer Irene Kral. Jackie Cain (born May 22, 1928, in Milwaukee) started out singing with Don Maya, Jay Burkhart, and Lee Konitz (1947–48). After Jackie and Roy met in 1947, they began working together, inspired by the team of Buddy Stewart and Dave Lambert.

Jackie and Roy rose to fame while with Charlie Ventura's "Bop for the People" band in 1948–49, singing unusual material (including pianist Lou Stein's "East of Suez" and "Euphoria") and turning older standards into Bebop romps. Since leaving Ventura and getting married, Jackie and Roy have worked steadily in jazz clubs. They had their own television show in Chicago in the early 1950s, were based in Las Vegas during 1957–60, moved to New York, and have appeared on some television commercials. They have recorded for many labels, including Atlantic, Coral, Storyville, ABC-Paramount, Columbia, Roulette, Verve, Capitol , CTI, Concord, Finesse, Discovery, Fantasy, Audiophile, Contemporary, Music Masters, and DRG. In addition to performing standards, Jackie and Roy have recorded songbook albums featuring the music of Stephen

Sondheim, Cy Coleman, and Alec Wilder and even a record of songs loosely connected to Humphrey Bogart.

9 *Forever / 1994 / Jazz Heritage 513934*
7 *The Beautiful Sea / July 15, 1998-Aug. 20, 1998 / DRG 8474*

Jackie and Roy's many early recordings are mostly out of print. *Forever* is a strong later effort, featuring the vocal duo on such numbers as Dave Brubeck's "The Duke," "Spring Can Really Hang You Up the Most," "The Continental," and "I Know That You Know." The rhythm section (which as usual includes Roy Kral's piano) is joined on some numbers by a horn section, a string quartet, and guitarist Gene Bertoncini. *The Beautiful Sea,* which is subtitled "Songs of Sun, Sand & Sea," features an eclectic batch of songs, including "On a Slow Boat to China," Dave Frishberg's "Zanzibar," Herbie Hancock's "Dolphin Dance," and "The Shining Sea." A few strings and Dave Samuels on marimba and vibes augment the rhythm section. Although not every song is equally successful, it is remarkable to hear how ageless the voices of Jackie and Roy still were after a half-century of performing together.

LPS TO SEARCH FOR

Sweet and Low Down (Columbia 1469), from 1960, finds Jackie and Roy in top form on the title cut, "They Can't Take That Away from Me," and "Mountain Greenery," while Jackie takes three solo features, including Cole Porter's worthy obscurity "Experiment." One of Jackie and Roy's most jazz-oriented dates is 1988's *Full Circle* (Contemporary 14046), an octet outing with Conte Candoli, Bill Watrous, Bob Cooper on tenor, and baritonist Bill Perkins; highlights include "Cherokee," Bob Dorough's "Never in a Single Year," and "Line for Lyons."

DAVE LAMBERT

b. June 19, 1917, Boston, MA. d. Oct. 3, 1966, Westport, CT

One of the first important Bebop singers, Dave Lambert is most famous for being part of the greatest jazz vocal group ever: Lambert, Hendricks, and Ross. Lambert brought the craziness of Leo Watson and the adventure of Louis Armstrong's scat singing into Bebop while being a much better singer than the jubilant Babs Gonzales.

Lambert worked as a drummer with the Hugh McGuinness Trio during three summers (1937-40), served in the Army (1940-43), and sang with Johnny Long's big band for a year. While with Gene Krupa's orchestra (1944-45), he frequently teamed up with Buddy Stewart, including on "What's This," the first recorded Bebop vocal. Lambert freelanced for the next decade, performing with Stewart on and off until the latter died in a 1950 car accident; they recorded a few selections for the Keynote and Sittin' In With labels and sang with Charlie Parker on a preserved radio broadcast from the Royal Roost in 1949. Lambert led a group of singers on unsuccessful (and rather bizarre) recordings of "Old Folks" and "In the Still of the Night" with Parker in 1953.

After a period of scuffling, Lambert (who had recorded a few songs with a vocal group in 1949) collaborated with Jon Hendricks in 1955 for a little-known recording of "Four Brothers." In 1957 he and Hendricks tried without much luck to audition singers to record vocalese versions of famous Count Basie recordings, but there were just not enough talented vocalists around who understood what was needed. However, Lambert and Hendricks were very impressed by Annie Ross, and, through overdubbing, they came up with *Sing a Song of Basie,* a classic album. Lambert, Hendricks, and Ross were quite active until 1962, when Ross dropped out due to bad health. Yolande Bavan was her replacement, and Lambert, Hendricks, and Bavan kept busy until the group's breakup in 1964. Lambert, who recorded a solo album in 1959 (long out of print), gigged a bit during 1964-66 as a soloist and can be heard in a scatting version of "Donna Lee" at a 1965 Charlie Parker memorial concert. Dave Lambert was killed in 1966 at the age of 49 when he was hit by a car while changing a tire, ending the career of one of Bebop's first singers.

ANITA O'DAY

b. Oct. 18, 1919, Kansas City, MO

Along with Ella Fitzgerald, Anita O'Day was one of the few female singers from the swing era who not only comprehended Bebop but was a pacesetter in the music. Unlike Ella, whose roots always remained clearly in swing, O'Day had just caught the tail end of the swing era and was clearly a Bopper at heart.

She was born Anita Belle Colton and took the name Anita O'Day while working in dance marathons in the 1930s, since O'Day was pig Latin for dough! After deciding to dedicate herself to singing jazz, O'Day performed with Max Miller in Chicago during 1939–40 and then caught on big as the singer with the Gene Krupa Orchestra during 1941–43. Unlike many other female vocalists of the time, O'Day never served as glamorous window dressing or felt satisfied merely to sing a song straight for a chorus and then sit down; she was always a creative improviser. While with Krupa she had hits in "Let Me Off Uptown," "Thanks for the Boogie Ride," "That's What You Think," "Bolero at the Savoy," and "Massachusetts," sometimes teaming up with trumpeter Roy Eldridge. After Krupa was framed and busted for marijuana possession and forced to break up his band in 1943, O'Day sang with Woody Herman (briefly) and Stan Kenton's orchestra (1944–45). "And Her Tears Flowed Like Wine" was her most popular number with Kenton, but O'Day was not happy in that situation; she preferred swinging to being weighed down by the complex charts and loud ensembles. Her legacy lived on with Kenton, however, for her successor, June Christy, was originally strongly influenced by her.

O'Day was part of Krupa's new band during 1945–46, having popular recordings in "Opus No. 1" and "Boogie Blues." She became a single in 1946 but largely struggled during the Bebop era, working steadily but not building on her fame. Unlike other singers who graduated from the big bands, O'Day mostly avoided recording pop music and stuck to the music that she loved most. Her only recordings of the 1947–51 period were titles for the tiny Signature, Gem, and London labels, including "What Is This Thing Called Love," the eccentric "Hi Ho Trailus Boot Whip," and "How High the Moon."

Anita O'Day's golden age was the 1952–63 period, when she recorded for Verve. During that period she was one of the top singers in jazz. She appeared at the 1958 Newport Jazz Festival (being quite sensational in the film of that event, *Jazz on a Summer's Day*) and also the movie *The Gene Krupa Story*. Both her voice and her creativity can be heard at their peak on her recordings for Verve.

However, during the 1950s O'Day also became a heroin addict, and, although her career continued at a high level into the early 1960s, things fell apart after that. She spent time off the scene, almost died from an overdose, and was off records altogether during 1964–69. But against the odds, she made a full comeback in the 1970s, almost reaching her earlier heights, as can be heard on an MPS album from 1970 and a 1975 set for the Japanese Trio label. Her very honest autobiography, *High Times, Hard Times,* gave her addi-

tional recognition. Unfortunately though, in the 1980s Anita O'Day's voice seriously declined, and alcohol abuse did not help her career. However, she sang on an occasional basis in the 1990s, performing at Carnegie Hall in 1999.

7 *The Complete Recordings 1949–1950 / Jan. 18, 1945–Dec. 27, 1950 / Baldwin Street Music 302*
Although the Bebop era was not that prosperous a time for Anita O'Day, she had found her voice. All of her studio recordings of 1949–50, four songs from a radio show in 1945, and five radio transcriptions from that same year with the Nat King Cole Trio are on this well-conceived disc. Not all of the material from 1949–50 material is classic; there is no need to revive "Poor Simple Simon," "Your Eyes Are Bigger Than Your Heart," or "Yea Boo!" Fortunately most of the other tunes are on a higher level (particularly "Them There Eyes," "You Took Advantage of Me," and the numbers with Cole), making this set easily recommended to Anita O'Day fans and collectors.

* *The Complete Anita O'Day Verve/Clef Sessions / Jan. 22, 1952–Oct. 15, 1962 / Mosaic 9-188*
8 *This Is Anita / Dec. 6–8, 1955 / Verve 829 261*
8 *Pick Yourself Up with Anita O'Day / Dec. 15 + 17, 1956 / Verve 314 517 329*
9 *Anita Sings the Most / Jan. 31, 1957 / Verve 829 577*
7 *Anita Sings the Winners / Apr. 2–3, 1958 / Verve 837 929*
6 *Swings Cole Porter / Jan. 22, 1952–Aug. 17, 1960 / Verve 849 266*
9 *All the Sad Young Men / Oct. 16, 1961 / Verve 314 517 065*

Anita O'Day was at the peak of her powers during her Verve years, being one of the top Bebop-oriented singers around. Happily, a nine-CD limited-edition Mosaic box set was put out in 1999 that has every one of her recordings for Verve. Get it while you can; do not hesitate! O'Day is heard both with combos and with orchestras led by arrangers Buddy Bregman, Russ Garcia, Marty Paich, Billy May, Jimmy Giuffre, Bill Holman, Johnny Mandel, and Gary McFarland; in addition, there is a reunion with Gene Krupa and Roy Eldridge.

For those whose budget cannot justify the purchase, six of the individual sets are available as single CDs from Verve. On *This Is Anita,* the singer is wonderful on "You're the Top" (which has updated lyrics), "Honeysuckle Rose," and an emotional rendition of "A Nightingale Sang in Berkeley Square." Buddy Bregman's orchestra and writing is on that

CD and also featured on *Pick Yourself Up*. On the latter project, O'Day is heard in a variety of settings: with a chamber string orchestra, a big band, and a small combo. The swing standards include "Don't Be That Way," "Stompin' at the Savoy," "There's a Lull in My Life," and "Sweet Georgia Brown."

Anita Sings the Most is a particularly special set, for O'Day is accompanied by Oscar Peterson, Herb Ellis, Ray Brown, and drummer John Poole. A very fast "Them There Eyes" and the warm ballads are most memorable, although it is regretful that there is only 34 minutes of playing time on this disc; but what is here is great! *Sings the Winners* (which utilizes the Russ Garcia Orchestra) has as its hook the singer's interpretations of songs made famous by other musicians. "Take the 'A' Train," "Four," "Four Brothers," and "The Peanut Vendor" work best. *Swings Cole Porter,* which is mostly from 1959 with Billy May's orchestra, suffers from the brevity of the performances, despite O'Day's appealing voice. The dozen Cole Porter songs include five that are under two minutes. Six other "O'Day Sings Porter" selections from other Verve dates are "bonus" tracks. *All the Sad Young Men* owes its strong success to Gary McFarland's complex yet colorful arrangements, unusual material (including the title cut, "You Came a Long Way from St. Louis," "Senor Blues," and a surprisingly different version of "Boogie Blues"), and the fact that Anita O'Day rose to the challenge in inspiring fashion.

7 *I Get a Kick Out of You / Apr. 25, 1975 / Evidence 22054*
6 *In a Mellow Tone / Mar. 13–15, 1989 / DRG 5209*
3 *At Vine St. Live / Aug. 2–3, 1991 / DRG 8435*
1 *Rules of the Road / 1993 / Pablo 2210–950*

O'Day recorded very little after 1963 (other than a fine set in 1970), until 1975. There would be a variety of so-so recordings for her private Emily label, but *I Get a Kick Out of You* is much better. O'Day at 55 still had some power left, and her Evidence CD (recorded originally for the Japanese Trio label) finds her in top form on "Opus One," "A Song for You," "Undecided," "When Sunny Gets Blue," and a lengthy "Gone with the Wind." Pianist Ronnell Bright's quartet is fine in support. On *In a Mellow Tone,* from 1989, O'Day sounds quite a bit older, but this set was well planned and O'Day pushes herself, successfully. She is assisted by a sextet that has Gordon Brisker on tenor, and the singer's versions of "I Cried for You," "A Sleepin' Bee," "Like Someone in Love," and "More Than You Know" hold up fairly well.

But that project would be her last worthwhile hurrah. *At Vine St. Live* shows how weak her live shows had become (redoing standards that she had sung much better in the 1950s). And *Rules of the Road* is unspeakably bad, for by then O'Day no longer had much of a voice. Despite their best efforts, the big band, Buddy Bregman's charts, and trumpeter Jack Sheldon's spots only point out that Anita O'Day should no longer have been recording at that point. But Anita O'Day's classic Verve recordings are available to show listeners just how exciting a jazz singer she was in her prime.

LPS TO SEARCH FOR

Anita O'Day's ten Signature recordings of 1947–48 are on *Hi Ho Trailus Boot Whip* (Bob Thiele Music 1–0595). Highlights include chance-taking versions of "What Is This Thing Called Love," "Sometimes I'm Happy," "How High the Moon," and the eccentric title cut. *Anita O'Day in Berlin* (MPS 20750), from 1970, was the singer's comeback record and her first recording in seven years. The repertoire includes some recent songs, a medley of "Yesterday" and "Yesterdays," and "Honeysuckle Rose." *Mello'Day* (GNP/ Crescendo 2126) is one of Anita O'Day's best albums from her later period. The 1978 set, which includes the Lou Levy Trio and saxophonist Ernie Watts, shows that (at least for a little while) O'Day had made a full comeback.

FILMS

Anita O'Day's two big hits with Gene Krupa, "Let Me Off Uptown' and "Thanks for the Boogie Ride," were fortunately filmed as Soundies in 1942; the latter song is done in particularly entertaining fashion. The highpoint of O'Day's career, her exciting versions of "Sweet Georgia Brown" (done in a lowdown fashion) and "Tea for Two" (during which she scats up a storm) from the 1958 Newport Jazz Festival, was luckily filmed and is available in *Jazz on a Summer's Day* (New Yorker Video 16590). In addition, O'Day pops up in *The Gene Krupa Story* (1959) singing "Memories of You," has a small acting role in *Zigzag* (1970), and performs "I Concentrate On You" in *The Outfit* (1973).

JACKIE PARIS

b. Sept. 20, 1927, Nutley, NJ

Jackie Paris has had a strangely episodic career, never really catching on or rising above the level of a little-known cult figure throughout his long career. Originally a guitarist,

Paris worked with a trio in the early 1940s, served in the Army (1944–46), and made his recording debut in 1947. He freelanced (including performing with Charlie Parker) and sang with Lionel Hampton's band during 1949–50. In 1949 Paris recorded the first-ever vocal version of "'Round Midnight." He recorded a few albums during the 1950s (one apiece for Brunswick, Wing, and East-Wind and in 1960 for Time), including a guest appearance with Gigi Gryce and Donald Byrd in 1957. But, after making an obscure record for Impulse in 1962, Paris was off records altogether until 1981, other than singing "Duke Ellington's Sound of Love" with Charles Mingus in 1974. Jackie Paris, who has also worked as a tap dancer and as a teacher, remains an occasional performer up to the present day.

LPS TO SEARCH FOR

Jackie Paris's self-titled 1981 album (Audiophile 158) is an excellent outing in which the singer is accompanied by pianist Carlos Franzetti, bassist Marc Johnson, and drummer Joe LaBarbera. Highlights of the ballad-oriented set include "Detour Ahead," "Everything Must Change," and "Young and Foolish."

BUDDY STEWART

b. Sept. 22, 1922, Derry, NJ, d. Feb. 1, 1950, NM
One of the earliest of the Bebop singers, Buddy Stewart would be much better known today were it not for his early death. Stewart grew up in show business and was singing in vaudeville by the time he was eight. He formed a vocal trio when he was 15 and began working in New York in 1940. Stewart sang with a vocal group, the Snowflakes, that was briefly associated with Glenn Miller before becoming part of the Claude Thornhill Orchestra. He served in the Army during 1942–44 and then began teaming up regularly with Dave Lambert. Together the duo sang "What's This" on a recording with Gene Krupa's orchestra, the first Bop vocal record. Stewart also sang some ballads with Krupa in 1946 (he had a warm voice) and worked with Charlie Ventura (where he often sang wordless lines in ensembles), Red Rodney, Kai Winding, and Charlie Barnet's Bebop band (1949), having several reunions with Lambert. Buddy Stewart, who recorded five songs as a leader for the SIW label in 1948 (four have been reissued by Spotlite), died in a car accident at the age of 27.

SARAH VAUGHAN

b. Mar. 27, 1924, Newark, NJ, d. Apr. 3, 1990, Los Angeles, CA
The most important singer to emerge from the Bebop era, Sarah Vaughan had one of the greatest voices ever heard. She had such a wide range and such control over her voice that she could have been an opera singer, and she consistently gave the impression that nothing was impossible for her to accomplish. Vaughan grasped the intricacies of Bop early on, and throughout her long career the influence of Bop (although less overt after the early '50s) was always felt in her singing.

Sarah Vaughan ranked up there with Ella Fitzgerald as arguably the top female jazz singer of all time (although some listeners would hold out for the more charismatic, though limited, Billie Holiday). She sang in church while quite young and had extensive piano lessons throughout the 1930s. In 1943, after winning an Apollo Theatre amateur contest, she was hired by Earl Hines as singer and second pianist. Sassy (her lifelong nickname) was part of the famous 1943 Earl Hines Bebop Orchestra, where she was influenced by Billy Eckstine (who became a lifelong friend), Dizzy Gillespie, and Charlie Parker. Unfortunately that group did not record due to the Musicians Union recording strike. When Eckstine decided to form his own big band the following year, Vaughan joined him, picking up additional experience. On December 31, 1944, she had her recording debut as a leader, cutting four songs with a group that included Dizzy Gillespie. The musical high point was "Interlude," a vocal version of Gillespie's "A Night in Tunisia." The following year Vaughan recorded with Gillespie and Charlie Parker on two occasions (including "Lover Man"), and during part of 1945–46 she sang with John Kirby. Otherwise, Sarah Vaughan worked as a single throughout the rest of her lengthy career.

During 1946–48, Vaughan recorded for Musicraft and recorded such numbers as "If You Could See Me Now," "You're Not the Kind" (both from a date that also included Freddie Webster and Bud Powell), "Tenderly," "It's Magic," and even "The Lord's Prayer." She also was involved in several all-star Bebop radio broadcasts and concerts during the second half of the 1940s. In 1949 Vaughan signed with Columbia, and her recordings of the next few years alternated between classic jazz dates (including one with Miles Davis) and more commercial outings. From that point on, Sarah

The most important singer to emerge from the Bebop years,
Sarah Vaughan had an incredible voice throughout her entire career.

Vaughan worked steadily and was considered one of the most famous of all jazz singers; her voice could not be denied, even with the changes the music world underwent during the next three decades. In the 1950s she recorded pop-oriented dates for Mercury and jazz sessions (including one with Clifford Brown) for its subsidiary Emarcy. A regular at jazz festivals and a world traveler who never seemed to show fatigue or age in her voice, Vaughan recorded for Roulette and Mercury in the 1960s, was off records altogether during 1968–70 (when she could not find the right situation), and then returned with strong dates for Mainstream and Pablo (1977–82).

Though she was sometimes accused of indulging in vocal gymnastics and could get a bit carried away, to the end of her life Sarah Vaughan's voice remained in wondrous form. She was able to overcome potentially weak material (often by strangling unworthy tunes to death!) and consistently uplifted superior songs to the stars.

5 *Time After Time / Dec. 31, 1944–Dec. 29, 1947 / Drive Archives 41021*

8 *Sarah Vaughan/Lester Young: One Night Stand / Nov. 8, 1947 / Blue Note 32139*

9 *In Hi-Fi / Dec. 21, 1949–Jan. 5, 1953 / Columbia/ Legacy 65117*

8 *I'll Be Seeing You / 1949–1962 / Vintage Jazz Classics 1015*

7 *Perdido! / 1951–Apr. 21, 1953 / Natasha Imports 4004*

Other than a couple of sessions made for the Continental label during 1944–45, Sarah Vaughan's first recordings as a leader were cut for Musicraft during 1946–48. Unfortunately those valuable sessions (which are now owned by Discovery) have not been coherently reissued in recent times on CD. The Drive Archives CD is a sampler that jumps around chronologically but has some of the high points from that period, including "East of the Sun" (from Sassy's first Continental session), "Tenderly," and a couple of sacred pieces. Missing are such gems as "Interlude" (a vocal version of "A Night in Tunisia"), "If You Could See Me Now," and "You're Not the Kind."

Sarah Vaughan had a remarkable voice from the beginning of her career and sounded quite mature even while still in her early twenties. *One Night Stand* has a 1947 Town Hall concert split evenly between Sassy and the Lester Young Sextet. Young plays well on his seven numbers (which includes "Just You, Just Me" and "Lester's Bebop Boogie"), although his backup group sometimes sounds a little unsteady; the combination of pianist Sadik Hakim and bassist Rodney Richardson has its awkward moments, while the Boppish trumpeter Shorty McConnell was not on the tenor's level. However, the main reason to acquire this set is for Sarah Vaughan's eight numbers. Her voice sounds quite beautiful and her improvisations take plenty of chances during the ballad-oriented program. Vaughan and Pres meet up successfully on the final number, "I Cried for You."

On the sessions of May 18–19, 1950, Sarah Vaughan recorded eight delightful numbers, usually with the assistance of Miles Davis, Benny Green, Budd Johnson on tenor, and Tony Scott; their rendition of "Ain't Misbehavin'" has exquisite eight-bar solos from each of the four horns. *In Hi-Fi* reissues that project, adds seven alternate takes, and includes six unrelated jazz numbers from 1949 and 1951–53. Vaughan is in particularly inspired form on the Miles Davis date, with the other highlights including "Mean to Me," "Nice Work If You Can Get It," and "East of the Sun." The 1990 CD *I'll Be Seeing You* has a variety of previously unreleased concert and radio performances featuring Sarah Vaughan in quite a few different situations from a 13-year period. In addition to her work with her trio and backed by an orchestra, Vaughan is joined by Woody Herman's clarinet on "On Green Dolphin Street" and "Just One of Those Things," is accompanied by Duke Ellington on two numbers, duets with Nat King Cole on "Love You Madly," and shares the spotlight with Joe Williams on "Teach Me Tonight." Other than two primitively recorded numbers from 1951, *Perdido!* features Vaughan from Birdland in 1953, singing her usual repertoire of the time (including "Tenderly,"

"I Get a Kick Out of You," and "You're Mine You") with her trio; Dizzy Gillespie sits in on a few numbers.

* ***The Complete Sarah Vaughan on Mercury Vol. 1 / Feb. 10, 1954–June 21, 1956 / Mercury 826 320***
* ***The Complete Sarah Vaughan on Mercury Vol. 2 / Oct. 29, 1956–July 12, 1957 / Mercury 826 327***
* ***The Complete Sarah Vaughan on Mercury Vol. 3 / Aug. 6, 1957–1959 / Mercury 826 333***
10 ***Sarah Vaughan with Clifford Brown / Dec. 16 + 18, 1954 / Emarcy 814 641***
9 ***In the Land of Hi-Fi / Oct. 25–27, 1955 / Emarcy 826 454***
7 ***The George Gershwin Songbook, Volume 1 / Apr. 2, 1954–1957 / Emarcy 846 895***
7 ***The George Gershwin Songbook, Volume 2 / Oct. 26, 1955–Aug. 15, 1964 / Emarcy 846 896***
9 ***At Mister Kelly's / Aug. 6–8, 1957 / Emarcy 832 791***
10 ***No Count Sarah / Dec. 1958 / Emarcy 824 057***

During 1954–59, Sarah Vaughan recorded exclusively for the Mercury label, and its jazz-oriented subsidiary Emarcy, everything from swinging jazz dates to sessions with string orchestras and big bands. On 17 CDs packaged as three boxes (*Vol. 1* and *Vol. 3* have six discs, while *Vol. 2* is "just" five CDs), every recording by the singer from this period has been reissued. Although this is the perfect way to acquire Vaughan's Mercury and Emarcy recordings, not every interested listener will be able to afford these or necessarily even be able to find each of these increasingly difficult-to-locate sets. *Vol. 1* is overall the best of the trio, since it includes Vaughan's set with Clifford Brown, an outing with the Ernie Wilkins Orchestra (the *In the Land of Hi-Fi* date), and many jazz-oriented sessions. *Vol. 2* has Vaughan's Gershwin project, her 13 vocal duets with Billy Eckstine, and lots of orchestra sides (usually using Hal Mooney's arrangements). *Vol. 3* is highlighted by 21 songs from the singer's engagement at Mister Kelly's in Chicago with her trio, Vaughan's initial recording of "Misty," her album with the Count Basie Orchestra, some combo dates, and lots of commercial sets, some arranged by Quincy Jones.

Fortunately, six of Sarah Vaughan's better Emarcy projects are also available individually. Everything works on the singer's one collaboration with trumpeter Clifford Brown; the all-star group also includes Paul Quinichette on tenor, flutist Herbie Mann, and Sassy's regular accompanist of the period, pianist Jimmy Jones. Their versions of "Lullaby of

Birdland," "He's My Guy," and "You're Not the Kind" are particularly memorable, making this an essential acquisition. Almost on the same level is *In the Land of Hi-Fi,* an outing with an 11-piece all-star group arranged by Ernie Wilkins. Altoist Cannonball Adderley has many strong solos, and Vaughan sounds quite happy swinging away on such numbers as "Soon," "Cherokee," "How High the Moon," and "An Occasional Man." Nearly all of the selections on the two volumes of her *George Gershwin Songbook* were recorded in 1957 with pianist Jimmy Jones and a studio orchestra arranged by Hal Mooney. *Vol. 1,* which also has three performances from 1954–55, finds Vaughan's voice sounding beautiful on such numbers as "Embraceable You," "He Loves and She Loves," "A Foggy Day," and "Love Walked In." *Vol. 2,* which adds three unrelated recordings of Gershwin songs (from 1955, 1957, and 1964), includes such gems as "But Not for Me," "Someone to Watch Over Me," "I've Got a Crush on You," and "Fascinatin' Rhythm."

At Mister Kelly's gave Sarah Vaughan a rare opportunity to be heard live with her regular trio, a group consisting of Jimmy Jones, bassist Richard Davis, and Roy Haynes. A strong example of Sassy's live show of the era, she is heard digging into a variety of standards, including "September in the Rain," "Honeysuckle Rose," "Poor Butterfly," and "Sometimes I'm Happy," contrasting quite favorably with her more commercial studio recordings of the era. *No Count Sarah* features Vaughan singing with the 1958 Count Basie Orchestra but with Ronnell Bright on piano rather than Basie (thus the album's title!). This is a real classic, with definitive versions of Horace Silver's "Doodlin'," the wordless "No Count Blues," and "Cheek to Cheek."

7 *Linger Awhile / July 7, 1957–Mar. 1, 1982 / Pablo 2312-144*

6 *The Roulette Years / Apr. 19, 1960–1964 / Roulette 94983*

5 *The Singles Sessions / May 5, 1960–Feb. 1962 / Roulette 795331*

7 *Count Basie & Sarah Vaughan / July 1960–Jan. 1961 / Roulette 37241*

9 *After Hours / July 18, 1961 / Roulette 55468*

5 *You're Mine, You / Jan. 1962–Feb. 1962 / Roulette 57157*

7 *The Benny Carter Sessions / Aug. 1962–Jan. 1963 / Roulette 28640*

5 *Sarah Slightly Classical / May 1963–July 1963 / Roulette 95977*

9 *Sarah Sings Soulfully / June 6 ¦ 12, 1963 / Roulette 98445*

Released for the first time in 1999, *Linger Awhile* has Sassy's set at the 1957 Newport Jazz Festival in which she is backed by Jimmy Jones, Richard Davis, and Roy Haynes. She is in fine form, singing her usual repertoire of the era (including "The Masquerade Is Over," "All of Me," and "Poor Butterfly") and sounding quite boppish in spots. In addition, this CD has seven alternate takes from five of the singer's Pablo albums of 1978–82, versions that do not have any noticeable flaws and are quite jazz-oriented.

In 1960 Sarah Vaughan switched labels, going over to Roulette, where she would record exclusively into 1963. Unlike the situation with Mercury, her complete output has not yet been reissued, although a variety of her sessions have been put out on individual CDs. *The Roulette Years* is a 24-song sampler that draws its material from ten different albums, a few of which have not been reissued yet. Complete personnel and dates are lacking, but listeners cannot complain about not getting enough selections! Vaughan is heard in settings ranging from a guitar-bass duo to the Count Basie big band and a studio orchestra. But most of the singer's fans will prefer to get the complete dates whenever possible.

Vaughan recorded some titles for Roulette during 1960–62 that were meant for the singles market, in hopes of having a hit. Fourteen of the rather brief songs (only one exceeds three minutes) are included on *The Singles Sessions,* but since the CD contains only 35 minutes of music, this one is of minor interest. Vaughan's versions of "Them There Eyes," "Don't Go to Strangers," "Love," "One Mint Julep," and "Mama, He Treats Your Daughter Mean" are fun, but more music should have been included on this rather skimpy CD. As with *No Count Sarah,* Count Basie does not actually appear on *Count Basie & Sarah Vaughan,* even though his name is listed first and his picture is on the album cover! Actually the Basie band (with Kirk Stuart in Count's spot) is heard almost exclusively in a supportive role, even on such jazz songs as "Perdido," "Mean to Me," and "Until I Met You." Sassy is in fine form, although the lack of much interplay between her and the big band is unfortunate. There are three "bonus cuts" added to the CD, including delightful Vaughan-Joe Williams vocal duets on "Teach Me Tonight" and "If I Were a Bell."

After Hours is a very intimate date, with Vaughan accompanied just by guitarist Mundell Lowe and bassist George Duvivier. Since Lowe has only one solo, the focus is entirely on the singer during this ballad-oriented recording, and she proves more than equal to the task on such songs as "Ev'ry Time We Say Goodbye," "Easy to Love," and "Ill Wind." She also recorded a similar date in 1962 (with Barney Kessel and bassist Joe Comfort), but that has not been reissued yet. *You're Mine, You* has Vaughan backed by an orchestra arranged by Quincy Jones. The singer sounds a bit mannered in spots (her over-the-top rendition of "Maria" may be too much for some listeners), and the arrangements are actually more suitable for a Frank Sinatra date than for Sassy, as are such numbers as "The Best Is Yet to Come," "Witchcraft," and "The Second Time Around." The last two songs (which are also available in *The Singles Sessions*) are the high points: "One Mint Julep" and "Mama, He Treats Your Daughter Mean."

The Benny Carter Sessions combines two former albums (*The Explosive Side of Sarah Vaughan* and *The Lonely Hours*) that feature arrangements by Carter but unfortunately no playing by the altoist. The first set, which has Vaughan joined by some of the members of Count Basie's orchestra, boasts a strong repertoire and excellent versions of "Honeysuckle Rose," "The Lady's in Love with You," "The Trolley Song," and "I Can't Give You Anything but Love." *The Lonely Hours* is a ballad session with a string orchestra, mostly swing-era standards, and, despite the lack of variety, the beauty of Vaughan's voice makes it all worthwhile. *Sarah Slightly Classical,* however, is much more of an acquired taste. Sassy sings semi-operatic versions of such numbers as "Be My Love," "Full Moon and Empty Arms," and "Ah, Sweet Mystery of Life," pouring an excessive amount of emotion into most of the songs. Though it is difficult not to be very impressed by the potential of her voice, this is actually much more recommended to opera fans than to jazz listeners! But in contrast, *Sarah Sings Soulfully* is a gem. Although such songs as "A Taste of Honey," "What Kind of Fool Am I," and "The Good Life" may not promise much, Vaughan (still just 39 at the time) is heard throughout in peak form and she uplifts the material. Her versions of "Sermonette," "Gravy Waltz," "Moanin'," "'Round Midnight," and "Midnight Sun" are definitive, and the backup sextet (which includes Teddy Edwards and trumpeter Carmell Jones) is excellent. A perfect close to Sarah Vaughan's Roulette years.

* *The Complete Sarah Vaughan on Mercury Vol. 4 / July 19, 1963–Jan. 1967 / Mercury 830 714*

9 *Sassy Swings the Tivoli / July 18–21, 1963 / Mercury 832 788*

8 *Jazzfest Masters / July 1969 / Scotti Bros. 72392 75244*

10 *Live in Japan / Sept. 24, 1973 / Mobile Fidelity 2-844*

All of Sarah Vaughan's recordings during her second period with Mercury are available on the six-CD set titled *Vol. 4.* This includes *Vaughan with Voices* (in which she is backed by the Svend Saaby Choir), *The Mancini Songbook, Sassy Swings Again* (a big band outing with trumpeter Freddie Hubbard), and the greatly expanded trio set *Sassy Swings the Tivoli* along with some miscellaneous items and many orchestral dates. While completists will want *Vol. 4,* the two-CD *Sassy Swings the Tivoli* has her finest performances from the second Mercury period, a 1963 live set with pianist Kirk Stuart, bassist Charles Williams, and drummer George Hughes that ranks with her finest work of the decade. "Poor Butterfly," "I'll Be Seeing You," and "Black Coffee" are among the more memorable selections.

After permanently leaving Mercury in 1967, Sarah Vaughan did not record again in the studio until late 1971. In 1992 the Scotti Bros. label came out with Sassy's performance from the 1969 New Orleans Jazz Festival, virtually the only recording released from this unusually quiet period in the singer's career. Nine selections are performed with an all-star quintet that includes Clark Terry, tenor saxophonist Zoot Sims, and pianist Jaki Byard, there are three cuts with a big band, plus a version of "A Closer Walk with Thee" that is performed with a Dixieland band and a gospel choir. Throughout, Sassy sounds in fine form, mostly singing her usual repertoire.

During 1971–74, Vaughan recorded regularly for Mainstream, including several not-so-hot commercial projects that found her performing current pop songs. However, the two-CD *Complete Sarah Vaughan Live in Japan* (reissued by the audiophile Mobile Fidelity label) is a definite exception. Age 49 at the time, Sassy rarely sounded better than she does on the 27 selections, which include "Poor Butterfly," "'Round Midnight," "Misty," "The Nearness of You," and "Bye Bye Blackbird." She is assisted by pianist Carl Schroeder, bassist John Gianelli, and drummer Jimmy Cobb. For whatever reason, she was inspired that night, not only scatting well and showing off her phenomenal voice but really digging into the lyrics. Essential music.

- **5** *I Love Brazil! / Oct. 31, 1977–Nov. 7, 1977 / Pablo 2312–101*
- **8** *How Long Has This Been Going On? / Apr. 25, 1978 / Pablo 2310–821*
- **8** *The Duke Ellington Songbook One / Aug. 15, 1979– Sept. 13, 1979 / Pablo 2312–111*
- **9** *The Duke Ellington Songbook Two / Aug. 15, 1979– Sept. 13, 1979 / Pablo 2312–116*
- **8** *Send in the Clowns / Feb. 16, 1981–May 16, 1981 / Pablo 2312–130*
- **9** *Crazy and Mixed Up / Mar. 1–2, 1982 / Pablo 2312– 137*
- **2** *The Mystery of Man / June 30, 1984 / Kokopelli 1301*

After a recording absence during 1975–76, Vaughan cut a series of interesting albums for Norman Granz's Pablo label during 1977–82, the last significant recordings of her career. Actually, *I Love Brazil* is a mixed success. Although Sassy's voice is typically wonderful and she is joined by a group of Brazilian all-stars (including keyboardist Jose Roberto Bertrami, Milton Nascimento, Dori Caymmi, and, on two songs, Antonio Carlos Jobim on piano), the music never really takes off. *How Long Has This Been Going On?* is a more typical Granz production that has Vaughan swinging with Oscar Peterson, Joe Pass, Ray Brown, and Louie Bellson on ten standards. Among the highlights are "Midnight Sun," "More Than You Know, " "Teach Me Tonight," and "I've Got the World on a String."

The singer's two CDs of Duke Ellington material are quite successful. *Songbook One* has her joined by either Jimmy Rowles or Mike Wofford on piano, Joe Pass or Bucky Pizzarelli on guitar, bassist Andy Simpkins, drummer Grady Tate, and sometimes horn soloists (including her husband of the time, trumpeter Waymon Reed) plus an occasional string orchestra arranged by Billy Byers. The emphasis is on ballads, including "In a Sentimental Mood," "All Too Soon," and "Sophisticated Lady." *Songbook Two* (the better of the two discs) has more variety in tempo, contributions from Reed, flutist Frank Wess, and altoist Eddie "Cleanhead" Vinson (who takes a vocal), and such songs as "I Ain't Got Nothin' but the Blues," "Tonight I Shall Sleep," "Rocks in My Bed," and "It Don't Mean a Thing."

Send in the Clowns finds Vaughan backed by the Count Basie Orchestra (with George Gaffney filling in on piano) performing arrangements by Sammy Nestico and Allyn Ferguson. The band is mostly in the background (though there is one solo apiece for trombonist Booty Wood and tenorman Kenny Hing), but Sassy sounds in superb form on such numbers as "I Gotta Right to Sing the Blues," "I Hadn't Anyone Till You," and "When Your Lover Has Gone." Even her version of "Send in the Clowns," a song she loved that she always turned into an overdramatic display of her voice, can be excused. Vaughan was delighted to have the opportunity with *Crazy and Mixed Up* to produce her own album. Backed by pianist Roland Hanna, Joe Pass, bassist Andy Simpkins, and drummer Harold Jones, Sassy is heard in top form on eight tunes, including "Autumn Leaves," "The Island," and "You Are Too Beautiful." She sounds (a month shy of her 58th birthday) as if she would be going on forever.

But sadly, *Crazy and Mixed Up* was her last worthwhile jazz album. Later in 1982 she recorded a Gershwin set for Columbia with the Los Angeles Philharmonic Orchestra that is of little interest. In 1984 Sassy was the lead voice on a highly unusual project in which Gene Lees translated the philosophical poems of Pope John II into English and set them to music. Vaughan performed these poems with the backing of a huge orchestra and chorus conducted by Lalo Schifrin, but the results are quite ponderous, overly serious, pompous, and nearly unlistenable, despite the best intentions of everyone concerned. Other than an indifferent Brazilian album in 1987 (*Brazilian Romance*), this would be the final recording in the long and mostly brilliant career of Sarah Vaughan.

LPS TO SEARCH FOR

Sarah Vaughan's important Musicraft recordings are long overdue to be reissued complete and in chronological order on CD. *The Divine Sarah* (Musicraft 504), *The Man I Love* (Musicraft 2002), and *Lover Man* (Musicraft 2006) contain the majority of these valuable titles. The two-LP set, *The Columbia Years 1949–1953* (Columbia 44165), has most of Sassy's best recordings for Columbia, including the eight from her Miles Davis session and her early versions of "Black Coffee," "You're Mine, You," "Perdido," and "After Hours."

FILMS

Sarah Vaughan is featured on five numbers from 1951 that have been released on *The Snader Telescriptions – The Vocal-*

ists (Storyville 6007). The singer pops up briefly in *Disc Jockey* (1951). *The Divine One* (BMG Video 80066) is a fine documentary covering her life. *Sarah Vaughan & Friends* (A Vision 50209) teams Sassy in the 1980s with a rather odd trumpet section: Dizzy Gillespie, Al Hirt, Maynard Ferguson, Don Cherry, and Chuck Mangione!

Arrangers

There had been major arrangers in jazz since Don Redman wrote charts for Fletcher Henderson's orchestra in 1923, and arrangers were the underrated heroes of the swing era. During the classic Bebop era, most big bands were in the process of breaking up. But, although Bop was primarily thought of as a player's music , there was a need for arrangers who understood the new style and could orchestrate it for larger ensembles. Ralph Burns's work helped make Woody Herman's orchestra into one of the top big bands of 1944-46, George Handy's radical charts made history for Boyd Raeburn (even if commercial success never came), Gil Fuller was an important part of Dizzy Gillespie's orchestra, Pete Rugolo took Stan Kenton's ideas to their logical extreme, Nat Pierce had his own regional ensemble, and Chico O'Farrill helped out several big bands (including those of Gillespie, Machito, and Benny Goodman). Probably the most talented Bebop writer of the era was Tadd Dameron, whose compositions and arrangements for smaller ensembles were more significant than his fairly basic piano playing.

Other important writers of the period who made significant contributions to later periods, including Gil Evans and Shorty Rogers, will be covered in other books in this series.

RALPH BURNS

b. June 29, 1922, Newton, MA

One of the key writers for Woody Herman's First and Second Herds, Ralph Burns wrote inventive charts for Herman that were connected to both swing and Bebop. He started on piano when he was seven and studied at the New England Conservatory during 1938-39. After moving to New York, Burns worked with Nick Jerret, Charlie Barnet (for whom he wrote "The Moose"), and Red Norvo (1943). He joined Woody Herman in 1944 as a pianist, but his writing soon became more significant; after a year he stopped touring with the band to concentrate on arranging and composing. Among his compositions for Herman were the riotous "Apple Honey," "Bijou" (Bill Harris's big showcase), and the four-part "Summer Sequence"; one movement from the last soon became "Early Autumn," a hit ballad feature for Stan Getz. By the early 1950s, Burns was more involved in writing for radio, television, and the studios than for jazz, but he did lead eight jazz-oriented albums during the decade for Verve, MGM, Period, and Decca, playing piano on most of the dates. Burns left jazz altogether by the 1960s and has since written for films and Broadway shows, including 1977's *New York, New York*.

8 *Bijou* / 1955 / *Original Jazz Classics 1917*
Ralph Burns's only combo date as a leader is also his only in-

print jazz CD as a leader (except for 1951's *Free Forms*, which has been reissued as part of a Lee Konitz/Jimmy Giuffre Verve set). For this rare outing, Burns is showcased as a pianist in a quartet with Tal Farlow, bassist Clyde Lombardi, and drummer Osie Johnson. The first six songs all have "spring" or "sprang" in their titles (including "Spring Sequence," "It Might As Well Be Spring," and Willie "the Lion" Smith's "Echo of Spring"), and the other five selections include his tricky "Perpetual Motion" and "Bijou." Throughout, Burns plays thoughtfully, sounding very much like an arranger but displaying an impressive amount of technique and swing.

FILMS

Ralph Burns can be seen with Woody Herman's Orchestra in *Earl Carroll Vanities* (1945)

TADD DAMERON

b. Feb. 21, 1917, Cleveland, OH, d. Mar. 8, 1965, New York, NY

Even if Bebop is thought of as first and foremost a soloist's music, it also spawned a few very talented writers. Tadd Dameron was arguably the definitive arranger/composer of the Bebop era; particularly if one thinks of Thelonious Monk as really belonging to a later period. Dameron's compositions (which include "Hot House," "Good Bait," "Our

Delight," "Lady Bird," "Half Step Down, Please," "Cool Breeze," and "If You Could See Me Now") gave musicians challenging pieces to play and kept the music fresh and exciting.

Dameron's roots were in the swing era. He worked with Zack Whyte and Blanche Calloway, wrote for Vido Musso, and contributed arrangements for Harlan Leonard's Kansas City Orchestra, some of which were recorded in 1940. In the early '40s Dameron wrote arrangements for Jimmy Lunceford and Count Basie, and he helped fill in the library of the Billy Eckstine Orchestra and Georgie Auld's big band. During the classic Bebop era, Dameron was one of the top writers for the Dizzy Gillespie Big Band (1945 and 1946–47), and he wrote for Sarah Vaughan (who recorded "If You Could See Me Now"). Although a fairly basic pianist who was shy to solo, Dameron was a member of Babs Gonzales's Three Bips and a Bop (1947) and led a sextet at the Royal Roost (1948–49) that included, at various times, Fats Navarro (who recorded extensively with Dameron), Miles Davis, Allan Eager, and Kai Winding.

Dameron and Miles Davis performed at the 1949 Paris Jazz Festival with a quintet that included James Moody. Dameron stayed in Europe for a few months, writing for Ted Heath, and then back in the United States he contributed some charts for Artie Shaw's Bebop Orchestra, toured with Bull Moose Jackson's R&B group (1951–52), and, in 1953, had a nonet that featured Clifford Brown. Unfortunately drug abuse and the jazz world's change in musical styles led to less work during the next few years, although Dameron recorded *Fontainebleau* in 1956 and *Mating Call* with John Coltrane in 1958. Due to drug convictions, Dameron spent most of 1959–61 in jail. After his release he resumed writing, including for Blue Mitchell (some of those charts were actually written while in prison), Sonny Stitt, Milt Jackson, and Benny Goodman. Tadd Dameron recorded a final record in 1962 before passing away from cancer, three years later, at the age of 48. Years after his death, Dameron's music was used as the basis for Dameronia, a group headed by drummer Philly Joe Jones.

7 *Fontainebleau / Mar. 9, 1956 / Original Jazz Classics 055*

8 *Mating Call / Nov. 30, 1956 / Original Jazz Classics 212*

9 *The Magic Touch of Tadd Dameron / Feb. 27, 1962–Apr. 16, 1962 / Original Jazz Classics 143*

Tadd Dameron's Blue Note, Savoy, Jazzland, and Capitol dates of 1947–49 have been reissued as part of Fats Navarro CDs, and his 1953 Prestige set has reappeared under Clifford Brown's name! After 1953, Dameron led only three full albums, resulting in this trio of CDs. *Fontainebleau* has some excellent music from a 1956 octet that includes Kenny Dorham, altoist Sahib Shihab, and Cecil Payne, but unfortunately the playing time is barely 30 minutes. The five Dameron originals that are heard include "Delirium," "The Scene Is Clean," and the 11-minute blues "Bula-Beige." *Mating Call* is a bit unusual, for it is a quartet with tenor saxophonist John Coltrane and finds Dameron (who wrote all six numbers, including "On a Misty Night" and "Soultrane") in the role of featured pianist. He does fine (assisted by John Simmons and drummer Philly Joe Jones), although his playing would never intimidate Oscar Peterson!

Best of the trio is *The Magic Touch,* which does a superb job of summing up Tadd Dameron's career. "On a Misty Night," "Fontainebleau," "If You Could See Me Now," "Our Delight," and "Dial B for Beauty" are among Dameron's ten compositions, there are three previously unreleased alternate takes on the CD reissue, and Dameron had an opportunity to arrange his music (on some selections) for a 14-piece orchestra. Bill Evans is heard on piano, and other key players include Clark Terry, Jimmy Cleveland, Julius Watkins, Johnny Griffin, and singer Barbara Winfield (who is on two cuts). Highly recommended.

GIL FULLER

b. Apr. 14, 1920, Los Angeles, CA, d. May 26, 1994, New York, NY

Gil Fuller is best known for his writing for the Dizzy Gillespie big band. Never a soloist, Fuller stuck to composing and arranging throughout his career. He studied engineering at New York University, wrote in Los Angeles for the big bands of Les Hite and Floyd Ray, and served in the Army (1942–45). After his discharge, Fuller wrote charts for Billy Eckstine, Jimmie Lunceford, Woody Herman, Charlie Barnet, Count Basie, Artie Shaw, Machito, Tito Puente, and others. He really made his mark on Bebop by contributing arrangements during 1946–49 for Dizzy Gillespie, including "Manteca," "Oop-Bop-Sh-Bam," "One Bass Hit," "Ray's Idea," and especially the futuristic "Things to Come."

After having led a four-song date for Savoy in 1949 (including taking a vocal on "Mean to Me"), Fuller worked outside of music (in real estate and engineering), had a few music publishing firms, and freelanced. In 1962 he arranged a country album for Ray Charles, and he became more active by the mid-1960s, when he led two albums (one with Gillespie and one with James Moody) for Pacific Jazz. Fuller also helped Dizzy Gillespie with his reunion big band in 1968. But Gil Fuller eventually dropped out of music again, and his contributions to Bebop have since tended to be underrated.

LPS TO SEARCH FOR

Other than four songs for Savoy in 1949 (which are invariably reissued as part of a sampler) and his 1965 date with Dizzy Gillespie (generally reissued under Dizzy's name), Gil Fuller's only other date as a leader is *Night Flight* (Pacific Jazz 10101). That album was made with an orchestra assembled for the 1965 Monterey Jazz Festival, featuring James Moody on tenor as the dominant soloist. Fuller's originals (half of the program) and arrangements are excellent, making one wonder why he did not record much more through the years.

GEORGE HANDY

b. Jan. 17, 1920, Brooklyn, NY, d. Jan. 8, 1997, Harris, NY

George Handy was one of the most adventurous arrangers of the Bebop era, and his writing for the Boyd Raeburn Orchestra was radical, jarring, quite dissonant, and a bit nuts—but always colorful. Handy's period in the spotlight was actually quite brief. He studied piano with his mother from the age of five, attended the Juilliard School of Music, and took lessons with Aaron Copland. After playing with Michael Loring (1938–39), Handy was in the Army in 1940 and then wrote music for Raymond Scott (1941). Handy played piano and wrote for Boyd Raeburn during 1944 (when the orchestra was gradually changing from a swing band to a more Bop-oriented outfit). He left to write for Paramount Studios and recorded in a quartet also including guitarist Arv Garrison, bassist-vocalist Vivian Garry, and drummer Roy Hall. Handy soon returned to Raeburn and during 1945–46 did his greatest work, including such numbers as "Tonsillectomy," "Dalvatore Sally," and "Rip Van Winkle" plus rather remarkable transformations of "Over the Rainbow," "Body and Soul," and "Temptation." The latter two charts have all kinds of dissonant effects going on "behind" the vocals of David Allyn and Ginnie Powell, while "Over the Rainbow" is quite satirical. He also had the opportunity to record his "Diggin' for Diz" on piano with Charlie Parker and Dizzy Gillespie.

Unfortunately a personality conflict led Handy to quit Raeburn in August 1946. The rest of his career was anticlimactic. He wrote for other bands (including those of Ina Ray Hutton, Herbie Fields, and Alvino Rey), but drug abuse caused him to spend a lot of time off the scene. During 1954–55, Handy led two now-obscure albums for RCA's X subsidiary. He also played and recorded with Zoot Sims during 1956–57 and in the late 1960s worked as a record reviewer for *Downbeat*. But George Handy spent most of his final 40 years as a freelance arranger in obscurity, a strange ending to a once-promising career.

CHICO O'FARRILL

b. Oct. 28, 1921, Havana, Cuba

Chico O'Farrill was an important writer during the Bebop era, although he made his most significant contributions as a pioneer of Afro-Cuban jazz. Born in Cuba, O'Farrill began playing trumpet while in military school in Gainesville, Georgia from 1936 to 1940), a period of time when he became very interested in jazz. Back in Havana, O'Farrill switched to piano, studied composition, and freelanced. In 1948 he moved to New York and was soon writing for Benny Goodman's Bebop Orchestra (including "Undercurrent Blues"), Stan Kenton, Machito, Dizzy Gillespie, and Charlie Parker (including the "Manteca Suite" and the "Afro-Cuban Jazz Suite"). He recorded a series of exciting Latin jazz big band dates for Clef and Norgran during 1951–54 that mixed Bebop with Latin rhythms and are quite definitive of the idiom. Active in the United States during the 1950s, when he often led a big band, O'Farrill eventually moved to Mexico City, where, during the first half of the '60s, he worked locally. In 1965 he returned to New York, writing for the television series *Festival of the Lively Arts* and contributing arrangements for Count Basie, Machito, Stan Kenton, Cal Tjader, Clark Terry, Gato Barbieri, and Dizzy Gillespie, among many others. Off records as a leader during 1966–94 (other than one date for a Japanese label in 1976), Chico O'Farrill led an exciting album for Milestone in 1995 and has had a more prominent profile during the years since, being rightfully recognized as a legend. His son Arturo O'Farrill is a fine pianist and arranger.

10 *Cuban Blues: Chico O'Farrill Sessions / Dec. 21, 1950–Apr. 16, 1954 / Verve 314 533 256*
9 *Pure Emotion / Feb. 1995 / Milestone 9239*

8 *Heart of a Legend / Dec. 1998–July 1999 /
Milestone 9299*

Cuban Blues has all of the music from six of Chico O'Farrill's former ten-inch LPs for Clef and Norgran plus a session by Machito's orchestra (playing O'Farrill's lengthy "Afro-Cuban Jazz Suite," which features Charlie Parker, Flip Phillips, and Buddy Rich). The resulting two-CD set has some of the finest Afro-Cuban music ever recorded, whether it be familiar numbers such as "Malagueña" and "The Peanut Vendor," original miniatures, or the six-part "Second Afro-Cuban Jazz Suite." Essential music that contains both Boppish solos and consistently stirring rhythms.

Pure Emotion, which features a 22-piece orchestra in 1995, is a near classic. O'Farrill contributed seven originals plus arrangements on all ten numbers (including "Perdido") for a band that includes such notables as tenor saxophonist Mario Rivera, trombonists Robin Eubanks and Papo Vasquez, trumpeters Victor Paz and Michael Mossman, a four-man percussion section that includes Jerry Gonzalez, and pianist Arturo O'Farrill. *Heart of a Legend,* featuring O'Farrill's big band and many guests (including bassist Cachao, tenor saxophonist Gato Barbieri, altoist Paquito D'Rivera, Arturo Sandoval, and, on "Sing Your Blues Away," singer Freddie Cole). Despite the shifting personnel, the infectious music holds together quite well, with O'Farrill's orchestra (which also has many strong soloists) serving as the nucleus for this happy project. Even in his late 70s, Chico O'Farrill still has a lot to contribute to modern music.

LPS TO SEARCH FOR

Nine Flags (Impulse 9135), from 1966, has O'Farrill paying tribute to nine different countries that at the time were represented by brands of Nine Flags fragrances. The ten originals (which also include "The Lady from Nine Flags") have O'Farrill leading three different groups (with eight to 16 pieces), and, although a bit lightweight, there are worthwhile solos from Art Farmer, Clark Terry, J. J. Johnson, and guitarist Larry Coryell, among others.

NAT PIERCE

*b. July 16, 1925, Somerville, MA, d. June 10, 1992,
Los Angeles, CA*

Nat Pierce had a piano style that could sound identical to Count Basie's, and for most of his career, he was closely associated with Mainstream swing. However, in the late 1940s in Boston he led a Bop-oriented big band; thus his inclusion in this book!

Pierce studied at the New England Conservatory and began playing professionally in the Boston area in 1943. After working with Shorty Sherock and Larry Clinton (1948), he put together a rehearsal band in 1949 that lasted two years and included altoist Charlie Mariano and singer Teddi King; Pierce supplied most of the arrangements in addition to playing piano. A Hep CD and an earlier Zim LP contain most of this fine orchestra's recordings. In 1951 Pierce broke up the big band to become pianist and arranger for Woody Herman's Third Herd (1951–55). During the second half of the 1950s, he worked in many different situations, including substituting for Count Basie on Mainstream swing dates with some of Count's alumni, arranging for singers and big bands, working with Ruby Braff, Lester Young, Coleman Hawkins, Pee Wee Russell, and Ella Fitzgerald, and writing all of the arrangements for the classic *The Sound of Jazz* telecast. Pierce was pianist with Woody Herman's swinging Herd of 1961–66, wrote for Anita O'Day and Carmen McRae, settled in Los Angeles in 1971, and worked with the big bands of Louie Bellson and Bill Berry. He also sometimes subbed for Count Basie with Count's orchestra when the leader was declining. In 1975 Pierce co-formed and co-led the Juggernaut (an all-star big band that sounded remarkably similar to Basie's) with drummer Frank Capp. In addition to his work with the Juggernaut, Nat Pierce spent his later years recording as a sideman for Concord and touring Europe as a member of the Countsmen.

9 *The Boston Bustout / Dec. 1947–Dec. 1950 / Hep 13*
7 *5400 North / May 21, 1978 / Hep 2004*

The Nat Pierce orchestra of 1949–51 was considered one of the finest based in Boston during the era. *The Boston Bustout* has selections featuring Pierce with the Ray Borden big band in 1947, with combos led by Serge Chaloff and Charlie Mariano, and on a few numbers with his own orchestra; Teddi King takes three vocals. Moving up to 1978, *5400 North* is by a Pierce-led quintet with trumpeter Dick Collins, tenor saxophonist Bill Perkins, and, most notably, singer Mary Ann McCall. The live outing is essentially a modern swing date that has touches of West Coast Cool Jazz.

LPS TO SEARCH FOR

Nat Pierce Orchestra (Zim 1005) has additional selections from Pierce's Boppish big band of 1949–50. Also of interest is *The Ballad of Jazz Street* (Zim 2003), which is by a more swing-oriented big band from 1961; Clark Terry and the tenors of Paul Quinichette and Paul Gonsalves get prominent solo space.

FILMS

Nat Pierce is seen playing piano during parts of 1957's *The Sound of Jazz* (Vintage Jazz Classics 2001).

PETE RUGOLO

b. Dec. 25, 1915, San Piero, Sicily, Italy

Pete Rugolo was to Stan Kenton what Billy Strayhorn was to Duke Ellington. His writing was very much in Kenton's style, but Rugolo extended the bandleader's ideas and was prolific during 1945-48. His writing, like the style of Kenton's band, does not really fall into Bop but stands apart, being both influenced by and acting as an indirect influence on the Bebop movement.

Rugolo moved to the United States with his family when he was five, growing up in Santa Rosa, California. He studied with Darius Milhaud at Mills College, spent time in the Army (1942-45), and then attracted the attention of Stan Kenton. During 1945-49, Rugolo wrote a large portion of Kenton's arrangements, some of which were bombastic and a bit classical-oriented; he shared Kenton's goal of creating modern concert music rather than dance band pieces. In 1949 Rugolo became the music director of Capitol Records, where he wrote arrangements for singers (including June Christy, Nat King Cole, Peggy Lee, Billy Eckstine, and Dinah Washington) and for pop music dates. Although he led a big band in 1954 and headed a series of big band recordings during 1954-61, Rugolo largely left jazz after that period, becoming a very busy writer for the Hollywood studios.

LPS TO SEARCH FOR

While Pete Rugolo's work for Stan Kenton is currently available mostly on Kenton's CDs, his own dates as a leader have become scarce. Most are quite creative and utilize some of the top West Coast jazz musicians of the 1950s, particularly *Adventures in Rhythm* (Columbia 604), *Introducing Pete Rugolo* (Columbia 635), *Rugolomania* (Columbia 689), *Percussion at Work* (Mercury/Wing 12229), *Rugolo Plays Kenton* (Mercury 36143), and *An Adventure in Sound—Reeds* (Mercury 60039).

Vibraphonists

The vibraphone was first heard on jazz recordings when Lionel Hampton played small spots behind Louis Armstrong in 1930 on "Shine" and "Memories of You." It had been preceded by the xylophone, which was used in the 1920s as a novelty instrument, although Jimmy Bertrand (who would be Hampton's teacher) did record a few short solos. Red Norvo emerged in the early 1930s as a very skilled jazz xylophonist. He led a big band during the swing era (usually featuring his wife, singer Mildred Bailey), switched permanently to vibes in 1943, and was quite versatile. In 1945 he not only recorded with Benny Goodman and Woody Herman's First Herd but also welcomed Charlie Parker and Dizzy Gillespie to one of his own recording dates.

After years spent playing in Los Angeles, Lionel Hampton (who was originally a drummer) emerged in 1936, when he became a member of the Benny Goodman Quartet. Despite the presence of Red Norvo and a few relatively minor players (including the former bass saxophonist Adrian Rollini), Hampton dominated the vibes prior to the Bebop era, whether with BG, on his own all-star recordings, or with his big band, which in 1942 had a major hit with "Flying Home."

Two major new vibraphonists began to rise to prominence during the Bebop era: Milt Jackson and Terry Gibbs. Both were Bop players from the start and, although acknowledging their predecessors, they quickly developed their own individual sounds. Jackson was soulful, lyrical on ballads, and very fluent on both blues and fast Boppish romps. Gibbs was always a very spirited and excitable soloist, playing double-time on ballads and enjoying improvising on uptempo pieces. Although there were a few other new vibraphonists, including Marjorie Hyams (featured with Woody Herman and George Shearing before retiring prematurely), Jackson and Gibbs, along with Hampton, Norvo, and Cal Tjader, would dominate the vibes throughout the 1950s.

Along with Milt Jackson, the hyper Terry Gibbs easily transferred
Bebop to the vibes.

TERRY GIBBS

b. Oct. 13, 1924, Brooklyn, NY

An exciting vibraphonist whose hard-charging solos tend to
be hyper and full of energy, Terry Gibbs fit in perfectly with
Woody Herman's Second Herd. Born Julius Gubenko, he
started out playing xylophone, drums, and tympani, winning Major Bowes's famous Amateur Hour contest when he
was 12. After serving in the military, Terry Gibbs was a fixture on 52nd Street, made his recording debut with Aaron
Sachs, was with Tommy Dorsey's Orchestra in 1946 (a
group also featuring his future musical partner, Buddy De-
Franco), toured Scandinavia with Chubby Jackson (1947–
48), had a second stint with TD, and played with Buddy
Rich (1948). Gibbs's quick mind, strong technique, and
sense of humor made him one of the more popular attrac-

tions of the Bop era. He was an important part of Woody
Herman's Second Herd (1948–49), where he was well featured.

After an unsuccessful attempt to have his own big band,
Gibbs was adaptable enough to play quite well with Benny
Goodman's sextet (1951–52), following in the tradition of Lionel Hampton but adding his own personality to the music.
After some freelancing, in 1957 he moved to Los Angeles,
where he worked in the studios and became closely associated with Steve Allen. Gibbs organized his Dream Band (a
big band with a swing repertoire but more modern soloists)
during 1959–62 and led combos during the remainder of the
'60s, '70s, and '80s, including one that in 1963 featured Alice McLeod (the future Alice Coltrane) on piano. Since the
early 1980s, Terry Gibbs has frequently teamed up with
Buddy DeFranco (they always inspire each other), and dur-

ing the past decade he has often used his son, the talented Gerry Gibbs, on drums.

8 *Dream Band / Mar. 17 + 19, 1959 / Contemporary 7647*

7 *The Sundown Sessions, Vol. 2 / Nov. 1959 / Contemporary 7652*

7 *Flying Home, Vol. 3 / Mar. 17 + 19, 1959 / Contemporary 7654*

7 *Main Stem, Vol. 4 / Jan. 20-22, 1961 / Contemporary 7656*

8 *The Big Cat, Vol. 5 / Jan. 20-22, 1961 / Contemporary 7657*

Terry Gibbs recorded as a leader as early as 1949 (his first date, which featured Stan Getz, has often been reissued under the tenor's name) and made records in the 1950s for Savoy, Brunswick, Emarcy, and Interlude, but very little of that music has yet appeared on CD.

During 1959–62, Gibbs led what he called his "Dream Band," a big band of top Los Angeles–based players. Although two of the orchestra's studio recordings (one apiece for Mercury and Verve) remain out of print, starting in 1986 the Contemporary label came out with five CDs' worth of material; the first three volumes were previously unreleased, while Vols. 4–5 were previously out on Mercury but long unavailable. The arrangements are by Bill Holman, Bob Brookmeyer, Manny Albam, Al Cohn, Med Flory, Marty Paich, and Lennie Niehaus. The first three volumes feature such soloists as Gibbs, valve trombonist Bob Enevoldsen, Holman on tenor, trumpeters Stu Williamson and Conte Candoli, altoists Joe Maini and Charles Kennedy, and pianist Pete Jolly. Although the solos are modern for the time (influenced by both Bop and Cool Jazz), the repertoire is primarily from the 1930s and '40s, swing-era standards. *Dream Band* (an excellent place to start with this series) has such tunes as "Don't Be That Way," "Cottontail," "Jumpin' at the Woodside," and even "Let's Dance." *Vol. 2* includes "The Song Is You," Artie Shaw's "Back Bay Shuffle," and "My Reverie," while the third set is highlighted by "Avalon," "Flying Home," and Sonny Rollins's "Airegin."

Vols. 4 and 5, recorded nearly two years later, have a similar lineup of musicians (with trombonist Frank Rosolino and the tenors of Richie Kamuca and Bill Perkins as important new additions) but a very different repertoire. Although there are some swing-era tunes, much of the repertoire is less familiar. In addition to "Day In, Day Out" and "Ja-Da,"

Vol. 4 has Holman's "Limerick Waltz," Cohn's "Nose Cone," and Gibbs's "T and S." The fifth and final volume is quite strong, particularly "Tico Tico," "Billie's Bounce," "Do You Wanna Jump, Children," and "The Big Cat."

8 *Air Mail Special / Oct. 4-5, 1981 / Contemporary 14056*

8 *The Latin Connection / May 9-10, 1986 / Contemporary 14022*

9 *Chicago Fire / July 24-26, 1987 / Contemporary 14036*

8 *Memories of You / Apr. 13-15, 1991 / Contemporary 14066*

8 *Kings of Swing / Apr. 13-15, 1991 / Contemporary 14067*

Terry Gibbs kept busy after his Dream Band broke up in 1962, recording for Mercury, Jazz Vault, Limelight, Time, Impulse, and Dot during 1962–66, although the 1970s found him leading only three sessions (one later released by Xanadu and two for Jazz à La Carte).

In 1981, Gibbs made his first combo recording with Buddy DeFranco, resulting in music released by the now-defunct Tall Trees and Palo Alto labels. *Air Mail Special* has selections from both of the albums (although it is not complete), but what is on this CD is excellent. With pianist Frank Collett, bassist Andy Simpkins, and drummer Jimmie Smith supporting the lead soloists, the music typically is exciting. Highlights include the title cut, "Blues for Brody" (which has the principals taking choruses in each of the 12 keys), "Love for Sale," and "Now's the Time." There would be many more collaborations in future years, some of which were issued under DeFranco's name.

The now out-of-print *The Latin Connection* is notable for teaming Gibbs with Frank Morgan and a Latin rhythm section that (on three songs) includes Tito Puente on timbales. Most of the songs are Bop or swing standards, including "Scrapple from the Apple," "Groovin' High," "Good Bait," and "Sing Sing Sing." This Afro-Cuban-oriented set is quite successful and now a bit scarce. *Chicago Fire,* by the Gibbs-DeFranco Quintet (with the powerful pianist John Campbell, bassist Todd Coolman, and drummer Gerry Gibbs), has its explosive moments. Their versions of "Rockin' in Rhythm," "Cherokee," "Giant Steps," and "52nd Street Theme" definitely generate plenty of heat.

Memories of You and *Kings of Swing* find Gibbs and DeFranco joined by guitarist Herb Ellis, pianist Larry Novak,

Milt Hinton, and drummer Butch Miles. In both cases, all of the songs (nine apiece) are associated to an extent with Benny Goodman, but Gibbs and DeFranco do not sound like Lionel Hampton and BG. The melodies are swing, but the hot solos are pure Bebop. Both sets are equally rewarding, even if the repertoire is not too challenging.

8	*Play That Song / Oct. 23-27, 1994 / Chiaroscuro 337*
8	*Wham / Oct. 26-29, 1997 / Chiaroscuro 356*
6	*Play Steve Allen / Sept. 2, 1998 / Contemporary 14089*

Play That Song features the Terry Gibbs Quartet (with pianist Uri Caine, bassist Boris Koslov, and Gerry Gibbs) playing seven of the vibraphonist's originals plus a speedy "Limehouse Blues" and "Moonray." Gibbs and Caine (who in this setting often sounds a bit like Oscar Peterson) work together quite well. *Wham* has Gibbs and DeFranco backed by a fine rhythm section (pianist Aaron Goldberg, bassist Darek Oles, and Gerry Gibbs) performing basic originals, "Sweet Georgia Brown," "Early Autumn," and a version of "Sweet and Lovely" that has Flip Phillips sitting in on tenor. Gibbs and DeFranco reunited in 1998 (with pianist Tom Ranier, bassist Dave Carpenter, and drummer Gibbs) to perform 13 Steve Allen songs. As one might expect, the tunes are not the greatest, but the co-leaders do their best to uplift the music while always swinging hard.

LPS TO SEARCH FOR

A Jazz Band Ball (VSOP 40) reissues a 1957 date for Mode that is a bit unusual. Gibbs, Victor Feldman, and Larry Bunker all play vibes (and sometimes marimba and xylophone) while joined by Lou Levy, bassist Max Bennett, and drummer Mel Lewis; there are plenty of colorful moments on this Bop date. *Launching a New Band* (Mercury 20440), from 1959, was the debut album by Gibbs's Dream Band, and it is quite similar in style (and content) to the first three volumes released by Contemporary. *That Swing Thing* (Verve 8447), from 1961, showcases Gibbs in a quartet with pianist Pat Moran. *El Nutto* (Limelight 82005) is most notable for having Alice McLeod playing in Gibbs's quartet; the Bop-based pianist would soon marry and become permanently known as Alice Coltrane. *Take It from Me* (Impulse 58), from 1964 (with guitarist Kenny Burrell, bassist Sam Jones, and drummer Louis Hayes), has Gibbs jamming on six of his originals (none of which caught on), "All the Things You Are," and "Honeysuckle Rose." *Bopstacle Course* (Xanadu 210) is an

underrated gem, a 1974 matchup between Gibbs and Barry Harris (along with Sam Jones and drummer Alan Dawson) that is consistently exciting, making one wish that Gibbs and Harris had teamed up much more extensively.

FILMS

Terry Gibbs appears in *Jazz on a Summer's Day* (1959), playing "All of Me" with Dinah Washington.

MILT JACKSON

b. Jan. 1, 1923, Detroit, MI, d. Oct. 9, 1999, New York, NY

One of the greatest vibraphonists of all time and the main influence on vibists after 1945, Milt Jackson seemed incapable of playing an uninspired or soulless chorus. With the Modern Jazz Quartet and as a star soloist, "Bags" appeared on a countless number of recordings as a leader and as a sideman during a 53-year period. His brand of Bop, blues, and soul never went out of style.

Jackson actually started out on guitar when he was seven and played piano from the time he was 11, also briefly trying violin and drums and singing gospel with the Evangelist Singers. As a teenager he switched to vibes, an instrument that at the time not only was dominated by Lionel Hampton but also had Hamp as its only giant (Red Norvo would not switch from xylophone until 1943). By slowing down the speed of the vibraphone's oscillator, Bags was able to achieve a distinctive and warm sound of his own that differed from that of his predecessors. Jackson was set to join the Earl Hines big band in 1942 but was drafted and spent two years in the military. During 1944-45 in Detroit he led the Four Sharps, and he made his recording debut with Dinah Washington. In 1945 Dizzy Gillespie heard Jackson playing in Detroit with his own group and immediately invited him to join his sextet (which would soon include Charlie Parker) and, the following year, his new big band. After Jackson made his first recordings with Dizzy in 1946, he was in great demand, and he remained a popular attraction throughout his entire career.

During the Bebop era, Jackson worked with Gillespie, Charlie Parker, Thelonious Monk, Howard McGhee, and in 1949 the Woody Herman Second Herd, among others. He was a member of Dizzy Gillespie's sextet (1950-52) and formed a quartet with John Lewis, Percy Heath, and Kenny

Clarke that soon became a co-op called the Modern Jazz Quartet.

Milt Jackson's main musical activity for the next 22 years (1952–74) would be as the lead voice in the MJQ, although John Lewis was the group's musical director. Jackson would over time become frustrated by Lewis's tightly arranged and classical-oriented arrangements, but he was always well featured and had opportunities to play blues (including his own "Bags Groove") and jazz standards. In addition, Jackson did have many chances through the years to record as a leader with more freewheeling groups, as a leader, sideman, and co-leader, including with Miles Davis, Thelonious Monk, Coleman Hawkins, John Coltrane, Ray Charles, Wes Montgomery, Jimmy Heath, Cannonball Adderley, Oscar Peterson, Ray Brown, and the Count Basie Orchestra, among others. In 1974 Jackson quit the MJQ, partly because he was disappointed that the band was not making more money. During the next seven years, Jackson was featured on many all-star jam session recordings on the Pablo label. In 1981 he relented, and the MJQ came back together on a part-time basis until its permanent breakup in 1995. Milt Jackson was at his prime throughout his career, which ended with a recording and some concerts with the Clayton-Hamilton Jazz Orchestra during 1998–99.

7 *In the Beginning / Apr. 1948 / Original Jazz Classics 1771*

9 *Early Modern / Jan. 25, 1949–Nov. 1, 1954 / Savoy 92862*

8 *Milt Jackson with Thelonious Monk / July 2, 1948 + Apr. 7, 1952 / Blue Note 81509*

6 *Milt Jackson Quartet / May 30, 1955 / Original Jazz Classics 001*

8 *Opus de Jazz / Oct. 28, 1955 / Savoy 0109*

9 *Bags's Opus / Dec. 28–29, 1958 / Blue Note 84458*

9 *Bean Bags / Sept. 12, 1958 / Koch 8530*

9 *Bags and Trane / Jan. 15, 1959 / Atlantic 1368*

In the Beginning, although not Milt Jackson's first recordings, has some fascinating early performances. Bags was temporarily back in Detroit, cutting sessions for the soon-defunct Galaxy label. He is heard on eight numbers in a sextet including Sonny Stitt, trumpeter Russell Jacquet, and pianist Lucky Thompson. There are also four tunes (four years before the Modern Jazz Quartet was formed) in a quintet with John Lewis, Kenny Clarke, bassist Al Jackson, and Chano Pozo on conga plus a septet session without Jackson that features Stitt, Jacquet, and J. J. Johnson. The recording

quality is just OK, but the rather rare music (mostly basic originals) is quite Boppish. *Early Modern* is particularly intriguing for the three four-song sessions from 1951–52 that led to the formation of the Modern Jazz Quartet. Starting with Jackson, John Lewis, Ray Brown, and Kenny Clarke on the earliest date, Brown and Clarke are replaced by Percy Heath and drummer Al Jones on the second session, and Clarke takes over for Jones on the final date. The music is looser than the classic group would soon be, but this version of "Softly as in a Morning Sunrise" definitely sounds like the MJQ. Also on this CD is Jackson's feature with a Kenny Clarke–led group in 1949 ("You Go to My Head"), all but one selection from a Bags date from the same year (most notable for the playing of Julius Watkins and the debut of Jackson's "Bluesology"), and four numbers by the 1954 Kenny Clarke All Stars with Jackson, Frank Morgan, and tenor saxophonist Walter Benton.

Milt Jackson with Thelonious Monk combines the vibraphonist's 1948 session with Monk (which resulted in the original versions of "Evidence" and "Misterioso") and a 1952 date in which altoist Lou Donaldson makes the early MJQ into a quintet. The latter set is particularly enjoyable, while the historic Monk date is also available under Thelonious's name elsewhere. The six selections on *Milt Jackson Quartet* team Bags, Percy Heath, and drummer Connie Kay with pianist Horace Silver, whose funky solos sound different than John Lewis's would in the same setting. Together they perform five standards and Jackson's "Stonewall," solid early Hard Bop music, but rather brief, with a total of under 31 minutes of playing time. The time on *Opus de Jazz* is also brief (under 34 minutes), but the music is memorable. Jackson, Frank Wess (on flute and tenor), Hank Jones, bassist Eddie Jones, and Kenny Clarke in 1955 perform two originals, "You Leave Me Breathless," and a definitive (and over-13-minute) version of Horace Silver's "Opus de Funk." *Bags's Opus* matches Jackson with the future co-leaders of the Jazztet (trumpeter Art Farmer and tenor saxophonist Benny Golson) plus Tommy Flanagan, bassist Paul Chambers, and Connie Kay. Highlights include early versions of Golson's "I Remember Clifford" and "Whisper Not."

The next two CDs are unique collaborations. *Bean Bags* has Jackson co-leading the date with the masterful veteran tenor Coleman Hawkins; "Stuffy" and "Get Happy" are joyous romps, while "Don't Take Your Love from Me" is quite lyrical; Flanagan, guitarist Kenny Burrell, Eddie Jones, and Connie Kay offer tasteful support. *Bags and Trane* is the one meeting on records by Milt Jackson and tenor saxophonist John Coltrane. They jam on the title cut (an original), Bags' "The Late Late Blues," and three standards (including "Three Little Words" and "Bebop") with the assistance of Hank Jones, Paul Chambers, and Connie Kay.

7	*Statements / Dec. 14, 1961 + Aug. 6, 1964 / GRP/ Impulse 130*	
8	*Bags Meets Wes! / Dec. 18–19, 1961 / Original Jazz Classics 234*	
7	*Big Bags / June 19, 1962–July 5, 1962 / Original Jazz Classics 366*	
8	*For Someone I Love / Mar. 18, 1963–Aug. 5, 1963 / Original Jazz Classics 404*	
7	*Invitation / Aug. 30, 1962–Nov. 7, 1962 / Original Jazz Classics 260*	
7	*Live at the Village Gate / Dec. 9, 1963 / Original Jazz Classics 309*	

Statements has the original eight selections from the LP of the same name (a quartet with Hank Jones, Paul Chambers, and Connie Kay from 1961) augmented by five songs from 1964 with Jimmy Heath, Flanagan, bassist Richard Davis, and Kay; the latter set formed half of the album *Jazz 'n Samba*. The music is a mixture of standards (including "Paris Blues," "The Bad and the Beautiful," and "I Got It Bad") plus blues and basic originals, typically well played. *Bags Meets Wes!* has Jackson sharing the spotlight with the brilliant guitarist Wes Montgomery (plus pianist Wynton Kelly, Sam Jones, and Philly Joe Jones); the vibes-guitar combination works very well.

Big Bags showcases Jackson as the lead voice with a big band arranged by either Tadd Dameron or Ernie Wilkins, with two alternate takes added to the original program. Cornetist Nat Adderley, Jimmy Cleveland, and both tenors (James Moody and Jimmy Heath) have solos, but this is mostly a showcase for Jackson on tunes such as "Old Devil Moon," "Star Eyes," and " 'Round Midnight." *For Someone I Love* also puts the spotlight on the vibraphonist to a big band format, this time playing inventive arrangements by Melba Liston for 11–13 brass plus a rhythm section. Jackson is the main soloist throughout on such songs as "Days of Wine and Roses," "Save Your Love for Me," and "Chelsea Bridge," with short spots for Clark Terry, trombonist Quentin Jackson, and Julius Watkins on French horn. Tasteful and melodic music full of subtle surprises.

Invitation has Jackson mostly playing with Kenny Dorham, Jimmy Heath, Flanagan, bassist Ron Carter, and Kay

in a sextet, with "Ruby, My Dear" and "Invitation" being among the better selections. The remaining two numbers feature two trumpets (Virgil Jones takes Heath's place) and gives the hard Bop-oriented date some added variety. *Live at the Village Gate* is by a quintet with Jimmy Heath, Hank Jones, bassist Bob Cranshaw, and drummer Al "Tootie" Heath. The music is predictably excellent, particularly the group's versions of "Bags of Blue," Heath's "Gemini," and "Gerri's Blues."

9	*At the Montreux Jazz Festival 1975 / July 17, 1975 / Original Jazz Classics 884*	
8	*The Big 3 / Aug. 25, 1975 / Original Jazz Classics 805*	
8	*At the Kosei Nenkin / Mar. 22–23, 1976 / Pablo 2620–103*	
7	*Soul Fusion / June 1–2, 1977 / Original Jazz Classics 731*	
7	*Montreux '77 / July 13, 1977 / Original Jazz Classics 375*	
6	*Soul Believer / Jan. 20, 1978–Sept. 19, 1978 / Original Jazz Classics 686*	
7	*Bags' Bag / 1979 / Original Jazz Classics 935*	

During 1975–85, Milt Jackson led an extensive series of mostly jam session-oriented sessions for Norman Granz's Pablo label in addition to appearing on quite a few dates as a sideman. The MJQ was "on vacation" during 1975–81, and the vibraphonist was delighted to be free to jam with his fellow greats on a regular basis.

The Montreux Jazz Festival CD, from 1975, teams Jackson with Oscar Peterson, Niels Pedersen, and drummer Mickey Roker for a particularly stimulating date that is highlighted by "Funji Mama," "Speed Ball," and "Mack the Knife"; in reality, all eight selections (which include a few ballads) are notable. *The Big 3,* featuring a pianoless vibes-guitar-bass trio with Bags, Joe Pass, and Ray Brown, includes such numbers as "The Pink Panther," "Blue Bossa," "Nuages," and "Wave," plenty of variety that inspires the virtuosi to play at their best. Originally an 11-song two-LP set, *At the Kosei Nenkin* drops two of the numbers so as to fit all the music on a single CD, but the quintet outing with Teddy Edwards, Cedar Walton, Ray Brown, and Billy Higgins still has plenty of meat left, including fine versions of "Killer Joe," "St. Thomas," "Bolivia," and "Bye Bye Blackbird."

Soul Fusion finds Jackson happily interacting with the Monty Alexander Trio (with bassist John Clayton and drummer Jeff Hamilton) on some obscure tunes plus Stevie

Wonder's "Isn't She Lovely" and Jobim's "Once I Loved." *Montreux '77* is a spontaneous outing in which a quintet co-led by Jackson and Ray Brown (including Monty Alexander, drummer Jimmie Smith, and Eddie "Lockjaw" Davis on tenor) were joined at the last minute by Clark Terry. "CMJ" (which has funny vocals by C. T. and Bags) and "Mean to Me" are among the more memorable tracks. *Soul Believer* is one of Milt Jackson's rare vocal albums, and it is superior to his rather weak 1976 Pablo date *Feelings* (Original Jazz Classics 448), although still not too essential. Jackson's vocals are OK, though his versions of "Ain't Misbehavin'," "Roll 'Em Pete," and "I've Got It Bad" would never be considered definitive! Cedar Walton helps lead the backing rhythm section. Milt Jackson closed the 1970s with *Bags' Bag*. The selections team Bags with Walton and Brown. Six of the eight numbers (mostly standards and blues) add Billy Higgins or Frank Severino on drums, with guitarists John Collins and Vaughn Andre appearing on one song apiece; best are "Slow Boat to China" and "The Rev."

9	*Night Mist / Apr. 14, 1980 / Original Jazz Classics 827*
5	*Big Mouth / Apr. 18, 1980–Feb. 27, 1981 / Original Jazz Classics 865*
8	*Ain't but a Few of Us Left / Nov. 30, 1981 / Original Jazz Classics 785*
8	*Mostly Duke / Apr. 23-24, 1982 / Pablo 2310-944*
8	*Memories of Thelonious Sphere Monk / Apr. 28, 1982 / Original Jazz Classics 851*
7	*Jackson, Johnson, Brown & Company / May 25-26, 1983 / Original Jazz Classics 907*
7	*Soul Route / Nov. 30, 1983–Dec. 1, 1983 / Pablo 2310-900*
7	*It Don't Mean a Thing If You Can't Tap Your Foot to It / July 18, 1984 / Original Jazz Classics 601*
7	*Brother Jim / May 17, 1985 / Pablo 2310-916*

Milt Jackson continued recording steadily for Pablo during the first half of the 1980s. His style did not change at all during this period, sticking to Bop standards, blues, and ballads, adding warmth and swing to each session. *Night Mist* is a particularly strong set of blues and near-blues due to the highly individual voices of the three horns: Harry "Sweets" Edison, Eddie "Lockjaw" Davis, and Eddie "Cleanhead" Vinson." *Big Mouth* tried something different, for Jackson is accompanied by electronic rhythm sections and as many as four vocalists, all of which gives a commercial feel to the music, even on such songs as "Bags' Groove," "The Days of Wine and Roses," and "I'm Getting Sentimental Over You." Brazilian guitarist Oscar Castro-Neves helps out on a few tunes, but the results overall are somewhat forgettable. More conventional but much more satisfying is *Ain't but a Few of Us Left*, which features Jackson with Oscar Peterson, Ray Brown, and drummer Grady Tate on such numbers as "Stuffy" "Body and Soul" and "A Time for Love" (taken as a piano-vibes duet).

Mostly Duke and *Memories of Thelonious Sphere Monk* were two of the three albums recorded by Jackson, Alexander, Brown, and Roker during a six-day period in 1982; *A London Bridge* has not yet been reissued on CD. The quality is consistent throughout the three sets, with the only significant difference being the repertoire. *Mostly Duke* has six songs associated with Duke Ellington (including "Main Stem," "Take the 'A' Train" and "Just Squeeze Me") plus a Jackson original and two other standards. *Memories of Thelonious Sphere Monk* was recorded two months after the pianist-composer's death and features four Monk compositions (including "'Round Midnight" and "In Walked Bud") plus three unrelated songs, including a ten-minute version of John Lewis's "Django."

Jackson, Johnson, Brown & Company teams Bags, J. J. Johnson, and Ray Brown with pianist Tom Ranier, guitarist John Collins, and drummer Roy McCurdy. The blend of vibes and trombone works quite well, and the repertoire (mostly standards) includes "Lament," "Our Delight," "Bags' Groove," and Jay McShann's "Jumpin' Blues." *Soul Route* matches Jackson with the Ray Brown Trio of the time (Brown, pianist Gene Harris and Mickey Roker), and the Harris-Jackson combination is a winner on five basic originals and such familiar standards as "In a Mellotone" and "My Romance." Substitute Cedar Walton for Harris and you have the quartet heard on *It Don't Mean a Thing If You Can't Tap Your Foot to It*. They perform four group originals and three vintage standards (including "If I Were a Bell"). Milt Jackson wrapped up his Pablo years with *Brother Jim* by what was called his "Gold Medal Winners," a sextet with Walton, Cranshaw, Roker, and both Jimmy Heath and Harold Vick on soprano and tenor. Several combinations of musicians are used, the two sopranos get to trade off, Joe Pass sits in on "Sudden Death," and Milt Jackson takes "Lullaby of the Leaves" as a rare accompanied vibraphone solo.

| 7 | *Bebop / Mar. 29-30, 1988 / Atlantic 90991* |
| 7 | *The Harem / Dec. 10-11, 1990 / Music Masters 5061* |

8 *Reverence and Compassion / 1993 / Qwest/Reprise 45204*

8 *The Prophet Speaks / 1994 / Qwest/Reprise 45591*

8 *Burnin' in the Woodhouse / 1995 / Qwest/Warner Bros. 45918*

6 *Sa Va Bella (For Lady Legends) / 1997 / Qwest/ Warner Bros. 46607*

9 *Explosive / 1998 / Qwest/Warner Bros. 47286*

Bebop features Bebop veterans Jackson, J.J. Johnson, and Jimmy Heath joined by Jon Faddis, Cedar Walton, John Clayton, and Mickey Roker for a run-through on nine veteran Bop songs. No real surprises occur on such tunes as "Au Privave," "Woody 'n You," and "Ornithology," but everyone plays well, and Faddis pops out some typically effortless high notes. Jackson, Heath (on tenor and soprano), James Moody (sticking to flute), Walton, Cranshaw, and drummer Kenny Washington perform six group originals and three standards (including Dizzy Gillespie's "Olinga") on *The Harem,* a typically swinging date; the soprano-flute blend is particularly appealing.

In 1993, Milt Jackson signed with the Qwest label, and he would record his final dates for Quincy Jones's company. *Reverence and Compassion* has Jackson backed by a six-piece horn section and a large string section, but his playing is unchanged and his rhythm section includes such old friends as Cedar Walton, John Clayton, and Billy Higgins. Jackson, Clayton, and Walton contributed originals, which alternate with such standards as "Young and Foolish," "This Masquerade," and "It Never Entered My Mind." The same basic quartet is on *The Prophet Speaks,* with guest tenor Joshua Redman on six of the 12 numbers and singer Joe Williams popping up on three of those songs (including "You Are So Beautiful" and his own blues "Five O'Clock in the Morning"). There is a definite happiness to this set, which also includes Thelonious Monk's "Off Minor" and "Ah, Sweet Mystery of Life." *Burnin' in the Woodside* continues the momentum as Jackson jams with the Benny Green Trio (pianist Green, bassist Christian McBride, and Kenny Washington), trumpeter Nicholas Payton, altoist Jesse Davis, and Joshua Redman, playing mostly lesser-known pieces and showing that Bags's abilities were undimmed despite the passing of a half-century. Jackson is also fine on *Sa Va Bella,* but the concept behind the project is a little confused. Jackson wanted to pay tribute to some of his favorite women (particularly singers from the past), but the liner notes do not make it clear which singers are being saluted with which song, although sometimes it is obvious. Etta Jones sings on a few tunes

(showing her age) but not the remake of her hit "Don't Go to Strangers," which is taken as an instrumental. There are some good moments (including the little bit of group singing on "A-Tisket, A-Tasket"), and the rhythm section (pianist Mike LaDonne, Bob Cranshaw, and Mickey Roker) is fine, but this CD could have been better.

Milt Jackson's final official recording as a leader, *Explosive,* serves as a brilliant end to his career. Jackson is matched with the Clayton-Hamilton Jazz Orchestra, and John Clayton's arrangements are perfect for the vibraphonist's style while not neglecting the strengths of the big band either. Among the other key soloists are tenor saxophonist Rickey Woodard, trombonist George Bohanon, and trumpeter Oscar Brashear. One of the album's high points is one of three songs that Jackson sits out on, a beautiful version of "Emily" that features Jeff Clayton's alto and John Clayton's bowed bass. But there is also plenty of Bags on this date during such numbers as "Revival Meeting," "The Nearness of You," "Evidence," and of course "Bags' Groove." A brilliant final act for Milt Jackson.

LPS TO SEARCH FOR

The two-LP *Second Nature* (Savoy 2204) has all of the music from two dates that team Jackson in 1956 with the great tenor Lucky Thompson, either Hank Jones or Wade Legge on piano, bassist Wendell Marshall, and Kenny Clarke (after he had left the MJQ). The music is often hard swinging and always high quality.

Many of Jackson's valuable Atlantic dates have not yet been reissued. From 1957, *Plenty Plenty Soul* (Atlantic 8811) has two separate dates that are equally rewarding: a sextet set with Horace Silver and Lucky Thompson, and a nonet that costars altoist Cannonball Adderley. *Soul Brothers* (Atlantic 1279) is an unusual project in that Ray Charles appears as a pianist and (on two fine numbers) an altoist; he does not take any vocals. Even odder is that Milt Jackson (who plays piano in spots) switches to guitar on "Bags' Guitar Blues"! Tenor saxophonist Billy Mitchell, guitarist Skeeter Best, Oscar Pettiford, and Connie Kay are also heard from during this little-known but enjoyable Bop date.

From 1964, *In a New Setting* (Limelight 82006) is most unusual for including pianist McCoy Tyner in Jackson's quintet (with Jimmy Heath, bassist Bob Cranshaw, and Connie Kay) and for the brevity of most of the selections; Jackson had hoped to get airplay for some of these melodic pieces. Fortunately the quality of the music was not impaired! *That's the Way It Is* (Impulse 9189) and *Just the Way*

It Had to Be (Impulse 9230) are a pair of good-humored and good-natured albums, both recorded at Shelly's Manne-Hole during August 1–2, 1969. Jackson and Ray Brown (who were the co-leaders) welcome Teddy Edwards, the young pianist Monty Alexander, and drummer Dick Berk to their swinging date. During 1972–74, Bags recorded three albums for the CTI label. Best is *Sunflower* (CTI 6024), due to the inclusion of the title cut and its composer-trumpeter Freddie Hubbard along with a fine rhythm section, strings, and woodwinds. *Goodbye* (CTI 6038) mostly has Jackson in a quintet with flutist Hubert Laws, Cedar Walton, bassist Ron Carter, and drummer Steve Gadd, playing standards such as "Detour Ahead" and "Old Devil Moon"; "SKJ," a leftover from the *Sunflower* album, adds Hubbard's trumpet. *Olinga* (CTI 6046) is highlighted by the ballad "Lost April" and a few recent songs by Jackson. He is joined by Cedar Walton (unfortunately on electric piano), Jimmy Heath on tenor and soprano, and a string section. Most of Milt Jackson's Pablo recordings have been reissued on CD but not *A London Bridge* (Pablo 2310–932), which finds Bags, Monty Alexander, Ray Brown, and Mickey Roker playing a different repertoire than usual, with four originals plus John Coltrane's "Impressions," "Flamingo," "Close Enough for Love," and just one Bebop standard, "Good Bait."

FILMS

Milt Jackson is featured with Dizzy Gillespie's Orchestra in *Jivin' in Bebop* (1947), a film that is included on the video *Things to Come* (Vintage Jazz Classics 2006).

Clarinetists

The clarinet was a major instrument in jazz for over 40 years, up until the Bebop era. Many New Orleans bands had a frontline of trumpet or cornet, trombone, and clarinet, with the last instrument weaving countermelodies and harmonies around the trumpet's lead. In the 1920s, the clarinet's pacesetters were Sidney Bechet (although he soon switched his main focus to soprano), Johnny Dodds, and Jimmie Noone. Benny Goodman emerged in the late '20s. After working as a studio musician during the first half of the 1930s, he became "the King of Swing," the most famous bandleader during the early part of the swing era.

Artie Shaw was BG's main competitor among clarinetists during the swing years, and Jimmy Dorsey and Woody Herman (both of whom doubled on alto) had important orchestras. Nearly every big band had a significant clarinet soloist (although not Count Basie's), and many of the saxophonists doubled on clarinet in ensembles. But ironically the instrument's great success during the swing era hurt it greatly when Bebop took over. The clarinet by 1945 was thought of as an old-fashioned instrument, one best suited to swing and Dixieland.

It did not help that the clarinet is a more difficult instrument to master than the saxophone and that Charlie Parker never played clarinet. Although Buddy DeFranco was thought of as the Bird of the clarinet, he did not have much of an impact or influence on younger players and was thought of more as an exception than as an important force. Tony Scott offered a cooler alternative (he could be thought of, in some ways, as the Lester Young of the clarinet), Stan Hasselgard had great potential and held his own with Benny Goodman himself, Aaron Sachs was a fine (but greatly underrated) player, and Jimmy Hamilton (whose style was certainly touched by Bop) was happy to spend most of his career with Duke Ellington.

But despite the rise of several important clarinetists in the decades since (most notably Eddie Daniels), the clarinet has not regained its former prominence and is still most closely associated with prebop styles.

BUDDY DeFRANCO

b. Feb. 17, 1923, Camden, NJ

A remarkable clarinetist and the first to adapt the instrument to Bebop, Buddy DeFranco has been a master for over 55 years as of this writing. Despite dominating his instrument for decades, DeFranco has never become even a fraction as famous as Benny Goodman or Artie Shaw, for the clarinet was going out of style just at the time that DeFranco was entering his prime. In fact, DeFranco sometimes found himself in the ironic position of winning jazz polls while struggling for work, and of participating in swing tribute bands while actually being a Bebopper.

Born Boniface Ferdinand Leonardo DeFranco, he began

playing the clarinet when he was nine, winning an amateur swing contest sponsored by Tommy Dorsey in 1937. De-Franco worked with the orchestras of Gene Krupa (1941–43), Charlie Barnet (1943–44), Tommy Dorsey (off and on during 1944–48), and Boyd Raeburn (1946), getting significant solo space with each of these big bands, particularly TD's. As early as 1944, DeFranco showed that he had transferred the innovations of Charlie Parker to the clarinet. After leaving Dorsey, DeFranco was with the Count Basie Septet during part of 1950 but otherwise led his own groups. He had a short-lived big band in 1951, a quartet with pianist Kenny Drew and Art Blakey, and a combo during 1954–55 that included Sonny Clark, bassist Eugene Wright, drummer Bobby White, and sometimes Tal Farlow. DeFranco was a participant on some of Norman Granz's most exciting JATP studio jam sessions in the '50s, recorded with Art Tatum and Lionel Hampton, settled in Los Angeles for a few years, and had a quartet during 1960–63 that costarred Tommy Gumina on accordion. In 1964 he recorded on bass clarinet with Art Blakey's Jazz Messengers.

However, work was scarce for him, so during 1966–74 De-Franco toured the world as leader of the Glenn Miller ghost band, even though he had never been part of Miller's orchestra. Since giving up that job (which after a time became a drudgery), DeFranco has led his own quartets, often teamed up with Terry Gibbs (including an impressive series of recordings), and has kept his position (although challenged by Eddie Daniels) as the number one clarinetist in jazz.

5   *Buddy DeFranco and Oscar Peterson Play George Gershwin / Dec. 6–7, 1954 / Verve 314 557 099*
6   *Free Fall / July 29, 1974 / Candid 71008*
8   *Gone with the Wind / Feb. 16, 1977 / Storyville 8220*
9   *The Buenos Aires Concerts / Nov. 27, 1980 / Hep 2014*

Early Buddy DeFranco records are frustratingly difficult to find. He recorded seven titles for Capitol during 1949, some of which have been reissued on samplers (*A Bird in Igor's Yard* is quite adventurous), and both his big band and his quartet recorded for MGM during 1951–52, but those have not yet been reissued. The same can largely be said for De-Franco's many recordings for the Norgran and Verve labels throughout the 1950s, except for his selections with Sonny Clark (which came out on a limited-edition Mosaic LP box set) and his tribute to George Gershwin. The latter, which has Oscar Peterson as the co-leader, does not live up to its expectations, due to the inclusion of a string orchestra, un-

adventurous arrangements by Russ Garcia, and an emphasis on slower tempos. The results are pleasant but lack the expected competitive fire.

DeFranco's recordings for Dot, Decca, and Mercury (1959–64), many done with Tommy Gumina, also remain out of print. After the long tour as leader of the Glenn Miller ghost band ended, DeFranco returned to jazz full time and by the mid-'70s was working regularly again. *Free Fall* finds him really stretching himself on his challenging originals (including the four-part "Threat of Freedom") along with two standards. DeFranco, keyboardist Victor Feldman, guitarist John Chiodini, bassist Victor Sproles, and drummer Joe Cocuzzo play well, but little all that memorable occurs.

Gone with the Wind finds the clarinetist tackling more conventional material (including "Like Someone in Love," "Billie's Bounce," and an uptempo "Love for Sale") with pianist Willie Pickens, bassist Todd Coolman, and drummer Jerry Coleman. This live date, not released for the first time until 1999, has long solos by DeFranco, with five of the seven selections exceeding ten minutes in length; he never seems to run out of ideas. *The Buenos Aires Concerts,* which combines the music from two former LPs recorded at the same gig, has DeFranco teaming up with a very good Argentinean rhythm section (pianist Jorge Navarro, guitarist Richard Lew, bassist Jorge Lopez-Ruiz, and drummer Osvaldo Lopez). The clarinetist sounds quite relaxed, even on the uptempo versions of "Billie's Bounce" and "Scrapple from the Apple," and very inspired; purchasers should be aware that "Scrapple from the Apple" and "The Song Is You" are in reverse order from how they are listed. A gem.

7   *Mr. Lucky / Jan. 5–6, 1981 / Original Jazz Classics 938*
8   *Nobody Else but Me / Dec. 15, 1981–June 20, 1989 / Hark*
9   *Hark / Apr. 30, 1985 / Original Jazz Classics 867*
9   *Holiday for Swing / Aug. 22–23, 1988 / Contemporary 14047*
8   *Chip off the Old Bop / July 28–29, 1992 / Concord 4527*
8   *Do Nothing Till You Hear from Us! / July 12–15, 1998 / Concord Jazz 4851*

Mr. Lucky, Buddy DeFranco's first of two albums led for Norman Granz's Pablo label, has him stretching out on such numbers as "Bye Bye Blackbird," the title cut, and some obscure but superior songs with guitarist Joe Cohn, pianist Albert Dailey, bassist George Duvivier, and drummer Ronnie Bedford. The privately issued *Nobody Else but Me* finds the clarinetist showcased from three different sessions with the Metropole Orchestra under the direction of either Rogier van Otterloo or Robert Pronk, mostly ripping through such standards as "Just Friends," "Autumn Leaves," and "Lover." The orchestra is supportive, and DeFranco is clearly inspired to have so many fine musicians playing behind him. *Hark* teams the clarinetist with Oscar Peterson, Joe Pass, Niels Pedersen, and drummer Martin Drew on three obscurities, "All Too Soon," "Summer Me, Winter Me," "By Myself," "This Is All I Ask," and a brilliant run-through on Clifford Brown's "Joy Spring."

Holiday for Swing is one of the few Buddy DeFranco-Terry Gibbs collaborations that was issued under the clarinetist's name. With pianist John Campbell, bassist Todd Coolman, and drummer Gerry Gibbs, the co-leaders race through such numbers as "Holiday for Strings," "Seven Come Eleven," "Yardbird Suite," "Parisian Thoroughfare," and Gibbs's "Fickle Fingers" with ease and hyper swing. A very exciting set. *Chip off the Old Block* is a little calmer in spots, but DeFranco still gets heated on much of this quintet outing with pianist Larry Novak, Joe Cohn, bassist Keter Betts, and drummer Jimmy Cobb. Highlights include "Groove Yard," "The Lamp Is Low," "Moon Song," and Flip Phillips's "Hashimoto's Blues." *Do Nothing Till You Hear from Us*, a follow-up to *You Must Believe in Swing* (which was released under the name of pianist Dave McKenna) is a second DeFranco-McKenna meeting, this time with Joe Cohn making the group a trio, except on the final two numbers. Listening to this swinging music, it is impossible to know that Buddy DeFranco (who contributed "Finegan's Walk" and "Skinnin' Rabbits") was 75. He sounds near his peak on such numbers as "You and the Night and the Music," "Speak Low," and "Gone with the Wind."

LPS TO SEARCH FOR

Very difficult to find but well worth the price is *The Complete Verve Recordings of the Buddy DeFranco Quartet/Quintet with Sonny Clark* (Mosaic 5-117), a five-LP set dating from 1954–55 also including bassist Gene Wright, drummer Bobby White, and, on the last third of the deluxe set, Tal Farlow. *Closed Session* (Verve 8382) has DeFranco paying tribute to the songs performed two decades earlier by Benny Goodman and Artie Shaw. The sidemen include Don Fager-

quist or Ray Linn on trumpet, Georgie Auld on tenor, vibraphonist Victor Feldman, and either Carl Perkins, Paul Smith, or Jimmy Rowles on piano; the music is more Boppish than it would have been if BG or Shaw were the clarinetist! *Cross Country Suite* (Dot 9006) has 11 originals and arrangements by Nelson Riddle for an orchestra. DeFranco is mostly in the lead, with assistance from Fagerquist and Herb Geller. DeFranco's musical partnership with accordionist Tommy Gumina was better than expected, as one can hear on *Presenting the Buddy DeFranco-Tommy Gumina Quartet* (Mercury 20685) and *The Girl from Ipanema* (Mercury 60900). *Boronquin* (Sonet 724), from 1975, has the veteran clarinetist utilizing a young group (pianist Ray Santisi, guitarist John Chiodini, bassist Mike Richmond, and drummer Randy Jones) and three of their harmonically advanced originals. However, it is the cooking versions of "The Song Is You" and "But Not for Me" that take honors. *Waterbed* (Choice 1017) is a decent but not essential meeting with accordionist Gordie Fleming in a quartet; the four Rob Adams/Al Baculis originals are advanced but not memorable, making this a lesser effort. *Like Someone in Love* (Progressive 7014), which has DeFranco in a quintet with Tal Farlow and pianist Derek Smith, features the three appealing lead voices on three standards and three originals in 1977.

FILMS

Buddy DeFranco appears with the Count Basie Septet (along with Clark Terry and Wardell Gray) on some Snader Telescriptions in 1950 that were made for television. He also appears in *The Wild Party* (1956).

JIMMY HAMILTON

b. May 25, 1917, Dillon, SC, d. Sept. 20, 1994, St. Croix, Virgin Islands

Of all of Duke Ellington's soloists of the mid-1940s, the one most affected by Bebop (other than Oscar Pettiford) was clarinetist Jimmy Hamilton. When he became Barney Bigard's permanent replacement with Ellington, the choice was controversial, since Hamilton had a much cooler sound and was much more advanced in his choice of notes than the New Orleans clarinetist. If he had instead sought a solo career, Hamilton might have been thought of as a competitor of Buddy DeFranco's, although chances are he would not have worked as often as he did with Ellington!

Hamilton was raised in Philadelphia and played baritone horn, reeds, piano, trumpet, and trombone. He actually played trumpet and trombone professionally with the bands of Frankie Fairfax (1935) and Lonnie Slappy before switching to clarinet and tenor. Hamilton picked up experience working with Lucky Millinder, Jimmy Mundy, Teddy Wilson's orchestra and sextet (1940–42), and Eddie Heywood's sextet. In May 1943 he succeeded Bigard's first replacement (Chauncey Haughton) with Duke Ellington and then spent 25 years with the orchestra. Hamilton was well featured with Duke ("Air Conditioned Jungle" was his most famous showcase), and he added a Bop sensibility to Ellington's music, even though his earlier influence had been Benny Goodman. And once in a while Hamilton had an opportunity to jam on tenor, where his tone was more R&B-oriented.

After leaving Ellington in mid-1968, Jimmy Hamilton moved to the Virgin Islands, playing and teaching locally. He would return to the United States on a few occasions to perform and record with Clarinet Summit (an avant-garde, a cappella clarinet quartet also including John Carter, Alvin Batiste, and David Murray). But other than that, he was content to play just now and then near his home and finally end his many years of endless traveling. As a leader, Jimmy Hamilton headed only a few sessions: four songs for Blue Note (1945), some titles for United (1953), two Urania albums (1954), a set for Everest (1960), two for Swingville (1961), and a final one for Who's Who (1985).

9   *Can't Help Swinging / Mar. 21, 1961–Apr. 4, 1961 / Prestige 24214*

There is not exactly an excess of sessions led by Jimmy Hamilton, so the reissue of his two Swingville dates in 1999 (on a single CD) was a happy occasion. Hamilton splits his time between his rarely heard tenor and his fluent clarinet on a sextet date with Clark Terry, trombonist Britt Woodman, and Tommy Flanagan, and a quartet outing with Flanagan's trio. The music, which includes both standards and Hamilton's originals, is mostly swing but hints at other styles. Hamilton plays so well throughout the two dates that it is surprising to realize that he would have only one other opportunity to lead his own record, and that would be decades later.

LPS TO SEARCH FOR

Rediscovered at the Buccaneer (Who's Who 21029), from 1985, features Hamilton on clarinet and alto (which he had

never played with Ellington) performing five Duke Ellington selections plus five laid-back love songs. A relaxed and well-played set that shows that Hamilton was always in fine form.

FILMS

In addition to his many filmed appearances as part of Duke Ellington's orchestra, Jimmy Hamilton appears with Teddy Wilson in *Boogie Woogie Dream* (1941).

STAN HASSELGARD

b. Oct. 4, 1922, Bollnas, Sweden, d. Nov. 23, 1948, Decatur, IL

Stan Hasselgard, the only clarinetist to play opposite Benny Goodman in a BG-led group, had the potential to be a giant of Bebop. Although he was not quite a virtuoso on Buddy DeFranco's level, his quick mind, strong technique, and creative ideas made him potentially the first major jazz musician to be born in Europe since Django Reinhardt and Stephane Grappelli.

Hasselgard recorded in his native Sweden as early as 1940, and his early influence was Benny Goodman. He played and recorded regularly in Sweden, working with the Royal Swinges, Arthur Osterwall (1944–45), Simon Brehm, and touring American trombonist Tyree Glenn. Hasselgard, whose first influence was Benny Goodman but who was looking with great interest toward Bebop, moved to the United States in 1947 to study art history at Columbia University. He freelanced (playing with Wardell Gray and Dodo Marmarosa) and recorded in December 1947 with a group that included Red Norvo and Barney Kessel. For a few months in 1948 Hasselgard was a member of the Benny Goodman Septet, a Boppish group (other than the leader) that also included Wardell Gray and either Teddy Wilson or Mary Lou Williams on piano. Although the band did not make any commercial records (due to the recording strike), radio broadcasts from their engagement at the Click in Philadelphia have since been released on record. After the band broke up (Goodman lost interest), Stan Hasselgard led a group that included Max Roach, and freelanced. Tragically, he died in a car crash at the age of 26, so we will never know how he would have developed in the 1950s or if he would have realized his great potential.

Four of the members of the historic, if short-lived, 1948 Benny Goodman Septet: guitarist Billy Bauer, tenor saxophonist Wardell Gray, clarinetist Stan Hasselgard, and BG.

8 *The Permanent Hasselgard* / *Oct. 11, 1945–Nov. 18, 1948* / *Phontastic 8802*

9 *At Click 1948* / *May 24, 1948–June 5, 1948* / *Dragon 183*

The Permanent Hasselgard has highlights from the clarinetist's last three years, including numbers in Sweden with the Kjeld Bonfils Orchestra and Trio, the Royal Swingers, Simon Brehms's sextet, Tyree Glenn, and the Bob Laine-Gosta Torner Sextett. In addition, Hasselgard leads a couple of swing-oriented dates in 1947 (one in America, with Louise Tobin taking two vocals), is on "Who Sleeps" with an all-star group that includes Red Norvo, and is featured on four numbers with the Goodman Septet (which are duplicated on the *At Click 1948* CD) and a V-Disc version of "Cottontop" from just five days before Hasselgard's death.

The short-lived (and commercially unrecorded) Benny Goodman Septet is heard on the Dragon CD during a two-week period when they played regularly at Philadelphia's Click. In addition to the two clarinetists, the band includes Wardell Gray, pianist Teddy Wilson, Billy Bauer, bassist Arnold Fishkind, and drummer Mel Zelnick. The music on the Dragon disc is often fascinating, allowing listeners to contrast the sounds and styles of Goodman and Hasselgard. Though BG does give Hasselgard a generous amount of solo space, he also takes a few surprisingly modern solos of his own.

LPS TO SEARCH FOR

Young Clarinet (Dragon 163) features Hasselgard at the beginning of his career, in 1940 (playing "Ain't She Sweet"), and traces his eight years on records, including a lot of rarities from the 1940–44 period. The final two selections (the only ones included that were cut in the United States) have the clarinetist heading a quintet for V-Disc versions of "You Took Advantage of Me" and "Patsy's Idea." *The Jazz Clarinet of Ake "Stan" Hasselgard* (Dragon 25) sticks to the 1945–48 period, when he quickly evolved from a Goodman-influenced swing clarinetist into an original modern voice of his own. Most of the music was previously unreleased, including a V-Disc alternate version of "Patsy's Idea" on which Hasselgard verbally imitates Goodman. *Jammin' at Jubilee* (Dragon 29) is completely from 1948, mostly recorded live, and has Hasselgard playing with the Jackie Mills Quintet (which includes Jimmy Rowles and Barney Kessel), with the International All Stars (featuring Wardell Gray and Dodo Marmarosa), and with a version of pianist Arnold Ross's quartet that on three numbers adds Billy Eckstine on vocals and valve trombone. In addition, there is a repeat of one number with the Benny Goodman Septet ("Mel's Idea") that is on the *At Click 1948* CD along with two slightly later performances with the band when Mary Lou Williams had taken over on piano.

AARON SACHS

b. July 4, 1923, Bronx, NY

A cool-toned clarinetist who was always able to play Bop fluently, Aaron Sachs (who doubled on tenor) had early jobs with Babe Russin (1941), Red Norvo (1941–42), Van Alexander (1942–43), Norvo again (1943–44), and Benny Goodman (1945–46). After showing great promise (which can be heard on four titles with Terry Gibbs that Sachs led in 1946 and were later reissued on an LP by Xanadu), a serious illness knocked Sachs out of action for much of 1948–49. By 1952 he was back to full force again, playing with Earl Hines (1952–53), Tito Rodriguez, and Louie Bellson's Big Band (1959). Aaron Sachs, who was married for a time to Helen Merrill, led albums for Bethlehem (1954), Dawn (1956), and Rama (1957), and recorded with Eddie Heywood, Sarah Vaughan (her December 31, 1944, session), and Shelly Manne. Since the early 1960s, Aaron Sachs has worked mostly as a teacher and freelancer, but he recorded with Tom Talbert's orchestra in the late 1990s.

8 *Clarinet and Co. / Feb. 18, 1957–Mar. 4, 1957 / Fresh Sound 113*

This Fresh Sound CD reissues Aaron Sachs's last recording as a leader (the Rama date). Sachs, heard on both clarinet and tenor, plays four numbers with a quintet that includes pianist Hall Overton and guitarist Jimmy Raney, and seven cuts with an octet that also includes four horns. With the exception of "Nancy with the Laughing Face" and Benny Golson's "Blue Sophisticate," all of the selections were composed by Sachs, trumpeter Phil Sunkel, Nat Pierce, or arranger Billy Ver Planck. The music is essentially 1950s Cool Jazz, with a strong look back at Bebop and swing; Sachs plays quite well throughout.

TONY SCOTT

b. June 17, 1921, Morristown, NJ

Tony Scott, the main alternative among Bebop-based clarinetists to Buddy DeFranco in the 1950s, had a very cool tone and a floating style (along with a command of the Bebop vocabulary) that should have made him a major name. However, the clarinet was out of style, and his decision to leave the United States after 1959 doomed him to obscurity.

Born Anthony Sciacca, Scott studied at Juilliard (1940–42), jammed at Minton's Playhouse, and then spent three years in the military. During the Bebop era he primarily freelanced, including playing with Buddy Rich, Ben Webster, Trummy Young, Charlie Ventura, Big Sid Catlett, and the Claude Thornhill Orchestra (1949). Scott led a 1946 record date that included Sarah Vaughan and Dizzy Gillespie (Dizzy under the pseudonym of "B. Bopstein"!). On a 1950 session led by Vaughan, Scott's tone was at its coolest, fitting in very well with Miles Davis in the backup group.

Scott mostly led his own groups in the 1950s, recording for Brunswick (1953), Victor (1954–57), Perfect, Seeco, Carlton, ABC-Paramount, Dot, Coral, and Signature, among other labels. In 1959, pianist Bill Evans was in his regular quartet. However, after the deaths of Billie Holiday (a close friend) and Lester Young, and due to his general frustration with the American jazz scene, Scott left the United States in 1960 and spent many years overseas in Europe and Asia, often playing ethnic music. His 1964 recording, *Music for Zen Meditation* (which teamed him in a trio with koto and shakuhachi), preceded the rise of both world music and New Age. In more recent times, Tony Scott (who lives mostly in Italy) has occasionally played Bebop, but by the 1990s he was clearly past his playing prime. His most significant years were prior to 1960.

Tony Scott's recordings from his prime are almost all currently out of print, a major omission. His three CDs for Philology were recorded when he was 71–74, and he does show his age. Scott's tone is still recognizable (although a little heavier than earlier), but his intonation is erratic and the Italian rhythm sections are fairly faceless. *The Clarinet Album* has Scott accompanied by pianist Massimo Farao, bassist Aldo Zunino, and drummer Giulio Capiozzo. The seven selections are all ballads, and, although there are some good moments, a 15 ½-minute version of "Speak Low" was a definite mistake! *Poets of Jazz* is a set of duets with pianist Renato Sellani (including such vintage tunes as "Stardust," "All of Me," and "Gone with the Wind" but surprisingly no Bebop standards), while *Homage to Lady Day* (with pianist Franco D'Andrea, bassist Attilio Zanchi, and drummer Gianni Cazzola) has eight songs that Billie Holiday recorded at one time or another. The latter date is a bit unusual in that Scott (for unknown reasons) chose to overdub his clarinet solos on all but one number (which meant that the rhythm section could not interact with him), yet that is never obvious. He plays as best he can (and this is the most rewarding of the trio of Philology discs), but this album should have been recorded in 1959!

LPS TO SEARCH FOR

Tony Scott recorded quite frequently during the second half of the 1950s. *The Touch of Tony Scott* (RCA 1353) has the clarinetist in 1956 with a big band, a tentette, and a quartet that includes Bill Evans. In addition to some standards, there are such numbers as "Rock Me but Don't Roll Me," "Aeolian Drinking Song," and "Vanilla Frosting on a Beef Pie"! *The Modern Art of Jazz* (Seeco 425) and *Free Blown Jazz* (Carlton 113) have the same personnel (Clark Terry, baritonist Sahib Shihab, trombonist Jimmy Knepper, Evans, Milt Hinton, or Henry Grimes on bass, and drummer Paul Motian, with Scott doubling on baritone) mixing standards with a few originals and swinging in a cool and fairly free fashion. *Tony Scott Plays Gypsy* (Signature 6001) is a little-known but high-quality quartet outing with guitarist Mundell Lowe, bassist Jimmy Garrison, and drummer Pete La Roca of music from the hit play *Gypsy*.

Shortly before he left the United States, Scott recorded several albums with trios that included Bill Evans and drummer Pete La Roca. Best is *Golden Moments* (Muse 5230), which (with Jimmy Garrison) has the quartet stretching out on four standards plus the "Free and Easy Blues." It hints strongly at the adventurous music that Scott might have played in the 1960s had he stayed in the United States. *I'll Remember* (Muse 5266) has the same quartet playing three standards and the blues "Garrison's Raiders." *Sung Heroes* (Sunnyside 1015) is, in contrast, a bit of a downer. With Scott LaFaro in Garrison's place, Scott (on clarinet, piano, guitar, and baritone) pays tribute to some of the people who had recently died (including Billie Holiday, Art Tatum, and Hot Lips Page), with much of the music being somber and taken at slower tempos, serving as an unintentional requiem for the classic clarinet style of Tony Scott.

Miscellaneous

JAZZ AT THE PHILHARMONIC

Jazz at the Philharmonic, which was run quite efficiently by producer Norman Granz, was essentially a traveling jam session. Because Granz was always more interested in individual jazz musicians who could swing than musicians who could fit only into a certain style, he freely mixed swing and Bebop All-Stars in his shows, allowing listeners an opportunity to hear Dizzy Gillespie and Roy Eldridge trading off, and Charlie Parker interacting with Lester Young or Coleman Hawkins. Critics often hated the performances (annoyed by the rambunctious audiences), but a great deal of rewarding music resulted, musicians were well paid (and largely protected from racism), and the public had an opportunity to see many jazz immortals playing together.

The first JATP concert was in 1944 at Philharmonic Auditorium and featured pianist Nat Cole, guitarist Les Paul, Illinois Jacquet, trumpeter Shorty Sherock, and the young J.J. Johnson inspiring each other on fairly basic material. Although future concerts were staged at other venues, Granz adopted the "Philharmonic" name to show that his music was full of class and prestige. JATP was at its prime during 1945–56, featuring an all-star jam on blues and standards (along with a ballad medley), and showcases for some of Granz's favorite combos and singers. Among the Bebop stars who had opportunities to play before the spirited audiences were Charlie Parker (whose spontaneous "Lady Be Good" solo was a classic), Dizzy Gillespie, Howard McGhee, J. J. Johnson, Bill Harris, trombonist Tommy Turk, Illinois Jacquet, Flip Phillips, Stan Getz, Hank Jones, Oscar Peterson (who was "discovered" by Granz), Barney Kessel, Herb Ellis, and Ray Brown, among many others. Swing was not neglected either, with strong participation by trumpeters Charlie Shavers, Roy Eldridge, Buck Clayton, and Harry "Sweets" Edison, the tenors of Coleman Hawkins, Lester Young, and Ben Webster, altoists Willie Smith and Benny Carter, guitarist Irving Ashby, and drummers Buddy Rich, Gene Krupa, Jo Jones, and Louie Bellson, among many others. Not to be left out was Ella Fitzgerald, who had her own separate sets during most of the 1950s shows. Norman Granz recorded many of the concerts and he also featured the all-stars in various combinations for studio recordings.

By 1956, the other parts of the show, particularly when Ella Fitzgerald was showcased, were getting more attention than the jam sessions, and attendance was declining. JATP toured Europe but not the U.S. during 1957–58 and then it ended. Norman Granz made future attempts to revive the format in 1967 and a few times in the 1970s, but the magic was gone. Instead he concentrated on managing Ella, booking concerts by regular bands, and running the Pablo label in the 1970s and '80s.

* **The Complete Jazz at the Philharmonic on Verve 1944–1949 / July 2, 1944–Mar. 1952 / Verve 314 523 893 2 JK101–05**
8 **The First Concert / July 2, 1944 / Verve 314 521 646**
6 **Frankfurt, 1952 / Nov. 20, 1952 / Pablo 5305**
7 **Hartford, 1953 / May 1953 / Pablo 2308–240**
8 **Live at the Nichigeki Theatre 1953 / Pablo 2620–104**
8 **Stockholm '55, the Exciting Battle / Pablo 2310–713**
9 **London, 1969 / Pablo 2620–119**
7 **Return to Happiness, Tokyo 1983 / Pablo 2620–117**

The Verve "Complete" box is a perfectly done ten-CD set that has every Jazz at the Philharmonic recording of the 1940s. If only the people at Polygram could be persuaded to do the same for the many JATP concerts of the 1950s! The 1940s set includes many previously unreleased numbers and quite a few classic performances. Some of the highlights are the humorous Nat Cole-Les Paul tradeoff on "Blues," Billie Holiday sounding near her peak in 1946, some craziness from Slim Gaillard, Charlie Parker's remarkable solo on "Lady Be Good" (which Eddie Jefferson years later would turn into vocalese), Flip Phillips and Illinois Jacquet taking solos on "Perdido," and Ella Fitzgerald's scatting. JATP really reached great heights during a 1949 concert that featured Charlie Parker, Lester Young, Flip Phillips, Roy Eldridge, Tommy Turk, and Buddy Rich. Obviously, get this priceless box while you can!

The very first JATP performance was highlighted by the Cole-Paul tradeoff and some screaming Illinois Jacquet tenor; the single-CD *The First Concert* has all of the music. *Frankfurt, 1952* is just ok, with some worthwhile solos by Roy Eldridge, Lester Young, and Flip Phillips on a blues, two standards, and a three-song ballad medley but with less fireworks than expected. *Hartford, 1953* has three features for Lester Young and performances by Oscar Peterson's quartet along with a 15-minute version of "Cotton Tail" with Eldridge, Charlie Shavers, Bill Harris, Ben Webster, Flip Phillips, Benny Carter, and Willie Smith. The two-CD *Live at the Nichigeki Theatre* is most notable for an exciting trumpet battle by Charlie Shavers and Roy Eldridge on "Cottontail" that Shavers wins. Also included are sets by Ella Fitzgerald, the Oscar Peterson Trio, and the Gene Krupa Trio (with Benny Carter). In contrast, Eldridge steals the show on *Stockholm '55* with a closing solo on the medium-slow blues "Little David" that is quite spectacular, even dwarfing the playing of Dizzy Gillespie, Flip Phillips, Bill Harris, and Oscar Peterson.

The two-CD *London, 1969* has highlights from an attempt to revive Jazz at the Philharmonic. The cast of characters is quite impressive and mostly plays up to their potential: trumpeters Dizzy Gillespie and Clark Terry, Zoot Sims and James Moody on tenors, Teddy Wilson, Louie Bellson, blues singer/guitarist T-Bone Walker (heard on three songs), Benny Carter, and Coleman Hawkins (who sounds much better at this late point in his life than expected). *Return to Happiness,* from 1983, celebrated the 30th anniversary of JATP's first visit to Japan. It was a final try at Jazz at the Philharmonic, featuring Granz's favorite survivors, some of whom had never played with JATP before but fit right in. Clark Terry, Harry "Sweets" Edison, J. J. Johnson, Zoot Sims, Eddie "Lockjaw" Davis, Al Grey, Oscar Peterson, Joe Pass, and Louie Bellson are among the solo stars, and there are also short sets by Peterson and Ella Fitzgerald plus a closing "Flying Home" that pays tribute to the spirit of JATP one last time.

LPS TO SEARCH FOR

Although Verve released quite a few JATP LPs in the early 1980s, most of the music from the 1950s is now out of print.

Well worth looking for are *Norgran Blues 1950* (Verve 815151), *The Trumpet Battle 1952* (Verve 815152), *Gene Krupa & Buddy Rich—The Drum Battle* (Verve 815146), *One O'Clock Jump 1953* (Verve 815153), *The Challenges* (Verve 815154), which has a very exciting Dizzy Gillespie-Roy Eldridge trumpet battle, and *Blues in Chicago 1955* (Verve 815155).

The Bebop-Era Big Bands

In 1946 the big band era officially ended. Many factors (including a ruinous entertainment tax, the rise of pop vocalists, competition from such styles as Dixieland, rhythm and blues, and the new Bebop music, and a certain predictability that had crept into swing) resulted in the breakup of a large number of jazz orchestras during 1945–46. The decline of swing-oriented big bands climaxed with the dissolution of eight orchestras (those of Tommy Dorsey, Les Brown, Harry James, Woody Herman, Jack Teagarden, Benny Goodman, Benny Carter, and Ina Ray Hutton) in December 1946. Although Dorsey, Brown, James, and Herman would soon have new orchestras, big bands were much scarcer in 1948 than they had been only two years before (both Glenn Miller and Jimmy Lunceford had passed away by then), and the trend would continue.

Most musicians of the classic Bebop era picked up important early training as members of big bands (including Charlie Parker with Jay McShann and Dizzy Gillespie with Cab Calloway), and some continued to play with jazz orchestras on an occasional basis on and off throughout the late 1940s. The surviving swing bands during 1945–49 often used some advanced arrangements and had a few soloists who were open to the influence of Bop. Even when the bandleader himself did not care much for the new music, it was difficult to keep the modern influence completely out of the music without stifling all creativity. And during 1948–49, when the major record labels suddenly discovered Bebop and hoped to make a killing from it, many unlikely swing bands (including those of Benny Goodman, Charlie Barnet, and Artie Shaw) gave Bop a chance, if briefly.

Bebop big bands (as opposed to those simply giving it a whirl) were not too common, since the music never caught on as popular music, and large ensembles became increasingly difficult to afford as the 1940s progressed. The most significant Bebop orchestras were those led by Billy Eckstine (1944–47) and Dizzy Gillespie (1945 and 1946–50), both of which are covered in different sections in this book (under the leader's name). Of the surviving swing bands that emphasized modern music, those led by Woody Herman (his first two Herds), Stan Kenton, Duke Ellington, and Count Basie were among the most important. But by 1950, many of the surviving big bands had either broken up altogether (including Woody Herman's Second Herd and the orchestras of Dizzy Gillespie, Benny Goodman, Charlie Barnet, Artie Shaw, and even Count Basie) or reverted to nostalgia swing.

This section deals not only with the big bands, such as Boyd Raeburn's, that emphasized Bebop, but also with the activities of the major swing orchestras during the classic Bebop era and the ways that many of the swing-era celebrities reacted to the new music.

LOUIS ARMSTRONG

b. Aug. 4, 1901, New Orleans, LA, d. July 6, 1971, New York, NY

Louis Armstrong was quoted in the March 1948 issue of *Metronome* as follows: "I'll never play this Bebop because I don't like it. Don't get me wrong; I think some of them cats who play it play real good, like Dizzy, especially. But bebop is the easy way out. Instead of holding notes the way they should be held, they just play a lot of little notes. They sorta fake out of it. You won't find many of them cats who can blow a straight lead . . . It doesn't come from the heart the way real music should."

The accomplishments of Louis Armstrong, the most important jazz soloist in history, are so vast as to be almost impossible to comprehend. His trumpet playing (cornet before 1927), though born in the New Orleans jazz tradition of ensemble playing, was so powerful that he became a primary factor in the emergence of jazz as a vehicle for virtuoso improvisers. Armstrong's relaxed phrasing was a major revelation (as opposed to the phrasing of the early players, who "got hot" by simply playing loud staccato runs), his ability to infuse the blues into the most sophisticated music turned many heads, and his genius at "telling a story" during his solos made his improvisations both accessible and logical. As a vocalist, Satch popularized scat singing and phrased like a horn (improving melodies with subtle creativity), and his gravelly voice became one of the most imitated in the world. And, due to his sunny personality, inventive wit, and comedic abilities, Louis Armstrong became the most beloved and famous jazz musician in the world; he still is!

Louis Armstrong first became a sensation in the 1920s. He practically outshone his idol, cornetist Joe "King" Oliver, in the 1923 Creole Jazz Band and spent a year amazing New York musicians while with Fletcher Henderson's orchestra (1924–25). His series of Hot Five and Hot Seven recordings (1925–28) found him taking one innovative solo after another on such numbers as "Cornet Chop Suey," "Potato Head Blues," "Wild Man Blues," "Struttin' with Some Barbeque," and in 1928 (with Earl Hines) "West End Blues" and "Weather Bird." Starting in 1929, Armstrong began leading a series of big bands, and he shifted his repertoire much more toward popular songs (rather than New Orleans jazz standards) while still remaining the leading jazz trumpeter and singer. Throughout the Swing era, Armstrong led a big band (the former Luis Russell Orchestra) that served mostly as a backdrop for his solos and singing without really developing much of a personality of its own. By 1942 both his band's repertoire and his own playing were thought of as passé, and he was overshadowed by the orchestras of Duke Ellington, Benny Goodman, and Glenn Miller and younger swing trumpeters (such as Harry James, Roy Eldridge, and Henry "Red" Allen) who were originally inspired by him. Although many fans and some friends advised him to get rid of his big band and cut back to a small group, Satch hated the idea of letting his sidemen go, and he kept the orchestra together into 1947 while occasionally having special appearances with combos. However, when he finally broke up the big band and formed the Louis Armstrong All-Stars

(initially with trombonist Jack Teagarden and clarinetist Barney Bigard as his key sidemen), Satch had the perfect vehicle for his talents, a freewheeling sextet that he used as his regular band to worldwide acclaim for the last 24 years of his life.

Bop musicians generally admired Armstrong's trumpet playing (Dizzy Gillespie, Miles Davis, and Howard McGhee always praised him), but they disliked his clowning on stage and felt that he did not treat his music with enough dignity. Armstrong, who always enjoyed putting on an entertaining show, in turn disliked the Boppers' de-emphasis on pretty melodies and the way they often ignored their audiences. He also felt hurt being criticized by the musicians whom he had indirectly influenced, and he was probably worried that he was no longer the pacesetting trumpeter. During 1947–48 Armstrong was engaged in an occasional war of words with some of the younger musicians. However, the great success of his All-Stars allowed him to largely ignore modern jazz after the classic Bebop era ended, and he became good friends with Dizzy Gillespie (they were neighbors). To the end of his life Louis Armstrong continued on his own magical musical path, no longer concerned about being the most "modern" player.

8 *From the Big Band to the All Stars (1946–1956) / Dec. 8, 1932–Aug. 1, 1956 / RCA 66605*

This two-CD set, which has the alternate take of Louis Armstrong's 1932 recording of "Hobo, You Can't Ride This Train" plus two orchestra numbers from 1956, sticks otherwise to the 1946–47 period. The program (which has been reissued several times in different ways) starts off with a pair of very interesting performances with the Esquire All-Americans, teaming Armstrong with advanced swing players on "Long Long Journey" and on "Snafu." The latter finds Satch taking one of his very few solos that actually hints at Bebop. The twofer also has the last dozen recordings by the Louis Armstrong Orchestra; Lucky Thompson is in the ensembles but has no solo space, similar to the role of Dexter Gordon in Armstrong's 1943 band. In addition, Armstrong is heard on three Dixieland numbers with Kid Ory and on a few sessions that led to the formation of his All-Stars. The highlights include "Jack-Armstrong Blues" (arguably Satch's finest recorded solo of the 1940s), "Rockin' Chair," "A Song Was Born," and "Please Stop Playing Those Blues" with Jack Teagarden often as the co-star.

GEORGIE AULD

b. May 19, 1919, Toronto, Canada, d. Jan. 8, 1990, Palm Springs, CA

Georgie Auld was nothing if not adaptable. Auld, who moved to the United States in the late 1920s with his family, started out as an altoist but switched to tenor after he first heard Coleman Hawkins. He was well featured with Bunny Berigan's orchestra during 1937–38, where he sounded almost identical to Charlie Barnet. Auld was a top soloist with Artie Shaw during 1938–39 (briefly leading the orchestra after Shaw fled to Mexico) and was an important soloist with Benny Goodman's orchestra and particularly his sextet during 1940–41, playing alongside Charlie Christian and Cootie Williams. By then, Auld's tone had been influenced by both Ben Webster and Lester Young. After a second stint with Artie Shaw in 1942, Auld put together his own orchestra.

Georgie Auld led three different big bands during 1942–46. In 1942 he had a swing orchestra for half a year before he was drafted; no recordings were made. From September 1943 to the end of 1944, McGhee led a very interesting transitional orchestra that was swing-based but looked toward Bebop. His sidemen included trumpeters Sonny Berman and Howard McGhee along with Al Cohn on tenor. After that orchestra broke up, Auld led a couple of big band sessions for Musicraft in early 1945 that featured such notable all-stars as trumpeters Dizzy Gillespie, Billy Butterfield, Freddie Webster, and Al Killian, trombonist Trummy Young, Al Cohn, Erroll Garner, and Chubby Jackson. Auld's touring big band of 1945–46 also fell between swing and Bop and never achieved much commercial success. The better-known sidemen were Cohn, Serge Chaloff, and highnote trumpeter Al Porcino, with Cohn, Tadd Dameron, and Neal Hefti providing many of the arrangements. However, the postwar period was not the ideal era to form a new big band, and the final Auld Orchestra did not make it to the end of 1946. Although he occasionally recorded with younger musicians in later years (including a 1949 tentet and a 1951 quintet date with trombonist Frank Rosolino, Lou Levy, and Tiny Kahn), most of Georgie Auld's later work found him playing swing.

9 *Jump, Georgie, Jump / Jan. 1940–July 1945 / Hep 27*

This CD has eight of the ten selections recorded by Georgie Auld with the nucleus of the Artie Shaw big band in 1940 after the clarinetist had spontaneously abandoned the swing business. Without Shaw's presence, the orchestra did not stand a chance, although during the few months that the 20-year-old Auld headed the outfit, it continued its high musical standards. Of much more interest from the Bebop standpoint are the other 15 performances. A radio transcription by the Auld Orchestra of 1944 (which otherwise had only one four-song studio date) includes some rare trumpet solos from Sonny Berman along with some strong tenor playing by the leader in a Coleman Hawkins vein. In addition, the CD has five selections from a July 1945 broadcast by the later Auld Orchestra, with fine solos from Porcino and Auld (on tenor, alto, and soprano).

LPS TO SEARCH FOR

During 1945–46, the Georgie Auld big band recorded nine sessions for Musicraft, 34 selections in all. Twenty-six were reissued on *Big Band Jazz, Vol. 1* (Musicraft 501) and *With Sarah Vaughan, Vol. 2* (Musicraft 509). *Big Band Jazz, Vol. 1* has six of the seven numbers from the two all-star big band sessions (with Dizzy Gillespie, Trummy Young, and Erroll Garner) and is highlighted by "Georgie Porgie," "In the Middle," "Co-Pilot," and "Jump, Georgie, Jump." The second album includes two early vocals by Sarah Vaughan and a variety of instrumentals (plus two Auld vocals) from his short-lived working band, an important but now largely-forgotten outfit.

CHARLIE BARNET

b. Oct. 26, 1913, New York, NY, d. Sept. 4, 1991, San Diego, CA

Throughout much of his musical career, Charlie Barnet was able to do pretty much whatever he wanted. His parents were millionaires, and, although they would have preferred him to be a lawyer rather than a musician, they supported him in the 1930s as he struggled to find his sound, both on tenor and with his orchestra. In 1939 the Charlie Barnet Orchestra finally caught on (after several years of struggling) and made Ray Noble's "Cherokee" into a standard five years before Charlie Parker and the Beboppers adopted that song as a test piece for up-and-coming players. Barnet, whose band often emulated Duke Ellington's, played tenor, alto, and occasional soprano, and his orchestra had many instrumental hits during 1939–42. After switching from the Blue-bird label to Decca in 1942, Barnet led one of his strongest bands, one that not only featured trumpeter-vocalist Peanuts Holland and singer Kay Starr (plus guest trumpeter Roy Eldridge on a few sessions), but also Barney Kessel and Dodo Marmarosa. In addition, Howard McGhee and Oscar Pettiford (who, with Chubby Jackson for a period, gave Barnet two bassists) had brief stints with the band. Although few now realize it, Marmarosa can be heard prominently on Barnet's 1944 hit "Skyliner."

Barnet kept his mind open toward more modern jazz, featuring trumpeter Clark Terry in 1947. In 1948 he decided to wholeheartedly embrace Bebop. By 1949 he was using arrangements by Manny Albam, Gil Fuller, and Pete Rugolo among others, had a rhythm section made up of Claude Williamson, Eddie Safranski, and Cliff Leeman or Tiny Kahn on drums and, at one point in time, a trumpet section that included Rolf Ericson, Doc Severinsen, Maynard Ferguson, and Ray Wetzel; the last three were all screamers. Although Barnet's own style was mostly unchanged, he was certainly open to the newer music, as can be heard during Maynard Ferguson's radical playing on "All the Things You Are," and in the singing of guest artists Dave Lambert and Buddy Stewart on "Bebop Spoken Here."

Unfortunately Barnet's Bebop band was a commercial flop despite its tie-in with the Capitol label. At the end of 1949, Charlie Barnet broke up his last significant orchestra, returning to swing, and eventually semi-retiring.

10 *Drop Me Off in Harlem / Apr. 30, 1942–June 16, 1946 / GRP/Decca 612*

9 *The Capitol Big Band Sessions / Aug. 9, 1948–Dec. 4, 1950 / Capitol 21258*

7 *Swell & Super / June 22, 1949–Oct. 1949 / Drive Archive 42446*

Drop Me Off in Harlem has 20 of the 44 selections that the Charlie Barnet Orchestra cut for Decca during the 1942–46 period. The stars include Peanuts Holland, Roy Eldridge, Al Killian (a top high-note trumpeter), Buddy DeFranco, Barney Kessel, Dodo Marmarosa, guest trombonist Lawrence Brown, and vocalists Kay Starr and Francis Wayne. In general, the music is high-quality swing, with only slight hints of Bebop. Barnet's 1946–47 recordings for Apollo and Clef (which followed his Decca period) are long overdue to be reissued. His band, by the time he had signed with Capitol, sounded a decade more advanced than his Decca ensem-ble. All 22 of Barnet's Capitol recordings are on a single CD, and the results are quite modern and often futuristic. "Red-skin Rhumba" (the lone title from 1948) and four dance band numbers from 1950 (after he gave up Bebop) sandwich the 17 songs from 1949. In addition to the mighty trumpet section, Barnet's Bebop Orchestra also featured trombonist Herbie Harper, altoist Vinnie Dean, tenor saxophonist Dick Hafer (whose cooler tone was a contrast from Barnet's), and Claude Williamson. Manny Albam, Gil Fuller, Pete Rugolo, Dave Matthews, Johnny Richards, Tiny Kahn, and Paul Villepigue provided the adventurous arrangements. Highlights include "Cu-Ba," two versions of "Charlie's Other Aunt," Matthews's "Portrait of Edward Kennedy Ellington," "Bebop Spoken Here" (with Dave Lambert and Buddy Stewart), "Claude Reigns" (Claude Williamson's feature), and "Really?" *Swell & Super* adds to this band's discography with music taken from four radio broadcasts (formerly out as an Alamac budget LP), including alternate versions of "Bebop Spoken Here," Maynard Ferguson's feature on "All the Things You Are," and "Portrait of Edward Kennedy Ellington" plus other songs not otherwise recorded by this near-classic, if short-lived, outfit.

CAB CALLOWAY

b. Dec. 25, 1907, Rochester, NY, d. Nov. 18, 1994, Hockessin, DE

Cab Calloway made three main contributions to the Bebop era. His often crazy singing and scat style influenced Leo Watson, Slim Gaillard, Dave Lambert, and Babs Gonzales among other adventurous vocalists. During 1939–41, Calloway's orchestra featured the young trumpeter Dizzy Gillespie. And Calloway called Dizzy's radical solos "Chinese music," a term that stuck!

Cab Calloway became a hit after he took over the Missourians in 1930 and began appearing regularly at the Cotton Club. His recording of "Minnie the Moocher" on March 3, 1931, made him immortal, and he was one of the best-known personalities in show business for the next 20 years. In 1939, when Dizzy Gillespie (then 22) joined Cab, the singer was at the height of his fame, whereas Gillespie was a young unknown still heavily influenced by Roy Eldridge. Although Calloway had doubts about Dizzy's chance-taking solos (which often contained odd notes that did not fit smoothly with the swing-oriented rhythm section), he did feature him on quite a few choruses during his two-year stint with the band. Gillespie's exit from Calloway's orchestra was sudden. Hit by a spitball while in the middle of a performance, Cab blamed Dizzy (who was known as a practical joker); a fight ensued and Gillespie nicked Calloway with a knife. Decades later, it was revealed that Jonah Jones (a favorite of Cab's) was actually the guilty one.

Calloway kept his orchestra together until April 1948, and it remained a swing outfit that largely avoided the influence of Bebop. However, in 1949 (when he was heading a septet called the Cab Jivers), Cab recorded a hilarious version of "I Beeped When I Shoulda Bopped," poking fun both at Bop and his "hi-de-ho" style. This rendition (which is far superior to the more famous version cut earlier by Dizzy Gillespie's orchestra) is available on the two-CD set *Cab Calloway & Co.* (French RCA 66496), which otherwise mostly sticks to Cab's vintage 1932–34 recordings.

9 *1939–1940 / Mar. 28, 1939–Mar. 8, 1940 / Classics 595*

8 *1940 / Mar. 8, 1940–Aug. 28, 1940 / Classics 614*

7 *1940–1941 / Aug. 28, 1940–July 24, 1941 / Classics 629*

7 *1941–1942 / July 24, 1941–July 27, 1942 / Classics 682*

7 *1942–1947 / Feb. 2, 1942–Dec. 11, 1947 / Classics 996*

All of Dizzy Gillespie's recordings with the Cab Calloway Orchestra are on the first four of these Classics CDs, a complete chronological reissue of Calloway's studio sides; there are a dozen CDs in the full Calloway series. Although the rhythm section was about as modern as possible for that time (pianist Bennie Payne, guitarist Danny Barker, bassist Milt Hinton, and drummer Cozy Cole) and the lineup included tenor saxophonist Chu Berry and future Afro-Cuban jazz pioneer Mario Bauza on trumpet, in reality Gillespie had few musical allies in the band as he sought to form his own style. Dizzy did get quite a few solos during his Calloway stint, including "Pickin' the Cabbage," "Pluckin' the Bass," and "A Bee Gezindt" on *1939–1940.* "Bye Bye Blues" has Dizzy's most interesting spot on *1940,* and he also arranged the Cozy Cole feature "Paradiddle." *1940–1941* finds Gillespie at his early best on "Take the 'A' Train." *1941–1942* contains Gillespie's last seven performances with Calloway (although no memorable solos) before his quick departure. By then, Cab's orchestra was often playing swinging arrangements by Buster Harding and Andy Gibson and the

musicianship was quite high; Jonah Jones was Calloway's new trumpet star.

1942–1947 covers a nearly six-year period and consists of the final recordings by the Cab Calloway Orchestra. There are touches of Bop in some of the later charts, but, in general, Calloway was successful in avoiding the influence of the "Chinese music" that his former trumpeter, Dizzy Gillespie, helped found.

BENNY CARTER
b. Aug. 8, 1907, New York, NY

Benny Carter's remarkable career has spanned from the 1920s into the beginning of the 21st century. He ranked with Johnny Hodges as the top altoist of the Swing era, playing in a style that has changed little in the many decades since. Carter has also been a superior swing trumpeter, recorded on clarinet, tenor, and piano and even taken a few vocals (proving on this last that even he is not flawless!). His arranging has been influential, and, as a composer, Carter has written such songs as "When Lights Are Low," "Blues in My Heart," and "Cow Cow Boogie," among many others. His most important early associations were with Charlie Johnson's orchestra (1927), Fletcher Henderson (1928–31), and McKinney's Cotton Pickers (1931–32), heading the last during its declining period.

Carter led several big bands of his own, including one during 1932–34 (before a five-year period spent working steadily in Europe) another during 1938–41, and a third ensemble that he started in 1943. None were commercially successful, but each was quite musical. In 1943, Carter was in Los Angeles working on the score of the film *Stormy Weather.* The West Coast orchestra that he formed at the time was based mostly in L. A. for the next five years. Many top young players passed through his big band, including J. J. Johnson (who had his first recorded solo on "Love for Sale" with Carter in 1943), Freddie Webster, Curly Russell, Max Roach, Idrees Sulieman, Al Grey, Dexter Gordon, Lucky Thompson, and Miles Davis. Davis joined Carter when the altoist was on a crosscountry tour in late 1945, principally to get to Los Angeles to become part of Charlie Parker's quintet. The Benny Carter Orchestra made some studio recordings for Capitol and Deluxe during 1943–46, and several radio broadcasts from the period have been released.

Benny Carter, who was quite aware of Charlie Parker,

never changed his own style (growing within himself rather than making any major alterations), which made sense because he was such a personal player that there was little point of his becoming an imitation Bird. Since breaking up his last big band in 1948, the classic jazzman has remained quite busy and productive as a major swing stylist, arranger, and composer, in the studios and in jazz itself.

- **10** *Further Definitions / Nov. 13, 1961–Mar. 4, 1966 / GRP/Impulse 229*
- **7** *Carter, Gillespie, Inc. / Apr. 27, 1976 / Original Jazz Classics 682*
- **8** *My Man Benny/My Man Phil / Nov. 21–22, 1989 / Music Masters 5036*

Throughout his career, Benny Carter has often played with young modernists while staying true to his own musical vision. The GRP/Impulse CD reissue has all of the music from 1961's *Further Definitions* and 1966's *Additions to Further Definitions*. The former set is a classic that features Carter's arrangements and solos in an octet with fellow altoist Phil Woods and tenors Coleman Hawkins and Charlie Rouse. Their versions of "Honeysuckle Rose," "Crazy Rhythm," "Cotton Tail," and "Doozy" in particular are memorable, and Hawkins is featured on a fresh remake of "Body and Soul." The later date has similar instrumentation but different players, with Carter and Bud Shank on altos and Teddy Edwards plus either Buddy Collette or Bill Perkins on tenors. There are some very good moments on this date too, including "Fantastic, That's You," "If Dreams Come True," and a remake of "Doozy."

Benny Carter and Dizzy Gillespie were old friends by the time they teamed up for a 1976 recording. The playing is worthwhile (particularly on "Broadway" and "A Night in Tunisia") but not that many fireworks result; too much mutual respect and not enough competitiveness! The two-CD set *My Man Benny/My Man Phil* finds Carter (then 82) and Phil Woods (just 58) battling it out in fiery fashion. Carter takes two trumpet solos, brought in six of the ten songs, and sings "My Man Phil." But it is his interplay on alto with Woods that is most memorable, showing that he really is an ageless improviser.

LPS TO SEARCH FOR

The 1943–48 Benny Carter big band is best represented on several LPs. *1944* (Hindsight 218) has the ensemble performing live in Southern California with spots for J. J. John-son and guest clarinetist Barney Bigard, plus three trumpet solos by Carter. *In Hollywood 1944–46* (Jazz Society 502) comprises music from three radio broadcasts. *Jazz off the Air Vol. 3* (Spotlite 147), spanning the entire life of the orchestra (1944–48), has some rare solos from J.J., Miles Davis, and Dexter Gordon. From 1946, Carter primarily leads specially assembled all-star big bands on *The Deluxe Recordings* (Swingtime 1013), mixing together swing veterans and up-and-coming Beboppers plus singer Maxine Sullivan.

JIMMY DORSEY

b. Feb. 29, 1904, Shenandoah, PA, d. June 12, 1957, New York, NY

Like Benny Carter, Jimmy Dorsey had his roots in the 1920s and matured during the Swing era. A brilliant alto saxophonist and clarinetist, Dorsey was a top musician by 1925; he appeared on countless studio dates, recording with the bands of Red Nichols, Jean Goldkette, Frankie Trumbauer, and Paul Whiteman and, starting in 1928, leading occasional recording dates with his younger brother, Tommy Dorsey. After they co-led the Dorsey Brothers Orchestra during 1934–35, the constantly bickering siblings went their separate ways. The Jimmy Dorsey Orchestra worked steadily during the second half of the 1930s but did not really hit the big time until the early 1940s, when the joint vocal records of Helen O'Connell and Bob Eberly gave JD many best-sellers, including "Green Eyes," "Tangerine," "Amapola," and "Brazil." Ironically enough, Dorsey was almost reduced to a cameo player on these recordings, and his alto playing was underrated by many swing fans.

However, Charlie Parker always spoke highly of Dorsey, and Jimmy kept his mind open toward bebop while not strongly affected by it. He used a Gillespie arrangement in 1944 ("Grand Central Getaway"), Serge Chaloff was his baritonist for a period in 1946, and his 1947 rhythm section (guitarist Herb Ellis, pianist Lou Carter, and bassist Johnny Frigo) broke away to become the fine King Cole Trio-inspired group, Soft Winds. In 1949 Maynard Ferguson spent a few months in Dorsey's trumpet section, but no studio recordings resulted (although some radio broadcasts appeared on LPs). Otherwise, Dorsey focused mostly on trying, unsuccessfully, to keep the Swing era alive, and he had fun during 1949–50, occasionally jamming with a Dixieland combo taken out of his big band called "The Original Dorseyland Jazz Band." After he reluctantly broke up his big band in 1953, he spent his final three years co-leading the nostalgic Dorsey Brothers Orchestra with Tommy. It was while watching one of their television shows and laughing at a comedy routine that Charlie Parker died.

LPS TO SEARCH FOR

1942–44 Vol. 2 (Hindsight 153) is primarily World War II swing, but there are V-Disc versions of "Grand Central Getaway" (listed as a Dizzy Gillespie-Jimmy Dorsey composition) and some surprisingly Boppish (if brief) trumpet from Ray Linn on "All the Things You Are." *Diz Does Everything* (Big Band Archives 1216), from 1949, has the Boppish title cut and a few spots for the young Maynard Ferguson but is otherwise a swing set with occasional Dixieland-flavored solos from trumpeter Charlie Teagarden.

TOMMY DORSEY

b. Nov. 19, 1905, Shenandoah, PA, d. Nov. 26, 1956, Greenwich, CT

Tommy Dorsey made no bones about it: he hated Bebop! The "Sentimental Gentleman of Swing" (who could actually be quite profane) was famous for having a very beautiful tone on trombone, which was best displayed on ballads. He often played with his older brother, Jimmy, in the early days, when TD was also an effective trumpeter. After spending much of 1925–33 as a studio musician, he co-led the Dorsey Brothers Orchestra (1934–35) with Jimmy before their many musical arguments (most quite trivial) led TD to form his own big band.

Tommy Dorsey believed in putting on a well-rounded program that included swinging instrumentals, ballad vocals, dance music, and occasional bits of Dixieland. His orchestra became one of the most popular in the world in 1937 (after "Marie" and "Song of India" caught on), and his early 1940s band had not only the leader's trombone, drummer Buddy Rich, and trumpeter Ziggy Elman but also the hip arrangements of Sy Oliver (whom TD had lured away from Jimmy Lunceford) and a full team of vocalists that included Frank Sinatra, Jo Stafford, Connie Haynes, and the Pied Pipers. Buddy DeFranco became Dorsey's clarinet soloist for a time, and a string section added to TD's prestige.

And then it all changed. The strings were gone by 1946, swing was considered old hat, and Dorsey was no longer considered at the cutting edge of pop music. Although he

had trumpeter Charlie Shavers and tenor saxophonist Boomie Richman as major soloists, business was drastically falling off; Dorsey blamed Bebop primarily. He felt that the Beboppers were neglecting dancers with their rapid tempos, lack of hummable melodies, and general disdain for the audience, killing off the dance band business. Dorsey broke up his big band late in 1946 but was soon back on the road again. By sticking exclusively to swing (even if his band included Shavers and Louie Bellson), Dorsey turned his band into a formula—a nostalgia band that received the most applause whenever it recreated his earlier hits. Although only 41 in 1947, Tommy Dorsey would never again lead a creative group. After 1952, he spent the last few years of his life as co-leader of the Dorsey Brothers Orchestra, trying unsuccessfully to make nostalgic swing seem relevant to audiences in the mid-1950s.

6 *The Post War Era / Jan. 31, 1946–June 13, 1950 / Bluebird 66156*

Tommy Dorsey's post-1945 recordings are rarely reissued. Ironically TD is barely on most of the 22 songs included on this CD (other than his feature on "Trombonology"), although there are some good spots for Charlie Shavers and Boomie Richman. The arrangements are mostly by Bill Finegan, with a few charts from Sy Oliver, Tommy Todd, Sid Cooper, and Charlie Shavers. The later recordings (predictable dance music) tend to lack much enthusiasm, and any search for Bebop on these mostly jazz-oriented selections will come up fruitless.

DUKE ELLINGTON

b. Apr. 29, 1899, Washington DC, d. May 24, 1974, New York, NY

Duke Ellington was never really a part of the Bebop era (or even the Swing era), for he was in his own musical world. As a bandleader during 1925–74, a composer of thousands of songs (hundreds of which became standards), an innovative arranger, and a talented pianist, Ellington was at the top of his field by 1927 and never declined. He was also one of the few big bandleaders able to keep his orchestra together throughout (and far beyond) the classic Bebop era.

Edward Kennedy "Duke" Ellington started playing and composing music in his native Washington, D.C., as early as 1917. He first went to New York in 1922, had better luck on his second visit the following year, worked with the Washingtonians under the leadership of banjoist Elmer Snowden, and by 1924 (after a money dispute) was leading the band himself. During a long period at the Kentucky Club, Ellington and his musicians found their own unique sound (which can be heard emerging on records in 1926). In 1927, after securing a regular job at the Cotton Club, Duke Ellington's orchestra was on its way to fame.

In 1945, when Bebop began to be noticed, Duke Ellington was not worried. He had 20 years of major successes behind him, "I'm Beginning to See the Light" was his latest song to become a hit (for Harry James), and he was a household name. Ellington's main contributions to Bop were in several areas. His bassist of 1939–41, Jimmy Blanton, largely liberated his instrument from a pure timekeeping role; he was the main inspiration for Oscar Pettiford (who played with Duke during 1945–48), Ray Brown, and the many bassists to follow. Duke, who was originally a stride pianist inspired by James P. Johnson and Willie "The Lion" Smith, had become a more percussive player and a major influence on Thelonious Monk (and in later years Roland Hanna, Randy Weston, Mal Waldron, and even Cecil Taylor). Probably the biggest impact that Ellington had on the Bebop era was in the way he presented and thought of himself. Rather than being just an entertainer (although he continued playing dances on a regular basis), Ellington carried himself as a dignified artist, and his big band was one of the first to regularly perform at concerts (rather than dance halls) for a sit-down audience. Its series of Carnegie Hall concerts (starting in 1943) were historic, as were Ellington's longform works, including the 50-minute suite "Black, Brown and Beige," "The Liberian Suite," and "Harlem."

After only a few changes during the 1929–42 period, the Ellington orchestra's personnel went through more turnover than usual during the next decade. Although most of the soloists would still be swing oriented, a few (the highnote trumpeters Al Killian and Cat Anderson, Jimmy Hamilton, and Oscar Pettiford) were much more open to Bop. Legend has it that Ellington offered a job to Charlie Parker, who asked for so much money that Duke said if Bird could pay him that kind of salary, he would join Bird's group instead! Bird never did play with Ellington, nor did Fats Navarro (who was also offered a position), although Dizzy Gillespie subbed for a few weeks with Duke in 1943. At the end of the 1940s, Paul Gonsalves (who had a swing-oriented sound but was as harmonically advanced as the Bebop players) became Ellington's permanent tenor saxophonist, and,

shortly after, trumpeter Clark Terry joined up to increase the Bop quotient in Ellington's orchestra.

As the Bebop era ended at the end of 1949, Duke Ellington was at just the halfway point of his remarkable 50-year career.

10 *The Carnegie Hall Concerts (January 1943) / Jan. 23–28, 1943 / Prestige 34004*
9 *Black, Brown and Beige / Dec. 1, 1944–Sept. 3, 1946 / Bluebird 86641*
10 *Ellington Uptown / Dec. 7, 1951–Aug. 10, 1952 / Columbia 40836*

Duke Ellington's January 23, 1943, Carnegie Hall concert was a major event, debuting his "Black, Brown and Beige" suite (which, despite mixed reviews during the era, comes across very well today). Although Jimmy Blanton and clarinetist Barney Bigard had already departed, the classic 1940–42 Ellington Orchestra was still very much intact. The Prestige two-CD set also contains quite a few notable versions of Ellington standards, including Billy Strayhorn's advanced "Johnny Come Lately" and "Cotton Tail."

Black, Brown and Beige, a three-CD set, has all of the 1944–46 Duke Ellington Orchestra's recordings (master takes only) on Victor. The many gems, which include "I Ain't Got Nothin' But the Blues," "I'm Beginning to See the Light," exciting remakes (particularly "It Don't Mean a Thing"), the "Perfume Suite," and excerpts from "Black, Brown and Beige," do not even hint at Bebop but, due to the consistently high quality, should be of strong interest to Bop collectors.

Ellington Uptown is a classic. Betty Roche takes a famous Bebop vocal on "Take the 'A' Train," Clark Terry is featured on a modernized version of "Perdido" (which has a colorful Gerald Wilson arrangement), Louis Bellson stretches out on "Skin Deep," "Harlem" is heard in its definitive treatment, and "The Mooche" contrasts the cool Bebop clarinet of Jimmy Hamilton with the more New Orleans-flavored clarinet of Russell Procope. Most intriguing is "Controversial Suite," which in its two sections looks back to New Orleans jazz and forward to a very cold and mechanized future (that happily never took place).

8 *Piano Duets—Great Times / Sept. 13, 1950–Nov. 1950 / Original Jazz Classics 108*
9 *Piano Reflections / Apr. 13, 1953–Dec. 3, 1953 / Capitol 92863*

Duke Ellington's piano playing through the years is well worth tracing. Starting with his variations of James P. Johnson's stride style, Ellington gradually left more space, became a more dramatic player, and, although often hinting at stride, his voicings and rhythms were quite modern by the mid-1940s. *Piano Duets—Great Times* has Ellington and Billy Strayhorn in a two-piano quartet that performs eight numbers (including "Tonk," "Cottontail," and "Johnny Come Lately"). There are also four additional cuts in which Oscar Pettiford (on cello) is the star; he is backed by Ellington in a trio/quartet that sometimes includes Strayhorn on celeste. *Piano Reflections,* from 1953, is an excellent showcase for Duke's piano (in a trio with bassist Wendell Marshall and drummer Butch Ballard), playing mostly his own songs, some of which are lesser-known.

For a recording date in 1962, that would not be released until 1984 as *Featuring Paul Gonsalves,* Ellington decided to reward his longtime sideman by featuring the tenor as the only soloist on eight numbers, including "C Jam Blues," "Take the 'A' Train," "Jam with Sam," and "Paris Blues." Gonsalves shows off his roots in both swing and Bop.

Duke Ellington had several summit meetings in the early 1960s, including recordings with Louis Armstrong, the Count Basie Orchestra, Coleman Hawkins, and John Coltrane. *Money Jungle,* a trio date with Max Roach and bassist Charles Mingus, finds Ellington being pushed but rising to the occasion and sounding more modern than his younger sidemen; the influence that he had on Thelonious Monk is quite apparent. From the last stage of his career, *This One's for Blanton* features Ellington playing duets with Ray Brown on five standards and the four-part "Fragmented Suite for Piano and Bass" that recall the earlier Ellington-Blanton duets. And on *Duke's Big 4,* recorded when he was 73, Ellington joins in joyfully with Joe Pass, Brown, and Louie Bellson in a quartet on such numbers as "Cotton Tail," "Love You Madly," and "Everything but You."

LPS TO SEARCH FOR

A perfectly done six-LP set that has not been reissued on CD, *The Complete Duke Ellington 1947–1952* (CBS 66607)

features all of Ellington's recordings during the second half of the Bebop era. Among the 76 performances are the "Liberian Suite," the "Controversial Suite" (which is also included on *Ellington Uptown*), some novelty vocal numbers, Hamilton's showcase on "Air Conditioned Jungle," the beautiful "On a Turquoise Cloud," and the humorous "Boogie Bop Blues."

BENNY GOODMAN

b. May 30, 1909, Chicago, IL, d. June 13, 1986, New York, NY

Benny Goodman, the "King of Swing," was confused by Bebop and never really understood it, even though he flirted with the new music for a year. Goodman started on the clarinet when he was 11, and playing his horn would be the most important thing in BG's life for the next 66 years. Goodman developed quickly and at 16 was featured with the Ben Pollack Orchestra. A technically brilliant player, BG was a very busy studio musician during 1929–34, until he decided to form his own swinging big band. It was a struggle to keep his orchestra together at first, but he was able to secure a job as one of the three big bands featured on the *Let's Dance* radio series. When that job ended, BG went on a legendary cross-country tour that had its ups and downs, with some near-disasters. Reaching California, the band did well in Oakland and then created a sensation on August 21, 1935, at the Palomar Ballroom in Los Angeles, a gig that was the symbolic beginning for the Swing era. Within a short time the 26-year-old clarinetist was famous and his big band was the number-one jazz orchestra in the world. Success would follow success, including recordings and performances by the integrated Benny Goodman Trio and Quartet (featuring pianist Teddy Wilson, drummer Gene Krupa, and vibraphonist Lionel Hampton), the addition of Harry James to the trumpet section in 1937, and the clarinetist's Carnegie Hall concert (January 16, 1938), which served as the climactic point of Benny Goodman's career.

Although other swing bands were soon challenging, and sometimes surpassing, Goodman's in popularity (including those of Artie Shaw, Glenn Miller, and Harry James), BG continued to produce significant music. His 1939–41 sextets and septets featured the innovative electric guitarist Charlie Christian, and Eddie Sauter's arrangements for Goodman's big band during 1940–42 were often radical and way ahead of their time. In 1944 BG was in top form on some sextet sessions with Red Norvo, Teddy Wilson, and Slam Stewart, and he had a new big band during 1945–46. The only problem was that the Swing era was ending, and Goodman, who was considered a musical symbol of youth in 1935, was by 1945 thought of as old-fashioned, despite being only 36. He broke up his big band near the end of 1946, led a new orchestra in Los Angeles for a time the following year, and started listening a bit to Bebop.

In 1948 Goodman put together a Boppish septet and, for the only time in his career, shared the front line with another clarinetist, Stan Hasselgard. Also in the band were Wardell Gray, and either Teddy Wilson or Mary Lou Williams on piano. Unfortunately, a recording strike kept this group completely off records, and after a few months Goodman lost interest; ticket sales had been disappointing. Luckily, some of the septet's radio broadcasts from Philadelphia's Click were documented, and the surviving music has been released under Stan Hasselgard's name (where it is also reviewed in this book). The one Goodman studio recording of the year, "Stealin' Apples," is quite Boppish and features solos from Wardell Gray and Fats Navarro in addition to Goodman, although Hasselgard had departed by then.

Later in 1948, Goodman formed his last "permanent" big band and, with the support of the Capitol label, some of its recordings from the following year emphasized the Bebop arrangements of Chico O'Farrill. Soloists included Doug Mettome, Eddie Bert, Gray, and pianist (soon to be singer) Buddy Greco. A septet date from that year finds Greco singing Mary Lou Williams's "In the Land of Oo-Bla-Dee," and has rather modern ensembles on "Bedlam" and "Blue Lou." The more adventurous big band recordings include "Undercurrent Blues," "Bop Hop," and "Egg Head." Goodman's clarinet solos occasionally utilized Boppish phrases but in some cases he sounds a little out of place in his own band!

In 1950 Benny Goodman gave up both the orchestra and any further interest in Bebop, returning to the classic swing music that he had made famous.

* ***The Complete Capitol Small Group Recordings /
June 12, 1944–Dec. 14, 1955 / Mosaic 4-148***
9 ***Undercurrent Blues / Jan. 28, 1947–Oct. 15, 1949 /
Capitol 32086***

The limited-edition four-CD Mosaic box set has a version of "After You've Gone" from 1944, Goodman jams from 1954–55 (with contributions from pianist Mel Powell, Lionel

Hampton, and trumpeters Ruby Braff and Charlie Shavers) plus Goodman's combo dates of 1947–49. Actually the selections from 1947 are primarily swing (including solos by Teddy Wilson and Red Norvo, appearances by many musicians then based in Los Angeles, and a funny duet vocal with Stan Kenton on "Happy Blues"). The only Bop to be heard is 1948's "Stealin' Apples" and four songs from Goodman's 1949 septet with Gray and Mettome.

Of more relevance to this book is *Undercurrent Blues*, which could be given the subtitle "The Complete Bebop Benny Goodman Studio Sides." This intriguing CD has virtually all of Goodman's non-Hasselgard Bop performances. Included are three advanced pieces from 1947 (highlighted by Mary Lou Williams's "Lonely Moments"), 1948's "Stealin' Apples," three of the four songs from the 1949 septet date, and all of the big band numbers mentioned earlier in the Goodman biography, plus a few previously unreleased performances. But the King of Swing did not succeed in becoming the King of Bebop!

LPS TO SEARCH FOR

Long overdue to be reissued on CD, *Presents Eddie Sauter Arrangements* (Columbia 523) has some of the most radical Sauter charts for the Goodman bands of 1940–45, including "Love Walked In," "Moonlight on the Ganges," "La Rosita," and "Superman." Music well worth reviving.

LIONEL HAMPTON
b. Apr. 12, 1908, Louisville, KY

Lionel Hampton always loved to put on a colorful show using enthusiastic groups of young musicians. When he formed and directed his big bands in the 1940s, Hamp did not care so much if a musician was primarily a swing, Bop, or R&B stylist; he was more concerned with how excitingly they played. No one ever accused Hampton of being a dull performer! Originally a drummer in Chicago, Hampton had a few lessons from Jimmy Bertrand, a pioneer drummer who doubled on xylophone. After moving to Los Angeles in 1927, Hampton played and recorded with Paul Howard's Quality Serenaders (1929–30) and was with Les Hite's orchestra in 1930 when they accompanied Louis Armstrong on a few recording dates. Satch noticed a vibraphone in the studio and suggested that Hampton play a few notes on it. Hamp's brief spots on "Shine" and "Memories of You" were the first jazz vibes solos on records. After six additional years in Los Angeles, working with Hite and his own orchestra, Hampton was discovered by Benny Goodman in 1936 and was soon part of the Benny Goodman Quartet. Four years with the clarinetist made the vibist famous. He led an extensive series of recordings with many of the top stars of swing during this period before Hampton went out on his own in the summer of 1940.

The vibraphonist was quite well known before forming his big band and, after his orchestra's third recording session (which resulted in a classic version of "Flying Home," featuring an Illinois Jacquet solo that helped launch R&B), Hampton's big band was one of the most popular in the country. Although Hampton's vibes playing was not very influential during the Bebop era (other than on Terry Gibbs), and Milt Jackson soon became the pacesetter, he remained a major force. Among the many notable players to spend time in Hampton's band in the 1940s were trumpeters Fats Navarro, Kenny Dorham, Cat Anderson, Ernie Royal, Snooky Young, and Benny Bailey, trombonist Fred Beckett, tenors Jacquet, Arnett Cobb, and Johnny Griffin, altoist Earl Bostic, guitarist Wes Montgomery, pianist Milt Buckner, bassist Charles Mingus, and singers Dinah Washington, Little Jimmy Scott, and Betty Carter. Although Hampton's music was often exhibitionistic (with its screaming trumpets and honking tenors), and closer to R&B than to bebop, his mind was open toward the new music—and he recorded Charles Mingus's rather adventurous "Mingus Fingers" in 1947.

Hampton's last important big band was the one he took on a European tour in 1953; in its personnel were trumpeters Clifford Brown and Art Farmer, arranger-trumpeter Quincy Jones, altoist Gigi Gryce, pianist George Wallington, electric bass pioneer Monk Montgomery, and singer Annie Ross. But unfortunately conflicts within the band (for some reason Hamp did not want his sidemen to record overseas) resulted in the group's breakup and no studio recordings. The vibraphonist would continue alternating between leading young orchestras, having reunions with Benny Goodman, and appearing in all-star settings through the 1990s, never tiring of playing "Flying Home."

10 *Hamp! / May 26, 1942–Mar. 20, 1963 / GRP/Decca 652*

9 *Midnight Sun / Jan. 29, 1946–Nov. 10, 1947 / GRP/ Decca 625*

Hamp! is a definitive two-CD sampling of Lionel Hampton's 1940s band, mostly from 1942–50 (with two selections

from a 1963 date with trumpeter Charlie Teagarden). Its many highlights include "Flying Home," "Hamp's Boogie Woogie," "Red Cross" (with guest Dizzy Gillespie), "Evil Gal Blues" (Dinah Washington's first hit), Hampton's famous solo on "Stardust" (possibly the high point of his career), "Blow Top Blues," "Hey! Ba-Ba-Re-Bop," "Red Top," "Mingus Fingers," "Midnight Sun," and "Rag Mop." About the only major recording missing is "Flying Home #2," which features Arnett Cobb's tenor in Jacquet's place. *Midnight Sun* repeats eight selections but adds a dozen more from the 1946–47 period, including a two-part "Air Mail Special," "Cobb's Idea," "Goldwyn Stomp," and "Giddy Up."

LPS TO SEARCH FOR

Lionel Hampton's big band of 1948 did not record, but luckily a few radio broadcasts exist, last out as the budget LP *1948* (Alamac 2419). Among the players featured are trumpeters Fats Navarro (heard on "Hot House"), Teddy Buckner, Bennie Bailey, and the odd high-note player Leo "The Whistler" Shepherd, trombonists Britt Woodman and Al Grey, tenorman Johnny Sparrow, Milt Buckner, Charles Mingus, and a very early taste of guitarist Wes Montgomery.

WOODY HERMAN

b. May 16, 1913, Milwaukee, WI, d. Oct. 29, 1987, Los Angeles, CA

Woody Herman was already an established big bandleader before the rise of Bebop. However, the two orchestras that he led during the classic Bebop era (the First and Second Herds) would overshadow his earlier swing band. They became his most famous and beloved big bands, influencing and casting a long shadow over his later orchestras.

Woody Herman was an important force in the jazz world for over 50 years. A fine swing clarinetist and an altoist who was influenced most by Johnny Hodges, Herman was most significant as a bandleader, a talent scout, and an encourager of young talent. He hated nostalgia and was always most interested in playing new music, constantly encouraging his sidemen to write fresh material and introduce new voices and ideas into the band. Although some initially doubted the sincerity of his change in musical direction during 1944–45 (a view that Charlie Barnet expressed in his memoirs), the consistency of Herman's open-minded approach throughout his career was one of his greatest strengths.

Woody Herman's Second Herd at New York's Commodore Hotel in 1948 included singer Mary Ann McCall, Stan Getz (the first tenor on the left), the clarinet-holding leader, and baritonist Serge Chaloff.

He began his performing career quite early, as a child singer and dancer in vaudeville. Herman started on alto saxophone before his teenage years and at 14 began doubling on clarinet. He picked up early experience working with the bands of Myron Stewart, Joe Lichter (1928), Tom Gerun (1929–34), Harry Sosnick, and Gus Arnheim. As a member of the Isham Jones big band (1934–36), Herman was well featured, both on the radio and on records, as a singer, and on clarinet, alto, and baritone, including with Isham Jones's Juniors, a combo taken out of the orchestra.

When Isham Jones broke up his orchestra in the summer of 1936, the 23-year-old Herman formed his own big band, using several of Jones's players. At first the leader was featured on records mostly as a ballad singer and, although he had a good voice, the Woody Herman Orchestra struggled for a couple years. But in 1939 Herman had a hit with "Woodchoppers' Ball," and he was soon recording such hot instrumentals as "Dallas Blues," "Blues Downstairs," and

"Blues Upstairs." This change led to Herman's orchestra's being nicknamed "The Band That Plays the Blues" and sometimes having a Dixieland feel during its more heated numbers.

During 1942–44, the Woody Herman Orchestra went through many more changes. Dave Matthews's arrangements, which were influenced by Duke Ellington, were often utilized, and such guests as tenors Ben Webster, Budd Johnson, and Georgie Auld, trumpeter Ray Nance, and altoist Johnny Hodges reinforced the Ellington flavor on Herman's records. Dizzy Gillespie's futuristic "Down Under" was recorded in 1942, and Herman was clearly looking forward (although his advice to Gillespie to give up playing trumpet and stick to writing was off the mark!). Chubby Jackson, who became Herman's bassist in 1943, helped persuade the bandleader to use new and colorful players, advice seconded by Ralph Burns, who joined as chief arranger and pianist the following year. During the 1943–44 period, the Woody

Herman Orchestra went through an almost complete change of personnel, and, by the end of '44, Herman had the most exciting new big band in jazz.

Soon known as Herman's Herd, the orchestra featured major soloists in tenor saxophonist Flip Phillips and trombonist Bill Harris, a trumpet section that included Sonny Berman, Neal Hefti (who soon became an important arranger), and Pete Candoli (with his 17-year-old brother Conte sometimes joining too), and a rhythm section made up of pianist Tony Aless (after Burns became a full-time writer), guitarist Billy Bauer, Chubby Jackson, and drummer Dave Tough (eventually replaced by Don Lamond). Although Herman occasionally sang (having a hit with "Laura" and helping to make "Caldonia" a standard), as did Frances Wayne, and the band tried to fit into the commercial swing world, the Herd was best known for its rambunctious and often crazy up-tempo romps. Among its classic numbers were "Apple Honey," "Northwest Passage," "The Good Earth," "Your Father's Moustache," "Wild Root," and "Blowin' Up a Storm," Bill Harris's famous showcase on "Bijou," "Let It Snow, Let It Snow, Let It Snow," "Sidewalks of Cuba," and "Fan It," with the last recorded by the Woodchoppers (a nonet taken out of the orchestra). Other top musicians who were with the Herd during this era included trumpeter-arranger Shorty Rogers, pianist Jimmy Rowles, vibraphonist Red Norvo (who had been preceded by Margie Hyams), and guitarist Chuck Wayne. The height of the Herd's success was perhaps its 1946 Carnegie Hall concert, which found the orchestra debuting "Ebony Concerto," a special work composed by Igor Stravinsky, who enjoyed the band's music.

So it was a major surprise when, at the end of 1946, Woody Herman broke up the Herd. Years later, it was revealed that it was due to his wife's health and drinking problems. The decision was regrettable, for the Herd (soon to be remembered as the First Herd) was the only big band that Herman led that was really financially successful. After a year of freelancing, making occasional record dates in a variety of settings, Woody Herman returned to the big band field with his Second Herd. While its predecessor had fallen between swing and Bop, there was no doubt that the new band was quite modern. Originally, Shorty Rogers and Don Lamond were the only holdovers from the earlier group, although Chubby Jackson and Bill Harris would join the Second Herd later in 1948. However, the most distinctive feature of the group, and one that Herman retained in his later bands,

was the use of three cool-toned tenors (Stan Getz, Zoot Sims, and Herbie Steward) rather than the usual two, voiced closely with baritonist Serge Chaloff. Jimmy Giuffre's "Four Brothers" (which became a hit) featured the four saxes, and the Second Herd became informally known as the Four Brothers Band. A few months later, Al Cohn replaced Steward. Other musicians who were with the Second Herd during part of 1948 included Red Rodney, Lou Levy, and Terry Gibbs along with singer Mary Ann McCall. In addition to "Four Brothers," the Second Herd's notable recordings included "I've Got News for You" (which, in Shorty Rogers's arrangement, quoted Charlie Parker's solo from "Dark Shadows"), "Keen and Peachy," "The Goof and I," and the fourth part of Ralph Burns's "Summer Sequence," which was later recorded independently as "Early Autumn," a lyrical ballad that brought initial fame to Stan Getz.

But, although the Second Herd sometimes brought back the craziness of the First Herd, financially it was a difficult struggle. The big band era had ended, the orchestra failed to catch on commercially, and the drug abuse that was rampant among some of his sidemen caused Herman a lot of grief. The 1949 version of the group still had Rogers, Harris, Chaloff, and Levy, but Gene Ammons, Buddy Savitt, and Jimmy Giuffre as the tenors, with Milt Jackson, Oscar Pettiford, and Shelly Manne spending time with the mighty orchestra. "More Moon" (featuring Ammons), Johnny Mandel's "Not Really the Blues," and "Lollypop" were that year's best recordings. However, having already lost a lot of money, Woody Herman was forced to break up the Second Herd before the end of 1949.

Because he had to fulfill some commitments, Herman reorganized a big band in 1950, and this ensemble (the Third Herd) survived into the fall of 1955. The Third Herd was similar to the Second (including using three tenors) but also had a dance book that featured much more melodic and safer music. Although not an overly distinctive unit, the Third Herd left behind some fine recordings. Among the musicians who passed through the group were trumpeters Conte Candoli, Don Fagerquist, Doug Mettome, Stu Williamson, and Al Porcino, trombonists Bill Harris, Urbie Green, Carl Fontana, and Kai Winding, tenors Al Cohn, Phil Urso, Bill Perkins, Dick Hafer and Richie Kamuca, baritonist Jack Nimitz, pianists Dave McKenna and Nat Pierce, bassist Red Mitchell, and drummer Chuck Flores.

Herman was between big bands for a few years in the late 1950s when he had a sextet that featured cornetist Nat

Adderley and guitarist Charlie Byrd. He headed short-term orchestras full of alumni for recordings and special occasions (including the 1959 Monterey Jazz Festival). In 1960 Herman formed what would have been the Fourth (or perhaps Fifth) Herd but was instead better known as the Swingin' Herman Herd (and later the Young Thundering Herd). At first, the Bebop-oriented group featured the high-note work of Bill Chase, trumpeters Rolf Ericson and Don Rader, and Don Lanphere on tenor. By 1962, Chase was joined by trombonist Phil Wilson, pianist-arranger Nat Pierce, drummer Jake Hanna, and the hard-driving tenor of Sal Nistico as the key members of one of the most exciting big bands of the era, as can be heard on their recordings for the Philips label. The orchestra remained largely intact into 1965, and, despite regular personnel changes, Herman would lead big bands for the remainder of his life.

By 1968, Woody Herman's orchestra began playing more pop tunes as Herman tried his best to introduce current pieces into his band's book. The 1968–71 era is considered an off-period by veteran fans who did not want to hear Herman playing such unsuitable material as "Light My Fire," "Hey Jude," and "Aquarius"! But by 1972, with the recording of *The Raven Speaks* for Fantasy, Herman's band was back to performing mostly swinging jazz, including more modern works by John Coltrane, Chick Corea, and the young band members. There were reunions with alumni (including a notable 40th anniversary Carnegie Hall concert in 1976), and the 1970s found Herman featuring such sidemen as trumpeter Tom Harrell, the tenors of Gregory Herbert and Joe Lovano, baritonist Gary Smulyan, keyboardists Alan Broadbent, Andy Laverne, and Lyle Mays, guitarists Pat Martino and Joe Beck, and drummer Jeff Hamilton. Most important among the newer players was tenor saxophonist Frank Tiberi (who occasionally played bassoon), for, over time, he would become Herman's right-hand man.

By 1980, when he was 67, Woody Herman (who had added soprano to his horns) would probably have liked to semi-retire or at least to spend some time off the road. However, his manager had gambled away the band's withholding taxes a few years earlier, and the Internal Revenue Service hounded Herman for the rest of his life; retirement was out of the question. Throughout the 1980s, Herman mostly toured endlessly. His orchestra, which was more Bop-oriented than it had been since the mid-'60s, continued playing "Four Brothers," "Early Autumn," and "Apple Honey" on a regular basis in addition to newer works that appealed to the bandleader. After Herman celebrated his 50th anniversary as a leader in 1986, his health began to seriously decline. In 1987 he passed away at the age of 74. Since his death, the Woody Herman Orchestra has continued to tour on a part-time basis under the direction of Frank Tiberi, not growing much but continually paying tribute to its late leader's open-mindedness and dedication to swinging Bebop.

4 *1936–1937 / Feb. 3, 1936–Aug. 10, 1937 / Classics 1042*

9 *Blues on Parade / Apr. 26, 1937–July 24, 1942 / GRP/Decca 606*

1936–1937 has the first recordings by the Woody Herman Orchestra, 16 selections that primarily feature Herman's ballad vocalizing. Although a few numbers are swinging (including "Doctor Jazz" and "It Happened Down in Dixieland"), the emphasis is on ballads, and there is only one instrumental. Also on this CD is "Stompin' at the Savoy" from Isham Jones's orchestra (with Herman well featured) and six numbers by an octet taken from that big band which was called Jones's Juniors. While *1936–1937* is for completists, *Blues on Parade* is a superior sampler of Woody Herman's early big band, with most of the best jazz numbers reissued, including "Woodchopper's Ball," "Blue Prelude," "Blues Downstairs," "Chip's Blues," Dizzy Gillespie's "Down Under," "Blues in the Night," and two versions of "Blues on Parade."

10 *The Thundering Herds, 1945–1947 / Feb. 19, 1945–Dec. 27, 1947 / Columbia 44108*

4 *Best of the Big Bands / Feb. 26, 1945–Dec. 22, 1947 / Columbia 45340*

7 *Vol. 1: Live in 1944 / Aug. 2, 1944–Aug. 21, 1944 / Jass 621*

6 *Vol. 2: Live in 1945 / Feb. 18, 1945–Aug. 22, 1945 / Jass 625*

8 *At Carnegie Hall, 1946 / Mar. 25, 1946 / Verve 314 559 833*

The First Herd's Columbia recordings are long overdue to be reissued complete and in chronological order, but it will probably be up to the European Classics series to eventually do it right. In the meantime, *The Thundering Herds* is the definitive single-CD sampling of the Herd. All but two of the 16 selections are from 1945–46, including "Apple Honey," "Northwest Passage," "Your Father's Moustache," and "Bijou" plus a remake of "Woodchopper's Ball." The two later tracks ("The Goof and I" and "Four Brothers") are by the Second Herd. Unfortunately, *Best of the Big Bands* is largely a dud. Twelve of its 16 numbers differ from the ones on *The Thundering Herds*, but, other than "Caldonia," none of the additional material is essential. Worse yet, recording dates and personnel are not included, making one wonder who this release was aimed at.

The two Jass CDs feature radio broadcasts, live performances, and one rehearsal by the First Herd that add to the legendary big band's legacy. *Vol. 1* has eight vocals by Herman, six from Francis Wayne, plus 11 instrumentals, several of which were never recorded by the band. *Vol. 2* consists mostly of alternate live versions of familiar numbers, but it is always fun to hear "new" renditions of such tunes as "Red Top," "Bijou," "Apple Honey," and "Northwest Passage."

Woody Herman's 1946 Carnegie Hall concert has been expanded a bit on a 1999 two-CD set that includes previously unreleased versions of "I'll Get By," "I Surrender Dear," "1–2–3–4 Jump," "With Someone New," "Summer Sequence," and "Ebony Concerto"; the last two are unfortunately incomplete. Soundwise, this version is a big improvement over previous releases (although far from flawless), and the unissued selections help make the release into more of an event. Other highlights include "Bijou" and extended versions of "Blowin' Up a Storm," "Our Father's Moustache," and "Wildroot."

8 *The Second Herd 1948 / Mar. 12, 1948 + May 12, 1948 / Storyville 8240*

10 *Keeper of the Flame / Dec. 29, 1948–July 21, 1949 / Capitol 98453*

The Second Herd's first recordings were made for Columbia at the end of 1947, shortly before the second recording strike kept Herman off records during nearly all of 1948. The Storyville release has three radio broadcasts and shows listeners how strong a band Herman had during 1948. Herman and Mary Ann McCall take vocals on 10 of the 22 selections, but it is the other tunes (including "Half Past Jumping Time," "Non-Alcoholic," "Apple Honey," "The Goof and I," and "Four Brothers") that are of greatest interest. At the time the key soloists included Shorty Rogers, Al Cohn, Stan Getz, Zoot Sims, and Serge Chaloff.

The single-disc *Keeper of the Flame* has all of the Four Brothers band's studio recordings for Capitol, including three selections that were previously unreleased. The seven months covered by this set resulted in the last sides by the

original personnel plus other numbers by the band when Gene Ammons and Oscar Pettiford were aboard. The highlights include the Beboppish "Lemon Drop," "Early Autumn," "More Moon," "Not Really the Blues," and "Lollipop." A more extensive "complete on Capitol" box set is due to be released by Mosaic that will duplicate this CD plus have some of Woody Herman's work of the 1950s.

7 *The Third Herd / May 15, 1951 / Storyville 8241*

6 *Songs for Hip Lovers / Jan. 11, 1957–Mar. 19, 1957 / Verve 314 559 872*

7 *The Herd Rides Again . . . In Stereo / July 30, 1958–Aug. 1, 1958 / Evidence 22010*

8 *Herman's Heat & Puente's Beat / Aug. 1958 / Evidence 22008*

7 *The Fourth Herd & the New World of Woody Herman / July 31, 1959–Dec. 27, 1962 / Mobile Fidelity 630*

8 *Big New Herd at the Monterey Jazz Festival / Oct. 3, 1959 / Koch 8508*

Most of the recordings by Woody Herman's Third Herd (which were made for his Mars label and Capitol) are not currently available on CD, although the Capitol dates will soon be returning in a Mosaic box set. Partly filling the gap is a Storyville CD that features the Third Herd live at the Hollywood Palladium. The music (which includes arrangements by Ralph Burns, Shorty Rogers, and Neal Hefti) is more melodic in general than that of the Second Herd, with more even tempos and a bit less excitement. However, it was still a fine jazz band, featuring solos from trumpeters Don Fagerquist, Doug Mettome, and Rogers, trombonist Urbie Green, Phil Urso on tenor, and pianist Dave McKenna along with occasional vocals by Herman and Dolly Houston.

Songs for Hip Lovers has its charming moments. Herman is heard strictly as a singer, either backed by a sextet (with trumpeter Harry "Sweets" Edison and Ben Webster on tenor) or with a ten-piece group (including Charlie Shavers and Bill Harris) arranged by Marty Paich. Herman sticks to swing standards and shows that he was an underrated singer who, in terms of style, really belonged to the 1930s. However his horns are missed during these concise (under-four-minute) performances.

The Herd Rides Again . . . In Stereo finds Herman in 1958 revisiting the repertoire of the First Herd with a studio group that includes some alumni of his bands plus other sympathetic players. Surprisingly, Flip Phillips and Bill

Harris are not present. Heard on such songs as "Northwest Passage," "Caldonia," "Blowin' Up a Storm," and "Bijou" as the main soloists are tenors Al Cohn and Sam Donahue, valve trombonist Bob Brookmeyer, and high-note trumpeter Ernie Royal. This "recreation" largely works.

Herman's Heat & Puente's Beat has the altoist leading a pair of studio orchestras on a dozen songs, six of which also include the rhythm section of Tito Puente's Afro-Cuban jazz group to exciting effect (including "Mambo Herd," "Cha-Cha Chick," and "Tito Meets Woody"). The Mobile Fidelity CD contains a very rare Jazzland release (originally called *The Fourth Herd*) from 1959 with an all-star studio group that includes the tenors of Zoot Sims, Al Cohn, and Don Lanphere plus trumpeters Nat Adderley and Red Rodney, and transcriptions from 1962 (*The New World of Woody Herman*), which are most notable for featuring Paul Gonsalves on tenor rather than an absent Sal Nistico. For his appearance at the 1959 Monterey Jazz Festival, Woody Herman headed an all-star orchestra. The band's set at Monterey (originally released by Atlantic and now available on a Koch CD) was considered a bit of a "comeback" for Woody Herman. In addition to two ballad features for trombonist Urbie Green, there is solo space for tenors Zoot Sims, Bill Perkins, and Richie Kamuca (including on "Four Brothers"), Conte Candoli, and guitarist Charlie Byrd. A joyous set.

8 *Jazz Masters 54 / Oct. 15, 1962–Sept. 9, 1964 / Verve 314 529 903*

3 *Keep on Keepin' on 1968–1970 / GRP/Chess 818*

Woody Herman's Swingin' Herd recorded a series of gems for Philips (1962–64) and Columbia (1964–67), but extremely little of it has been reissued on CD. The *Jazz Masters* release has some of the highlights from the Philips period, including "Sister Sadie," Charles Mingus's "Better Get It in Your Soul," "Caldonia," "The Good Earth," and "Dr. Wong's Bag," but it barely skims the surface of what the orchestra (with Sal Nistico, Phil Wilson, Bill Chase, Nat Pierce, and drummer Jake Hanna) accomplished.

Keep on Keepin' on is drawn from three of Woody Herman's rather weak recordings for the Cadet label, when he was trying to transform pop/rock songs into material suitable for his big band. Unless listeners have the desire to hear what Herman and his musicians did to "Light My Fire," "I Say a Little Prayer," "My Cherie Amour," "Aquarius," and "A Time for Love," this date can be skipped; only an exten-

sive version of "Blues in the Night" (arranged by Alan Broadbent) is worthwhile.

9 *The Raven Speaks / Aug. 28–30, 1972 / Original Jazz Classics 663*

8 *Giant Steps / Apr. 9–12, 1973 / Original Jazz Classics 8344*

6 *Feelin' So Blue / Apr. 11, 1973–Jan. 7, 1975 / Original Jazz Classics 953*

7 *Thundering Herd / Jan. 2–4, 1974 / Original Jazz Classics 841*

6 *Herd at Montreux / July 6, 1974 / Original Jazz Classics 991*

8 *Live in Warsaw / Feb. 25, 1976 / Storyville 8207*

7 *Featuring Stan Getz / Nov. 20, 1976 / RCA 9026-68702*

Woody Herman's orchestra recorded regularly for Fantasy during 1971–75. Fortunately the best of these releases, *The Raven Speaks,* is back on CD. "Reunion at Newport" (featuring Herman's clarinet, pianist Harold Danko, Frank Tiberi on tenor, and Bill Stapleton's flügelhorn) is a near-classic, and the other numbers include memorable versions of "Alone Again (Naturally)," "Watermelon Man," and the title cut. *Giant Steps* finds Herman's band showcasing modern tunes, including Chick Corea's "La Fiesta," "Freedom Jazz Dance," "A Child Is Born" and the title cut. Key soloists include Stapleton and both Tiberi and Greg Herbert on tenors. *Feelin' So Blue* draws its material from three different sessions (and overlapping Herman bands) from 1973–75. Despite having the feel of leftovers, there are a few strong tracks, including most notably "Brotherhood of Man" and "Sombrero Sam." *Thundering Herd* features the 1974 Herman Herd really stretching itself by playing music by John Coltrane ("Lazy Bird" and "Naima,"), Carole King, Frank Zappa, Michel Legrand, and Stanley Clarke plus two other recent pieces. Due to the generally strong arrangements of Stapleton, Broadbent, and Tony Klatka, and fine soloing (from trumpeter Klatka, Tiberi, Stapleton, Gregory Herbert, and keyboardist Andy Laverne), this is a successful effort, even if few of these songs stayed long in Herman's repertoire. *Herd at Montreux* also has some material that did not last long in the Herman book ("Superstar," Billy Cobham's "Crosswind," and a dirge that served as a tribute to Duke Ellington), but Aaron Copland's "Fanfare for the Common Man" caught on. Gregory Herbert and Andy Laverne are the most significant soloists, although Herman is barely heard from.

Live in Warsaw has the 1976 version of Woody Herman's orchestra running through its usual repertoire, including spirited versions of "Four Brothers," "Early Autumn," "Opus de Funk," "Fanfare for the Common Man," and a lengthy "Caldonia." There were no big names in the band at the time (Frank Tiberi on tenor and bassoon, and Pat Metheny's future keyboardist, Lyle Mays, come the closest), but the band sounds quite enthusiastic during this fine concert. Also in 1976, Woody Herman celebrated the 40th anniversary of leading his first band by performing at Carnegie Hall. The music was originally released as a two-LP set, featuring both Herman's current band and many of his former sidemen. Unfortunately, *Featuring Stan Getz,* a single CD, has just nine of the 18 selections, shuffles the order around, and misses a few of the high points. What is here is fine (including appearances by tenors Stan Getz, Zoot Sims, Al Cohn, Jimmy Giuffre, Flip Phillips, and Joe Lovano) with the highlights including "Four Brothers," "Early Autumn," and "Caldonia," but there is a lot of music missing. Look for the two-LP set instead!

8   *Woody and Friends / Sept. 1979 / Concord Jazz 4170*
7   *Volume 1 . . . A Concord Jam / Aug. 1980 / Concord Jazz 4142*
7   *Volume 2 . . . Four Others / July 1981 / Concord Jazz 4180*
7   *Live at the Concord Jazz Festival / Aug. 15. 1981 / Concord Jazz 4191*
7   *World Class / Sept. 1982 / Concord Jazz 4240*
8   *Volume 3: A Great American Evening / Apr. 1983 / Concord Jazz 4220*
9   *50th Anniversary Tour / Mar. 1986 / Concord Jazz 4302*
8   *Woody's Gold Star / Mar. 1987 / Concord Jazz 4330*
8   *A Tribute to the Legacy of Woody Herman / June 21–22, 1996 / NYJAM 1996*

Woody Herman's final eight years were spent recording for the Concord label. Several of the outings were all-star dates. *Woody and Friends* (from the 1979 Monterey Jazz Festival) has appearances by Slide Hampton, Dizzy Gillespie, and trumpeter Woody Shaw on "Woody 'n You" and "Manteca," although Stan Getz practically steals the show on "What Are You Doing the Rest of Your Life?" Four other songs feature the Herman Orchestra, including "Caravan,"

John Coltrane's "Countdown" (with tenor solos from Frank Tiberi and Bob Belden), and Charles Mingus's "Better Git It in Your Soul." *Volume 1* has Herman (on clarinet) jamming with a variety of players, including cornetist Warren Vache, altoist Dick Johnson, clarinetist Eiji Kitamura, pianist Dave McKenna, vibraphonist Cal Tjader, and tenorman Scott Hamilton; best is McKenna's feature on "My Melancholy Baby" and the no-holds-barred closer, "Apple Honey." For *Volume 2,* Herman presented four of his former tenor saxophonists, each of whom played with him in different eras: Flip Phillips, Al Cohn, Bill Perkins, and Sal Nistico. Cohn's arrangements for such tunes as "Not Really the Blues," "Tiny's Blues," "Four Others," and "The Goof and I" uplift the music. Herman makes his only appearance playing alto on "Tenderly."

Al Cohn (on "Lemon Drop" and "Things Ain't What They Used to Be") and Stan Getz (playing "The Dolphin") guest on *Live at the Concord Jazz Festival,* but otherwise this is a showcase for Woody Herman's 1981 band. The best-known sidemen are flugelhornist Bill Stapleton, trombonist John Fedchock, and pianist John Oddo (who contributed four originals and six of the nine arrangements); the band sounds tight and powerful. *World Class* has four of Herman's former tenors (this time around Flip Phillips, Al Cohn, Med Flory, and Sal Nistico) playing on four of the eight numbers with the big band, including "Four Brothers," Phillips's "The Claw," and "Perdido," easily the high points of the set, which was recorded live in Japan. *Volume 3* finds Herman presenting almost too many all-stars on a spontaneous jam: trumpeter-singer Jack Sheldon (who is humorous on "Leopard-Skin Pill-Box Hat"), trombonist George Masso, clarinetist Eiji Kitamura, Scott Hamilton on tenor, whistler Ron McCroby (heard on "Wave"), guitarist Cal Collins, pianist Nat Pierce, bassist Bob Maize, and drummer Jake Hanna. Somehow everything works. Herman takes two vocals (including leading off a group jam on "Caldonia") and is featured on "I've Got the World on a String."

In 1986 Woody Herman celebrated his 50th year as a bandleader. The album that resulted was the strongest of his Concord recordings, one performed without any guests. With John Fedchock contributing all but one of the arrangements, and such soloists as Fedchock, baritonist Mike Brignola, tenors Frank Tiberi and Jerry Pinter, and trumpeters Mark Lewis and Ron Stout, this was a particularly strong big band. Highlights include "It Don't Mean a Thing," "Blues for Red," "Central Park West," and "Fried Buzzard." Woody Herman's final recording, *Woody's Gold Star,* is better than expected. Herman, who was ailing, is not on the album much, but such soloists as Tiberi, Pinter, Fedchock (who again contributes most of the arrangements), and Ron Stout return, and three percussionists (including Poncho Sanchez and Pete Escovedo) make three of the nine numbers really cook. A strong ending to Woody Herman's very productive career.

Since Herman's death, his orchestra has been kept together on a part-time basis under the leadership of Frank Tiberi. The band did not record again until 1996 but still had a few of the same key players, including Tiberi, baritonist Mike Brignola, and Fedchock. The NYJAM CD also adds such guests as tenor saxophonist Frank Foster, Buddy DeFranco, alumnus Terry Gibbs, Urbie Green, Pete Candoli, Tom Harrell, and Alan Broadbent to play such Herman favorites as "Four Brothers," "Woodchopper's Ball," "Bijou," "Lemon Drop," and a lengthy "Woody's Whistle."

LPS TO SEARCH FOR

The pre-Herd Woody Herman Orchestra is heard on radio broadcasts from 1936–41 on *Blues in the Night* (Sunbeam 206) and performing radio transcriptions on *The First Session* (Circle 95) and *1937* (Hindsight 116). *Dance Time— Forty Three* (First Head 34) has the otherwise-undocumented 1943 Woody Herman Orchestra, featuring trumpeters Billie Rogers and Billy May, Vido Musso on tenor, and Jimmy Rowles in addition to Herman. *The Turning Point* (Decca 79229) contains music from the very interesting November 1943–December 1944 period, documenting the months when "The Band That Plays the Blues" evolved into the First Herd. Dave Matthews's arrangements gave Herman's ensemble the sound of Duke Ellington, and such guests as tenors Ben Webster, Allen Eager, and Georgie Auld, valve trombonist Juan Tizol, and altoist Johnny Hodges are heard from. The First Herd emerged in time for *1944 Vol. II* (Hindsight 134), a set of dress rehearsals that Herman led in mid-1944 prior to broadcasting on the *Old Gold Show.* Flip Phillips and Bill Harris are the main soloists along with the leader, and the music falls between swing and the new Bop music.

The Thundering Herds (Columbia C3L 25) is a superb three-LP box set that unfortunately has not appeared on CD except in piecemeal fashion. The First Herd is heard on its best 37 selections (including seven from the 1946 Wood-

choppers), and there are also eight songs by the Second Herd. Virtually all of the high points are here, including "Apple Honey," "Caldonia," "Northwest Passage," "The Good Earth," "Bijou," "Your Father's Mustache," "Fan It," "Let It Snow, Let It Snow, Let It Snow," the four-part "Summer Sequence," "I've Got News for You," and "Four Brothers." Valuable broadcasts of the 1948 Second Herd are heard on *Hollywood Palladium* (Jazz Anthology 5237) and *Woody Herman Roadband 1948* (Hep 18).

Some of the studio recordings that Woody Herman's band made for his short-lived Mars label are on *The Third Herd, Vol. 1* (Discovery 815) and *Vol. 2* (Discovery 845), while live performances from October 20 and November 10, 1951 are on *Live in New Orleans* (Giants of Jazz 1022). *The Woody Herman Band* (Capitol 560) features mostly dance tunes but also includes a classic version of "Wild Apple Honey." *Jackpot* (Capitol 748) spotlights Herman's first group after the breakup of the Third Herd, an octet with two trumpets (including Dick Collins), Cy Touff on bass trumpet, and Richie Kamuca on tenor.

The Woody Herman Quartet (Philips 20-004) is a rare small-group-date showcase for Herman's clarinet in 1962, playing swing standards and showing that he was generally underrated as a soloist. The Philips big band recordings of Herman are all well worth acquiring (and should be reissued), including *1963* (Philips 200-065), *Encore* (Philips 200-092), *Woody's Big Band Goodies* (released on Mercury/ Wing 16329), *1964* (Philips 200-118), and *The Swinging Herman Herd Recorded Live* (Philips 200-131). The Herman Orchestra's Columbia dates are a bit streakier. The gem of the lot is *Woody's Winners* (Columbia 2436), which includes "Northwest Passage" (featuring Sal Nistico) and a lengthy "Opus de Funk." Other soloists include trumpeters Bill Chase, Dusko Goykovich, and Don Rader, tenorman Gary Klein, pianist Nat Pierce, and Herman himself. *My Kind of Broadway* (Columbia 2357) has its moments, while *Jazz Hoot* (Columbia 32530) and *East and West* (Columbia 9493) are both consistently exciting sets that serve as the close of this era in Woody Herman's long history.

Brand New (Fantasy 8414) is an intriguing date, for on three numbers blues/rock guitarist Michael Bloomfield guests with the Herman band (the combination works well), and other key soloists include keyboardist Alan Broadbent (who arranged five of the eight numbers), the young Frank Tiberi on tenor, trumpeter Tony Klatka, and Herman on soprano and clarinet. *Cobra* (Fantasy 9499), from 1975, is on and off (Herman's vocal on "Jazzman" is forgettable) but most notable for having an excellent big band version of Chick Corea's "Spain." The two-LP *40th Anniversary Carnegie Hall Concert* (RCA 2–2203) has been only partially reissued on CD. Such alumni as Flip Phillips, Nat Pierce, Don Lamond, Chubby Jackson, Jimmy Giuffre, Stan Getz, Al Cohn, Zoot Sims, Conte and Pete Candoli, Ralph Burns, Mary Ann McCall, Phil Wilson, and Jimmy Rowles are heard from along with Herman's band of 1976 (which includes both Frank Tiberi and Joe Lovano on tenors). Even with Herman sometimes shouting out soloists' names over the music (particularly on "Four Brothers"), the music overall is quite rewarding, making one wish that RCA had reissued the full set instead of half the program.

While between the Fantasy and Concord periods, Woody Herman recorded three rather diverse sets for the Century label in 1978. *Chick, Donald, Walter & Woodrow* (Century 1110) has the orchestra playing music by Steely Dan and Chick Corea. A mixture of old tunes ("Woodchopper's Ball" and "I Got News for You") and new ("Isn't She Lovely?" and "Duke Ellington's Sound of Love") are on *Road Father* (Century 1080) while a reunion with Flip Phillips emphasizes ballads, *Together* (Century 1090).

FILMS

Woody Herman's Orchestra appears in *Wake Up and Dream* (1942), *Wintertime* (1943), *Sensations of 1945* (1944), *Earl Carroll Vanities* (1945), *Hit Parade of 1947* (1947), and, briefly, *New Orleans* (1947). *1960s The Swingin' Singin' Years* (Vintage Jazz Classics 2003) has Herman singing and joking around with his big band on "Your Father's Mustache." *Woody Herman Remembered* (Leisure Video) includes a variety of later performances by Herman's orchestra, dating from the 1970s and '80s.

EARL HINES

b. Dec. 28, 1903, Duquesne, PA, d. Apr. 22, 1983, Oakland, CA

Earl Hines led the first Bebop orchestra, but tragically no recordings or even radio broadcasts exist of this very significant band. Hines, who has been called "the first modern jazz pianist," ironically never played Bebop himself. One of the greatest of all jazz improvisers, Hines back in the 1920s was one of the first pianists to get away from stating every beat in a stride pattern with his left hand. Instead, he enjoyed suspending time, implying the rhythm for a few beats while playing a virtuosic pattern with his left hand, before "finding" the beat again a moment before it would have been too late. His right hand often played octaves in a "trumpet style" so it could be heard over an orchestra, and the net effect was an original style that sometimes bordered on the reckless but never seemed to lose its way. Hines worked with singer Lois Deppe back in 1922, moved to Chicago and met up with Louis Armstrong, both in live performances and on records. In 1928, Hines was heard on records with Jimmie Noone's Apex Club Orchestra and Louis Armstrong's Savoy Ballroom Five (including "Weather Bird" and "West End Blues"), on a dozen remarkable unaccompanied piano solos, and later in the year with his own new big band. The Earl Hines Orchestra would be a fixture at the Grand Terrace Ballroom in Chicago during 1928–40.

In the early 1940s, Hines's big band often featured the vocals of Billy Eckstine and the tenor playing of Budd Johnson (who also contributed some of the arrangements). The orchestra had hits in "Boogie Woogie on St. Louis Blues" and "Jelly Jelly" and was quite strong during 1941–42. In 1943 Eckstine and Johnson persuaded Hines to start hiring some promising young players, including Charlie Parker (who switched to tenor since that was the position that was open), Dizzy Gillespie, and Sarah Vaughan (used as a featured singer and second pianist). Unlike most other major name big bands of the time, the Hines Orchestra did not cut any V-discs, and not a single radio air check has been discovered, so it can only be imagined what this orchestra sounded like. It was while with Hines that Gillespie wrote "A Night in Tunisia." The closest radio broadcast that has been discovered is from October 1944, and by then Eckstine, Vaughan, Gillespie, and Parker were gone; each had left to join the Billy Eckstine Big Band.

Hines's orchestra did not record in the studio again until January 1945. Wardell Gary was the featured tenor saxophonist, but the band's music was essentially advanced swing. Hines kept his big band together until early 1948 (singer Johnny Hartman was his main discovery) before giving up and becoming a member of the Louis Armstrong All-Stars for three years. Earl Hines would play primarily Dixieland in the 1950s, was rediscovered in 1964, and kept very busy during his final 19 years, often playing with a quartet (that included old friend Budd Johnson) or creating wondrous solo concerts. But it is a mystery why no one thought of recording his 1943 band's arrangements at a later time or tried to recreate the now-permanently lost style and sound of the first Bebop orchestra.

9 *1942–1945 / Mar. 19, 1942–Jan. 12, 1945 / Classics 876*

8 *1945–1947 / Sept. 1945–Dec. 1947 / Classics 1041*

It is a musical tragedy that the 1943 Earl Hines Orchestra did not record. There are virtually no clues in listening to the recordings that Hines made before and after that year as to how his Bop big band sounded. *1942–1945* starts off with Hines's last orchestra date (which includes "Second Balcony Jump" and Billy Eckstine's vocal on "Stormy Monday Blues") before the recording strike. That CD also includes four trio numbers (with guitarist Al Casey and Oscar Pettiford) from a Fats Waller tribute date, six selections with an all-star swing combo that includes cornetist Ray Nance, altoist Johnny Hodges, Flip Phillips, Casey, Pettiford, and drummer Sid Catlett (Betty Roche takes three vocals), and the Hines big band's first session of 1945. By then the Bebop phase had passed, although Wardell Gray plays well. *1945–1947* has all kinds of obscure material, most of the final recordings by the Earl Hines Orchestra. Wardell Gray is the main star on many of the first 14 numbers, while the later tracks include Johnny Hartman's first four vocals. Ironically some of the arrangements are a little Boppish, but these sound awkward. Most of the other vocals (by the high-toned Lord Essex, Dorothy Parker, Melrose Colbert, and Hines) are forgettable, although there are some solid swing instrumentals to make this a worthwhile acquisition for jazz collectors.

HARRY JAMES

b. Mar. 15, 1916, Albany, GA, d. July 5, 1983, Las Vegas, NV

During 1943–46, Harry James had the most popular swing orchestra in the world, and he was (along with Louis Armstrong) the most famous trumpeter. Because he had quite a few pop hits and has long symbolized swing, few probably realize that he liked Bebop, was friends with Dizzy Gillespie and Miles Davis, and was quite capable of playing an inventive Bop solo.

James was a strong improviser with a very warm tone, but tends to be underrated in jazz history books due to his commercial success and his generally predictable post-1950 work. His father, who conducted and played with circus bands, taught Harry to play trumpet, and the youth gained his earliest experience playing alongside the elder James. As a teenager, he worked with territory bands and in 1935 was "discovered" by Ben Pollack, with whom he made his recording debut. Benny Goodman heard James when he was still 20 and hired him for his pacesetting band in January 1937. For two years James was a sparkplug for Goodman, taking exciting solos and being part of a very highly rated trumpet section that also included Ziggy Elman and Chris Griffin. In early 1939, the 23-year-old formed his first big band, but it would be a struggle for two years, despite his fame. However, after "You Made Me Love You" caught on in 1941, James rocketed to stardom. Soon his orchestra had a full string section and James had other hits ("I'll Get By," "Cherry," and the three Helen Forrest specialties "I Don't Want to Walk Without You," "I Cried for You," and "I Had the Craziest Dream"). Glenn Miller's decision to enlist in the Army meant that James was at the top of the band business by mid-1942 without any close competition. He made headlines by marrying actress Betty Grable, appeared in films himself, and, as World War II closed, had another major hit in "It's Been a Long Long Time."

As with many other bandleaders, things changed drastically in 1946. Singers took over the pop charts, and, although James had a popular band (with altoist Willie Smith and Corky Corcoran on tenor as the two main soloists among his sidemen), the decline of the band business led him to break up his orchestra at the end of the year. However, he came back five months later, dropped the strings in 1948, and showed some interest in Bebop. His extended recorded version of "Tuxedo Junction" from November 3, 1947, has a remarkable trumpet solo in which James shows that he could play Bop with the best of them. Such a pity that he never recorded with Dizzy Gillespie!

There are also a few Boppish touches to both the arrangements and James's solos through 1949. But by 1950 Harry James was back to playing strictly swing again. He would be content for the remainder of his career to stand still musically, having a big band that sounded like Count Basie's and playing countless versions of his 1940s hits while turning down offers to record with Jazz at the Philharmonic and with potentially stimulating modernists.

9 *Snooty Fruity / Nov. 21, 1944–Feb. 15, 1955 / Columbia 45447*

This CD has 18 jazz-oriented numbers from Harry James covering a ten-year period, with plenty of solo space for altoist Willie Smith (who strangely enough gets first billing). Along with the many hot swing numbers is the Boppish rendition of "Tuxedo Junction" that hints at what Harry James could have accomplished had he stuck to that course.

LPS TO SEARCH FOR

With most of Harry James's valuable Columbia recordings remaining out of print, fans should look for Hindsight's six James LPs taken from radio transcriptions and live appearances: *Vol. 1 1943–1946* (HSR 102), *Vol. 2 1943–1946* (HSR 123), *Vol. 3 1948–1949* (HSR 135), *Vol. 4 1943–1946* (HSR 141), *Vol. 5 1943–1953* (HSR 142), and *Vol. 6 1947–1949* (HSR 150). Most of the music is swing, but there are some selections on *Vol. 3* and *Vol. 6* that show the temporary influence that Bop had on James's musical thinking during the era.

STAN KENTON

b. Dec. 15, 1911, Wichita, KS, d. Aug. 25, 1979, Los Angeles, CA

Stan Kenton stood apart from the Swing and Bop eras in which he matured, performing music that he termed "Progressive Jazz." He may very well have been just about the only big band leader who was actually happy that the Swing era ended, for his ambition was to have a jazz concert orchestra as opposed to a popular dance band. Since his career and recordings will be discussed in full in a future book on West Coast Jazz, this entry only deals with his career up until the early 1950s.

Kenton, who grew up in California, began on piano while in his teens. Among his early employers were Everett Hoagland (1933–34), Russ Plummer, Hal Grayson, Gus Arnheim (1936), and Vido Musso. While working with these orchestras, Kenton (a decent pianist most influenced by Earl Hines but never a virtuoso) began to devise plans for his own big band, an orchestra that he hoped would uplift jazz to the realm of "serious" music. In 1940 he organized a rehearsal band with local players ("Etude for Saxophones" is the one existing recording from that period), and then in the summer of 1941 he gained a strong following while playing regularly at the Rendezvous Ballroom in Balboa Beach. At this point, Kenton did most of the writing for the band, including composing his permanent theme song, "Artistry in Rhythm." Inspired by Jimmy Lunceford's screaming brass, Kenton's orchestra also had virile-sounding tenors and

could be quite bombastic yet oddly sentimental. Due to its success in Los Angeles, the Stan Kenton Orchestra recorded nine selections for Decca during 1941–42, but none made a stir. A period of struggle followed, including a stint as Bob Hope's backup band on his radio shows that did not allow the orchestra to do much; Les Brown would end up getting the position later on, with much greater success.

Things began to change when Stan Kenton signed with Capitol. On November 19, 1943, he began a 25-year association with the label by recording "Artistry in Rhythm," "Do Nothin' Till You Hear from Me," "Harlem Folk Dance," and a hit, "Eager Beaver." Trumpeter Buddy Childers and Art Pepper were the most notable names in the band at that time, and there would be short-term stints by Anita O'Day (her recording of "And Her Tears Flowed Like Wine" sold well, although she was unhappy in this style of music) and the young tenor Stan Getz. While the big band era was collapsing during 1945–46, Stan Kenton's ensemble was growing in popularity, attracting a listening audience that was quite impressed by the unusual sounds they were hearing. Starting in late 1945, Pete Rugolo (who arranged and composed initially in Kenton's style) was invaluable, not only transforming Kenton's basic ideas into reality, but building and extending upon the bandleader's dreams. Among the soloists who starred with Kenton during the 1945–47 period were Art Pepper, tenors Vido Musso and Bob Cooper, Kai Winding, Ed Safranski, Shelly Manne, and such screaming trumpeters as Ray Wetzel and Al Porcino.

With June Christy (Anita O'Day's replacement) having hit vocal records (especially "Tampico" and "Across the Alley from the Alamo") and a few instrumentals (including "Intermission Riff" and "The Peanut Vendor") selling quite well, Kenton was able to afford to perform such noncommercial works as "Elegy for Alto," "Monotony," "Chorale for Brass, Piano and Bongo," and "Concerto to End All Concertos." Although much of his orchestra's music from this era could be called pompous, bombastic, and unswinging, Kenton would not consider those terms to be insults!

After the orchestra worked steadily during 1948 (the year of the second recording strike), Kenton was quite weary and broke up the band, ironically just before he would have been free to resume making recordings. After a long rest and much planning, in 1950 Kenton put together the Innovations Orchestra, his most ambitious project. Now his ensemble consisted of five trumpets (including Maynard Ferguson and Shorty Rogers), five trombones, tuba, two French horns, five saxophonists (including Bud Shank, Art

Pepper, and Bob Cooper), a four-piece rhythm section (with guitarist Laurindo Almeida and Shelly Manne), conga, and a 16-piece string section! The big band era may have been long over, but Kenton had the biggest of all of his bands, a 39-piece orchestra! Not only was the Innovations Orchestra extremely expensive to operate, but with few exceptions the music it played was highly advanced, difficult, and dense. The most radical charts were written by Bob Graettinger, including the four-part "City of Glass" and "This Modern World," although even the more swinging pieces by Shorty Rogers were far from simple.

Stan Kenton went on two major tours with the Innovations Orchestra during 1950–51, using a smaller orchestra on other occasions. Then, having made his point, by 1953 Kenton was leading a much more swinging big band. He would head distinctive orchestras full of top all-stars through the early 1960s, make major contributions to jazz education, and go on endless tours with big bands full of relative youngsters during his final 15 years until his death in 1979. Until bad health slowed him down, Stan Kenton lived on the road, tirelessly fighting for the "progressive jazz" that he believed in.

* ***The Complete Capitol Studio Recordings of Stan Kenton 1943-47 / Nov. 19, 1943-Dec. 22, 1947 / Mosaic 7-163***
10 ***Retrospective / Nov. 19, 1943-July 18, 1968 / Capitol 97350***

The seven-CD limited edition Mosaic box has all 153 studio recordings that Stan Kenton's orchestra made during 1943–47, all of its studio recordings (other than the nine earlier titles for Decca) that Kenton's orchestra cut before 1950. From "Eager Beaver," "Monotony" and "Tampico" to "Concert to End All Concertos," it is all here. Other highlights include "Artistry in Rhythm," "Southern Scandal," "Artistry Jumps," "Intermission Riff," "Come Back to Sorrento," "Artistry in Percussion," "Artistry in Bolero," "Opus in Pastels," "Elegy for Alto," "The Peanut Vendor," "Thermopolae," and "Interlude" plus 18 previously unreleased performances. The four-CD *Retrospective* is a superb "best of" collection that spans Kenton's entire 25-year-period with Capitol. There are 21 selections from 1943–47 (duplicating the Mosaic box), ten from 1950–51, and 41 other pieces from 1952–68 that give an excellent sampling of Stan Kenton's musical legacy.

6 ***In Hollywood / May 20, 1944-Dec. 6, 1944 / Mr. Music 7007***

7 ***From Coast to Coast / Sept. 15, 1945-Nov. 13, 1945 / Jazz Unlimited 2055***
9 ***Tampico / May 4, 1945 Oct. 22, 1947 / Memoir 526***

In Hollywood and *From Coast to Coast* consist of radio broadcasts by the Stan Kenton Orchestra. The former set has a dozen vocals by either Anita O'Day or Gene Howard and just eight instrumentals. The main soloists are Stan Getz, Dave Matthews or Emmett Carls on tenor, and trumpeter Buddy Childers, but no real surprises occur. *From Coast to Coast* is less commercial, with just nine vocals on the 22 cuts and such numbers as "Taboo," "Southern Scandal," "Eager Beaver," "Opus in Pastels," and "Artistry Jumps" *Tampico* has 25 June Christy vocals (practically all of her studio sides with Kenton during this era), including "Tampico," "Shoo Fly Pie and Apple Pan Dowdy," "Easy Street," "Rika Jika Jack," "His Feet's Too Big for de Bed," "Across the Alley from the Alamo," and "He Was a Good Man As Good Men Go."

10 ***The Innovations Orchestra / Feb. 3, 1950-Aug. 24, 1950 / Capitol 59965***
10 ***City of Glass / Dec. 6, 1947-May 28, 1953 / Capitol 32084***
8 ***Stan Kenton and His Innovations Orchestra / 1950-1951 / Laserlight 15 70***
8 ***Live at Cornell University, 1951 / Oct. 14, 1951 / Jazz Unlimited 2008***

Stan Kenton's Innovations Orchestra is definitely an acquired taste, his most radical band. The two-CD reissue called *The Innovations Orchestra* has all of the music originally issued as *Innovations in Modern Music* and *Stan Kenton Presents* plus 14 other selections. Such soloists as Maynard Ferguson, Shorty Rogers, Art Pepper, and Bob Cooper get their spots to star on difficult arrangements by Pete Rugolo, Bill Russo, Shorty Rogers, Chico O'Farrill, and Bob Graettinger. Well worth exploring. The music on this twofer, however, sounds conservative compared to the Graettinger arrangements for *City of Glass,* which has virtually all of the eccentric writer's work for Kenton. Whether it be the pieces that comprise "This Modern World," the remarkable, dense "Thermopylae," or even his version of "You Go to My Head," the music is quite avant-garde and mostly atonal.

The Laserlight and Jazz Unlimited CDs contain live music from the Innovations Orchestra during its two tours. The Laserlight set is excellent even if the playing time is a bit brief (38 minutes); the repertoire includes four pieces named after bandmembers ("Shelly Manne," "Conte Candoli," "Art Pepper," and "Bob Cooper"); the last three were composed by Shorty Rogers. *Live at Cornell University* is taken from the string orchestra's second and final tour. The exciting group performs a few numbers that they otherwise never recorded plus alternates of "Shelly Manne," "Maynard Ferguson," "Opus in Pastels," and "Halls of Brass."

FILMS

In addition to many band shorts, Stan Kenton's Orchestra appears in *Talk About a Lady* (1946).

GENE KRUPA

b. Jan. 15, 1909, Chicago, IL, d. Oct. 16, 1973, Yonkers, NY

Gene Krupa was the most famous drummer of the Swing era, but, although he did not alter his style, he kept his mind open toward Bebop and hired many talented young sidemen for his big band during the 1945–49 period. Starting in 1925, Krupa freelanced in Chicago with a variety of groups, first appearing on records in 1927 with the McKenzie-Condon Chicagoans. He moved to New York two years later, worked in the studios, and in December 1934 became a member of the Benny Goodman Orchestra. A flamboyant player who made every simple move on stage look complex and colorful, Krupa became a star with Goodman, whether playing "Sing Sing Sing" with the big band or jamming with BG's trio and quartet. A personality conflict with the clarinetist and his own rapidly growing popularity led Krupa to go out on his own shortly after Goodman's famous 1938 Carnegie Hall concert. The Gene Krupa Big Band struggled for a time as it tried to find its own musical personality beyond the leader's drum solos. During 1941–42 the Krupa orchestra finally broke through, thanks to the vocals of Anita O'Day and the trumpet solos of Roy Eldridge. Their hits included "Let Me Off Uptown," "After You've Gone," "Rockin' Chair," "Thanks for the Boogie Ride," "That's What You Think," and "Massachusetts." But the first Gene Krupa big band was forced to break up in May 1943 when the drummer was framed on a marijuana rap and briefly jailed.

After being cleared and released, Krupa at first rejoined Benny Goodman for a few months and then spent seven months in 1944 with Tommy Dorsey's orchestra. In mid-1944, the new Gene Krupa Orchestra debuted. The large ensemble initially included ten strings, a four-voice vocal group called the G-Noters (which included Dave Lambert and Buddy Stewart), and a second drummer for when Krupa felt obliged to conduct the ensemble. The strings were dropped within a year and the vocal group went nowhere, but on January 22, 1945, Lambert and Stewart recorded "What's This" with Krupa, the earliest example of a Bop vocal with a big band. Buddy Stewart would remain with Krupa as his ballad singer and male jazz singer through 1946. Anita O'Day rejoined the band for a time in 1945 (having a hit with her vocalized version of "Opus #1"), and the highly expressive tenor saxophonist Charlie Ventura proved to be a major asset. Krupa, Ventura, and pianist Teddy Napoleon often recorded separately as the Gene Krupa Trio, and their colorful interplay resulted in a popular recording of "Dark Eyes." The year 1945 also brought such additions to the ensemble as trumpeter Don Fagerquist and Charlie Kennedy (the first Charlie Parker-influenced altoist to be featured in a big band), and the following year the Boppish trumpeter Red Rodney was a key soloist while the young Gerry Mulligan was contributing arrangements (most notably "Disc Jockey Jump").

Although Gene Krupa would never be thought of as a Bebopper, his 1946 orchestra (with Rodney, Ventura, and Kennedy) has to rank as one of the most interesting Bebop-oriented big bands of the time. 1947 found Krupa recording "Calling Dr. Gillespie," and in 1949 (when Roy Eldridge had temporarily rejoined the band and Buddy Wise was in Ventura's former solo spot) Krupa was playing such numbers as "Bop Boogie" and "Lemon Drop" (a feature for trombonist Frank Rosolino's scatting). But, despite the leader's star appeal, by 1950 his big band was struggling (the Bop charts were gone by then), and in 1951 he reluctantly broke up the orchestra. During the remainder of his career Gene Krupa worked with swing combos, toured with Jazz at the Philharmonic, and had frequent reunions with Benny Goodman, leaving his Bop band of 1945–49 as a little-known footnote in jazz history.

5   *Leave Us Leap / Jan. 11, 1945–1948 / Vintage Jazz Classics 1047*

*   *The Complete Capitol Recordings of Gene Krupa & Harry James / Feb. 20, 1946–July 1, 1958 / Mosaic 7-192*

With the exception of the final selection (a version of "Disc Jockey Jump" from 1948), *Leave Us Leap* consists of radio broadcasts by the Gene Krupa Orchestra (often with a string section) from 1945. The music is primarily swing-oriented, with arrangements by Ed Finckel, vocals by Buddy Stewart (on "Summertime" and "Laura"), Lillian Lane, and the G-Noters (which includes Stewart and Dave Lambert). Charlie Ventura and pianist Teddy Napoleon have their spots and are featured with Krupa on "Dark Eyes," but there are a fair number of throwaway selections too.

The seven-CD limited-edition Mosaic box set is split between two very different bands. The final three discs feature the Harry James Orchestra of 1955–58 and is of interest mostly to swing fans, featuring both recreations of James's hits (made for "Hi-Fi") and arrangements that make the ensemble sound like Count Basie's. However, it is the first four CDs that are of greatest interest, for they feature the obscure (and mostly unreleased to the public) Capitol radio transcriptions of the 1946–47 Krupa big band. Seven numbers showcase the Ventura-Napoleon-Krupa trio, Buddy Stewart and Caroline Grey have some vocals, and there are plenty of solos by Red Rodney, Dan Fagerquist, Charlie Kennedy, Ventura, and Buddy Wise.

LPS TO SEARCH FOR

Ace Drummer Man (Giants of Jazz 1006) has quite a few rarities from Krupa. Two numbers from 1943 ("Liza" and "Hodge Podge") feature Buddy DeFranco, Dodo Marmarosa, and Krupa in a trio and are among the clarinetist's very first recordings. "Dark Eyes" and "Wire Brush Stomp" feature a different trio (with Ventura and pianist George Walters), there are two vocals by Anita O'Day with the 1945 big band, and the remainder of the LP has a miniset by the 1947 Krupa Orchestra, with Kennedy and Wise well featured.

FILMS

Gene Krupa and his big band of the classic Bop era appear in *George White's Scandals* (1945), *Beat the Band* (1947), *Glamour Girl* (1948), and *Make-Believe Ballroom* (1949).

MACHITO

b. Feb. 16, 1912, Tampa, FL, d. Apr. 15, 1984, London, England

Machito led an influential orchestra that mixed Cuban music with Bebop, helping to pioneer Latin jazz. Born Frank Grillo, Machito was a singer, a conductor, and an occasional percussionist (often playing maracas) who was a perfect frontman for his orchestra. He was raised in Cuba and worked in Havana during 1928–37 with many of the top Cuban bands. Machito moved to the United States in 1937 as a singer with La Estrella Habañera and performed with a variety of Latin bands in the late 1930s, including Xavier Cugat. In 1940 Machito formed the Afro-Cubans, and in 1941 his brother-in-law, trumpeter Mario Bauza, became the orchestra's musical director, persuading Machito to hire jazz-influenced arrangers. Machito first recorded in 1941, and two years later his orchestra played its first Afro-Cuban jazz piece, "Tanga." It took a few years for Machito's brand of Afro-Cuban jazz to catch on, but a January 24, 1947, Town Hall concert that also featured Stan Kenton's orchestra was a major success. So impressed was Kenton with Machito that he used the bandleader on maracas during his popular recordings of "The Peanut Vendor" and "Cuban Carnival."

Also impressed was producer Norman Granz, who began recording Machito for his Clef label. In addition to recordings by the 13-piece group (which comprised three trumpets, including Bauza, four saxophonists, piano, bass, and four percussionists), Machito's orchestra during 1948–60 recorded with such guests as Charlie Parker, Dizzy Gillespie, Howard McGhee, Harry "Sweets" Edison, Flip Phillips, Johnny Griffin, Brew Moore, trombonist Curtis Fuller, flutist Herbie Mann, altoist Cannonball Adderley, and Buddy Rich.

Machito was based at New York's Palladium from the 1950s into the '80s, and his Latin jazz band managed to retain its popularity through the decades, until Machito had a fatal stroke in 1984.

10 *Mucho Macho / 1948–1949 / Pablo 2625-712*
9 *Kenya / Dec. 17–24, 1957 / Roulette 22668*
8 *1983 Grammy Award Winner / Feb. 6–7, 1982 / MCA/Impulse 33106*

The best-known recordings by Machito's orchestra are the ones made with Charlie Parker (which have been released under Bird's name) and with various guests. *Mucho Macho* is quite valuable, for it features the early Machito band without any outsiders, performing stirring Afro-Cuban jazz at the height of the Bebop era. Most of the pieces are obscurities by Cubans (including two pieces by Chico O'Farrill), but there are also Latinized renditions of seven standards, including "At Sundown," "Why Do I Love You?" "Tea for Two," and "St. Louis Blues," that show what a powerhouse band Machito led. Moving up nearly a decade, *Kenya* from 1957 features songs and arrangements by Mario Bauza, A. K. Salim, and Rene Hernandez plus Chano Pozo's "Tin Tin Deo." Cannonball Adderley and trumpeter Joe Newman are guest soloists throughout and also heard from are trumpeter

Doc Cheatham, Eddie Bert on trombone, and several of Machito's sidemen. The music is both stirring and infectious.

The Impulse disc was recorded two years before Machito's death but finds the leader using the same instrumentation as his earlier 13-piece group except that he had added a fourth trumpeter. Machito's vocals are still powerful, he is assisted by his daughter Paula on vocals and son Mario on timbales, and trumpeter Chocolate Armenteros is among the main soloists in this accessible and highly rhythmic program.

LPS TO SEARCH FOR

Afro-Cubop (Spotlite 138) has valuable live performances of Machito's orchestra from the Royal Roost in 1949, with guest spots for Howard McGhee, Brew Moore, Milt Jackson (on "Boppin' the Vibes"), and Harry Belafonte (singing "Lean on Me"). In addition, there are three obscure numbers from 1950 that find Charlie Parker playing with an Afro-Cuban band in 1950 that might be Machito's; Bird solos on "Mambo" and "Lament for the Congo."

RAY McKINLEY

b. June 18, 1910, Fort Worth, TX, d. May 7, 1995, Largo, FL

Ray McKinley is best known for his work in the Swing era as a solid drummer and as a good-natured singer. He gained recognition for his work with the Dorsey Brothers Orchestra (1934–35) and the Jimmy Dorsey big band (1935–39) and was an unofficial co-leader of the Will Bradley Orchestra (1939–42), where he sang on some of Bradley's best-selling records (including "Beat Me Daddy, Eight to the Bar" and the eccentric "Celery Stalks at Midnight"). McKinley led his own big band for a few months in 1942 before going into the military, where he worked with Glenn Miller's Army Air Force Band (1943–45), which he led after Miller's death.

During 1946–50, Ray McKinley had his own big band and, although not Bop-oriented, the orchestra featured many of Eddie Sauter's rather adventurous arrangements. Billed as "The Most Versatile Band in the Land," McKinley's ensemble is remembered today mostly due to Sauter's charts. Although the personnel at times included Rusty Dedrick or Nick Travis on trumpet, Peanuts Hucko on tenor and clarinet, pianist Lou Stein, and guitarist Mundell Lowe, there was not that much solo space, and Sauter's music developed parallel to but independent of Bebop. In 1950

McKinley broke up the band and, after freelancing for a few years, in 1956 he organized and then led for a decade the new Glenn Miller Orchestra, playing nostalgia swing until his retirement.

7 *Borderline / Mar. 7, 1946–Nov. 1947 / Jazz Heritage 514914*

A dozen of the Ray McKinley's Savoy and Majestic recordings are on this CD, but the music is more rewarding than the packaging. The dates are not given, the composer credits are wrong in at least three cases (Jelly Roll Morton did not write "Mint Julep," nor did M. Franko compose "Over the Rainbow"!), and the personnel listing (which mistakenly includes Bud Freeman on tenor) is quite incomplete. The 12 performances on this LP-length program (at least ten of which are on the Savoy twofer LP listed under LPs to Search For) are excellent and give a fine overview of the unusual orchestra's sound. Highlights include "Hangover Square," "Borderline," and "Howdy Friends" (which was McKinley's theme song). However, this music deserves to be treated better.

LPS TO SEARCH FOR

The Most Versatile Band in the Land (Savoy 2261) is a two-LP set that has 28 selections from 1946–47, 18 of which feature Eddie Sauter arrangements. The most important sidemen are Rusty Dedrick, Peanuts Hucko, and Mundell Lowe; Sam Butera takes a tenor solo on "Mint Julep." Also of strong interest is *Ray McKinley* (Golden Era 15030), which features his orchestra playing a dozen instrumentals on radio broadcasts from 1949, including seven Sauter charts.

FILMS

Ray McKinley appears in *Make-Believe Ballroom* (1949).

JAY McSHANN

b. Jan. 12, 1916, Muskogee, OK

Jay McShann led one of the last significant big bands to emerge out of Kansas City, an excellent blues-based outfit most notable for including among its personnel Charlie Parker. McShann, who started playing piano when he was 12, worked in the Southwest, settled in Kansas City in the mid-1930s, and was part of the legendary after-hours jam sessions. In 1937 McShann formed his orchestra, which for a few years was a fixture in Kansas City. Bird became a member near its beginning and was with McShann on and off for the next five years.

McShann, who recorded some small-group sides in 1940 (released on the CD *Early Bird* and reviewed under Charlie Parker's name), brought his band east in 1941. Signed to Decca, the McShann Orchestra had three recording sessions during 1941–42, with "Confessin' the Blues" (featuring Walter Brown's vocal) becoming a minor hit. Because Decca preferred that McShann stick to recording blues, some of the orchestra's better swing charts were never documented. Charlie Parker has short solos on four of the recordings: "Swingmatism," "Hootie Blues," "The Jumpin' Blues," and "Sepian Bounce." Although Bird's solo spots are brief (often just a chorus), they made a strong impression on younger musicians, as did his lengthier improvisations on radio broadcasts by the McShann band. No one else in the band was as advanced as Parker (trumpeter Buddy Anderson was the closest), but Bird's strong blues sensibility allowed him to fit in better than Dizzy Gillespie did with Cab Calloway.

Parker went on his own later in 1942. McShann's orchestra (with Paul Quinichette featured on tenor) lasted until 1944, when the leader was drafted. After his discharge, McShann led groups that made the transition from swing to early R&B, featuring singer Jimmy Witherspoon, but he never really explored Bebop himself, sticking to his likable swing-and-blues style (and becoming a fine blues vocalist himself) during the next half-century.

9 *Blues from Kansas City / Apr. 30, 1941–Dec. 1, 1943 / GRP/Decca 614*

Jay McShann recorded 21 selections for Decca during 1941–43 and all of them are on this CD, including the four with Charlie Parker solos. In addition to Bird, the stars include the pianist-leader, singers Walter Brown and Al Hibbler, and (on the session from 1943) Paul Quinichette. In addition to the 11 big band numbers, ten of the songs are actually played by small groups (from a trio up to a septet), and these put the focus more on the underrated pianist.

BOYD RAEBURN

b. Oct. 27, 1913, Faith, SD, d. Aug. 2, 1966, Lafayette, IN

Boyd Raeburn was never much of a musician and he did not write or arrange music, but for a few years he led one of the most adventurous big bands in jazz. Raeburn, who origi-nally played tenor sax in the ensembles but was rarely audible and later switched to baritone and finally bass sax, headed a series of nondescript commercial big bands in the 1930s, none of which made much of an impression or recorded. In 1944 he became interested in playing swing and his orchestra that year featured altoist Johnny Bothwell (who sounded quite close to Johnny Hodges), Roy Eldridge, Sonny Berman, trombonist Trummy Young, Benny Harris, Al Cohn, Oscar Pettiford, Shelly Manne or Don Lamond on drums, and the young Serge Chaloff at various times. Raeburn's pianist George Handy contributed some of the arrangements, as did George Williams and Eddie Finckel. Raeburn's orchestra was influenced most at the time by Count Basie but was also the first to make a commercial recording of Dizzy Gillespie's "A Night in Tunisia," with the composer guesting on trumpet.

In 1945 the band took a major turn to the left and became much more radical. George Handy became the main arranger, and his charts were often very dissonant, dense, and eccentric, even having explosions occur behind the relatively straight vocals of David Allyn and Ginnie Powell. With the big band era collapsing and Raeburn's music being so undanceable, it probably made little sense for the orchestra to continue, but it actually grew in size during 1946, with French horns and a harp added. Lucky Thompson, Dodo Marmarosa, tenorman Frankie Socolow, bassist Harry Babasin, and Buddy DeFranco were among the bigger names to spend time with the big band. In mid-1946, a personality conflict led Handy to leave Raeburn, but Johnny Richards effectively carried on as the main arranger for a time. The band (which was up to 21 pieces) survived as long as it could, although (with even the Harry James and Benny Goodman orchestras breaking up) the odds were certainly against it! To his credit, Raeburn struggled on to the end of 1947 before finally giving up. Raeburn made other attempts to lead similar orchestras during 1948–49, but those ventures quickly flopped. He went back to performing dance music and in 1956–57 recorded three rather straight dance dates for Columbia that went nowhere. Boyd Raeburn ended up outside of music, working in the furniture business and living for periods in Nassau and the Bahamas.

6 *1944 / June 13, 1944–Aug. 21, 1944 / Circle 22*
7 *1944–1945 / June 22, 1944–Jan. 17, 1945 / Circle 113*
10 *Jubilee Broadcasts: 1946 / Dec. 29, 1945–Apr. 1946 / Hep 1*

Although the rather radical Boyd Raeburn Orchestra never stood a chance commercially, it made some unique music before its inevitable collapse.

The radio transcriptions on the two Circle discs feature the short-lived Boyd Raeburn swing band of 1944–45, a unit that was a transition before George Handy's radical arrangements transformed the orchestra. Eddie Finckel and George Williams contributed most of the arrangements to these dates, there are so-so vocals from Don Darcy and Marjorie Wood, and the main soloists are Johnny Bothwell, Benny Harris, and trombonist Earl Swope. *1944,* which has an early rendition of "A Night in Tunisia," includes such numbers as "Hep Boyds," "March of the Boyds," "Early Boyd," "Boyd Meets the Duke," "Boyd Meets Girl," and "Little Boyd Blue"! *1944–1945* has guest appearances by Dizzy Gillespie (on "Barefoot Boy with Cheek" and a vocal version of

"A Night in Tunisia" that is called "Interlude") and trombonist Trummy Young (who sings "Is You Is or Is You Ain't My Baby?").

Jubilee Broadcasts is from the prime period of the Boyd Raeburn Orchestra. The radio appearances feature trumpeter Ray Linn, trombonist Ollie Wilson, Lucky Thompson, and Dodo Marmarosa as the key soloists. Dizzy Gillespie sits in for "A Night in Tunisia," Mel Torme and the Mel-Tones guest on "That's Where I Came In," and "Caravan" features the Ray Linn septet (taken out of the band) with a rare early flute solo by Harry Klee. George Handy contributed 12 of the arrangements, including "Tonsillectomy," rather dense vocal "accompaniments" on "Temptation," and "Body and Soul," "Rip Van Winkle," and "Dalvatore Sally." Until Raeburn's studio recordings from the period (owned by Savoy) are reissued in coherent order on CD, the Hep disc is his best available release.

LPS TO SEARCH FOR

Experiments in Big Band Jazz (Musicraft 505) has a dozen titles that the Boyd Raeburn Orchestra made for the Musicraft label in 1945, when it was still essentially a swing band. Dizzy Gillespie guests on "Night in Tunisia" and "March of the Boyds," and the other key soloists are Johnny Bothwell, trumpeter Tommy Allison, and Frankie Socolow. The most significant Boyd Raeburn studio recordings are on the two-LP set *Jewells* (Savoy 2250), music from 1945–47 (plus four songs led by singer David Allyn in 1949) that has been reissued on CD thus far in piecemeal fashion. The most significant, colorful, and crazy Boyd Raeburn recordings are all here, including "Tonsillectomy," "Rip Van Winkle," "Temptation," "Dalvatore Sally," "Boyd Meets Stravinsky," a hilarious reworking of "Over the Rainbow," "Body and Soul," "Hep Boyd's," and "Duck Waddle."

A variety of collector's records also document the Boyd Raeburn Orchestra on the radio. These include *One Night Stand* (Joyce 1131), which has a broadcast from as early as January 1944, *Rare 1944–46 Broadcast Performances* (IAJRC 48), *Instrumentals Never Before on Record* (First Time 1515), *The Unissued Boyd Raeburn—1945* (Joyce 1210), *Hep Boyds* (Golden Era 15014), *Rhythms by Raeburn* (Aircheck 20), *Boyd Raeburn's Jubilee* (Joyce 5010), *Boyd Raeburn's Second Jubilee* (Joyce 5011), and the two best ones: *Where You At* (Hep 3) and *Memphis in June* (Hep 22).

BUDDY RICH

b. Sept. 30, 1917, Brooklyn, NY, d. Apr. 2, 1987, Los Angeles, CA

"The world's greatest drummer," Buddy Rich had no competition in technique, speed, drive, or volume; he was the most explosive of drummers for decades. Although he was not a Bebop drummer (having formed his style in the Swing era), Rich made a strong attempt to lead a Bebop orchestra in 1945.

A genius, Rich taught himself drums when he was 1½, playing in vaudeville shows with his parents at the time and getting a high salary by the time he was 3. He was billed as "Traps the Drum Wonder" when he was 6 and grew up in show business, drumming, tap dancing, and singing in vaudeville until he was 18 and started playing jazz. Rich's remarkable technique was noticeable from the start in the jazz world, and he quickly graduated from Joe Marsala's group (1937–38) to the orchestras of Bunny Berigan (1938), Artie Shaw (1939), and Tommy Dorsey (1939–42). After serving in the Marines (1942–44), he had a second stint with Dorsey (1944–45) and then put together his own big band, which debuted in October 1945.

Rich's original group lacked any big names, although the trombone section had Earl Swope (later with Woody Herman) and future composer Johnny Mandel while Tony Scott played clarinet and alto. As was true of his later bands, there was constant turnover. Altoist Aaron Sachs and trumpeter Red Rodney were with Rich for a period before he broke up the band in late 1946 to go on a Jazz at the Philharmonic tour. In early 1947 Rich put together another orchestra, which for a time had Al Cohn on tenor and George Handy playing piano; Cohn and Handy were among the main arrangers. In 1948 vibraphonist Terry Gibbs and tenorman Jimmy Giuffre were key soloists with Rich. However, the economic difficulties of keeping the boppish band together, the lack of an original identifying sound for the Buddy Rich Orchestra, and the leader's volatility led him to give up altogether before 1949—for the time.

Buddy Rich would work with various all-star groups, Jazz at the Philharmonic, and Harry James's big band and with his own combos up until 1966, when Rich successfully formed a new big band. He never relinquished the title of "the world's greatest drummer."

7 *Buddy Rich / Jan. 1946–Sept. 1948 / V-Disc*
The Buddy Rich big band's 1946 recordings for Mercury (its only official studio sides) have not yet been reissued coherently on CD. This disc from the budget V-Disc series has nine of the Rich Orchestra's V-Disc performances. But since it only adds up to around 32 minutes of music, it seems a waste that Rich's six other V-Discs were not also included so as to make this a complete set. The packaging (which does not list dates or personnel) is also a waste, but the music (highlighted by "Quiet Riot," "Daily Double," "Nellie's Nightmare," and "Just You, Just Me") is Boppish and spans almost the entire existence of Rich's two orchestras.

LPS TO SEARCH FOR

A Young Man and His Dreams (Giants of Jazz 1019) has three radio appearances by Rich's orchestra (dating from December 24, 1945, to March 27, 1946). *Live Sessions at the Palladium, Hollywood* (Jazz Anthology 5206) is from March 27–28, 1946, and repeats three of the Giants of Jazz selections but otherwise comprises mostly fresh material. The two-LP set *Both Sides* (Emarcy 2-402) starts out with four of the Rich big band's Mercury studio numbers from 1946 (Red Rodney solos on "Oop Bop Sh'Bam"). Rich is also featured with a big band in 1959 arranged by Ernie Wilkins (and featuring Harry Sweets Edison and the tenors of Benny Golson and Al Cohn), on five numbers from a session (fully reissued on CD) that combines his 1959 combo (including Phil Woods) with that of Max Roach, and on three numbers with his 1960 septet.

FILMS

The Buddy Rich big band appears in *Earl Carroll Sketchbook* (1946).

ARTIE SHAW

b. May 23, 1910, New York, NY

Artie Shaw was always curious about Bebop, and he was one of the few swing big bandleaders who had no difficulty improvising in the new style. Shaw began playing music when he was 12, and within three years the clarinetist (who early on doubled on other reeds) was out on the road playing with territory bands. He initially recorded in the late 1920s, moved to New York in 1930, and became a studio musician. In 1934 Shaw retired for the first time (living on a farm in hopes of becoming inspired to write a novel) but returned to the studios when his money ran out. After he was a surprise sensation at a major big band concert on April 8, 1936 (surprising the audience by playing "Interlude in B-Flat" with a string quartet and a rhythm section), he formed the first of his many big bands. Although that orchestra (made up of four horns, a string quartet, and a four-piece rhythm section) failed, his second big band (which had more conventional instrumentation) caught on big in 1938, helped by his giant hit recording, "Begin the Beguine."

In 1939 Shaw had the most popular band in the country (featuring Georgie Auld, Buddy Rich, and singer Helen Forrest), but the pressures of being a celebrity got to him and he fled the bandstand one night. As Shaw vacationed in Mexico, his orchestra struggled and then broke up. The clarinetist came back a few months later to appear in the Fred Astaire movie *Second Chorus,* recorded "Frenesi" with a large

ensemble, and soon had another large hit. Shaw put together his third orchestra, the "Stardust" band (getting its nickname from its perfect recording of that standard), which had a full string section and several major jazz stars, including trumpeter Billy Butterfield. The clarinetist's Gramercy Five (a sextet taken out of his orchestra and including Johnny Guarnieri on harpsichord) had a million seller in "Summit Ridge Drive." By early 1941, Shaw had become bored again and he broke up this orchestra. A few months later he had a fourth band, which featured trumpeter-singer Hot Lips Page and some of his favorite alumni (including Georgie Auld and Johnny Guarnieri) but which, after the attack on Pearl Harbor, disbanded so he could join the Navy in the spring of 1942.

Shaw led an unrecorded service band while in the military, became ill, and was given a medical discharge in February 1944. A few months later he was back with his fifth big band, one that featured Roy Eldridge, Dodo Marmarosa, and Barney Kessel. At his 1945 recording of "Easy to Love," Shaw's solo is quite Boppish, so it is obvious that, even at that early stage, he was quite aware of the new music. In 1946 Shaw ended his fifth orchestra, although he recorded fairly often with studio bands, utilizing Mel Torme and the Mel-Tones on some numbers (including a hip version of "What Is This Thing Called Love?"). Shaw was mostly inactive during 1947–48, and then in September 1949 he surprised everyone by putting together a Boppish big band, his sixth and final orchestra. The personnel included such fine young players as trumpeter Don Fagerquist, trombonist Porky Cohen (who decades later would be with Roomful of Blues), Frank Socolow, and Herbie Steward on altos, the tenors of Al Cohn and Zoot Sims, Dodo Marmarosa, and guitarist Jimmy Raney. The arrangements (by Cohn, Tadd Dameron, Johnny Mandel, Gene Roland, and George Russell) were modern and up to date. Unfortunately the band did not catch on and lasted only a few months. The public wanted to hear Shaw play "Begin the Beguine," and it would not let him escape his past successes.

Unlike some of the other swing big bandleaders who tried Bop for a short time, Artie Shaw was quite sincere in his interest in the music. He recorded in a variety of settings during 1950–52 and, even when the arrangements were commercial, Shaw's solos showed the influence of Bop. In September 1953 he recorded for the first time with his final Gramercy Five (which had Hank Jones, Tal Farlow, Tommy Potter, drummer Irv Kluger, and Joe Roland on vibes). With

Joe Puma sometimes in Farlow's place and Roland occasionally absent, Shaw worked with the group during 1954 and played some of the finest clarinet solos of his life. But he became frustrated with the music business, with a public who wanted him to continue acting as if it were still 1939, and possibly with his own quest for perfection. In 1955 Artie Shaw (who was still just 45) put down the clarinet permanently and has not played since.

- **9**   *The Complete Gramercy Five Sessions / Sept. 3, 1940–Aug. 2, 1945 / Bluebird 7637*
- **8**   *1949 / 1949 / Music Masters 0234*
- **9**   *The Last Recordings / Feb. 1954–June 1954 / Music Masters 65071*
- **9**   *More Last Recordings / Feb. 1954–June 1954 / Music Masters 65101*

Although it only recorded eight selections in 1940, Artie Shaw's Gramercy Five is well remembered because of both its hit "Summit Ridge Drive" and the harpsichord playing of Johnny Guarnieri. *The Complete Gramercy Five Sessions* is included in this book because the final seven performances (which include an alternate take), which feature Shaw and Roy Eldridge as the lead voices, also have short solos from Dodo Marmarosa and Barney Kessel.

Artie Shaw's short-lived Bebop orchestra is showcased on *1949,* a 1990 CD that makes unclear the exact dates or whether these performances were released previously; they probably were not. In addition to Shaw, the main soloists are Don Fagerquist, Al Cohn (Zoot Sims only has one spot), and either Sonny Russo or Fred Zito on trombone. The versions of "Stardust," "They Can't Take That Away From Me," "I Get a Kick Out of You," and some more recent songs fit quite well into the Bebop mainstream and even look a bit toward Cool Jazz of the 1950s. It is a shame that the band did not last. Both *The Last Recordings* and *More Last Recordings* are two-CD sets that feature Shaw's final band, his Gramercy Five with Tal Farlow or Joe Puma on guitar, Hank Jones, Tommy Potter, drummer Irv Kluger, and sometimes vibraphonist Joe Roland. Some of the performances were previously unreleased, while others were put out by Verve but soon forgotten. Both sets contain many strong clarinet solos, with *More Last Recordings* being of particular interest due to Shaw playing rather boppish solos on such earlier hits as "Begin the Beguine," "Stardust," "Summit Ridge Drive," and "Frenesi," all of which he makes sounds quite modern for 1954. It is also a pleasure to hear Shaw stretching out during the performances, many of which are over seven minutes long ("Grabtown Grapple" exceeds ten minutes). These recordings show that Artie Shaw really did retire at the peak of his powers.

LPS TO SEARCH FOR

The Pied Piper (First Heard 1005) has live selections from Artie Shaw's 1949 Bebop band that do not duplicate the Music Masters release; three numbers feature Shaw, Fagerquist, and the rhythm section jamming in a different version of the Gramercy Five. The collectors' Joyce label came out with seven LPs in their "Later Artie Shaw" series that trace his obscure recordings of 1949–54. *Vol. 1* (Ajaz 291) has Shaw on the only six originally released studio sides with the Bebop orchestra plus a couple of numbers with Fagerquist in the Gramercy Five backing Mary Ann McCall's singing and a few selections with a string section.

TOM TALBERT
b. Aug. 4, 1924, Crystal Bay, MN

A long-underrated arranger, Tom Talbert has had his own style since the mid-1940s. Inspired to write by hearing the big bands on the radio, Talbert played piano and began writing arrangements for bands that he organized while in high school. He served in the Army (where he arranged for a military dance band), was discharged, freelanced, and, after moving to California, led a part-time Bop-influenced orchestra during 1946–49. Among the musicians who passed through his big band were Dodo Marmarosa, Art Pepper, Claude Williamson, and tenors Babe Russin and Warne Marsh. After struggling for a few years to keep the ensemble going (reaching a creative height in 1949), the Tom Talbert Orchestra disbanded in 1950, and Talbert began writing for Stan Kenton's Innovations Orchestra, moving to New York. He also wrote for Claude Thornhill, Tony Pastor, Johnny Smith, Oscar Pettiford, and Don Elliott, among others. Talbert, who recorded a classic album in 1956 (*Bix Duke Fats*) which has been reissued by Sea Breeze and will be covered in another book in this series, lived in the Midwest during the second half of the 1960s. In 1975, he returned to Los Angeles, where he has led a part-time orchestra ever since, recording several fine albums for Sea Breeze.

- **9**   *Tom Talbert Jazz Orchestra—1946–1949 / June 25, 1946–Nov. 1949 / Sea Breeze 2069*

The majority of the 16 selections on this CD (all of which have arrangements by Talbert) were previously unreleased, until this disc came out in the 1990s. The writing is as modern as that heard played by the big bands of Stan Kenton and Boyd Raeburn. Among the sidemen who have solo space are trumpeter Frank Beach, Babe Russin, Dodo Marmarosa, Lucky Thompson, Art Pepper, Jack Montrose on tenor, and Claude Williamson. The writing is quite original, and even the occasional vocal numbers are of great interest. Highly recommended.

CLAUDE THORNHILL

b. Aug. 10, 1909, Terre Haute, IN, d. July 1, 1965, New York, NY

Claude Thornhill's band is certainly a difficult one to place, for it was significant in swing (where it was thought of as a borderline sweet band), in Bebop, and as a direct predecessor and influence on Cool/West Coast jazz. Thornhill started playing piano as a youth and, from the early 1930s on, he worked with many bands in the New York area, including Benny Goodman (1934), Leo Reisman, and Ray Noble. He was Maxine Sullivan's musical director when she first began to be noticed (becoming famous for her recording of "Loch Lomond") and worked in the Hollywood studios as a pianist and arranger.

In 1940 Claude Thornhill formed a big band whose ensembles emphasized long, floating tones and unusual tone colors, employing almost no vibrato. Its repertoire included many ballads and some vocals but stood apart from dance bands of the era in the atmosphere that it evoked; sometimes the six reeds all played clarinets in unison. Thornhill and Bill Borden did most of the writing in the early days. The orchestra often played adaptations of classical themes, it introduced the haunting "Autumn Nocturne," its theme "Snowfall" was quite memorable, and "Where or When" was its main hit. In 1942 Gil Evans began to contribute arrangements to Thornhill (including "There's a Small Hotel" and "Buster's Last Stand") and two French horns were added to the band along with a vocal group called the Snowflakes. Then a three-year interruption took place as Thornhill joined the Navy, where for a time he played with Artie Shaw's service band.

After his discharge in late 1945, Claude Thornhill formed his second orchestra, resuming where he had left off. A hit record of "A Sunday Kind of Love" (featuring singer Fran

Warren) helped keep the band in business, and Gil Evans emerged as the main arranger. The 1946 orchestra (which again had two French horns) did not have any major names among the sidemen (guitarist Barry Galbraith was the closest). But in 1947 (when a tuba was added to the group) Red Rodney, altoist Lee Konitz, and clarinetist Danny Polo became the main soloists in addition to the leader on piano. Thanks to Evans, such songs as "Anthropology," "Robbin's Nest," "Yardbird Suite," and "Donna Lee" were added to the repertoire, making the Thornhill Orchestra one of the most modern big bands of the time. Miles Davis first met Gil Evans when he inquired about the "Donna Lee" arrangement, and his 1948–50 Nonet (which also used French horn and tuba) would be based to an extent on a scaling down of the Claude Thornhill Orchestra.

The Claude Thornhill Orchestra lasted until late in 1950 (altoist Herb Geller and tenors Brew Moore and Dick Hafer were with the big band for short periods). Thornhill occasionally put together later big bands for short-term projects (including a 1953 recording of Gerry Mulligan arrangements) but mostly played in obscurity until his death from a heart attack in 1965 when he was 55.

8 *Snowfall / Sept. 20, 1940–July 9, 1941 / Hep 1058*
7 *Best of the Big Bands / Mar. 10, 1941–Dec. 17, 1947 / Columbia 46152*
8 *Transcription Performances / Sept. 25, 1947–Dec. 17, 1947 / Hep 60*
8 *The 1948 Transcription Performances / Apr. 1948–Oct. 1948 / Hep 17*

Snowfall has the first 25 recordings of the Claude Thornhill Orchestra. The music is only of slight interest from the Bop standpoint, but listeners can hear the genesis of the Thornhill sound in the moody instrumentals and atmospheric ensembles. Thornhill, clarinetist Irving Fazola, trumpeter Rusty Dedrick, and tenor saxophonist Hammon Russum are the main soloists, and the highlights include "Snowfall," "Hungarian Dance No. 5," "Traumerei," "Portrait of a Guinea Farm," and "Where or When." *Best of the Big Bands* has poor packaging (no personnel or recording dates) and skips around, but it does have some of the best Thornhill recordings from both of his bands. Included are repeats of "Snowfall," "Where or When," and "Portrait of a Guinea Farm" plus "Buster's Last Stand," "A Sunday Kind of Love," "Robbin's Nest," "Yardbird Suite," and "Anthropology." However, this important and enjoyable music does deserve to be reissued complete and in chronological order, so hopefully Hep will eventually cover the band's entire history.

The two other Hep CDs feature Claude Thornhill's radio transcriptions, and both contain a generous amount of music. The 1947 big band features trumpeters Red Rodney and Ed Zandy, Lee Konitz, Danny Polo, and trombonist Tak Takvorian, lots of Gil Evans charts, and such songs as "Robbins' Nest," "Polka Dots and Moonbeams," "Anthropology," "Early Autumn," "I Get the Blues When It Rains," "Sorta Kinda," and "Donna Lee." The 1948 big band (with trumpeter Gene Roland, Polo, Konitz, and Brew Moore) repeats some of the same charts (although the solos are different) and also has arrangements by Gerry Mulligan; highlights include "Poor Little Rich Girl," "Spanish Dance," "Royal Garden Blues," "There's a Small Hotel," "Godchild," and "La Paloma."

LPS TO SEARCH FOR

The two-LP set *Tapestries* (Affinity 1040) is a definitive "best of" sampler of Thornhill's 1941–47 recordings (plus a Maxine Sullivan number from 1937) and has 17 Gil Evans arrangements. Other than the regretful absence of "Where or When," virtually every significant Thornhill recording is on this twofer. *1941 & 1947* (Circle 19) and *1947* (Hindsight 108) both contain additional radio transcriptions and do not duplicate the Hep 1947 set. The Circle set is of minor interest to Bop collectors (the only Evans arrangement is "Sorta Kinda"), but the Hindsight album does have more Evans charts and additional solos from Rodney and Konitz.

COOTIE WILLIAMS

b. July 24, 1910, Mobile, AL, d. Sept. 14, 1985, New York, NY

A major trumpeter who matured during the Swing era, Charles Melvin "Cootie" Williams is best known for his two long periods with Duke Ellington. However, he also led a significant big band of his own in the 1940s. Williams played trombone, tuba, and drums in a school band before teaching himself the trumpet. He worked locally in the South as a teenager, and in 1928 Williams moved to New York, where he played with Chick Webb and Fletcher Henderson. In February 1929 he became Bubber Miley's replacement with Duke Ellington's orchestra and for the next 11 years was a major soloist with the band, mastering mutes (as Miley had)

to create a variety of unique sounds, but also taking open-trumpet solos influenced a bit by Louis Armstrong. Cootie's decision in November 1940 to leave Ellington and join Benny Goodman was considered big news in the music business. Williams spent a year with Goodman, featured with both the big band and Goodman's septet (alongside Charlie Christian and Georgie Auld). When he left BG, Williams asked for his former job back with Ellington, but Duke (who now had Ray Nance in Cootie's spot) wisely suggested that he form his own big band instead.

The Cootie Williams Big Band became a fixture at the Savoy Ballroom in New York and worked steadily for the next five years. The group's one recording session of 1942 resulted in the first waxing of a Thelonious Monk tune, "Epistrophy" (which was originally titled "Fly Right"). At the time Joe Guy, altoist-singer Eddie "Cleanhead" Vinson, and pianist Ken Kersey were among Williams's sidemen. After the recording strike, Williams's initial session in 1944 was with a sextet taken from his big band, one including Vinson, tenor saxophonist Eddie "Lockjaw" Davis, and (making his recording debut) Bud Powell. The full orchestra also recorded frequently during 1944–45, including the earliest version of Monk's "'Round Midnight" and several numbers that included Powell piano solos, showing that Bud's trailblazing Bop style was already well developed at that early stage. By early 1945 Powell and Davis had departed (the new tenor soloist was Sam "The Man" Taylor). But Vinson was still a major attraction, and Charlie Parker sat in with the band at the Savoy in February 1945, soloing with a sextet from the orchestra on "Floogie Boo." The Cootie Williams Orchestra during 1946–47 became more R&B-oriented (in order to satisfy its dancing audience) before the trumpeter cut back to an octet later in 1947. In 1948, with Willis "Gator" Jackson on tenor, Williams had an R&B hit with "'Gator Tail."

But after Jackson went out on his own, Williams was largely forgotten in the 1950s, still working at the Savoy but hardly recording. That all changed when he rejoined Duke Ellington in 1962 (after a 22-year absence). Cootie Williams spent the next dozen years touring the world with Ellington's orchestra, staying in the big band even after Mercer Ellington took over the band upon Duke's death in 1974, before retiring in the mid-1970s. By then, few remembered Cootie Williams' important connection to the development of Bebop.

LPS TO SEARCH FOR

The recordings of the Cootie Williams Orchestra are long overdue to be reissued coherently on CD. *Big Band Bounce & Boogie* (Affinity 1031) has all 16 of the studio selections from 1944, featuring the trumpeter with a sextet and with his full big band. Eddie "Cleanhead" Vinson and Pearl Bailey have a few vocals, Vinson, Lockjaw Davis, and Bud Powell get solo space, and the highlights include "'Round Midnight," "Echoes of Harlem," "Blue Garden Blues," and "Somebody's Gotta Go." *Typhoon* (Contact 1003) has most of Williams's more important recordings from 1945–50. The titles are more R&B-oriented but quite fun with passionate solos from the tenors of Sam "The Man" Taylor, Weasel Parker, and Willis "Gator" Jackson.

GERALD WILSON

b. Sept. 4, 1918, Shelby, MS

Gerald Wilson is best known for his early association with Jimmy Lunceford and for the many fine big bands that he has led since 1960, but he also had a notable (if now largely forgotten) Bebop-oriented orchestra in Los Angeles during 1944–47. In 1932 Wilson moved with his family to Detroit, where he studied music and played with the Plantation Music Orchestra. His big break was joining Lunceford's Orchestra in 1939, where he played trumpet and contributed occasional arrangements (including "Yard Dog Mazurka," and "Hi Spook") that were swinging yet advanced. Wilson moved permanently to Los Angeles in 1942 (he loved the weather) and freelanced with the bands of Les Hite, Phil Moore, Willie Smith, and Benny Carter. After serving in the Navy, in 1944 Gerald Wilson formed his first big band.

Because he was an advanced writer, Wilson had no difficulty with Bebop. Such players as trumpeters Snooky

Young, Emmett Berry, Hobart Dotson, trombonists Vic Dickenson and Melba Liston, tenor saxophonist Vernon Slater, pianists Jimmy Bunn and Gerald Wiggins, and bassist Red Callender were part of his orchestra at various times. However, in 1947 Wilson reluctantly gave up struggling to keep the big band together, for the time being. He wrote for and played with the big bands of Dizzy Gillespie (to whom he contributed "Dizzier and Dizzier") and Count Basie, and had occasional short-term bands in the 1950s (recording an obscure album for Audiolab in 1954). In 1961 he signed with the Pacific Jazz label and began recording a series of significant big band albums (which will be covered in this series' Hard Bop book). Although Gerald Wilson has long since given up playing trumpet, he has remained quite active as an arranger and bandleader in the Los Angeles area up to the present time.

8 *1945–1946 / May 6, 1945–1946 / Classic 976*

The first Gerald Wilson Big Band recorded 32 selections for the Excelsior, Exclusive, Black & White, United Artists, and Aladdin labels. The 20 earliest cuts (11 of which have vocals) are on this CD, which reissues quite a bit of obscure material. The soloists include Snooky Young, Hobart Dotson, altoist Gus Evans, Vernon Slater, and Eddie Davis (not the same player as "Lockjaw") on tenors and Jimmy Bunn. This Bop-oriented band had roots in Jimmy Lunceford-type swing. The colorful music is highlighted by "Synthetic Joe," "Puerto Rican Breakdown," "Groovin' High," "Skip the Gutter," and "Cruisin' with Cab."

LPS TO SEARCH FOR

Cruisin' with Gerald (Sounds of Swing 121) repeats nine of the selections from the Classics CD but also has seven slightly later cuts by the Gerald Wilson Orchestra; all but one number are instrumentals.

BOP SINCE 1949

In 1950 Bebop was declared dead by the major record labels. Most of the few remaining big bands (including those led by Dizzy Gillespie, Benny Goodman, Charlie Barnet, and Count Basie), broke up and Woody Herman's Second Herd was replaced by the more conservative Third Herd. Gillespie, on his own Dee Gee label, soon began recording material that put more of an emphasis on novelty vocals and R&B effects. Fats Navarro died, Bud Powell was institutionalized during part of 1951–53, J.J. Johnson spent 1953 outside of music, and Charlie Parker passed away in 1955. Was Bebop really dead?

The answer was No. The only thing dead was the interest of the bigger labels in documenting the music. Much more money could be made by middle-of-the-road pop vocalists and rhythm & blues bands. However, Bebop survived as a major influence on the next two styles of jazz, both of which could be considered direct outgrowths of Bop: Cool Jazz and Hard Bop.

Unlike the collapse of the big band era in 1946 and Bebop's quick replacement of swing as jazz's mainstream music, Bop did not suddenly get superceded by another style. Throughout the 1950s, even when Cool Jazz and Hard Bop caught on, Bebop continued to grow and evolve as a powerful force in jazz. Dizzy Gillespie led a major big band during 1956–57, Thelonious Monk (after a decade of struggle) suddenly became a star in 1957, Clifford Brown rose quickly to prominence before his tragic death, J.J. Johnson did some of his finest work later in the decade, and Bud Powell was the main influence on younger pianists. The Eisenhower era was a conservative period and jazz did not really move much beyond Bop until the beginnings of free jazz and the avant-garde near the end of the 1950s.

Cool (or West Coast) jazz (which was intially inspired by the Miles Davis Nonet recordings of 1948–50 and the work of pianist Lennie Tristano) smoothed down some of the rough edges of Bop, emphasizing softer tones, more even rhythms, and tightly arranged ensembles, bringing back the lightness of Count Basie's rhythm section and some aspects of swing. Hard Bop, which emerged by the mid-1950s, infused its music with "soul" and gospel chord voicings, sometimes utilized a more active role for the bassist (rather than just sticking to four-to-the-bar bass lines), and often had lengthier melody statements. The rise of the LP (which allowed recordings, which had formerly been largely restricted to three-minutes, to potentially stretch on for over 20 minutes) gave musicians the opportunity to take longer solos and be more adventurous than they had previously.

Both Cool Jazz and Hard Bop overlapped with Bebop, which made putting together this section a bit of a dilemma. Nearly every jazz musician to rise to prominence since 1949 has at one time or other played and usually recorded some Bop, even if that musician is associated more closely with another style. While seeking to duplicate as little from future books as possible, it is also apparent that there are some major jazz musicians from the post-1949 period that have to be included in any book on Bebop. So the criteria for inclusion in this section is that (1) the individual musicians and singers have spent a large portion of their career performing Bebop and (2) they have to have been influenced chiefly by the music's giants (particularly Charlie Parker, Dizzy Gillespie, and Bud Powell). All of the musicians and singers in this part of the book have essentially been "keepers of the flame," whether it be the Gillespie-inspired trumpeter Jon Faddis, Bebop-oriented saxophonists (such as Johnny Griffin and Richie Cole), pianists who have been strongly touched by Bud Powell (Barry Harris, Sonny Clark, and Tommy Flanagan), or vocalese singers such as Jon Hendricks and Annie Ross. A few of the musicians who continued evolving beyond Bop have only part of their careers discussed (including Sonny Rollins and Art Pepper) and will be dealt with further in other books. And a few of the choices are bound to be considered a little controversial, particularly the inclusion of singers Betty Carter, Mark Murphy, Sheila Jordan, and Kurt Elling, all of whom grew beyond Bop but seem to fit best in this genre.

As has been stated elsewhere, the very best jazz musicians and singers do not perform in a rigid style but instead express themselves in an individual manner. Charlie Parker did not play "Bebop," he played Charlie Parker music. Be that as it may, this Bebop book would not be complete without these important later contributors to Bop who have kept the "message from Bird" alive and relevant up to the present time.

GREG ABATE

b. May 31, 1947, Fall River, MA

A hero of the New England jazz scene and a veteran Bebop soloist, Greg Abate did not begin recording as a leader until 1991, when he was 44, but he has made up for lost time ever since. Abate's most notable associations prior to the 1990s were with the Ray Charles Orchestra in the 1970s (where he succeeded David "Fathead" Newman) and with the Artie Shaw Orchestra (led by clarinetist Dick Johnson) during 1985–87. Abate is best known for his alto playing (he considers Charlie Parker, Paul Desmond, and Phil Woods to be his main influences), but he is also a strong soloist on tenor, flute, and soprano. Since 1991, Greg Abate has recorded a consistently satisfying string of Bebop records as a leader for Seaside, Candid, and Blue Chip Jazz.

8   *Bop City—Live at Birdland! / July 28, 1991 / Candid 79513*

7   *My Buddy / Dec. 13, 1994 / Seaside 132*

8   *Broken Dreams / Feb. 15, 1996 / Seaside 144*

9   *Bop Lives! / May 6, 1996 / Blue Chip Jazz 4001*

8   *Happy Samba / Dec. 3-4, 1997 / Blue Chip Jazz 4004*

Greg Abate's recordings as a leader have been quite consistent, featuring swinging straight-ahead jazz but mostly new and fresh material rather than Bebop standards. *Bop City* has Abate (on alto, soprano, tenor, and flute) playing seven of his originals, two tunes by trombonist Hal Crook, and three well-known songs, assisted by an all-star rhythm section (pianist James Williams, bassist Rufus Reid, and drummer Kenny Washington). *My Buddy* features Abate joined by some fine local players (most prominent is pianist Mac Chrupcala, trumpeter Paul Fontaine, and, on three cuts, singer Donna Byrne). Although veteran altoist Jack Stevens contributed seven of the 13 cuts and Abate brought in three, the music is mostly very much in the classic Bebop tradition, even though the leader's soprano on "Expresso" is quite modern.

Broken Dreams is a quartet/quintet date with pianist Chrupcala, bassist Dave Zinno, drummer John Anter, and (on four of the ten numbers) tenor saxophonist Frank Tiberi. This time around the repertoire is split between originals (by Abate, Chrupcala, and Stevens) and vintage tunes, including "Boulevard of Broken Dreams," "After You've Gone," and "It Had to Be You." It seems strange that a CD called *Bop Lives!* does not have any Bebop standards (the closest is "Basting the Bird," which is based on "Confirmation," Thelonious Monk's haunting "Ask Me Now," and Hank Mobley's "This I Dig of You"), but Abate's solos (he sticks here exclusively to alto) are classic Bebop; he is assisted by pianist Kenny Barron, bassist Rufus Reid, drummer Ben Riley, and (on five of the nine numbers) trumpeter Claudio Roditi. *Happy Samba* lives up to its name, for the 11 obscurities (eight by Abate, who is heard mostly on alto, with three appearances on soprano and one on flute) feature the leader backed by Brazilian rhythms provided by pianist Mark Soskin, bassist Harvie Swartz, drummer Ed Uribe, and Wilson Corniel on conga.

Greg Abate, who deserves to be much better known, has yet to record an unworthy CD.

KARRIN ALLYSON

b. Great Bend, KS

Karrin Allyson, who has recorded for the Concord label steadily since 1992, has the ability to scat sing with the very best yet can also dig into a ballad such as "Everything Must Change" and interpret the words with great sensitivity. Allyson grew up in Omaha, Nebraska, and the San Francisco Bay area. She graduated from the University of Nebraska in 1987 and then picked up important experience performing jazz regularly at a Minneapolis nightclub. After moving to Kansas City in the late 1980s, she quickly became an important part of the local scene. Since signing with Concord, Allyson (who also plays piano now and then) has been gradually becoming much better known, appearing at major festivals and touring Europe several times while using a nucleus of Kansas City musicians in her group. Karrin Allyson, who occasionally sings in Portuguese, French, or Italian, is a well-rounded vocalist whose ability to improvise in Boppish settings makes her one of the most consistently exciting Bop-oriented jazz singers of today.

8   *I Didn't Know About You / 1992 / Concord Jazz 4543*

9   *Sweet Home Cookin' / June 9-10, 1993 / Concord Jazz 4593*

9   *Azure-Te / Nov. 14-16, 1994 / Concord Jazz 4641*

10   *Collage / Jan. 5-10, 1996 / Concord Jazz 4709*

8   *Daydream / Jan. 5, 1996–Apr. 25, 1997 / Concord Jazz*

7 *From Paris to Rio / Mar. 15-28, 1999 / Concord Jazz 4865*

From the opening song of her first CD ("Nature Boy"), it was obvious that Karin Allyson was a bright new talent. Each of her six Concord releases has its classic moments. *I Didn't Know About You* includes a duet with drummer Todd Strait on "What a Little Moonlight Can Do," a rapid "'S Wonderful," and a samba version of "It Might As Well Be Spring." *Sweet Home Cookin'* (which features such players as pianist Alan Broadbent, trumpeter Randy Sandke, and tenor saxophonist Bob Cooper) is highlighted by highly appealing versions of "One Note Samba," "I Cover the Waterfront," "Social Call," and "Dindi." *Azure-Te* (which features guest spots for violinist Claude Williams and flugelhornist Mike Metheny, as does *Collage*) is notable for "How High the Moon/Ornithology," a touching "Blame It on My Youth," "Yardbird Suite," and "Some Other Time."

Collage is a classic. Karrin Allyson is heard in prime form on a variety of superior material, the frameworks and arrangements are colorful, and there is a lot of variety to this outing. Among the selections that Allyson uplifts are "It Could Happen to You/Fried Bananas," "Autumn Leaves" (which she sings in French), Clifford Brown's "Joy Spring," "Ask Me Now," and "Cherokee." *Daydream* (which has spots for trumpeter Randy Brecker and vibraphonist Gary Burton) has more of an emphasis on ballads than usual, including a haunting version of "Everything Must Change" (which is introspective yet emotional), "My Foolish Heart," "Daydream," and a happy "So Danco Samba" that perfectly fits Allyson's voice. *From Paris to Rio* is a definite change of pace, for on the great majority of the songs, Karrin Allyson sings in French, Portuguese, or Italian! In most cases, the emphasis is on the lyrics and the melodies rather than on scatting or improvising, but the infectious and good-natured date (which features Gil Goldstein on accordion along with the singer's usual Kansas City crew) is still quite worthwhile; among the songs are "O Pato," "O Barquinho," "Parisian Thoroughfare," and "That Day."

GABE BALTAZAR

b. Nov. 1, 1929, Hilo, HI

One of the last great players to emerge from Stan Kenton's orchestra, Gabe Baltazar has long been a hard-charging altoist with an appealing sound and the ability to keep Charlie Parker's innovations fresh decades after Bird's death. A resident of Hawaii, Baltazar first spent time on the mainland of the United States in the mid-1950s. He recorded with Paul Togawa (1957), was with the Lighthouse All-Stars in 1960 (that version of the band never recorded), and then spent an important five years as part of Kenton's orchestra (1960–65), being well featured on quite a few of the bandleader's records.

After leaving Kenton, Baltazar worked with Terry Gibbs, recorded with the orchestras of Gil Fuller and Oliver Nelson, and freelanced, including with Shelly Manne, pianist Victor Feldman, and trumpeter Don Ellis. He returned to Hawaii in 1969, mostly playing locally but visiting the mainland now and then, including for a 1979 album in which he was "presented" by Stan Kenton. After appearing at the 50th anniversary celebration of Stan Kenton's orchestra in 1991, Gabe Baltazar started spending more time in California. He has since recorded some very rewarding dates for V.S.O.P. and Fresh Sound, including debuting an original he is certainly entitled to play, "Birdology 101!"

9 *Back in Action / Oct. 18-19, 1992 / V.S.O.P. 85*
10 *Birdology / Oct. 24-25, 1992 / Fresh Sound 5001*

Gabe Baltazar cut two exciting quartet dates within a week in October 1992, and both made observers wonder why he has not recorded much more often. *Back in Action,* which finds Baltazar joined by pianist Tom Ranier, bassist Richard Simon, and drummer Steve Houghton, alternates originals and standards with highlights including Boppish transformations of "Is It True What They Say About Dixie" and "The Birth of the Blues." *Birdology* is even better, matching Baltazar (who plays clarinet on "Memories of You") with pianist Frank Strazzeri, bassist Andy Simpkins, and drummer Nick Martinis. The title cut fuses together a lot of Charlie Parker licks to form an original song, and other memorable performances include "If There Is Someone Lovelier Than You," "One Morning in May," and "Autumn Nocturne." Highly recommended.

LPS TO SEARCH FOR

Stan Kenton Presents Gabe Baltazar (Creative World 3005) was the altoist's long-overdue debut as a leader. Baltazar is heard in 1979 backed by a big band and strings arranged by Don Menza, performing such numbers as "What's New," "Take the 'A' Train," and Menza's "Spanish Boots."

Gabe Baltazar is one of the main soloists in the 1962 special *Stan Kenton* (Vintage Jazz Classics 2007).

BEBOP & BEYOND

Bebop & Beyond is a part-time band that is both a repertory group (paying tributes to jazz greats) and a creative jazz outfit that features creative new solos. Its leader, Mel Martin (b. June 7, 1942, Sacramento, CA), first played professionally as a saxophonist when he was 14. He attended San Francisco State University but dropped out to work as a musician and has been based in the San Francisco Bay Area ever since. Martin worked in the studios, performed with a variety of rock groups (including Santana, Azteca, Cold Blood, Boz Scaggs, and Van Morrison), and had a fusion band during 1977–78 called Listen; steel drum master Andy Narell was a sideman and two albums for the Inner City label resulted. In 1983 Martin made a duet album with guitarist Randy Vincent for Catero and then formed his first version of Bebop & Beyond.

Since then, Bebop & Beyond has recorded tribute projects to Thelonious Monk and Dizzy Gillespie (Dizzy himself played on the latter) and featured such players as Vincent, pianist George Cables, trumpeter Warren Gale, drummer Eddie Marshall, tenor saxophonist Joe Henderson, altoist John Handy, Howard Johnson on tuba and baritone, and Martin on alto, tenor, and soprano. In recent times Bebop & Beyond has also paid tribute to Charles Mingus. Mel Martin on his own also recorded an album of Benny Carter compositions.

9   *Plays Thelonious Monk / Feb. 13 + 15, 1990 / Bluemoon 79154*
7   *Plays Dizzy Gillespie / May 23–24, 1991 / Bluemoon 79170*

Bebop and Beyond's Monk project, which resulted in colorful renditions of nine of Thelonious Monk's tunes, is a gem. Martin (on tenor, soprano, and flute) is joined by Warren Gale, Randy Vincent, bassist Jeff Chambers, either Donald Bailey or Eddie Marshall on drums, and three guests on some tracks: George Cables, Joe Henderson, and Howard Johnson. Among the songs uplifted are "San Francisco Holiday," "Brilliant Corners," and "Gallop's Gallop"; both "Think of One" and "Who Knows" has the group performing transcriptions of Monk's original piano solos. *Plays Dizzy Gillespie,* from the following year, has the core band (Martin, Vincent, Gale, Cables, Chambers, and Bailey or Vince Lateano on drums) joined by the great trumpeter himself. Unfortunately, by 1991 (in what would be his final studio recording), Gillespie was way past his prime, but he does get off a couple of decent solos along with a vocal on "I Waited For You." Martin (heard on soprano, alto, tenor, and flute), Vincent, and Gale are the solo stars on such numbers as "Wheatleigh Hall," "That's Earl, Brother," and Martin's "Rhythm Man."

LPS TO SEARCH FOR

Bebop and Beyond (Concord Jazz 244), the group's debut album, was recorded in 1984 and features a sextet with Martin, Gale, Cable, Marshall, bassist Frank Tusa, and altoist John Handy. They perform four group tunes, Tadd Dameron's "On a Misty Night," Monk's "Evidence," and "Monk's Mood." Martin (on tenor and soprano) and Handy work well off each other throughout this enjoyable effort.

EDDIE BERT
b. May 16, 1922, Yonkers, NY

Considering how long and productive a career he has had, it is surprising that trombonist Eddie Bert is so little known by the jazz public. Inspired originally by trombonists Benny Morton, Miff Mole, and Trummy Young (all of whom gave him lessons), Bert became a member of the Sam Donahue Orchestra in 1940. In 1941 he joined Red Norvo, with whom he recorded his first solo the following year ("Jersey Bounce"). Bert was with the Charlie Barnet (1943) and Woody Herman orchestras, played at a notable Town Hall concert in 1944 with Red Norvo, and then went into the military. After his discharge, he worked with Herbie Fields, Stan Kenton (1947–48), Benny Goodman's Bebop Orchestra (1948–49), Herman and Kenton again (1950–51), Ray McKinley, Les Elgart, and Kenton a third time (1955). Bert's fluent style easily made the transition between swing and Bop, and he was always technically skilled enough to fit in well with studio bands.

During 1952–55, Bert recorded as a leader for Discovery, Savoy, Jazztone, and Trans-World, using such notable sidemen as Sal Salvador, Duke Jordan, Hank Jones, Kenny Clarke, guitarist Joe Puma, and Oscar Pettiford. Among Bert's more notable associations since then have been projects with Charles Mingus (1955), Benny Goodman (1957), and Tom Talbert, the Miles Davis-Gil Evans recordings, Thelonious Monk (his big band concerts of 1959 and 1963), Elliot Lawrence, Chubby Jackson, the Dick Cavett television band under the direction of drummer Bobby Rosengarden (1968–72), the Thad Jones-Mel Lewis Orchestra, the New York Jazz Repertory Orchestra, Lionel Hampton, the American Jazz Orchestra, Loren Schoenberg's big band, and T. S. Monk (1997). Eddie Bert recorded as a leader during the past 25 years for the Danish Backbone label, Molshajala, Mothlight, and Fresh Sound, all obscure but worthy releases from an ageless if largely unknown Bebop survivor.

8 *Encore / Sept. 1, 1955 / Savoy 0229*
9 *Walk on the Roots / Aug. 2, 1985–Aug. 9, 1989 / Mothlight 3805*
8 *A Eddie Bert-Gabe Baltazar Quintet / Feb. 6-7, 1999 / Woofy 92*

The main fault with *Encore* is the brevity of the seven-song program (under 35 minutes), but the music is excellent. Bert is heard as the lead voice in a quartet with guitarist Joe Puma, bassist Clyde Lombardi, and Kenny Clarke and in a quintet with tenor saxophonist J. R. Monterose, Hank Jones, Lombardi, and Clarke. The tunes (all originals by Bert or Puma) are excellent examples of cool-toned Bop and find Bert in fine form.

Moving ahead 30 years, *Walk on the Roots* showcases Bert on duets from 1985 with bassist Stephen Roane and in trios from four years later with Roane and guitarist James Chirillo. Bert's trombone playing, still in its prime, was largely unchanged from the 1950s; he was a Bebopper touched a bit by J. J. Johnson but with his own sound. Among the more interesting selections on this set (which has a few standards mixed in with the originals) are "Little Train," Benny Golson's "Out of the Past," "Bongo Bop," "Social Call," "Foolin' Myself," and an eccentric version of "Lazy Butterfly." Bert's collaboration with Gabe Baltazar has an appealing trombone-alto frontline with backing by pianist Ross Tompkins, bassist Richard Simon, and drummer Paul Kreibich. Essentially a jam session (with fairly long versions of "Jumpin' with Symphony Sid," "All the Things You Are," Al Cohn's "P Town," and "Body and Soul" among the nine numbers), the superior song selection, the fairly concise solos, and the excellent playing uplift the set. Bert (who certainly does not sound as if he was 76 at the time) takes a surprise vocal on "He Ain't Got Rhythm," which he had recorded previously in the mid-1950s.

LPS TO SEARCH FOR

Kaleidoscope (Savoy 1186) features Bert with two quintets during 1953–54, a set with Duke Jordan and Sal Salvador, and one in which he shares the frontline with altoist Vinnie Dean. Bert first vocal version of "He Ain't Got Rhythm" is here, and he plays quite fluently on such tunes as "Love Me or Leave Me," "Broadway," and "Cherokee."

CLIFFORD BROWN

b. Oct. 30, 1930, Wilmington, DE, d. June 27, 1956, Bedford, PA

The death of Clifford Brown, one of the greatest jazz trumpeters of all time, in a car accident along with pianist Richie Powell and Powell's wife (who was driving in a rainstorm), was possibly the greatest tragedy in jazz history. Brownie had already amassed a substantial recorded legacy, but the trumpeter (who was ironically a clean-living person) was still only 25 and surely would have had decades of accomplishments in the future.

Clifford Brown started playing trumpet when he was 13 and by 1948 was performing in Philadelphia-area clubs. He was strongly influenced by Fats Navarro, who, along with Charlie Parker and Dizzy Gillespie, encouraged the young trumpeter. Brown went to Maryland State University for a year before a serious car accident in June 1950 knocked him out of action until mid-1951. He made his recording debut in 1952 with Chris Powell's Blue Flames (a rhythm and blues band) but really began to gain attention in 1953. At 22 he was considered the brightest new trumpeter in jazz and a natural successor to Fats Navarro (who had died in 1950 at the age of 26, just 14 months older than Brown would be at his own death). Brownie worked and recorded with Tadd Dameron and during the second half of 1953 was with Lionel Hampton's orchestra, touring Europe. Although he did not make any studio recordings with Hamp, while overseas Brown led a series of impressive recordings of his own with a quartet, a sextet, and a big band.

In early 1954, Brown was featured on a memorable engagement at Birdland with a quintet also including drummer Art Blakey (the leader), Lou Donaldson, pianist Horace Silver, and Curly Russell, playing quite brilliantly. Brownie came out to Los Angeles, where he joined forces with Max Roach, forming a quintet that at first consisted of Teddy Edwards, pianist Carl Perkins, and bassist George Bledsoe. Brownie starred at several recorded jam sessions while in L.A., and by the middle of the year the Brown/Roach Quintet had stabilized, with Harold Land on tenor, Richie Powell, and bassist George Morrow. The band can be considered either the last classic Bebop group or one of the first important hard Bop units. It would be a perfect vehicle for Brownie's playing for the last two years of his life, recording regularly for Emarcy.

Brown, who wrote such songs as "Joy Spring" and "Daahoud," continued to grow in fame and power during 1955, and his tone became even more beautiful. By early 1956 Sonny Rollins was in Land's place and the super group had limitless potential. Clifford Brown's playing was caught on record the very last night of his life, as he played "Walkin'," "A Night in Tunisia," and a stunning version of "Donna Lee" at a Philadelphia jam session. But then came the car accident that ended the career of one of the all-time greats.

Clifford Brown's influence on the trumpeters that came after him has been dominant, particularly affecting the sound and styles of such major soloists as Lee Morgan, Freddie Hubbard, and Woody Shaw, all of whom had a lot of Brownie in their playing.

* ***The Complete Blue Note and Pacific Jazz Recordings / June 9, 1953–Aug. 13, 1954 / Pacific Jazz 34195***
8 ***Clifford Brown Memorial / June 11, 1953 + Sept. 15, 1953 / Original Jazz Classics 017***
7 ***Clifford Brown Big Band in Paris / Sept. 28, 1953–Oct. 11, 1953 / Original Jazz Classics 359***
8 ***The Clifford Brown Sextet in Paris / Sept. 29, 1953–Oct, 8, 1953 / Original Jazz Classics 358***
7 ***The Complete Paris Sessions Vol. 1 / Sept. 28–29, 1953 / Vogue 45728***
9 ***The Clifford Brown Quartet in Paris / Oct. 15, 1953 / Original Jazz Classics 357***

Clifford Brown gained the attention of the jazz world during 1953–54 before he started teaming up with Max Roach. The four-CD *The Complete Blue Note and Pacific Jazz Recordings* shows why he was rated so highly. Brownie is heard in a quintet led by Lou Donaldson (which also includes Elmo Hope, Percy Heath, and drummer Philly Joe Jones), with J. J. Johnson's Sextet (also comprised of Jimmy Heath, John Lewis, Percy Heath, and Kenny Clarke), and heading his own similar group (with altoist Gigi Gryce, tenor saxophonist Charlie Rouse, Lewis, Heath, and Art Blakey). In addition, Brown is the main soloist with a West Coast septet, playing the arrangements of Jack Montrose. The final two CDs of the box has all of the music from a marathon session

at Birdland with Lou Donaldson, Horace Silver, Curly Russell, and Blakey. This classic four-CD set has many high points, including Hope's "De-Dah," "Brownie Speaks," "Brownie Eyes," "Cherokee," "Turnpike," "Get Happy," "Daahoud," "Joy Spring," and "Wee Dot."

Clifford Brown Memorial combines two separate dates. Brown is heard as the key soloist with a nonet led by Tadd Dameron (and also including Gigi Gryce and tenor saxophonist Benny Golson) and in a looser setting in Sweden with the Swedish All-Stars (including altoist Arne Domnerus, baritonist Lars Gullin, and fellow Hampton trumpeter Art Farmer); among the more memorable numbers are "Philly J.J.," "Dial 'B' for Beauty," and "Stockholm Sweetnin'." While in Paris with Lionel Hampton's orchestra, Brownie was one of several sidemen who disobeyed Hamp's odd order not to record (even Hampton made a few dates). Many of Brown's sessions from this period featured the alto and the writing of Gigi Gryce. *Big Band in Paris* has a variety of odds and ends, with the better tracks being the nearly eight-minute-long "Chez Moi" and two takes apiece of "Brownskins" and "Keeping Up with Jonesy." Brown's work with Gryce in a sextet (in which they are joined by a French rhythm section consisting of pianist Henri Renaud, guitarist Jimmy Gourley, Pierre Michelot, and drummer Jean-Louis Viale) is on a high level, including such numbers as "All the Things You Are," "I Cover the Waterfront," and "Minority." *The Complete Paris Sessions, Vol. 1* was the first step in reissuing the big band and sextet material complete and in chronological order, and it includes "Brown Skins," "Keeping Up with Jonesy," and half of the sextet selections, but we are still waiting for Vol. 2!

The Clifford Brown Quartet in Paris has just six selections plus six alternate takes, but the playing by Brownie (who is backed by Renaud, Michelot, and drummer Benny Bennett) is on such a high level that the repetition holds one's interest. The trumpeter's renditions of "I Can Dream, Can't I," "The Song Is You," and "You're a Lucky Guy" are memorable, but the gem of the date is "It Might As Well Be Spring"; pity that there are no alternate takes of that one!

* ***The Complete Emarcy Recordings / Aug. 2, 1954–Feb. 25, 1956 / Emarcy 838 306***
9 ***Brown and Roach, Inc. / Aug. 2–6, 1954 / Emarcy 814 644***
9 ***Jordu / Aug. 2, 1954–Feb. 25, 1955 / Emarcy 814 645***
6 ***More Study in Brown / Aug. 3, 1954–Feb. 16, 1956 / Emarcy 814 637***

One of the finest jazz trumpeters of all time, Clifford Brown strongly
influenced most trumpeters who emerged after his 1956 death.

7 *Clifford Brown with Strings / Jan. 18–20, 1955 / Emarcy 814 642*

8 *A Study in Brown / Feb. 23–25, 1955 / Emarcy 814 646*

9 *At Basin Street / Jan. 4, 1956–Feb. 17, 1956 / Emarcy 814 648*

10 *The Beginning and the End / Mar. 21, 1952 + June 25, 1956 / Columbia/Legacy 66491*

The ten-CD *The Complete Emarcy Recordings* easily exhausts all superlatives and covers all of Brownie's work for the label, including every alternate take: all of the studio sides by the Brown/Roach Quintet (including the later dates with Sonny Rollins), Clifford's collaborations with Helen Merrill, Sarah Vaughan, and Dinah Washington (the last in an extensive jam session), heated jams with all-star groups, and the trumpeter's date with strings. This music belongs in every serious jazz collection.

But since the box will probably become increasingly difficult to find, and because it is not inexpensive, some listeners may be satisfied with a few of the individual sets instead. The Brown-Roach-Land-Powell-Morrow Quintet is featured on *Brown and Roach, Inc.* (which includes exciting versions of "Stompin' at the Savoy," "I Get a Kick Out of You," and a Brown showcase on "Ghost of a Chance"), *Jordu* has a memorable "Parisian Thoroughfare," "The Blues Walk," and famous Brown solos on "Daahoud" and "Joy Spring," and *More Study in Brown* mostly features alternate takes and previously unreleased material, including a version of "I'll Remember April" with Sonny Rollins.

Clifford Brown with Strings shows off the beautiful tone of the trumpeter on such tunes as "Portrait of Jenny," "Memories of You," and "Stardust." However, the dull Neal Hefti arrangements and the lack of any mood or tempo variation makes this set (considered a classic by some) recommended for selective tastes only. The last studio album by the original Brown/Roach Quintet, *A Study in Brown,* is most notable for a heated "Cherokee," "Sandu," and "Take the 'A' Train." The one official studio record of the quintet with Sonny Rollins resulted in *At Basin Street.* The near-miraculous renditions of "What Is This Thing Called Love" and "I'll Remember April" show off the tremendous potential of this super group.

The Beginning and the End is extraordinary in both a musical way and a historic way. Brown's first two recordings (brief versions of "I Come from Jamaica" and "Ida Red" with Chris Powell's Blue Flames in 1952) are here, as are the three songs that he played during his last night on earth. Performing in Philadelphia with pianist Sam Dockery, bassist Ace Tesone, drummer Ellis Tollin, and tenors Ziggy Vines (just on "Walkin'") and Billy Root (on "Walkin'" and "A Night in Tunisia"), Clifford Brown is heard throughout in miraculous form. He stretches out on "Walkin'," comes up with ideas on "A Night in Tunisia" that are much different than Dizzy Gillespie's, and races through a rapid quartet version of "Donna Lee." Brownie was even captured saying goodbye to the audience before he left on the fateful trip, definitely exiting on top.

LPS TO SEARCH FOR

The Best of Max Roach and Clifford Brown in Concert (GNP/Crescendo 18), from 1954, has two four-song dates that were the beginning of the Brown/Roach Quintet. The first numbers (with Teddy Edwards, Carl Perkins, and George Bledsoe) include "Sunset Eyes" and "All God's Chillun Got Rhythm," while the August 30 session with Land, Powell, and Morrow includes "I Get a Kick Out of You" and "Jordu." The poorly recorded double-LP *Live at the Bee Hive* (Columbia 35965), much of which sounds like a series of trumpet-drums duets (!), is a jam session in Chicago that has Sonny Rollins's first documented appearances with the group. *Pure Genius Volume One* (Elektra Musician 60026) is better although still not of studio quality. It is an additional album of Rollins in 1956 with the quintet, jamming on five numbers, including "I'll Remember April" and "Daahoud." There never was a second volume!

FILMS

Miraculously, more than 40 years after his death, the first discovered film of Clifford Brown was found, an episode of a Soupy Sales variety show from 1955 that has Brownie playing two numbers ("Memories of You" and "Indiana") with a rhythm section and saying a few words about an upcoming gig.

CONTE CANDOLI
b. July 12, 1927, Mishawaka, IN

One of the great Bebop trumpeters, Conte Candoli tends to get overlooked in jazz history books because he has spent much of his professional life in Los Angeles. The younger brother of trumpeter Pete Candoli (who made his biggest impression with Woody Herman's First Herd during 1944–46 before becoming primarily a studio musician), Conte (born Secondo Candoli) began playing jobs in South Bend, Indiana, as a teenager. He played with Woody Herman during summer vacation for the first time when he was just 16, and he was with Herman's First Herd during January–September 1945 before going into the Army. After his release, Candoli was a member of the Chubby Jackson Sextet (1947–48), touring Scandinavia. The trumpeter's other early jobs included periods with Stan Kenton (1948), Charlie Ventura (1949), Herman (1950), Charlie Barnet (1951), and most significantly a second stint with Kenton (1951–53). After freelancing in Chicago, in 1954 Candoli settled in Los Angeles, where during the remainder of the decade he was featured regularly with Howard Rumsey's Lighthouse All-Stars. In addition to playing in the studios and in spontaneous Bop-oriented groups, Candoli was with the Terry Gibbs Dream Band, Gerry Mulligan's Concert Jazz Band (1960–61), and Shelly Manne's Quintet, guesting with Stan Kenton's Neophonic Orchestra. Candoli has worked extensively on TV (including being with the *Tonight Show* band throughout the 1970s and much of the '80s) and with Supersax, Louie Bellson, his own combos, the reunited Lighthouse All-Stars of the 1980s (led by Shorty Rogers), and occasionally, with Pete in the Candoli Brothers.

Although he has recorded more often as a leader in recent times, Conte Candoli (who was offered a job with Charlie Parker in 1955 right before the altoist's death made that impossible) is still underrated as a Bebop trumpeter.

7   *Powerhouse Trumpet / July 26, 1955 / Bethlehem / Avenue Jazz 75826*
8   *Conte Candoli Quartet / June 1957 / V.S.O.P. 43*
8   *Sweet Simon / May 20-21, 1991 / Best Recordings 92101*

Conte Candoli led seven albums during 1954–60, of which *Powerhouse Trumpet* was his second. A fairly typical mid-1950s Bebop date, the outing matches Candoli with tenor saxophonist Bill Holman, Lou Levy, bassist Leroy Vinnegar, and drummer Lawrence Marable. Holman and Candoli contributed two songs apiece (including Conte's "Groovin' Higher," which is based on "Groovin' High") and they also perform three jazz standards. Nothing too unusual happens and the playing time is brief, but the music is swinging and satisfying. *Conte Candoli Quartet* has Candoli as the only horn in a group with pianist Vince Guaraldi, bassist Monty Budwig, and drummer Stan Levey. The repertoire (three rarely played standards, originals by Al Cohn, drummer Osie Johnson, and Pete Candoli plus Conte's "Mambo Blues") is fresh and the trumpeter's playing is consistently inspired.

Despite being continually active, Conte Candoli led only one record date during 1961–84. Fortunately the 1990s resulted in much more documentation. *Sweet Simon,* from 1991, teams the trumpeter with Pete Christlieb (a perfect partner in the frontline), pianist Frank Strazzeri, Monty Budwig, and Ralph Penland or Roy McCurdy on drums. Candoli sounds creative and swinging on such songs as Frank Rosolino's "Blue Daniel," "Woody 'n You," "I Should Care," and his own "Sweet Simon." The obscure JHM release is a quartet date with pianist Joe Haider, bassist Isla Eckinger, and drummer Wolfgang Haffner that has the feel of a jam session. Candoli expertly jams his way through seven Bebop standards, including "What Is This Thing Called Love?" "Confirmation," and "Tin Tin Deo," showing that he is a master of the style. Age 69 in 1996, Conte Candoli recorded his best all-around date as a leader for Fresh Sound, a quartet session with pianist Jan Lundgren, bassist Chuck Berghofer, and drummer Joe LaBarbera. On such songs as "Softly, As In a Morning Sunrise," "Star Eyes," "I'll Remember April," and his own "I Dig Fig," Conte Candoli shows how strong a player he has been during the past 50 years despite his lack of recognition beyond the city limits of Los Angeles! The more recent Woofy date is also quite successful, teaming Candoli with altoist Med

Flory (the founder of Supersax), Frank Strazzeri, bassist Tom Warrington, and drummer Dick Berk on "Count's Blues" and six standards, including "Confirmation," Jobim's "Corcovado" (mistakenly listed as being by Laurindo Almeida), and "It's You or No One." This CD is particularly valuable for its rare opportunity to hear Flory stretch out, although Candoli is also heard throughout in excellent form.

LPS TO SEARCH FOR

Conversations (RCA 1509), which Candoli co-led with trombonist Frank Rosolino, is a 1973 album in which they are joined by a fine Italian rhythm section that includes pianist Franco D'Andrea. The title track features the trombonist's scat singing, and the two horns have a ballad feature apiece and perform a pair of Rosolino's originals plus "Star Eyes." *Old Acquaintance* (Pausa 718) is a particularly exciting date in which Candoli is inspired by Phil Woods and a rhythm section comprising vibraphonist Charlie Shoemake, pianist Terry Trotter, Monty Budwig, and drummer Bill Goodwin; highlights include Bud Powell's "Wail," "Just You, Just Me," and Fats Navarro's "Nostalgia."

FILMS

Conte Candoli appears briefly in *Bell, Book and Candle* (1958).

BETTY CARTER

b. May 16, 1930, Flint, MI, d. Sept. 26, 1998, Brooklyn, NY

One of the most difficult parts of putting together this section is determining which significant jazz musicians and singers can be considered important primarily to Bebop and which performers fall into later styles. In the case of Betty Carter, she began singing in the Bebop tradition and then gradually extended the boundaries of Bop to the breaking point and beyond. An innovator throughout most of her career, Carter considered herself part of the Bop world and tended to dislike avant-garde jazz even though many of her more esoteric improvisations were as close to free jazz as to Bebop.

Born Lillie Mae Jones, she studied piano and starting in 1946 worked as a vocalist in Detroit, where she had an opportunity to sing with Charlie Parker. During 1948–51, Carter was with Lionel Hampton's orchestra, touring as Lor-

Arguably the most adventurous jazz singer (along with Mark Murphy) since 1970, Betty Carter was always proud of her roots in Bebop.

raine Carter. She was nicknamed Betty "Bebop" Carter by Hampton, a title that she disliked, although she ended up keeping the "Betty" part. After leaving Hampton, Carter freelanced around New York, was on King Pleasure's recording of "Red Top," and made her first record date as a leader in 1956 with Gigi Gryce and Ray Bryant. Her early recordings are much more conventional than what would come but even during the 1950s Carter had something of her own to offer, and her singing was never entirely predictable. She recorded an album of duets with Ray Charles in 1961 that gave her a little bit of attention, but many years of struggle and obscurity still lay ahead. Her singing became freer and esoteric (years later she would record an album titled *It's Not About the Melody*), and she loved extremes of tempo (very slow ballads and rapid romps), often changing speeds

and moods at unexpected moments. Carter did not record at all during 1966–68, and it was ultimately up to her to start her own label (Bet-Car) in 1970 so her progress would be documented the way she wanted.

An underground legend for years, Betty Carter had such a strong reputation that, by the time she recorded a set of duets with veteran Carmen McRae in 1987, it was as an equal. She signed with Verve in 1988 and finally gained the recognition she deserved during her final decade. Carter became a constant in jazz polls, worked regularly, had her earlier recordings reissued, became extremely influential on other singers, and was almost as well known as a talent scout. Through the years her pianists included John Hicks, Mulgrew Miller, Benny Green, Stephen Scott, Jacky Terrasson, and Cyrus Chestnut, all of whom benefited from working with the dynamic and always chance-taking performer. Up until the time of her death in 1998, Betty Carter came to be known as arguably the most important jazz singer after 1970.

8   *Meet Betty Carter and Ray Bryant / May 13, 1955–Apr. 25, 1956 / Columbia/Legacy 64936*

9   *I Can't Help It / Feb. 1958–Aug. 30, 1960 / GRP/Impulse 114*

7   *'Round Midnight / Aug. 10, 1962–Jan. 15, 1963 / Atco 80453*

8   *Inside Betty Carter / Apr. 1964–May 26, 1965 / Capitol 89702*

Meet Betty Carter and Ray Bryant has the singer's recording debut as a leader, although she also can be heard on a few earlier isolated titles (including "Red Top" with King Pleasure). The first 11 selections on this CD feature Carter either with a big band arranged by Gigi Gryce or with pianist Ray Bryant in a quartet also including Jerome Richardson on flute. Among the more memorable selections are the definitive version of Gryce's "Social Call" (Jon Hendricks wrote the lyrics), "Let's Fall in Love," "Moonlight in Vermont," "I Could Write a Book," and "Tell Him I Said Hello." Also on this CD are eight instrumentals by the Bryant trio (with bassist Wendell Marshall and drummer Philly Joe Jones). *I Can't Help It* reissues in full Carter's next two albums, dates recorded originally for Peacock and ABC-Paramount. The former set has Carter joined by either a sextet or a tentet with such backup players as Kenny Dorham, trumpeter Ray Copeland, Gigi Gryce, and Jerome Richardson (on tenor, flute, and bass clarinet); the latter project is with an unidentified orchestra arranged by Richard Wess. There was definite evolution in Betty Carter's style during these years. Her voice was always distinctive, and now her phrasing was getting less predictable, even if these 24 selections are mostly very concise. Her "I Can't Help It" discusses her musical philosophy, and other highlights include "You're Getting to Be a Habit with Me," "You're Driving Me Crazy," "What a Little Moonlight Can Do," "I Don't Want to Set the World on Fire," and "Jazz (Ain't Nothin' But Soul)."

'Round Midnight (the first of her two albums with the same title) features Carter backed by orchestras arranged and conducted by either Claus Ogermann or Oliver Nelson. One can sense that, after the success of her duets with Ray Charles, the label was trying to make Carter into a major name. She performs such songs as "Heart and Soul," "When I Fall in Love," "The Good Life," and "Everybody's Somebody's Fool." However, this set (which includes two songs originally released as a single) failed to become a bestseller, and the singer's style was already becoming a bit too eccentric for the mass public. Betty Carter's early period on records concludes with *Inside Betty Carter*. The CD reissues her original brief eight-song session from 1964 (with pianist Harold Mabern, bassist Bob Cranshaw, and drummer Roy McCurdy) and adds seven previously unreleased numbers from 1965 with a rhythm section that is unknown other than guitarist Kenny Burrell. High points include "This Is Always," "Some Other Time," "Spring Can Really Hang You Up the Most," and "You're a Sweetheart."

8   *Finally / Dec. 6, 1969 / Roulette 795332*
      'Round Midnight / Dec. 6, 1969 / Roulette 95999

7   *Live at the Village Vanguard / May 16, 1970 / Verve 835 681*

7   *The Betty Carter Album / 1972–1973 / Verve 835 682*

9   *The Audience with Betty Carter / Dec. 6–8, 1979 / Verve 835 684*

8   *Whatever Happened to Love / Mar. 17, 1982 / Verve 835 683*

After four years off records, Betty Carter recorded enough material during a concert at Judson Hall on December 6, 1969, to fill up two albums. *Finally* and *'Round Midnight* have the adventurous singer joined by pianist Norman Simmons, bassist Lisle Atkinson, and drummer Al Harewood. The dates are full of wild chance-taking, with unusually fast and slow tempos often occurring. *Finally* has three spontaneous medleys (including one of "Body and Soul" and "Heart and Soul"), "Girl Talk," and "You're a Sweetheart" among the songs, while *'Round Midnight* includes "Every Time We Say Goodbye," "My Shining Hour," and "Surrey with the Fringe on Top" among the more memorable selections. Age 39 at the time, Betty Carter had found her style. Pity that it would take another couple of decades before the jazz world fully recognized her talents.

In 1970 Betty Carter recorded a set at the Village Vanguard for her new Betcar label, with the same rhythm section as on *Finally*. Among the tunes that she alters and swings are "I Didn't Know What Time It Was," "I Could Write a Book," and Randy Weston's "Berkshire Blues." For *The Betty Carter Album,* the singer is joined by Daniel Mixon or Onaje Allen Gumbs on piano, bassist Buster Williams, and Chip Lyles or Louis Hayes on drums. Carter sings six originals (including a remake of "I Can't Help It") plus four standards

("You're a Sweetheart" is memorable again). Betty Carter recorded only two albums during the 1977–87 period. *The Audience with Betty Carter,* originally a two-LP set, gives an excellent example of what her live shows were like during the era. Beginning with a remarkable 25-minute improvisation on "Sounds (Movin' On)," Carter, pianist John Hicks, bassist Curtis Lundy, and drummer Kenny Washington perform unusual versions of "The Trolley Song," "Everything I Have Is Yours," "I Could Write a Book," "My Favorite Things," and Carter's originals. She really tears into some of the material and the results are consistently unpredictable. *Whatever Happened to Love* mixes three of her songs with a lengthy version of the title cut and such unlikely numbers as "Cocktails for Two," "Goodbye," and "I Cry Alone." Carter is joined by pianist Khalid Moss, Curtis Lundy, drummer Lewis Nash, and (on a few numbers) an unidentified tenor saxophonist plus a string section conducted by David Amram.

> **9** *Look What I Got! / 1988 / Verve 835 661*
> **8** *Droppin' Things / May 25, 1990–June 7, 1990 / Verve 843 991*
> **8** *It's Not About the Melody / 1992 / Verve 314 513 870*
> **9** *Feed the Fire / Oct. 30, 1993 / Verve 314 523 600*
> **8** *I'm Yours, You're Mine / Jan. 24–25, 1996 / Verve 314 533 182*

After being signed by Verve in 1988, Betty Carter finally received the exposure that she deserved. Her five albums for the label are all rewarding and find her consistently stretching herself. *Look What I Got* has her joined by two different rhythm sections (Benny Green or Stephen Scott on piano, Michael Bowie or Ira Coleman on bass, and Winard Harper, Lewis Nash, or Troy Davis on drums) plus (on four numbers) tenor saxophonist Don Braden. In addition to "That Sunday, That Summer," "The Man I Love," "Imagination," and "The Good Life," Carter performs obscurities and originals, but the individual songs matter much less than what she does to them. On *Droppin' Things,* there are workouts with pianist Marc Cary, bassist Tarus Mateen, and drummer Gregory Hutchinson with four of the numbers adding tenor saxophonist Craig Handy and trumpeter Freddie Hubbard. In addition, Carter performs a medley of "Star Dust" and "Memories of You" as duets with Geri Allen. The title of *It's Not About the Melody* sums up Betty Carter's singing style, for even when performing a well-known standard, a stating of the theme is optional. On the CD, she utilizes a trio of

different rhythm sections (with Cyrus Chestnut, Mulgrew Miller, or John Hicks on piano, Ariel J. Roland, Christian McBride or Walter Booker on bass, and Clarence Penn, Lewis Nash, or Jeff "Tain" Watts on drums) plus, occasionally, Craig Handy for fairly concise but unpredictable flights. Do not expect these renditions of "I Should Care," "You Go to My Head," and "When It's Sleepy Time Down South" to sound like any other version!

Feed the Fire differs from Betty Carter's other Verve releases in that, instead of using a young rhythm section, she teams up with famous names: pianist Geri Allen, bassist Dave Holland, and drummer Jack DeJohnette. However, the fire is still very much present on such tunes as "Lover Man," "If I Should Lose You," and a 12-minute rendition of "Day Dream"; no one is allowed to coast! The last album by the singer to be released to date, *I'm Yours, You're Mine,* finds the 65-year-old still taking wild chances and pushing her group (which consists of tenor saxophonist Mark Shim, pianist Xavier Davis, Curtis Lundy or Matt Hughes on bass, drummer Gregory Hutchinson, and, on "September Song," trombonist Andre Hayward). Betty Carter never played it safe musically.

LPS TO SEARCH FOR

The one Betty Carter album not yet reissued on CD is 1976's *Now It's My Turn* (Roulette 5005). Carter and her trio (John Hicks, bassist Walter Booker, and an unidentified drummer) do remarkable things with such unlikely material as "Music Maestro Please," "Wagon Wheels," and "Most Gentlemen Don't Like Love."

PETE CHRISTLIEB
b. Feb. 16, 1945, Los Angeles, CA

A hard-charging tenor saxophonist with a warm tone, Pete Christlieb has been a major player behind the scenes in the Los Angeles area (often playing with big bands and in the studios) since the 1970s. His father, Don Christlieb, was a classical bassoonist. Pete started playing violin when he was seven, switching to tenor when he was 13. Starting in the mid-1960s, Christlieb has worked with the who's who of straightahead jazz in Los Angeles, including Chet Baker (1964), Woody Herman (1966), Louie Bellson (with whom he has played on an occasional basis since 1967), Doc Severinsen's Tonight Show Orchestra, the Capp-Pierce Juggernaut, Bob Florence's Limited Edition, Bill Holman's orchestra, bassist John Leitham, the Anthony Wilson Nonet, and countless others. Pete Christlieb had his own label (Bosco) in the 1980s and has headed dates for Warner Bros. (a set co-led with fellow tenor Warne Marsh), Criss Cross, Capri, Woofy and CARS.

8 *Conversations with Warne, Vol. 1 / Sept. 15, 1978 / Criss Cross 1043*
8 *Conversations with Warne, Vol. 2 / Sept. 15, 1978 / Criss Cross 1103*
8 *Mosaic / Feb. 16, 1990 / Capri 74026*
8 *The Pete Christlieb-Andy Martin Quintet / Apr. 4-5, 1998 / Woofy 83*
10 *For Heaven's Sake / 1999 / CARS 0040*

The first three CDs covered in this section were particularly special occasions for Pete Christlieb. Warne Marsh was one of his heroes. Shortly after Christlieb had an opportunity to meet and befriend him in 1978, the two tenors recorded a pair of albums' worth of material in one day. Assisted by bassist Jim Hughart and drummer Nick Ceroli, the co-leaders clearly inspired each other, with Christlieb doing his best to keep up with the older saxophonist while Marsh rose to the occasion. All 17 selections that resulted are "originals" by the two tenors that are based on the chord changes of standards. *Vol. 1* has eight numbers and *Vol. 2* adds five more plus alternate takes of four pieces included on the first disc. Both *Conversations with Warne* are equally rewarding. For *Mosaic*, Christlieb had the opportunity to play with tenor great Bob Cooper, who had encouraged him earlier in his career. The rhythm section (pianist Mike Wofford, bassist Chuck Berghofer, and drummer Donald Bailey) is featured on "The Late, Late Show," Cooper has "Come Sunday" as his feature, and the other six songs (which include "Shaw 'Nuff," "Limehouse Blues," and "Rain") contrast Christlieb's hard tone with the cooler sound of Coop. Enjoyable music. The Woofy date is very much a jam session as the great tenor, trombonist Andy Martin, pianist Terry Trotter, bassist Jim Hughart, and drummer Dick Berk run through seven standards, including lengthy versions of "Just Friends," "What Is This Thing Called Love," and "Speak Low." Christlieb has no problem eating up the chord changes, Martin (who is developing into a major soloist) is an able foil, and the rhythm section swings away.

For Heaven's Sake is a particularly well-conceived effort. The personnel and instrumentation change a bit on each selection, and there are arrangements by Bill Holman, Johnny Mandel, John Bainbridge, Lou Levy, Tom Rainier, Jim Hughart, and Edward Karam. The sidemen include Conte Candoli, Andy Martin, Tom Ranier on piano, organ, and clarinet, Lou Levy, and guitarist Anthony Wilson. However, Christlieb is generally the lead voice, including on such numbers as "I Won't Dance," "For Heaven's Sake" (which has the tenor backed by six voices), the memorable "Capriole" (one of several numbers that includes a woodwind section), "Pernod," and a medium-tempo "My Ideal." Taken as a whole, this is Pete Christlieb's definitive recording to date and a real gem.

LPS TO SEARCH FOR

Apogee (Warner Bros. 3236), which was produced by the co-leaders of Steely Dan (Walter Becker and Donald Fagen), received a lot of attention in 1979 when it was released, teaming together Christlieb and Marsh (with backup by Lou Levy, Jim Hughart, and Nick Ceroli) on both standards ("Donna Lee" and "I'm Old Fashioned") and obscurities. Warner Bros. was not recording much jazz during that era, so this date had a bit of publicity before being allowed to drop out of sight! Also difficult to find but worth the search are Christlieb's projects for his Bosco label, including 1981's *Self Portrait* (Bosco 1) and *Going My Way* (Bosco 2). While the latter is a quartet date with guests (Donald Bailey on harmonica and Michael Melvoin's organ), the former features Pete with some of his favorite players in the L. A. area at the time, including Marsh, flugelhornist Steve Huffsteter, altoist Joe Roccisano, and even his father, Don Christlieb, on bassoon.

SONNY CLARK
b. July 21, 1931, Herminie, PA, d. Jan. 13, 1963, New York, NY

Sonny Clark was one of the best pianists to emerge in the 1950s who was directly influenced by Bud Powell. Although many of his records fit as much into Hard Bop as Bop, Clark's solo style would have been perfectly at home during the classic Bebop era.

Clark began his short professional life playing with Wardell Gray in Los Angeles and with tenor saxophonist Vido Musso and Oscar Pettiford in San Francisco. He made his recording debut with Teddy Charles and was a member of the Buddy DeFranco Quartet during 1953-56; all of their records were reissued by Mosaic in a limited-edition box set.

In Los Angeles during that era, Clark also freelanced, playing with Sonny Criss, Frank Rosolino, and the Lighthouse All-Stars, among others. He moved to New York and led a series of classic sets for Blue Note, including *Dial "S" for Sonny, Sonny's Crib* (which features John Coltrane in the cast), *Cool Struttin'*, and 1961's *Leapin' and Lopin'*. The pianist also recorded as a sideman with many top musicians, including Sonny Rollins, Dexter Gordon, guitarist Grant Green, trumpeter Lee Morgan, tenors Ike Quebec, Stanley Turrentine, and Hank Mobley, guitarist Jimmy Raney, and trombonist Curtis Fuller, working for a time as Dinah Washington's accompanist.

Unfortunately drug abuse fouled up and eventually greatly shortened Sonny Clark's life, for he died of a heart attack when he was just 31, cutting short a career that should have had many more decades to go.

6 *Oakland, 1955 / Jan. 13, 1955 / Uptown 27.40*
9 *Sonny's Crib / Sept. 1, 1957 / Blue Note 97367*
8 *Dial S for Sonny / Nov. 10, 1957 / Blue Note 56585*
8 *Sonny Clark Trio / Nov. 13, 1957 / Blue Note 46547*
9 *Cool Struttin' / Jan. 5, 1958 / Blue Note 46513*
7 *Standards / Nov. 16, 1958–Dec. 7, 1958 / Blue Note 21283*
8 *My Conception / Dec. 8, 1957 + Mar. 29, 1959 / Blue Note 22674*
7 *Sonny Clark Trio / Mar. 23, 1960 / Time 1044*
8 *Leapin' and Lopin' / Nov. 13, 1961 / Blue Note 84091*

With the exception of a live session from 1954, these nine CDs have every selection (including the alternate takes) from all of the dates led by Sonny Clark during his career. *Oakland, 1955* in 1995 released for the first time a live set featuring Clark in a trio with bassist Jerry Good and drummer Al Randall. The only minus to this valuable program is the so-so recording quality but one does get to hear Clark stretching out as the lead voice on a dozen selections including "There Will Never Be Another You," "Bags' Groove," "Night in Tunisia" and "Ow," sounding quite mature at age 23.

The recording dates given on the CD reissues of *Sonny's Crib* and *Dial S for Sonny* differ from the dates given on the previous issues, and now *Sonny's Crib* is in the position of being the pianist's debut set for Blue Note, where formerly it was considered the second one. Three alternate takes have been added to the original program, which gives listeners an opportunity to hear the often-remarkable sextet (which includes trumpeter Donald Byrd, trombonist Curtis Fuller, John Coltrane on tenor, bassist Paul Chambers, and drummer Art Taylor) at greater length. The title track and "News for Lulu" are Clark originals, while the other three pieces are standards: "With a Song in My Heart," "Speak Low," and "Come Rain or Come Shine." The frontline was one of the strongest ever on a Sonny Clark date. *Dial "S" for Sonny* is a bit cooler in sound (with trumpeter Art Farmer, Fuller, tenor saxophonist Hank Mobley, bassist Wilbur Ware, and drummer Louis Hayes joining Clark). The sextet performs four of Clark's underrated originals (plus an alternate take of "Bootin' It") and two standards. The music is spirited and relaxed yet often hard-swinging. *Sonny Clark Trio* (with Chambers and Philly Joe Jones) is pure Bebop as Clark romps through such numbers as Dizzy Gillespie's "Two Bass Hit," "Be-Bop," "Tadd's Delight," and "I'll Remember April"; three alternate takes expand the six-song program.

One of the most famous of Sonny Clark's Blue Note albums is *Cool Struttin'*, a quintet date with Farmer, altoist Jackie McLean, Chambers, and Jones. The LP had two Clark originals (the memorable title cut and "Blue Minor"), Miles Davis's "Sippin' at Bells," and the traditional "Deep Night." The CD adds two cuts (Clark's "Royal Flush" and "Lover") previously out only in Japan without lowering the high quality. Much less known is the music on *Standards* and *My Conception*, all of which was out before only in Japan or (in a few cases) on singles. *Standards* (with either Paul Chambers or Jymie Merritt on bass and drummer Wes Landers) has mostly shorter performances (all but two of the 14 selections are under five minutes), but Clark shows that he knew how to get the most out of every note. Keeping with the CD title, the great majority of the selections date from the swing era (including "Blues in the Night," "Somebody Loves Me," "I Cover the Waterfront," and "The Breeze and I"), but Clark's Boppish style was modern for the time. *My Conception* has six songs from a quintet date with Donald Byrd, Hank Mobley, Paul Chambers, and Art Blakey and three cuts played by tenor saxophonist Clifford Jordan (in 1957, shortly before he developed his distinctive sound), guitarist Kenny Burrell, Chambers, and drummer Pete LaRoca. Of particular interest is that all of the tunes are Clark originals, none of which have been revived since, even though several are quite catchy. Bebop revivalists in search of fresh material are particularly advised to get this disc!

After being quite busy during 1957-early 1959, Sonny

Clark's career slowed down, and he led only two further albums. *Sonny Clark Trio* (which has sometimes been issued under Max Roach's name) finds Clark performing eight of his originals (including an unaccompanied "My Conception") with Roach and bassist George Duvivier, including "Minor Meeting," "Blues Mambo," and "Junka." His final date as a leader, *Leapin' and Lopin'*, which was recorded exactly 14 months before Clark's death, shows no hint of decline despite the pianist's erratic lifestyle. Assisted by trumpeter Tommy Turrentine, tenor saxophonist Charlie Rouse, bassist Butch Warren, and drummer Billy Higgins, Clark introduced four of his originals on this set (including the previously unreleased "Zellmar's Delight") plus a tune apiece by Turrentine and Warren. The only standard, "Deep in a Dream," has a guest appearance by tenor saxophonist Ike Quebec, who would pass away three days after Clark in early 1963.

LPS TO SEARCH FOR

The only currently unavailable Clark session, *The Sonny Clark Memorial Album* (Xanadu 121), is an erratically recorded but interesting outing from January 15, 1954. On the pianist's first set as a leader, he is heard on several unaccompanied solos and a few trio numbers with bassist Simon Brehm and drummer Bobby White, working his way through the strong Bud Powell influence to find his own voice.

JIMMY CLEVELAND

b. May 3, 1926, Wartrace, TN

One of the most fluent trombonists of the 1950s, Jimmy Cleveland was in great demand during that decade for Bop-oriented dates. He started playing trombone when he was 16, served in the Army (1944–46), attended Tennessee State University, and was part of the Lionel Hampton Orchestra during 1950–53, touring Europe in 1953 and playing alongside Clifford Brown and Art Farmer. Influenced by J.J. Johnson but developing his own personal sound, Cleveland appeared on many record sessions during 1954–60 including with Dizzy Gillespie, Gil Evans, Oscar Pettiford, Johnny Richards, Lucky Thompson, Eddie "Lockjaw" Davis, Eddie Jefferson, Benny Golson, James Moody, and Gerry Mulligan. He returned to Europe with Quincy Jones's orchestra (1959–60) and was with the short-lived Thelonious Monk Octet in 1967 but otherwise worked pri-

marily in the studios in the 1960s and '70s. Cleveland relocated to Los Angeles to work with the orchestra of *The Merv Griffin Show,* recorded with Quincy Jones, and worked with the Gerald Wilson Orchestra and again with Hampton. He has kept a mostly low profile during the past couple of decades. Jimmy Cleveland remained semiactive up to the present time, although his last opportunity to lead his own record date was in 1959.

LPS TO SEARCH FOR

Jimmy Cleveland recorded four albums as a leader for Emarcy/Mercury and half of one for Epic during 1955–59. All have been long out of print, although two were reissued in the 1970s. *Introducing Jimmy Cleveland* (Emarcy 36066 and reissued by the Trip label) has the trombonist playing Quincy Jones arrangements with three overlapping medium-size groups. Among the key sidemen on the swinging material are trumpeter Ernie Royal, either Lucky Thompson or Jerome Richardson on tenor, baritonist Cecil Payne, and either Wade Legge, John Williams, or Hank Jones on piano. *Cleveland Style* (Mercury 1019) is most notable for Ernie Wilkins's colorful arrangements for a septet that makes prominent use of Jay McAllister or Don Butterfield on tuba in the ensembles; Cleveland shares the frontline with Art Farmer and Benny Golson. But listeners can only hope that these two albums and the other Jimmy Cleveland sessions will be reissued on CD someday.

FILMS

Jimmy Cleveland appears briefly in *The Hustler* (1961).

DOLO COKER

b. Nov. 16, 1927, Hartford, CT, d. Apr. 13, 1983, Los Angeles, CA

Charles "Dolo" Coker was a solid Bebop pianist who brought his own conception to the Bud Powell tradition. Although he played with Ben Webster in Philadelphia as early as 1946, Coker did not really emerge from the local jazz scene until the mid-1950s. After moving to New York, he worked with such saxophonists as Sonny Stitt (1955–57), Gene Ammons, Lou Donaldson, Art Pepper (recording *Intensity* in 1960), and Dexter Gordon (1960–61, in the play *The Connection*) plus Kenny Dorham and drummer Philly Joe Jones. Coker moved permanently to Los Angeles in 1961, performing mostly with his own trios and with local musicians.

In the 1970s his profile was raised a bit through a series of records for the Xanadu label, including the only four that he ever led (1976–78). During that era Dolo Coker worked with Stitt, Pepper, Supersax, Sonny Criss, Herb Ellis, trumpeter Blue Mitchell, Red Rodney, altoist Lee Konitz, Jack Sheldon, Teddy Edwards, and Harry "Sweets" Edison, among others. His Boppish solos were always a strong asset, making his passing at age 55 a major loss despite his lack of fame.

LPS TO SEARCH FOR

All four of Dolo Coker's Xanadu dates as a leader have yet to be reissued on CD. That is a pity, for each release is quite rewarding. *Dolo!* (Xanadu 139), from December 26, 1976, finds Coker, Blue Mitchell, tenor saxophonist Harold Land, bassist Leroy Vinnegar, and drummer Frank Butler performing four of the pianist's originals and a song by Mitchell; the rhythm trio explores "Never Let Me Go." The very next day, with Art Pepper in Land's place, the quintet performed four more group originals and "Gone with the Wind" for *California Hard* (Xanadu 142); this time the trio is showcased on "Gone Again." *Third Down* is mostly a trio session from 1977 with Vinnegar and Butler, other than two songs that add guest trumpeter Harry "Sweets" Edison. Overall this is one of Dolo Coker's best outings. His last date as a leader, 1979's *All Alone* (Xanadu 178), is a ballad-oriented set of unaccompanied piano solos that holds interest throughout. But when are these valuable sessions going to reappear on CD?

With his Alto Madness band, Richie Cole in the 1970s and '80s showed that Bebop still had a lot of life left.

RICHIE COLE

b. Feb. 29, 1948, Trenton, NJ

In the 1970s, when it was easy to get the impression that Bebop was becoming extinct (fusion was dominating the jazz landscape), altoist Richie Cole emerged with his "Alto Madness," adding his own flavor of craziness to Bop and helping to lead to its comeback. Cole always felt that any song could be transformed into Bebop, and he proved it on such tunes as "Hooray for Hollywood," "The Star Trek Theme," "Holiday for Strings," "Yakety Sax," the "I Love Lucy Theme," and "La Bamba." His emergence preceded the "Young Lions" movement by several years and showed that not all young jazz musicians were playing fusion or avant-garde music.

Cole's father owned a jazz club in New Jersey, so he heard jazz from an early age. He started playing alto when he was ten and, after attending Berklee for two years, he became a member of Buddy Rich's orchestra in 1969. After a stint with Lionel Hampton, Cole became a bandleader, and he has led various versions of "Alto Madness" ever since. Through the years he has collaborated with such players as altoist Eric Kloss, Phil Woods (an important early influence and his teacher as a teenager), Eddie Jefferson, Bruce Forman, the Manhattan Transfer, pianist Bobby Enriquez, Sonny Stitt, Art Pepper, altoist Hank Crawford, Paquito D'Rivera, and even Boots Randolph! Cole's string of records for Muse (1976–81) were among the finest of his career, although he has also recorded worthy dates for Palo Alto, Concord, Milestone, Heads Up, Music Masters, and his own label. Richie Cole, who on occasions in the past played tenor and baritone, spent periods off the scene in the 1990s, but whenever he returned, he still displayed great skill and enthusiasm for Bebop.

9 *New York Afternoon: Alto Madness / Oct. 13, 1976 / Muse 5119*

10 *Pure Madness / Dec. 1977–Apr. 25, 1979 / 32 Jazz 32162*

8 *Richie Cole Live / Oct. 1, 1978 / Just Jazz 1005*

7 *Side by Side / July 25 + 26, 1980 / Muse 6016*

8 *Richie and Phil & Richie / Oct. 13, 1976–Feb. 1, 1981 / 32 Jazz 32065*

Other than a couple of obscure releases from 1975–76 (for Progressive and Adelphi) and two albums co-led with fellow altoist Eric Kloss, Richie Cole's solo career really began with *New York Afternoon*. The finest work of his career was done for the now-defunct Muse label during 1976–81. Some of the music was reissued by Muse on CDs, but those are unfortunately now out of print and 32 Jazz, which owns the Muse catalog, is still in the early stages of reissuing Cole's valuable recordings.

New York Afternoon has Cole in his early prime, playing with a sextet that includes guitarist Vic Juris, keyboardist Mickey Tucker, bassist Rick Laird, drummer Eddie Gladden, and percussionist Ray Mantilla; Eddie Jefferson sings on two of the seven numbers. The highlights of the set include "Waltz for a Rainy Be-Bop Evening," "New York Afternoon," "Stormy Weather," and "Alto Madness."

Pure Madness is a two-CD set that reissues all of the music from the earlier LPs *Alto Madness* and *Hollywood Madness*, two of Richie Cole's finest recordings. The former set has the same basic band (with Harold Mabern on piano and either Laird or Steve Gilmore on bass) as *New York Afternoon*, showing that even the themes from *The Price Is Right* and *Last Tango in Paris* can be turned into Boppish jazz. Eddie Jefferson sings "The Common Touch" and "Moody's Mood '78." *Hollywood Madness* was one of Richie Cole's more adventurous projects, and it really shows off the potential of his Alto Madness concept. With a fine backup band (Bruce Forman, pianist Dick Hindman, bassist Marshall Hawkins and drummer Les DeMerle), Cole jams on "Hooray for Hollywood" and "Malibu Breeze." Eddie Jefferson, just two weeks before his premature death, is featured on "Hi-Fly" and "Relaxin' at Camarillo," while the Manhattan Transfer guests on "Tokyo Rose Sings the Hollywood Blues," "I Love Lucy," and "Waitin' for Waits." The last has

Tom Waits giving the piece an odd coda. Overall, the twofer *Pure Madness* is Cole's definitive release.

Richie Cole Live was first released in 1995. The altoist is heard live in Half Moon Bay with a San Francisco rhythm section (pianist Smith Dobson, bassist Bob Maize, and drummer Jeep Duquesne) and, on two numbers, altoist Bishop Norman Williams. Eddie Jefferson is also present to perform brief versions of "Summertime" and "Lester Leaps In"; the highlights of this spirited set are "Tokyo Rose," "As Time Goes By," and "Donna Lee."

On July 25–26, 1980, Richie Cole played next to his main influence Phil Woods, and the resulting joint recording (*Side By Side*) was their only one. Muse reissued the original six selections plus a Woods composition ("Rain Go Away") that was not on the original LP. *Richie and Phil & Richie* leaves out "Rain Go Away" and adds six other selections taken from other Muse dates (mostly not reissued elsewhere). It is kind of inexcusable that one tune was left off, driving completists crazy! Not too surprisingly, the Cole-Woods matchup is full of fire, with the two altoists battling it out on "Scrapple from the Apple" and "Donna Lee" and welcoming guest tenor Eddie "Lockjaw" Davis to "Save Your Love for Me." Pianist John Hicks, bassist Walter Booker, and drummer Jimmy Cobb keep the music (which includes the brief free-form "Naugahyde Reality" and the lengthy "Eddie's Mood/Side by Side") moving along. The extra six numbers are taken from four Muse LPs, with three selections drawn from *Some Things Speak for Themselves* (including "Cherokee"). It would have made sense to have all five numbers from that LP along with the missing cut from the Cole-Woods matchup included instead.

8 *Pure Imagination / Nov. 1986 / Concord Jazz 4314*

8 *Bossa International / July 16 1987 / Milestone 9180*

7 *Signature / July 1988 / Milestone 9162*

7 *Profile / Apr. 5–7, 1993 / Heads Up 3022*

8 *Kush—The Music of Dizzy Gillespie / Dec. 9, 1994 / Heads Up 3032*

7 *West Side Story / Mar. 28–29, 1996 / Music Masters 65115*

6 *Trenton Style / 1999 / Alto Madness Records 0002*

Richie Cole's one recording for Concord is an excellent one. *Pure Imagination* finds him showcased in a pianoless quartet with guitarist Vic Juris on such unlikely (but swinging) material as "There'll Be Bluebirds over the White Cliffs of Dover," "Come Fly with Me," and "Flying Down to Rio," displaying plenty of wit and Bebop chops. *Bossa International* is one of Richie Cole's more serious dates, with no real joking around. He teams up with fellow altoist Hank Crawford, guitarist Emily Remler, bassist Marshall Hawkins, and drummer Victor Jones for "Confirmation," "Fantasy Blues," "Snowfall," and "Cherokee" among others. *Signature* features Cole in several different groupings, including a duet with pianist Dick Hindman on "America the Beautiful," quintets with Vic Juris, and either Hindman or Ben Sidran on piano (including "Take the Cole Train"), with strings on "If Ever I Would Leave You," utilizing the steel drums of Andy Narell on two cuts, and performing as the "Mega-Universal Saxophone Orchestra" (overdubbing as two altos, two tenors, and two baritones) on a pair of selections. Overall it holds together.

After 1988, Richie Cole recorded much less frequently. *Profile* was his first release in nearly five years and Cole sounds quite unchanged, still using Dick Hindman in his quintet (along with guitarist Henry Johnson) and playing some offbeat material, including his own "Presidential Sax," Carroll Coates's "One for Monterey," and "Volare." The Dizzy Gillespie tribute CD, *Kush*, benefits greatly from Bob Belden's arrangements and ideas. Cole is showcased with groups ranging from a two-guitar trio ("This Is the Way") and a sextet with trumpeter Jack Walrath ("A Night in Tunisia") to some big band sides and an alto battle with Paquito D'Rivera on "Kush." All of the songs were composed by Dizzy Gillespie except "You Go to My Head," which is by Haven Gillespie!

West Side Story has Cole and a sextet with Vic Juris and pianist Lou Forestieri digging into seven of the main themes from West Side Story plus the altoist's "West Side Blues," bringing out the beauty in the melodies while transforming them into Bebop. After several more years off the scene, in 1999 Richie Cole introduced his own label and a nonet/tentet that he called the Alto Madness Orchestra. The group (which includes trumpeter Guy Fricano, tenor saxophonist Billy Ross, and both Vic Juris and Andrei Ryabov on guitars) is fine, but the arrangements and Cole's soloing sound a bit tired on this surprisingly safe effort, which mixes warhorses with a few lesser-known numbers. A predictable and not overly memorable date.

LPS TO SEARCH FOR

Keeper of the Flame (Muse 5192) is one of Richie Cole's finest recordings and is full of excitement. With his quintet of the time (featuring Vic Juris and Harold Mabern), Cole digs into such tunes as "As Time Goes By," "I Can't Get Started," and "Holiday for Strings," featuring Eddie Jefferson's singing on the rapid "Harold's House of Jazz" (based on "Cherokee") and a vocal version of "New York Afternoon." Three other out-of-print Muse LPs also deserve to be brought back. *Some Things Speak for Themselves* (Muse 5295), which has been partly reissued, features Cole in top form in Japan in 1981, jamming through three Bop standards, "Irish Folk Song" (based on "I Got Rhythm"), and "Tokyo Rose Sings the Hollywood Blues" with his quintet of the period (with Bruce Forman and pianist Smith Dobson). *Cool C* (Muse 5245), from the same week, has Cole playing five standards, "Cool C," and "Back to Bop" with a Japanese rhythm section eight brass and two percussionists. *Alive!* (Muse 5270) is definitely a wild session as Cole and the virtuosic pianist Bobby Enriquez (along with Bruce Forman, bassist Marshall Hawkins, and drummer Scott Morris) inspire each other to lots of craziness on "Punishment Blues," "Body and Soul," the pianist's feature on "Samba De Orfeu," "Yardbird Suite," "Alto Acres" (on which Cole ironically plays tenor!) and "Red Top."

Richie Cole was probably at the peak of his powers in 1982 when he recorded three now-out-of-print albums for Palo Alto. *Return to Alto Acres* (Palo Alto 8023) has him matching wits with Art Pepper and pianist Roger Kellaway not only on alto but also on tenor and baritone. *Alto Annie's Theme* (Palo Alto 8036) was one of Cole's best showcases, a quartet date with Dick Hindman in which he tears into "Jeannine," "Boplicity," "Alto Annie's Theme," and "Tangerine." A somewhat nutty date is *Yakety Madness!* (Palo Alto 8041) during which Cole teams up with tenor saxophonist Boots Randolph (best known for "Yakety Sax"). Randolph can play swinging tenor and he does in spots, but there is also quite a bit of silliness and corn on such tunes as "Yakety Sax," "Wabash Cannonball," "Barnyard Be-Bop," and a rather insipid medley of southern songs. Three years passed before Cole's next recording, a decent but unremarkable *Bossa Nova Eyes* (Palo Alto 8070). Cole is heard in a quintet with Dick Hindman and is best on "I Remember Sonny Stitt" and "Serenata"; singer Janis Siegel guests on the title cut. *Popbop* (Milestone 9152) finds Cole really stretching his repertoire with "La Bamba," "Spanish Harlem," "Star Trek," and Rudy Wiedoeft's early '20s "Saxophobia." The "violins of madness" are on a few numbers and "La Bamba" features a Latin band, but otherwise Cole is accompanied by a sextet with Vic Juris.

FILMS

Richie Cole is a featured soloist on Eddie Jefferson's *Live from the Jazz Workshop* (Rhapsody Films).

EDDIE COSTA

b. Aug. 14, 1930, Atlas, PA, d. July 28, 1962, New York, NY

A distinctive pianist who emphasized the lower register of his instrument, and a fluent vibraphonist, Eddie Coast had a great deal of potential. Costa, who was born to a coal-mining family, studied piano with his brother Bill and was self-taught on vibes. He moved to New York after high school, played with violinist Joe Venuti (1948), and spent two years in the Army. By the early to-mid 1950s, Costa was quite busy in New York, working in the studios and on jazz dates. He was an important part of the classic Tal Farlow Trio and worked and recorded with Sal Salvador, Don Elliott, Kai Winding, Woody Herman (1958–59), guitarist Johnny Smith, Oscar Pettiford, Gil Evans, flutist Herbie Mann, and (in the early 1960s) the Clark Terry-Bob Brookmeyer Quintet. Costa also led some small-group dates of his own for Jubilee, Mode (reissued by V.S.O.P.), Coral, and Dot. But Eddie Costa's life and career were cut short when he died in a car accident at the age of 31.

LPS TO SEARCH FOR

Of Eddie Costa's four dates as a leader, the only one that has been reissued in recent times is the one originally made for Mode, Eddie Costa 5 (V.S.O.P. 7). The high-quality Bop album from 1957 features Costa (who plays vibes on two of the seven numbers) with Art Farmer, Phil Woods, bassist Teddy Kotick, and drummer Paul Motian.

DAMERONIA

Drummer Philly Joe Jones and trumpeter Don Sickler (a master at transcribing arrangements from records) formed Dameronia in the early 1980s to pay tribute to the late great Bebop composer-arranger Tadd Dameron by reviving his music. Dameronia, which recorded two albums for the Uptown label during the 1982–83 period and performed at a few special concerts, was a nonet consisting of such veterans as

Sickler and either Johnny Coles or Virgil Jones on trumpets, Britt Woodman or Benny Powell on trombone, altoist Frank Wess, Charles Davis on tenor, Cecil Payne, Walter Davis Jr., bassist Larry Ridley, and Jones. The part-time group disbanded after Philly Joe's death in 1985 but came back together for a 1989 concert in France that was recorded and released by Soul Note; by then Clifford Jordan was the tenor saxophonist and Kenny Washington was in Jones's place. The short-term band succeeded in focusing attention on Dameron's timeless music.

8 *Live at the Theatre Boulogne / May 30, 1989 / Soul Note 121202*

Although the first two Dameronia releases have not come out on CD yet, their reunion concert of 1989 is readily available. Among the nine Tadd Dameron compositions performed by the nonet (only three of which also appeared on one of their earlier Uptown LPs) are "Hot House," "Good Bait," "Soultrane," and "Philly J.J." Since the time of this concert, Clifford Jordan and Walter Davis Jr. have passed away, so this enjoyable event can be thought of as a tribute to several jazz greats. Such a pity that Dameron could not have kept a group of this caliber and size together during his life.

LPS TO SEARCH FOR

To Tadd with Love (Uptown 27.11) and *Look Stop and Listen* (Uptown 27.15) bring back a total of 13 Tadd Dameron songs, avoiding the obvious picks (such as "Hot House") in favor of some lesser-known tunes, including "Fontainebleau," "The Scene Is Clean," "Choose Now," and "Theme of No Repeat." The earlier date is from 1982 while the second one (from 1983) includes one non-Dameron song (Benny Golson's "Killer Joe") and has guest appearances by Johnny Griffin on four selections.

WALTER DAVIS, JR.

b. Sept. 2, 1932, Richmond, VA, d. June 2, 1990, New York, NY

Walter Davis's piano style and career fell between Bebop and Hard Bop, and he was always proud of his roots in Charlie Parker's and Thelonious Monk's music. Davis worked in Newark, New Jersey, as a teenager, spent part of the classic Bebop era with Babs Gonzales's Three Bips and a Bop, and was a member of Charlie Parker's last regularly working quintet in 1952. Davis, whose style was most influenced by

Bud Powell, worked with Max Roach (1952–53), the Dizzy Gillespie Big Band (1956), Donald Byrd, Art Blakey's Jazz Messengers (1959), and Jackie McLean. In 1959 he recorded his lone Blue Note album as a leader, the classic *Davis Cup*.

Davis spent much of the 1960s outside of music but he was back in the 1970s, touring with Sonny Rollins (1973–74) and the Jazz Messengers (1975–77). The pianist participated in the soundtrack of the Clint Eastwood film *Bird* and made several records as a leader during 1977–79 and 1987–89. Walter Davis, Jr., was touring with Dizzy Gillespie's group when he died suddenly in 1990 at the age of 57.

10 *Davis Cup / Aug. 2, 1959 / Blue Note 32098*
9 *In Walked Thelonious / Apr. 19, 1987 / Jazz Heritage 512631*

Walter Davis, Jr.'s first date as a leader, *Davis Cup,* was so successful that it is strange that there was not a follow-up. Davis performs six of his originals (mostly medium- to fast-tempo pieces except for the ballad "Sweetness") in a quintet with trumpeter Donald Byrd (in prime form), altoist Jackie McLean, bassist Sam Jones, and drummer Art Taylor; everything works. However, Davis would not record as a leader again until 1977. During 1977–79 he recorded for Denon, Red, and Owl, there was a 1981 date for the Night and Day label and during 1987–89 he cut additional sessions for Jazz Heritage, Jazz City, and Steeplechase. *In Walked Thelonious* is special, for Davis is heard playing 14 Thelonious Monk compositions (performing "'Round Midnight" twice) as unaccompanied solos, including such difficult tunes as "Gallop's Gallop," "Trinkle Twinkle," and "Criss Cross." Walter Davis, Jr., who was a friend of Thelonious's, really knew Monk's music well, and these thoughtful improvisations certainly do justice to the classic songs.

BLOSSOM DEARIE

b. Apr. 28, 1926, East Durham, NY

Blossom Dearie is an odd combination of talents. Her voice sounds like a little girl's (particularly in her earlier recordings), yet her piano playing is Boppish and her lyrics and original compositions are quite sophisticated and worldly.

Dearie gained some early attention singing with the Blue Flames (a vocal group that for a time was featured with Woody Herman's big band) and the Blue Rey's (with Alvino Rey's orchestra). She can be heard on the original version of "Moody's Mood for Love" with King Pleasure. While living in Paris during 1952–56, Dearie sang with Annie Ross and formed the Blue Stars (for whom she wrote many arrangements); they had a hit version of "Lullaby of Birdland." Since moving back to New York in 1956, Blossom Dearie (yes, that is her real name!) has gained a cult following in the jazz and cabaret worlds, leading her own trios and becoming particularly well-known for her versions of Dave Frishberg's "Peel Me a Grape" and her own "Hey John." She made some records for Verve in the 1950s and a Capitol set in 1964 but has recorded mostly for her own Daffodil label since 1974.

9 *Blossom Dearie / Sept. 11, 1956–Apr. 9, 1959 / Verve 837 934*
8 *Give Him the Ooh-La-La / Sept. 12–13, 1957 / Verve 314 517 067*
7 *Verve Jazz Masters 51 / Sept. 12, 1956–Feb. 19, 1960 / Verve 314 529 906*

With the exception of sessions made in Paris for Barclay during 1955–56, the Verve CD titled *Blossom Dearie* has the singer-pianist's earliest dates as a leader. Assisted by Ray Brown and drummer Jo Jones, Dearie mostly plays her own fresh renditions of swing standards, including "Deed I Do," "Everything I've Got," "More Than You Know," and "I Won't Dance" plus two French songs. The CD reissue adds three selections from a 1959 quartet date with guitarist Kenny Burrell, Brown, and Ed Thigpen. *Give Him the Ooh-La-La* features Dearie with a similar group (Herb Ellis, Brown, and Jones) but this time mixing in standards with such obscurities as "Bang Goes the Drum," "The Middle of Love," "I Walk a Little Faster," and the title cut (which is heard on two takes). *Verve Jazz Masters 51,* a sampler, has five selections from these two CDs but also includes 11 selections from Dearie's other four Verve sets, which remain out of print. Among those highlights are "Once Upon a Summertime," "Little Jazz Bird," "Rhode Island Is Famous for You," "Down with Love," and "The Party's Over." In lieu of getting the complete sessions, *Verve Jazz Masters 51* serves as an excellent introduction to the unique Blossom Dearie.

LPS TO SEARCH FOR

Post-1960 Blossom Dearie recordings are scarce. She made a date for the Japanese DIW label in 1963 and a few for British Fontana during 1966–70 and since 1973 has recorded primarily for her own tiny Daffodil company. The only exception is *May I Come In* (Capitol 2086), a 1964 outing with an orchestra that finds her interpreting such sings as "I'm in

Love Again," "When Sunny Gets Blue," "I Wish You Love," and even "Charade" and "Put on a Happy Face."

LOU DONALDSON

b. Nov. 1, 1926, Badin, NC

Altoist Lou Donaldson, whose style has always been most influenced by Charlie Parker, developed his own tone and fairly accessible style in the 1950s and has excelled in Bebop, Hard Bop, and Soul Jazz settings through the years. He began on clarinet when he was 15 before switching permanently to alto. After college and the Navy (where he was fortunate enough to be in a military dance band), Donaldson moved to New York and played with Hot Lips Page (1948–49) and trumpeter Dud Bascomb. In 1952 he began a long-term association with the Blue Note label, recording as a leader for the first of many times. Donaldson appeared at Birdland in 1954 for a notable gig with Art Blakey and Clifford Brown that was extensively recorded. By then he was working primarily as a bandleader, although Donaldson did record fine dates as a sideman with others, including Thelonious Monk, Milt Jackson, and organist Jimmy Smith.

Donaldson played mostly Bebop in the 1950s, often utilizing a conga player after 1958. In 1961 he started using an organist in place of a pianist, and his music evolved into soul jazz and hard Bop. The altoist left Blue Note in 1963 to record for Cadet and Argo but returned in 1967 and, with the success of Alligator Boogaloo, began recording much more commercial records. For a time he often utilized an electronic Varitone sax, which watered down his sound, and his music was more funk- and soul-oriented. However, starting in 1981, Lou Donaldson returned to Hard Bop and soul jazz. He has remained quite active in the straight-ahead jazz field ever since, playing at major festivals and recording regularly.

9   *Quartet/Quintet/Sextet / June 20, 1952–Aug. 21, 1954 / Blue Note 81537*

9   *Blues Walk / July 28, 1958 / Blue Note 46525*

8   *Sunny Side Up / Feb. 5–28, 1960 / Blue Note 32095*

8   *Gravy Train / Apr. 27, 1961 / Blue Note 53357*

This section covers Lou Donaldson's recordings up to 1961, when he began using an organist regularly in his group and his music shifted toward Hard Bop and soul jazz; his later sessions will be covered in future books covering those styles. Donaldson recorded regularly for Blue Note, and it is

surprising that at this point seven of his albums from the 1952–61 period have not yet been reissued on CD; the one called *New Faces, New Sounds* has been reissued under Clifford Brown's name.

Quartet/Quintet/Sextet features the young altoist in three settings. He plays four numbers (plus three alternate takes) in 1952 with pianist Horace Silver, bassist Gene Ramey, and drummer Art Taylor; the same group, with trumpeter Blue Mitchell added, performs four other songs from later in the year; and Donaldson's last four tunes are from 1954 with Kenny Dorham, trombonist Matthew Gee, Elmo Hope, Percy Heath, and Art Blakey. Although obviously touched by Charlie Parker, Donaldson also displays a soulful tone of his own, and his solos are a bit more basic and funky in their own way than Bird's. Highlights include "Lou's Blues," "The Best Things in Life Are Free," "The Stroller," and "After You've Gone."

Blues Walk, from 1958, is pure Bebop, with Donaldson (backed by pianist Herman Foster, bassist Peck Morrison, drummer Dave Bailey, and Ray Barretto on conga) romping through "Move," "The Masquerade Is Over," "Callin' All Cats," his blues "Play Ray," and "Blues Walk" while sounding quite lyrical on the ballad "Autumn Nocturne." *Sunny Side Up* finds Donaldson (who is joined by trumpeter Bill Hardman, pianist Horace Parlan, either Sam Jones or Laymon Jackson on bass, and drummer Al Harewood) starting to lean more toward soulful Hard Bop, although his roots in Bebop would never completely disappear. Donaldson is in fine form on "Blues for J. P.," "It's You or No One," "The Truth," and "Softly As in a Morning Sunrise." *Gravy Train* was the last album by Donaldson's band with Foster (plus bassist Ben Tucker, Dave Bailey, and Alec Dorsey on conga) before he would begin using Big John Patton on organ. Donaldson sounds typically exuberant and cheerful on such tunes as "South of the Border," "Avalon," and "The Glory of Love." At that point, he had many decades of interesting and usually rewarding recordings still ahead of him.

LPS TO SEARCH FOR

Midnight Sun (Blue Note 1023), from 1960, was not released for the first time until 1980. Two of its seven tunes would a year later appear on *Gravy Train* and two others would be remade in future years, but these renditions (with Horace Parlan, Ben Tucker, Al Harewood, and Ray Barretto) are also fine. Highlights include "Candy," "Avalon," and "Exactly Like You."

BOB DOROUGH

b. Dec. 12, 1923, Cherry Hill, AR

Bob Dorough can in some ways be thought of as the male equivalent of Blossom Dearie, having a unique and oddly charming vocal style, being a Bop-oriented pianist, writing sophisticated songs, and gaining a cult following that has helped him weather long periods of neglect by the greater jazz public. Dorough, who played saxophone and clarinet when he first started out, performed with an Army band during 1943–45 and attended North Texas State University (1946–49) and Columbia University (1949–52). He was the musical director for boxer Sugar Ray Robinson for two years (1952–54) during a period when Robinson was involved in show business. Dorough was in Paris during 1954–55 (recording with Blossom Dearie) and, back in the United States, he made a classic album for Bethlehem in 1956. Dorough also recorded two numbers with Miles Davis in 1962.

Although otherwise recording only sporadically (including for his own Laissez-Faire label), Dorough has worked steadily with his own duets/trios ever since, using the late Bill Takas as his bassist for many years. Among Dorough's better-known songs are "Devil May Care" (recently revived by Diana Krall), "Comin' Home Baby" (a hit for Mel Torme), "I've Got Just About Everything," "I'm Hip" (cowritten with Dave Frishberg), "Nothin' Like You," "You're the Dangerous Type," the lyrics to Charlie Parker's "Yardbird Suite," and the many children's songs he wrote for Schoolhouse Rock starting in 1973. In 1997, it surprised everyone (including himself) when Bob Dorough was signed to Blue Note, recording for a major label for the first time in his career at the age of 73.

- **9** *Devil May Care / Oct. 1956 / Bethlehem 20-4004*
- **10** *Just About Everything / Mar. 17-21, 1966 / Evidence 22094*
- **8** *Beginning to See the Light / Apr. 1976 / Laissez-Faire 02*
- **6** *Right on My Way Home / Apr. 30, 1997–May 6, 1997 / Blue Note 57729*
- **8** *Too Much Coffee, Man / 1999 / Blue Note 99239*

Bob Dorough's debut recording in 1956 finds him introducing "Devil May Care" and performing such numbers as "You're the Dangerous Type," "Yardbird Suite" (Charlie Parker's tune, to which he gave new lyrics), and Hoagy Carmichael's sly "Baltimore Oriole." Dorough contributes Boppish piano and is joined by trumpeter Warren Fitzgerald, vibraphonist Jack Hitchcock, drummer Jerry Segal, and his longtime bassist, Bill Takas. Other than an odd poetry reading from 1958 and an album of tunes from the Broadway show *Oliver* in 1963, Dorough's next recording as a leader would not take place until Focus recorded him in 1966, music that has been reissued by Evidence. Dorough is even stronger on this set than on his first album, redoing "Baltimore Oriole," introducing four songs (including "I've Got Just About Everything" and "Baby, You Should Know It"), and singing fresh renditions of "'Tis Autumn" and "Lazy Afternoon." But despite the high quality of the music, Dorough would not record again for another decade, and the live music on *Beginning to See the Light* was released on his own label. Dorough and Takas play duets on their usual club program of the time, which contains a couple of children's songs and versions of "Better Than Anything," "I'm Hip," "Nothing Like You," and "I've Got Just About Everything."

Bob Dorough made recordings in the 1980s for Laissez-Faire, Bloomdido, Philology, Red, Pinnacle, and Orange Blue, but virtually all are difficult to find today. The release of *Right on My Way Home* was a major surprise, featuring Dorough with two rhythm sections (with Bill Takas or Christian McBride on bass, Grady Tate or Billy Hart on drums, and guest saxophonist Joe Lovano). However, Dorough's three new songs are not destined to be remembered, and his decision to record "Moon River" is a bit questionable. Best are "Whatever Happened to Love Songs," "I Get the Neck of the Chicken," and "Spring Can Really Hang You Up the Most." His second Blue Note session, which features Phil Woods's alto, a few rhythm sections, and a horn section, is particularly fun. The renditions of "The Coffee Song," "Too Much Coffee, Man," and "Yesterday, I Made Your Breakfast" are at times a bit riotous and almost over the top with joy. "Where Is the Song?" (which humorously does not have a real melody or logical chord changes) and "Wake Up Sally, It's Saturday" might eventually catch on and other highlights include a remake of "I've Got Just About Everything" and Dave Frishberg's "Oklahoma Toad." Recommended.

LPS TO SEARCH FOR

Skabadabba (Pinnacle 7781), from 1987, is a worthwhile if little-known effort by Dorough in a quintet with trumpeter Lee Katzman, Bill Takas (on electric bass), drummer Peter Grant, and percussionist Luther Rix. Dorough sings his words to "Bijou" and his "I Want to Prove I Love You," also performing a few standards in his unique manner.

DOUBLE SIX OF PARIS

Two years after Lambert, Hendricks, and Ross were formed, a French equivalent called the Double Six of Paris came together. Led by Mimi Perrin, the band at various times included Monique Aldebert-Guerin, Louis Aldebert, Christiane Legrand, Ward Swingle, and Roger Guerin among its vocalists. Featuring six singers, the Double Six received its name because each of the vocalists overdubbed his or her voice so the overall sound was that of a dozen vocalists. As with Lambert, Hendricks, and Ross, much of the music was vocalese, although with lyrics in French. The Double Six of Paris recorded four albums during 1959–64, including one set with Dizzy Gillespie and Bud Powell (which is reviewed under Gillespie's name), one that emphasized Quincy Jones tunes, and an out-of-print 1964 set that pays tribute to Ray Charles. The Double Six of Paris broke up in 1965. Mimi Perrin led a similar group with the same name for a year before that venture ended in late 1966.

9 *Les Double Six / 1959–1962 / RCA 65659*
The Double Six of Paris's first two albums are reissued in full on this single CD, along with a lengthy (and previously unreleased) version of "Walkin'." A lot of the arrangements are based on records originally arranged by Quincy Jones (either for his own orchestra or his work for Count Basie and Harry Arnold's orchestra), including "For Lena and Lennie," "Stockholm Sweetnin'," "Doodlin'," and "Meet Benny Bailey." In addition, the Double Six recreates the recordings of Woody Herman, Shelly Manne, John Coltrane, Gerry Mulligan, J. J. Johnson, Charlie Parker ("Scrapple from the Apple"), Miles Davis ("Boplicity"), and Stan Kenton. Although for specialized tastes (since all of the words are in French), this is a classic of its kind.

KENNY DREW

b. Aug. 28, 1928, New York, NY, d. Aug. 4, 1993, Copenhagen, Denmark

A superior pianist whose style was flexible enough to fit into swing, Bop, and Hard Bop settings, Kenny Drew became one of the top expatriate American jazzmen, a player who was always in demand by American musicians touring Europe. Drew started playing piano when he was five, and he made his recording debut in 1949 with Howard McGhee. He worked steadily in the 1950s, including with Charlie Parker (1950–51), Buddy DeFranco (1952–53), Lester Young,

Coleman Hawkins, Milt Jackson, Dinah Washington (1956), and Buddy Rich. During 1953–60 Drew led record dates for Blue Note, Norgran, Pacific Jazz, Riverside, and Judson and appeared on sessions with such all-stars as John Coltrane, Chet Baker, Toots Thielemans, Sonny Stitt, Sonny Rollins, Art Blakey, Johnny Griffin, Art Farmer, and Clifford Brown, among others. The pianist moved to Paris in 1961 and permanently to Copenhagen three years later. In addition to leading his own trio and for a time co-owning the Matrix label, Drew worked frequently with Dexter Gordon and for a time had a duo with Niels Pedersen. He backed Johnny Griffin, Jackie McLean, violinist Stuff Smith, and Ben Webster, made many record dates for Steeplechase in the 1970s, and was active up until his death at age 64. Kenny Drew's son, Kenny Drew Jr., was a major new piano discovery in the 1990s.

7 *Talkin' and Walkin' / Nov. 18, 1955–Dec. 1955 / Blue Note 84439*
8 *The Kenny Drew Trio / Sept. 20 + 26, 1956 / Original Jazz Classics 065*
8 *Plays the Music of Harry Warren and Harold Arlen / Feb. 1957 / Milestone 47070*
7 *This Is New / Apr. 3, 1957 / Original Jazz Classics 483*
8 *Pal Joey / Oct. 15, 1957 / Original Jazz Classics 1809*

Originally cut for Pacific Jazz, *Talkin' and Walkin'* features Drew's regular quartet of the period, a West Coast-based group that also includes the short-lived Joe Maini on alto and tenor, bassist Leroy Vinnegar, and drummer Lawrence Marable. The ensemble performs six Drew originals plus "Prelude to a Kiss," J. J. Johnson's "Wee Dot," and "I'm Old Fashioned." In addition, the CD features Drew with the same group but led by Jack Sheldon on three numbers (two of which are the pianist's originals), selections only previously out on samplers. *The Kenny Drew Trio* has Drew, bassist Paul Chambers, and drummer Philly Joe Jones (both of the latter at the time were members of the Miles Davis Quintet) jaming on six standards (including "Caravan," "Taking a Chance on Love," and "It's Only a Paper Moon") plus two of the pianist's tunes. Two complete albums originally recorded for the defunct Judson label are reissued on *Plays the Music of Harry Warren and Harold Arlen*. Drew performs 24 concise duets with bassist Wilbur Ware and a dozen songs apiece by Warren and Arlen; his renditions are melodic yet not totally predictable.

This Is New features Drew, Wilbur Ware, drummer G. T. Hogan, Donald Byrd, and (on four of the seven selections) Hank Mobley on a solid Hard Bop date. The group of late '50s "Young Lions" performs four standards (including "It's You or No One" and "Why Do I Love You"), a couple of originals, and Sonny Rollins's "Paul's Pal." *Pal Joey* has Drew, Wilbur Ware, and Philly Joe Jones interpreting five Rodgers and Hart songs written for the play of the same name plus three of standards that were also performed in the film version. Highlights include "Bewitched, Bothered and Bewildered," "I Could Write a Book," and "The Lady Is a Tramp."

| 9 | *Undercurrent / Dec. 11, 1960 / Blue Note 84059* |
| 8 | *Solo/Duo / 1966–Sept. 29, 1983 / Storyville 8274* |

Undercurrent, Kenny Drew's second Blue Note set as a leader (his first was in 1953), was one of the best recordings of his early period. The quintet date, with the young Freddie Hubbard on trumpet, Hank Mobley, bassist Sam Jones, and drummer Louis Hayes, consists of six Drew originals that cover a lot of moods and result in superior Hard Bop. None of the tunes (including "Undercurrent," "Lion's Den" and "Groovin' the Blues") caught on, but that was not because of their quality.

After moving to Paris in 1961, Kenny Drew would not lead a record date for a dozen years but he kept quite busy with his trio and formed a musical partnership with bassist Niels-Henning Orsted Pedersen. Starting in 1973 Drew recorded steadily for SteepleChase, Xanadu, Soul Note, the Japanese Baystate label, Timeless, and Alfa Jazz. *Solo/Duo* is a 1996 CD that consists of previously unreleased material from radio broadcasts in Copenhagen. Drew is heard on duets from 1966 with Pedersen (including on Oscar Pettiford's "Swingin' Till the Girls Come Home"), taking unaccompanied piano solos in 1978, and performing duets with bassist Bo Stief in 1983. A fine all-round showcase by an underrated but very talented Bop-based pianist.

LPS TO SEARCH FOR

Kenny Drew and His Progressive Piano (Norgran 1066) features the pianist in trios with bassist Eugene Wright and either Specs Wright or Lawrence Marable on drums during 1953–54, when Drew was with the Buddy DeFranco quartet. His two excellent Xanadu albums were recorded within a day of each other during October 15–16, 1978: *Home Is Where the Soul Is* (Xanadu 166), which is a trio outing with Leroy Vinnegar and Frank Butler, and *For Sure!* (Xanadu 167), which has the group joined by Charles McPherson and Sam Noto.

MADELINE EASTMAN
b. June 27, 1954, San Francisco, CA

Madeline Eastman, who has long had a strong reputation in the San Francisco Bay area as a major jazz singer, first began to be known in other parts of the world when she made her recording debut as a leader in 1990. From the start she proved to be a constantly improvising singer, a bit influenced by Betty Carter but with a style, wit, and conception of her own. She studied at the College of San Mateo, recorded with Full Faith & Credit (1983), and taught singing at workshops and clinics. Since 1989, Madeline Eastman has recorded three CDs for the Mad-Kat label (which she co-owns with Kitty Margolis), married drummer Vince Lateano, and appeared at many clubs and festivals, growing in stature each year.

8	*Point of Departure / 1990 / Mad-Kat 1002*
9	*Mad About Madeline! / 1991 / Mad-Kat 1003*
7	*Art Attack / June 1994 / Mad-Kat 10005*

When a singer debuts with a band consisting of trumpeter Tom Harrell, pianist Mike Wofford, bassist Rufus Reid, and drummer Vince Lateano and has liner notes written by Mark Murphy, she is definitely worth looking into. *Point of Departure* was an impressive start to Madeline Eastman's recording career. It includes such tunes as "Wild Is the Wind," a minor-toned version of "You Are My Sunshine" (inspired by Mose Allison's rendition), "Little Boat," Joe Henderson's "Inner Urge," Bobby Hutcherson's "Little B's Poem," and "The Island." Eastman improvises every note and certainly holds listeners' attention throughout the stimulating set. *Mad About Madeline* is even better, with contributions by Phil Woods, pianist Cedar Walton, bassist Tony Dumas, and Lateano plus a guest spot for Mark Murphy, who shares "You're the Dangerous Type" with Eastman in delightful fashion. Other highlights of the essential set include inventive versions of "Cheek to Cheek," "Freedom Jazz Dance," "Turn Out the Stars," "Get Out of Town," "All of You," and Miles Davis's "Four." Madeline Eastman generally sounds wonderful throughout *Art Attack,* too (assisted by pianist Kenny Barron, drummer Tony Williams, the Turtle Island String Quartet, and others), but not everything works equally well. "Gypsy in My Soul" is overly pushy, the lyrics of Blossom Dearie's "I Like You, You're Nice/I Like You" did not need to be revised, and Ivan Lins's "Sonhos" (taken in Portuguese) is a misfire. However, creative renditions of "Nefertiti," "The Thrill Is Gone," Thelonious Monk's "Evidence," and "My Heart Stood Still" easily compensate, and there are a lot of intriguing moments on this fine outing. Madeline Eastman is long overdue for a fourth recording!

KURT ELLING

b. Nov. 2, 1967, Chicago, IL

The most inventive new jazz singer of the 1990s, Kurt Elling can be thought of as an extension of Mark Murphy, whose sound he often resembles. Although not strictly a Bebop singer, Elling is a modern-day hipster, who (like Murphy) sometimes performs (and improvises) lyrics that recall Jack Kerouac. He became interested in jazz while attending college and eventually gave up his plan to become a professor in the philosophy of religion. Elling picked up experience jamming in Chicago clubs, where his willingness (in fact, eagerness) to take chances was appreciated. A demo tape of his found its way into the hands of Bruce Lundvall of Blue Note, and in 1994 Elling recorded his highly successful debut for the label. Kurt Elling has thus far recorded four CDs and ranks near the top of today's relatively small list of creative male jazz singers.

9 *Close Your Eyes / Feb. 14, 1994–Nov. 2, 1994 / Blue Note 30645*

10 *The Messenger / July 1994–Dec. 1996 / Blue Note 52727*

8 *This Time It's Love / Dec. 1997–Jan. 1998 / Blue Note 93543*

8 *Live in Chicago / July 14–16, 1999 / Blue Note 22211*

At a time when there were extremely few worthwhile new male jazz singers, Kurt Elling burst upon the scene in 1994, and he has led the field ever since. *Close Your Eyes* finds Elling joined by his longtime pianist, Laurence Hobgood, and a rhythm section, with guest appearances from tenors Edward Petersen and Von Freeman. There is not a dull moment throughout this very impressive debut. The highlights include Wayne Shorter's "Dolores," "Ballad of the Sad Young Man," "Married Blues," Herbie Hancock's "Hurricane," and "Never Never Land." Along the way are some impro-

vised lyrics, some spoken word sections, and a healthy dose of humor. *The Messenger* (which has Elling assisted by Hopgood's trio, a few guest horns, and singer Cassandra Wilson on "Time of the Season") includes all kinds of successful ideas. Elling revitalizes "Nature Boy," "April in Paris," and "Prelude to a Kiss," sings vocalese (a Dexter Gordon solo) on "Tanya Jean," indulges in some storytelling on "It's Just a Thing," and scats wildly on Jimmy Heath's "Gingerbread Boy."

The ballad-oriented set *This Time It's Love* displays Elling's continued growth, particularly on a tongue-in-cheek "Too Young to Go Steady," "My Foolish Heart," a charming "I Feel So Smoochie" (with violinist Johnny Frigo sitting in), and "Freddie's Yen for Jen" (which has vocalese for a lengthy and difficult Freddie Hubbard solo). *Live in Chicago* finds the singer really stretching himself. His vocalese to a Wayne Shorter solo on "Night Dreamer" is quite adventurous (nearly sounding impossible to sing), and his versions of "My Foolish Heart" and "Smoke Gets in Your Eyes" contain subtle surprises. Jon Hendricks drops by to share the vocals on "Don't Get Scared" and "Goin' to Chicago" (the former is more successful than the latter), and Elling creates a humorous monologue before an all-too-short blues jam featuring tenors Von Freeman, Eddie Johnson, and Ed Petersen. A fun set.

HERB ELLIS

b. Aug. 4, 1921, Farmersville, TX

Guitarist Herb Ellis's sound and style basically come from Charlie Christian, but, as with his friend Barney Kessel, his playing also has a slight country twang. Ellis attended North Texas State University and picked up experience playing with the Casa Loma Orchestra (1944–45) and Jimmy Dorsey (1945–47). While with Dorsey, he met up with pianist Lou Carter and bassist Johnny Frigo; they broke away in 1947 to form a swing-oriented trio called The Soft Winds. The group lasted until 1950 and, after some freelancing, Ellis replaced Kessel with the Oscar Peterson Trio, forming one-third of Peterson's greatest group (1953–58) along with Ray Brown. Ellis toured constantly with Peterson and worked with the pianist on Jazz at the Philharmonic tours. In addition to making countless recordings with O.P. (including dates backing everyone from Louis Armstrong, Billie Holiday, and Lester Young to Sonny Stitt and Stan Getz), Ellis led a few sessions of his own.

Tiring of the traveling, Ellis settled for a long period in Los Angeles, worked as a studio musician, went on tours with Ella Fitzgerald, and in the early 1960s was a member of the Dukes of Dixieland. Ellis recorded with violinist Stuff Smith and fellow guitarist Charlie Byrd in the 1960s but mostly had a low profile outside of the studios. In the 1970s he worked much more as a leader, recorded extensively for Concord (including meetings with Joe Pass), and was part of the Great Guitars along with Kessel and Byrd. Herb Ellis has since remained active on at least a part-time basis, recording as a leader for Concord, Justice, and Jazz Focus, inspiring Johnny Frigo to make a comeback (on violin), and having occasional reunions with Oscar Peterson.

10 *Nothing but the Blues / Oct. 11, 1957–May 1, 1958 / Verve 314 521 674*

7 *Herb Ellis Meets Jimmy Giuffre / Mar. 26, 1959 / Verve 314 559 826*

9 *Together! / Jan. 8, 1963 / Koch Jazz 7805*

Nothing but the Blues was Herb Ellis's second album as a leader (following the out-of-print *Ellis in Wonderland*) and it is still his personal favorite recording. The eight blues have more variety than one would think, featuring Ellis with trumpeter Roy Eldridge (whose explosive solos keep the proceedings from getting too relaxed), tenor saxophonist Stan Getz, Ray Brown, and drummer Stan Levey. A CD reissue adds four selections made by the JATP All-Stars for use in films; Getz, Eldridge, Coleman Hawkins, and Dizzy Gillespie (who steals the show) all get their licks in.

Ellis's meeting with Jimmy Giuffre is a solid success. Giuffre plays some tenor and baritone on the nonet date (which also includes altoists Art Pepper and Bud Shank, Richie Kamuca's tenor, Lou Levy, guitarist Jim Hall, bassist Joe Mondragon, and Stan Levey), contributed three of the eight selections, and wrote all of the arrangements. Ellis, who takes his own "Patricia" unaccompanied, is in fine form on the straight-ahead and swinging material. While the Giuffre date is a bit "cool" in tone, Ellis's encounter with the great swing violinist Stuff Smith on *Together!* is frequently explosive and quite "hot." No one could ever take the spotlight from Smith, who takes two vocals and also performs his own "Skip It" and "Hillcrest" on this driving and exciting set. Three alternate takes expand the program (originally recorded for Epic), which also has Lou Levy, Bob Enevoldsen (on tenor and valve trombone), Al McKibbon, and Shelly Manne in the sextet.

7 *Jazz/Concord / July 29, 1973 / Concord Jazz 6001*

8 *Seven Come Eleven / July 29, 1973 / Concord Jazz 6002*

8 *Two for the Road / Jan. 30, 1974–Feb. 20, 1974 / Original Jazz Classics 726*

8 *Soft Shoe / Aug. 1974 / Concord Jazz 6003*

9 *After You've Gone / Aug. 1974 / Concord Jazz 6006*

Herb Ellis recorded quite frequently for the Concord label during the 1970s, leading the company's first three releases. Some of his Concord albums are a bit lazy, almost to the sleepy point, but in general the most rewarding ones have been the albums that have been reissued on CD. *Jazz/Concord* and *Seven Come Eleven* both team Ellis with fellow guitarist Joe Pass (who was starting to be discovered at the time) in a quartet with Ray Brown and drummer Jake Hanna, recorded live at he 1973 Concord Jazz Festival. *Jazz/Concord* includes fine renditions of "Look for the Silver Lining," "Honeysuckle Rose," and "Stuffy," but *Seven Come Eleven* gets the edge due to stronger material, including the title cut, "In a Mellotone," "Perdido," and "Concord Blues." Ellis and Pass also teamed up a third time, but for the Pablo label and for duets rather than with a quartet. Although this setting was much different than usual for Ellis, he holds his own with Pass on such numbers as "Lady Be Good," "I've Found a New Baby" and two versions of "Cherokee."

Soft Shoe received a lot of attention when it was released in 1974, partly due to having a jazz version of "The Flintstones Theme," which is based on the chord changes of "I've Got Rhythm." One of the very few straight-ahead recordings by pianist George Duke (who has spent much of his career playing funk and R&B), the date also features the great swing trumpeter Harry "Sweets" Edison, drummer Jake Hanna, and co-leaders Ellis and Ray Brown. The same group, with Plas Johnson added on tenor, is heard on *After You've Gone*. Recorded at the 1974 Concord Jazz Festival, they get hot on such tunes as "After You've Gone," Edison's "Home Grown," and "Flintstones II." Ellis and Brown play a duet on "Detour Ahead."

5 *Rhythm Willie / 1975 / Concord Jazz 6010*

6 *Hot Tracks / 1975 / Concord Jazz 6012*

6 *Herb / Sept. 13, 1977 / Music Heritage Society 512686*

7 *Windflower / Oct. 1977 / Concord Jazz 4056*

8 *Soft & Mellow / Aug. 1978 / Concord Jazz 4077*

8 *Doggin' Around / Mar. 1988 / Concord Jazz 4372*

Although Herb Ellis and Count Basie's rhythm guitarist Freddie Green are listed as co-leaders for *Rhythm Willie*, Green does not take any solos and is merely a supportive part of the rhythm section. The musicians (which include pianist Ross Tompkins, Brown, and Hanna) play well enough on such numbers as "It Had to Be You," "A Smooth One," and "I Want a Little Girl," but nothing eventful occurs and no one sounds as if they are sweating. *Hot Tracks* is better, although not as fiery as would be hoped with the lineup (Edison, Ellis, Plas Johnson, Brown, Hanna, and electric keyboardist Mike Melvoin). Melvoin's keyboard sounds dated, and the six group originals were not destined to catch on, but the music is lightly swinging. *Herb* is a reissue of an obscure quartet date (with Billy Taylor, bassist Ron Carter, and drummer Danny Richmond) originally made for Japanese Sony. Despite the different personnel, the music is typical of Ellis's work from the period, including swinging but mostly relaxed and predictable versions of such songs as "When Your Lover Has Gone," "My Funny Valentine," and "There Is No Greater Love."

Windflower is notable for teaming Ellis with Remo Palmieri, a guitarist who was on some of the early Bebop records of Charlie Parker and Dizzy Gillespie before spending much of his life in the studios. Palmieri sounds fine in the quartet (with bassist George Duvivier and drummer Ron Traxler), and he inspires Ellis a bit on tunes such as "The Night Has a Thousand Eyes," "Walkin'," and "Groove Merchant." *Soft & Mellow* fortunately does not stick completely to its title, featuring an opening version of "Shine" and a closing "Rosetta" that are full of fire. Ellis, Ross Tompkins, bassist Monty Budwig, and Jake Hanna also sound fine on the ballads, "Wave" and "Jeff's Bad Blues," making this one of the guitarist's better Concord sessions. Off records (except for a couple of Japanese albums) for nearly seven years, Herb Ellis returned to Concord one last time with *Doggin' Around*, a set of duets with bassist Red Mitchell. Mitchell's wit, the interplay between the musicians on the likable swing standards, and a classic drawing by Gary Larson make this a CD well worth picking up.

9	*Roll Call* / 1991 / *Justice 1001*
8	*Down-Home* / Sept. 13, 1991 / *Justice 1003*
9	*Texas Swings* / 1992 / *Justice 1002*
8	*An Evening with Herb Ellis* / Feb. 19, 1995 / *Jazz Focus 019*

Herb Ellis's Justice recordings of 1991–92 found the veteran guitarist revitalized by having the opportunity to play with different musicians than usual. *Roll Call* has him jamming with organist Mel Rhyne and old friend Jake Hanna. There are also guest appearances from the great swing violinist Johnny Frigo (whose rediscovery began with this set) and Jay Thomas on tenor and flugelhorn. *Down-Home* is particularly unusual, for Ellis wrote all ten selections and plays with a much younger group made up of trumpeter Rebecca Franks, pianist Stefan Karlsson, bassist David Craig, and drummer Sebastian Whittaker. The music swings along and is typically Boppish but sounds fresher than normal.

Texas Swings is also a logical idea that had not been thought of before: putting Herb Ellis in a Western swing setting. Although the steel guitar of Herb Remington might sound a bit jarring at times to some listeners, the violin playing of Johnny Gimble and Bobby Bruce is quite welcome, and Willie Nelson makes a few guest appearances on second guitar. Although the material (which includes "Scrapple from the Apple," "Undecided," and "Rosetta") is not that different from a typical Ellis date, the very different instrumental colors clearly inspired him to some of his best playing.

An Evening with Herb Ellis features the guitarist in a more conventional setting (a quartet with pianist Bill MacDonough, bassist Chuck Israels, and drummer John Nolan), but Ellis sounds quite happy and stretches himself a bit. The repertoire is comprised of nine standards, including "Sweet Georgia Brown," a ten-minute "Things Ain't What They Used to Be," "I Love You," and "I Want to Be Happy," and overall Ellis is heard on a very good night, playing before fans in Bellingham, Washington.

LPS TO SEARCH FOR

Softly . . . But with That Feeling (Verve 2674) is a relaxed quartet outing from 1961 with vibraphonist Victor Feldman, bassist Leroy Vinnegar, and drummer Ronnie Zito, highlighted by "Like Someone in Love," "John Brown's Body," and "Gravy Waltz." *Guitar/Guitar* (Columbia 2330) was Ellis's first meeting on records with fellow guitarist Charlie Byrd. The 11 concise selections are mostly quite relaxed, but a few sparks are generated on "Carolina in the Morning," "Three Quarter Blues," and "So Danco Samba" (which is renamed "Jazz 'n Samba"). From the Concord years, *A Pair to Draw On* (Concord 17) is a pleasant and melodic outing from 1976, a set of duets by Ellis and pianist Ross Tompkins. *Herb Ellis at Montreux* (Concord Jazz 116), from 1979, has the guitarist showcased with two different rhythm sections (Ray Brown or Michael Moore on bass, Jeff Hamilton or Jake Hanna on drums, and sometimes pianist Ross Tompkins), digging into "Love Walked In," "Georgia on My Mind," and "I Love You"; unfortunately the playing time is under 32 minutes. In contrast, *Herb Mix* (Concord Jazz 181), from 1981, is pleasant but dull, with Ellis, bassist Bob Maize, and drummer Jimmie Smith mostly playing warhorses that had been heard too many times before!

FILMS

Herb Ellis is one of several guitarists who can be seen on *Legends of Jazz Guitar Vols. 1–3* (Vestapol 13009, 13033 and 13043). He is also well featured on the documentary *Detour Ahead* (Vestapol 13083), which includes quite a few performances.

ROLF ERICSON

b. Aug. 29, 1922, Stockholm, Sweden, d. June 16, 1997, Stockholm, Sweden

One of the top European Bop trumpeters, Rolf Ericson was able to hold his own with both Charlie Parker and the veterans of Duke Ellington's orchestra. Ericson began playing trumpet when he was eight and was initially inspired by seeing a Louis Armstrong concert in Stockholm (1933). He began working professionally in 1938. Ericson moved to New York in 1947 and was part of the Charlie Barnet Bebop Orchestra in 1949 and Woody Herman's Third Herd (1950) in addition to having short-term gigs with Benny Carter, Wardell Gray, and Elliot Lawrence. He returned to Sweden in time to work with Charlie Parker during Bird's European tour. Ericson first recorded as a leader in 1950 and also appeared on record with altoist Arne Domnerus and Leonard Feather's Swinging Swedes. Coming back to the United States in 1953, Ericson worked with Charlie Spivak, Harry James, the Dorsey Brothers, Les Brown, and the Lighthouse All-Stars. In 1956 he toured Europe with singer Ernestine Anderson and baritonist Lars Gullin. In the United States during the next decade he worked with Dexter Gordon, Harold Land, Stan Kenton, Woody Herman, Maynard Ferguson's orchestra (1960–61), Buddy Rich, Charles Mingus (1962–63), Benny Goodman, Gerry Mulligan, Charles Mingus, and Duke Ellington (off and on during 1963–71). Although he spent part of the 1970s in Germany as a studio musician, Ericson was constantly on the move during his

final 20 years, appearing now and then in the United States, including with Count Basie, the Juggernaut, the Clayton-Hamilton Orchestra, and Louis Bellson. Rolf Ericson's mellow tone, strong technical skills, and love for Bebop kept him in demand throughout virtually his entire musical career.

8   *Rolf Ericson & the American Stars 1956 / June 21, 1956 + July 30, 1956 / Dragon 255*
7   *My Foolish Heart / June 10, 1989 / Art Union 35*
8   *Ellington & Strayhorn by Ericson & Aberg / Jan. 25–26, 1995 / Sittel 9223*

In 1956, Rolf Ericson led a group of American All-Stars in a tour of his native Sweden, but unfortunately several of the musicians were drug addicts and Ericson ended up having to replace the entire band. A Dragon CD has the four studio sides from the quintet (which also included Cecil Payne, Duke Jordan, bassist John Simmons, and drummer Art Taylor) and also the only existing broadcast of the group he ended up with, one including the great baritonist Lars Gullin, pianist Freddie Redd, Tommy Potter, and drummer Joe Harris. Ernestine Anderson, who sings "You Go to My Head" with the first band, is featured on five of the 14 numbers with its successor, showing that she was already quite distinctive. "Dig," "Lady Be Good," and a 14-minute version of "A Night in Tunisia" are among the highlights.

Most of Rolf Ericson's recordings as a leader have been for lesser-known European and Japanese labels. *My Foolish Heart* finds him performing lyrical and swinging duets with pianist Lex Jasper in 1989, nine standards (including two Duke Ellington songs and Miles Davis's "Four") plus Bobby Shew's "Nadlin." Age 72 at the time of his Ellington/Strayhorn tribute for the Sittel label, Ericson (who still sounds excellent) performs a dozen songs from the Ellington book, the great majority of which (particularly "Sentimental Lady," "Serenade to Sweden," "Portrait of a Silk-Thread," and "Fleurette Africaine") are not played all that often. He is joined by Lennart Aberg on tenor, soprano, and flute, pianist Bobo Stenson, bassist Dan Berglund, drummer Egil Johansen, and (on two numbers) singer Rose-Marie Aberg.

LPS TO SEARCH FOR

Rolf Ericson recorded as a leader in Stockholm for the Artist (1950–52), Metronome (1956), Four Leaf Clover (1971 and 1978), and Dragon labels. *Stockholm Sweetnin'* (Dragon 78), from 1984, finds Ericson (a few days short of his 62nd birthday) still in prime form. He heads a quintet also including drummer Mel Lewis and three fellow Swedes (tenor saxophonist Nils Sandstrom, pianist Goran Lindberg, and bassist Sture Nordin) on a Bop-oriented date that has two originals plus such pieces as Thad Jones's "Bird Song," "Stockholm Sweetnin'," and "Without a Song."

JON FADDIS

b. July 24, 1953, Oakland, CA

It took over 30 years before any trumpeter could really duplicate the complex style of Dizzy Gillespie. Jon Faddis had the Gillespie approach mastered by the time he was 21, and he has since developed more of his own voice, even while constantly paying tribute to his idol. Faddis started playing trumpet when he was eight, and as a teenager his range was already quite astounding displaying the ability to hit high notes with ease. In 1971 he toured with Lionel Hampton and during 1972–73 appeared at a few concerts with Charles Mingus (filling in on "Little Royal Suite" for an ailing Roy Eldridge). He led two albums for Pablo while in his early twenties (including a duet date with Oscar Peterson) and sometimes played with Dizzy Gillespie (although their most exciting encounters do not seem to have been recorded). During 1977–84, not all that much was heard from Faddis as a soloist; he worked as a studio musician and played first trumpet with the Thad Jones/Mel Lewis Orchestra. However, Faddis re-emerged in 1985, recording for Concord, Epic, and Chesky in the years since. Jon Faddis, who can also sound like Eldridge and Louis Armstrong, has led the Carnegie Hall Jazz Orchestra since 1993. He is one of the top Bebop-oriented trumpeters around today, keeping the sound and style of Dizzy Gillespie very much alive.

10 *Legacy / Aug. 1985 / Concord Jazz 4291*
5 *Into the Faddisphere / May 2–8, 1989 / Epic 45266*
7 *Hornucopia / 1991 / Epic 46598*
7 *Remembrances / Oct. 13–15, 1997 / Chesky 166*

Jon Faddis's two Pablo albums have not yet been reissued on CD. After he returned to the jazz scene on a full-time basis in 1985, he recorded the classic *Legacy*. Faddis sounds like Louis Armstrong for part of "West End Blues," emulates Roy Eldridge closely on "Little Jazz," and pays tribute to Gillespie on "A Night in Tunisia" and "Things to Come." He also performs four other selections more in his own style. Assisted by tenor saxophonist Harold Land, pianist Kenny

Barron, Ray Brown, and drummer Mel Lewis, Jon Faddis has rarely sounded better, although he is capable of this level of greatness at any time.

Into the Faddisphere is a disappointment, for Faddis greatly overdoes it in the upper register, not just on the title cut but throughout this fairly modern set (which has six of his originals), even a modalized version of the Harry James-associated "Ciribiribin." Performing with a high-quality rhythm section (pianist Renee Rosnes, bassist Phil Bowler, and drummer Ralph Peterson), Faddis goes out of his way to show off his chops, but unfortunately his soul and taste are mostly missing on this effort. *Hornucopia* is erratic (with plenty of hits and misses) but is consistently colorful and on a much higher level. Faddis is featured on an orchestra piece ("High Five") in which he sails high above five lower brass; he plays a wa-wa plunger mute behind Vivian Cherry's singing on "Reckless Blues," is silly on "Ahbeedunseedja," and raps about Dizzy Gillespie ("Repartee") before the two trumpeters (unfortunately muted) briefly jam "Cherokee." A tribute to Miles Davis ("Dewey's Dance") does not work too well, "March That Thang" has the feel of a funky marching band, "Dizzy Atmosphere" is brief but fiery, and "I Surrender All" features Faddis playing a gospel-oriented duet with pianist James Williams. Definitely an intriguing set, well worth checking out.

Remembrances is a mostly melancholy affair as Faddis (who plays a lot on flugelhorn on this date) primarily performs a variety of ballads. He is accompanied by woodwinds (including Paquito D'Rivera, who solos on "In Your Own Sweet Way"), a French horn, and a rhythm section (with pianist David Hazeltine), arranged by Carlos Franzetti. Among the selections are "Sophisticated Lady," Herbie Hancock's "Speak Like a Child," "In Your Own Sweet Way," and "Goodbye." A tasteful and wistful affair that is much different than the trumpeter's usual Bop session.

LPS TO SEARCH FOR

Jon Faddis's debut as a leader was *Jon & Billy* (Black-Hawk 80532), a date from 1974 co-led with the intense tenor saxophonist Billy Harper that is sometimes abrasive (the two horns do not blend that well) but that has its intriguing moments. Pianist Roland Hanna (who doubles here on electric piano), bassist George Mraz, and drummer Motohiko Hino assist the co-leaders on six obscurities, four written by Hanna. *Youngblood* (Pablo 2310–765), from 1976, is long overdue to be reissued on CD. Faddis (who was 22 at the time) stretches out on Gillespie's "Here 'Tis," "Bebop," a haunting version of "Gershwin Prelude #2," "'Round Midnight," and "Samba de Orpheus" in spirited fashion. Kenny Barron, Mraz, and drummer Mickey Roker are stimulating in support on this near-classic date. The trumpeter's other out-of-print Pablo album, a superior duet date with Oscar Peterson, is reviewed under the pianist's name.

DON FAGERQUIST

b. Feb. 6, 1927, Worcester, MA, d. Jan. 24, 1974, Los Angeles, CA

Don Fagerquist was a very promising trumpeter whose mellow sound and fluent style fit easily into both Bebop and Cool. He gained recognition for his work with the big bands of three swing greats during the Bebop era: Gene Krupa (1944–45 and 1948), Artie Shaw (his Bebop Orchestra and Gramercy Five during 1949–50), and Woody Herman's Third Herd (1951–52). Fagerquist was with a fourth swing bandleader, Les Brown (1953), when he became a member of the Dave Pell Octet (1953–59), one of the top Cool Jazz combos. Don Fagerquist, who also recorded with Pete Rugolo, Mel Torme, Shelly Manne, and Art Pepper, became a studio musician in 1956 (a member of the staff of Paramount Films) and ended his career outside of jazz, dying of kidney disease shortly before his 47th birthday.

8 *Eight by Eight / Sept. 1957 / V.S.O.P. 4*

Other than three songs from 1955, Don Fagerquist led only this one album during his career. Fortunately it is a very good one, showcasing the trumpeter with a nonet arranged by Marty Paich (who also plays piano). Altoist Herb Geller and valve trombonist Bob Enevoldsen get plenty of solo space in addition to the leader, and the band consists of baritonist Ronnie Lang, trumpeter Ed Leddy, Vince DeRosa on French horn, bassist Buddy Clark, and drummer Mel Lewis. Fagerquist plays beautifully throughout, including on "Aren't You Glad You're You," "Smoke Gets in Your Eyes," "The Song Is You," and "Easy Living."

TAL FARLOW

b. June 7, 1921, Greensboro, NC, d. July 25, 1998, Sea Bright, NJ

Tal Farlow was one of the great jazz guitarists of the 1950s. His huge hands, light touch, and ability to play rapid solos quite cleanly made him the envy of other musicians. However, Farlow spent much of his life running away from and avoiding success. He spent his final 40 years as a part-time player, often working as a sign painter in New England and playing guitar just for the fun of it!

Farlow did not actually start on the guitar until he was 21, when he taught himself the instrument, inspired by Charlie Christian and Lester Young. A year later he began his professional career. After working with pianist-vibraphonist Dardanelle (1947), vibraphonist Marjorie Hyams (1948), and Buddy DeFranco (1949), Farlow came to fame as a member of the Red Norvo Trio. The vibes-guitar-bass group, which also included either Charles Mingus or Red Mitchell on bass, was a perfect vehicle for Farlow's fast lines during 1949–53. He was a member of Artie Shaw's Gramercy Five in 1953–54, had a return engagement with Norvo (they would have several reunions through the years), and then led his own classic trio, which featured pianist Eddie Costa and bassist Vinnie Burke. Farlow recorded regularly for Verve in the 1950s, making quite a few brilliant recordings.

However, in 1958 Farlow settled in New England, became a full-time sign painter, and played music only on an occasional basis from then on. He made one record as a leader during 1960–75 (also appearing on a Sonny Criss date) and in the late 1960s occasionally worked with the Newport All-Stars; otherwise he was barely heard from in the jazz world. Farlow was more active during 1976–84 but then during his final decade was in and out of music. Whenever he did appear in public, it was newsworthy. Tal Farlow showed that, even in his mid-70s, he could swing harder yet with a lighter touch than just about any other guitarist around.

9 *The Swinging Guitar of Tal Farlow / May 31, 1956 / Verve 314 559 515*

8 *The Return of Tal Farlow: 1969 / Sept. 23, 1969 / Original Jazz Classics 356*

Tal Farlow's first date as a leader, cut for Blue Note in 1954, has been reissued as part of a Howard McGhee CD and is reviewed there. He recorded nine albums as a leader for Verve during 1954–59 (the finest work of his career), but relatively little of the material has thus far been reissued on CD. *The Swinging Guitar* features the classic (if relatively short-lived) trio of Farlow, Eddie Costa, and bassist Vinnie Burke romping on such numbers as "Yardbird Suite," "You Stepped Out of a Dream," and "I Love You." The original seven selections are joined by two alternate takes and two versions of "Gone with the Wind" that were previously unreleased. Farlow is in brilliant form throughout, and he sounds inspired by his sidemen.

The Return of Tal Farlow was just a temporary return, a 1969 quartet date with pianist John Scully, bassist Jack Six, and drummer Alan Dawson that was practically Farlow's only recording of the 1960–75 period. Fortunately he had been playing privately on a daily basis and had lost nothing in the interim, as he shows on such numbers as "Straight No Chaser," "I'll Remember April," and "My Romance."

☐ **7** *A Sign of the Times / Aug. 2, 1976 / Concord Jazz 4026*

☐ **7** *On Stage / Aug. 1976 / Concord Jazz 4143*

☐ **6** *Chromatic Palette / Jan. 1981 / Concord Jazz 4154*

☐ **8** *Cookin' on All Burners / Aug. 1982 / Concord Jazz 4204*

Tal Farlow recorded six albums for the Concord label during 1976–84. Although he had slowed down just a little and was not always as flawless as he had been previously, he was still a major guitarist whenever he was persuaded to play. Four of the Concords have been reissued on CD. *A Sign of the Times* features Farlow in a drumless trio with Hank Jones and Ray Brown, jamming on such tunes as "Fascinating Rhythm," a relaxed "Stompin' at the Savoy," Dave Brubeck's "In Your Own Sweet Way," and Brown's "Bayside Blues." *On Stage,* from the same month, is a reunion of Farlow and Red Norvo, who are joined by Jones, Brown, and drummer Jake Hanna. The live set (from the 1976 Concord Jazz Festival) has its moments (including Norvo's feature on "The One I Love Belongs to Somebody Else" and "Lullaby of Birdland"), but there are also some overly loose spots. Still, the happy feelings dominate. *Chromatic Palette* matches Farlow with Tommy Flanagan and bassist Gary Mazzaroppi on a relaxed outing, performing melodic versions of seven standards (including Django Reinhardt's "Nuages," "If I Were a Bell," and "St. Thomas") plus Farlow's blues "Blue Art, Too." It is a pity that a fire was not lit under the talented players on that particular day. *Cookin' on All Burners,* which teams Farlow with Mazzaroppi, pianist James Williams, and drummer Vinnie Johnson, cooks quite a bit more. The highlights include "You'd Be So Nice to Come Home To," "I've Got the World on a String," and "Lullaby of the Leaves;" overall this is the most highly recommended of Tal Farlow's Concord sets.

LPS TO SEARCH FOR

At least three of Tal Farlow's Verve albums from 1954–56 were reissued by either Japanese or French Verve in the 1980s. *The Tal Farlow Album* (Verve 2584) has the guitarist joined either by rhythm guitarist Barry Galbraith, Oscar Pettiford, and drummer Joe Morello or by Claude Williamson and bassist Red Mitchell. The results are swinging versions of 11 standards (including Pettiford's "Blues in the Closet," "You and the Night and the Music," and "Stompin' at the Savoy") plus the guitarist's "Gibson Boy." Farlow, pianist Gerald Wiggins, Ray Brown, and drummer Chico Hamilton stretch out on eight mostly relaxed songs (including "Strike Up the Band," "Have You Met Miss Jones?" and a speedy "Cherokee") on *Autumn in New York* (Verve 2304 321), while *Tal* (Verve 2565) is a particularly strong outing from the Farlow-Costa-Burke trio including heated versions of "There Is No Greater Love," "Yesterdays," and "Broadway." All of Farlow's Verve albums deserve to be reissued on CD.

Adding to the legacy of the Farlow-Costa-Burke group are exciting and rather extended live performances from 1956, issued as *Fuerst Set* (Xanadu 109) and *Second Set* (Xanadu 119). All eight numbers exceed eight minutes in length and three are longer than 14. The double-LP *Poppin' and Burnin'* (Verve 815 236) reissued five of the ten songs from the 1955 set *The Interpretations of Tal Farlow,* four of the eight from 1958's *This Is Tal Farlow,* and a previously unissued five-song session from 1956. Among Farlow's sidemen on these joyful performances are pianists Claude Williamson, Eddie Costa, and Hank Jones, bassists Red Mitchell, Bill Takas, Knobby Totah, and Ray Brown, drummers Stan Levey, Jimmy Campbell, and Louie Bellson plus Oscar Pettiford on cello. *Triology* (Inner City 1099) is a solid outing from 1976 with pianist Mike Nock and bassist Lynn Christie (originally released by Japanese Sony), while *Tal Farlow 78* (Concord Jazz 57), a date with bassist Gary Mazzaroppi and drummer Tom Sayek, offers few surprises but is swinging. Also not yet reissued is *The Legendary Tal Farlow* (Concord Jazz 266), a 1984 project that gives Farlow the rare opportunity to interact with a horn (Sam Most on flute and tenor) on five of the eight standards, including "You Stepped Out of a Dream" and "When Lights Are Low."

FILMS

Tal Farlow appears with the Red Norvo Trio in one scene of *Texas Carnival* (1951). Farlow plays alongside Herb Ellis and Charlie Byrd on *Great Guitarists of Jazz* (Vestapol 13075), from the 1980s, and he is the subject of *Talmage Farlow,* a superior 1981 documentary (Rhapsody Films).

TOMMY FLANAGAN

b. Mar. 16, 1930, Detroit, MI

Although he could always swing hard, Tommy Flanagan (like Hank Jones) is also known for his tasteful and flawless playing, staying creative within the confines of the straight-ahead Bebop music that he loves. Flanagan played clarinet when he was six, switching to piano when he was 11. Other than time spent away during his stint in the Army (1951–53), the pianist was an important part of the very fertile Detroit jazz scene of 1945–55. In 1956 Flanagan moved to New York, and his talent was recognized from the start. The pianist appeared on many record dates during 1956–62 as a sideman plus led several of his own albums for New Jazz, Prestige, Savoy, and Moodsville. He worked with Oscar Pettiford, J.J. Johnson (1956–58), Miles Davis (1957), Harry "Sweets" Edison, and Coleman Hawkins (1961 and 1965), fitting in well in both swing and Bebop settings. Flanagan spent two periods (1963–65 and 1968–78) as Ella Fitzgerald's accompanist and, although he was kept busy touring the world with the singer, he ended up being greatly underrated as a soloist. That began to change in 1975, when he resumed leading record dates.Since leaving Ella, Flanagan has worked mostly with his own trios. He has recorded quite prolifically during the past 25 years, including for Pablo, Enja, Denon, Galaxy, Phontastic, Progressive, Uptown, Timeless, Enja, Verve, and several European and Japanese labels. Although he has become somewhat frail in recent times, Tommy Flanagan is still one of the top Bebop-oriented pianists around today.

8 *Overseas / Aug. 15, 1957 / Original Jazz Classics 1033*

7 *Plays the Music of Rodgers & Hammerstein / Sept. 23 + 30, 1958 / Savoy 4429*

6 *The Tommy Flanagan Trio / May 18, 1960 / Original Jazz Classics 182*

Other than a coop date called *The Cats* that is sometimes reissued under his name, Tommy Flanagan's first set as a leader is a trio album with bassist Wilbur Little and drummer Elvin Jones that was cut in Stockholm, Sweden. Most recently reissued as *Overseas* (it had been formerly released by Metronome and Dragon), the music (six originals, "Re-

laxin' at Camarillo," "Chelsea Bridge," "Willow Weep for Me," and three alternate takes) is swinging Bebop. Even at that early stage, Flanagan's style is quite recognizable. The *Rodgers & Hammerstein* set (eight songs from "The King and I" plus three alternate takes) was originally issued under trumpeter Wilbur Harden's name and also includes bassist George Duvivier and drummer G. T. Hogan. Among the songs that the quartet swings are "Getting to Know You," "We Kiss in a Shadow," and "Hello Young Lovers." The reissue simply known as *The Tommy Flanagan Trio* was cut for the Prestige subsidiary Moodsville, and the seven songs (other than the pianist's "Jes' Fine") are purposely played at slow tempos, including a solo piano version of "Come Sunday." Fine music by Flanagan, Tommy Potter, and Roy Haynes, but often a bit sleepy.

9 *The Tokyo Recital / Feb. 15, 1975 / Original Jazz Classics 737*

8 *Montreux '77 / July 13, 1977 / Original Jazz Classics 372*

9 *Our Delights / Jan. 28, 1978 / Original Jazz Classics 752*

7 *Something Borrowed, Something Blue / Jan. 30, 1978 / Original Jazz Classics 473*

7 *Ballads and Blues / Nov. 15, 1978 / Enja 3031*

8 *Together / Dec. 6, 1978 / Jazz Heritage 515205L*

7 *Super Session / Feb. 4, 1980 / Enja 3059*

6 *Giant Steps / Feb. 17–18, 1982 / Enja 79646*

7 *Thelonica / Nov. 30, 1982–Dec. 1, 1982 / Enja 79615*

Tommy Flanagan did not lead any record dates during 1962–74, and he was in danger of being taken for granted by the mid-1970s. *The Tokyo Recital,* his "comeback" record (he had not really been away), is a high-quality exploration of Duke Ellington and Billy Strayhorn tunes with bassist Keter Betts and drummer Bobby Durham (who were also in Ella Fitzgerald's trio at the time). Among the highlights of the live set are "UMMG," "Mainstem," "The Intimacy of the Blues," and "Take the 'A' Train." *Montreux '77* features the same trio two years later performing a pair of medleys and four other numbers, including Charlie Parker's "Barbados" and Dizzy Gillespie's "Woody 'n You."

Tommy Flanagan and Hank Jones, two complementary pianists, recorded a duet set on January 28, 1978. Originally the music was released as two albums: *Our Delights* and *More Delights.* The latter program had six alternate takes plus two additional songs. Now the former release has been reissued with an alternate version of "Robbins' Nest" added. The music comprises Bebop standards (including "Our Delight," "Jordu," and "Confirmation"), and the pianists leave plenty of room for each other, making this a successful outing.

Virtually every Flanagan CD is well worth picking up, for he is among the most consistent of pianists. *Something Borrowed, Something Blue* (the name of one of his originals) is a trio date with Keter Betts and drummer Jimmie Smith that includes Thad Jones's "Bird Song," "Good Bait," and "Groovin' High" among its selections. *Ballads and Blues,* duets with bassist George Mraz, also includes some swinging Bebop standards, such as "Scrapple from the Apple" and "Star Eyes," that are neither ballads nor blues; however, most of the other numbers are more relaxed. *Together* is a frequently exciting duet project with fellow pianist Kenny Barron that is made up of six standards, including Miles Davis's "Dig," "Stella by Starlight," and "The Way You Look Tonight." Flanagan reunited with fellow Detroiter Elvin Jones along with bassist Red Mitchell on *Super-Session,* performing two of his best originals ("Minor Perhaps" and "Rachel's Rondo") plus four familiar standards (including John Lewis' "Django" and "I Love You"). The playing (with its close interplay) is as exquisite as is expected from the personnel. Flanagan had played with John Coltrane on the original version of "Giant Steps," although at the time he did not take much of a solo. The CD *Giant Steps,* with George Mraz and drummer Al Foster, has Flanagan interpreting six of 'Trane's songs, including "Mr. P. C.," "Naima," and the title cut. The music is fine, but nothing too adventurous occurs because the danger of Coltrane's performances is lacking. *Thelonica,* a double tribute to Thelonious Monk and the Baroness Pannonica de Koenigswarter (a good friend of many Bebop musicians) has Flanagan's title cut along with mostly relaxed renditions of eight of Monk's tunes, including "Off Minor," "Ask Me Now," and "Ugly Beauty." The pianist is joined by George Mraz and Art Taylor for this pleasing session.

8   *Nights at the Vanguard / Oct. 18–19, 1986 / Uptown 27.29*
7   *Jazz Poet / Jan. 17–19, 1989 / Alfa/Compose 7102*
9   *Beyond the Bluebird / Apr. 29–30, 1990 / Timeless 350*
8   *Flanagan's Shenanigans / Apr. 2, 1993 / Storyville 4191*
10   *Let's Play the Music of Thad Jones / Apr. 4, 1993 / Enja 8040*
7   *Lady Be Good . . . For Ella / July 30–31, 1993 / Verve 314 521 617*
7   *Sea Changes / Mar. 11–12, 1996 / Evidence 22191*
8   *Sunset and the Mockingbird / Mar. 16, 1997 / Blue Note 93155*

Tommy Flanagan has kept quite busy during the past 25 years, recording many albums (mostly trio), virtually all of which are excellent examples of his playing. *Nights at the Vanguard,* performed with George Mraz and Al Foster, includes such tunes as Thelonious Monk's "San Francisco Holiday," Phil Woods's "Goodbye Mr. Evans," "More Than You Know," and Bud Powell's "I'll Keep Loving You" plus a pair of Thad Jones songs. *Jazz Poet* is a mostly lightly swinging effort with Mraz and drummer Kenny Washington that is highlighted by "Caravan," "I'm Old Fashioned," and Billy Strayhorn's "Raincheck." *Beyond the Bluebird* finds Flanagan sounding more inspired than normal; perhaps it was due to the presence of guitarist Kenny Burrell (along with Mraz and drummer Lewis Nash). The songs are quite superior and include "Yesterdays," Charlie Parker's "Barbados," Barry Harris's "Nascimento," and two numbers by the pianist.

Flanagan's Shenanigans was recorded in Denmark when Tommy Flanagan was awarded the 1993 Jazzpar Prize. He plays four songs with a trio (bassist Jesper Lundgaard and Lewis Nash), "For Lena and Lennie" with tenor saxophonist Jesper Thilo, and three other numbers with the trio and a six-piece horn section. The music (which includes his tunes "Eclypso," "Beyond the Bluebird," and Minor Mishap") does a fine job of summing up the pianist's career up to that point. However, it is a pity that the full group could not have not been utilized for an entire set of Flanagan's music, since their numbers are the high point. *Let's Play the Music of Thad Jones,* from two days later, is one of the pianist's finest recordings. Flanagan (along with Lundgaard and Lewis Nash) explores 11 Thad Jones songs, few of which had ever been played by a piano trio before. In addition to "Mean What You Say," "A Child Is Born," and "Three in One," there are quite a few superb obscurities on this memorable date, a classic of its kind. *Lady Be Good* is a fine tribute set (with bassist Peter Washington and Lewis Nash) to Flanagan's longtime employer, Ella Fitzgerald. The pianist performs eight songs that he fondly remembered playing with Ella, including "How High the Moon," "Smooth Sailing,"

"Angel Eyes," and two versions of "Lady Be Good." *Sea Changes* is another outing by the Flanagan-Washington-Nash trio, this time performing five Flanagan originals and six standards, including "Between the Devil and the Deep Blue Sea" and "Relaxin' at Camarillo." *Sunset and the Mockingbird* was recorded on Flanagan's 67th birthday, live at the Village Vanguard with Washington and Nash. For the fun occasion, Flanagan avoids any warhorses and instead plays tunes by Thad Jones, Tom MacIntosh, Dizzy Gillespie, and Duke Ellington (the little-known title cut, which is quite haunting) plus the closing "Good Night My Love."

LPS TO SEARCH FOR

It's Magic (Savoy 1158) has four forgotten originals and a three-song ballad medley played in 1957 (the liner notes mistakenly say 1947) by a fine hard Bop quintet consisting of Flanagan, altoist Sonny Redd, trombonist Curtis Fuller, bassist George Tucker, and drummer Louis Hayes. *Trinity* (Inner City 1084) is a superior trio outing from 1975 with bassist Ron Carter and Roy Haynes that includes such numbers as "52nd Street Theme," "Ruby, My Dear," and several Flanagan originals. *Plays the Music of Harold Arlen* (Inner City 1071) matches Flanagan with bassist George Mraz and drummer Connie Kay on nine Arlen tunes, with Helen Merrill taking a guest vocal on "Last Night When We Were Young." *The Magnificent Tommy Flanagan* (Progressive 7059), from 1981, also features Mraz along with Al Foster; Flanagan plays seven standards (including "Speak Low," "Change Partners," and "Just in Time") plus Thad Jones's "Blueish Grey."

FILMS

Tommy Flanagan appears briefly in the 1973 jazz documentary *Born to Swing* (Rhapsody Films). He also plays an exciting version of "Fascinating Rhythm" with Tal Farlow and Red Mitchell in 1981's *Talmage Farlow* (Rhapsody Films).

CARL FONTANA

b. July 18, 1928, Monroe, LA

Until recent times, trombonist Carl Fontana had mostly an underground reputation among his fellow musicians, for he was barely represented on records. His father played saxophone and Fontana played in his dad's dance band as a youth during 1941–45. He attended Louisiana State University (graduating in 1950) and then gained some recognition for his work with Woody Herman's orchestra (1951–53). Fontana played with Lionel Hampton (1954), Hal McIntyre's big band (1954–55), and Stan Kenton (1956–57), showing that he was a master of Bebop and a technical wizard of the trombone. But after playing with Kai Winding's four-trombone septet (1956–57), Fontana moved to Las Vegas, where he has worked primarily with show bands up to the present time.

Fontana has played jazz on various occasions through the years, including touring with Woody Herman (1966), making a record with Supersax (1973), playing with Louie Bellson, co-leading the Hanna-Fontana Band with drummer Jake Hanna (1975), gigging with the World's Greatest Jazz Band, and recording with trumpeter Bobby Shew (1995). Most recently, Carl Fontana has been featured on some recorded jam sessions for the Woofy label, displaying his technically skilled, very fluent and swinging approach to Bebop and standards, one that always amazes other trombonists.

9 *The Great Fontana / Sept. 5-6, 1985 / Uptown 27.28*
8 *The Carl Fontana-Arno Marsh Quintet / Aug. 2-3, 1997 / Woofy 51*
8 *The Carl Fontana Quartet / Feb. 7-8, 1998 / Woofy 72*
8 *The Carl Fontana-Andy Martin Quintet / Dec. 5-6, 1998 / Woofy 87*

Despite his strong reputation, Carl Fontana did not record his first album as a leader until he was 57. Joined by tenor saxophonist Al Cohn, pianist Richard Wyands, bassist Ray Drummond, and drummer Akira Tana in 1985, the trombonist plays brilliantly throughout *The Great Fontana*. He digs into three obscure but worthy songs (Sonny Clark's "Shoutin' on a Riff," Charlie Shavers's "Showcase," and Eddie Higgins's "Expubident") plus a variety of standards, four of which were released for the first time on the CD version of this former LP.

The three Woofy CDs are all essentially jam sessions, offering listeners some valuable examples of the too rarely heard Carl Fontana horn. The date with tenor saxophonist Arno Marsh (a little-known player who had stints with the Woody Herman and Stan Kenton bands that overlapped with Fontana's periods) also feature pianist Brian O'Rourke, bassist John Leitham, and drummer Dick Berk. The seven standards include such offbeat choices as "Milestones," Gerry Mulligan's "Disc Jockey Jump," and "Apple Honey." The quartet date (with O'Rourke, bassist Tom Warrington, and drummer Dom Moio) has Fontana well showcased as the only horn. The six songs include "Look for the Silver Lining," the underrated "If I Only Had a Brain," and "The Flintstones." Later in 1998, he was teamed up with the same rhythm section and fellow trombonist Andy Martin, whose speed and quick ideas puts him on Fontana's level, no easy feat! They stretch out on six songs (which clock in between 9 and 14 minutes long) on their Woofy CD, including "I Thought About You," Benny Carter's "Only Trust Your Heart," and "Caravan." Although little planning went into the three Woofy releases, there was no need for rehearsals. Carl Fontana was simply allowed the opportunities to stretch out. Why didn't some other label think of that 30 years earlier?

BRUCE FORMAN

b. May 14, 1956, Springfield, MA

Bruce Forman has long been a hard-swinging Bebop guitarist, one who excels at playing chorus after chorus of creative ideas over common chord changes. Forman had piano lessons for six years before deciding to switch to the guitar in 1970. He moved with his family to San Francisco in 1971 and has been a fixture in Northern California ever since, appearing regularly at the Monterey Jazz Festival. Forman was a regular member of Richie Cole's band during 1978–82 but otherwise has mostly led his own groups in addition to being quite active as a jazz educator. Bruce Forman has headed albums for the Choice, Muse, Concord, and Kamei labels and has recorded as a sideman with Cole, Eddie Jefferson, Mark Murphy, Freddie Hubbard, Ray Brown, Bobby Hutcherson, and others.

7	*There Are Times / Aug. 1986 / Concord Jazz 4332*
8	*Pardon Me! / Oct. 1988 / Concord Jazz 4368*
9	*Still of the Night / 1991 / Kamei 7000*
9	*Forman on the Job / 1992 / Kamei 7004*

Bruce Forman recorded four albums for the Concord label during 1984–88, but the earliest two (which have pianist George Cables as a co-leader) are currently available only as cassettes! *There Are Times* once again has Cables joining Forman, along with bassist Jeff Carney, drummer Eddie Marshall, and the great vibraphonist Bobby Hutcherson. Each of the eight selections has its intriguing moments, including a version of Dizzy Gillespie's "Con Alma" that is in 5/4, "Strike Up the Band," Thelonious Monk's "Little Roo-

tie," and "All the Things You Are." *Pardon Me!* is actually better, due to the participation of pianist Billy Childs (who is in particularly creative form) in a quartet with Carney and Marshall. The material is challenging, including John Coltrane's "Count Down" and Dave Liebman's "Once Again" plus four Forman originals and a pair of familiar standards. Throughout, Forman makes every note count and swing.

The small San Francisco label Kamei has featured primarily guitarists, and its first release showcases Forman in a trio with bassist John Clayton and drummer Albert "Tootie" Heath. The group performs three of the leader's tunes and such heated numbers as "In the Still of the Night," "Cherokee," and "Lady Be Good." Also very much in the straight-ahead vein is *Forman on the Job*, which has the trio of Forman, Clayton, and drummer Vince Lateano joined on eight of the 11 numbers by pianist Mark Levine, with four appearances by tenor saxophonist Joe Henderson, five from percussionist John Santos, and two by Andy Narell on steel drums. The repertoire is particularly strong, including Bud Powell's "Un Poco Loco," "Autumn Nocturne," Forman's "Last Minute Calypso," and "A Night in Tunisia."

LPS TO SEARCH FOR

Bruce Forman's debut as a leader, 1978's *Coast to Coast* (Choice 1026), is quite scarce. During 1981–82 he led four dates for Muse, including *20/20* (Muse 5273), a quartet outing with pianist Albert Dailey that has two guest appearances by trumpeter Tom Harrell, and *In Transit* (Muse 5299). The latter has Forman interacting with Ed Kelly (on organ) and drummer Eddie Marshall on five of the guitarist's songs plus "Mood Indigo," "Peace," and "Waltzing Matilda." *Dynamics* (Concord Jazz 279), a duet date with George Cables, features some surprisingly passionate but quiet performances, including "Mutt & Jeff," "Doxy," "Be My Love," and "I Mean You."

HERB GELLER

b. Nov. 2, 1928, Los Angeles, CA

Herb Geller was an important part of the Los Angeles jazz scene in the 1950s yet is today playing with fire and brilliance that he only hinted at in his early days, despite how strong he was then! Geller initially picked up experience working with Joe Venuti's orchestra (1946) and Claude Thornhill (1949). After a period in New York, he moved back to his native Los Angeles in 1951, married the talented

Bop pianist Lorraine Walsh, and became quite busy. During 1951–58, Geller worked with Billy May, Maynard Ferguson, Shorty Rogers, Bill Holman, Chet Baker, and Shelly Manne, was associated with Lenny Bruce, recorded on jam sessions with Clifford Brown and Max Roach, and led a quartet that included his wife. His sound, although influenced by Charlie Parker with bits of Benny Carter, was a bit heavier and he knew his Bebop extremely well.

The sudden death of Lorraine Geller in 1958 was a major shock that took him years to get over. Herb Geller played with Benny Goodman (off and on during 1958–61), was in Brazil for a time, moved to Berlin in 1962, and three years later settled permanently in Hamburg, Germany. Geller worked regularly with German radio orchestras for 30 years and, although he continued to grow as a musician, he was largely forgotten in the United States. However, starting in the early 1990s, Geller began appearing more regularly in his native country, and his recordings (for Enja, V.S.O.P., Fresh Sound, and Hep) and live appearances (mostly on the West Coast) show that he is still improving with age. In addition to his powerful alto playing and his doubling on soprano, Herb Geller, who presented his autobiography as a musical show, also occasionally sings.

8	*Stax of Sax / 1958 / Fresh Sound 75*
6	*A Jazz Song Book / Dec. 1988 / Enja 79655*
9	*The Herb Geller Quartet / Aug. 5-6, 1993 / V.S.O.P. 89*
10	*Plays the Al Cohn Songbook / June 11-12, 1994 / Hep 2066*
8	*Playing Jazz / Jan. 16-20, 1995 / Fresh Sound 5011*
8	*I'll Be Back / Aug. 23-24, 1996 / Hep 2074*
9	*You're Looking at Me / Feb. 25-26, 1997 / Fresh Sound 5018*

During 1953–59, Herb Geller led a four-song session for Imperial, three albums for Emarcy, two for Jubilee, and one for Atco. One of his few sessions that is currently available is *Stax of Sax,* a reissue of the second Jubilee date. The altoist is joined by vibraphonist Victor Feldman, pianist Walter Norris (who would also move permanently to Europe), bassist Leroy Vinnegar, and drummer Anthony Vazley for three excellent originals, "Change Partners," and "It Might As Well Be Spring." Fine West Coast Bebop.

After relocating to Europe, Herb Geller did not lead any other record dates until one misfire (the rather odd *View from Here*) in 1975 and then nothing until 1984. *A Jazz Song Book* comprises instrumental versions of nine songs from Geller's musical autobiography. These early versions (performed by Geller on alto and soprano, Walter Norris, guitarist John Schroder, bassist Mike Richmond, and drummer Adam Nussbaum) contain strong solos by Geller that easily overshadow the often-forgettable themes.

The Herb Geller Quartet is a better buy. Inspired by pianist Tom Ranier, bassist John Leitham, and drummer Louie Bellson, Geller shows just how exciting a player he had become, whether performing Zoot Sims's "The Red Door," Jimmy Rowles's "The Peacocks" (with the composer guesting on piano), "This Is New," or one of his five originals. On "Stand-Up Comic" (from his autobiography), Geller takes a personable vocal. However, *Herb Geller Plays the Al Cohn Songbook* is the altoist's most essential release to date. Geller performs a dozen of the late tenor's songs plus his original tribute, "Mr. Music," and Johnny Mandel's "El Cajon." Geller (on alto and soprano) plays magnificently throughout the well-conceived set, Tom Ranier is heard not only on piano but also on tenor, clarinet, and bass clarinet, bassist John Leitham and drummer Paul Kreibich are excellent in support, and Ruth Price contributes a few vocals. The material is made up of mostly lesser-known tunes, and the creative performances would certainly have pleased Al Cohn.

Playing Jazz was the recorded realization of Geller's dream, 19 songs that form his musical autobiography (including a remake of "Stand-Up Comic"). In addition to the composer's quartet (with Ranier, Leitham, and drummer Paul Kreibich), the performances feature Geller, Lothar Atwell, Mike Campbell, Stephanie Haynes, Polly Podewell, and Rich Crystal in speaking and, usually, singing parts. Geller focuses mostly on his early years before he moved to Europe, paying tribute to Lenny Bruce, Charlie Parker, Joe Albany, Chet Baker, and Al Cohn, among others, while telling his life story. The chronology does jump around a lot, but the unusual audio show will hold listeners' interest.

I'll Be Back features Geller in Germany with his local working unit (guitarist Ed Harris, bassist Thomas Biller, and drummer Heinrich Kobberling), performing four originals, one song by Harris, and superior standards, including "Dream Dancing," "You're Laughing at Me," and Hoagy Carmichael's "One Morning in May." Back in the United States in 1997, Geller recorded a particularly rewarding set, *You're Looking at Me,* with pianist Jan Lundgren, bassist Dave Carpenter, and drummer Joe LaBarbera. The first ten selections are all mostly veteran standards, including several that are not performed all that often ("Summer Night," "Changes," Billy Strayhorn's "Orson," and "All Through the Night"). The final four numbers are taken from "The Josephine Baker Suite," original pieces from a musical in Europe for which Geller wrote the score.

LPS TO SEARCH FOR

Herb Geller Plays (Emarcy 36045) is by the Gellers in 1954, a Boppish mixture of standards and originals with Curtis Counce or Leroy Vinnegar on bass and Lawrence Marable or Eldridge Freeman on drums. *Herb Geller Sextet* (Emarcy 36040 and last available as Trip 5539) has a sextet with both Gellers, Conte Candoli, and the barely documented but swinging cool-toned tenor saxophonist Ziggy Vines (whose only other recording was at Clifford Brown's final gig). *Hot House* from 1984 (Circle 241184/30) was the beginning of the second half of Herb Geller's recording career. The live date teams the altoist with a fine German rhythm section on six standards, including "Hot House," "Well, You Needn't," and "Donna Lee," showing that Herb Geller's Bebop chops were still quite sharp.

PAUL GONSALVES

b. July 12, 1920, Boston, MA, d. May 15, 1974, London, England

Several of Duke Ellington's sidemen of the 1950s were strongly influenced by Bebop, particularly Jimmy Hamilton, Clark Terry, and Duke's longtime tenor saxophonist soloist, Paul Gonsalves. Gonsalves's harmonically advanced style (which was somewhat unpredictable) always sounded modern even with his big Ben Webster-influenced tone, and he was an influence years later on avant-gardist David Murray.

Gonsalves first played guitar when he was 16 before switching to tenor, working early on with Sabby Lewis's band. After a term in the Army, Gonsalves was one of the more Boppish soloists in Count Basie's orchestra during 1946–49, where he was Illinois Jacquet's successor. His Bop credentials were further established during his stint with the Dizzy Gillespie Orchestra (1949–50). However, Gonsalves will always be best known for his 24 years with Duke Ellington (1950–74). Ellington loved the fact that Gonsalves could play marathon solos at a driving speed (in addition to warm ballads) and he featured him often. At the 1956 Newport Jazz Festival in the transition between "Diminuendo in Blue"

and "Crescendo in Blue," Ellington spontaneously urged Gonsalves on as he took a 27-chorus solo that caused a sensation (practically inspiring a riot) and led to Duke's commercial renaissance. Although Gonsalves occasionally led record dates of his own (including a classic meeting with Sonny Stitt) and was used as a sideman on some sessions, he was never tempted to leave Ellington's band. Paul Gonsalves passed away nine days before Duke Ellington and was considered a valuable sideman to the very end.

7 *Ellingtonia Moods & Blues / Feb. 29, 1960 / RCA 63562.*
8 *Getting Together! / Dec. 20, 1960 / Original Jazz Classics 203*
7 *Just a-Sittin' and a-Rockin' / Aug. 28, 1970 + Sept. 3, 1970 / Black Lion 760148*
8 *Paul Gonsalves Meets Earl Hines / Dec. 15, 1970 + Nov. 29, 1972 /. Black Lion 760177*
8 *Mexican Bandit Meets Pittsburgh Pirate / Aug. 24, 1973 / Original Jazz Classics 751*

Starting in 1956 (shortly after his big Newport success), Paul Gonsalves led albums for Emarcy, Argo, RCA, Jazzland, British Vocalion, Impulse, the British World Record Club, Storyville, Catalyst, French Riviera, Black Lion, and Fantasy. *Ellingtonia Moods* has Paul Gonsalves as the leader, although altoist Johnny Hodges and trumpeter Ray Nance (who makes several majestic statements) often steal solo honors. Trombonist Booty Wood is also in fine form, while the rhythm section comprises pianist Jimmy Jones (probably responsible for the arranged ensembles), bassist Al Hall, and drummer Oliver Jackson. Gonsalves wrote the two best numbers (the medium-tempo blues "Chocataw" and a catchy "I Got Rhythm" derivative called "The Line-Up"), Hodges brought in four others, and the septet also plays "Daydream" (which, contrary to the liner notes, is not one of the altoist's originals). The ensembles could have been much more freewheeling but the results are excellent.

Getting Together is a Boppish date on which Gonsalves heads a quintet also featuring cornetist Nat Adderley (on four of the seven tunes), pianist Wynton Kelly, bassist Sam Jones, and drummer Jimmy Cobb. Among the best selections are "Hard Groove," "I Cover the Waterfront," and "Walkin'." For *Just a-Sittin' and a-Rockin'*, Gonsalves shares the frontline with two Ellingtonians (Ray Nance on trumpet, violin, and vocals and altoist Norris Turney), assisted by a fine rhythm section with Hank Jones or Raymond Fol on piano. Most of the selections are relaxed, with "Stompy Jones" generating the most heat. The tenor's collaboration with pianist Earl Hines, bassist Al Hall, and drummer Jo Jones has five extended standards, including "It Don't Mean a Thing," "Moten Swing," and "I Got It Bad." The music dates from 1970, other than an unrelated piano solo ("Blue Sands") from 1972.

Mexican Bandit Meets Pittsburgh Pirate features the potent team of Gonsalves and trumpeter Roy Eldridge. Joined by pianist Cliff Smalls, Sam Jones, and drummer Eddie Locke, the two horns perform three heated pieces and a few ballads. Eldridge takes a rare vocal on "Somebody Loves Me," and other highlights include Gonsalves's warm tone on "I Cover the Waterfront," "5400 North," and "C Jam Blues." It may have been late in their careers, but Paul Gonsalves and Roy Eldridge never lost their competitive spirit.

LPS TO SEARCH FOR

Tell It the Way It Is (Impulse 55), from 1963, is most notable for a superb version of "Body and Soul"; Ray Nance, Johnny Hodges, and Rolf Ericson are also major assets. *The Buenos Aires Sessions* (Catalyst 7913), from five years later, has Gonsalves and trumpeter Willie Cook with an Argentinean rhythm section and is quite inspired and swinging.

GREAT GUITARS

Herb Ellis, Barney Kessel, and Charlie Byrd were all quite familiar with each other's playing throughout their careers. Ellis and Byrd had recorded together in 1963, and back in 1953 Ellis became Kessel's replacement with the Oscar Peterson Trio when Kessel decided to leave the road to settle in the studios. The three guitarists each shared a strong love for Charlie Christian's music, although Byrd gained his reputation in the early 1960s playing bossa nova on the acoustic guitar. In 1973 the trio came together as Great Guitars, a quintet that also utilized Byrd's rhythm section. During 1974–82 Great Guitars recorded five albums for Concord and performed occasionally in clubs. Although the musicians had individual features, the high points were invariably when the three guitarists were romping on an uptempo Bebop or swing standard.

In 1992, a decade after the group's last joint record, Barney Kessel had a major stroke that ended his career. Great Guitars (with Ron Eschete in Kessel's place) played a concert in 1995, and in 1996, with Mundell Lowe joining Ellis and

Byrd, Great Guitars made their final record; Larry Coryell gave the group four guitarists on some selections. Charlie Byrd's death in 1999 permanently ended the band.

9   *Great Guitars / July 28, 1974 / Concord Jazz 6004*
8   *Great Guitars II / July 1976 / Concord Jazz 4023*
7   *Straight Tracks / 1978 / Concord Jazz 4421*
8   *Great Guitars at the Winery / July 1980 / Concord Jazz 4131*
6   *Great Guitars at Charlie's Georgetown / Aug. 1982 / Concord Jazz 4209*
8   *The Return of the Great Guitars / Feb. 14-15, 1996 / Concord Jazz 4715*

Each of the Great Guitars's recordings are enjoyable. The first five have Byrd, Ellis, and Kessel joined by bassist Joe Byrd and either John Rae, Wayne Phillips, Jimmie Smith, or Chuck Redd on drums. The initial *Great Guitars* release was recorded live at the 1974 Concord Jazz Festival and has a little more of the "sound of surprise" than the later ones, since the setting was a new one for the three guitarists. Among the more notable selections are "Undecided," "Topsy," and "Benny's Bugle." There are also four numbers showcasing Kessel and Ellis (three are duets) and two Byrd features. *Great Guitars II,* recorded in the studio, has its exciting moments, including "Lover," a witty "Cow Cow Boogie," and a three-song medley that resolves into a heated "Flying Home." *Straight Tracks* emphasizes mostly lazier tempos and includes "I'm Putting All My Eggs in One Basket," "Gravy Waltz," and the hotter "Little Rock Getaway." *Great Guitars at the Winery* has more variety and heat, being highlighted by swinging versions of "Broadway," "Air Mail Special," "So Danco Samba," and "Sheik of Araby." *Great Guitars at Charlie's Georgetown,* the last outing by the original group, includes "Where or When," "Change Partners," "Opus One," and "Get Happy." But, other than the last piece, the emphasis is on slower tempos and a bit too much taste!

Fourteen years later, Charlie Byrd and Herb Ellis had a reunion with a new and short-lived version of the group, with Mundell Lowe in Kessel's place plus bassist John Goldsby and drummer Tim Horner. On eight of the 13 pieces, Larry Coryell gives the band a fourth guitarist. The old magic between Byrd and Ellis is rekindled one last time on such numbers as "Things Ain't What They Used to Be," "A Smooth One," "Bernie's Tune," and "Seven Come Eleven," a last hurrah for this enjoyable Bebop group.

FILMS

The Great Guitars fortunately can be seen on several videos: *Great Guitars* (Rhapsody 9036), *Great Guitars* (Shanachie 6305), and *Jazz at the Maintenance Shop* (Shanachie 6309). The later version of the group, with Tal Farlow in place of Kessel, is featured as *Great Guitarists of Jazz* (Vestapol 13075).

BENNIE GREEN

b. Apr. 16, 1923, Chicago, IL, d. Mar. 23, 1977, San Diego, CA

J.J. Johnson was such a dominant influence on Bebop-oriented trombonists that only two major players emerged during 1945–55 who had a different sound: Bill Harris and Bennie Green. Green's witty style and tone (which was fat and expressive) made him instantly recognizable. He was able to straddle the boundaries between swing, Bop, and early R&B throughout his career. Green was part of the Earl Hines's Orchestra during 1942–48 (other than two years in the military), including the period when Dizzy Gillespie and Charlie Parker were among Hines' sidemen. After playing with Charlie Ventura's combo during 1948–50, he rejoined Hines, who had a small swing band during 1951–53. Green became a bandleader in 1953, and his sidemen during the next decade included tenors Charlie Rouse, Johnny Griffin, Eddie "Lockjaw" Davis, Eric Dixon, and Jimmy Forrest, pianists Cliff Smalls, Sonny Clark, and Gildo Mahones, bassist Paul Chambers, and drummer Louis Hayes, among others.

Green recorded often as a leader during 1951–61 (making albums for Prestige, Decca, Blue Note, Vee-Jay, Time, Bethlehem, and Jazzland) and occasionally as a sideman, including with Charles Mingus, Miles Davis, and Buck Clayton, but his glory period was over after 1961. There was just one additional record date as a leader, when he teamed up with Sonny Stitt in 1964. Benny Green was in Duke Ellington's orchestra for a few months during 1968–69 and appeared at the 1972 Newport Jazz Festival in New York jam sessions (which were recorded) five years before his death, but he mostly languished in obscurity during his final 15 years, playing in Las Vegas.

8   *Blows His Horn / June 10, 1955 + Sept. 22, 1955 / Original Jazz Classics 1728*

7   *Bennie Green with Art Farmer / Apr. 13, 1956 / Original Jazz Classics 1800*

7   *Walking Down / June 29, 1956 / Original Jazz Classics 1753*

9   *Soul Stirrin' / Apr. 28, 1958 / Blue Note 59381*

5   *The Swingin'est / Nov. 12, 1958 / Vee-Jay 905*

8   *Glidin' Along / Mar. 9 + 22, 1961 / Original Jazz Classics 1869*

Bennie Green always conveyed a feeling of fun in his music. *Blows His Horn,* a sextet outing with Charlie Rouse, pianist Cliff Smalls, bassist Paul Chambers, drummer Osie Johnson, and Candido on conga, has group vocals on two songs, several jumping numbers, and a mixture of basic originals and appealing standards. The Green-Rouse blend works well, and among the better pieces are "Sometimes I'm Happy," "Body and Soul," and "Hi Yo Silver." Green's meeting with trumpeter Art Farmer (along with Smalls, bassist Addison Farmer, and drummer Philly Joe Jones) is a bit more serious (although the trombone solos are quite cheerful) as the two horns dig into three group originals, "My Blue Heaven," and "Gone with the Wind." Unfortunately the playing time is less than 34 minutes, but what is included is excellent. *Walking Down* finds Green in a quintet with Eric Dixon (who would become best known for his long association with Count Basie, although here he sounds a lot like Paul Gonsalves), pianist Lloyd Mayers, bassist Sonny Wellesley, and drummer Bill English. Some of the music is a bit loose, but the arrangements contain a few surprises, including change of tempos on "Walkin' " and "The Things We Did Last Summer," and a cooking version of "It's You or No One."

Bennie Green leads a particularly intriguing group on *Soul Stirrin',* a sextet with both Gene Ammons and Billy Root on tenors, Sonny Clark, bassist Ike Isaacs, and a young Elvin Jones on drums. Two songs (the title cut and "Lullaby of the Doomed") have vocals by Green and Babs Gonzales, and the full group joins in (glee club style) on "We Wanna Cook." All of the horns and Clark get in their solos, a wide variety of tempos are employed, and the overall result is one of the trombonist's strongest recordings. Unfortunately *The Swingin'est,* which also has an all-star group (with Green, Ammons, and Frank Foster on tenors, Frank Wess on flute and tenor, cornetist Nat Adderley, Tommy Flanagan, bassist Ed Jones, and drummer Albert "Tootie" Heath), does not live up to its potential. Nearly all of the songs (originals by band members) are blues, and the inclusion of three alternate takes adds to the sameness of the overly basic material. There are some good moments, but this CD should be heard only in small doses! *Glidin' Along,* Green's last date as a leader (other than the later set shared with Sonny Stitt), is an excellent one, with the trombonist teamed with the competitive tenor of Johnny Griffin plus pianist Junior Mance, Paul Chambers or Larry Gales on bass, and drummer Ben Riley. Other than "Stardust" (the project's only ballad), the emphasis is on medium-tempo originals, all of which were contributed by either Green, Griffin, or Babs Gonzales (although the singer is absent from the session). The music is typically joyous and swinging.

LPS TO SEARCH FOR

Bennie Green (Bainbridge 1046), from 1960, has plenty of spirited solos from Green, tenor saxophonist Jimmy Forrest, and Sonny Clark, with the pianist contributing three of the six songs, including a remake of his "Cool Struttin'." *Catwalk* (Bethlehem 6018), also from 1960, featuring Green jamming blues, ballads, and basic originals with Forrest in a sextet with organist Skip Hall and with a septet that adds altoist Lem Davis and has pianist Mal Waldron in Hall's place.

AL GREY

b. June 6, 1925, Aldie, VA; d. Mar. 24, 2000, Phoenix, AZ

Throughout his career, trombonist Al Grey was best known for his mastery of the plunger mute, but he was also able to sound quite at home in Bebop settings. Grey started on the baritone horn when he was four and soon started studying trombone with his father (who played both brass and reed instruments). He served in the Navy during World War II (playing with a service dance band) and then spent the Bebop era working with the orchestras of Benny Carter (1945–46), Jimmie Lunceford (1946–47), Lucky Millinder, and Lionel Hampton. Grey played for a time with tenor saxophonist Arnett Cobb's jump combo. He was a major asset with the Dizzy Gillespie big band of 1956–57. Grey's rambunctious solo on "Cool Breeze" at the 1957 Newport Jazz Festival held its own with the exciting statements of Gillespie and tenor saxophonist Billy Mitchell. After working briefly with Oscar Pettiford, Grey became a key soloist with the Count Basie Orchestra (1957–61). He co-led a sextet with Billy Mitchell that featured the up-and-coming vibraphonist Bobby

Hutcherson, and then rejoined Basie (1964–66). After a few years of freelancing, Grey was back with Count for a third time (1971–77), making his biggest impression during this stint. When he left Basie for the final time, Grey and Jimmy Forrest (Count's other top soloist of the 1970s) co-led a quintet, which lasted until Forrest's death in 1980. During his last 20 years, Al Grey (whose "wa-wa" sound is a throwback to the 1930s) appeared in many all-star groups, including with Clark Terry, the Statesmen of Jazz, and Lionel Hampton, and in a band with his son, Mike Grey, on second trombone.

9 *Truly Wonderful! / July 19-21, 1978 / Stash 552*
8 *Night Train—Revisited / July 19-21, 1978 / Storyville 8293*
7 *Al Grey and Jesper Thilo Quintet / Aug. 1986 / Storyville 4136*
7 *Al Meets Bjarne / Aug. 5, 1988 / Gemini 62*
6 *Fab / Feb. 4 + 7, 1990 / Capri 74038*
7 *Live at the Floating Jazz Festival / Oct. 22-25, 1990 / Chiaroscuro 313*
8 *Me 'n Jack / 1993 / Pullen Music 2350*
9 *Centerpiece / Mar. 23-26, 1995 / Telarc 83379*
7 *Matzoh and Grits / Apr. 22-23, 1996 / Arbors 19167*
7 *Echoes of New Orleans / Oct. 20, 1997 / Progressive 7108*

The Al Grey-Jimmy Forrest Quintet was a perfect setting for both trombonist Grey and tenor saxophonist Forrest during the latter's last few years. *Truly Wonderful!* reissues four of the seven selections from an Aviva LP (*Live at Rick's*), plus it adds five other numbers. Assisted by pianist Shirley Scott (who is normally an organist), bassist John Duke, and drummer Bobby Durham, the two horns sound spirited on such numbers as "Jumpin' Blues," "Blues Everywhere," and a $14\frac{1}{2}$-minute version of "Misty." Additional material from the same engagement is heard on *Night Train—Revisited,* including the other three numbers from the LP, plus seven other cuts. A few titles are repeated, but these solos are quite different, adding to the legacy of this short-lived band.

The next two sets team Grey with a European saxophonist. While Jesper Thilo looks toward Zoot Sims for inspiration, Bjarne Nerem sounds closer to Coleman Hawkins. The Thilo date includes "A Night in Tunisia," "On the Sunny Side of the Street," and Grey's "I'm Hungry, Sabrina." *Al Meets Bjarne* also has some fine solos from pianist Norman Simmons (who contributed two songs) and such heated jam numbers as "Things Ain't What They Used to Be," "Lester Leaps In," and "Stompin' at the Savoy."

Fab features Grey with his son, Mike Grey, on second trombone, Norman Simmons, guitarist Joe Cohn (son of Al Cohn), bassist J.J. Wiggins (son of Gerald Wiggins), and Bobby Durham plus a variety of guests. Clark Terry helps out on flugelhorn and scats wildly with Grey on "Cotton Tail," altoist Virginia Mayhew is heard on one of her earliest recordings, Jon Hendricks sings the so-so (and rather echoey) "Save the Grease," and trombonist Delfeayo Marsalis sits in on one song. The music is fun if not too essential. *Live at the Floating Jazz Festival* is a loose but coherent live date in which Grey welcomes his son, Mike Grey, saxophonist Rickey Woodard (mostly playing alto), guitarist Cohn, bassist Steve Novosel, and Durham. Both trumpeter Marcus Belgrave and a mysterious figure called "Gabriel Armstrong" (actually Jon Faddis) make guest appearances. Throughout the jam (which includes "Mood Indigo," "Lester Leaps In," "Perdido," and "Jumpin' at the Woodside"), Al Grey is the main solo star. The closing eight-minute "Jazzspeak" is valuable as he verbally discusses his plunger technique.

Gray meets organist Jack McDuff on *Me 'n Jack*. Most of the selections are blues and basic originals, with some solo space taken by Joe Cohn and tenor saxophonist Jerry Waldon. *Centerpiece* is a particularly strong outing (recorded live at the Blue Note) and teams Gray with veteran trumpeter Harry "Sweets" Edison (on one of his last good recordings), tenor saxophonist Jerome Richardson (who sometimes takes solo honors), pianist Junior Mance, bassist Ben Brown, and Bobby Durham. Among the high points are the trombonist's "Diz Related," "Homage to Norman," "I Wish I Knew" (Edison's charming feature), "Lester Leaps In," and "Centerpiece." The varied program works quite well, with everyone sounding in fine form.

By the time he recorded *Matzoh and Grits* in 1996, Grey was 70 and just beginning to show his age. For this project he performs eight familiar tunes and three originals with a band that includes altoist-flutist Cleve Guyton, pianist Randolph Noel, Joe Cohn, J.J. Wiggins, and Durham, ranging in style from swing to hard Bop. *Echoes of New Orleans* has a few numbers that look toward Dixieland (including "Basin Street Blues" and "Struttin' with Some Barbecue") but is mostly in the modern swing to Bop genre, where Al Grey always felt most comfortable. Grey performs with New Orleans-based musicians (Rick Trolsen on second trom-

bone, tenor saxophonist Tony Dagradi, pianist Red Atkins, bassist James Singleton, and drummer Ossie Davis), including on a remake of "Diz Related," "Cottontail" (on which Grey takes a scat vocal), and "Caravan," showing that his infectious blend of humor, bent notes, plunger mastery, and Boppish ideas was always quite potent.

LPS TO SEARCH FOR

The two-LP set *Basic Grey* (Chess 9220) has highlights from four of Grey's 1959–62 albums for Cadet, with solo space taken by tenor saxophonist Billy Mitchell, trumpeters Joe Newman, Henry Boozier, Dave Burns, and Donald Byrd, trombonist Benny Powell, vibraphonist Bobby Hutcherson, and pianist Herbie Hancock. In addition to the swing standards, there are modern originals by Thad Jones, Frank Foster, Randy Weston, and Melba Liston. *Key Bone* (Classic Jazz 103), from 1972, has Grey interacting happily with altoist-singer Eddie "Cleanhead" Vinson and organist Wild Bill Davis on basic originals. *Grey's Mood* (Classic Jazz 118) consists of two dates from 1975 with different groups: an octet with tenor saxophonist Hal Singer and a quintet with Jimmy Forrest and Tommy Flanagan. *O. D.* (Grey Forrest 1001), from 1980, was Forrest's final recording and is a long-out-of-print effort by the group that he co-led with Al Grey; organist Don Patterson helps out with the swinging.

JOHNNY GRIFFIN

b. Apr. 24, 1928, Chicago, IL

Johnny Griffin is one of the great tenor saxophonists, and his speed (he was sometimes billed as "the world's fastest saxophonist"), original sound (an inspiration to Rahsaan Roland Kirk), command of the language of Bebop, and consistency have all been equally impressive. He worked early on with Lionel Hampton's orchestra (1945–47) and trumpeter Joe Morris's R&B group (1947–50), being known as "Little Johnny Griffin" with the latter. After gigging with Arnett Cobb (1951) and spending time in the Army (1951–53), Griffin played in Chicago during 1953–60 and began recording quite regularly. He easily held his own against fellow tenors John Coltrane and Hank Mobley in 1957's *A Blowing Session*, was a member of Art Blakey's Jazz Messengers for part of that year, and was perfect for the Thelonious Monk Quartet in 1958. Griffin teamed with the equally competitive tenor Eddie "Lockjaw" Davis in a quintet that they co-led in New York during 1960–62.

In 1963 the tenor moved to Europe, where he still lives. Griffin, who has resided in Paris and the Netherlands, jammed with Bud Powell, was in Thelonious Monk's short-lived nonet in 1967, and was a featured soloist with the Kenny Clarke-Francy Boland Big Band (1967–72). Johnny Griffin played with the Paris Reunion Band for a time in the 1980s and had reunions with Eddie "Lockjaw" Davis and Arnett Cobb but has mostly led a variety of quartets during the past three decades. He still records fairly regularly (both as a leader and as a sideman) and visits the United States now and then, having lost none of the fabled speed in his playing.

9 *Introducing Johnny Griffin / Apr. 17, 1956 / Blue Note 46536*

10 *A Blowing Session / Apr. 6, 1957 / Blue Note 81559*

9 *The Congregation / Oct. 13, 1957 / Blue Note 89383*

7 *Johnny Griffin Sextet / Feb. 23, 1958 / Original Jazz Classics 1827*

8 *Way Out! / Feb. 26–27, 1958 / Original Jazz Classics 1855*

7 *The Little Giant / Aug. 4–5, 1959 / Original Jazz Classics 136*

Introducing Johnny Griffin was not Griffin's very first date as a leader (since he cut a few titles for Okeh in 1953 and a full album for Argo earlier in 1956), but it is the set that gained him a great deal of initial recognition. On three originals, two ballads, and rapid renditions of "The Way You Look Tonight" and "Cherokee," Griffin is heard in his early prime, assisted by pianist Wynton Kelly, Curly Russell, and Max Roach. *The Blowing Session* has four jam tunes that match the very different tenor styles of Griffin, John Coltrane, and Hank Mobley. They are quite fiery on a very fast version of "The Way You Look Tonight," "All the Things You Are," and two basic Griffin tunes along with Wynton Kelly, bassist Paul Chambers, and Art Blakey; each of the tenors (each of whom had their own sound) fares quite well on this classic encounter. *The Congregation* (with Sonny Clark, Paul Chambers, and drummer Kenny Dennis) is most notable for the jubilant title tune, which is reminiscent of Horace Silver's "The Preacher." Other highlights include "I'm Glad There Is You," "It's You or No One," and "I Remember You."

In 1958 Johnny Griffin signed with the Riverside label. All but two of his dozen albums have been reissued thus far in the Original Jazz Classics series, and as a whole they add up

to some of the finest work of his career. On *Johnny Griffin Sextet,* the tenor performs three obscurities (including his original "Catharsis"), "What's New," and "Woody 'n You" with a young all-star group including trumpeter Donald Byrd, baritonist Pepper Adams, Kenny Drew, bassist Wilbur Ware, and Philly Joe Jones. *Way Out!* has Griffin as the only horn with the same rhythm section, playing five originals by fellow Chicagoans plus a roaring version of "Cherokee." *The Little Giant* returns Griffin to a sextet format with trumpeter Blue Mitchell, trombonist Julian Priester, Wynton Kelly, bassist Sam Jones, and drummer Albert "Tootie" Heath. The date is a little unusual in that all of the material (including Griffin's "63rd Street Theme") is obscure, and pianist Norman Simmons contributed three of the six songs along with all of the horn arrangements. Griffin excels as usual.

7 *The Big Soul Band / May 24, 1960–June 3, 1960 / Original Jazz Classics 485*

8 *Johnny Griffin's Studio Jazz Party / Sept. 7, 1960 / Original Jazz Classics 1902*

9 *Looking at Monk / Feb. 7, 1961 / Original Jazz Classics 1911*

9 *Change of Pace / Feb. 7 + 16, 1961 / Original Jazz Classics 1922*

7 *White Gardenia / July 13–17, 1961 / Original Jazz Classics 1877*

8 *Tough Tenor Favorites / Feb. 5, 1962 / Original Jazz Classics 1861*

8 *Do Nothing 'Til You Hear from Me / June 26, 1962 / Original Jazz Classics 1908*

7 *In Copenhagen / Apr. 16, 1964–Dec. 12, 1964 / Storyville 8300*

8 *The Man I Love / Mar. 30, 1967 / Black Lion 760107*

The Big Soul Band has Griffin joined by a ten-piece group for a set that contains several spirituals, including "Wade in the Water" (heard in two takes), "Nobody Knows the Trouble I've Seen," and "Deep River." Norman Simmons again arranged all of the music, in addition to contributing three originals, and there are some solos from Clark Terry and trombonists Matthew Gee and Julian Priester along the way. *Studio Jazz Party* is a loose and fun set as Griffin jams on a variety of standards (including "Good Bait" and "There Will Never Be Another You") and basic material with trumpeter Dave Burns (a veteran of Dizzy Gillespie's 1940s big

Once billed (not inaccurately) as "the world's fastest tenor,"
Johnny Griffin had his own sound and a competitive edge that
made him impossible to defeat in tenor battles.

band), Norman Simmons, bassist Victor Sproles, and drummer Ben Riley.

Most of the recordings by the quintet that Griffin co-led with Eddie "Lockjaw" Davis were issued under Lockjaw's name, but there were a few exceptions. *Looking at Monk* was one of the first full-length albums of Thelonious Monk's music performed by other musicians: Griffin, Davis, pianist Junior Mance, bassist Larry Gales, and Ben Riley (the last two would be joining Monk's quartet in the future). The quintet explores such numbers as "In Walked Bud," "Rhythm-a-ning," and "Well You Needn't," paying respect to Thelonious's melodies while generating a great deal of competitive heat.

Change of Pace is an atmospheric date in which Griffin is joined by both Bill Lee and Larry Gales on basses, drummer Ben Riley, and (on five of the nine numbers) the French horn

of Julius Watkins. The music is often haunting, the blend between the tenor and the French horn is memorable, and Lee's bowed bass (over Gales's walking bass lines) is a major asset. Well worth several listens. Also on the lyrical side is *White Gardenia,* a Billie Holiday tribute set that was completed on the second anniversary of her death. Backed by seven brass instruments, a string section dominated by cellos, and a four-piece rhythm section, Griffin puts plenty of feeling into such songs as "Gloomy Sunday," "Good Morning Heartache," "Don't Explain," and "Travelin' Light." Melba Liston and Norman Simmons provided the tasteful arrangements.

Tough Tenor Favorites is another match-up between Griffin and Lockjaw, with support provided by pianist Horace Parlan, bassist Buddy Catlett, and Ben Riley. Best are fiery renditions of "Blue Lou," "Ow," and "From This Moment

On." Closing the Riverside period is *Do Nothing 'Til You Hear from Me,* a quartet set with pianist Buddy Montgomery (who switches to vibes on two of the four songs), Monk Montgomery (heard on a rare appearance on acoustic rather than electric bass), and Art Taylor. Griffin alternates hard swingers (including "Slow Burn") with warm ballads (such as "The Midnight Sun Will Never Set").

Although his move to Europe resulted in his receiving less publicity in the United States, Griffin has remained in prime form up to the present day. The music on *In Copenhagen* was not released for the first time until 1998. Griffin jams on five standards (some quite lengthy, including "What Is This Thing Called Love?") with Kenny Drew, Niels Pedersen, and Art Taylor plus a 19-minute rendition of his "Doctor's Blues," during which he takes a good-humored vocal. *The Man I Love,* from three years later, uses Drew and Pedersen in the rhythm section along with Al "Tootie" Heath. Griffin tears into such numbers as "The Man I Love," "Blues for Harvey," and a memorable rendition of "The Masquerade Is Over" while displaying warmth on "Sophisticated Lady."

8 | *Return of the Griffin / Oct. 17, 1978 / Original Jazz Classics 1882*
7 | *Tough Tenors Back Again / July 10, 1984 / Storyville 8298*
9 | *Catharsis / July 15, 1989 / Storyville 8306*
7 | *The Cat / Oct. 26–29, 1990 / Antilles 422 848 421*
7 | *Dance of Passion / Apr. 29–30, 1992 / Antilles 314 512 604*
8 | *Chicago, New York, Paris / Dec. 4–5, 1994 / Verve 314 527 367*

During 1978–79 and 1983 Johnny Griffin recorded five albums for Galaxy while visiting the United States. The only one thus far reissued on CD is *Return of the Griffin.* Joined by pianist Ronnie Mathews, bassist Ray Drummond, and drummer Keith Copeland, Griffin is typically exuberant on "Autumn Leaves," his "Fifty- Six," and "A Monk's Dream." In 1984 Griffin had one of his last reunions with "Lockjaw" Davis (who would pass away two years later). *Tough Tenors Back Again* (which was not released until 1997) has the two saxophonists matching wits and power on "Blues Up and Down," "Call It What You Wanna," and "Lester Leaps In," with the assistance of pianist Harry Pickens, bassist Curtis Lundy, and drummer Kenny Washington, live at the Montmartre in Copenhagen. *Catharsis* also has music not released at the time of its performance (not for a decade).

Griffin jams on the traditional "Hush-A-Bye," his own medium-tempo "Slukefter Blues" (which he really rips into), and four standards (including "Just Friends" and "Rhythm-a-ning"), performed live in Copenhagen with Kenny Drew, bassist Jens Melgaard, and drummer Ole Streenberg. It is a perfect example of how exciting the tenor saxophonist generally sounds in clubs.

The Cat features mostly slower tempos and Griffin's sly melodies (all nine selections are his), although he shows on a blazing "63rd Street Theme" that he can still outrace any other saxophonist. Otherwise he is assisted at a more relaxed pace by trombonist Curtis Fuller, vibraphonist Steve Nelson, pianist-arranger Michael Weiss, bassist Dennis Irwin, and Kenny Washington; several of his originals have memorable melodies, particularly the title cut. *Dance of Passion* also puts the emphasis on Griffin's tunes (a blazing "All Through the Night" is the only standard among the eight songs), and many of the songs (with a few exceptions) are played at laid-back tempos. The colorful arrangements by Weiss (who is on piano) are for a septet, with Dave Bargeron on tuba, John Clark on French horn, trombonist Steve Turre (whose plunger work on the eerie title cut is outstanding), bassist Peter Washington, and Kenny Washington.

Chicago, New York, Paris came out in 1995, celebrating Johnny Griffin's first 50 years as a professional saxophonist. Trumpeter Roy Hargrove (in tasteful and superior form) helps out on three of the nine songs, and Griffin is joined by one of two rhythm sections: Kenny Barron or Peter Martin on piano, Christian McBride or Rodney Whitaker on bass, and Victor Lewis or Gregory Hutchinson on drums. It is to Griffin's great credit that he still sounded at the peak of his powers at the age of 66, whether caressing "My Romance," contributing a few originals (including the catchy "The Jamfs Are Coming"), or enthusiastically ripping through "Without a Song."

LPS TO SEARCH FOR

Some of Johnny Griffin's best recordings with the Joe Morris Orchestra of 1947–49 are on *Fly Mister Fly* (Saxophonograph 504). Although ostensibly R&B, these jump titles are quite jazz-oriented and also feature fine trumpet solos by Morris and appearances by Elmo Hope, Percy Heath, and Philly Joe Jones. Even at that early stage (he was 19), Griffin had full command of the Bebop vocabulary, a distinctive tone, and plenty of enthusiasm. The two-LP set *Live in To-*

kyo (Inner City 6042), from 1976, has Griffin playing long versions of "All the Things You Are," "The Man I Love," and two originals (clocking in between 16 and 20 minutes apiece) plus a brief, hot version of "Wee," with the assistance of Horace Parlan, bassist Mads Vinding, and Art Taylor. The Galaxy albums of 1978–79 and 1983 that have not yet been reissued (all are rewarding) are *Bush Dance* (Galaxy 5126), which has a remarkable version of "A Night in Tunisia," *NYC Underground* (Galaxy 5132), *To the Ladies* (Galaxy 5139), and *Call It Whachawana* (Galaxy 5146).

SLIDE HAMPTON

b. Apr. 4, 1932, Jeanette, PA

A solid Bop trombonist, Slide Hampton has also been a top arranger for many Bop-oriented ensembles during the past 40 years. Born Locksley Wellington Hampton, "Slide" came from a very musical family in which his mother, father, four brothers, and four sisters all played music, although he is the only one that became famous. Hampton worked with the family band (1945–52), Buddy Johnson's orchestra, and Lionel Hampton, making his first big impact playing and writing for Maynard Ferguson's big band (1957–59). Hampton led a few octets in the 1960s, and among his sidemen were trumpeters Freddie Hubbard and Booker Little, and tenor saxophonist George Coleman. He also appeared in a Dizzy Gillespie big band in 1960 and worked with Art Blakey's Jazz Messengers and the Thad Jones-Mel Lewis Orchestra. Hampton traveled to Europe with Woody Herman's orchestra in 1968 and stayed nine years, writing music for radio orchestras and occasionally playing throughout the continent. Since returning to the United States in 1977, he has been involved in many projects. Slide Hampton has headed the World of Trombones (a 12-piece group with nine trombones), co-led Continuum (a quintet with Jimmy Heath that plays the music of Tadd Dameron), freelanced as both a writer and a player, and often worked in Dizzy Gillespie tribute projects, including with Jon Faddis and with his Jazz Masters.

8   *Mellow-Dy / 1967–1968 / Laserlight 17 115*
8   *World of Trombones / Jan. 8–9, 1979 / 1201 Music 9015*
9   *Roots / Apr. 1985 / Criss Cross 1015*
7   *Dedicated to Diz / Feb. 6–7, 1993 / Telarc 83323*

Slide Hampton led albums for Strand (1959), Atlantic (four during 1960–62), the Charlie Parker label, Epic, and Phillips (the last three all during 1962) and at least eight dates during his European years. The most readily available of the latter albums is *Mellow-Dy,* an excellent program recorded in Paris. Three songs showcase Hampton's trombone playing with a quartet that includes pianist Martial Solal, while the other three tracks are with a sextet that also features tenor saxophonist Nathan Davis, vibraphonist Dave Pike, and Hampton Hawes. Though Hampton contributed four of the six numbers, it is his very fluent trombone playing that takes honors.

The multitrombone dates of Kai Winding tended to be commercial and mundane, but Slide Hampton's *World of Trombones* was a different matter. Utilizing nine trombonists (all of whom get to solo on "Lester Leaps In"), including Curtis Fuller and Steve Turre, Hampton's arrangements really swing, particularly on such numbers as "Lester Leaps In," "Donna Lee," and John Coltrane's "Impressions." *Roots* is a high-quality blowing date in which Hampton (along with tenor saxophonist Clifford Jordan, pianist Cedar Walton, bassist David Williams, and drummer Billy Higgins) digs into four standards (including Charlie Parker's "Barbados") and three group originals. In case there is any doubt how strong a soloist Hampton is, this CD can easily serve as proof.

Dedicated to Diz, by Slide Hampton's Jazz Masters, is a well-played if somewhat predictable tribute to Dizzy Gillespie, who had recently passed away. With the exception of "Lover Man" (which is a bit out-of-place), all of the selections were composed by Gillespie, including "Bebop," "Tour de Force," and "A Night in Tunisia." The all-star cast is quite impressive (Jon Faddis, Roy Hargrove, and Claudio Roditi on trumpets, Hampton and Steve Turre on trombones, the reeds of Antonio Hart, David Sanchez, and Jimmy Heath, pianist Danilo Perez, bassist George Mraz, drummer Lewis Nash, and Douglas Purviance on bass trombone and tuba), but the biggest surprise to the reasonably enjoyable date is how few surprises there are!

BARRY HARRIS

b. Dec. 15, 1929, Detroit, MI

When it came to keeping Bebop piano fresh, relevant, and exciting in the 1960s and '70s, few did more than Barry Harris, who has since survived into an era when his style is finally recognized as classic. His playing has always been very close to Bud Powell's, yet Harris can also emulate Thelonious Monk, and is an expert interpreter of Tadd Dameron's music. One of the many major jazz pianists to emerge from Detroit, Harris followed Hank Jones and, with Tommy Flanagan, preceded Roland Hanna. A significant part of the Detroit jazz scene in the 1950s, he worked with the house band at Detroit's Blue Bird club, backing many top Bebop musicians passing through town. Harris played with Max Roach for a brief time in 1956, made his recording debut as a leader in 1958, and for a few months in 1960, was a member of Cannonball Adderley's Quintet, moving to New York. Harris played with Coleman Hawkins on and off throughout the 1960s, and recorded with many top artists, including Yusef Lateef, Dexter Gordon, Hank Mobley, Illinois Jacquet, trumpeter Lee Morgan ("The Sidewinder"), and Charles McPherson, making records as a leader for Riverside and Prestige. Harris did some of his finest work in the 1970s, being an inspiring sideman on two of Sonny Stitt's greatest recordings (*Tune Up* and *Constellation*) and sounding at the peak of his powers on his own Xanadu releases. Since that time, Barry Harris has remained active with his trio and become an important jazz educator (founding and teaching at the Jazz Cultural Center during 1982–87), always going out of his way to keep the legacy of Bebop piano alive.

8 *At the Jazz Workshop / May 15–16, 1960 / Original Jazz Classics 208*

8 *Preminado / Dec. 21, 1960 + Jan. 19, 1961 / Original Jazz Classics 486*

7 *Listen to Barry Harris . . . Solo Piano / July 4, 1961 / Original Jazz Classics 999*

9 *Chasin' the Bird / May 31, 1962 + Aug. 23, 1962 / Original Jazz Classics 872*

8 *Luminescence! / Apr. 20, 1967 / Original Jazz Classics 924*

8 *Magnificent! / Nov. 25, 1969 / Original Jazz Classics 1026*

7 *For the Moment / Mar. 2, 1984 / Uptown 27.47*

7 *Live at Maybeck Recital Hall, Volume Twelve / Mar. 1990 / Concord Jazz 4476*

9 *Confirmation / Sept. 1, 1991 / Candid 79519*

8 *First Time Ever / Oct. 1–2, 1996 / Evidence 22192*

Barry Harris made his recording debut as a leader for Cadet in 1958, but that trio outing has not yet been reissued. However, most of his output for Riverside (1960–62) and Prestige (1967–69) has returned. *At the Jazz Workshop* is a trio date with bassist Sam Jones and drummer Louis Hayes, who

were his rhythm mates with Cannonball Adderley at the time. Harris's classic Bebop style was already quite mature, as can be heard on "Star Eyes," "Moose the Mooche," "Woody 'n You," and three of his originals; a trio of alternate takes has been added to this fine CD reissue. On *Preminado,* Harris is joined by bassist Joe Benjamin and pushed by drummer Elvin Jones on such numbers as "My Heart Stood Still," "There's No One but You," and "What Is This Thing Called Love?"; the pianist takes "I Should Care" as an unaccompanied feature. *Listen to Barry Harris* consists of ten solos. Although Harris plays well, alternating Boppish originals with standards, he shows throughout that he really sounds best in a trio! An emotional "Londonderry Air" and "I Didn't Know What Time It Was" are highlights.

Chasin' the Bird (with bassist Bob Cranshaw and drummer Clifford Jarvis) is one of Harris's finest recordings of the era; he performs three originals and such numbers as "Chasin' the Bird," "Indiana," and "The Way You Look Tonight" very much in the style of Bud Powell. Also easily recommended is *Luminescence!,* a rare Bebop album from 1967 (when the music was thought of as being passé) that has Harris leading a sextet consisting of baritonist Pepper Adams, tenor saxophonist Junior Cook, Slide Hampton, Cranshaw, and drummer Lenny McBrowne. The group performs three Harris tunes, "My Ideal," and swinging versions of two Bud Powell songs ("Dance of the Infidels" and "Webb City"); everyone plays up to par. *Magnificent!,* a trio set with bassist Ron Carter and drummer Leroy Williams, lives up to its title, with such rarely performed Bop titles as "Bean and the Boys," "Ah-Leu-Cha," and "Dexterity" alternating with four Harris tunes and "These Foolish Things Remind Me of You." Barry Harris has long been an underrated composer, and quite a few of his obscure songs deserve to be revived by others.

Harris's classic Xanadu albums have yet to be reissued on CD. *For the Moment,* from 1984, shows that his enthusiasm for Bebop has been quite consistent through the years. Teamed with bassist Rufus Reid and Leroy Williams, Harris performs a four-song Thelonious medley, "Shaw 'Nuff," a remake of "Bean and the Boys," "I Love Lucy," "My Heart Stood Still," and seven of his originals, including two versions of "To Monk with Love." Volume Twelve of the fabled *Maybeck Recital Hall* series features Harris performing ten piano solos, including "It Could Happen to You," a few tunes purposely in Bud Powell's style," "Parker's Mood," "Cherokee," and on odd medley of "It Never Entered My Mind," "Flintstones," and "I Love Lucy"! The music on

Confirmation is quite fun, for Harris is joined by Kenny Barron on second piano along with bassist Ray Drummond and drummer Ben Riley. The two pianists really romp on eight Bebop standards (including "On Green Dolphin Street," "All God's Chillun' Got Rhythm," and "Oleo") plus Harris's catchy "Nascimento." Even if the ensembles sometimes get a bit crowded, the constant joy of these encounters makes this set a gem.

The title of *First Time Ever* does not refer to the uniqueness of its music but to this as apparently the first time that Barry Harris recorded with bassist George Mraz; Leroy Williams completes the trio. Harris performs six of his tunes (including "To Walter Davis Jr. With Love" and "Nascimento"), "Smoke Gets in Your Eyes," and "You Go to My Head" in his unchanged and still-enthusiastic Bebop style.

LPS TO SEARCH FOR

Barry Harris did some of the finest work of his career for the Xanadu label in the 1970s, both as a sideman and as a leader. *Barry Harris Plays Tadd Dameron* (Xanadu 113) teams him with bassist Gene Taylor and Leroy Williams on eight of Dameron's best songs. *Tokyo: 1976* (Xanadu 177) is a jam on six Bebop classics with Sam Jones and Leroy Williams plus (on "Groovin' High" and "Blue 'n Boogie") Charles McPherson and guitarist Jimmy Raney. *Live in Tokyo* (Xanadu 130) has more titles from the same occasions with Jones and Williams, and *Barry Harris Plays Barry Harris* (Xanadu 154) is a rare all-original set with bassist George Duvivier and Williams. Although *The Bird of Red and Gold* (Xanadu 213), a set of a dozen piano solos with a very rare Harris vocal on the title cut, says that it was recorded in 1989, logic argues that this LP is from 1979, since it was released in 1982!

FILMS

3 Piano Portraits (Rhapsody Films), in addition to features on pianists Jaki Byard and Cyrus Chestnut, includes Barry Harris's *Passing It On* (1985), a 23-minute short film that has Harris talking to students about jazz and playing a bit of his classic Bebop piano.

HAMPTON HAWES

b. Nov. 13, 1928, Los Angeles, CA, d. May 22, 1977, Los Angeles, CA

Hampton Hawes was originally a Bud Powell-influenced pianist, but his later work sometimes stretched into Hard Bop and early Crossover jazz, although he always kept his own sound, along with a connection to the Bop tradition. One of the top pianists in Los Angeles, Hawes was a major part of the Central Avenue scene from the mid-1940s on, playing with Big Jay McNeely (1944), Dexter Gordon, Wardell Gray, Sonny Criss, the main local musicians, and even Charlie Parker briefly in 1947. Hawes was part of Howard McGhee's group (1950–51), worked with Shorty Rogers, Art Farmer, Art Pepper, and the Lighthouse All-Stars, was in the Army (1952–54), and then began recording frequently for the Contemporary label, often with his own trio. He kept quite busy (including record dates with Sonny Rollins, Barney Kessel, and Art Farmer) until he was arrested on his 30th birthday for heroin possession in 1958, and given a ten-year prison sentence because he refused to become an informer.

Pardoned by President Kennedy in 1963, after five years behind bars, Hawes at first resumed playing in his earlier style, but soon there was a harder edge to his music that fit in well with the period. For a time in the early 1970s, Hawes often played electric piano (his longtime fans were not pleased) and kept his music open to pop influences. However, by 1975 he was playing mostly acoustic piano again. Hampton Hawes's fascinating and frank autobiography, *Raise Up Off Me,* came out in 1974, three years before his death from a stroke at age 48.

8. *Piano: East/West / Dec. 1952 + Feb. 28, 1955 / Original Jazz Classics 1705*
9. *The Trio, Vol. 1 / June 28, 1955 / Original Jazz Classics 316*
9. *The Trio, Vol. 2 / Dec. 3, 1955–Jan. 26, 1956 / Original Jazz Classics 318*
9. *The Trio, Vol. 3 / Jan. 25, 1956 / Original Jazz Classics 421*
8. *All Night Session, Vol. 1 / Nov. 12, 1956 / Original Jazz Classics 638*
8. *All Night Session, Vol. 2 / Nov. 12–13, 1956 / Original Jazz Classics 639*
8. *All Night Session, Vol. 3 / Nov. 13, 1956 / Original Jazz Classics 640*

Piano: East/West is split between two unrelated sessions. Eight numbers have Hawes, vibraphonist Larry Bunker, bassist Clarence Jones, and drummer Lawrence Marable showing plenty of fire, particularly on "Terrible T," "I'll Remember April," "Buzzy," and a brief but explosive rendition of "Move." The second half of this set features Freddie Redd, a talented pianist and composer, on four extended numbers in a 1955 trio with bassist John Ore and drummer

Ron Jefferson. The expected difference between East Coast and West Coast Bop playing cannot be heard in a comparison of these two players!

Hampton Hawes's string of recordings for the Contemporary label (mostly reissued in the OJC series) made him famous in the jazz world. Teamed with bassist Red Mitchell and drummer Chuck Thompson in his *Trio* series, Hawes is in brilliant form on these three volumes, sounding like Bud Powell to an extent but with a little more funk and a little less danger. *Vol. 1* includes "I Got Rhythm," "What Is This Thing Called Love?" and "Hamp's Blues," *Vol. 2* has such notable performances as "Stella by Starlight" Charlie Parker's "Steeplechase," and "Autumn in New York," and *Vol. 3* is highlighted by "Somebody Loves Me," "Night in Tunisia," and "Coolin' the Blues." The trio of volumes is equally rewarding and among Hawes's finest recordings; he sounds inspired and consistently creative throughout.

The same can be said for the three-CD *All Night Session* series, in which Hawes is joined by guitarist Jim Hall, Red Mitchell, and drummer Bruz Freeman. Recorded during one long session and released in the same order as they were played, the selections find the quartet often really stretching out. *Vol. 1* includes "Jordu," "Groovin' High," and the 11-minute-long "Hampton's Pulpit." *Vol. 2* is highlighted by "I'll Remember April," "Will You Still Be Mine," and "Blue 'n Boogie." *Vol. 3* originally only had four numbers (including "Blues #3" and "Blues #4"), but the CD reissue adds "Blues of a Sort." Hall has occasional solos with the group, one of the few times that Hawes worked with a guitarist.

7 *Bird Song / Jan. 18, 1956–Mar. 1958 / Original Jazz Classics 1035*

9 *Four! / Jan. 27, 1958 / Original Jazz Classics 165*

8 *For Real! / Mar. 17, 1958 / Original Jazz Classics 713*

8 *The Green Leaves of Summer / Feb. 17, 1964 / Original Jazz Classics 476*

6 *Here and Now / May 12, 1965 / Original Jazz Classics 178*

7 *The Séance / Apr. 30, 1966–May 1, 1966 / Original Jazz Classics 455*

7 *I'm All Smiles / Apr. 30, 1966–May 1, 1966 / Original Jazz Classics 796*

The music on *Bird Song*, performances with Paul Chambers and Lawrence Marable from 1956 plus three numbers with bassist Scott LaFaro and drummer Frank Butler in 1958, was released for the first time in 1999. The earlier set in particular is rewarding, with Hawes exploring such numbers as "Big Foot," "Ray's Idea," "Just One of Those Things," and Charlie Parker's "Cheryl." *Four!* has Hawes in a quartet with Barney Kessel, Red Mitchell, and Shelly Manne, performing nine selections (two released for the first time on the CD reissue), including "Yardbird Suite," "There Will Never Be Another You," and "Love Is Just Around the Corner." Despite the fact that his life was becoming very erratic, Hawes (like Art Pepper) was remarkably consistent on records. *For Real!* was the pianist's next-to-last recording before his period in prison, but there is no sense of decline or dread in the music. Hawes is joined by LaFaro, Butler, and tenor saxophonist Harold Land on three originals plus "Wrap Your Troubles in Dreams," "Crazeology," and "I Love You." Strangely enough, this was the pianist's only date as a leader in the 1950s in which he used a horn player.

A few months after his release from prison, Hampton Hawes, on *The Green Leaves of Summer,* showed that he had lost nothing in his playing in the interim. Joined by bassist Monk Montgomery and drummer Steve Ellington, Hawes sounds largely unchanged and swinging on such tunes as "Vierd Blues," "Secret Love," and "G. K. Blues." On *Here and Now,* Hawes for the first time tries his best to uplift current pop tunes, including "Fly Me to the Moon," "What Kind of Fool Am I," and even "People." His trio (with bassist Chuck Israels and drummer Donald Bailey) plays quite well, but the material is too inflexible and generally not worth the effort.

Hampton Hawes's interrupted Contemporary period ended with two albums cut at the same sessions: *The Séance* and *I'm All Smiles.* Performing with Red Mitchell and Donald Bailey, Hawes sticks to jazz tunes and a few originals ("The Shadow of Your Smile" is the only pop song), hints at the avant-garde in his extensive improvisations, and sounds as if he is constantly stretching himself. *The Séance* includes "Oleo" and "My Romance," while *I'm All Smiles* is notable for "Manha de Carnaval" and Hawes's "Searchin'."

8 *Blues for Bud / Mar. 10, 1968 / Black Lion 760126*

4 *Plays Movie Musicals / Aug. 1969 / Fresh Sound 65*

6 *High in the Sky / 1970 / Fresh Sound 59*

7 *Trio at Montreux / June 1971 / Fresh Sound 133*

8 *Live at the Jazz Showcase in Chicago, Vol. One / June 1973 / Enja 3099*

6 *Something Special / June 10, 1976 / Contemporary 14072*

7 *At the Piano / Aug. 14, 1976 / Original Jazz Classics 877*

While Beboppers unanimously praise Hampton Hawes's classic Contemporary recordings, feelings are more mixed about the work from his final decade. The pianist switched between record labels, recorded in a variety of settings, and sometimes was heard on electric piano. However, no one will have any problems with *Blues for Bud* (a reissue of *Spanish Steps*), which is a trio outing with bassist Jimmy Woode and Art Taylor. Hawes's playing on this date sometimes moves beyond Bebop toward Hard Bop, McCoy Tyner, and modal jazz, but there are no bows to commercialism; the CD reissue adds five performances (mostly alternate takes) to the original program. *Plays Movie Musicals* has Hawes with bassist Bob West, drummer Larry Bunker, and a string section performing just 28 minutes of music. The eight songs (all of which debuted in movies) include a few decent numbers but also such duds as "As Long As She Needs Me" and "People." *High in the Sky*, with Leroy Vinegar and Donald Bailey, is better. Hawes explores five post-originals (including "Evening Trane" and "Carmel") and the 11-minute title cut plus "The Look of Love," showing that he was quite aware of more modern forms of jazz even if he had not yet found his place in it.

Trio at Montreux is a bit unusual as Hawes, bassist Henry Franklin, and drummer Mike Carvin perform a 26-minute version of the pianist's "High in the Sky" and a rendition of Burt Bacharach's "This Guy's in Love with You" that lasts over 31 minutes! However, despite some wandering moments, the trio comes up with many creative ideas, indulging in close interplay, and the music is much better than expected. Although Hawes often played electric piano in the early 1970s, the music on *Live at the Jazz Showcase in Chicago, Vol. 1* finds him sticking to the acoustic piano on four trio numbers with bassist Cecil McBee and Roy Haynes. These versions of "Stella by Starlight," Charlie Parker's "Bluebird," "Spanish Moods," and "St. Thomas" show that, although Hawes had stretched past Bebop, he was still quite capable of playing long stretches in his older, classic style. Less than a year before his death, Hawes appeared at the Douglas Beach House at Half Moon Bay, California, performing with Leroy Vinnegar, guitarist Denny Diaz, and drummer Al Williams. The music, first released in 1994, consists of three originals, two pop tunes ("Sunny" and

"Fly Me to the Moon"), and "St. Thomas." Nothing all that unusual occurs but the music is pleasing.

The pianist's final recording found him returning to the Contemporary label, interacting with two veterans (Ray Brown and Shelly Manne), and, while not recreating the past, also not being shy to show off his roots in Bebop. Hawes performs two originals, a couple of worthwhile current pop tunes, "Blue in Green," and "When I Grow Too Old to Dream." It is a pity that the still-evolving Hampton Hawes story had to stop here.

LPS TO SEARCH FOR

The Hampton Hawes Memorial Album (Xanadu 161), other than a date from 1951, has the pianist's first recordings as a leader. There are a dozen selections with bassist Joe Mondragon and either Shelly Manne or Larry Bunker on drums from 1952, and these live performances (released for the first time in 1982) have decent recording quality and feature Hawes already playing in his recognizable Bud Powell-inspired Boppish style. The last three selections ("All the Things You Are," "I Got Rhythm," and "How High the Moon") showcase the mature Hawes in 1956 with Red Mitchell and drummer Chuck Thompson. *The Sermon* (Contemporary 7653) was recorded a week after Hawes's 1958 arrest while he was awaiting his sentence. Joined by bassist Leroy Vinnegar and drummer Stan Levey, Hawes is heard performing seven spirituals (including "Just a Closer Walk with Thee," "Nobody Knows the Trouble I've Seen," and "Go Down Moses") plus a blues, his last work of the 1950s. *The Challenge* (Storyville 1013), from 1968, was a bit of a challenge for Hawes, since this was his first set of unaccompanied solos. The nine standards (including "It Could Happen to You," "My Romance," and "Bag's Groove") and three originals mostly work quite well, swinging without the assistance of bass and drums.

Live at the Montmartre (Freedom 1020), from September 2, 1971, has Hawes, Henry Franklin, and drummer Michael Carvin forming an adventurous trio on four originals and a fairly concise version of "This Guy's in Love with You." *A Little Copenhagen Night Music* (Freedom 1043) is from the same club date and is more Bebop-oriented, with just one original ("Spanish Way"), trio renditions of "Now's the Time," "'Round Midnight," and Charlie Parker's "Cheryl" plus a version of "Dexter's Deck" that has Dexter Gordon sitting in.

Hampton Hawes's Prestige recordings have not yet resurfaced. *Universe* (Prestige 10046) is somewhat pop oriented, with Hawes on various electric keyboards for seven of his originals, but this set has its moments and some worthwhile solos from tenorman Harold Land and trumpeter Oscar Brashear. *Blues for Walls* (Prestige 10060) has more of the same but is more commerical and less interesting despite decent spots for Brashear and saxophonist Hadley Caliman. *Playin' in the Yard* (Prestige 10077) is a trio outing with electric bassist Bob Cranshaw and Kenny Clarke that is a bit more straight-ahead, but Hawes shows that he lost a lot of his musical personality whenever he played electric piano; he is not distinctive at all. Much better is 1975's *Recorded Live at the Great American Music Hall* (Concord Jazz 222), which has surprisingly creative duet versions of "Fly Me to the Moon" and "Sunny" with bassist Mario Suraci, and a three-part original suite for solo piano called "The Status of Maceo" that hints at a creative future for Hampton Hawes that would never be.

FILMS

Hampton Hawes can be seen on several numbers from the early 1970s with *The L.A. All Stars* (Rhapsody Films) and from the same era as part of the *Shelly Manne Quartet* (Rhapsody Films).

TUBBY HAYES

b. Jan. 30, 1935, London, England, d. June 8, 1973, London, England

Most of England's top modern jazz soloists fit more into the Hard Bop vein (and will be covered in a future book), but Edward "Tubby" Hayes was a classic Bebopper. A tenor saxophonist who was also skilled on flute and vibraphone, Hayes originally played violin when he was eight, switching to tenor four years later, and becoming a professional when he was 15. During 1951–55 he worked with Kenny Baker, Ambrose, Vic Lewis, and Jack Parnell. At 20, Hayes formed his own Bop-oriented octet, doubling on vibes starting in 1956. He co-led the Jazz Couriers with tenor saxophonist Ronnie Scott (1957–59), became well known in his native England, played at many European festivals, led a big band (contributing many of the arrangements), and visited the United States on several occasions during 1961–65. Unfortunately Tubby Hayes had a weak heart, which made him inactive during much of 1969–70 and led to his death during an operation, when he was just 38. Hayes did record fairly often, including a 1961 session with Clark Terry and a 1962 meeting with James Moody and Rahsaan Roland Kirk, in which he held his own with his fellow tenors.

9 | *The New York Sessions / Oct. 3–4, 1961 / Columbia 45446*
8 | *Night and Day / Nov. 7, 1963–Aug. 9, 1966 / Ronnie Scott's Jazz House 013*
7 | *Tubby Hayes-Tony Coe / Nov. 18, 1966 / Progressive 7079*
8 | *In Scandinavia / Feb. 18, 1972 / Storyville 8251*

In 1961 Tubby Hayes made his first visit to New York, and a recording from that time teams him with Horace Parlan, bassist George Duvivier, drummer Dave Bailey, Clark Terry (on four of the ten selections), and vibraphonist Eddie Costa (on two others). The CD reissue adds four previously unreleased tracks (including two with extra appearances by Terry) and shows that Hayes could compete favorably with his American counterparts. Among the songs performed are a couple of Sonny Rollins tunes ("Airegin" and "Doxy"), "Pint of Bitter," and a lyrical "You're My Everything." Hayes, who early on was most influenced by Zoot Sims and Al Cohn, by 1963 was also touched by Johnny Griffin, Rahsaan Roland Kirk, and (to a smaller degree) John Coltrane. *Night and Day* has five lengthy jams (all but one are over 13 minutes long) taken from five different appearances that Hayes made at Ronnie Scott's club in England. Jimmy Deuchar plays trumpet and mellophonium on one song apiece, but otherwise these are quartet performances with either Terry Shannon or Mike Pyne on piano. Hayes, who plays three standards, Clark Terry's "The Simple Waltz," and his own "Half a Sawbuck," is heard mostly on tenor, other than doubling on flute on "The Simple Waltz" and taking "Spring Can Really Hang You Up the Most" on vibes. The recording quality is quite good and Hayes is in excellent form throughout.

The Progressive CD has a 1966 concert shared by tenors Hayes and Tony Coe. Actually Hayes appears on only the first two songs ("Freedom Monday" and the ballad "When My Baby Gets Mad"), which totals 19 minutes, performing in a quintet also including trumpeter Les Condon, Mike Pyne, bassist Ron Matthewson, and drummer Tony Levin. Coe (heard with trombonist John Picard in a quintet) is well showcased on three numbers (including "The Jeep Is Jumpin'"), and guitarist Frank Evans has two features with a trio, so Tubby Hayes's contributions are actually relatively minor to this mostly swinging CD.

Following his serious health problems of 1969–70, Hayes was able to make a brief comeback. *In Scandinavia* is a quartet outing with pianist Staffan Abeleen, Niels Pedersen, and drummer Alex Riel, recorded live in Stockholm. Hayes interprets two fine originals plus "Without a Song," "Vierd Blues," "I Thought about You," and "Rhythm-a-ning." His playing was still very much in the modern mainstream, boppish but not derivative of his early influences. Tubby swings hard during what would be his last full session to be documented, 16 months before his early death.

LPS TO SEARCH FOR

England's Late Jazz Great (IAJRC 50) has live performances by Tubby Hayes from the 1957–72 period. There are two numbers with his Jazz Couriers (with Hayes on vibes and Ronnie Scott on tenor), two songs with the Harry South Orchestra, quartet, quintet, and big band selections from the 1960s, and a version of "I Thought About You" from April 1972, which is Hayes's final appearance on records. *A Tribute: Tubbs* (Spotlite 902) has four lengthy selections (three swinging originals plus "All of You") from a December 1963 gig with Jimmy Deuchar, pianist Terry Shannon, bassist Freddy Logan, and drummer Allan Ganley.

FILMS

Tubby Hayes is seen briefly with a band in Charlie Chaplin's *A King in New York* (1957). Hayes appears with Charles Mingus and Dave Brubeck in the British film *All Night Long* (1961). He is also in *The Beauty Jungle* (1964) and *Dr. Terror's House of Horrors* (1965). For contractual reasons, Tubby Hayes is probably the tenor soloist heard throughout Sonny Rollins's film score of *Alfie* (1966).

ROY HAYNES

b. Mar. 13, 1925, Roxbury, MA

Roy Haynes has had a long career, spanning several styles of jazz, and has played with virtually everyone. Although overshadowed throughout his musical life by Max Roach, Art Blakey, Tony Williams, Elvin Jones, and Buddy Rich, Haynes has finally been receiving much more recognition in recent times, and he ranks up there with the greats. Haynes actually began his career near the end of the swing era, playing with the big bands of Sabby Lewis and Luis Russell

(1945–47). He worked regularly with Lester Young's group during 1947–49 and was a longtime member of the Charlie Parker Quintet (1949–52). The Bird connection gave him a strong reputation in the jazz world. Haynes recorded with Bud Powell, Kai Winding, Wardell Gray, and Stan Getz, was a member of Sarah Vaughan's trio during 1953–58, worked with Thelonious Monk, Miles Davis (for a short while in 1958), pianist Phineas Newborn, altoist Lee Konitz, George Shearing, Lennie Tristano, altoist Eric Dolphy, and Stan Getz (1961); he was never unemployed for long! Haynes subbed for Elvin Jones with the classic John Coltrane Quartet on several occasions (some of which were recorded) and toured with Stan Getz (1965–67) and Gary Burton (1967–68). Starting in 1969, Haynes led his own Hip Ensemble, but he has also worked on many occasions with pianist Chick Corea (including his Bud Powell Tribute band in the 1990s), guitarist Pat Metheny, Dizzy Gillespie, Art Pepper, and virtually every top musician in modern jazz. He first led his own record dates back in 1954 (for Emarcy and Swing) and has headed sessions for New Jazz (1958 and 1960), Impulse (an album that utilized Rahsaan Roland Kirk), Pacific Jazz, Mainstream, Galaxy, Dreyfus, Evidence, Freelance, and Storyville, among other labels. Although currently in his mid-70s, the apparently ageless Roy Haynes (whose résumé is quite wondrous), at this writing, still looks as if he could pass for 50! His son, Graham Haynes, is a fine cornetist.

8 *We Three / Nov. 14, 1958 / Original Jazz Classics 196*
7 *Just Us / July 5, 1960 / Original Jazz Classics 879*
7 *Cracklin' / Apr. 10, 1963 / Original Jazz Classics 818*

Roy Haynes led obscure albums for Emarcy and Swing in 1954, but otherwise 1958's *We Three* was his first record as a leader. This trio date with pianist Phineas Newborn and bassist Paul Chambers is most notable for the playing of Newborn, a virtuoso who was on the level of Oscar Peterson. Best known among the six selections (which contain some obscurities) are "After Hours" and Tadd Dameron's "Our Delight." Haynes does not solo much on *We Three* or *Just Us,* a different trio date that features the Red Garland-influenced piano of Richard Wyands and bassist Eddie DeHaas, being content to take the brief "Well Now" as his showcase. *Cracklin'* has the intense tenor saxophonist Booker Ervin as the main star of a quartet that also includes

Haynes, pianist Ronnie Mathews, and bassist Larry Ridley; together they perform "Under Paris Skies" and five originals.

- **8**   *True or False / Oct. 30, 1986 / Evidence 22171*
- **9**   *Homecoming / June 27, 1992 / Evidence 22092*
- **9**   *When It's Haynes It Roars / July 25–26, 1992 / Dreyfus 36556*
- **8**   *Te-Vou! / 1994 / Dreyfus 36569*
- **8**   *My Shining Hour / Mar. 10–13, 1994 / Storyville 4199*
- **9**   *Praise / May 3–5, 1998 / Dreyfus 36598*

Roy Haynes led sessions for Pacific Jazz (1964), Japanese Victor (1968 and 1973), Mainstream (1971), Horo (1975), Galaxy (1977), and French Blue Marge (1979), but all are quite scarce these days. In terms of style, Haynes's groups on record (starting in 1986) generally fall between Hard Bop and post-Bop while occasionally looking back toward his roots in Bebop. *True or False,* a date not released domestically until 1997, has Haynes, the John Coltrane-inspired tenor of Ralph Moore, pianist David Kikoski, and bassist Ed Howard playing two songs by Chick Corea (including one called "Bud Powell") and others by Wayne Shorter, Sonny Rollins ("The Everywhere Calypso"), Thelonious Monk ("Played Twice"), Charlie Parker ("Big Foot"), and Duke Ellington plus "Limehouse Blues" and a Haynes original.

Homecoming and *When It's Haynes It Roars* both feature the quartet of Haynes, Kikoski, Howard and the talented tenor saxophonist Craig Handy. Handy's playing is consistently inspired. *Homecoming* has fairly lengthy versions of six standards (all at least nine minutes long), including Monk's "Green Chimneys," "Star Eyes," and a remake of "Bud Powell." From a month later, *When It's Haynes It Roars* finds Handy doubling on soprano and performing much more concise renditions of such songs as "I Thought about You," Monk's "Bye Ya," and Miles Davis's "Sippin' at Bells." Both sets are gems.

Te-Vou! is more of an all-star date than a working band, yet the quintet (Haynes, altoist Donald Harrison, Pat Metheny, Kikoski, and bassist Christian McBride) sounds very much as if they had been playing together regularly. Haynes takes only one solo, and the other musicians also pay more attention to the group sound than to trying for individual heroics. The repertoire consists of three Metheny tunes and one apiece by Chick Corea ("Like This"), Harrison, Ornette Coleman, Charlie Haden, and Thelonious Monk ("Trinkle Twinkle"). In 1994 Roy Haynes won the prestigious Jazzpar

prize. He flew to Denmark to accept the award, recording a quartet date (*My Shining Hour*) with tenor saxophonist Tomas Franck, pianist Thomas Clausen, and Niels Pedersen. They perform five standards (including long versions of "My Shining Hour" and "All Blues") plus an original apiece from Clausen and Franck, both of whom deserve to be better known in the United States. Solid straight-ahead jazz.

Leading a particularly impressive group in 1998 (a sextet with flugelhornist Graham Haynes, altoist Kenny Garrett, tenor saxophonist David Sanchez, David Kikoski, bassist Dwayne Burno and, on one song, percussionist Daniel Moreno), Roy Haynes sounds decades younger than his 73 years on *Praise*. He is showcased on "Shades of Senegal," plays a heated duet with Garrett on "My Little Suede Shoes," has a couple trio numbers with Kikoski, and swings such tunes as Chick Corea's "Mirror Mirror," "Israel," and "Blues on the Corner."

LPS TO SEARCH FOR

Out of the Afternoon (Impulse 23), from 1962, has Haynes, Tommy Flanagan, and bassist Henry Grimes all overshadowed by the remarkable Rahsaan Roland Kirk on tenor, manzello, and stritch. Haynes contributed three originals, but it is Kirk's playing on "Moon Ray," "Snap Crackle," and "If I Should Lose You" that consistently steals the show. *Thank You, Thank You* (Galaxy 5103), from 1977, has plenty of variety by groups ranging from a duet (a drum-percussion feature with Kenneth Nash on "Processional") and a quartet with vibraphonist Bobby Hutcherson to a septet; the music ranges from a bit poppish to post-Bop. *Vistalite* (Galaxy 5116), from 1978, is an up-and-down affair, flirting with electronics and funkier rhythms but also featuring tenor saxophonist Joe Henderson on four numbers, including an acoustic quartet rendition of "Invitation."

FILMS

Roy Haynes plays with Red Rodney, Frank Morgan, pianist Monty Alexander, and bassist Rufus Reid in a 1990 quintet featured on *A Tribute to Charlie Parker Vol. 1* (Storyville 6048).

JON HENDRICKS
b. Sept. 16, 1921, Newark, OH

When it comes to writing lyrics to recorded jazz solos, the art known as "vocalese," Jon Hendricks has long been at the top of his field. The genius of vocalese and a skillful singer,

The "genius of vocalese," Jon Hendricks (an entertaining singer and a brilliant lyricist) has championed Bebop throughout his career.

Hendricks has made important contributions to Bebop for 45 years. He grew up in Toledo, Ohio as one of 17 children, sang locally as a youth with Art Tatum, and performed on the radio. Hendricks served in the military (1942–46) and studied law, but he also played drums for two years and had hopes of being a performer. He was particularly inspired when Charlie Parker urged him to come to New York and be a jazz singer. In 1952 Hendricks did just that, and his "I Want You to Be My Baby" was recorded by Louis Jordan. In 1955 he recorded "Four Brothers" and "Cloudburst" with the Dave Lambert Singers but also worked outside of music for several years, singing only on a part-time basis. In 1957 Hendricks and Dave Lambert teamed up in hopes of recording their vocalese versions of some of Count Basie's vintage recordings, utilizing a vocal group. Unfortunately the other singers were not up to their level, other than Annie Ross. So instead it was decided to overdub their voices as Lambert, Hendricks, and Ross; the resulting album (*Sing a Song of Basie*) was so successful that they became a vocal group, arguably the finest in jazz history. In addition, in 1960 Hendricks wrote, produced, and starred in the show *Evolution of the Blues* for the Monterey Jazz Festival; he would revive it on several occasions in the future, including in the mid-1990s for Monterey. He also wrote the English lyrics for Antonio Carlos Jobim's "Desafinado."

Lambert, Hendricks, and Ross worked and recorded steadily up to 1962, when Ross departed due to erratic health, being replaced by Yolande Bevan. Lambert, Hendricks, and Bevan lasted until their breakup in 1964. Dave Lambert's death in 1966 permanently ended any chance of a future reunion. Since the breakup of Lambert, Hendricks, and Bevan, Hendricks has had a very successful solo career. He lived in Europe during 1968–72, settled near San Francisco (where he taught and for a time wrote about jazz for the *San Francisco Chronicle*), had a new version of *Evolution of the Blues,* which ran for five years in San Francisco, and in the late 1970s organized Hendricks & Company (also known as The Hendricks Family). The latter group, usually featuring his wife, Judith, his daughter, Michelle Hendricks, and a fourth voice (for a time it was Bobby McFerrin), allowed Jon Hendricks to revive the music of Lambert, Hendricks, and Ross, which he has continued to champion. He also contributed the vocal arrangements for The Manhattan Transfer's *Vocalese* album, had a major part in Wynton Marsalis's *Blood on the Fields,* and during 1998–99 participated in a series of reunions with Annie Ross, although the years have taken its toll on both of their voices. Still, in his late seventies, Jon Hendricks remains quite masterful.

9   *Recorded in Person at the Trident / 1963 / Smash 314 510 601*

8   *Love / Aug. 1981–Feb. 1982 / Muse 5258*

10   *Freddie Freeloader / June 7, 1989–Mar. 20, 1990 / Denon 81757 6302*

9   *Boppin' at the Blue Note / Dec. 23-26, 1993 / Telarc 83320*

Recorded in Person at the Trident, Jon Hendricks's fourth album as a leader (following one set for World Pacific and two for Columbia) is his earliest to be reissued on CD thus far. Performing with San Francisco-based musicians (tenor saxophonist Noel Jewkes, pianist Flip Nunez, bassist Fred Marshall, and drummer Jerry Granelli), Hendricks does a fine job of summing up his musical life up to 1963. Among the selections he performs are "Watermelon Man," "Old Folks," his humorous "Gimme That Wine," "Cloudburst," "Shiny Stockings," and "Stockholm Sweetnin'." Jumping ahead 18 years, *Love,* the first recording by Hendricks & Company, finds Jon joined by wife Judith, daughter Michele, and Bob Gurland (or sometimes Leslie Dorsey) on vocals. All of the lyrics are Jon Hendricks's except for "Angel Eyes" (a solo feature for Michele). Harry "Sweets" Edison and tenor saxophonist Jerome Richardson make guest appearances. Among the many exciting vocalese numbers are "Royal Garden Blues," "Bright Moments," "Groove Merchant," and "Harlem Airshaft."

There are quite a few remarkable selections on *Freddie*

Freeloader. Jon Hendricks is joined by The Manhattan Transfer, the Count Basie Orchestra, trumpeter Wynton Marsalis, Al Grey, tenor saxophonist Stanley Turrentine, Tommy Flanagan, bassists George Mraz and Rufus Reid, drummer Jimmy Cobb, and The Jon Hendricks Vocalstra. But even with such numbers as "Jumpin' at the Woodside," "Sugar," Thelonious Monk's "Trinkle Tinkle," and "Sing Sing Sing," the title cut takes honors. Recreating the famous 1959 Miles Davis recording, Hendricks welcomes Bobby McFerrin (who emulates pianist Wynton Kelly), Al Jarreau (who takes the role of Davis), and George Benson (filling in for a jubilant Cannonball Adderley), saving the most difficult vocalese solo for himself: John Coltrane. Judith Hendricks's singing of Louis Armstrong solos on "Stardust" and "Swing That Music" is also noteworthy. A classic.

Boppin' at the Blue Note is quite fun. The first seven selections of the live set mostly emphasize scatting rather than vocalese, with Jon Hendricks showing plenty of enthusiasm on "Get Me to the Church on Time," "Do You Call That a Buddy," and "Roll 'Em Pete." Joined by an all-star horn section (Wynton Marsalis, Al Grey, Red Holloway on alto, and tenor saxophonist Benny Golson), Hendricks sounds much younger than his 72 years. "Everybody's Boppin'" has heated scat singing not only by the leader and Michele Hendricks but by Marsalis (in his vocal debut). Michele is featured on "Almost Like Being in Love" and "Since I Fell for You." Together with Kevin Burke and Judith, Michele, and Aria Hendricks, Jon Hendricks concludes the CD by performing vocalese versions of three Count Basie charts ("It's Sand, Man," "Shiny Stockings," and "One O'Clock Jump"), bringing back the spirit of Lambert, Hendricks, and Ross one more time.

LPS TO SEARCH FOR

Jon Hendricks's first album as a leader, *A Good Git-Together* (World Pacific 1283), from 1959, has not been reissued since its original release. Teamed with altoist Pony Poindexter, guitarist Wes Montgomery, altoist Cannonball Adderley, and cornetist Nat Adderley, Hendricks performs such spirited numbers as "Everything Started in the House of Lord," "Social Call," and the title cut plus two songs he had written a few years earlier for Louis Jordan. *Tell Me the Truth* (Arista 4043), from 1975, is a real obscurity, with Hendricks performing his own personal versions of "Flat Foot Floogie," John Coltrane's "Naima," and Gil Evans's "Blues for Pablo."

Jon Hendricks leads a vocal group on eight numbers during *A Tribute to Charlie Parker, Vol. 2* (Storyville 6049), from 1990.

ERNIE HENRY

b. Sept. 3, 1926, Brooklyn, NY, d. Dec. 29, 1957, New York, NY

Ernie Henry's premature death must have been a major shock, for he had accomplished a great deal during his final two years. Influenced by Charlie Parker, Henry had developed his own sound and proved flexible and skilled enough to play with the top Bop musicians. He started on violin when he was eight, switching to alto four years later. Henry worked with Tadd Dameron (1947), Fats Navarro, Charlie Ventura, Max Roach, and the Dizzy Gillespie big band (1948–49) during the classic Bebop era. He toured with Illinois Jacquet's band (1950–52) and then, after a few years off the scene, returned in 1956. Henry recorded with Thelonious Monk (*Brilliant Corners*) and Kenny Dorham, gigged with Charles Mingus, and was part of the 1956–57 Dizzy Gillespie big band. Ernie Henry led three albums of his own for the Riverside label during 1956–57, with the final one being recorded just three months before his death at age 31.

8 *Presenting Ernie Henry* / Aug. 23–30, 1956 / *Original Jazz Classics 102*
8 *Seven Standards and a Blues* / Sept. 30, 1957 / *Original Jazz Classics 1722*
7 *Last Chorus* / Aug. 30, 1956–Nov. 13, 1957 / *Original Jazz Classics 1906*

Ernie Henry's initial session as a leader, *Presenting Ernie Henry,* is a particularly strong outing, teaming the altoist with Kenny Dorham, Kenny Drew, bassist Wilbur Ware, and drummer Art Taylor on five of his originals (including "Orient" and "Cleo's Chant"), "Gone with the Wind," and "I Should Care." The great potential that Henry had is on full display throughout this date, which falls between Bop and Hard Bop. *Seven Standards and a Blues* has Henry showcased in a quartet with Wynton Kelly, Wilbur Ware, and Philly Joe Jones, digging into such songs as "I Get a Kick Out of You," "I've Got the World on a String," and "Like Someone in Love," contributing the original blues "Specific Gravity." Henry plays with such enthusiasm that it is difficult to believe he had only three months left to live.

Last Chorus was originally put out posthumously as a tribute. There are four songs from an incomplete project from September 23, 1957, with an octet also showcasing trumpeter Lee Morgan, trombonist Melba Liston, Benny Golson on tenor, Cecil Payne, Wynton Kelly, bassist Paul Chambers, and Philly Joe Jones, including "Autumn Leaves" and "All the Things You Are." In addition there is an alternate take from Henry's very last session (a quartet date from November 1957 that was headed by Kenny Dorham), an excerpt from "Ba-Lue Bolivar Ba-Lues-Are" with Thelonious Monk, and one alternate take apiece from Henry's two other dates as a leader. By acquiring these three CDs (*Presenting Ernie Henry* unfortunately has gone out of print), listeners will essentially have "The Complete Ernie Henry." There should have been so much more.

RED HOLLOWAY

b. May 31, 1927, Helena, AZ

A good-humored and hard-swinging improviser, James "Red" Holloway has long had original sounds on both tenor and alto saxophones, being able to play Bebop, blues, and R&B with equal facility and enthusiasm. Holloway's first important musical job was working in Chicago with Eugene Wright's big band (1943–46). After serving in the Army, he played with blues singer-pianist Roosevelt Sykes (1948), Nat Towles (1949–50), and Lionel Hampton plus with his own groups, often appearing on records behind other acts, particularly from the blues and R&B worlds. After years as a valuable background player, Holloway had a higher profile while with organist Jack McDuff's band (1963–65) at a time when guitarist George Benson was also in the group. Since then, Red Holloway has generally been a leader (including heading the house band at the Parisian Room in Los Angeles during 1969–84), although he did find time to tour and record with Sonny Stitt (on and off during 1977–82) and make appearances with the Juggernaut, the Cheathams, Horace Silver (with whom he recorded in 1993), Harry "Sweets" Edison, Clark Terry and with all-star groups.

8 *Legends of Acid Jazz* / Oct. 10, 1963 + Dec. 1965 / *Prestige 24199*
8 *Brother Red* / Feb. 6–7, 1964 / *Prestige 24141*

Legends of Acid Jazz reissues all of the music from Red Holloway's first and fourth albums as a leader (respectively *The Burner* and *Red Soul*). While the former set matches Holloway (who is on tenor throughout) on all but one cut with organist John Patton, guitarist Eric Gale, trumpeter Paul Serrano, bassist Leonard Gaskin, and drummer Herbie Lovelle ("Moonlight in Vermont" has a completely different personnel), the later session teams Holloway in a quintet with George Benson and either organist Lonnie Smith or pianist Norman Simmons. Most of the music is basic originals by either Holloway or Benson and fits well into soul jazz. *Brother Red* reissues all of the music from the tenor's *Cookin' Together* album and adds three cuts from a Jack McDuff date and a selection out previously only on a sampler. The personnel is essentially the McDuff band (with the organist, who switches to piano on two cuts, Benson, bassist Wilfred Middlebrooks, and drummer Joe Dukes). The hot combo is joined by an orchestra arranged by Benny Golson on three songs, with most of the material (which includes a few blues) sounding quite soulful.

- **8** *Red Holloway & Company / Jan. 1987 / Concord Jazz 4322*
- **9** *Locksmith Blues / June 1989 / Concord Jazz 4390*
- **7** *In the Red / Nov. 27, 1997 / High Note 7022*
- **7** *Live at the 1995 Floating Jazz Festival / Nov. 5–9, 1995 / Chiaroscuro 348*

After his Prestige period ended, Red Holloway did not record as a leader again until 1982, when he made an album for Jam. After a 1984 effort for Steeplechase, he cut two dates as a leader for Concord (also appearing with several Concord all-star bands). *Red Holloway & Company* finds the saxophonist (with pianist Cedar Walton, bassist Richard Reid, and drummer Jimmie Smith) playing more complex material than usual, including "Caravan," "Passion Flower," and Thelonious Monk's "Well You Needn't," showing that he is a masterful Bop musician. *Locksmith Blues* (with Gerald Wiggins, guitarist Phil Upchurch, Reid, and drummer Paul Humphrey) has the magical combination of Holloway and Clark Terry. The co-leaders both take humorous vocals on the title cut and romp on a variety of standards (including "Red Top" and "Cotton Tail") plus some of Holloway's jump tunes and blues. *In the Red* is a quartet outing with Norman Simmons, bassist Peter Washington, and drummer Kenny Washington that features some offbeat material, including Dexter Gordon's "The Chase," "Watermelon Man," and Harold Land's "Rapture." Red's appearance at the 1995 Floating Jazz Festival (along with pianist Dwight Dickerson, Richard Reid, and Paul Humphrey) finds him playing a variety of standards and soulful tunes, with Harry "Sweets" Edison making three worthwhile appearances. A couple of numbers are jokey throwaways that did not need to be included, but there are some strong moments. The set is rounded off by a 6½-minute "Jazzspeak" in which Red Holloway talks humorously and informatively about his life in music.

LPS TO SEARCH FOR

Hittin' the Road Again (JAM 014), from 1982, has Holloway playing tenor, alto and baritone in addition to taking a happy blues vocal on "Sylvia Is Her Name." He wrote five of the six selections and jams joyfully with an L.A.-based group that includes Dwight Dickerson, guitarist Shuggie Otis, Richard Reid, and drummer Gerryck King. *Nica's Dream* (Steeplechase 1192) is a no-nonsense straight-ahead date from 1984 with pianist Horace Parlan, bassist Jesper Lundgaard, and drummer Aage Tanggaard that features Holloway digging into five standards (including "Love for Sale" and "Wee") and two of his basic originals.

ELMO HOPE

b. June 27, 1923, New York, NY, d. May 19, 1967, New York, NY

A major Bop pianist and a creative composer, Elmo Hope was underrated and undervalued throughout his career, overshadowed by his friends Bud Powell and Thelonious Monk. Hope played with trumpeter Joe Morris's early R&B band (1948–51) alongside Johnny Griffin. He began to record as a leader in 1953 and worked with Clifford Brown, Sonny Rollins, Lou Donaldson, and Jackie McLean among others, but drug problems led to the loss of his cabaret card and long periods of scuffling. Hope toured with Chet Baker in 1957 before moving to Los Angeles, staying for four years. He worked with Lionel Hampton (1959) and made records with Harold Land and Curtis Counce. But after returning to New York in 1961, he was briefly jailed for drug abuse. Hope struggled during his final years, although his last records (from 1966) found him still sounding at the peak of his powers. Elmo Hope died at the age of 43, largely forgotten by the jazz world. His wife, Bertha Hope, recorded a few numbers with him in 1961, and in the 1990s began to gain a strong reputation on her own as a fine pianist.

9 *Trio and Quintet / June 18, 1953–Oct. 31, 1957 / Blue Note 84438*

8 *Meditations / July 28, 1955 / Original Jazz Classics 1751*

7 *Hope Meets Foster / Oct. 4, 1955 / Original Jazz Classics 1703*

9 *The All-Star Sessions / May 7, 1956–Nov. 14, 1961 / Milestone 47037*

7 *Homecoming / June 22 + 29, 1961 / Original Jazz Classics 1810*

Trio and Quintet has Elmo Hope's first recordings as a leader and all of the music that he recorded for Blue Note and Pacific Jazz, including two alternate takes. A trio date with Percy Heath and drummer Philly Joe Jones from 1953 is a perfect showcase for Hope's Boppish, yet distinctive, style. He is also heard in a 1954 quintet with tenor saxophonist Frank Foster, the obscure trumpeter Freeman Lee, Percy Heath, and Art Blakey, and on three numbers from 1957 with a West Coast group consisting of tenorman Harold Land, trumpeter Stu Williamson, bassist Leroy Vinnegar, and drummer Frank Butler. This valuable CD includes 14 rarely played Elmo Hope songs, just ripe to be rediscovered and revived.

Meditations is a fine trio date with bassist John Ore and drummer Willie Jones that includes five Hope originals (mostly based on the chord changes of earlier tunes) among the 11 songs, but is most notable for Hope's piano playing. *Hope Meets Foster* is a second meeting of Hope with both Foster and (on three of the six songs) Freeman Lee, joined this time by John Ore and Art Taylor. They perform three songs by Hope, two by Foster (including "Fosterity"), and an uptempo version of "Georgia on My Mind." Other than one alternate take, *The All-Star Sessions* has all of the music that was previously out on a two-LP set. The generous reissue features Hope in three different settings. He stretches out on four relatively lengthy songs in a jam session setting with trumpeter Donald Byrd, both John Coltrane and Hank Mobley on tenors, bassist Paul Chambers, and drummer Philly Joe Jones. Hope performs three of his originals in a different sextet with trumpeter Blue Mitchell, Jimmy Heath, and Frank Foster on tenors, Percy Heath, and Philly Joe Jones. And finally he, Heath, and Jones dig into four trio numbers. This CD is a perfect place to start experiencing the music of Elmo Hope, both as a contributor to catchy songs and as a Bop-based pianist. *Homecoming* has the same music as the second half of *The All Star Sessions,* with two

alternate takes substituting for the four cuts with John Coltrane.

8 *Elmo Hope Trio / Feb. 8, 1959 / Original Jazz Classics 477*

7 *Hope-Full / Nov. 9 + 14, 1961 / Original Jazz Classics 1872*

9 *The Final Sessions / Mar. 8, 1966 + May 9, 1966 / Evidence 22147*

Elmo Hope, along with bassist Jimmy Bond and drummer Frank Butler, performs seven of his obscure originals and "Like Someone in Love" with spirit and swing on *Elmo Hope Trio*. *Hope-Full* is a unique set in two ways. Hope is heard on five unaccompanied piano solos (he otherwise always played in trios) and, in addition to originals, he performs Boppish versions of "When Johnny Comes Marching Home" and "Liza." In addition, three songs are successful piano duets with his young wife, Bertha Hope, including "Yesterdays" and "My Heart Stood Still."

Although only a year away from his death when he recorded *The Final Sessions*, Elmo Hope was still in prime form. This double CD includes all of the music from the original two LPs (trios with John Ore and either Clifford Jarvis or Philly Joe Jones on drums) plus three alternate takes and five songs (formerly edited) heard in their complete form for the first time. A strong closing act to a much-too-brief life.

LPS TO SEARCH FOR

Here's Hope (V.S.O.P. 2) and *High Hope!* (V.S.O.P. 3) are reissues of trio sets (mostly with Paul Chambers and Philly Joe Jones) from 1961 that add to the legacy of Elmo Hope. When these two brief sets are eventually reissued on CD, hopefully they will be combined on one disc.

EDDIE JEFFERSON

b. Aug. 3, 1918, Pittsburgh, PA, d. May 9, 1979, Detroit, MI

The earliest example of vocalese on records is Bee Palmer in 1929 singing words to the recorded solo of Bix Beiderbecke on "Singin' the Blues." But since that performance went unreleased until the 1990s, it obviously had no influence on Eddie Jefferson's work!

Otherwise, Jefferson can be considered the founder of vocalese. Early on he played tuba, guitar, and drums and was active in show business as a dancer and as a singer, although he never had that great a voice. Jefferson, who appeared with Coleman Hawkins in 1939, developed fairly late as a vocalist, not being caught on records until he was in his thirties. He began writing vocalese lyrics in the early 1940s, and broadcasts from 1949 find him already singing his lyrics to Charlie Parker's solo on "Parker's Mood" and Lester Young's on "I Cover the Waterfront." However, in 1952, King Pleasure stole some of Jefferson's thunder, making the vocalese breakthrough with his hit recordings of Jefferson's "Moody's Mood for Love" (a classic that used the notes from a James Moody alto solo) and his own words to "Parker's Mood."

Jefferson made his first official recordings (including one based on Coleman Hawkins's famous solo on "Body and Soul") in 1952 and then spent 1953–57 singing with James Moody's octet. Jefferson worked and recorded on and off during the next decade, was again with Moody during 1968–73, co-led a band (The Artistic Truth) with drummer Roy Brooks (1974–75), and during the mid- to late '70s teamed up regularly with Richie Cole. Among his other lyrics were his words to "Jeannine," "Lady Be Good," "So What," and "Freedom Jazz Dance." Eddie Jefferson was shot to death for unknown reasons outside a Detroit club shortly after a performance in 1979, when he was 60.

9 *The Jazz Singer / Jan. 19, 1959–Oct. 29, 1965 / Evidence 22062*

9 *Letter from Home / Dec. 18, 1961–Feb. 8, 1962 / Original Jazz Classics 307*

8 *Body and Soul / Sept. 27, 1968 / Original Jazz Classics 396*

8 *Come Along with Me / Aug. 12, 1969 / Original Jazz Classics 613*

8 *Things Are Getting Better / Mar. 5, 1974 / Muse 5043*

7 *Godfather of Vocalese / Mar. 17, 1976 / Muse 6013*

Although Eddie Jefferson was captured on record as early as 1949 (two titles put out on a Spotlite LP sampler) and there was a pair of four-song sessions made for Savoy (1952) and Prestige (1953), his first album was not cut until 1959–60. The Evidence CD collects all of Jefferson's 1959–61 recordings (other than the titles on *Letter from Home*) and adds a couple of odds and ends from 1964–65. On most selections Jefferson is backed by groups ranging from a sextet to a nonet, with such sidemen as altoist Sahib Shihab, Howard McGhee, and James Moody. Included is his vocalese version

of "So What," his initial recording of "Moody's Mood for Love," and such titles as "Now's the Time," "Body and Soul," and "Honeysuckle Rose." There are a couple of unusual duets: one apiece with pianist Tommy Tucker and blues guitarist Louisiana Red. Historic and highly enjoyable music.

Letter from Home is a real gem. Eddie Jefferson is backed by a medium-size band that includes James Moody (on alto) and Johnny Griffin. The CD reissue (which adds two alternate takes to the original program) has such numbers as "I Cover the Waterfront," "A Night in Tunisia," "Body and Soul," and "Parker's Mood" (using different lyrics than King Pleasure's famous version). Other than a few isolated titles, Jefferson would not have the opportunity to record again until 1968. For *Body and Soul*, Jefferson is teamed with James Moody (on tenor this time), trumpeter Dave Burns, and the Barry Harris trio, performing both classics ("Body and Soul," "So What", and "Now's the Time") and his lyrics to newer tunes ("Mercy, Mercy, Mercy," "Filthy McNasty," and "Psychedelic Sally"). *Come Along with Me* has solo space for trumpeter Bill Hardman, Charles McPherson, and Barry Harris but is most notable for Jefferson's lyrics to "The Preacher," "Yardbird Suite," "Dexter Digs In," "Baby Girl" (based on "These Foolish Things"), and "When You're Smiling," among others.

Things Are Getting Better jumps ahead five years. Jefferson does his best to update the vocalese tradition, performing such "impossible" vocal pieces as "Bitches Brew" (a Miles Davis fusion number) and "Freedom Jazz Dance" in addition to the jubilant title tune, "A Night in Tunisia," and "I Just Got Back in Town" (based on James Moody's solo on "I Cover the Waterfront"). He is assisted by a quintet that includes trumpeter Joe Newman and the reeds of Billy Mitchell. *Godfather of Vocalese* (a reissue of an album that was ironically titled *Still on the Planet*) is from Jefferson's last period, when he was often teaming up with Richie Cole. Cole, trumpeter Wayman Reed, and keyboardist Mickey Tucker have some solo space, and singer Betsy Fesmire helps out on two numbers. Jefferson sounds typically enthusiastic on such tunes as "I Got the Blues," "Ornithology," and Herbie Hancock's "Chameleon," creating yet another easily recommended set.

LPS TO SEARCH FOR

Most of Eddie Jefferson recordings have been reissued on CD, but not his last two albums: *The Live-liest* (Muse 5127) and *The Main Man* (Inner City 1033), which date from

1976–77. In both cases the emphasis is on vocalese and Bop, with even the many remakes sounding fresh and swinging. At 60, the innovative singer still had a lot of life left in him.

FILMS

Eddie Jefferson—Live from the Jazz Workshop (Rhapsody Films) is a definitive performance with Richie Cole from 1979, filmed just two days before the singer's tragic death.

OLIVER JONES

b. Sept. 11, 1934, Montreal, Canada

Although he started playing piano at an early age, Oliver Jones certainly qualifies as a late-bloomer in the jazz world. Jones began on the piano when he was seven and started lessons with Oscar Peterson's sister Daisy when he was nine. That probably accounts for the strong Oscar Peterson influence that can still be felt in his playing. Jones spent many years working with show bands, and with pop singer Ken Hamilton, often in Puerto Rico. In fact, he did not commit himself to jazz until he returned to Montreal in 1980, when he was already 46. Jones debuted on records three years later (at age 49), starting a long-term association with the Justin Time label in 1983. During the next 15 years, he toured regularly with his trio and also played solo concerts, impressing listeners with his swinging style and brilliant technique. As the 21st century began, Oliver Jones talked of retiring, although he still plays in public now and then.

- **8** *Lights of Burgundy / Apr. 3-5, 1985 / Justin Time 6*
- **7** *Speak Low/Swing Hard / July 3, 1985 + Sept. 9, 1985 / Justin Time 17*
- **8** *Cookin' at Sweet Basil / Sept. 3, 1987 / Justin Time 25*
- **8** *Just Friends / Jan. 1989 / Justin Time 31*
- **7** *Northern Summit / June 1990 / Justin Time 34*
- **8** *A Class Act / Mar. 1991–May 1991 / Justin Time 79376*
- **9** *Just 88 / Oct. 1992-Feb. 1993 / Justin Time 51*
- **7** *Yuletide Swing / May 1994 / Justin Time 71*
- **7** *From Lush to Lively / May 31, 1995-Mar. 5-6, June 1, 1995 / Justin Time 73*
- **9** *Have Fingers, Will Travel / Mar. 5-6, 1997 / Justin Time 102*
- **8** *Just in Time / Nov. 20-22, 1997 / Justin Time 120/1*

The Justin Time label was initially founded specifically to record Oliver Jones, and their first three releases were sets

by the pianist. A consistent performer who cannot help but sound a lot like Oscar Peterson, Jones has yet to record an indifferent record or an unswinging chorus. *Lights of Burgundy,* which won the Juno award for best Canadian jazz record of 1986, finds Jones performing four originals and nine standards (including "Oleo," "In a Mellow Tone," and "Broadway") with the cool-toned tenor saxophonist Fraser MacPherson, guitarist Reg Schwager, bassist Michel Donato, and drummer Jim Hillman. *Speak Low/Swing Hard* is a trio outing with bassist Skip Beckwith and Jim Hillman that includes such numbers as "On the Trail," "Up Jumped Spring," "I'm An Old Cowhand," and "Speak Low." *Cookin' at Sweet Basil,* performed with bassist Dave Young and drummer Terry Clarke, has a few Jones tunes (including "Snuggles" and "Bossa for CC") plus a heated version of "If I Were a Bell" and an emotional "My Funny Valentine." *Just Friends* is quite fun, for Jones's trio (with Dave Young and drummer Nasyr Abdul Al-Khabyyr) is joined by flugelhornist Clark Terry; Jones and Terry perform a duet version of "Georgia on My Mind."

For *Northern Summit,* Jones teams up with Oscar Peterson's former guitarist, Herb Ellis, and bassist Red Mitchell, alternating new tunes with such jam favorites as "I Love You," "I Want to Be Happy," "Pennies from Heaven," and "Lester Leaps In." Jones easily steals solo honors and although few surprises occur, the music is at a high level. *A Class Act* has another former Peterson sideman, drummer Ed Thigpen, playing with Jones and bassist Steve Wallace on a program that is a bit more modern than usual, with songs by trumpeter Kenny Wheeler and pianist Bill Evans, quite a few group originals, and Peterson's "Hymn to Freedom." On *Just 88,* a set of solo piano, Oliver Jones shows that he does not really need other musicians in order to sound complete. He brings in three new tunes (including "Dizzy-Nest") and uplifts such standards as "It Could Happen to You," "But Not for Me," and "How High the Moon." Jones makes superior use of space on some numbers since there is not a bassist or drummer to fill in the rhythm, and this excellent recital finds him sounding more individual than usual.

Yuletide Swing is a Christmas album in which Jones (with guitarist Richard Ring, Dave Young, and drummer Wali Muhammad) swings hard on ten Christmas favorites, including "Santa Claus Is Coming to Town," "Let It Snow, Let It Snow, Let It Snow," and "Winter Wonderland." *From Lush to Lively* has some of Canada's best musicians (including a few members of Rob McConnell's Boss Brass) plus a string section arranged by Rick Wilkins backing the pianist. Jones performs four Oscar Peterson tunes, three of his originals, and four familiar standards (including "The Way You Look Tonight" and "The Very Thought of You"). The emphasis is on slower tempos, but there are some heated moments and Jones plays beautifully as usual. *Have Fingers, Will Travel* has the other famous member of the Oscar Peterson Trio (Ray Brown) joining the pianist and drummer Jeff Hamilton for a particularly strong program. "If I Were a Bell," "I'm Through with Love," "Without a Song," and "My Romance" are uplifted, and Jones also contributed six songs (including two blues).

The music on *Just in Time* (it was about time that a Justin Time release was named that!) is typically excellent. This two-CD set with Dave Young and drummer Norman Marshall Villeneuve differs from the previous sets only in that nearly all of the songs are standards (just one song apiece from Jones and Peterson plus two obscurities). Among the high points are a lengthy "Falling in Love with Love," a heartfelt "Little Girl Blue," "Green Dolphin Street," "Oleo," and an eight-song George Gershwin medley. The pianist demonstrates throughout this double disc (as with the other releases) that there is no such thing as an unworthy Oliver Jones recording.

QUINCY JONES

b. Mar. 14, 1933, Chicago, IL

A giant in the music industry, Quincy Jones made his greatest impact to Bebop-oriented jazz with his late-1950s big band. He grew up in Seattle, learned to play trumpet (although he was not a soloist), and became a distinctive arranger. Jones worked with Lionel Hampton's orchestra (1951–53), where he sat in the trumpet section next to Clifford Brown and Art Farmer. He soon gave up trumpet altogether but was a busy freelance arranger throughout the 1950s, writing for such top artists as Clifford Brown, Oscar Pettiford, Art Farmer, altoists Gigi Gryce and Cannonball Adderley, Dinah Washington, Tommy Dorsey, and Count Basie. Jones was with the Dizzy Gillespie Big Band in 1956 (the year that he began recording as a leader), spent 1957–58 in Paris as an arranger and producer for the Barclay label, and wrote for the Harry Arnold Orchestra in Sweden.

In 1959 Jones put together an all-star orchestra to tour Europe as part of Harold Arlen's show *Free and Easy*. The big band included trumpeters Clark Terry and Benny Bailey,

trombonists Jimmy Cleveland and Quentin Jackson, Julius Watkins on French horn, Phil Woods, and Budd Johnson. The show soon collapsed, but Jones managed to keep the big band together throughout 1960 before it broke up. In 1961 Jones became the head of Mercury's A&R department, being promoted to vice president in 1964. Although he led some jazz dates in the '60s (and wrote for Count Basie, Sarah Vaughan, and Billy Eckstine), Jones became much busier writing for films and television, and his recordings (which often utilized jazz players) gradually became much more commercial. He worked for A&M during 1969–81 and made his last real jazz sessions during 1969–70 (the albums *Walking in Space* and *Gula Matari*). Jones, who during his jazz prime wrote such songs as "Stockholm Sweetnin'," "For Lena and Lennie," "Quintessence," and "The Midnight Sun Never Sets," has worked primarily as a pop producer since the early 1970s, turning his back on jazz. To be fair, his Qwest label (founded in 1980) released fine jazz dates in the 1990s by Milt Jackson, singer Ernestine Anderson, and avant-garde altoist Sonny Simmons. Jones headed the orchestra that, at the 1991 Montreux Jazz Festival, accompanied Miles Davis on a revival of Gil Evans charts. But "Q," who has in recent times equated rap with jazz, has done little else for jazz during the past 30 years other than take bows for his earlier accomplishments!

8   *This Is How I Feel About Jazz / Sept. 14, 1956–Feb. 25, 1957 / GRP/Impulse 115*

9   *Live in Paris Circa 1960 / Feb. 14, 1960 / Qwest/ Warner Bros. 46190*

8   *Swiss Radio Days Jazz Series, Vol. 1 / June 27, 1960 / TCB 2012*

7   *The Quintessence / Nov. 29, 1961–Dec. 22, 1961 / Impulse 222*

8   *Walking in Space / June 18–19, 1969 / A&M 801*

8   *Gula Matari / Mar. 25, 1970–May 12, 1970 / A&M 820*

Other than one four-song date in Stockholm from 1953, the music on *This Is How I Feel About Jazz* was Quincy Jones's recording debut as a leader. The first six selections (which include his "Stockholm Sweetnin'" and "Evening in Paris") formed Jones's first album and features such fine players as Art Farmer, Jimmy Cleveland, Phil Woods, and Lucky Thompson. The other six selections are actually from a 1957 album that Jones produced but did not arrange, a type of West Coast jazz summit. Three songs feature four altoists playing together (Benny Carter, Art Pepper, Herb Geller, and Charlie Mariano), while the other numbers have three tenors (Buddy Collette, Bill Perkins, and Walter Benton) plus baritonist Pepper Adams; pity that the remaining three tunes (featuring four trumpeters!) were not included too. Interesting music overall, but the earlier album is the reason to acquire this disc.

Unfortunately Jones's *The Birth of a Band* (Emarcy 822496), the best-known studio album by his late 1950s big band, has been out of print for a while, and his other Mercury dates (including an appearance at the 1961 Newport Jazz Festival) have been scarce for years. Partly filling the gap are the Qwest and TCB releases, both of which feature his big band live in Europe. The Paris date boasts such soloists as Clark Terry (who also sings on "Everybody's Blues"), Benny Bailey, Phil Woods and the tenors of Budd Johnson, and Jerome Richardson. Terry and Budd Johnson had departed by the time of the Swiss broadcast, but the music (which also includes arrangements by Ernie Wilkins, Billy Byers, Melba Liston, Phil Woods, and Al Cohn) was still quite Boppish (including versions of "Cherokee," Bud Powell's "Parisian Thoroughfare," and "The Phantom's Blues") and swinging. This was Quincy Jones's finest orchestra.

By the time he recorded *The Quintessence* back in New York, the big band was history. However, this set is one of his better jazz dates, hurt only by the brevity of the music (totaling around just 30 minutes). Jones utilizes a big band that includes a few of his alumni (including Woods) for such numbers as "Straight No Chaser," "For Lena and Lennie," and "Invitation," but only one performance is longer than 4½ minutes.

Throughout the 1960s, Quincy Jones occasionally recorded jazz, although by then he was balancing short creative solos with commercialism. Two of his most successful outings before he gave up jazz altogether were *Walking in Space* and *Gula Matari*. In both cases, he used the sounds of some of his favorite jazz musicians. The former date included the tenor of Rahsaan Roland Kirk, flutist Hubert Laws, Jerome Richardson on soprano, guitarist Eric Gale, trumpeter Freddie Hubbard, Jimmy Cleveland, and Toots Thielemans's harmonica, while the latter had Laws, Richardson, Gale, and Hubbard plus bassist Major Holley humming along with his bowed bass (á la Slam Stewart), Al Grey, and Toots Thielemans whistling along with his guitar. Both sets are quite interesting and have colorful arrangements. It is a pity that Quincy Jones would soon permanently change direction, leaving jazz for more lucrative areas.

SHEILA JORDAN
b. Nov. 18, 1929, Detroit, MI

Sheila Jordan, like Betty Carter, has really transcended Bebop, using Bop as her frame of reference as she continually stretches herself into other areas of music. Her voice may be relatively small, but her range of emotions, ability to improvise lyrics, and friendly unpredictability make Jordan a giant. She studied piano from the age of 11, was raised in Pennsylvania, returned to Detroit with her family when she was 14, and gained experience singing in a vocal group. She moved to New York in 1951 after having sung with Charlie Parker and been encouraged by him. She was married to one of Bird's best pianists (Duke Jordan) for a decade (1952–62), studied with Lennie Tristano, and appeared in clubs now and then in the 1950s. Arranger George Russell had her record an unusual and very atmospheric version of "You Are My Sunshine" with his sextet in 1962, and that year she was one of the few singers ever to be given the opportunity to lead a record date for Blue Note during its classic years.

Despite her promising beginning, Sheila Jordan spent many years working at a conventional day job outside of music, not recording again until the early 1970s. In the '70s she worked with pianist-composer Carla Bley and trombonist Roswell Rudd, and co-led a group with pianist Steve Kuhn. In 1977 she recorded a duo album with Arild Andersen that led to many other voice-bass collaborations with Harvie Swartz in the years since. Since the 1980s, Jordan has been able to perform full time in music, sometimes collaborating on special projects with pianist-bandleader George Gruntz but generally working as a single. Although some of her albums border on the avant-garde, Sheila Jordan has never lost sight of her roots in Bebop or her initial love for the music of Charlie Parker.

9 *Portrait of Sheila / Sept. 19, 1962 + Oct. 12, 1962 / Blue Note 89002*
9 *Sheila / Aug. 27-28, 1977 / Steeplechase 31081*
8 *The Very Thought of Two / Feb. 4, 1988 / M-A 005*
8 *Songs from Within / Mar. 1989 / M-A 014*

Sheila Jordan's debut as a leader resulted in a classic Blue Note session. Accompanied by guitarist Barry Galbraith, bassist Steve Swallow, and Denzil Best throughout *Portrait* of *Sheila*, Jordan is cool, subtle, constantly creative, and adventurous on a variety of standards (including "Falling in Love with Love," "Am I Blue," "Baltimore Oriole," and "I'm a Fool to Want You") plus Oscar Brown, Jr.'s "Hum Drum Blues." The music is quite haunting. But, despite her recording's artistic success, Jordan would not lead her second record date until 1975.

After obscure efforts for the Japanese East Wind label (1975) and Grapevine (1976), Jordan recorded her first duet album with bass. *Sheila* teams her with European bassist Arild Andersen for a set of quite intuitive music. The duo performs such numbers as "Lush Life," "On Green Dolphin Street," "Better Than Anything," "Please Don't Talk About Me When I'm Gone," and more modern pieces; their communication is frequently remarkable. During the next decade Jordan recorded with Steve Kuhn on ECM and led dates for Palo Alto (1982), Black Hawk (1984), and Japanese CBS (1986). The Palo Alto album found her for the first time recording duets with bassist Harvie Swartz, and they teamed up as a duo again on *The Very Thought of Two* and *Songs from Within,* both for the tiny M-A label. The former album includes such tunes as "The Very Thought of You," "Dat Dere," "Lost in the Stars," a medley of "The Bird" and "Quasimodo," and the autobiographical "Sheila's Blues." *Songs from Within* is highlighted by "Waltz for Debby," "St. Thomas," "You Don't Know What Love Is," and a medley of "I Got Rhythm" and "Anthropology." As is true of most M-A releases, there is an extra cut taken from a different release tacked onto the end. *The Very Thought of Two* has a duet by pianist Milcho Leviev and bassist Dave Holland, while *Songs from Within* has a feature for Marty Krystall's bass clarinet.

8	*Lost and Found / Sept 28–29, 1989 / Muse 5390*
10	*One for Junior / Sept. 1991 / Muse 5489*
8	*Heart Strings / Mar. 5–6, 1993 / Muse 5468*
8	*Jazz Child / Apr. 1–2, 1998 / High Note 7029*

Jordan, Swartz, pianist Kenny Barron, and drummer Ben Riley form a superior quartet on *Lost and Found.* The singer digs into such songs as "The Very Thought of You," "Anthropology," and "I Concentrate on You," making each tune sound brand new while bringing out some hidden meanings in the lyrics. The same band (with Bill Mays on occasional synthesizers) is used to accompany Sheila Jordan on *One for Junior* as she shares a set of vocal duets with Mark Murphy in their only recorded meeting to date. Everything works on this classic encounter, whether it be the hipster conversation on George Handy's "Where You At," a Charlie Parker tribute, "The Best Thing for You," or a medley of "Don't Like Goodbyes" and "Difficult to Say Goodbye." The success of this unique set makes it regretful that Mark Murphy never met up with Betty Carter on record.

Heart Strings also has its special moments as Jordan is joined by the Hiraga String Quartet, pianist Alan Broadbent (who arranged the music), Swartz, and drummer Marvin "Smitty" Smith. Although the emphasis is on ballads, there is a fair amount of variety along with several touching moments. Highlights include "Haunted Heart," "Look for the Silver Lining," and a medley of "Inchworm" and "The Caterpillar Song."

Sheila Jordan has yet to record a set under her own name that cannot be considered at least a near-gem. On *Jazz Child* she has a reunion with Steve Kuhn and is also assisted by bassist David Finck, drummer Billy Drummond, and (on three tunes) fellow vocalist Theo Bleckmann. Some of the material is definitely offbeat (including "The Moon Is a Harsh Mistress," Don Cherry's "Art Deco," Kuhn's "The Zoo," Gil Fuller's "Oh Henry," and trumpeter Tom Harrell's "Buffalo Wings"), but it all works. Also among the highlights are Abbey Lincoln's "Bird Alone," Jordan's title cut, and a medley of the singer's "Ballad for Miles" and "My Funny Valentine."

LPS TO SEARCH FOR

Old Time Feeling (Palo Alto 8038), from 1982, was the first set of Sheila Jordan-Harvie Swartz duets (including "Sleeping Bee," "Quasimodo," "Lazy Afternoon," and "Some Other Time"). *The Crossing* (Black Hawk 50501), with Kenny Barron, Swartz, Ben Riley, and flugelhornist Tom Harrell in 1984, is most notable for "Inchworm," a different version of "Sheila's Blues," Miles Davis's "Little Willie Leaps," and "Suite for Lady and Prez."

KING PLEASURE

b. Mar. 24, 1922, Oakdale, TN, d. Mar. 21, 1981, Los Angeles, CA

Of all of the male vocalese singers of the 1950s (including Eddie Jefferson, Dave Lambert, and Jon Hendricks), King Pleasure (who was born Clarence Beeks) had the best voice and the most mysterious life. Little is known of his early years other than that he grew up in Cincinnati. In 1951 Beeks won a talent contest at the Apollo Theatre singing Eddie Jefferson's words to "Moody's Mood for Love." The following year, he recorded it (before Jefferson had the chance) as King Pleasure (with Blossom Dearie taking the brief female part), and his version made the piece a standard. In 1953 Pleasure had a second hit in "Parker's Mood"; the lyrics predicted Charlie Parker's death, which did not please Bird much! Pleasure also recorded a few other vocalese classics, including "Red Top" (with Betty Carter), Lester Young's "D. B. Blues," and "Jumpin' with Symphony Sid." He moved to the West Coast in 1956, cut a few singles that year, and made full albums in 1960 and 1962. But then King Pleasure drifted into complete obscurity; upon his death in 1981, many were surprised that he had not passed on many years before!

10 *King Pleasure Sings/Annie Ross Sings / Feb. 19, 1952–Dec. 7, 1954 / Original Jazz Classics 217*

9 *Moody's Mood for Love / 1955–Sept. 5, 1962 / Blue Note 84463*

It is easy to acquire every single King Pleasure recording, for all he left was the music on these two CDs plus a Hi Fi LP. *King Pleasure Sings/Annie Ross Sings* has all dozen of his 1952–54 recordings, including the original versions of "Moody's Mood for Love" and "Parker's Mood," "Red Top" (with Betty Carter), "Sometimes I'm Happy," "Don't Get Scared" (with Jon Hendricks), and two instrumentals by his backup band (which includes J.J. Johnson, Kai Winding, and Lucky Thompson). The music overall is consistently classic, as is the one Annie Ross date that is included, a four-song session that has her initial renditions of "Twisted" and "Farmer's Market."

Moody's Mood for Love has all of Pleasure's other recordings other than the Hi Fi date. The six songs from 1955–56 were originally put out as singles, and there are also two numbers from those sessions that were previously unreleased. Included is "D. B. Blues," a remake of "Moody's Mood for Love" and "All of Me." In addition, the ten selections from 1962 that formed King Pleasure's final album are here. The singer is joined by tenor saxophonist Seldon Powell and (on a remake of "Don't Get Scared") Jon Hendricks, but otherwise the personnel is unknown. Among the tunes sung are "Sometimes I'm Happy," "This Is Always," and a final rendition of "Moody's Mood for Love." Only 40 at the time, King Pleasure would never record again, disappearing permanently from the jazz scene.

LPS TO SEARCH FOR

In 1960 King Pleasure recorded an album for Hi Fi that was last reissued by Everest. *King Pleasure* (Everest 262) has the singer joined by trombonist Matthew Gee, Teddy Edwards, and Harold Land on tenors and a West Coast rhythm section with Gerald Wiggins. The majority of the songs are remakes (including "Moody's Mood for Love," "The New Symphony Sid," "Parker's Mood," and "Don't Get Scared"), but these renditions hold their own with the earlier versions.

LAMBERT, HENDRICKS, AND ROSS

The greatest jazz vocal group since the Boswell Sisters and possibly the best of all time, Lambert, Hendricks, and Ross was the natural extension of the vocalese music of Eddie Jefferson, King Pleasure, and the three singers who formed the group: Dave Lambert, Jon Hendricks, and Annie Ross. In 1957 Lambert and Hendricks planned a project in which they would recreate some of Count Basie's earlier recordings by having a large group of vocalists sing Hendricks's lyrics to the arranged ensembles and solos from the original sessions. However, the rehearsals were frustrating because the other singers were not flexible or swinging enough to bring the notes of Lester Young, Buck Clayton, and Harry "Sweets" Edison back to life; only Annie Ross was up to the level that Lambert and Hendricks wanted. Soon they realized that, by overdubbing their three voices, they could create the music the way they wanted with just the three of them. The resulting album, *Sing a Song of Basie,* was a hit and the group Lambert, Hendricks, and Ross was born.

During the next five years, Lambert, Hendricks, and Ross became one of the most popular attractions in jazz. They appeared at festivals and recorded a total of six albums, including an actual collaboration with Count Basie, a set of Duke Ellington songs, and such numbers as "Going to Chicago" (with Joe Williams and the Basie band), "Li'l Darlin'," "Jackie," a remake of Ross's "Twisted," "Cloudburst," "Gimme That Wine," "Come on Home," and "Cookin' at the Continental."

In 1962 bad health forced Annie Ross to quit the group. Her replacement was Yolande Bavan, who was better in ensembles than as a soloist. Lambert, Hendricks, and Bavan continued for two years, recording three albums. In 1964, when both Lambert and Bavan quit, the classic ensemble came to an end, but its influence is still felt on virtually every jazz vocal group that has risen since, including The Manhattan Transfer.

10 *Sing a Song of Basie / Aug. 26, 1957–Nov. 26, 1957 / GRP/Impulse 112*

9 *Sing Along with Basie / May 26, 1958–Sept. 3, 1958 / Roulette 7953322*

8 *The Swingers! / Oct. 1, 1958–Mar. 1959 / EMI 46849*

10 *The Hottest New Group in Jazz / Aug. 6, 1959–Mar. 9, 1962 / Columbia/Legacy 64933*

All six recordings by Lambert, Hendricks, and Ross are included on these four sets. *Sing a Song of Basie* launched the group. The three singers, using overdubbing, recreate ten Count Basie recordings while backed by just a rhythm section (pianist Nat Pierce, rhythm guitarist Freddie Green, bassist Eddie Jones, and drummer Sonny Payne). All of the performances are brilliant in their own way, whether it be the individual singing or Hendricks's lyrics, with the high points including "Everyday," "One O'Clock Jump," "Little Pony," "Fiesta in Blue," and "Avenue C." *Sing Along with Basie* has the vocalists actually joined by the Basie Orchestra on such numbers as "Jumpin' at the Woodside," "Swingin' the Blues," and "Lil' Darlin'." This version of "Going to Chicago Blues" is rather remarkable as Joe Williams sings his regular part while Lambert, Hendricks, and Ross sing the earlier horn lines around his vocal! *The Swingers!* is a comparatively obscure release, matching the singers with tenor saxophonist Zoot Sims, pianist Russ Freeman, and a rhythm section on a variety of tunes, including "Jackie" (Ross's feature), Sonny Rollins's "Airegin," Miles Davis's "Four," "Now's the Time," and Oscar Pettiford's "Swingin' Till the Girls Come Home."

The best buy of all is *The Hottest New Group in Jazz,* for this double CD has three complete projects (*The Hottest New Group in Jazz, Sings Ellington,* and *High Flying*) plus four previously unreleased titles and three songs out previously only on singles. Among the classics are "Charleston Alley," "Moanin'," a remake of "Twisted," "Cloudburst," John Hendricks's hilarious "Gimme That Wine," "Summertime" (based on the Miles Davis/Gil Evans recording), "All Too Soon," "Come on Home," "Farmer's Market," "Cookin' at the Continental," the humorous "Halloween Spooks," and "Poppity Pop." Essential.

7 *Swingin' Till the Girls Come Home / Sept. 6, 1962– Dec. 21, 1963 / Bluebird 6282*

8 *Live at Newport '63 / July 5, 1963 / RCA 68731*

Lambert, Hendricks, and Bevan recorded three albums during their two-year existence. *Swingin' Till the Girls Come Home* is a sampler that draws its music from each of the dates, live performances at Basin Street East, the 1963 Newport Jazz Festival, and the Village Gate. Among the numbers are spirited versions of "One O'Clock Jump," "Doodlin'," "Cloudburst," "Jumpin' at the Woodside," and "It's Sand, Man!" Four of the 15 selections are taken from the Newport date, which has been reissued in full as *Live at Newport '63,* including a previously unreleased version of "Bye Bye Blackbird" on which Hendricks emulates Miles Davis's 1956 solo. Also heard from during the excellent performance (which includes "Watermelon Man," "Gimme That Wine," and "Walkin'") are Coleman Hawkins, Clark Terry, and the Gildo Mahones Trio.

LPS TO SEARCH FOR

The two other Lambert, Hendricks, and Bevan albums that have not yet been reissued in full on CD are *Live at Basin Street East* (RCA 2635) (which has spots for Pony Poindexter on alto and soprano) and *Havin' a Ball at the Village Gate* (RCA 2861), with guest cornetist Thad Jones and Booker Ervin on tenor.

CHUCK MANGIONE

b. Nov. 29, 1940, Rochester, NY

Flugelhornist Chuck Mangione had a series of best-selling records in the 1970s, music that could be called pop/jazz and (when utilizing a string orchestra and singer Esther Satterfield) tended to be lightweight. However, few listeners probably realize that, early in his career, Mangione was a Dizzy Gillespie-inspired trumpeter who played straightahead jazz in his native Rochester with the Jazz Brothers.

Mangione's father was a big jazz fan who often took Chuck and his brother, keyboardist Gap Mangione, out to see concerts; Dizzy Gillespie became a family friend and gave the youth a trumpet in the early '50s. Chuck studied at the Eastman School and during 1960–61 co-led the Jazz Brothers with Gap, a quintet that also included tenor saxophonist Sal Nistico and, at times, bassist Steve Davis and drummer Roy McCurdy. The band recorded three albums for Riverside during that period, the recording debut for all of the musicians. In 1962 Mangione had his first solo record date, *Recuerdo,* which teamed him with an all-star quintet and found the trumpeter in his early prime as a full-fledged Bebopper.

Chuck Mangione had stints with Kai Winding and the big bands of Woody Herman and Maynard Ferguson (the latter two both in 1965) and was with Art Blakey's Jazz Messengers (1965–67). This was an important transitional period before he began emphasizing the soft-toned flugelhorn, formed his own quartet, and began his series of melodic and poppish projects, climaxing in the 1977 hit "Feels So Good." At the height of his fame, in 1980, Chuck Mangione recorded the two-LP set *Tarantella,* which on a few selections (including "Things to Come," "'Round Midnight," and "Manteca") welcomed guest Dizzy Gillespie and paid tribute to Mangione's little-known Bebop roots.

- **7** *The Jazz Brothers / Aug. 8, 1960 / Original Jazz Classics 997*
- **7** *Hey Baby! / Mar. 8, 1961 / Original Jazz Classics 668*
- **7** *Spring Fever / Nov. 28, 1961 / Original Jazz Classics 767*
- **8** *Recuerdo / July 31, 1962 / Original Jazz Classics 495*

The Jazz Brothers, also known as the Mangione Brothers, recorded three albums for Jazzland and Riverside during 1960–61, all reissued in the Original Jazz Classics series. Although the musicians were not yet original voices (Mangione was obviously influenced by Gillespie, and tenor saxophonist Sal Nistico is heard in his pre-Woody Herman period), they are heard playing Bop with plenty of spirit. The initial release, *The Jazz Brothers* (which includes drummer Roy McCurdy), is highlighted by "Secret Love," "Struttin' with Sandra," and "Girl of My Dreams." *Hey Baby!* (with bassist Steve Davis completing the quintet) includes "Bags Groove," "The Night Has a Thousand Eyes," and "Just You, Just Me." Davis and McCurdy were gone by the time the Mangiones recorded *Spring Fever,* but Nistico was still there and the style of the band (heard on "What's New" and "Softly As in a Morning Sunrise") was largely unchanged.

Chuck Mangione's debut as a leader is a standards-oriented set, *Recuerdo,* features Mangione with altoist Joe Romano, pianist Wynton Kelly, bassist Sam Jones, and drummer Louie Hayes on such numbers as "Big Foot," "So-

lar," and "If Ever I Would Leave You." The CD reissue adds two alternate takes to this important early effort by the future pop/jazz star.

MANHATTAN TRANSFER

Throughout its long history, The Manhattan Transfer has been well-known for its eclectic shows, which range from swing to doo-wop, straight-ahead jazz to Brazilian and rock and roll. Tim Hauser led the first short-lived version of the group (1969–71), and then in 1972 he teamed up with Alan Paul, Janis Siegel, and Laurel Masse with much greater success. Cheryl Bentyne took Masse's place in 1979, and the personnel has not changed since. The Transfer started as an open-minded swing group, became much more successful after beginning their longtime association with Atlantic Records in 1975, and have performed a wide variety of music since, never losing their great popularity.

Jazz has always been part of The Manhattan Transfer's music, including a version of "You Can Depend on Me" from 1975 that featured tenor saxophonist Zoot Sims, a 1977 rendition of "Four Brothers," their hit version of "Birdland" two years later, 1981's "Confirmation," and their recording of Eddie Jefferson's lyrics on "Body and Soul." Although its roots are more in swing than in Bop (as best heard in 1997's *Swing* CD), in 1985 The Manhattan Transfer's *Vocalese* album found them singing Jon Hendricks's lyrics with the power and creativity of Lambert, Hendricks, and Ross.

- **7** *Extensions / 1979 / Mobile Fidelity 578*
- **10** *Vocalese / 1985 / Atlantic 81266*
- **10** *Swing / 1997 / Atlantic 83012*

Of The Manhattan Transfer's many Atlantic albums, these three are among the standouts. *Extensions* is actually a mixed bag. Mobile Fidelity reissued an audiophile version of what was The Transfer's breakthrough set, a program that includes their hit version of "Birdland," "Body and Soul" (a tribute to Eddie Jefferson), and Spyro Gyra's "Shaker Song" along with some pop material. The Manhattan Transfer's most significant Bop-oriented album is *Vocalese,* which features the vocal group singing the vocalese lyrics of Jon Hendricks. In addition to Hendricks, the participants include the Count Basie Orchestra, the Four Freshmen, James Moody, singer Bobby McFerrin, Richie Cole, and Dizzy Gillespie (on "Joy Spring"). Among the selections are "Killer

Joe," "Airegin," "Night in Tunisia," "Move," and several tunes formerly recorded by Count Basie.

In 1997 The Manhattan Transfer returned to their swing roots. On *Swing* they are heard with small groups (since their voices assume the role of a big band) with guest violinist Stephane Grappelli (on "Nuages"), the remarkable Rosenberg Trio (young gypsies who play in the Django Reinhardt tradition), and some Western swing players. The music is primarily vocalese versions of swing classics, including Benny Goodman's 1935 version of "King Porter Stomp," "Moten Swing," "Down South Camp Meetin'," and Charlie Barnet's "Skyliner."

KITTY MARGOLIS

b. Nov. 7, 1955, San Mateo, CA

One of the top jazz singers of current times, Kitty Margolis has stretched and broken through the boundaries of Bebop frequently throughout her career. She started playing guitar when she was 12, performing in folk-rock groups as a teenager. Margolis sang in a Western swing band while attending Harvard, finishing her schooling at San Francisco State University. In 1978 she started working as a jazz singer, and in the early 1980s she often collaborated with singer/guitarist Joyce Cooling, trumpeter Eddie Henderson, and tenor saxophonist Pee Wee Ellis. By the second half of the 1980s she was considered one of the San Francisco Bay Area's most significant jazz singers, and in 1989 she made her recording debut, starting the Madkat label, which she shares with Madeline Eastman. Since then Kitty Margolis (who is most inspired by Betty Carter and Mark Murphy) has recorded two additional albums, visited Europe regularly, and continued to grow as an adventurous singer.

7 *Live at the Jazz Workshop / 1989 / Madkat 1001*
9 *Evolution / 1993 / Madkat 1004*
9 *Straight Up with a Twist / 1997 / Madkat 1006*

Live at the Jazz Workshop is Kitty Margolis's most Bop-oriented set, a fairly conventional but spirited and creative outing with pianist Al Plank, bassist Scott Steed, and drummer Vince Lateano. The singer uplifts eight veteran standards, including "I Concentrate on You," "All Blues," "All the Things You Are," and "Too Marvelous for Words," showing off both her scatting and her interpretive skills. *Evolution* is on a higher level. Utilizing a few different rhythm sections and such players as tenor saxophonist Joe

Henderson, pianist Dick Hindman, blues guitarist Joe Louis Walker, trumpeter Tom Peron, and tenor saxophonist Kenny Brooks, Margolis stretches from Bop ("Anthropology") and Brazilian music to her fresh lyrics for Wayne Shorter's "Footprints" and Cedar Walton's "Firm Roots," lowdown blues, and ballads. Everything works.

Straight Up with a Twist takes lots of chances and has its eccentric moments. Assisted by Charles Brown (who sings on two numbers, including an odd version of "The In Crowd"), trumpeter Roy Hargrove, and Kenny Brooks, Kitty Margolis shows how much she has grown through the past few years. "Getting to Know You" is slow and sensuous, "Fever" is taken in $\frac{7}{4}$ time, Thelonious Monk's "In Walked Bud" is turned funky and renamed "In Walked Bean," "My Romance" is boppish," "Today I Sing the Blues" is lowdown, and "Speak Low" concludes with Kitty's wordless vocalizing over the closing vamp, which shows the influence of Indian music. An intriguing set by a major jazz singer.

ROB McCONNELL

b. Feb. 14, 1935, London, Ontario, Canada

A swinging big band arranger and one of the finest valve trombonists in jazz history, Rob McConnell has been leading his Boss Brass in Canada since 1968. McConnell has spent most of his career working in the studios of Canada. In fact, his only extensive time in the United States was a stint with Maynard Ferguson (1963–64) and a period in the late 1980s when he lived in Los Angeles. McConnell played with a group led by Phil Nimmons during 1965–69 called Nimmons 'n Nine Plus Six. When he originally formed the Boss Brass in 1968, it consisted solely of brass instruments plus a rhythm section. Even after adding a saxophone section in 1971, this was primarily a pop-oriented studio group. However, starting in 1976, the Boss Brass became a swinging Bop-oriented jazz orchestra featuring many of the top Canadian players. Among the musicians who have starred with the big band have been trumpeters Guido Basso and Sam Noto, trombonist Ian McDougall, saxophonists Moe Koffman, Eugene Amaro, and Rick Wilkins, guitarist Ed Bickert, bassist Don Thompson, and drummer Terry Clarke plus the leader, who writes most of the arrangements. Other than during the leader's Los Angeles "vacation," the Boss Brass has been together continuously for over 30 years, although, in reality, the influential big band works only around 30 days a year!

8 *Live in Digital / Dec. 1-3, 1980 / Sea Breeze 106*

9 *Brassy & Sassy / Feb. 3, 1992 / Concord Jazz 4508*

8 *Our 25th Year / Mar. 29-30, 1993 / Concord Jazz 4559*

7 *Overtime / May 9-10, 1994 / Concord Jazz 4618*

8 *Don't Get Around Much Anymore / Apr. 3-4, 1995 / Concord Jazz 4661*

7 *Even Canadians Get the Blues / Apr. 23-24, 1996 / Concord 4722*

8 *Play the Jazz Classics / May 26-27, 1997 / Concord Jazz 4784*

4 *Big Band Christmas / Apr. 27-28, 1998 / Concord Jazz 4844*

The only early album by Rob McConnell's Boss Brass that is easily available is 1980's *Live in Digital.* Such soloists are featured as McConnell, tenors Rick Wilkins and Eugene Amaro, trombonist Ian McDougall, altoist Moe Koffman, and trumpeter Sam Noto (showcased on "I Love You"), among others; all but Noto would still be in the band when their Concord period began. Highlights include "T. O." (which covers several jazz styles from Dixieland to free), "Groovin' High," a modernized "Louisiana," and the funky "Squib Cakes." *Brassy & Sassy* was recorded over 11 years later, but there was no real change in the Boss Brass's sound or in McConnell's swinging and witty charts. The music still fell between Bop and modern swing and had become very influential on stage bands and college orchestras (although it was difficult for either of the latter to gather together solo strength on the level of McConnell's group). *Brassy & Sassy* has a lengthy "Strike Up the Band," "Things Ain't What They Used to Be," an 11-minute version of "Scrapple from the Apple," and Ian McDougall's three-part "Blue Serge Suite(e)" among its memorable performances.

Our 25th Year has its share of surprises and solid swing. "4 B.C." is a bit eccentric, "Riffs I Have Known" pays tribute to arranger Bob Florence, "What Am I Here For?" and "Flying Home" are transformed a bit, and "Broadway" really moves. *Overtime* includes a feature for Rick Wilkins and McConnell on "The Touch of Your Lips," some fine Guido Basso trumpet on "Stella By Starlight," Moe Koffman's alto showcased on the ballad "After You," a superior Ed Bickert solo during "Alone Together," and a tribute to Al Cohn and Zoot Sims on "This May Be Your Lucky Day." *Don't Get Around Much Anymore* has the Boss Brass coming up with fresh renditions of the title cut, "Crazy Rhythm," "Gee Baby, Ain't I Good to You," "Rockin' in Rhythm" (the last

has clarinet solos by Moe Koffman and Bob Leonard), and "Donna Lee." Among the solo stars throughout the CD are guitarist Lorne Lofsky (temporarily filling in for Ed Bickert, who had broken both arms in an accident), Koffman, Wilkins, Basso, trumpeter John MacLeod, altoist Jerry Johnson, and trombonist Alastair Kay.

The three most recent Boss Brass recordings all have themes. *Even Canadians Get the Blues* is allegedly a blues album, but a few of the pieces actually are bluish rather than being technically blues; some chords have been altered, and the closer is a brief version of the Canadian national anthem! In addition to the usual soloists, the reeds play clarinets on "The Clarinet Is Black and Blue," tenor saxophonist Alex Dean and Bickert are featured on "Blue Hodge," and Doug Riley sits in on organ for "The Shuffle Boogie Swamp Groove Blues." *Play the Jazz Classics* is a standards date, but, typically, not all of the songs are that famous (particularly the 1920s "Santa Claus Blues") or are treated in predictable fashion. *Big Band Christmas* is a bit of a disappointment, for McConnell and his band are overly respectful toward the Yuletide favorites. Five of the 11 performances are medleys, and few of the pieces ever get away much from just merely stating the melodies. Only "My Favorite Things," with its solos from Pat LaBarbera on soprano (who fills in during the album for Rick Wilkins) and Alex Dean's tenor, generates any real excitement. But with this one exception, it can be said without exaggeration that fans of one Boss Brass album will be able to easily enjoy all of them!

7 *The Rob McConnell Jive 5 / Aug. 1990 / Concord Jazz 4437*

8 *Trio Sketches / May 20-21, 1993 / Concord Jazz 4591*

8 *Three for the Road / Oct. 11-12, 1996 / Concord Jazz 4765*

On an occasional basis through the years, Rob McConnell has featured his valve trombone in small-group settings, including these three Concord releases. The *Jive 5* set teams him with Ed Bickert, Rick Wilkins, bassist Neil Swainson, and drummer Jerry Fuller. Other than "Them There Eyes," the tunes are taken at a relaxed pace, with several of the songs being quite obscure, including McConnell's "4 B.C.," which was written in tribute to Benny Carter. *Trio Sketches* matches McConnell with Bickert and Swainson in a set that has quiet volume, subtle interplay, and lots of swinging. Among the selections that the trio performs are "Snow White," "Can't We Be Friends," "Long Ago and Far Away," and "'Deed I Do." McConnell, Bickert, and Don Thompson (mostly on bass) form the trio on *Three for the Road*. The material is particularly intriguing, including an "Old Medley," a "Young Medley," a three-song Henry Mancini medley (with Thompson switching to piano), "A Sleeping Bee," and a lengthy "I Don't Know Enough About You." The emphasis is generally on slower tempos, but the interplay will keep listeners from dozing off!

LPS TO SEARCH FOR

With one exception, all of the Boss Brass's pre-1990 recordings are rather scarce. Ironically, the band's now-out-of-print LPs from the 1976–85 period are on the same level as the readily available Concords, with McConnell's writing style and the solo talents of his players (some of whom have been with him for many years) being top-notch from the start. So all of these LPs are recommended: *The Jazz Album* (Attic 1015), which really launched the orchestra, *Big Band Jazz Vol. 1* (Pausa 7140), *Again Vols. 1 & 2* (Pausa 7148 and 7149), *Present Perfect* (Pausa 7067), *Tribute* (Pausa 7106), *All in Good Time* (Palo Alto 8074), *Atras da Porta* (Innovation 0010), and *Boss Brass & Woods* (Innovation 0011), which features guest altoist Phil Woods. In addition, *Old Friends/New Music* (Unisson 1001) is an excellent small-group date from 1984 by McConnell with Basso, Wilkins, Bickert, bassist Steve Wallace, and drummer Terry Clarke.

MARIAN McPARTLAND

b. Mar. 20, 1918, Slough, England

Justly famous for her *Piano Jazz* radio series, Marian McPartland has been an important pianist since the 1950s. Like her idol, Mary Lou Williams, McPartland has remained quite modern throughout her career without losing her musical individuality. Born Marian Turner, she studied at the Guildhall School of Music in London (1937–38). Early on, Marian played in a group with three other pianists in vaudeville and performed for British troops throughout Europe during World War II. She met cornetist Jimmy McPartland in Belgium, and they were soon married. Although her husband was a Dixieland player, Marian was more swing-oriented and open to the innovations of Bebop and beyond. In 1946 they moved to the United States, where she often gigged with him, being flexible enough to fit into his trad groups.

McPartland had formed her own trio by 1950 when she played at the Embers, and she had a long residency (1952–60) at the Hickory House; Joe Morello was her drummer until he left to join Dave Brubeck in 1957, and Bill Crow (preceded by Bob Carter and Vinnie Burke) was her regular bassist. McPartland worked steadily throughout the 1960s (including in 1963 with Benny Goodman) and '70s. And although she and Jimmy McPartland were divorced, they remained good friends and remarried shortly before his death in 1991. She formed and recorded for her own Halcyon label during 1969–77 before signing with Concord in 1978. The long-term association with Concord (which continues to this day) has proven to be a perfect outlet for her recording career.

In 1978, *Piano Jazz* began its now-legendary and still-continuing run on National Public Radio. In each edition of her *Piano Jazz* shows, McPartland not only interviews another top pianist but plays duets with him or her. Her guests have ranged from ragtimer Eubie Blake to avant-gardist Cecil Taylor and have included virtually all of the top active pianists during the past couple of decades. Over 30 of the shows have been released as individual CDs by The Jazz Alliance label. In addition, McPartland has been active as an educator, as an author (some of her writings are included in the Oxford University Press book *All in Good Time*), and occasionally as a touring musician.

Still a harmonically sophisticated pianist (who particularly loves interpreting the songs of Billy Strayhorn), Marian McPartland in her early eighties remains a vital and ageless force.

9   *On 52nd Street / Apr. 27, 1953–Oct. 1953 / Savoy 92880*

7   *Ambiance / July 1970 / The Jazz Alliance 10029*

8   *Plays the Music of Alec Wilder / June 20–21, 1973 / The Jazz Alliance 10016*

7   *A Sentimental Journey / 1973–1974 / The Jazz Alliance 10025*

The only live set that documented the Marian McPartland Trio at the Hickory House was made for Savoy in October 1953, when her group included bassist Vinnie Burke and drummer Joe Morello. *On 52nd Street* has a dozen selections from that occasion (all standards, including "A Foggy Day," "Manhattan," "Four Brothers," and "Just Squeeze Me"). In addition, the disc concludes with five studio numbers by McPartland and Morello from a few months earlier when Bob Carter was on bass. The McPartland Trio with Morello and bassist Bill Crow cut three studio albums for Capitol, but those have never been reissued.

After the earlier Savoy and Capitol dates, Marian McPartland made records for Argo (1958), Time (1960 and 1963), Sesac (1964), and Dot (1968). In 1969 she felt motivated to start her own record company, Halcyon, and (other than three sets for Tony Bennett's Improv label) Halcyon would be her musical home until she signed with Concord in 1978. The Jazz Alliance (a Concord subsidiary) has thus far reissued a few of the pianist's Halcyon albums on CD. *Ambiance* is unusual in that the improvising by McPartland, bassist Michael Moore, and either Jimmy Madison or Billy Hart on drums is quite spontaneous and very free, bordering on the avant-garde, even on the two standards ("Three Little Words" and "What Is This Thing Called Love"). The eccentric but talented composer Alec Wilder became a close friend of McPartland's in his later years. On her 1973 *Wilder* set, McPartland (in duets with Michael Moore or trios with bassist Rusty Gilder and drummer Joe Corsello) performs Wilder's two "hits" ("I'll Be Around" and "It's So Peaceful in the Country") plus eight other lesser-known tunes, including "Lullaby for a Lady," "Homework," and "Where Are the Good Companions?" A fascinating set of rare music.

During 1973–74, Marian recorded two albums with her former husband, Jimmy McPartland, sets filled with Dixieland and swing standards that have mostly been reissued as *A Sentimental Journey*. These were some of the cornetist's better late-period performances, as he shows on such numbers as "Royal Garden Blues," "Dinah," "Avalon," "Perdido," and "Wolverine Blues." Joining the McPartlands on these happy dates are either trombonist Hank Berger and clarinetist Jack Maheu or trombonist Vic Dickenson and tenor saxophonist Buddy Tate.

6 ***From This Moment on* / Dec. 1978 / Concord Jazz 4086**

7 ***Portrait of Marian McPartland* / May 1979 / Concord Jazz 4101**

7 ***At the Festival* / Aug. 1979 / Concord Jazz 4113**

7 ***Personal Choice* / June 1982 / Concord Jazz 4202**

7 ***Willow Creek* / Jan. 1985 / Concord Jazz 4272**

9 ***Plays the Music of Billy Strayhorn* / Mar. 1987 / Concord Jazz 4326**

8 ***Plays the Benny Carter Songbook* / Jan. 1990 / Concord Jazz 4412**

Marian McPartland debuted on Concord with *From This Moment On*, a relaxed trio outing with bassist Brian Torff and drummer Jake Hanna. Other than a remake of "Ambi-

ance," the music is comprised of familiar standards, including "You and the Night and the Music," "Lullaby of the Leaves," and "There Is No Greater Love"; only two songs exceed 4½ minutes in length. *Portrait of Marian McPartland* has the same trio plus the underrated altoist and flutist Jerry Dodgion. The repertoire is particularly wide-ranging, including a few older tunes, Herbie Hancock's "Tell Me a Bedroom Story," Chick Corea's "Matrix," and McPartland's "Time and Time Again." *At the Festival* (recorded at the 1979 Concord Jazz Festival) has the McPartland-Torff-Hanna trio stretching out quite winningly on five ,numbers including "I Love You," "Cotton Tail," and Chick Corea's "Windows." The last three selections find the group growing to a quartet with the addition of the promising young altoist Mary Fettig Park, who is particularly strong on "On Green Dolphin Street" and "Oleo."

After nearly three years largely off records (other than a collaboration with George Shearing), Marian McPartland returned to Concord with *Personal Choice,* a trio session that included Jake Hanna and bassist Steve LaSpina. Highlights of the fine all-round set include "I Hear a Rhapsody," Oscar Pettiford's "Tricotism," and Marian's "Melancholy Mood." *Willow Creek* is a set of unaccompanied solos, with all ten pieces being ballads. McPartland puts plenty of feeling into such tunes as "Long Ago and Far Away," Noel Coward's "Someday I'll Find You," "I've Got a Crush on You," and Billy Strayhorn's "Blood Count."

McPartland has always had a special affinity for Strayhorn's music, so it was logical that she would eventually record a full set of his music. Assisted by altoist Dodgion, LaSpina, and drummer Joey Baron, the pianist digs into such songs as "Isfahan," "Lotus Blossom," "Lush Life," "Daydream," and "Take the 'A' Train," infusing them with understated but heartfelt emotion. For her Benny Carter tribute, McPartland was joined not only by bassist John Clayton and drummer Harold Jones but the great altoist Carter himself. This is a melodic and rather happy set of swinging music, which includes 11 of Benny's originals, highlighted by "When Lights Are Low," "Key Largo," "Doozy," and "Easy Money." Benny Carter, 82 at the time, could pass musically for a man half his age.

8 ***Live at Maybeck Recital Hall, Vol. 9* / Jan. 20, 1991 / Concord Jazz 4460**

8 ***In My Life* / Jan. 1993 / Concord Jazz 4561**

7 ***Plays the Music of Mary Lou Williams* / Jan. 17–18, 1994 / Concord Jazz 4605**

7 *Live at Yoshi's Nitespot / Nov. 11-12, 1995 / Concord Jazz 4712*

5 *Silent Pool / June 11-12, 1996 / Concord Jazz 4745*

8 *Just Friends / Sept. 4, 1997–Jan. 26, 1998 / Concord Jazz 4805*

9 *Reprise / Sept. 16-17, 1998 / Concord Jazz 4853*

Marian McPartland put on a strong and well-rounded performance during her *Maybeck Recital Hall* solo concert. She is heard on two originals (including her impressionistic "Theme from Piano Jazz"), plays a few Duke Ellington tunes (highlighted by "Clothed Woman"), and swings lightly and thoughtfully on such numbers as "This Time the Dream's on Me," Ornette Coleman's "Turn Around," and "It's You or No One." *In My Life,* a trio/quartet date with bassist Gary Mazzaroppi, drummer Glenn Davis, and (on half the numbers) Chris Potter on alto and tenor, has quite a few special moments. McPartland certainly shows off her diverse musical interests by performing "Groove Yard," the Beatles' "In My Life," two John Coltrane songs, "Gone with the Wind," her own "For Dizzy," and a touching version of "Singin' the Blues" that she dedicated to the late Jimmy McPartland.

It was only right that McPartland would record a set of Mary Lou Williams-associated tunes since Williams was long one of her heroes. Joined by bassist Bill Douglass and drummer Omar Clay, the pianist performs 11 Williams compositions (including "Lonely Moments," "What's Your Story, Morning Glory," "In the Land of Oo Bla Dee," and "Cloudy") plus two songs that the older pianist enjoyed and McPartland's "Threnody." The tribute is heartfelt, although it does not catch fire all that often; it would have benefited from some striding and perhaps a hot version of Williams's "Roll 'Em." *Live at Yoshi's Nitespot* is a relaxed trio outing with bassist Bill Douglass and Glenn Davis. As usual, McPartland performs a program that covers a wide range, from Ellington ("In a Sentimental Mood") to Stephen Sondheim ("Pretty Women"), Charlie Parker ("Steeplechase") to Ornette Coleman ("Turn Around"). Many of the songs had been recorded by her previously, but McPartland has never lost her enthusiasm for creating thoughtful improvisations. Both Douglass and Davis are quite sensitive in their accompaniment of her, and there are a few harder-swinging numbers tossed in for variety.

Although Marian McPartland clearly enjoyed having the opportunity to record with a string section on *Silent Pool,* in truth Alan Broadbent's arrangements are rather sleepy, much closer to mood music than to jazz. McPartland plays well on a dozen of her originals (including "For Dizzy," "Ambiance," and "Melancholy Mood"), but the lack of mood variation and adventure in the charts make this just a so-so effort, rather forgettable despite the good intentions.

The two most recent Marian McPartland CDs are both special events. After 19 years of interviewing pianists on her radio show and playing duets with them, she was long overdue to have a duet piano album. *Just Friends* is particularly unusual, for McPartland performs two duets apiece with Tommy Flanagan, Renee Rosnes, George Shearing (the best matchup of the bunch), Geri Allen (including a free improvisation), Dave Brubeck (highlighted by a ten-minute "Gone with the Wind"), and Gene Harris. Concluding the special set is McPartland's tender solo rendition of "When the Saints Go Marching In," dedicated to her late husband.

Reprise is a very happy reunion of McPartland's Hickory House Trio, the version with Bill Crow and Joe Morello. The repertoire is fresher than usual, there are some hot pieces along the way, and these renditions of "I Hear Music," "I Thought About You," "Falling in Love with Love," "Tickle Toe," and "Things Ain't What They Used to Be" show that the musical magic the trio displayed more than 40 years earlier was still intact.

LPS TO SEARCH FOR

The double LP *At the Hickory House* (Savoy 2248) has all of the music included in the single-CD *On 52nd Street* plus eight additional trio numbers from 1952 with bassist Max Wayne and either Mousie Alexander or Mel Zelnick on drums. *Marian McPartland* (Bainbridge 1045) is a fine 1963 trio date with bassist Ben Tucker and drummer Dave Bailey (and sometimes a percussionist) that includes "Love for Sale," Tucker's "Comin' Home Baby," and "Straight No Chaser." And from the Halcyon label but not yet reissued are *A Delicate Balance* (Halcyon 105), which is a trio outing from 1971–72 with bassist Jay Leonhart and drummer Jimmy Madison, *Solo Concert at Haverford* (Halcyon 111), and a fine 1977 jam session with altoist Vi Redd and guitarist Mary Osborne called *Now's the Time* (Halcyon 115).

FILMS

Marian McPartland jams with husband Jimmy, trombonist Spiegle Willcox, and the great violinist Joe Venuti (who steals the show) in 1976's hour-long show *Jazz at the Top* (Rochester Ave. Educational).

CHARLES McPHERSON

b. July 24, 1939, Joplin, MO

In some ways, altoist Charles McPherson was to Bebop of the 1960s what Sonny Stitt was in the '50s: a latter-day disciple of Charlie Parker who, although having a slightly different tone, could sound awfully close to Bird. McPherson gained early experience playing in Detroit in the mid- to late 1950s (including working with his teacher pianist Barry Harris), moving to New York in 1959. In 1960 he and trumpeter Lonnie Hillyer succeeded Eric Dolphy and Ted Curson as members of the Charles Mingus Quartet. McPherson played with Mingus off and on during 1960–74, adding the sound of Bird to the bassist's ensembles and always being one of Mingus's most reliable sidemen. He briefly co-led a group with Hillyer in 1966 but worked mostly as a sideman until forming his own band in 1972. In 1978 McPherson moved to San Diego, which has been his home base ever since. Charles McPherson remains quite active as a performer today, with his son, Chuck McPherson, sometimes playing drums in his quartet.

9 *Bebop Revisited! / Nov. 20, 1964 / Original Jazz Classics 710*

8 *Con Alma! / Aug. 6, 1965 / Original Jazz Classics 1875*

8 *The Quintet/Live! / Oct. 13, 1966 / Original Jazz Classics 1804*

7 *From This Moment On! / Jan. 31, 1968 / Original Jazz Classics 1899*

8 *Horizons / Aug. 27, 1968 / Original Jazz Classics 1912*

Charles McPherson led six dates for Prestige during 1964–69; all but the final one (*McPherson's Mood*) has thus far been reissued on CD in the Original Jazz Classics series. Bebop may have been considered out of style during the second half of the 1960s, when the avant-garde was getting many of the headlines, soul jazz was selling the most records, and fusion was around the corner, but McPherson went on his own singular path. Age 25 at the time of *Bebop Revisited!*, McPherson is heard in superior form in a quintet with trumpeter Carmell Jones, Barry Harris, Nelson Boyd, and drummer Al "Tootie" Heath. Together they perform six Bebop standards (including "Hot House," "Nostalgia," and Bud Powell's "Wail") plus a tune called "Variations on a Blues by Bird." *Con Alma!* is in a similar vein except that McPherson's

frontline partner, tenor saxophonist Clifford Jordan, was looking beyond Bop. Barry Harris is back, along with bassist George Tucker and drummer Alan Dawson, and the repertoire includes a song apiece by Thelonious Monk, Duke Ellington, Charlie Parker, Dizzy Gillespie, Dexter Gordon, and McPherson himself ("I Don't Know").

The short-lived Charles McPherson-Lonnie Hillyer Quintet (with Harris, bassist Ray McKinney, and drummer Billy Higgins) sounds fine on *The Quintet/Live!* other than a few loose melody statements (Hillyer has difficulty on "Shaw 'Nuff"). The altoist contributed two of the six songs, and the four standards include an emotional rendition of "Never Let Me Go." *From This Moment On!* finds McPherson adjusting his playing a bit as he jams with younger players: pianist Cedar Walton, up-and-coming guitarist Pat Martino, bassist Peck Morrison, and drummer Lenny McBrowne. Even though there are no Bop standards on the date (the closest one is the title cut), McPherson still sounds quite comfortable essaying the chord changes, even as the other musicians push the music toward Hard Bop. *Horizons* has McPherson again joined by Walton and Martino plus the obscure vibraphonist Nasir Hafiz, bassist Walter Booker, and drummer Billy Higgins. The liner notes (the original ones are duplicated in the reissue) make it clear that the altoist was tired of being compared to Charlie Parker and was going out of his way to avoid older Bop tunes. He contributed four of the six songs, although the high point is the McPherson–Martino duet on "Lush Life."

6 *Siku Ya Bibi / 1972 / Jazz Heritage 513102*

9 *Beautiful! / Aug. 12, 1975 / Xanadu 1230*

8 *First Flight Out / Jan. 25-26, 1994 / Arabesque 113*

9 *Come Play with Me / Mar. 2, 1995 / Arabesque 117*

8 *Manhattan Nocturne / Apr. 24-25, 1997 / Arabesque 134*

After the Prestige period ended, McPherson recorded three rather diverse sets for Mainstream during 1971–73. *Siku Ya Bibi* is a reissue of the second one, a tribute to Billie Holiday. McPherson performs eight songs associated with Lady Day. Four are played with a fine Bop rhythm section (Barry Harris, bassist Sam Jones, and drummer Leroy Williams), while the other four have the altoist joined by a string section arranged by Ernie Wilkins. The emphasis on ballads (including "Lover Man," "God Bless the Child," and "Good Morning Heartache") and the distracting strings keep this from being the success it could have been, although it has its moments.

Much more rewarding was the altoist's association with the Xanadu label in the mid-1970s, which resulted in four albums under his leadership and many sideman appearances. Unfortunately, the Xanadu recordings have not been reissued on CD yet, other than the altoist's first date for the company. *Beautiful* teams him with Duke Jordan, Sam Jones, and Leroy Williams on freewheeling versions of such songs as "It Could Happen to You," "Lover," and "This Can't Be Love." The CD reissue adds a previously unreleased trio version of "All God's Chillun Got Rhythm" that was performed while the rhythm section was waiting for McPherson to show up! This CD was put out by the Artistic Music Distribution in 1995 and will probably be difficult to find.

Other than an obscure date for Discovery in 1984, Charles McPherson went a long time between records. However, his three sets for Arabesque find him still in prime form. *First Flight Out* teams him with a modern jazz group (trumpeter Tom Harrell, pianist Michael Weiss, bassist Peter Washington, and drummer Victor Lewis), alternating swinging originals with a couple Charles Mingus tunes, Monk's "Well You Needn't," "Deep Night," and "My Funny Valentine." *Come Play with Me* is particularly strong, a quartet date with pianist Mulgrew Miller, bassist Santi Debriano, and drummer Lewis Nash that has six of McPherson's originals (several of which are blues, with "Fun House" based on "Limehouse Blues"), "Get Happy," "Darn That Dream," and Charlie Parker's "Bloomdido." Still just 57 at the time of *Manhattan Nocturne*, Charles McPherson shows no sign of running out of gas on this set. Joined by Mulgrew Miller, bassist Ray Drummond, Victor Lewis, and percussionist Bobby Sanabria, the altoist pours plenty of Boppish ideas and emotion into such songs as Monk's "Evidence," "You're My Thrill," "Blue 'n Boogie," and four spirited originals. Certainly in Charles McPherson's sound and ideas, Bebop Lives!

LPS TO SEARCH FOR

Charles McPherson's other Xanadu albums are all gems: a meeting with Barry Harris, Sam Jones, and Leroy Williams called *Live in Tokyo* (Xanadu 131), *New Horizons* (Xanadu 149), with pianist Mickey Tucker, bassist Cecil McBee, and drummer Freddie Waits, and a sextet date with guitarist Peter Sprague, Lou Levy, bassist Monty Budwig, Chuck McPherson on drums, and percussionist Kevin Jones humorously titled *Free Bop* (Xanadu 170).

FILMS

Charles McPherson plays on the soundtrack for Dick Gregory (who portrays a character loosely based on Charlie Parker) in 1966's *Sweet Love, Bitter* (Rhapsody 9019). McPherson also appears briefly in the eccentric 1968 documentary *Mingus* (Rhapsody Films) and filled in some of the parts for Charlie Parker on the soundtrack of *Bird* (1988).

CARMEN McRAE

b. Apr. 8, 1920, New York, NY, d. Nov. 10, 1994, Beverly Hills, CA

One of the top jazz singers of all time, Carmen McRae may not have had quite the range and depth of an Ella Fitzgerald or a Sarah Vaughan but she had something of her own to offer, including her influential behind-the-beat phrasing. McRae studied piano as a youth, wrote the song "Dream of Life" (recorded by Billie Holiday in 1939), and sang with the Benny Carter big band in 1944. But it would not be until 1954 that she began to get much notice. In the meantime she married and divorced Kenny Clarke, had brief associations with Count Basie and Mercer Ellington (during 1946–47, when she was known as Carmen Clarke), and worked as an intermission pianist and singer at lower-level New York clubs. In 1954 she made her recording debut as a leader (for Bethlehem), and her Decca recordings of 1955–59 gave her a strong reputation. McRae's voice was higher during that era than it would be later on, and she was influenced by Billie Holiday and (to a lesser extent) Sarah Vaughan, but she was already quite distinctive, often adding irony to the lyrics that she interpreted. Although sometimes stuck recording weak material in the 1960s and '70s, McRae remained a popular singer throughout her career. She was a participant in Dave Brubeck's the Real Ambassadors in 1961 (alongside Louis Armstrong), recorded dates with Brubeck, George Shearing, Cal Tjader, and Betty Carter, and ended her career on a high level with *Carmen Sings Monk* (1988) and *Sarah: Dedicated to You* (1990). Unfortunately Carmen McRae refused to quit smoking and was forced to retire in 1991 due to emphysema, passing away three years later.

6 *Carmen McRae / Oct. 6, 1954–Dec. 1954 / Avenue Jazz/Bethlehem 75990*
I'll Be Seeing You: A Tribute to Carmen McRae / June 14, 1955–Mar. 10, 1959 / GRP/Decca 647
9 *Here to Stay / June 14, 1955–Nov. 12, 1959 / GRP/Decca 610*

With her behind-the-beat phrasing, constant creativity, and ironic delivery, Carmen McRae found her own niche even while Ella and Sarah Vaughan gained most of the headlines.

8 *Sings Great American Songwriters / June 16, 1955– Mar. 4, 1959 / GRP/Decca 631*

Carmen McRae's debut as a leader resulted in a fine (if brief) album for Bethlehem: *Carmen McRae.* The original eight songs (totaling just 25 minutes) are joined by five alternate takes on the CD reissue. Half of the music has the singer joined by accordionist Mat Mathews's quintet (with flutist Herbie Mann), while the other cuts have a small group with clarinetist Tony Scott (who switches to piano on "Misery"). The emphasis is on ballads.

During 1955–59 McRae recorded regularly for Decca. A little over half of the selections have been reissued thus far. The attractive two-CD set *I'll Be Seeing You* starts off with her singing "Something to Live For" while backed by pianist-composer Billy Strayhorn. The music continues in chronological order as McRae is joined by middle-of-the-road string orchestras, the Ray Bryant Trio in 1957, and some more jazz-oriented big bands during her later record-

ings. Although not all of the music on this set is essential, there are enough highlights (including "Star Eyes," "Whatever Lola Wants," "Skyliner," "East of the Sun," "Exactly Like You," and "If I Were a Bell") to make this an excellent acquisition. *Here to Stay* has most of the music from McRae's 1955 album *By Special Request* and 1959's *Something to Swing About.* The latter is a big band date with arrangements by Ernie Wilkins and some solos for Zoot Sims on tenor, trumpeter Richard Williams, and pianist Dick Katz; highlights include "A Sleepin' Bee," "Comes Love," and "That's for Me." The earlier date has McRae assisted by Mat Mathews's quintet with Herbie Mann or a four-piece rhythm section. An emotional "Suppertime" has McRae accompanying herself on piano. Also from her Decca years is *Sings Great American Songwriters,* 20 selections drawn from ten separate sessions. With the exception of four numbers (three with the Ray Bryant Trio), the singer is backed by orchestras throughout. Among the better performances are "You Took Advantage of Me," "I Was Doing All Right," "My Man's Gone Now," and "When I Fall in Love." But a complete reissue of Carmen McRae's Decca recordings has not yet taken place.

9 *Sings "Lover Man" and Other Billie Holiday Classics / June 29, 1961 + July 26, 1961 / Columbia/Legacy 65115*

6 *Alive! / 1965 / Columbia/Legacy 57887*

8 *The Great American Songbook / Oct. 1972 / Atlantic 904*

8 *Velvet Soul / 1972–1973 / Laserlight 17 111*

After leaving Decca, Carmen McRae recorded for Columbia (1961–62), Focus (1964), Mainstream (1962–66), Atlantic (1967–70), Black Lion (1970), Groove Merchant (1973), Catalyst (1973), Buddha (1978), and several real turkeys (worst was *I Am Music* and *Can't Hide Love*) for Blue Note (1975–76). While Sarah Vaughan could overwhelm weak material and Ella Fitzgerald tended to uplift everything (the deserving as well as the undeserving), McRae tended to be sunk when she was pushed into performing rotten ditties. The 1960s and '70s were somewhat erratic for her in the recording studio, but there were some good moments. In 1961 McRae paid tribute to her early idol, Billie Holiday, by recording a dozen of her songs for Columbia with the Norman Simmons trio, cornetist Nat Adderley, tenor saxophonist Eddie "Lockjaw" Davis, and guitarist Mundell Lowe. The CD reissue, which includes her fresh renditions of such tunes as "Them There Eyes," "Miss Brown to You," "Some Other Spring," and "What a Little Moonlight Can Do," adds two somewhat-out-of-place selections from the same sessions: "If the Moon Turns Green" and "The Christmas Song." On "Strange Fruit" (in which she is backed by just Lowe's guitar), McRae's coolness is very effective.

Alive!, which was originally put out by Mainstream, has McRae performing at the Village Gate with Simmons's trio, guitarist Joe Puma, flutist Ray Beckenstein, and Jose Mangual on bongos. The flute and bongos make the music seem a bit dated in spots, and the material is diverse, ranging from Billie Holiday songs and "Perdido" to "The Shadow of Your Smile," several recent show tunes, and some long-forgotten items like "Run Run Run" and "Woman Talk." *The Great American Songbook* is a much better set. McRae, joined by pianist Jimmy Rowles, Joe Pass, bassist Chuck Domanico, and drummer Chuck Flores, performs a jazz-oriented program of some of her favorite songs. Even with

the inclusion of such fine numbers as "If the Moon Turns Green," "I Only Have Eyes for You," "Sunday" and "I Thought About You," McRae's version of Rowles's humorous "The Ballad of Thelonious Monk" (which is about a country fan discovering Monk) is the main reason that this live set is remembered.

The budget Laserlight label reissued all of the music from McRae's two Groove Merchant albums on *Velvet Soul*. The singer is heard with pianist Dick Shreve, vibraphonist Larry Bunker, Joe Pass, Ray Brown, drummer Frank Severino, and sometimes brass and string sections on the first ten selections. The other nine cuts have tenorman Zoot Sims, pianist Tom Garvin, guitarist Bucky Pizzarelli, bassist Paul West, and drummer Jimmy Madison in the group. Unlike her often horrible Blue Note dates of the mid-1970s, McRae sounds quite comfortable on this reissue, singing songs that interest her. Highlights include "Nice Work If You Can Get It," her classic rendition of Blossom Dearie's "Hey John," "Straighten Up and Fly Right," "You're Mine, You" and "Exactly Like You."

8 *You're Looking at Me / Nov. 1983 / Concord Jazz 235*

8 *For Lady Day, Volume 1 / Dec. 31, 1983 / Novus 63163*

9 *Any Old Time / June 23, 1986 / Denon 1216*

7 *The Carmen McRae-Betty Carter Duets / Jan. 30, 1987–Feb. 1, 1987 / Verve 314 529 579*

7 *Fine and Mellow—Live at Birdland West / Dec. 1987 / Concord Jazz 342*

10 *Carmen Sings Monk / Jan. 30, 1988–Apr. 1988 / Novus 3086*

7 *Dream of Life / June 21–24, 1989 / Qwest/Warner Bros. 46340*

9 *Dedicated to You / Oct. 12–14, 1990 / Novus 3110*

Carmen McRae's final decade of performing was a bit of a golden age for her. McRae's voice was lower than it had been previously, but it was still very much under control; her ironic interpretations of lyrics could be sarcastic, and her often-halting phrasing really stood out. *You're Lookin' at Me* is a tribute to the songs of Nat King Cole, although McRae makes no attempt to sound like him. She wisely utilized his former guitarist, John Collins, in her quartet (with pianist Marshall Otwell, bassist John Leftwich, and drummer Donald Bailey), and her versions of "I'm an Errand Girl for Rhythm," "The Frim Fram Sauce," and "You're Lookin' at Me" are memorable and probably influenced Diana Krall.

The one misfire was performing "Sweet Lorraine" without changing the words. Another tribute, McRae's second set of Billie Holiday songs, *For Lady Day, Volume 1,* did not get released until after her death. Performed live at the Blue Note and broadcast on the radio, this first of two sets (Volume 2 has not been released yet) has McRae, Otwell, Leftwich, Bailey, and (on some songs) guest Zoot Sims interpreting a dozen songs associated with Lady Day, including "I'm Gonna Lock My Heart and Throw Away the Key," "Fine and Mellow," "I Cried for You," and "God Bless the Child." McRae is also caught speaking movingly about Billie Holiday.

Any Old Time (recorded with John Collins, pianist Eric Gunnison, bassist Scott Colley, drummer Mark Pulice, and tenor saxophonist Clifford Jordan) is a well-rounded studio set in which McRae performs 13 veteran standards, including "Tulip or Tulip," "Have You Met Miss Jones?," "Mean to Me," and "I'm Glad There Is You" plus a few songs associated with Billie Holiday.

McRae's duet album with Betty Carter (they are joined by Gunnison, bassist Jim Hughart, and drummer Winard Harper) is certainly unusual, for the two very individual singers try their best to blend as they sing quite spontaneously and crack jokes. Carter usually sounds the best while McRae has the wittiest wisecracks. The results (which include "What's New," "Am I Blue," "Sometimes I'm Happy," and three selections added to the reissue that are without Carter) are ragged but generally fun. *Fine And Mellow* (recorded in 1987, when McRae was 67) is full of spirit and swing as the singer is happily joined by a cooking group consisting of Red Holloway, organist Jack McDuff, guitarist Phil Upchurch, bassist John Clayton, and drummer Paul Humphrey; best are "What Can I Say Dear After I Say I'm Sorry," "These Foolish Things," and "My Handy Man Ain't Handy No More."

Carmen Sings Monk is a classic, one of the great recordings of her career. She performs 13 Thelonious Monk tunes (plus second live versions of two songs), half of which have lyrics by Jon Hendricks. Joined by Clifford Jordan, Eric Gunnison, bassist George Mraz, and drummer Al Foster (with tenor saxophonist Charlie Rouse and pianist Larry Willis on the live tracks), McRae makes the tricky selections (which include "Ruby, My Dear," "Well You Needn't," "Pannonica," "Rhythm-a-ning," "Ask Me Now," and "Ugly Beauty") sound effortless and swinging. *Dream of Life,* not released until 1998, features the vocalist with the WDR Big Band performing John Clayton arrangements of some of the songs that she often sang in clubs, including "Sunday," "For All We Know," "A Song for You," and "I Didn't Know What Time It Was." Carmen McRae's final album, *A Tribute to You,* was recorded in memory of the recently deceased Sarah Vaughan. It is almost on the same level as the Monk songbook. Backed by the Shirley Horn Trio (it is a pity that Horn could not have been coaxed into performing a vocal duet), McRae performs a variety of songs that Sassy enjoyed, including "Poor Butterfly," "Misty," "Black Coffee," "Tenderly," and "It's Magic." Carmen McRae succeeds in bringing back the spirit of Sarah Vaughan while still sounding as individual and unique as she always was.

LPS TO SEARCH FOR

Additional selections from her Decca period (with some duplications) can be heard on *Blue Moon* (Decca 8347) and the two-LP set *The Greatest of Carmen McRae* (MCA2–4111).

FILMS

Carmen McRae sings in *The Subterraneans* (1960) and *Hotel* (1967) and has a strictly acting role in *Roots: The Next Generations* (1978).

DON MENZA

b. Apr. 22, 1936, Buffalo, NY

A forceful and hyper tenor saxophonist, influenced by Sonny Rollins and Don Byas but quite familiar with (and able to emulate) all styles of saxophone playing, Don Menza deserves much more recognition. He started on clarinet when he was 12, began on tenor the next year, served in the Army (1956–59), and gained some recognition for his solos and arrangements with the Maynard Ferguson big band (1960–62). Menza had a short period with Stan Kenton's orchestra, led a quintet in his native Buffalo for a year that featured Sam Noto, and then spent 1964–68 living and working in Germany. After he returned to the United States, Menza was with Buddy Rich's big band in 1968, recording a famous solo on "Channel One Suite" (included on Rich's *Mercy, Mercy, Mercy* CD) that shows off his expertise with circular breathing and is considered a classic. However, Don Menza never became more famous than he was at that time. He moved to California, worked with drummer Elvin Jones (1969), the Juggernaut, Bill Berry, Benny Carter, and Louie Bellson's groups (with whom he frequently recorded), and became a studio musician and educator, eventually settling in Las Vegas.

8 *Live at Claudio's / Aug. 24, 1991 / Sackville 3052*
Don Menza first recorded as a leader (other than a single in 1963) for the German Saba label in 1965, and other dates were cut for Catalyst (1976), Discwasher (1979), Realtime (1981), and Palo Alto (1981). Good luck finding any of those! The one easily available Don Menza CD is this straight-ahead quartet date with co-leader Pete Magadini on drums, pianist Wray Downes, and bassist Dave Young. Recorded live in Montreal, Menza performs "Confirmation," Thelonious Monk's "I Mean You," Tadd Dameron's "On a Misty Night," "These Foolish Things," two Magadini blues, and his own "Rose Tattoo." A fine showcase for the extroverted tenor. But why are there not many more Don Menza CDs out?

LPS TO SEARCH FOR

Don Menza's earlier dates include a 1976 meeting with trombonist Frank Rosolino, *First Flight* (Catalyst 7617), *Horn of Plenty* (Discwasher 005), which features a Los Angeles sextet, *Burnin'* (Realtime 301), by Menza's little-known big band of the early '80s (highlighted by his exciting "Dizzyland"), and an encounter with Sal Nistico and Sam Noto in 1981 on *Hip Pocket* (Palo Alto 8010) during which Menza (in a change of pace) plays alto and baritone.

PIERRE MICHELOT

b. Mar. 3, 1928, Saint Denis, France
The No. 1 Bebop bassist of France, Pierre Michelot has been in demand by visiting American jazzmen for decades, adding support and swing (along with concise solos) to every situation in which he is hired. Michelot began playing piano when he was seven, switching to bass at the age of 16. Among his countless associations from the late-1940s on have been cornetist Rex Stewart, Django Reinhardt, Coleman Hawkins, James Moody, Clifford Brown, Stephane Grappelli, Don Byas, Miles Davis (1956–57), Thelonious Monk, Lester Young, Stan Getz, Bud Powell (The Three Bosses with Kenny Clarke), Dexter Gordon, pianist Martial Solal, Zoot Sims, Dizzy Gillespie, and Chet Baker. It is fitting that Michelot appeared in the film *'Round Midnight,* since that movie dealt with American jazz musicians in Paris!

8 *Bass and Bosses / Dec. 10–11, 1989 / Emarcy 842 531*

Despite being very active for decades, Pierre Michelot has led very few recording dates: a half-album for Polydor (1958), a Mercury big band date (1963), and this project from 1989. Michelot heads a colorful and unusual quintet also including Toots Thielemans on harmonica, violinist Pierre Blanchard, pianist Maurice Vander, and drummer Billy Higgins. Michelot contributed two straightahead pieces, is showcased on "Blues in the Closet," and performs Jimmy Rowles's "The Peacocks," "Godchild," "The Jitterbug Waltz," and "A Child Is Born." Although the bassist is typically in a supportive role much of the time, his playing stimulates the others and the overall results are quite rewarding.

FRANK MORGAN

b. Dec. 23, 1933, Minneapolis, MN
A disciple of Charlie Parker's in the early days, altoist Frank Morgan followed Bird's example in his personal life much too closely and ended up with a career divided into two periods. The son of guitarist Stanley Morgan (who worked with the Ink Spots), Morgan played clarinet at seven, switching to alto when he was ten. In 1947 his family moved to Los Angeles, where he won a talent contest that led to his actually recording a solo at the age of 15 with bandleader Freddie Martin. Morgan was part of the Los Angeles Bebop scene of the early 1950s, participating in jam sessions and recording with Wardell Gray/Teddy Charles (1953) and Kenny Clarke (1954) before leading his own album the following year. But by then he was a heroin addict. He was arrested in 1955 for drug possession and spent the next 30 years in and out of prison.

Amazingly, in 1985 Frank Morgan began a complete comeback, kicking drugs and becoming an inspiration to others. At first he sounded quite close to Charlie Parker, but soon he had developed his own sound within the Bebop tradition. In the 1990s Frank Morgan was one of the leading alto saxophonists in jazz, having beat the rather formidable odds, recording consistently stimulating dates for Contemporary, Antilles, and Telarc.

9 *Easy Living / June 1985 / Original Jazz Classics 833*
9 *Lament / Apr. 21–22, 1986 / Contemporary 14021*
7 *Double Image / May 21–22, 1986 / Contemporary 14035*

8 *Bebop Lives / Dec. 14-15, 1986 / Contemporary 14026*

7 *Quiet Fire / Mar. 26-28, 1987 / Contemporary 14064*

9 *Major Changes / Apr. 27-29, 1987 / Contemporary 14039*

8 *Yardbird Suite / Jan. 10-11, 1988 / Contemporary 14045*

8 *Reflections / Jan. 11-12, 1988 / Contemporary 14052*

After 30 years off records, Frank Morgan made an unlikely comeback in 1985. He had been on records with trombonist Benny Powell and violinist L. Subramaniam in 1979 (and a second record with Subramaniam in 1984), but those were only temporary returns. In 1985, on *Easy Living,* a quartet date with pianist Cedar Walton, bassist Tony Dumas, and drummer Billy Higgins, the 51-year-old altoist showed that he had lost nothing through the decades and was ready to start growing again. He performs two songs associated with Charlie Parker ("Embraceable You" and "Now's the Time") and a variety of numbers (by Jobim, Wayne Shorter, Walton, and McCoy Tyner) that had not been written at the time he had left the jazz scene. *Lament* (with Walton, Higgins, and bassist Buster Williams) is on the same level, with Morgan finding fresh ideas to express on such tunes as Lee Morgan's "Ceora," "Perdido," Miles Davis's "Half Nelson," and J.J. Johnson's "Lament." *Double Image* is a fine set of alto piano duets with George Cables consisting of three originals, three obscurities, "All the Things You Are," and "After You've Gone." Cables's sensitive playing (he would later record duets with Art Pepper) inspires Morgan to play quite emotionally. *Bebop Lives* documents Morgan's triumphant debut in New York, playing live at the Village Vanguard with flugelhornist Johnny Coles, Walton, Williams, and Higgins. The six standards include an intense ballad feature for Morgan on "Come Sunday," "Parker's Mood," and "All the Things You Are."

Quiet Fire teams Frank Morgan with Bud Shank. Both of the altoists had (after very different careers) ended up on similar paths, pushing in adventurous and intense fashion at the boundaries of Bebop. With George Cables, bassist John Heard, and drummer Jimmy Cobb, they perform four quintet pieces (including "Solar" and "The Night Has a Thousand Eyes") and have a ballad feature apiece (Shank on "Emily" and Morgan gets "What's New"). There is no coasting on this live date and, although the playing is not flawless (too many chances are taken for that), the results are

often quite exciting. *Major Changes* is a collaboration by Morgan with the McCoy Tyner Trio (pianist Tyner, bassist Avery Sharpe, and drummer Louis Hayes). It is proof, if any were needed, that Morgan had moved beyond Bop to post-Bop. On three Tyner originals (including "Frank's Back"), the "Theme from 'Love Story'," and a trio of standards, Morgan sounds quite lyrical and emotional, fitting in quite well with Tyner's dense chords. In contrast, *Yardbird Suite* has Morgan returning to a strictly Bebop repertoire (including "A Night in Tunisia," "Star Eyes," and "Scrapple from the Apple") with the assistance of pianist Mulgrew Miller (whose playing is coincidentally most influenced by McCoy Tyner), bassist Ron Carter, and drummer Al Foster. From the same week, *Reflections* features Morgan leading an all-star group (tenor saxophonist Joe Henderson, vibraphonist Bobby Hutcherson, Miller, Carter, and Foster) through a solid Hard Bop date that includes "Caravan," Thelonious Monk's "Reflections," "Sonnymoon for Two," and four originals by band members (including Henderson's "Black Narcissus").

7 *Mood Indigo / June 26-27, 1989 / Antilles 91320*

6 *A Lovesome Thing / Sept. 5-6, 1990 / Antilles 422-848 213*

7 *You Must Believe in Spring / Mar. 10-11, 1992 / Antilles 314 512 570*

7 *Listen to the Dawn / Apr. 19, 1993–Nov. 27, 1993 / Antilles 314 518 979*

8 *Love, Lost & Found / Mar. 7-9, 1995 / Telarc 83374*

8 *Bop! / Aug. 19-21, 1996 / Telarc 83413*

Unlike his Contemporary recordings, Frank Morgan has frequently emphasized ballads in his Antilles and Telarc sets. On his debut for Antilles, *Mood Indigo,* he performs four duets with George Cables, one with Buster Williams, a trio with Williams and Al Foster, a quartet number with Cables, Williams, and Foster, two quartets with Ronnie Mathews in Cables's place, and a pair of quintets that include trumpeter Wynton Marsalis with Mathews, Williams, and Foster. The music includes Morgan's emotional renditions of such selections as "This Love of Mine," "Bessie's Blues," "Up Jumped Spring," and Cables's "Lullaby." *A Lovesome Thing* is also taken mostly at slower tempos. Morgan, Cables, bassist David Williams, and drummer Lewis Nash welcome trumpeter Roy Hargrove to three of the nine songs (including "Footprints" and "Everything Happens to Me"), and Abbey Lincoln sings a so-so version of "Ten

Cents a Dance" and her own "Wholey Earth." Overall, this set is not without interest but falls short of being essential.

Morgan's third straight ballad album, *You Must Believe in Spring,* is a bit unusual. The altoist plays two duets apiece with Barry Harris and Hank Jones and one apiece with Kenny Barron, Tommy Flanagan, and Roland Hanna; all of the pianists but Barron were originally from Detroit. Each pianist is introduced before his duet(s) with Morgan by playing an unaccompanied solo that often lasts as long as the collaborations. So out of the dozen selections, Morgan is present for only seven, totaling around 38 minutes. The music is frequently exquisite (including "You've Changed," "Embraceable You," and "You Must Believe in Spring"), but there are no fireworks to be heard!

On *Listen to the Dawn,* three of the songs are duets with guitarist Kenny Burrell, but otherwise Morgan is joined by Burrell, bassist Ron Carter, and drummer Grady Tate to form a sparse and laid-back quartet. The highlights include "Grooveyard," "It Might As Well Be Spring," and "I Didn't Know About You," all tastefully played. Switching to the Telarc label, Morgan is in excellent form on *Love, Lost & Found,* a set of quietly played standards (including "The Nearness of You," "Skylark," "It's Only a Paper Moon," and "Someday My Prince Will Come") with pianist Cedar Walton, Ray Brown, and Billy Higgins; this thoughtful version of "What Is This Thing Called Love" is a highlight. Age 62 in 1996, Frank Morgan (joined by pianist Rodney Kendrick, either Curtis Lundy or Ray Drummond on bass and drummer Leroy Williams) on *Bop!* plays what producer John Snyder accurately called "Bop without clichés." On this high-quality date, Morgan mostly pays tribute to Charlie Parker, not by copying him but by displaying his own individuality on such songs as "Well You Needn't," "52nd Street Theme," and a lengthy version of Miles Davis's "Half Nelson." He had every right to sound celebratory, for his 11-year comeback was successful after 30 years of darkness.

LPS TO SEARCH FOR

Frank Morgan (GNP/Crescendo 9041) is a reissue of the altoist's first record as a leader. He is heard in 1955 on a set split between songs with Machito's rhythm section, Conte Candoli, and organist Wild Bill Davis, and a Bop date with Candoli, Wardell Gray (on his last session), and a fine rhythm section featuring pianist Carl Perkins. The performances show off Morgan's strong potential, which would not be realized for another 30 years.

FILMS

Frank Morgan is featured on a 1990 concert with Red Rodney, Monty Alexander, Rufus Reid, and Roy Haynes that has been released as *A Tribute to Charlie Parker Vol. 1* (Storyville 6048).

LANNY MORGAN

b. Mar. 30, 1934, Des Moines, IA

A brilliant Bebop altoist often overlooked because he lives in Los Angeles rather than New York, Lanny Morgan is one of the underrated greats; few can rip through "Cherokee" with his flow of ideas. Morgan grew up in Los Angeles and, starting in 1954, played with the big bands of Charlie Barnet, Si Zentner, and Bob Florence. He was set to join Stan Kenton's orchestra but instead had to serve in the military. After his discharge, Morgan gained some recognition while being a key soloist with Maynard Ferguson's big band (1960–65). He freelanced in New York for several years and then in 1969 returned to L.A. Since then he has been a busy studio musician, a longtime member of Supersax, and a fixture in the big bands of Bill Holman, Bob Florence, and occasionally Bill Berry. He also toured with Natalie Cole and has popped up in countless musical situations, occasionally leading his own combo. Lanny Morgan has recorded as a leader for Palo Alto (1981), VSOP (1993), Contemporary (1996), and Fresh Sound (1997).

10 *The Lanny Morgan Quartet / June 11 + 13, 1993 / V.S.O.P. 92*

9 *Pacific Standard Time / Sept. 1996–Oct. 1996 / Contemporary 14084*

8 *A Suite for Yardbird / Sept. 30, 1997–Oct. 1, 1997 / Fresh Sound 5023*

The Lanny Morgan Quartet, Lanny Morgan's second date as a leader finds him in superb form, digging into eight standards (including Lee Konitz's "Subconscious Lee," "Joy Spring," "Bloomdido," and a definitive "Cherokee") with the assistance of pianist Tom Ranier, bassist Bob Maize, and drummer Frank Capp. Although obviously well versed in Charlie Parker, Morgan has his own sound and his own approach to Bebop, as he shows throughout this consistently fine date.

Pacific Standard Time is on a similar level. Morgan jams on ten standards with Ranier, bassist Dave Carpenter, and drummer Joe LaBarbera. Among the hotter numbers are

"Stella By Starlight," "I'll Remember April," "Spring Can Really Hang You Up the Most" (taken as a heated samba), and "It's You or No One." *A Suite for Yardbird* (with Lou Levy, bassist Tom Warrington, and drummer Paul Kreibich) finds Morgan also playing quite well. But because he performs a dozen songs closely associated with Charlie Parker (including "Ornithology," "Ko Ko," "Yardbird Suite," "Donna Lee," and even "Klact-oveeseds-tene"), the altoist naturally has to come in second place to Bird. However, sometimes it is a close second!

LPS TO SEARCH FOR

Lanny Morgan's debut as a leader, 1981's *It's About Time* (Palo Alto 8007), is long overdue to be reissued. The altoist (who also plays a bit of soprano) is joined by Bruce Forman, Lou Levy, bassist Monty Budwig, and drummer Nick Ceroli for a mixture of standards (including "Ko Ko" and "Easy Living") and originals, with his "Friends Again" being a new line on "Just Friends."

MARK MURPHY

b. Mar. 14, 1932, Syracuse, NY

One of the most consistently creative of all jazz singers, Mark Murphy is an eccentric performer whose wild jumps between low notes and falsetto can be both startling and exciting. He seems unable to sing anything completely straight for long, scats masterfully, and sometimes performs vocalese, yet is quite capable of wringing emotion out of ballads. Murphy began singing professionally when he was 16, although his recording debut was not until he was 24. His Riverside dates were successful, displaying a great deal of potential. After a period of struggle as the music industry changed, Murphy spent 1963–72 mostly in London, performing on radio, television, and at European jazz festivals. After returning to the United States, he quickly became popular in the jazz world, recording regularly for Muse and becoming an influential force on other singers (including Kurt Elling). Since 1972, Mark Murphy has gradually evolved from a vocalist with an underground reputation to a poll-winning jazz singer, and he still never coasts.

6   *Crazy Rhythm / June 26, 1956–Aug. 15, 1957 / GRP/ Decca 670*

8   *Rah / Sept. 1961–Nov. 1961 / Original Jazz Classics 141*

Mark Murphy's unwillingness to play it safe has inspired countless singers during the past 30 years.

8   *That's How I Love the Blues / Oct. 1, 1962–Dec. 28, 1962 / Original Jazz Classics 367*

Mark Murphy's long-elusive debut on records (*Crazy Rhythm*) was reissued in 1999. Backed by an orchestra arranged by Ralph Burns, Murphy sings mostly veteran standards (including "Exactly Like You," "Pick Yourself Up," and "Taking a Chance on Love"). Although his interpretations are generally melodic and concise, already he was improvising in subtle ways. After cutting three Capitol records during 1959–60 (long out of print), Murphy recorded two albums for Riverside that have fortunately been reissued in the Original Jazz Classics series. *Rah* has a brass section arranged by Ernie Wilkins that gives drive and power to some interesting Murphy variations on such songs as "Angel Eyes," "Spring Can Really Hang You Up the Most," "Out of This World," "Doodlin'," and "Li'l Darlin'." *That's How I Love the Blues* has Murphy singing a dozen tunes that have "blue" or "blues" in their titles, the majority of which are actually blues. Al Cohn provided arrangements for the two trumpets, organ, pianist Roger Kellaway, and a rhythm section. Murphy sounds quite enthusiastic during the set which includes "Going to Chicago Blues," "Señor Blues," "Blues in My Heart," "Blues in the Night," and "Everybody's Crazy 'Bout the Doggone Blues."

10 ***Stolen . . . And Other Moments / Nov. 20, 1972–Dec. 17, 1991 / 32 Jazz 32036***
Mark Murphy Sings / June 17–19, 1975 / Muse 5078
9 ***Stolen Moments / June 1, 1978 / Muse 5102***
8 ***Bop for Kerouac / Mar. 12, 1981 / Muse 5253***
8 ***Kerouac, Then and Now / Nov. 1986 / Muse 5359***
9 ***Beauty and the Beast / Sept. 10, 1985–Nov. 23, 1986 / Muse 5355***

During his many years overseas, Mark Murphy recorded a few isolated dates for Fontana, Immediate, and Saba, but none of those recordings have been made available domestically on CD. However, shortly after his return to the United States in 1972, the singer began to record regularly for Muse. His long string of recordings for that label is the finest work of his career. Muse reissued some of the music on CD before it was purchased by 32 Jazz. Thus far, other than the two-CD sampler *Stolen . . . And Other Moments,* the individual sets have not been reissued, although some of the Muse CDs might still be found. The 32 Jazz twofer does have many of the high points from Murphy's Muse years and is a perfect way to get introduced to his music. The most adventurous male jazz singer in the years since 1972, Murphy can be heard on this definitive sampler performing unique versions of "I'm Glad There Is You," "Young and Foolish," "Where You At," "Time on My Hands," "Red Clay," his classic rendition of "Stolen Moments," "Parker's Mood," and "Ballad of the Sad Young Men."

Two of the best of his Muse sets are *Mark Murphy Sings* (which includes such numbers as John Coltrane's "Naima," "Body and Soul," "Maiden Voyage," "Cantaloupe Island," and Freddie Hubbard's "Red Clay") and *Stolen Moments,* which is highlighted by the title cut, "Farmer's Market," "Waters of March," and "We'll Be Together Again." *Bop for Kerouac* is particularly unusual, because Murphy alternates Bop-oriented improvising with readings from the works of Jack Kerouac (who loved Bebop). He is assisted by Richie Cole and Bruce Forman in a fine combo on such pieces as "Boplicity," "Parker's Mood," and "Ballad of the Sad Young Men." *Kerouac, Then and Now* has Murphy singing songs that he thinks Jack Kerouac would have liked (including

"Blood Count," "Ask Me Now," and "Lazy Afternoon"), reading two long excerpts from Kerouac's works, and recreating a routine by the odd hipster Lord Buckley. *Beauty and the Beast* has lots of adventurous moments, including Murphy reciting the words he wrote to Wayne Shorter's "Beauty and the Beast" before he sings the song, unearthing some rare Ira Gershwin lyrics to "I Can't Get Started," turning a Rachmaninoff melody into "Vocalise," and performing rare vocal versions of McCoy Tyner's "Effendi" and Sonny Rollins's "Doxy."

6 ***September Ballads / Sept. 15–17, 1987 / Milestone 9154***
7 ***What a Way to Go / Sept. 1990 / Muse 5419***
5 ***Night Mood / Dec. 31, 1991 / Milestone 9145***
7 ***Song for the Geese / 1997 / RCA 44865***
10 ***Some Time Ago / Dec. 27–28, 1999 / High Note 7048***

September Ballads is an attempt by Mark Murphy to uplift fairly recent songs, but unfortunately his singing is usually much better than the material. There are tunes by Pat Metheny, Michael Franks, Gary McFarland, Chick Corea, and Elian Elias, but few of the themes are memorable. However, Murphy sings well and he is assisted in spots by flugelhornist Art Farmer and guitarist Larry Coryell. *What a Way to Go* has Murphy overcoming a somewhat generic electric rhythm section (though tenorman Danny Wilensky sounds good) and coming up with fine versions of Lee Morgan's "Ceora," "I Fall in Love Too Easily," and "All My Tomorrows." *Night Mood* is weaker. For the songs of Ivan Lins, Murphy is assisted by Frank Morgan, flugelhornist Claudio Roditi, and the rhythm section called Azymuth, but he does not sound all that comfortable on the mostly unfamiliar material. *Song for the Geese* has a more conventional repertoire (including "You Go to My Head," Stanley Turrentine's "Sugar," "Baltimore Oriole," "You're Blasé," and J.J. Johnson's "Lament"), but Murphy (backed by a standard rhythm section) never plays it safe, goes over the top now and then, and succeeds in keeping listeners on the edge of their seats.

Age 67 at the time *Some Time Ago* was made, Mark Murphy is heard at the peak of his creative powers on that 1999 recording. Joined by a quintet consisting of trumpeter Dave Ballou, altoist Allan Mezquida, pianist-arranger Lee Musker, drummer Winard Harper, and either Steve LaSpina or Sean Smith on bass, Murphy swings "There's No More Blue Time," puts plenty of feeling into Jimmy Rowles's "The Peacocks," and records the first vocal version of Oscar Pettiford's "Bohemia After Dark." Other selections include "You're My Alter Ego," Cedar Walton's "Mosaic" (retitled "Life's Mosaic"), a very fast "That Old Black Magic," and a somber medley of "Why Was I Born?" and "I'm a Fool to Want You." Highly recommended.

LPS TO SEARCH FOR

This Could Be the Start of Something Big (last out as Pausa 9042) features Murphy near the beginning of his recording career in the late 1950s, being joined on six standards and an unusual seven-song medley by some West Coast jazz all-stars. Bill Holman's arrangements and Murphy's enthusiasm help overcome the brevity of some of the tracks. Also from the Capitol period (and benefiting from Holman's charts) is *Playing the Field* (Capitol 1458), which includes such numbers as "Put the Blame on Mame," "Love Is a Many Splendored Thing," "As Long As I Live," and "I Didn't Know About You." But compared to what would be coming, this effort is rather safe. Of the out-of-print Muse dates, *The Artistry of Mark Murphy* (Muse 5286) includes "The Odd Child" (his lyric to George Wallington's "Godchild"), "Moody's Mood," "Autumn Nocturne," and a "Trilogy for Kids" made up of "Babe's Blues," "Little Niles," and "Dat Dere." *The Nat King Cole Songbook Volume One* (Muse 5308) and *Volume Two* (Muse 5320) find Murphy paying tribute to the pianist-singer by performing a total of 22 songs associated with Cole. What is odd is that, instead of utilizing a piano-guitar-bass trio, Murphy sings duets with guitarist Joe LoDuca, keyboardist Gary Schunk, or bassist Bob Magusson. Somehow it works, even though the musicians never meet up and play together. *Living Room* (Muse 5345) has lots of variety, from Dave Frishberg's "Our Love Rolls On," "Charleston Alley," and "There'll Be Some Changes Made" to a humorous version of "Ain't Nobody Here but Us Chickens." Trumpeter Ted Curson and tenor saxophonist Gerry Niewood help out with some concise solos.

FILMS

Mark Murphy appears in the British film *Just Like a Woman* (1966).

SAL NISTICO

b. Apr. 12, 1940, Syracuse, NY, d. Mar. 3, 1991, Berne, Switzerland

Woody Herman's top soloist of the 1960s, Sal Nistico was a hard-charging and frequently explosive tenor saxophonist who added excitement to most sessions in which he appeared. Nistico started on alto but switched to tenor when he was 16. He worked with R&B bands for a few years and was part of Chuck Mangione's Jazz Brothers during 1959–61, making his recording debut with Mangione. Nistico became well known while with Woody Herman's big band (1962–65), recording several notable solos during the period. He spent five months with the Count Basie Orchestra in 1965, was back with Basie in 1967, and returned to Herman's band during 1968–70, 1971, and finally 1981–82. He also played with the big bands of Don Ellis, Tito Puente, and Buddy Rich but mostly spent his later years jamming with smaller combos. Unfortunately Sal Nistico never really fulfilled his potential, was mostly obscure in the 1970s and '80s (although he led albums for the Horo, Ego, Bee Hive, Steam, and Red labels) and had largely faded away by the time of his death, a month short of his 51st birthday.

8   *Sal Nistico Live / Feb. 1, 1981 / Just Jazz 1003*

Virtually the only Sal Nistico recording currently available on CD, this set was not initially released until 1995. Fortunately it is a good one. Nistico jams on three standards ("How Deep Is the Ocean," "You Stepped Out of a Dream," and "I Can't Get Started"), Hank Mobley's "Stella Wise," and his own "Backlog" with pianist Mark Levine, bassist Peter Barshay, and drummer Bobby Rosenstein. Nistico still had his strong sound, he really stretches out (all but one song is over ten minutes), and the music swings hard. Recommended.

LPS TO SEARCH FOR

It is surprising that Sal Nistico's first two dates as a leader (from 1961–62) have not yet been reissued in the Original Jazz Classics series. Both *Heavyweights* (Jazzland 66), a quintet outing with cornetist Nat Adderley, Barry Harris, bassist Sam Jones, and drummer Walter Perkins, and *Comin' on Up* (Riverside 457), with trumpeter Sal Amico, Harris, bassist Bob Cranshaw, and drummer Vinnie Ruggiero, are excellent early examples of Nistico. 1978's *Neo/Nistico* (Bee Hive 7006) teams the tenorman with trumpeter Ted Curson, baritonist Nick Brignola, pianist Ronnie Mathews, Sam Jones, and Roy Haynes on two Nistico originals (including a Kenny Dorham tribute called "Blues for K. D."), Wayne Shorter's "Fee-Fi-Fo-Fum," and three standards. A roaring "Anthropology" has the horns playing the melody harmonized in fourths, not an inspired idea (!), but the rest of this blowing date works quite well.

SAM NOTO

b. Apr. 17, 1930, Buffalo, NY

Although not a Canadian, trumpeter Sam Noto has spent many years up north, moving to Toronto in 1975. Early on, Noto played with the big bands of Stan Kenton (1953–58), Louis Bellson (1959), Kenton again (1960), and Count Basie (two periods during 1964–67). The years 1969–75 were spent mostly in the anonymity of Las Vegas. Noto recorded with Red Rodney (another jazzer in Vegas during that era) in 1974, and that led to his long-overdue discovery as a superior trumpeter who considered his main influences to be Dizzy Gillespie, Fats Navarro, and Miles Davis. Sam Noto was well documented by the Xanadu label during 1975–78, both as a leader and as a sideman, but unfortunately none of those dates have been reissued yet on CD. In the decades since, he was a member of Rob McConnell's Boss Brass, worked in the studios, and every once in a while popped up on a Bop recording, although never often enough.

LPS TO SEARCH FOR

During 1975–78, Sam Note led four highly enjoyable Bop-oriented dates for Xanadu, all of which are scarce these days. *Entrance* (Xanadu 103), his first session ever as a leader, found the 44-year-old playing both standards and Boppish originals (including "Fats Flats," "Make Believe," and Fats Navarro's "Nostalgia") with Barry Harris, bassist Leroy Vinnegar, and drummer Lenny McBrowne. *Act One* (Xanadu 127) reunited Noto with tenor saxophonist Joe Romano (an old friend who was in his undocumented group in the 1960s), Harris, bassist Sam Jones, and drummer Billy Higgins on five of Noto's originals (most of which are based on the chord changes of standards) and a lyrical three-song ballad medley. *Notes to You* (Xanadu 144) brings back Romano and Jones and adds baritonist Ronnie Cuber, pianist Jimmy Rowles, and drummer Freddie Waits. They perform one lone standard ("'Round Midnight") and five Noto tunes, including a couple ("Quasinoto" and "Cross Chris") whose titles look like other songs (Bird's "Quasimodo" and Monk's "Criss Cross") but actually have no relation! *Noto-Riety* (Xanadu 168) features the appealing blend of Noto and flutist Sam Most on six of the trumpeter's Boppish originals, assisted by Dolo Coker, bassist Monty Budwig, and drummer Frank Butler.

2-4-5 (Unisson 1007), from 1986–87, gets its name because Noto is heard on three duets with bassist Neil Swain-son, a pair of quartets with pianist Gary Williamson, bassist Steve Wallace, and drummer Bob McLaren, and four quintets that add tenor saxophonist Pat Labarbera. Noto contributed three songs, and among the other tunes are "Beautiful Love," Bud Powell's "Dance of the Infidels," and Sonny Stitt's "Sonny Side."

JOE PASS

b. Jan. 13, 1929, New Brunswick, NJ, d. May 23, 1994, Los Angeles, CA

Joe Pass was a conservative revolutionary, a guitarist with such brilliant technique that he could play an uptempo version of "Cherokee" unaccompanied and sound like a self-sufficient orchestra. Pass stayed within the Bop tradition throughout his life, but was at such a high level that he towered above most other jazz guitarists even while playing mostly standards from decades earlier.

Born Joseph Passalaqua, he took a long time to get his career going. Pass played with the Tony Pastor Orchestra while still in high school, was in Charlie Barnet's big band in 1947, and served in the military. But he wasted the 1950s as a drug addict and scuffled for the entire decade, spending some time in prison. However, in 1962 Pass finally got his career underway. He emerged with a recording made at Synanon, and during the remainder of the decade he recorded frequently for Pacific Jazz and World Pacific, including two classic dates (*Catch Me* and *For Django*). Pass also worked with the Gerald Wilson Orchestra, pianist Les McCann, Bud Shank, pianist-arranger Clare Fischer, Bill Perkins, organist Groove Holmes, the George Shearing Quintet (1965–67), Herb Ellis, and Benny Goodman (1973).

In 1973 Pass started recording for Norman Granz's Pablo label, and his album *Virtuoso* became a sensation. No guitarist previously had played uptempo tunes such as "How High the Moon," "Cherokee," and "The Song Is You" unaccompanied, creating bass lines, melodies, harmonies, and heated solos simultaneously. Pass recorded prolifically for Pablo up to 1992, including many more solo dates, sessions with quartets and larger groups, and meetings with such all-stars as Oscar Peterson, Ella Fitzgerald, Milt Jackson, Dizzy Gillespie, Count Basie, and even Duke Ellington. He worked constantly, and his later, post-Pablo dates show that he never did decline. Joe Pass remained active almost to the end, passing away from cancer at age 65.

Joe Pass showed that it really is possible to play an uptempo "Cherokee" unaccompanied on the guitar, without leaving out the melody, harmony, chords, and a rapid solo.

8 *The Best of Joe Pass / Feb. 1961–Sept. 1964 / Pacific Jazz 54944*

9 *Joy Spring / Feb. 6, 1964 / Pacific Jazz 35222*

6 *Joe's Blues / 1967 / Laserlight 21094*

There are literally dozens of Joe Pass CDs currently available and pretty much all are listed in this entry. However, his pre-Pablo period has been greatly neglected. In fact, his two early classics, *Catch Me* (1963) and *For Django* (1964), have not been reissued in full by Blue Note, which is rather surprising. *The Best of Joe Pass* draws its 16 selections from seven albums, including *Sound of Synanon,* four cuts from *For Django, 12 String Guitar Movie Themes,* just one cut from *Catch Me,* and sideman dates with the Gerald Wilson Orchestra, Richard "Groove" Holmes, and Les McCann.

This sampler is well done, but it would be nice if all of the material was currently available.

Joy Spring has five standards (including "The Night Has a Thousand Eyes" and Charlie Parker's "Relaxin' at Camarillo") played by Pass with pianist Mike Wofford, bassist Jim Hughart, and drummer Colin Bailey. Substitute rhythm guitarist John Pisano for Wofford and you would have the *For Django* band, a quartet that Pass utilized extensively much later in his career. *Joe's Blues* is a complete obscurity, and the estimated date might be inaccurate. This release from a budget label has Pass interacting with Herb Ellis (they teamed up for a few albums released under Ellis's name in the early 1970s), bassist Monty Budwig, and Colin Bailey. They perform a variety of old standards (including "Look for the Silver Lining" and "When You're Smiling") plus "What Have They Done to My Song?" in swinging fashion. A potentially intriguing album from 1966 that has never been reissued is *The Stones Jazz* (World Pacific 1854), which has Pass playing ten songs from the Rolling Stones songbook! Has any guitarist sounded less like a rock player than Joe Pass?

* *Guitar Virtuoso / Jan. 8, 1973–Aug. 12, 1992 / Pablo 4423*

Guitar Virtuoso is an excellent four-CD sampler of Joe Pass's work for the Pablo label. There are no previously unreleased performances included, so this box is recommended primarily to listeners wanting to get some of the high points of this very productive period in the guitarist's life. The four CDs are not programmed in chronological order, but, since Pass's style did not change much during this period, it really does not matter. The four discs are divided into *Solo Guitar/ Studio Recordings, Group Studio Recordings, Live Solo Guitar and Group Recordings,* and *Vocal & Duo Studio Recordings.* Duke Ellington, Oscar Peterson, Herb Ellis, Ella Fitzgerald, Sarah Vaughan, and Zoot Sims make appearances, and some of the 63 performances showcase Pass as a featured sideman.

10 *Virtuoso / Dec. 1973 / Pablo 2310-708*

9 *Virtuoso #2 / Sept. 14, 1976 + Oct. 26, 1976 / Pablo 2310-788*

7 *Virtuoso #3 / May 27, 1977 + June 1, 1977 / Original Jazz Classics 684*

8 *Virtuoso #4 / Nov. 1973 / Pablo 2640-102*

9 *At the Montreux Jazz Festival 1975 / July 17-18, 1975 / Original Jazz Classics 934*

7 *Montreux '77 / July 15, 1977 / Original Jazz Classics 382*

7 *I Remember Charlie Parker / Feb. 17, 1979 / Original Jazz Classics 602*

8 *Blues Dues (Live at Long Beach City College) / Jan. 20, 1984 / Original Jazz Classics 964*

7 *University of Akron Concert / Mar. 1986 / Pablo 2308-249*

7 *Blues for Fred / Feb. 2-3, 1988 / Pablo 2310-931*

8 *Virtuoso Live! / Sept. 13-15, 1991 / Pablo 2310-948*

7 *Songs for Ellen / Aug. 7-20, 1992 / Pablo 2310-955*

7 *Unforgettable / Aug. 7-20, 1992 / Pablo 2310-964*

All 14 of these CDs (*Virtuoso #4* is a double disc) feature Joe Pass as an unaccompanied guitar soloist. While other guitarists in the past have occasionally played ballads as a solo piece, Pass was one of the very first to rip his way through uptempo numbers and manage to sound both driving and relaxed. Even the most devoted Bop guitar fan probably will not need all of these releases, but then again none of them are throwaways. The original *Virtuoso* set (which includes "Night and Day," "How High the Moon," "Cherokee," "All the Things You Are," and "The Song Is You") is the one that caused a major stir and gave a great deal of momentum to Pass's career. All of the others discs are close to the same level. *Virtuoso #2* finds Pass somehow playing John Coltrane's complex "Giant Steps" and a pair of Chick Corea tunes solo along with some older songs, while *Virtuoso #3* consists of a dozen of his originals. *Virtuoso #4* was actually recorded before the original Virtuoso and is unusual in that Pass plays acoustic guitar throughout. At the time of his appearance at the 1975 Montreux Jazz Festival, his only solo guitar record that had been released was *Virtuoso,* so the audience sounds not only appreciative but a bit surprised at his wizardry. The *1977 Montreux* set is primarily blues, with a few exceptions. The *Charlie Parker* tribute focuses mostly on songs from the "Bird with Strings" sessions rather than Bop standards; Pass is quite lyrical throughout. Despite its title, *Blues Dues* actually has only two blues on the set and finds Pass tackling such tunes as "Wave," "'Round Midnight," and "Honeysuckle Rose," among others.

By the time he performed at the University of Akron in 1986, Pass's solo concerts were both legendary and a bit taken for granted; his repertoire for *University of Akron Concert* includes Clifford Brown's "Joy Spring" and a seven-song Duke Ellington medley. *Blues for Fred* was dedicated to Fred Astaire and has Pass exploring ten songs from Astaire's musical output; many of them (such as "Night and Day," "Lady Be Good," and "The Way You Look Tonight") had been in the guitarist's repertoire for a long time anyway. *Virtuoso Live!* is a hodgepodge of favorites (including "Stompin' at the Savoy," "Beautiful Love," and "Mack the Knife"). *Songs for Ellen* is an acoustic set of mostly swing standards (with the emphasis on slower tempos) dedicated to Pass's wife, and *Unforgettable* (from the same sessions) is also acoustic and of the same quality.

Whether swinging or simply sounding beautiful, Joe Pass' solo recitals were classic. A healthy sampling of these recordings belongs in every jazz collection.

8 *Portraits of Duke Ellington / June 21, 1974 / Pablo 2310-716*

8 *Quadrant / Feb. 2, 1977 / Original Jazz Classics 498*

7 *Tudo Bem! / May 8, 1978 / Original Jazz Classics 685*

9 *Chops / Nov. 19, 1978 / Original Jazz Classics 786*

7 *Checkmate / Jan. 12, 1981 / Original Jazz Classics 975*

7 *Ira, George and Joe / Nov. 23, 1981 / Original Jazz Classics 828*

9 *We'll Be Together Again / Oct. 23, 1983 / Original Jazz Classics 909*

6 *Whitestone / Feb. 28, 1985–Mar. 1, 1985 / Pablo 2310-912*

8 *One for My Baby / Dec. 28, 1988 / Pablo 2310-936*

9 *Summer Nights / Dec. 1989 / Pablo 2310-939*

8 *Appasionato / Aug. 9-11, 1990 / Pablo 2310-946*

8 *Duets / Feb. 16-17, 1991 / Pablo 2310-959*

8 *Joe Pass Quartet Live at Yoshi's / Jan. 30, 1992-Feb. 1, 1992 / Pablo 2310-951*

8 *Nuages, Live at Yoshi's, Vol. 2 / Jan. 30, 1992-Feb. 1, 1992 / Pablo 2310-961*

Even without counting his many sideman appearances, Joe Pass was involved in quite a few group projects while on the Pablo label. *Portraits of Duke Ellington* was recorded a month after Ellington's death, and it has Pass, Ray Brown, and drummer Bobby Durham interpreting nine warhorses associated with Duke, including "Satin Doll," "In a Mellotone," and "Caravan." The guitarist's playing uplifts the music.

Quadrant has Pass interacting with Milt Jackson, Ray Brown, and drummer Mickey Roker on a modern Bop date that includes four originals, Carl Perkins's "Grooveyard," and a pair of Gershwin tunes. Pass and Jackson always did blend together well. *Tudo Bem!* is a bit unusual, for it finds Pass performing with modern Brazilian musicians (including guitarist Oscar Castro-Neves, electric bassist Octavio Bailly, drummer Claudio Slon, and percussionist Paulinho Da Costa plus keyboardist Don Grusin) on three Jobim tunes (including "Wave" and "Corcovado") and a program dominated by Brazilian standards. For *Chops* it was back to Bebop as Pass engages in heated duets with bassist Niels Pedersen, including "Oleo," "Tricotism," and "Yardbird Suite." Pass's duets with the tasteful and subtle pianist Jimmy Rowles on *Checkmate* are generally much more relaxed, laid back, and intimate. *Ira, George and Joe* is a set of 11 Gershwin tunes performed by Pass, rhythm guitarist John Pisano, bassist Jim Hughart, and Shelly Manne. Nothing

unusual happens, but the treatments as usual are of consistent high quality.

We'll Be Together Again is possibly the only full-length album ever of guitar-trombone duets. Pass and J.J. Johnson prove to be highly compatible players, and, even when the songs are familiar (such as "Limehouse Blues," "Nature Boy," and "When Lights Are Low"), obviously their versions sound very much different than all the previous ones. It is a pleasure to hear J.J. in such an exposed setting; he sounds quite brilliant. *Whitestone* is a pleasant if so-so Brazilian date in which Pass is joined by Pisano, Don Grusin, and a rhythm section. There are some nice moments on the date (including "Estate"), but overall the results do not rise much above the level of background music.

One for My Baby has Pass with a conventional quintet (which for him was not too conventional!) and performing with three musicians with whom he had not played before: the soulful tenor saxophonist Plas Johnson, pianist Gerald Wiggins (who makes some rare appearances here on organ too), and drummer Albert "Tootie" Heath in addition to bassist Andy Simpkins. Three blues (two by Pass) alternate with five vintage tunes, and the results are typically swinging.

Summer Nights reunited Joe Pass with his *For Django* quartet of 1963, and the 26 years that had passed did not dull the group's tightness. Pass would use rhythm guitarist John Pisano, bassist Jim Hughart, and drummer Colin Bailey as his regular group on and off during his last few years. *Summer Nights* could actually be called "For Django 2," for all of the songs (except for the title cut and three basic originals) were played by Reinhardt, including "I Got Rhythm," "Them There Eyes," and four songs written by the classic guitarist. *Appasionato* has the same musicians in 1990 interpreting a more Bop-oriented repertoire, including "Relaxin' at Camarillo," "Nica's Dream," "That's Earl, Brother," and "Stuffy." John Pisano is one of the most modest of all guitarists, and he loved accompanying Pass. Duets was a dream come true in ways for him because the project (not released until after Pass's death) has the two guitarists playing quite spontaneously. With the exception of "Alone Together" and Horace Silver's "Lonely Woman," the ten songs were all made up on the spot, and Pisano fares very well (following Pass's every idea closely) even though he was always shy to solo. Pass, Pisano, and Bailey return for both volumes of *Live at Yoshi's,* this time with bassist Monty Budwig on one of his final dates before his death. The music ranges from exciting (such as "Doxy" and "Oleo" on Vol. 1 and "Cherokee" on the second disc) to relaxed, with Pass clearly enjoying playing with these musicians one more time.

6	*Joe Pass in Hamburg / Apr. 23, 1990–Feb. 21, 1992 / ACT 9100*
8	*Six String Santa / Feb. 4, 1992 / Laserlight 15 470*
7	*Finally / Feb. 15, 1992 / Verve 314 512 603*
7	*My Song / Feb. 2–4, 1993 / Telarc 83326*
9	*Roy Clark and Joe Pass Play Hank Williams / 1994 / Buster Ann Music*

Joe Pass's final Pablo album was recorded in 1992, but he was not quite finished yet. *Joe Pass in Hamburg* has him joined by the NDR big band in 1990 and 1992. A few of the ballads get a bit sleepy, but the exciting "Fragments of Blues" and a medium-tempo "More Than You Know" wake the music up. Pianist Walter Norris and trombonist Jiggs Whigham have some brief spots, but this is Pass's show, and he was apparently quite pleased to be playing with a big band. *Six String Santa* (with the Pisano-Hughart-Bailey group) is quite fun as Pass plays quartets, guitar duets with Pisano, and unaccompanied solos on ten Yuletide favorites (including "Let It Snow," "Santa Claus Is Coming to Town," and "Winter Wonderland") plus his own "Happy Holiday Blues."

Joe Pass and bassist Red Mitchell first met in 1952 but had only three brief opportunities to play together during the next 40 years, until they "finally" made a duet album for Verve in 1992: *Finally*. The combination works well (Mitchell always had very fast reactions), and the bassist (who is featured on "Pennies from Heaven") even takes a vocal on his "Finally," although it is surprising that there were not more romps included on this tasteful set. *My Song* once again has the Pisano-Hughart-Bailey group, although this version differs from their previous projects in that Tom Ranier makes the group a quintet, playing piano and having one appearance apiece on clarinet, tenor, and soprano. Ranier's participation gives the date its own personality; highlights include "Rockin' in Rhythm," "Keepin' Out of Mischief Now," and "Ain't Misbehavin'."

Joe Pass's final recording is an oddity in ways, but it is also quite logical. He teams up with country guitarist Roy Clark to play a set of Hank Williams tunes. However, Clark loves playing swing and Williams's songs tended to have appealing chord changes, including "Hey, Good Lookin'," "Your Cheatin' Heart," and "There'll Be No Teardrops Tonight." Pisano, Hughart, and Bailey assist Joe Pass one last time on this surprising final chapter to his career.

LPS TO SEARCH FOR

Most of Joe Pass's early recordings are unfortunately out of print. *The Complete "Catch Me" Sessions* (Blue Note 1053), from 1963, is a reissue of Pass's first set as a leader (adding two additional performances), and it is considered a classic. He plays a variety of standards (many of which would stay in his repertoire throughout his career) and the title cut in a quartet with Clare Fischer (doubling on piano and organ), bassist Albert Stinson, and Colin Bailey. *For Django* (World Pacific 85) is even better, a tribute to Django Reinhardt (mostly Reinhardt-associated songs plus John Lewis's "Django" and Pass's title cut) with the Pisano-Hughart-Bailey quartet. *A Sign of the Times* (World Pacific 21844) has Pass backed by an orchestra arranged by Bob Florence in 1965. Even with its commercial touches, it has some strong solos along the way. *Guitar Interludes* (Discovery 776) is a strange if moderately intriguing set from 1969–70 that finds Pass and a rhythm section joined by a seven-voice horn section. The guitarist plays five "Interludes," "Joey's Blues," two obscurities, and five songs by the unknown Irwin Roseman. His last record before joining Pablo was *Intercontinental* (MPS 20738), an excellent trio date with bassist Eberhard Weber and drummer Kenny Clare.

And for those Joe Pass fanatics who do not feel that enough of the guitarist's Pablo dates are on CD, the two-LP *Live at Dante's* (Pablo 2620 114), a 1974 set with Jim Hughart and drummer Frank Severino, gives listeners 13 additional numbers. Also out of print are a set of duets with Niels Pedersen from 1979 called *Northsea Nights* (Pablo 2308–221), *All Too Soon* (Pablo 2312–117), which has the group Quadrant (Pass, Milt Jackson, Ray Brown, and Mickey Roker) playing Duke Ellington songs in 1980, and 1982's *Eximious* (Pablo 2310–877). Pass, Pedersen, and drummer Martin Drew perform standards and an original by the guitarist called "A Foxy Chick and a Cool Cat" on the last. *Sound Project* (Polytone 1600–101), from 1987, is a true obscurity, a trio date with Tommy Gumina on accordion and drummer Jimmie Smith. Gumina is one of the great accordionists (here his instrument is called a polycorus), and his matchup with Pass is a surprise success.

FILMS

Joe Pass is on a few numbers apiece on *Legends of Jazz Guitar Vol. 1* (Vestapol 13009) and *Vol. 2* (Vestapol 13033). He is seen at greater length at a solo concert on *Brecon Jazz Festival, 1991* (Vestapol 13025).

NIELS-HENNING ORSTED PEDERSEN

b. May 27, 1946, Osted, Denmark

Niels Pedersen developed very early in life as a talented Bop-based bassist, and he has been in great demand ever since. A virtuoso soloist and a stimulating accompanist, Pedersen has played with the who's who of straight-ahead jazz ever since he was a teenager. He had some piano lessons, switched to bass when he was 14, and developed so quickly that he was performing with major jazz artists by the time he was 16. Pedersen reluctantly had to turn down a chance to join Count Basie's orchestra when he was 17 due to his age. However, he worked as the house bassist at the Club Montmartre, where he accompanied such jazz musicians as Bud Powell, Brew Moore, Don Byas, Dexter Gordon, Johnny Griffin, Sonny Rollins, pianists Bill Evans, and Tete Montoliu, saxophonist Rahsaan Roland Kirk, and even avant-gardist Albert Ayler, among many others. Pedersen, who also worked with the Danish Radio Orchestra, in the 1970s had a longtime duo with Kenny Drew. He recorded quite a bit for the Pablo label in the 1970s and '80s, including with Oscar Peterson (often touring with his trio), Joe Pass, Count Basie, and quite a few all-stars. Niels-Henning Orsted Pedersen has recorded several dates as a leader for Steeplechase, Pablo, and Da Capo (his own sessions tend to be much more modern than Bebop), and he has remained quite busy up to the present time.

7 *Ambiance / Dec. 13–14, 1993 / Dacapo 9417*

Although this CD has the Danish Radio Big Band, the main soloist throughout is Niels Pedersen; there is another accompanying bassist in the ensembles. It is a bit of a novelty, having an orchestra accompany a bassist, but the arrangements contain a fair amount of variety, there are a few spots for tenor saxophonist Bob Rockwell, and the material (six songs by NHOP, "Donna Lee," and two traditional Danish themes) is fresh. One song is a duet by Pedersen and pianist Ole Kock Hansen, who is also the arranger and conductor of the orchestra.

LPS TO SEARCH FOR

Dancing on the Tables (SteepleChase 1125), from 1979, has strong post-Bop playing by Pedersen in a quartet with saxophonist Dave Liebman, guitarist John Scofield, and drummer Billy Hart. The Viking (Pablo 2310–894), from 1983, is

a set of intriguing duets with guitarist Philip Catherine, who on this date is not shy to show off the influence of Django Rcinhardt.

ART PEPPER

b. Sept. 1, 1925, Gardena, CA, d. June 1, 1982, Panorama City, CA

Art Pepper had an erratic and often-dark life full of harrowing episodes and drug addiction. But quite remarkably, his playing was consistent throughout his career. Virtually all of his recordings were at least at a brilliant level (despite the shape he was frequently in), and he was one of the great alto saxophonists of all time. Because his career was split into two periods and his later years found him playing post-Bop rather than Bebop, this entry deals with his pre-1961 life and work, leaving the later part of his remarkable career for another book in this series.

Pepper was initially inspired by Benny Carter and Charlie Parker and was one of the few altoists from his generation (along with Lee Konitz and Paul Desmond) who did not sound like a close relative of Bird's. He played for a short time with Gus Arnheim's orchestra and had stints with the Benny Carter and Stan Kenton big bands before serving in the military (1944–46). After his discharge, he was back with Kenton again during 1947–48 and 1950–51, being one of the band's star soloists no matter how complex the music. Unfortunately, by the early 1950s Pepper was a heroin addict, and his habit would make his lifestyle quite unstable and at times dangerous; he spent three periods in jail during 1951–56. But musically, the 1950s were a golden age for Pepper. He recorded as a leader for several labels, including most notably Contemporary (starting in 1956), and among his many fine Bop-oriented dates were two classics: *Meets the Rhythm Section* and *Art Pepper + Eleven*. Pepper also did some studio work and was utilized as a sideman on a variety of West Coast jazz sessions, some under the leadership of arranger Marty Paich.

But then it stopped. Most of the 1961–74 period was taken up by jail time, brief periods of recovery (including a 1968 stint with the Buddy Rich big band), and scuffling. Miraculously, in 1975, Art Pepper began making a comeback, and his final seven years were full of musical triumphs that dwarfed even his earlier accomplishments. His playing had changed and opened up to include many expressive and emotional sounds, although Pepper often still played standards; he also enjoyed wailing on the clarinet now and then.

His autobiography, *Straight Life,* frankly discusses his up-and-down life, and it helped lead to his long overdue recognition. By the time he passed away in 1982, Art Pepper had achieved his once-impossible goal of becoming the top altoist in jazz.

8 *The Discovery Sessions / Mar. 4, 1952–Aug. 25, 1953 / Savoy 92846*

3 *Surf Ride / Mar. 4, 1952–Aug. 25, 1953 / Savoy 0115*

5 *Art Pepper Quartet, Vol. 1 / Mar. 30, 1953 / Time Is 9805*

7 *The Art Pepper Quartet / Nov. 23, 1956 / Original Jazz Classics 816*

8 *The Way It Was! / Nov. 26, 1956–Nov. 23, 1960 / Original Jazz Classics 389*

8 *The Artistry of Pepper / Dec. 11, 1956–Aug. 12, 1957 / Pacific Jazz 97194*

On three sessions for Savoy during 1952–53, Art Pepper recorded 16 selections plus 25 alternate takes. All of the music (except for the four songs from the first date which were issued elsewhere) came out as part of a two-LP set and a single album back in the LP era. *The Discovery Sessions* has all 16 master takes plus six alternates. *Surf Ride,* in contrast, was put out by Japanese Nippon in 1991, and it is quite chintzy (with only 12 cuts) and its dates inaccurate; skip it! *The Discovery Sessions* features Pepper in a quartet with Hampton Hawes, bassist Joe Mondragon, and drummer Larry Bunker, with another combo that includes pianist Russ Freeman, bassist Bob Whitlock, and drummer Bobby White, and matching wits and harmonies with tenor saxophonist Jack Montrose, assisted by Claude Williamson, bassist Monty Budwig, and either Paul Vallerina or Larry Bunker on drums. Other than the alternate take of "The Way You Look Tonight," the music is concise (rarely more than $3\frac{1}{2}$ minutes apiece) but full of ideas; highlights include "Surf Ride," "Chili Pepper," "Suzy the Poodle," "Tickle Toe," "Deep Purple," and "Straight Life."

The erratic recording quality of *Art Pepper Quartet, Vol. 1* (there never was a Vol. 2) makes the otherwise fine club date with Sonny Clark, Harry Babasin on bass and cello, and drummer Bobby White of interest mostly to collectors. Pepper is heard in excellent form on "Brown Gold," "Tickle Toe," "Strike Up the Band," and four other numbers, live from the Lighthouse. The music on *Art Pepper Quartet* has also been issued as *Val's Pal* (V.S.O.P. 61) by another label. Pepper, and a quiet rhythm section (Russ Freeman, bassist

Ben Tucker, and drummer Gary Frommer) perform seven songs and five alternate takes. Although the set as a whole is not quite essential, Pepper's renditions of "Diane" and "Besame Mucho" (two songs that would stay in his repertoire to the end) are memorable. *The Way It Was!* has four tunes and two alternate takes from a session that was never completed despite its high quality. Pepper and tenor saxophonist Warne Marsh weave lines around each other on veteran standards (including "I Can't Believe That You're in Love with Me" and "Tickle Toe"), with backing from pianist Ronnie Ball, Ben Tucker, and Gary Frommer. To complete this release are three extra numbers, one tune apiece from the dates that resulted in *Art Pepper Meets the Rhythm Section, Intensity,* and *Gettin' Together* that were not released with the original sets.

The Artistry of Pepper has four fine selections in which the altoist is teamed with tenor saxophonist Bill Perkins, pianist Jimmy Rowles, Ben Tucker, and drummer Mel Lewis. However, the reason to get this CD is for a lesser-known but classic nonet session in which Shorty Rogers contributed all of the pieces (including "Didi," "Powder Puff," and "Popo") and arrangements. Featured along with Pepper are Bill Holman on tenor, trumpeter Don Fagerquist, and Stu Williamson on valve trombone.

8 *The Return of Art Pepper, Volume 1 / Jan. 3, 1956–Aug. 6, 1956 / Pacific Jazz 46863*

8 *Modern Art, Volume 2 / Dec. 28, 1956–Apr. 1, 1957 / Blue Note 46848*

8 *The Art of Pepper, Vol. 3 / Apr. 1, 1957 / Blue Note 46853*

10 *Meets the Rhythm Section / Jan. 19, 1957 / Original Jazz Classics 338*

10 *Art Pepper + Eleven: Modern Jazz Classics / Mar. 14, 1959–May 12, 1959 / Original Jazz Classics 341*

The first three CDs in this section are subtitled "The Complete Art Pepper Aladdin Recordings." Actually the music was originally put out by Jazz West, Intro, Liberty, Onyx, and the Japanese Trio label! Formerly scattered about, it is good to have the performances coherently reissued. *Volume 1* features Pepper in a quintet with Jack Sheldon, Russ Freeman, bassist Leroy Vinnegar, and Shelly Manne and on five numbers actually led by drummer Joe Morello that also includes Red Norvo, Gerald Wiggins, and Ben Tucker. Pepper dominates the music, particularly on "Straight Life," "Pepper Steak," "Tenor Blooz" (which finds him taking a rare solo on tenor), "You Go to My Head," "Patricia," and "Pepper Returns" (celebrating his release from prison).

Volume 2 showcases Pepper in quartets with either Russ Freeman or Carl Perkins on piano, bassist Tucker, and drummer Chuck Flores. The altoist flies through such songs as "When You're Smiling," "Stompin' at the Savoy," "Blues In," "Blues Out," and "Webb City." The April 1, 1957, session, which is completed on *Vol. 3* (featuring Perkins, Tucker, and Flores), was put out originally on stereo tapes but not on LPs until the 1970s. The music did not deserve to be so obscure! Highlights of *Vol. 3* include "Too Close for Comfort," a different version of Bud Powell's "Webb City," "Fascinating Rhythm," and "Surf Ride."

Art Pepper Meets the Rhythm Section and *Art Pepper + Eleven* were not only two of the best recordings of Pepper's career but two of the finest jazz dates of the 1950s. Although Pepper was apparently not in good shape for either one of them (particularly the former set), he sounds brilliant throughout. He had not played during the previous two weeks and did not even know that he was supposed to record with Miles Davis's rhythm section (pianist Red Garland, bassist Paul Chambers, and drummer Philly Joe Jones) until that morning! No matter, *Art Pepper Meets The Rhythm Section* features the altoist in peak form on such numbers as "You'd Be So Nice to Come Home To," "Straight Life," "Star Eyes," and "Birks Works." *Art Pepper + Eleven* is even better. Marty Paich arranged a dozen modern jazz classics (including "Move," "Groovin' High," "Four Brothers," "'Shaw Nuff," "Anthropology," and "Donna Lee") for a 12-piece group of West Coast jazz all-stars, with Pepper as the main soloist. Jack Sheldon has a few spots, but the focus is mostly on Pepper, who really rises to the occasion, making this a historic recording. The CD reissue adds three alternate takes to the original set.

- 9 **Gettin' Together** / Feb. 29, 1960 / Original Jazz Classics 169
- 8 **Smack Up** / Oct. 24–25, 1960 / Original Jazz Classics 176
- 9 **Intensity** / Nov. 23–25, 1960 / Original Jazz Classics 387

The last year that the classic early Art Pepper could be heard was 1960. He would soon be serving a series of prison terms and entering a 15-year period of darkness that ended in 1975 with the beginning of his unlikely comeback. *Gettin' Together* finds Pepper engaged in a sequel of sorts as he again utilizes Miles Davis's current rhythm section (which in 1960 consisted of pianist Wynton Kelly and drummer Jimmy Cobb in addition to Paul Chambers), having Conte Candoli make the group a quintet on half of the selections. Pepper splits the music between originals and standards, with the high points including "Bijou the Poodle," "Rhythm-a-ning," and "Diane." *Smack Up* is an ironic title for Pepper's October 1960 album. Although the song was actually written by tenor saxophonist Harold Land, it did express a large part of Pepper's problems. Despite that, he is in top form on a set of obscure material (including Ornette Coleman's "Tears Inside" and Buddy Collette's "A Bit of Basie") in a quintet with Jack Sheldon, pianist Pete Jolly, bassist Jimmy Bond, and drummer Frank Butler. *Intensity* was Pepper's final album before his long prison term, and it is remarkable how strong and emotional he sounds throughout this standards-oriented date. Pepper really digs deep into such songs as "I Love You," "Come Rain or Come Shine," and "Gone with the Wind." Dolo Coker, Jimmy Bond, and Frank Butler help bring this once bright chapter of Art Pepper's life to a close on a high level.

LPS TO SEARCH FOR

On February 12, 1952, shortly after serving his first brief term in jail, Art Pepper was captured live at the Surf Club in Hollywood. *The Early Show* (Xanadu 108) and *The Late Show* (Xanadu 117) are decently recorded on a private tape recorder and offer valuable early glimpses of Pepper in a quartet with Hampton Hawes, bassist Joe Mondragon, and Larry Bunker (on drums and vibes) playing Bop standards and such originals as "Suzy the Poodle," "Patty Cake," "Spiked Punch," and "Chili Pepper." Art Pepper's second and third sessions for Savoy were reissued in full (with many alternates takes) on the twofer *Discoveries* (Savoy 2217) and *Rediscoveries* (Savoy 1170). The limited-edition three-LP *Complete Pacific Jazz Small Group Recordings of Art Pepper* (Mosaic 3–105) features the altoist in two sextets and a quintet actually led by trumpeter Chet Baker plus a big band title ("Tenderly") with a Baker-led group; only six numbers from August 12, 1957 (reissued on the CD the Artistry of Pepper), are actually led by the altoist.

FILMS

Notes from a Jazz Survivor (Shanachie 6316) is a very frank and sometimes scary documentary on Art Pepper.

P. J. PERRY

b. Dec. 2, 1941, Calgary, Alberta, Canada

In jazz, geography often counts for far too much. P. J. Perry, a hard-swinging altoist influenced by Phil Woods and Art Pepper, could be considered the Sonny Stitt of Canada, but, unlike Stitt, he has made relatively few recordings. The son of tenor saxophonist Paul Guloien (who was known as Paul Perry), P. J. played in his father's band when he was 14. He soon became a busy freelancer in Vancouver, working steadily if not gaining any real recognition outside of his native country. Perry has turned down several offers to work with American bands (including one from Terry Gibbs when he was 18), preferring to stay in Canada and play with local jazz musicians and in the studios. He did spend time in Europe during 1963–66, working with Annie Ross and organist Brian Auger before returning to Vancouver. P. J. Perry has played with Tommy Banks's various groups and Rob McConnell's Boss Brass, and on gigs with Dizzy Gillespie, Red Rodney, Slide Hampton, trumpeter Tom Harrell, and Woody Shaw. His most widely available CDs are for Unity (1989) and Jazz Alliance (1990).

8   *My Ideal / Oct. 1989 / Unity 128*
9   *Worth Waiting for / Dec. 1990 / Jazz Alliance 10007*

P. J. Perry's playing on these two CDs is so strong that these are excellent sets by an altoist who deserves to be much better known. On *My Ideal,* he holds his own with pianist Mulgrew Miller, bassist Neil Swainson, and drummer Victor Lewis, contributing three originals and playing two obscurities plus "If I Should Lose You," "My Ideal," "Easy to Love," and Charlie Parker's "Cheryl." *Worth Waiting For,* with pianist Kenny Barron, bassist Chuck Deardorf, and Victor Lewis, is even better. There are no originals this time, just a dozen veteran standards. Barron has "Star Crossed Lovers" as a piano solo, Perry switches to tenor on three songs, and he sounds in top form on such numbers as "I Cried for You," "Easy to Love," and "Dig." Recommended.

OSCAR PETERSON

b. Aug. 15, 1925, Montreal, Canada

One of the greatest jazz pianists of all time, Oscar Peterson has remarkable technique (on the level of his idol, Art Tatum), can play extremely fast, and can outswing anyone. His sound is distinctive and his style does not fit securely into any one idiom, falling between swing and Bop. Because he has long been such a phenomenal technician, plays a lot of notes, has not radically changed his style since the mid-1950s, and has recorded an enormous number of records, Peterson has sometimes been overly criticized by jaded listeners and been taken for granted. But in reality, few jazz pianists have ever been on his level, whether playing with a trio, jamming with an all-star group, backing a singer, or taking frequently astonishing unaccompanied solos.

Peterson began taking classical piano lessons at age six (his father and his sister Daisy were his first teachers), and he took to the piano from the start. At 14 he won a talent show and began starring on a weekly radio show in Montreal. As a teenager, OP played with Johnny Holmes' big band in Canada. During 1945–49 Peterson recorded 32 numbers for the Victor label in Montreal with his early trio, showing the influence of Teddy Wilson and Nat King Cole and also displaying a love for boogie-woogie. Although his sound was not quite fully developed, Peterson was already a virtuoso who could play remarkable solos. Surprisingly his playing was not touched by Bebop yet.

That would soon change. In 1949 producer Norman Granz heard Peterson, was very impressed, and presented him as a surprise guest at a Jazz at the Philharmonic concert. He was an immediate sensation, and within a few years Peterson was a household name, first in jazz circles and then to a lesser extent among the general public. His style opened up a bit and took elements from Bebop that interested him (a lighter and sparser left hand, harmonic complexity, a greater possibility in his choice of notes) while still retaining his roots in swing. Peterson had a minor hit in "Tenderly," recorded duets with either Ray Brown or Major Holley on bass, added guitarist Irving Ashby to his first trio, and then in 1952 had a notable group with Barney Kessel and Brown. Kessel returned to the studios after a year but, with Herb Ellis taking over the guitar spot, Peterson had his greatest trio during 1953–58. The complex frameworks and arrangements along with the competitiveness among the three players resulted in plenty of fireworks and surprises. In addition to their own tours and recordings, the Oscar Peterson Trio worked with JATP and (often augmented by drums) backed many veteran all-stars, including Lester Young, Louis Armstrong, Ella Fitzgerald, and Roy Eldridge. Granz (who became Peterson's long-term manager) recorded the pianist constantly for his Clef and Verve labels.

In 1958 Ellis left the band and it was decided that, instead

An unclassifiable pianist whose quantity of outstanding recordings through the years is enormous, Oscar Peterson can outswing anyone.

of adding a different guitarist, the spot would be filled by a drummer. Gene Gummage briefly took Ellis's place before Ed Thigpen became a longtime member of the Oscar Peterson Trio. The Peterson-Brown-Thigpen combination lasted until 1965, with Peterson completely dominating the music and still growing in popularity. The successors of Brown and Thigpen included bassists Sam Jones (1966–70) and George Mraz (1970) and drummers Louis Hayes (1965–66), Bobby Durham (1967–70), and Ray Price (1970). In addition to his constant work with the trio, Oscar Peterson established and taught at the Advanced School of Contemporary Music in Toronto (1960–63), developed as a composer (including the "Canadiana Suite"), and even recorded an effective vocal album, *With Respect to Nat,* on which his voice sounds remarkably similar to that of Nat King Cole.

He also recorded notable dates with Milt Jackson and Clark Terry.

In the 1970s Peterson became one of the stars of Norman Granz's Pablo label, recording countless dates as a leader and as a sideman, often working with Joe Pass and Niels Pedersen. He also cut a series of two-piano sessions with Count Basie, led five duet albums with trumpeters Dizzy Gillespie, Roy Eldridge, Clark Terry, Harry "Sweets" Edison, and Jon Faddis, and appeared on many overlapping all-star sets. The gradual phasing out of Pablo during the 1980s resulted in less recordings after 1983, but in 1990 a two-day reunion with Herb Ellis and Ray Brown (along with drummer Bobby Durham) was documented on four CDs for Telarc. A serious stroke in 1993 knocked the pianist out of action for two years. Since his return, his left hand has been reduced to almost nothing in his playing. Peterson rarely plays any unaccompanied passages anymore, but he has resumed touring the world with a quartet and recording regularly. And incredibly, even though largely one-handed in his playing, Oscar Peterson is still one of the world's top pianists.

9 *The Complete Young Oscar Peterson / Apr. 30, 1945-Nov. 14, 1949 / RCA 66609*

8 *1951 / Just a Memory 9501 / Mar. 8, 1951-July 13, 1951*

Oscar Peterson has recorded an uncountable number of records during his productive career; nearly all of his CDs are covered in this extensive section. The earliest examples of OP on records are two songs from a radio broadcast in December 1944 (put out on a Harlequin sampler LP called *Jazz and Hot Dance in Canada*). Otherwise, his first 32 recordings are on the two-CD RCA set, *The Complete Young Oscar Peterson*. Just 19 when he recorded the first session, Peterson is heard during 1945–49 with his Canadian trios that have either Bert Brown, Albert King, or Austin Roberts on bass and Franck Gariepy, Roland Verdon, Russ Dufort, Wilkie Wilkinson, or Clarence Jones on drums or (on the final four numbers) guitarist Ben Johnson. At the time, Peterson's style was more swing-oriented; and the main difference from how he would soon sound in the near future is that Oscar also clearly enjoyed boogie-woogie, as he shows on a few numbers. But by and large these are swing piano sessions, with OP showing off his roots in the style of Nat King Cole.

Peterson's first recordings for Norman Granz (duets with either Ray Brown or Major Holley for the Clef label in 1950–51) have not yet been reissued on CD. The *Just a Memory* disc finds him returning to Montreal in 1951 for 20 duets with bassist Austin Roberts that were originally released as radio transcriptions. Although still playing mostly swing standards, Peterson sounds much more Bop-oriented in his solos than he had previously. He really rips into the uptempo pieces including, "Flying Home," "Seven Come Eleven," and "Get Happy." It must have been very clear that a new giant of the piano had arrived.

7 *The Song Is You: Best of the Verve Songbooks / Dec. 1952-Aug. 1, 1959 / Verve 314 531 558*

7 *The Gershwin Songbooks / Nov. 1, 1952-Aug. 1, 1959 / Verve 314 529 698*

7 *Plays the Duke Ellington Songbook / Dec. 1952-Aug. 9, 1959 / Verve 314 559 785*

9 *The Oscar Peterson Trio at Zardi's / Nov. 8, 1955 / Pablo 2620-118*

9 *Plays Count Basie / Dec. 27, 1955 / Verve 314 519 811*

10 *Stratford Shakespearean Festival / Aug. 8, 1956 / Verve 314 513 752*

9 *At the Concertgebouw / Sept. 29, 1957 + Oct. 9, 1957 / Verve 314 521 649*

Norman Granz loved to record Oscar Peterson, as he showed during Peterson's association with him for Verve and Clef and later at Pablo. The most extensive project was a series of albums featuring the work of specific composers. During 1952–54 Peterson and his trio recorded ten songbook albums (113 songs), and then in 1959 (with Thigpen's drums instead of the guitar of Ellis or Kessel) the newer trio cut nine more albums (108 songs) in that vein, repeating some of the same tunes. This was in addition to the OP Trio's other recordings! Unfortunately, as with Art Tatum's marathon solo sessions for Verve, not much planning went into these performances (no real arrangements), and it was just a matter of the group's sitting down and playing one song after another. The results are respectful to the original melodies and swinging but do not come up with any real surprises or revelations. *The Song Is You* has 22 of the earlier recordings and ten of the later ones, a good sampling of the two giant projects. *The Gershwin Songbooks* and *Plays the Duke Ellington Songbook* are both single CDs that contain all of the music from two original LPs, both the earlier and later Gershwin and Ellington sets (from 1952 and 1959). In general the earlier sets are of greater interest, and the music clocks in at around three minutes apiece; both CDs have 24 numbers. Nice music but not too essential. The other songbooks, which have not yet been reissued in full, are of the music of Richard Rodgers, Cole Porter, Irving Berlin, Jerome Kern, Vincent Youmans, Harry Warren, Harold Arlen, and Jimmy McHugh. All were done twice (once apiece with the two different trios) except the Youmans, which was not repeated in 1959.

Much more rewarding are the four other sets in this section by the Peterson-Ellis-Brown Trio. Ellis and Brown often practiced together independent of Peterson so they could challenge the pianist and constantly surprise him. The competitiveness between the players resulted in plenty of exciting moments. The two-CD *At Zardi's* (music that was unreleased until 1994) contains lots of telepathic moments between the three masterful musicians. *Plays Count Basie* is a relaxed outing (with Buddy Rich adding some tasteful and quiet drums) that has Peterson showing a surprising use of space; these renditions of "Easy Does It," "9:20 Special," "Broadway," and "One O'Clock Jump" are quite memorable.

The Peterson-Ellis-Brown Trio is heard at the peak of its powers on *Stratford Shakespearean Festival* (which has been named by each of the musicians as his personal favorite from this period), with many incredible worked-out passages and heated solos. *At the Concertgebouw* (actually recorded at the Civic Opera House in Chicago rather than in Amsterdam) is practically on the same level and has five added numbers by the group from a Los Angeles concert that formerly formed half an album that was shared with the Modern Jazz Quartet. Brilliant documents from one of jazz's greatest working bands.

6 *A Jazz Portrait of Frank Sinatra / May 18, 1959 / Verve 825 769*

8 *The Jazz Soul of Oscar Peterson/Affinity / July 21, 1959–Sept. 27, 1962 / Verve 314 533 100*

7 *Plays Porgy and Bess / Oct. 12, 1959 / Verve 314 519 807*

8 *Bursting Out with the All-Star Big Band/Swinging Brass / Nov. 5, 1959–June 24, 1962 / Verve 314 529 699*

7 *Live at CBC Studios, 1960 / Jan. 27, 1960 / Just a Memory 9507*

7 *Oscar Peterson / Feb. 28, 1961–Nov. 18, 1969 / RTE 1002*

* *The London House Sessions / July 27, 1961–Aug. 6, 1961 / Verve 314 531 766*

9 *Very Tall / Sept. 15 + 18, 1961 / Verve 314 559 830*

7 *West Side Story / Jan. 24-25, 1962 / Verve 821 575*

8 *Night Train / Dec. 15-16, 1962 / Verve 821 724*

Although the Peterson-Ellis-Brown Trio was quite prolific, the Peterson-Brown-Thigpen Trio soon surpassed it in output, even after Norman Granz sold the Verve label. Not all of their recordings were classic (the interplay between Peterson and Ellis was missed), but nearly all of the dates were quite rewarding. *A Jazz Portrait of Frank Sinatra* is an easy-listening set of a dozen songs associated with Sinatra; all are under four minutes long and can be considered superior background music despite Peterson's obvious virtuosity. Two excellent trio albums are reissued on *The Jazz Soul of*

Oscar Peterson/Affinity, highlighted by the pianist's versions of "Liza," "Woody 'n You," "Waltz for Debby," "Tangerine," and Ray Brown's most famous song, "Gravy Waltz." Peterson's renditions of ten themes from *Porgy and Bess* do not reach the heights of the famous Miles Davis/Gil Evans album of the year before, but his playing does succeed in bringing out the beauty of the classic melodies

Oscar Peterson's first two albums with big bands are reissued in full on the single-CD *Bursting Out with the All-Star Big Band/Swinging Brass.* Ernie Wilkins and Russ Garcia provided the arrangements for the horns on such tunes as Peterson's "Blues for Big Scotia," Clifford Brown's "Daahoud," "Tricotism," "Manteca," and "Con Alma." James Moody and altoists Norris Turney and Cannonball Adderley have a few short solos, but Peterson and his trio are in the lead most of the time. Colorful music. After recording many albums in 1959, Peterson did not cut any regular studio dates in all of 1960. *Live at CBC Studios* is a set of ten radio transcriptions made for Canadian stations that were released for the first time in 1997, nine standards (including "My Heart Stood Still," "How About You," and "I Didn't Know What Time It Was") plus Peterson's "Blues for Big Scotia." The RTE disc, *Oscar Peterson,* has music from six different concerts from 1961–69 that were broadcast over European radio. Twelve of the cuts are by the trio with Brown and Thigpen, with trumpeter Roy Eldridge sitting in on "But Not for Me" and "Main Stem." The later selections have Sam Jones and either Louis Hayes or Bobby Durham. The playing features typical hard swinging from Peterson; no surprises, but no throwaway tracks, either.

An engagement at Chicago's London House in 1961 resulted in music originally released as four LPs: *The Trio* (which is available individually as Verve 823 008), *The Sound of the Trio, Put on a Happy Face,* and *Something Warm* (the last two are also available as *Live at the London House,* Verve 422 847 569). The five-CD *The London House Sessions* reissues those four albums plus adds 30 previously unreleased selections! There is a definite sameness about the music if heard in one setting (with some repetition of titles), but the playing is on a high level and Oscar Peterson fanatics will have to get this set.

Very Tall is an inspiring date in which the trio is joined by Milt Jackson; this is the first time that Bags and OP met on record. Although only six songs resulted, each of the numbers is wonderful, particularly the romps on "On Green Dolphin Street," "Work Song," "John Brown's Body," and

"Reunion Blues." *West Side Story* is more conventional but enjoyable. The CD reissue (which has six songs from the play plus a reprise) is a bit brief but includes solid swinging versions of "Jet Song," "Tonight," and "I Feel Pretty." *Night Train* has the trio playing its usual repertoire (including "Bags' Groove," "Easy Does It," and "C Jam Blues") but finds the musicians sounding more inspired than usual. Two of the best tracks are Duke Ellington's "Band Call" and Peterson's "Hymn to Freedom."

* ***Exclusively for My Friends / 1963–Apr. 1968 / Verve 314 513 830***
10 ***Oscar Peterson Trio Plus One / Aug. 17, 1964 / Verve 818 840***
9 ***Canadiana Suite / Sept. 9, 1964 / Limelight 818 841***
6 ***We Get Requests / Oct. 19–20, 1964 / Verve 810 047***
* ***Exclusively for My Friends, the Lost Tapes / May 10, 1965–Oct. 30, 1968 / Verve 314 529 096***
7 ***Eloquence / May 29, 1965 / Limelight 818 842***
7 ***Blues Etude / Dec. 3, 1965 + May 4, 1966 / Limelight 818 844***
6 ***Tristeza on Piano / 1970 / MPS 817 489***
7 ***Two Originals / Nov. 1970–Dec. 1970 / Verve 314 533 549***
8 ***Reunion Blues / July 1971 / Verve 817 490***

Oscar Peterson has often said that he considers his series of recordings for the MPS label to be among his personal favorites. The four-CD set *Exclusively for My Friends* reissues in full six former LPs: *Action, Girl Talk, the Way I Really Play, My Favorite Instrument, Mellow Mood,* and *Travelin' On.* Peterson is heard in 1963 with Ray Brown and Ed Thigpen and quite a bit during 1967–68 with Sam Jones and either Louis Hayes or Bobby Durham on drums. However, it is the fourth CD, Peterson's first set of unaccompanied piano solos (originally forming *My Favorite Instrument*), that is classic. Strange that Norman Granz had not thought of featuring Peterson in this format at all in the 1950s!

Oscar Peterson Trio Plus One has flugelhornist Clark Terry making the group a quartet. The chemistry between CT and OP is obvious, and there are many jubilant moments throughout the date, including "Brotherhood of Man," "Mack the Knife," "They Didn't Believe Me," and "I Want a Little Girl." However, this set is best known for the initial version of Terry's "Mumbles," introducing his hilarious brand of scat singing.

Canadiana Suite was considered a major surprise when it came out because it has Peterson and his trio performing eight of his compositions, written in tribute to his native Canada. OP had not been thought of as a composer previously, but he clearly has talent in that area, as can be heard on such numbers as "Hogtown Blues" and "Wheatland." In contrast, *We Get Requests* features a lot of tired material that Peterson must have received constant requests for (including "The Days of Wine and Roses," "People," and "The Girl from Ipanema") although he wisely adds a couple of better tunes ("D. & E." And "Goodbye J. D.") that no one has ever heard of!

The Lost Tapes has a dozen songs cut for MPS that were previously unreleased. Four are with Brown and Thigpen in 1965 and the remainder are from 1967–68 with Sam Jones and Bobby Durham. Best are "Gravy Waltz," "Three O'Clock in the Morning," and an 11-minute version of "Tenderly." *Eloquence* was the final recording by the trio with Ed Thigpen, a live set with fine versions of John Lewis's "Django," "Younger Than Springtime," and "Autumn Leaves." Nothing unusual occurs, but the swinging music is typical of the output of this fine band. *Blues Etude* is a transitional CD in which Peterson, Brown, and Louis Hayes perform five numbers (including "If I Were a Bell" and "Stella by Starlight") in 1965, and Peterson, Sam Jones, and Hayes are heard on some selections from 1966. Because the pianist was the dominant voice in his trios anyway, there was no major change in his group's sound or style. *Tristeza on Piano,* despite its exotic name, has Peterson (along with Jones and drummer Bobby Durham) mostly performing standards, although sometimes with the feel of a bossa nova rhythm. In reality, Peterson overwhelms the gentle title cut and sounds a bit hyper on some of the other tunes, perhaps finally getting a bit bored with the format.

Two Originals reissues all of the music (except for a version of "Just Friends") originally on *Oscar's Choice* and *Walkin' the Line,* the only recordings by Peterson's 1970 trio with bassist George Mraz and drummer Ray Price. OP had become even a more powerful pianist during the 1960s than he had been earlier, and he sometimes overwhelms the other musicians on this excellent outing. The only real surprise in the repertoire is the inclusion of James P. Johnson's "Carolina Shout." *Reunion Blues* teams Peterson with Milt Jackson, Ray Brown (who had left the trio six years earlier), and Louis Hayes for six sensitive ballads and swinging standards (including "Red Top" and Benny Carter's "Dream of You") and an odd version of the Rolling Stones' "I Can't Get

No Satisfaction" (nice try!). Despite this last song, there is plenty of chemistry on the happy date.

9 *History of an Artist / Dec. 27, 1972–May 25, 1974 / Pablo 2625-702*

10 *The Trio / May 16–19, 1973 / Original Jazz Classics 992*

8 *The Good Life / May 16–19, 1973 / Original Jazz Classics 627*

8 *Oscar Peterson in Russia / Nov. 17, 1974 / Pablo 2625-711*

7 *The Giants / Dec. 7, 1974 / Original Jazz Classics 858*

10 *Á la Salle Pleyel / Mar. 17, 1975 / Pablo 2625-705*

8 *Oscar Peterson and Dizzy Gillespie / Nov. 28–29, 1974 / Pablo 2310-740*

9 *Oscar Peterson and Roy Eldridge / Dec. 8, 1974 / Original Jazz Classics 727*

8 *Oscar Peterson and Harry Edison / Dec. 21, 1974 / Original Jazz Classics 738*

9 *Oscar Peterson and Clark Terry / May 18, 1975 / Original Jazz Classics 806*

9 *Oscar Peterson and Jon Faddis / June 5, 1975 / Original Jazz Classics 1036*

7 *Jousts / Nov. 28, 1974–June 5, 1975 // Original Jazz Classics 857*

Oscar Peterson's Pablo years were extremely busy. Thus far 31 sets of his dates as a leader (totaling 36 CDs) have been reissued, and not all of his LPs have returned yet; this is not counting dozens of sessions as a sideman. Most of the activity took place during 1972–83, when it seemed as if every month would see the release of another Peterson album.

History of an Artist (originally three LPs and now a two-CD set) was the perfect way for Peterson to launch his Pablo period, for it summed up his previous 22 years quite nicely. The pianist is heard on a couple of duets with Ray Brown, with Brown and Irving Ashby (brought out of retirement), with Brown and Barney Kessel, in a reunion with Brown and Herb Ellis, in trios with Sam Jones, George Mraz, Louis Hayes, or Bobby Durham, solo on "Lady of the Lavender Mist," and in his most recent combo with Joe Pass and Niels Pedersen. Everything works, including a lengthy remake of "Tenderly."

It is remarkable how brilliant Oscar Peterson could play in the 1970s. Liberated from having a regular group, he challenges Joe Pass and Niels Pedersen throughout *The Trio*,

playing some stride and boogie-woogie on "Blues Etude," ripping into "Secret Love," often sounding stunning on "Easy Listening Blues" and "Chicago Blues," and showing lots of sensitivity on "Come Sunday." A perfect introduction to the pianist, heard at the peak of his powers. *The Good Life* (initially released a decade later) is from the same live sessions at the London House that resulted in *The Trio* and is almost as remarkable, with the highlights including Peterson's "Wheatland" and the blues "For Count." Despite the exotic locale of the two-CD *Oscar Peterson in Russia*, there is no change in the pianist's usual repertoire (15 standards and three originals). Peterson takes four songs as unaccompanied solos, plays four duets with Pedersen, has nine numbers with Pedersen and drummer Jake Hanna, and concludes with a solo version of "Someone to Watch Over Me." *The Giants* is a solid trio date with Pass and Brown featuring a few basic originals and veteran standards in typically swinging fashion. The one surprise is that Peterson switches to organ on "Blues for Dennis" and "Sunny."

The playing on *Á la Salle Pleyel* (a double CD) is so brilliant as to be almost shocking in spots. Peterson is heard solo on seven selections (including rapid renditions of "Indiana" and "Sweet Georgia Brown") plus a five-song Duke Ellington medley, while Joe Pass has five unaccompanied solos of his own. However, it is their six duets (especially "Honeysuckle Rose" and "Blues for Bise") that are most remarkable, full of fire, rapid reactions, and creative ideas that make it obvious that they are two of the truly classic masters.

During 1974–75, Norman Granz recorded Oscar Peterson on five duet albums with various trumpeters. Each is well worth owning. Dizzy Gillespie at 57 was in excellent form for his meeting with Peterson, particularly on "Autumn Leaves," "Blues for Bird," "Dizzy Atmosphere," and "Con Alma." Roy Eldridge did not still have the range of his prime years by 1974, but his competitiveness makes his encounter with Peterson particularly fiery. Highlights include "Little Jazz," "Sunday," and "Between the Devil and the Deep Blue Sea." The set with Harry "Sweets" Edison was comparatively friendly and easy-going, a little reminiscent of the date 20 years earlier that matched Art Tatum with Ben Webster. Edison makes every note count and lets Peterson fill in the space on such tunes as "Easy Living," "Mean to Me," and "The Man I Love." Clark Terry's approach is somewhere between that of Edison and that of Eldridge, friendly and playful but also challenging Peterson in spots. Their delightful pairing (the most satisfying of the five projects) includes

"Slow Boat to China," Dizzy Gillespie's "'Shaw 'Nuff," "No Flugel Blues," and "Mack the Knife." The pianist's duet album with Jon Faddis (who was not quite 22 at the time) is a gem. Faddis shows off both his impressive range and his love for Dizzy Gillespie's style on such numbers as "Things Ain't What They Used to Be," "Lester Leaps In," and "Blues for Birks," and does not seem awed by his meeting with the great Peterson. *Jousts* has nine additional duets from these sessions; two from each of the dates with Gillespie, Eldridge, Edison, and Terry, plus one with Faddis. A heated "Crazy Rhythm" with Eldridge" and "Oakland Blues" with Faddis are the high points.

8 *The Oscar Peterson Big 6 / July 16, 1975 / Original Jazz Classics 931*

4 *Porgy and Bess / Jan. 26, 1976 / Original Jazz Classics 829*

8 *Oscar Peterson Jam—Montreux '77 / July 14, 1977 / Original Jazz Classics 378*

7 *Oscar Peterson and the Bassists—Montreux '77 / July 15, 1977 / Original Jazz Classics 383*

7 *The Paris Concert / Oct. 5, 1978 / Pablo 2620-112*

7 *The London Concert / Oct. 21, 1978 / Pablo 2620-111*

6 *Night Child / Apr. 11-12, 1979 / Original Jazz Classics 1030*

8 *Skol / July 6, 1979 / Original Jazz Classics 496*

7 *Digital at Montreux / July 16, 1979 / Pablo 2308-224*

7 *The Personal Touch / Jan. 28, 1980-Feb. 19, 1980 / Pablo 2312-135*

8 *Live at the Northsea [AQ24] Jazz Festival / July 13, 1980 / Pablo 2620-115*

It is easy to become numb when listening to one Oscar Peterson recording after another, for he is so technically strong and consistently swinging, never showing any real weakness during his Pablo years. Peterson was frequently teamed with fellow all-stars during this period, sometimes under his own leadership. *The Oscar Peterson Big 6* (with Milt Jackson, Joe Pass, Niels Pedersen, and drummer Louie Bellson) is most noteworthy for the inclusion of Toots Thielemans, whose harmonica solos on the four lengthy numbers keep up with the speedy pianist. *Porgy and Bess* fails, not because of Peterson's playing but because of the strange concept. The set of duets finds Joe Pass playing acoustic guitar and Peterson sticking exclusively to the clavichord, an instrument from the 1600s that preceded the piano and sounds like a primitive harpsichord. Once the novelty of its sound passes, the music becomes somewhat tedious.

Better to stick to *Montreux '77*, an exciting five-song jam session in which Peterson, Pedersen, and Durham are joined by Dizzy Gillespie, Clark Terry, and Eddie "Lockjaw" Davis. There are plenty of fireworks ("Lockjaw" really pushes the two trumpeters) on OP's basic "Ali and Frazier," "If I Were a Bell," and "Bye Bye Blues." At another Montreux concert, the following day, Peterson led a trio with both Ray Brown and Niels Pedersen on basses, simply for the fun of it. There are many bass solos throughout this set (with Pedersen's speedy lines contrasting with Brown's huge tone) as Peterson plays standards and a pair of blues. Both *The Paris Concert* (with Pass and Pedersen) and *The London Concert* (with bassist John Heard and Louie Bellson) have their moments (Pass is heard unaccompanied on "Lover Man") and alternate ballads with romps, but the results overall are predictable excellence. *Night Child* is different than usual because Peterson performs six of his originals and spends the majority of his time on electric rather than acoustic piano; his personality is still distinctive but not as strong as usual. Pass, Pedersen, and Bellson help out.

Skol was Peterson's third meeting on record with violinist Stephane Grappelli (in a quintet with Pass, Pedersen, and drummer Mickey Roker). Peterson is both sympathetic and driving behind the masterful swing violinist on such numbers as "How About You?" "Skol Blues," and "Nuages." The title of *Digital at Montreux* is meaningless, but the music (duets by Peterson and Pedersen, including "Indiana," "Soft Winds," "On the Trail," and a Duke Ellington medley) is quite worthwhile. *The Personal Touch* is a real rarity in that Peterson (for the only time during his Pablo years) sings on the majority of the 13 selections. Also unusual about the quintet date (with Clark Terry, either Peter Leitch or Ed Bickert on guitar, bassist Dave Young, and drummer Jerry Fuller) is that all of the songs were written by Canadians, including such well-known standards as "Some of These Days," "I'll Never Smile Again," and "The World Is Waiting for the Sunrise." And to be consistent, the Canadian-born Peterson (whose voice still sounded like Nat King Cole's) adds two songs of his own. *Live at the Northsea Jazz Festival* was formerly an 11-song double-LP before re-emerging as a ten-song single CD, leaving out "Like Someone in Love." It features four virtuosi (Peterson, Thielemans, Pass, and Pedersen) in top form on the pianist's "City Lights" and a variety of superior standards, including "Caravan," "You Stepped Out of a Dream," and "There Is No Greater Love."

6 *A Royal Wedding Suite / Apr. 15-25, 1981 / Original Jazz Classics 973*

7 *Nigerian Marketplace / July 16, 1981 / Pablo 2308-231*

8 *Two of the Few / Jan. 20, 1983 / Original Jazz Classics 689*

7 *A Tribute to My Friends / Nov. 8, 1983 / Original Jazz Classics 908*

7 *If You Could See Me Now / Nov. 9, 1983 / Pablo 2310-918*

8 *Oscar Peterson + Harry Edison + Eddie "Cleanhead" Vinson / Nov. 12, 1986 / Pablo 2310-927*

7 *Oscar Peterson Live / Nov. 12 + 14, 1986 / Pablo 2310-940*

7 *Time After Time / Nov. 12 + 14, 1986 / Pablo 2310-947*

To celebrate the marriage of Prince Charles and Lady Diana of England, Oscar Peterson wrote a ten-song suite. *A Royal Wedding Suite* features his piano and electric piano with a string orchestra arranged by Rick Wilkins. None of the songs caught on, but the music is enjoyable enough and proved to be more timeless than the marriage! *Nigerian Marketplace,* recorded at the 1981 Montreux Jazz Festival, has Peterson, Pedersen, and drummer Terry Clarke playing two of his originals, "Au Privave," a pair of standards, and a medley of "Misty" and "Waltz for Debbie" in swinging fashion.

Two of the Few is a duet set with Milt Jackson. Although it might be expected that a piano-vibes date would be dominated by ballads, it is the romps that are most memorable, including "Lady Be Good," "Limehouse Blues," "Reunion Blues," and "Just You, Just Me." On *A Tribute to My Friends* (with Pass, Pedersen, and drummer Martin Drew), Peterson performs a song apiece dedicated to Louis Armstrong ("Blueberry Hill"), Lester Young, Coleman Hawkins, Dizzy Gillespie ("Birk's Works"), Ben Webster ("Cottontail"), Billie Holiday, Ella Fitzgerald, Roy Eldridge, and Charlie Parker ("Now's the Time"). *If You Could See Me Now* has the same quartet (from the following day) and is highlighted by "Weird Blues," two Peterson originals, and an extremely

fast version of "Limehouse Blues," which is played as a Peterson-Pass duet.

Norman Granz stopped recording new dates for Pablo during 1984–85 but came back temporarily in 1986. In typical fashion, Oscar Peterson recorded three albums within a three-day period. His meeting with Harry "Sweets" Edison and Eddie "Cleanhead" Vinson (along with Pass, bassist Dave Young, and Martin Drew) is most valuable for being a strictly instrumental set that really shows how strong (and Boppish) an altoist Vinson was. The blowing date includes "Stuffy," "Broadway," and the lengthy "Slooow Drag." *Oscar Peterson Live* and *Time After Time* were recorded with Pass, Young, and Drew (but unfortunately no Vinson) live at the Westwood Playhouse in Los Angeles. The former set has Peterson's three-part "Bach Suite," "If You Only Knew," and "City Lights" plus a hot medley of "Perdido" and "Caravan." *Time After Time* has two additional originals, a ballad medley, and, to close off his Pablo years, a burning rendition of "On the Trail."

7 *Live at the Blue Note / Mar. 16, 1990 / Telarc 83304*

7 *Saturday Night at the Blue Note / Mar. 17, 1990 / Telarc 83306*

7 *Last Call at the Blue Note / Mar. 18, 1990 / Telarc 83314*

7 *Encore at the Blue Note / Mar. 16-18, 1990 / Telarc 83356*

7 *The More I See You / Jan. 15-16, 1995 / Telarc 83370*

6 *An Oscar Peterson Christmas / Jan. 15, 1995-July 30, 1995 / Telarc 83372*

7 *Meets Roy Hargrove and Ralph Moore / June 11-12, 1996 / Telarc 83399*

7 *Oscar in Paris / June 25, 1996 / Telarc 83414*

8 *Live at the Town Hall / Oct. 1, 1996 / Telarc 83401*

7 *Oscar and Benny / Sept. 10-11, 1997 / Telarc 83406*

7 *A Summer Night in Munich / July 22, 1998 / Telarc 83450*

8 *The Very Tall Band / Nov. 24-26, 1998 / Telarc 83443*

Over three years, after the Pablo period ended, Oscar Peterson was signed to record with the Telarc label. His reunion engagement at the Blue Note with Herb Ellis, Ray Brown, and Bobby Durham resulted in four CDs. The inclusion of Durham on drums made it easier for the other players but took some of the potential danger and excitement away from the music. And unlike his trio's work in the

1950s, this was more of a jam session, without the tricky arrangements that Peterson's trio had once used. The results (36 songs in all) are certainly excellent if not essential, mixing standards in with occasional originals by the pianist, and the musicians sound quite happy to be playing together again.

The Blue Note gig is the last time (unless other recordings are unearthed) that Oscar Peterson can be heard on records at the peak of his powers. In 1993 he suffered a serious stroke that knocked him out of action. When he finally started to come back, in 1995, it was with a greatly weakened left hand, and he remains largely a one-handed pianist today. However, Peterson still plays more notes than most any pianist, and he has covered his handicap very well, although it is doubtful that he will be recording any more unaccompanied solo recitals. His first recording after his stroke, *The More I See You,* is a happy affair with Benny Carter (then 87 but sounding half his age), Clark Terry, guitarist Lorne Lofsky, Ray Brown, and drummer Lewis Nash. They jam through seven standards (including "In a Mellow Tone," "When My Dreamboat Comes Home," and "Squatty Roo") and two blues. *An Oscar Peterson Christmas* is quite relaxed, with Peterson, vibraphonist Dave Samuels, flugelhornist Jack Schantz, Lofsky, bassist David Young, drummer Jerry Fuller, and a 20-piece string ensemble arranged by Rick Wilkins playing 14 Christmas songs. The music swings lightly but is rather predictable, although it serves its purpose as Yuletide background music.

Peterson's date with trumpeter Roy Hargrove and tenor saxophonist Ralph Moore (plus Pedersen and Lewis Nash) was a good idea, for it gives him an opportunity to play with different musicians than usual. The music is strictly straight-ahead (including Dizzy Gillespie's "Tin Tin Deo," "Just Friends," and "My Foolish Heart") but fresh, since it includes seven swinging Peterson originals. Hargrove has some hot moments along the way. On the two-CD set *Oscar in Paris,* a quartet outing with Lofsky, Pedersen, and Drew, it would be impossible to know that Peterson is in any way "handicapped" from the music alone. His heated solos and comping behind Lofsky sound very complete; out of the 13 songs, nine are his originals, although "Sweet Georgia Brown" is the definite highlight.

Live at the Town Hall documents a special concert that paid tribute to Oscar Peterson. The pianist plays "Anything Goes" in a quartet with Ellis, Brown, and Lewis Nash, the quartet becomes a quintet with the addition of Benny Green on second piano for two songs, and Peterson also gets to play with Milt Jackson and Clark Terry (including "Mumbles" and "Mack the Knife"), behind Shirley Horn's vocal, and with tenor saxophonist Stanley Turrentine, Roy Hargrove, and the Manhattan Transfer ("Route 66"). Peterson has a full-length meeting with Benny Green (plus Brown and drummer Gregory Hutchinson) on *Oscar and Benny.* Since Green has the ability (and the technique) to sound very similar to Peterson at times, and the two pianists leave plenty of space for each other, this combination works quite well. Highlights include "When Lights Are Low," "Limehouse Blues," "Easy Does It," and "Scrapple from the Apple." *A Summer Night in Munich* documents Peterson's regularly working band of 1998, which includes guitarist Ulf Wakenius, Pedersen, and Drew. The guitar and the bass easily fill in for the pianist's largely absent left hand, and all of the music (other than "Satin Doll") consists of Peterson's underrated originals.

The Very Tall Band, recorded live at the Blue Note, has Peterson joined by Milt Jackson, Ray Brown, and drummer Karriem Riggins. This would be the vibraphonist's final recording, but that can be not ascertained from the happy playing heard on the reunion set. There is a medley for Brown's bass, an original apiece by the three principals, and joyous versions of "Ja-Da," "Sometimes I'm Happy," and the concluding "Caravan."

Listeners do not need to own all of these Oscar Peterson albums, but there are obviously far too many worthy CDs to choose from!

LPS TO SEARCH FOR

Oscar Peterson's earliest projects for Norman Granz have long been unavailable. *Tenderly* (Clef 696) has a dozen of the rare 1950 duets with Ray Brown or Major Holley and *An Evening with Oscar Peterson* (Clef 2048) includes a dozen more with Brown from August 1950. Irving Ashby's album with Peterson and Brown from January 1952 has long been scarce. *The Trio Set* (Verve 825 099) contains exciting Carnegie Hall performances by the trio from the JATP concerts with Barney Kessel (September 13, 1952) and from a year later (September 19, 1953), with Herb Ellis in Kessel's place. *The Newport Years Vol. III* (Verve 8828) features the Peterson-Ellis-Brown Trio romping on four songs (including "52nd Street Theme") and joined by Sonny Stitt, Roy Eldridge, and drummer Jo Jones on two jams and a pair of ballads, all from the 1957 Newport Jazz Festival.

Oscar Peterson and Nelson Riddle (Verve 8562), also known as *The Special Magic,* has the Peterson Trio assisted by a string orchestra arranged by Nelson Riddle in 1963 for easy-listening versions of standards. *The Oscar Peterson Trio Plays* (Verve 8591), despite some typical songs (including "Satin Doll" and "Fly Me to the Moon"), finds the Peterson-Brown-Thigpen group in 1964 in fine form on "The Strut" and speedy versions of "Shiny Stockings" and "You Stepped Out of a Dream." Shortly after Thigpen left the trio, Peterson, Brown, and their new drummer, Louis Hayes, were heard on *The Canadian Concert of Oscar Peterson* (Can-Am 1400). This LP contains 52 minutes of music and has Hayes easily fitting in on such numbers as "The Reunion Blues," "Hallelujah Time," and "Yours Is My Heart Alone." *With Respect to Nat* (Limelight 1030) is an unusual entry in Peterson's discography. Teamed with Brown and Herb Ellis plus an orchestra, OP pays tribute to the recently deceased Nat King Cole by not only playing but often singing on a dozen songs associated with Cole. Peterson, who had recorded a vocal album in the 1950s, sounds tone-wise remarkably identical to Cole, making this album great for blindfold tests! It is a pity that OP has rarely felt motivated to sing since. *Motions & Emotions* (MPS 20713) is one of his least important MPS albums, a set from 1969 with Claus Ogerman's orchestra that is weighed down by commercial material (including "By the Time I Get to Phoenix"!) and dull arrangements. *Hello Herbie* (MPS 15262) is a happy reunion with Herb Ellis in 1969, and some of the old magic was recaptured during this quartet set with Sam Jones and Bobby Durham.

The No. 1 Oscar Peterson album not yet reissued on CD is *Tracks* (MPS 20879), a marvelous set of solos from 1970. Peterson is absolutely brilliant on such numbers as "Give Me the Simple Life," "Honeysuckle Rose," and "A Little Jazz Exercise," making it obvious that he is really heard at his absolute best when free to be spontaneous without worrying about other musicians. Essential, if temporarily hard-to-find, music.

Recorded just prior to his association with the Pablo label, *Great Connection* (MPS 21281) is in a similar vein, a trio outing with Niels Pedersen and Louis Hayes that finds Peterson and Pedersen challenging each other, particularly on "Soft Winds" and "On the Trail." *Oscar Peterson/Stephane Grappelli* (Prestige 24041) is a two-LP set with violinist Stephane Grappelli, Niels Pedersen, and Kenny Clarke that swings as hard as expected; Grappelli in particular sounds inspired.

The Silent Partner (Pablo 2312–103), which features eight songs that Peterson wrote for the score of the movie of the same name, is more notable for the fine soloists (which include Benny Carter, Clark Terry, Zoot Sims, and Milt Jackson) than for the themes. Also not yet out on LP is the two-LP set *Freedom Song* (Pablo 2420–101), a quartet date with Pass, Pedersen, and drummer Martin Drew that is of greater interest than usual due to the inclusion of six of Peterson's originals along with the usual standards.

FILMS

Music in the Key of Oscar is a definitive 106-minute documentary from 1995, with many performances by Oscar Peterson (View Video 1351).

HERB POMEROY

b. Apr. 15, 1930, Gloucester, MA

Herb Pomeroy, a fine Bop trumpeter, would certainly have had a more significant playing career had he not spent many years as a top educator at Berklee. Pomeroy had gained his own musical education from Berklee (when it was known as the Schillinger House) in the early 1950s. The trumpeter gigged with Charlie Parker when Bird came to New England (a few live performances have been released on CD), Lionel Hampton, Stan Kenton (1954), and Serge Chaloff. He recorded with Chaloff and as a leader in 1955. That year, Pomeroy began four decades of teaching at Berklee, where he became a highly influential teacher and led a local big band of his students, recording with the student orchestra for Roulette and United Artists (1957–58). He also taught at the Lenox School of Music for a few years and worked with Orchestra USA (1962–63).

With his retirement from Berklee in 1995, Herb Pomeroy became more active as a playing musician again, recording with singer Donna Byrne and leading dates for the Daring and Arbors labels.

8   *Walking on Air / Nov. 17 + 20, 1996 / Arbors 19176*
Freed of his teaching duties, Herb Pomeroy began to perform more often as a freelance trumpeter starting in 1996. This fine set falls between swing and Bop, with Pomeroy joined by pianist Dave McKenna, guitarist Gray Sargent, bassist Marshall Wood, drummer Jim Gwin, and (on seven of the dozen selections) singer Donna Byrne, who is listed as co-leader. Pomeroy at 66 still displays strong trumpet

chops on such swinging tunes as "Doxy," "Taps Miller," "Just One of Those Things," and "Do Nothing Till You Hear from Me."

RICHIE POWELL

b. Sept. 5, 1931, New York, NY, d. June 27, 1956, Bedford, PA

The younger brother of Bud Powell, Richie Powell had strong potential as a Bebop pianist. He worked with several R&B groups, baritonist Paul Williams (1952), Johnny Hodges (1953–54), and the Clifford Brown/Max Roach Quintet (1954–56), doing much of the arranging for the last group. Years later, McCoy Tyner would credit Powell with being an influence on his chord voicings. Tragically, Richie Powell died in the same car crash that killed his wife and Clifford Brown, cutting short a promising career at the age of 24. He never led his own record date.

FILMS

Richie Powell briefly appears in *Carmen Jones* (1954).

THE REAL GROUP

Since the breakup of Lambert, Hendricks, and Ross/Bevan in 1964, quite a few short-lived vocal groups have tried to duplicate their magic. The Real Group is a bit different in that the ensemble is from Stockholm, Sweden, they consist of five rather than three singers (three men and two women), and they perform a capella. Formed in the mid-1980s and still active today, The Real Group was originally inspired by Jon Hendricks and Bobby McFerrin. They have recorded dates in Sweden for Edenroth and Town Crier, utilizing a repertoire full of Bebop and vocalese, with some swing, originals, and Scandinavian folk music too.

8 *Debut / Mar. 1987 / Edenroth 001*
9 *Unreal! / 1991–1994 / Town Crier 519*
9 *Live in Stockholm / 1996 / Passport/Town Crier 522*

The Real Group consists of singers Margareta Jalkeus, Katarina Nordstrom, Anders Edenroth, Peder Karlsson, and Anders Jalkeus. All three of their CDs are easily recommended to fans of vocal jazz, Lambert, Hendricks & Ross, scat singing, or vocalese. *Debut* has eight jazz standards (including "All of Me," "Joy Spring," and "Li'l Darlin' "), a few obscurities and originals, and the rock-and-rollish "Who

Put the Bomp?" *Unreal!* includes adaptations of two Swedish folk songs, the Beatles' "Come Together," and a few originals (including "A Cappella in Acapulco") along with such fun tunes as "Flight of the Foobirds," "Walkin'," "I've Found a New Baby," and "It Don't Mean a Thing." It is quite understandable why Jon Hendricks enthusiastically wrote the liner notes! *Live in Stockholm* has one folk song and one pop tune ("Strawberry Fields Forever") but otherwise sticks to jazz, including "Splanky," "Good Bait," "There Will Never Be Another You," and another version of "I've Found a New Baby." Definitely a group well worth checking out.

SONNY ROLLINS

b. Sept. 7, 1930, New York, NY

In 1944 there were two ways to play the tenor: the Coleman Hawkins approach or the one favored by Lester Young. A few new tenors emerged during that period who combined aspects of both of their styles (most notably Illinois Jacquet and Dexter Gordon). The rise of the "cool school" in the late 1940s (including the saxophonists in Woody Herman's Second Herd) resulted in many saxophonists adopting the Lester Young approach. But one young player who favored Coleman Hawkins came up with his own fresh new style: Sonny Rollins.

Sonny Rollins began his career in Bebop and would later venture into Hard Bop, Free Jazz, and his own unusual mixture of R&B, Bop, and calypsos. This entry covers his career up to his legendary sabbatical of 1959–61. Theodore "Sonny" Rollins started on piano, learned alto, and switched permanently to tenor in 1946. He made an impact near the end of the classic Bebop era in 1949 when he made his recording debut with Babs Gonzales, appeared next to Fats Navarro on a classic date with Bud Powell, and recorded with J.J. Johnson. Rollins freelanced in the early 1950s, making notable contributions to sessions with Miles Davis (including one on which the other tenor saxophonist was Charlie Parker) and Thelonious Monk (1953). He had his first date as a leader in 1951 and also played with Tadd Dameron and Art Blakey. However, Rollins dropped out of music during 1954–55 to kick drugs and get in better physical shape.

Rollins emerged from retirement in late 1955 to replace Harold Land with the Clifford Brown/Max Roach Quintet. He was quickly recognized as the top young tenor in jazz,

In the 1950s, Sonny Rollins competed favorably with Coleman Hawkins, Lester Young, and the up-and-coming John Coltrane as jazz's top tenor.

although John Coltrane was soon challenging him; in 1956 they made their only joint recording on "Tenor Madness." Rollins stayed with Max Roach's quintet after Clifford Brown's and Richie Powell's tragic deaths in a car accident, leaving in 1957 to lead his own group. During 1956–58, Rollins recorded some of the finest dates of his career, including such albums as *A Night at the Village Vanguard, Way Out West, Freedom Suite,* and *Sonny Rollins and the Contemporary Leaders.* He also wrote such jazz standards as "Airegin," "St. Thomas," "Doxy," and "Oleo" and appeared on albums with Thelonious Monk (Brilliant Corners) and Dizzy Gillespie. Rollins's method of soloing, like Monk's to an extent, found him often improvising off of a song's mel-ody rather than just running through the chord changes. His tone was distinctive, there was often humor in his ideas (and his choice of offbeat material), and he was quite capable of playing fascinating 10- or 15-minute solos.

Sonny Rollins's decision to retire in 1959, when he was at the height of his fame and influence, was a major surprise to the jazz world. He felt as if he were in a rut and, with the innovations of John Coltrane and Ornette Coleman, he also believed that it was time to reevaluate his life. When Rollins came back in 1962 with a pianoless quartet featuring guitarist Jim Hall (recording a classic album, *The Bridge*), his batteries were recharged. He explored increasingly adventurous improvising in the 1960s, flirting with the avant-garde.

Another period off the scene (1968–71) preceded his permanent return. Since then, Rollins has adopted a grittier tone and used tonal distortions more while building upon his earlier ideas, mixing together standards, ballads, and calypsos in his repertoire. He remains one of the most consistently exciting soloists in jazz.

* *The Complete Prestige Recordings / May 26, 1949–Dec. 7, 1956 / Prestige 4407*
  With the Modern Jazz Quartet / Jan. 17, 1951–Oct. 7, 1953 / Original Jazz Classics 011
7 *Moving Out / Aug. 18, 1954–Oct. 25, 1954 / Original Jazz Classics 058*
8 *Worktime / Dec. 2, 1955 / Original Jazz Classics 007*
8 *Plus 4 / Mar. 22, 1956 / Original Jazz Classics 243*
9 *Tenor Madness / May 24, 1956 / Original Jazz Classics 124*
10 *Saxophone Colossus / June 22, 1956 / Original Jazz Classics 291*
7 *Rollins Plays for Bird / Oct. 5, 1956 / Original Jazz Classics 214*
5 *Sonny Boy / Oct. 5, 1956 + Dec. 7, 1956 / Original Jazz Classics 348*
7 *Tour de Force / Dec. 7, 1956 / Original Jazz Classics 095*

During 1951–56 (particularly during 1954–56) Sonny Rollins recorded regularly for Prestige. *The Complete Prestige Recordings,* a seven-CD set, has not only all of the music included on the nine other Original Jazz Classics discs covered in this section but Rollins's dates as a sideman with J. J. Johnson (1949), Miles Davis (1951, 1953–54, and 1956), Thelonious Monk (1953), and Art Farmer (1954). The music is often classic and never less than interesting as Rollins is heard quickly evolving from a promising newcomer into a giant.

With the Modern Jazz Quartet does not have that accurate a title. Rollins is heard on "I Know" (based on "Confirmation") from the tail end of a Miles Davis set; Davis comps behind the tenor on piano. There are eight numbers in which Rollins is backed by Kenny Drew, Percy Heath, and Art Blakey, and then just four with the MJQ (Milt Jackson, John Lewis, Heath, and Kenny Clarke). The music (which includes "Almost Like Being in Love," "With a Song in My Heart," and "On a Slow Boat to China") is excellent straight-ahead Bop. *Moving Out* has the four selections re-corded by Rollins in a quintet with Kenny Dorham, Elmo Hope, Percy Heath, and Art Blakey plus his ballad feature on "More Than You Know" with Thelonious Monk, Tommy Potter, and Art Taylor. After his first "retirement" ended, Rollins returned with his first really major date as a leader, *Worktime.* Backed by pianist Ray Bryant, bassist George Morrow, and Max Roach, Rollins digs into five songs, including "It's Alright with Me" and a jubilant version of "There's No Business Like Show Business," showing that his method of improvising was both fresh and constantly intriguing.

Plus 4 finds Rollins heading the Clifford Brown/Max Roach Quintet (with Richie Powell and George Morrow) in what would be their last studio date as a unit. The super group romps on "I Feel a Song Coming On" and Rollins's "Pent-Up House," with the tenor saxophonist having "Count our Blessings" as his feature. *Tenor Madness* is most notable for the title cut, the only meeting on record between Rollins and John Coltrane. The tenors' contrasting solos and lengthy tradeoffs are quite memorable. The remainder of the set (with pianist Red Garland, bassist Paul Chambers, and drummer Philly Joe Jones) are quartet numbers featuring Rollins, including "The Most Beautiful Girl in the World" and "When Your Lover Has Gone."

Saxophone Colossus lives up to its name. On one of the greatest Sonny Rollins recordings ever, the tenor saxophonist (joined by Tommy Flanagan, bassist Doug Watkins, and Max Roach) performs the original (and definitive) version of his jazz calypso "St. Thomas," is searching on "You Don't Know What Love Is" and "Strode Rode," fully explores "Moritat" (the "Mack the Knife" theme) and plays a classic solo on "Blue Seven," one that would be analyzed by scholars in future years.

Rollins Plays for Bird was an intriguing concept, but the results are just OK. Rollins, Kenny Dorham, pianist Wade Legge, George Morrow, and Max Roach perform a seven-song medley plus "Kids Know" and a warm version of "I've Grown Accustomed to Your Face." The medley is interesting, although Rollins is on only four of those songs, and overall this is just an above-average release. *Sonny Boy* and *Tour de Force* have overlapping sets and should have been combined as one CD. *Tour de Force* has six songs recorded on December 7, 1956, by Rollins with Kenny Drew, George Morrow, and Max Roach; Earl Coleman sings "Two Different Worlds." *Sonny Boy* has four of the same songs plus one number ("The House I Live In") from the *Plays for Bird* session that was not included on that album or any other until the comprehensive Prestige box set came out. Kind of a mess!

■* **The Complete Blue Note Recordings / Dec. 16, 1956–
    Nov. 3, 1957 / Blue Note 21371**
■7 **Sonny Rollins, Vol. 1 / Dec. 16, 1956 / Blue Note
    81542**
■7 **Sonny Rollins, Vol. 2 / Apr. 14, 1957 / Blue Note
    81558**
■8 **Newk's Time / Sept. 22, 1957 / Blue Note 84001**
■10 **A Night at the Village Vanguard / Nov. 3, 1957 /
    Blue Note 99795**

Sonny Rollins recorded five albums for Blue Note during 1956–57. All of the music (which includes the two volumes from his legendary Village Vanguard performance) is on *The Complete Blue Note Recordings. Vol. 1* has Rollins, trumpeter Donald Byrd, pianist Wynton Kelly, bassist Gene Ramey, and Max Roach performing four of the tenor's lesser-known originals (none of which caught on) and most memorably "How Are Things in Glocca Morra." *Vol. 2* teams Rollins with J. J. Johnson, pianist Horace Silver, Paul Chambers, and Art Blakey on four numbers (including "You Stepped Out of a Dream" and "Poor Butterfly"). Most unusual about the set is that Thelonious Monk takes Silver's place on "Reflections" and that both pianists have solos on Monk's blues "Misterioso." *Newk's Time* is an excellent quartet outing with Wynton Kelly, Doug Watkins, and Philly Joe Jones that is highlighted by "Tune Up," "The Surrey with the Fringe on Top," and "Namely You." But as rewarding as those three Blue Note sets are, the double-CD *A Night at the Village Vanguard* (which has all of the music that was captured from one day and night) is the most exciting of Rollins's work for the label. With bassist Wilbur Ware and drummer Elvin Jones (other than on one of the two versions of "A Night in Tunisia," which has bassist Donald Bailey and drummer Pete La Roca) giving him stimulating support, Rollins performs 16 selections, really pushing himself. Among the highlights of the set (which could be subtitled "A Giant at Work") are "Four," "Woody 'n You," a 14-minute version of "What Is This Thing Called Love," "Sonnymoon for Two," and "Get Happy."

■* **The Freelance Years—The Complete Riverside &
    Contemporary Recordings / Dec. 1956–Oct. 22,
    1958 / Riverside 4427**

■10 **Way Out West / Mar. 7, 1957 / Original Jazz
    Classics 337**
■8 **The Sound of Sonny / June 11-19, 1957 / Original
    Jazz Classics 029**
■10 **Freedom Suite / Feb. 11, 1958 + Mar. 7, 1958 /
    Original Jazz Classics 067**
■9 **Sonny Rollins and the Contemporary Leaders / Oct.
    20-22, 1958 / Original Jazz Classics 340**
■8 **Sonny Rollins and the Big Brass / July 10-11, 1958 /
    Verve 557 545**
■7 **Aix-en-Provence 1959 / Mar. 11, 1959 / Jeal 502**

After leaving Prestige late in 1956, Sonny Rollins had a busy two years recording for several labels: Riverside, Contemporary, Period (which resulted in just three titles), Blue Note, and Verve. The Riverside, Contemporary, and Period titles are all on the five-CD set *The Freelance Years,* a box that is overflowing with classics. In addition to all of the music from *Way Out West, The Sound of Sonny, Freedom Suite,* and *Sonny Rollins and the Contemporary Leaders,* this box has the Period date and sideman sessions with Thelonious Monk (*Brilliant Corners*), Kenny Dorham (*Jazz Contrasts*), and Abbey Lincoln (*That's Him!*). This essential set was released in 2000.

Taking the projects individually, *Way Out West* is great fun. On a trio outing with Ray Brown and Shelly Manne, Rollins romps through such numbers as "I'm an Old Cowhand," "Wagon Wheels," and the rapid "Come, Gone" (based on "After You've Gone"); his pose as a cowboy on the album jacket is a justly famous William Claxton photo. *The Sound of Sonny* is most notable for the tenor's unaccompanied rendition of "It Could Happen to You." The other selections feature pianist Sonny Clark, Percy Heath or Paul Chambers on bass and Roy Haynes, with the highlights including "Just in Time," "Dearly Beloved," "Funky Hotel Blues," and the rather unlikely "Toot, Toot, Tootsie." *Freedom Suite,* which features Rollins in an unbeatable trio with Oscar Pettiford and Max Roach, has four standards (including "Someday I'll Find You" and "Shadow Waltz" and an alternate take). However, it is most notable for the 19 1/2-minute multisectioned "Freedom Suite," which has Rollins and his group really stretching out. Its title was a dig at the racism of the time.

On *Sonny Rollins and the Contemporary Leaders* (which also includes Hampton Hawes, Barney Kessel, bassist Leroy Vinnegar, Shelly Manne, and, on the two takes of "You," vibraphonist Victor Feldman), Rollins shows that he can turn seemingly any song into creative jazz. In his repertoire, in addition to "How High the Moon," "I've Found a New Baby," and "The Song Is You," are "In the Chapel in the Moonlight," "I've Told Ev'ry Little Star," and "Rock-a-Bye Your Baby with a Dixie Melody!" *Sonny Rollins and the Big Brass* was his lone date for Verve, featuring the tenor on three songs with a trio (bassist Henry Grimes and drummer Charlie Wright) and on four other tunes with a 13-piece group that includes eight brass instruments, arranged by Ernie Wilkins. Although those numbers are fine, best is Rollins's unaccompanied version of "Body and Soul." The last existing recordings of Sonny Rollins before his long sabbatical were some live concert dates made in Europe in March 1959. *Aix en Provence* finds Rollins stretching out on very lengthy versions of "Woody 'n You," "But Not for Me," and "Lady Bird" (clocking in between 15:50 and 18:35 apiece) with Henry Grimes and Kenny Clarke. The recording quality is fine, and Rollins manages to play these long improvisations without running out of ideas, making this CD worth bidding on.

LPS TO SEARCH FOR

All of Sonny Rollins's studio recordings from the 1950s have been reissued on CD. *In Stockholm* (Dragon 73), from March 4, 1959 (a week before the Jeal CD), features Rollins, Henry Grimes, and Pete La Roca performing fairly concise renditions of seven songs, including "St. Thomas," "I've Told Every Little Star," "Oleo," and "How High the Moon" (the longest piece, at just under 11 minutes).

ANNIE ROSS

b. July 25, 1930, Surrey, England

Annie Ross would be considered a major Bebop singer if only for contributing the vocalese of "Twisted" to jazz history in 1952. Born Annabelle Lynch, she moved at the age of three with her aunt (singer Ella Logan) to Los Angeles, where she appeared as a child actor in the *Our Gang* series and in bit parts in films. When she was a teenager, she studied acting in New York and then, back in England, she became a nightclub singer. Ross returned to the United States in 1950, writing and recording the vocalese lyrics of "Twisted," "Farmer's Market," and "Jackie," based on the solos of Wardell Gray and Art Farmer. After going back to Europe with Lionel Hampton's big band in 1953, she stayed for a few years, singing in clubs and acting in plays. In the

United States in 1957, Ross was hired by Dave Lambert and Jon Hendricks along with a group of other singers to record vocalese renditions of Count Basie recordings. But when the other vocalists proved unequal to the task, Lambert and Hendricks decided to overdub their voices along with Ross instead. The great success of the resulting *Sing a Song of Basie* led Lambert, Hendricks and Ross to become a regular group, appearing at festivals and clubs and recording a series of timeless albums.

Bad health caused Ross to drop out of the classic group in 1962. She moved back to England, ran a club (Annie's Room) for a couple of years, and worked mostly as an actress, rarely singing jazz after the mid-1960s. When she moved back to the United States in 1985, it was primarily to act in movies, although every once in a while she would sing in clubs. During 1998–99 Annie Ross had a series of reunions with Jon Hendricks. But, nostalgia value aside, age had taken its toll, and they were unable to reach their former heights.

7   *Skylark / Aug. 27-28, 1956 / DRG 8470*
9   *Sings a Song with Mulligan / Feb. 11, 1958–Sept. 25, 1958 / EMI-Manhattan 46852*
9   *A Gasser! / Feb. 1959–Mar. 1959 / Pacific Jazz 46854*
6   *Gypsy / 1959 / Pacific Jazz 33574*
7   *Annie Ross Sings a Handful of Songs / July 26 1963–July 1, 1964 / Fresh Sound 61*
4   *Music Is Forever / Dec. 1995 / DRG 91446*

Annie Ross first recorded in 1952, a pair of sessions that included the first versions of "Twisted" and "Farmer's Market." While in London during 1954–56, she recorded six titles, a duet album with Anthony Newley and the fine music that comprises *Skylark*. On this fairly conventional date (no scatting), Ross tastefully interprets a dozen standards (including "I Love Paris," "The Lady's in Love with You," "Between the Devil and the Deep Blue Sea," and "Skylark") with backing from pianist Tony Crombie, clarinetist Bob Burns, guitarist Roy Plummer, and bassist Lennie Bush. The swing-oriented date is a little reminiscent of what Susannah McCorkle would be doing 20 years later.

During her period with Lambert, Hendricks, and Ross, Annie Ross recorded three solo albums. She was at the peak of her powers during this era, as can be heard throughout *Sings a Song with Mulligan*. Ross is joined by baritonist Gerry Mulligan, either Art Farmer (on six songs) or Chet Baker (for the other ten) on trumpet, Bill Crow or Henry

Grimes on bass, and drummer Dave Bailey. Ross's interplay with Mulligan is memorable, and she uplifts such songs as "I've Grown Accustomed to Your Face," "All of You," "This Is Always," "How About You?" and "You Turned the Tables on Me." *A Gasser!* is on the same level, featuring either Zoot Sims or (for two numbers) Bill Perkins on tenor, pianist Russ Freeman, Jim Hall or Billy Bean on guitar, bassist Monty Budwig, and Mel Lewis or Frankie Capp on drums. Ross's twelve vocals are excellent (particularly "I'm Nobody's Baby," "You Took Advantage of Me," and "I Didn't Know About You"). In addition, there are five instrumentals from the same date that were originally issued on samplers, and these have fine playing by Sims and Freeman.

Gypsy is a very obscure but now-in-print Annie Ross set. She sings seven songs from the score of *Gypsy* while backed by a tentet arranged by Buddy Bregman. Herb Geller and trombonist Frank Rosolino have a couple of spots, and there is an opening instrumental "Overture" that introduces many of the themes, but in general the musicians are in the background. Ross sounds spirited on such numbers as "Everything's Coming Up Roses," "Some People," and even "Let Me Entertain You," swinging but not improvising much.

After leaving Lambert, Hendricks, and Ross, Annie Ross returned to acting. *A Handful of Songs* was her second album back in England. Backed by the Johnnie Spence Orchestra, Ross swings but mostly sings fairly straight on such songs as "All of You," "Nature Boy," "Let Me Love You," and "Like Someone in Love." The high point is one of the darkest, most desperate, and scariest versions of "Love for Sale" ever recorded.

After 1966 there is very little of Annie Ross on records. In 1995, when she was 65, she recorded *Music Is Forever*. It was a nice try, a jazz date with pianist Mike Renzi (Tommy Flanagan sits in on two numbers), a fine rhythm section, tenor saxophonist Frank Wess, and trombonist Al Grey. The repertoire is strong (with remakes of "Going to Chicago Blues," "Twisted," "Jackie," and "Farmer's Market" plus a few standards and a dramatic "One Meat Ball") and the inclusion of "Where Do You Start?" and Ross's sappy original "Music Is Forever" could be forgiven. But the problem is that her voice was definitely going (30 years largely off the scene made her pipes rusty), and there is no reason to listen to Ross's versions of her earlier hits when the original recordings are readily available. Get Annie Ross's classic performances from the 1950s instead!

FILMS

Annie Ross has had acting roles in many movies, including 1943's *Presenting Lily Mars* (where she played Judy Garland's younger sister), *Straight on Till Morning* (1972), *Dead Cert* (1974), *Alfie Darling* (1975), and *Yanks* (1979).

SAL SALVADOR

b. Dec. 21, 1925, Monson, MA, d. Sept. 22, 1999, Stamford, CT

A fine Bop guitarist who maintained a low profile after the 1950s, Sal Salvador had an appealing sound and a swinging style. Salvador started playing jazz as a teenager, was working professionally as a teenager (including with Phil Woods and drummer Joe Morello), and moved to New York in 1949. Salvador played with Terry Gibbs and guitarist Mundell Lowe in addition to doing studio work. He gained recognition for his period with Stan Kenton (1952–53) and then primarily led his own groups during the remainder of the decade. Although Salvador had a big band (Colors in Sound) during 1960–65, he was mostly involved in teaching by then and wrote several jazz guitar instructional books. He backed middle-of-the-road pop singers during the last half of the 1960s but otherwise mostly just played in the New England area. In 1978 Salvador returned to records, leading albums for Bee Hive, Stash, and JazzMania over the next 20 years. Sal Salvador had a quintet (Crystal Image) from 1989 on that explored rather adventurous music, but he never lost his enthusiasm for playing creative Bebop.

9 *Kenton Presents Sal Salvador / Dec. 24, 1953–Oct. 9, 1954 / Blue Note 96548*

7 *Sal Salvador and Crystal Image / 1989 / Stash 17*

The Blue Note CD reissues all of the music formerly on *Sal Salvador Quartet/Quintet* and *Stan Kenton Presents*. These 18 concise performances (only two songs are over $3\frac{1}{2}$ minutes long) are superior showcases for Salvador's guitar. He is heard in a quintet with tenor saxophonist Frank Socolow, pianist Johnny Williams, bassist Kenny O'Brien, and drummer Jimmy Campbell, a quartet with Eddie Costa (on piano and vibes), O'Brien, and drummer Joe Morello, and a different quartet with Costa, bassist Jimmy Gannon, and drummer Campbell. The music is essentially cool-toned Bop and it serves as a perfect introduction to Sal Salvador's playing.

Salvador recorded three sets for Bethlehem (1956–57),

two for Decca (1958–60), and an album apiece for Golden Crest (1961) and Dauntless (1963). Then, after 15 years off records, he was active from 1978 on. *Crystal Image* often utilizes three lead voices: the guitars of Salvador and Mike Giordano plus singer Barbara Oakes, who is an important part of the ensembles. With bassist Phil Bowler and drummer Greg Burrows completing the group, the band plays music far beyond Bebop, utilizing complex harmonies, arrangements by Salvador and Hank Levy, and tricky originals plus Chick Corea's "Got a Match?" Sal Salvador's work with Crystal Image showed that he still had an active musical curiosity as he sought to continue developing his original voice. The Stash CD is a fine example of his later period.

LPS TO SEARCH FOR

Many of Sal Salvador's most interesting later recordings have not yet been reissued on CD. *Parallelogram,* from the obscure GP label (GP 5016), has him performing originals and obscurities (plus "There Will Never Be Another You," "I'm Old Fashioned," and "Lush Life") with a local trio (keyboardist Neil Slater, bassist Rick Petrone, and drummer Joe Corsello). *Starfingers* (Bee Hive 7002) is a modern Bop date with Eddie Bert, baritonist Nick Brignola, pianist Derek Smith, bassist Sam Jones, and drummer Mel Lewis. *Juicy Lucy* (Bee Hive 7009) is a particularly strong outing with Billy Taylor, bassist Art Davis, and drummer Joe Morello that includes "Opus de Funk," an intense guitar-drums duo on "Tune for Two," and Salvador's "Northern Lights." The guitarist's three Stash albums of 1982–84 all have their memorable moments. *In Our Own Sweet Way* (Stash 224) consists of six standards (including "Anthropology," "Blue Monk," and "Over the Rainbow") played by Salvador, Nick Brignola (often stealing the show on baritone, alto, and soprano), pianist Don Friedman, bassist Garry Mazzaroppi, and drummer Butch Miles. Salvador plays 11 familiar tunes on *The World's Greatest Jazz Standards* (Stash 234) with vibraphonist Paul Johnson, Mazzaroppi, and Miles, including "All the Things You Are," "Just Friends," and "Cherokee." Best of the Stash dates is *Plays Gerry Mulligan* (Stash 251), which showcases Salvador in a quartet (with Johnson, Mazzaroppi, and Miles), a quintet (adding trumpeter Randy Brecker), and a sextet (with the addition of baritonist Brignola). Together they perform eight of Mulligan's finest songs, including "Bernie's Tune," "Walkin' Shoes," and "Line for Lyons."

FILMS

Sal Salvador appears with Sonny Stitt's group at the Newport Jazz Festival in *Jazz on a Summer's Day* (1958).

ARTURO SANDOVAL

b. Nov. 6, 1949, Artemisa, Cuba

A tremendous trumpet virtuoso, Arturo Sandoval is a dazzling player with a remarkable range and the technique to play anything. His accomplishments have not yet been on the same level as his great potential, but he is capable of playing something wondrous at any time.

Sandoval started classical trumpet lessons in his native Cuba when he was 12, attending the Cuban National School of the Arts as a teenager. He was one of the founding members of the Orquesta Cubana de Musica Moderna, which in 1973 became Irakere, Cuba's leading band. In 1977 Dizzy Gillespie visited Cuba and met Sandoval, who greatly impressed him. Sandoval was able to occasionally travel abroad, and in 1982 he recorded an album in Europe with Gillespie. Feeling stifled by the restrictions of Cuba's communist system, in 1990 Sandoval defected when his wife and son were with him in Rome. He settled in Florida, signed with GRP, formed his own group, and immediately became a popular attraction. A Bebop-based trumpeter, Sandoval often utilizes Cuban rhythms and plays a diverse repertoire in his performances. He worked with Dizzy Gillespie's United Nation Orchestra (even before his defection) and the GRP All-Star Big Band and made appearances with classical orchestras, but mostly he has led his own high-powered band. Arturo Sandoval is also a skilled pianist and a humorous scat singer in addition to being a spirited timbale player.

7 *Tumbaito / 1986 / Messidor 15974*
8 *No Problem / Aug. 7-8, 1986 / Jazz House 014*
6 *Just Music / Aug. 15-16, 1986 / Jazz House 018*
9 *Straight Ahead / Aug. 1988 / Jazz House 008*

Prior to his defection, Arturo Sandoval was caught on record with Irakere, with Dizzy Gillespie (*To a Finland Station*), and showcased on several small-group dates, including these four. In general, Sandoval does not show a great deal of restraint on these sessions, particularly on the cookers. He does show that he really can play anything effortlessly. *Tumbaito* includes five originals and "A Night in Tunisia" performed with a sextet that includes pianist Hilario Duran and guitarist Jorge Chicoy. *No Problem* starts out with a ferocious uptempo blues ("Nuestro Blues"), uses electric keyboards on some numbers, has a heavy dose of Latin percussion by Reinaldo Del Monte, and includes in its repertoire "Donna Lee," Dizzy Gillespie's "Fiesta Mojo" (which is really stretched out), and a different version of "A Night in Tunisia." *Just Music* has the same sextet (which includes keyboardist Duran, guitarist Chicoy, bassist Jorge Hernandez, and drummer Bernard Carreras), also caught live at Ronnie Scott's in England, performing group originals, "Georgia on My Mind," and Paul McCartney's "My Love." However, much of that performance is rock- and funk-oriented and quite erratic, with taste sometimes in short supply! *Straight Ahead* is much better. Sandoval is heard in a basic quartet with the remarkable pianist Chucho Valdes, bassist Ron Matthewson, and drummer Martin Drew playing some blues, basic originals, "My Funny Valentine," and "Blue Monk." The trumpeter displays the ability to rip through the lower register of his horn in speedy fashion á la Al Hirt and then jump into the upper register higher than Maynard Ferguson. Not for the faint-hearted!

- **8** | *Flight to Freedom* / 1991 / GRP 9634
- **10** | *I Remember Clifford* / 1992 / GRP 9668
- **8** | *Dream Come True* / 1993 / GRP 9701
- **6** | *Danzon* / Oct. 10, 1993–Nov. 24, 1993 / GRP 9761
- **9** | *The Latin Train* / 1995 / GRP 9818
- **9** | *Swingin'* / Jan. 6–9, 1996 / GRP 9846
- **6** | *Hot House* / 1998 / N2K 10023

Flight to Freedom was Arturo Sandoval's first recording after his move to the United States. The trumpeter is heard in a variety of settings, ranging from combos to an orchestra that utilizes a string section and, on "Caprichosos de la Habana," a Latin glee club vocal group. Most of the music is Boppish jazz with Latin percussion (including Mario Bauza's "Tanga") and occasional bits of rock and funk. Tenorman Ed Calle, guitarist Rene Toledo, and guest pianist Chick Corea (who is on three songs) are most notable among the supporting cast. Beboppers will be most interested in *I Remember Clifford*, Sandoval's tribute to Clifford Brown. Sandoval performs ten songs associated with Brownie (including "Daahoud," "Joy Spring," "Cherokee," and "Jordu") plus his own "I Left This Space for You." Sandoval is reasonably restrained and shows that he can play Bop with the best of them. His band features Ernie Watts, David Sanchez, or Ed Calle on tenor, pianist Kenny Kirkland, bassist Charnett Moffett, and drummer Kenny Washington.

Dream Come True mostly has Sandoval accompanied by one of two orchestras conducted by Michel Legrand and has more than its share of ballads, including "Once Upon a Summertime," Freddie Hubbard's "Little Sunflower," "To Diz With Love," and a touching duet with pianist Legrand on a brief "Con Alma." However, there is some definite fire displayed on a brief but explosive version of "Giant Steps" and a 10¼-minute rendition of "Dahomey Dance" in a sextet with Bill Watrous and tenor saxophonist Ernie Watts. There are also some strong moments on Danzon. But considering that the guests include Gloria Estefan, Vicki Carr, and Bill Cosby (!), there are also a few odd stretches. Actually this is primarily a high-powered Latin jazz date, with Sandoval also welcoming flutist Dave Valentin, pianist Danilo Perez, and saxophonists Ed Call and Kenny Anderson plus lots of percussionists. Most of the music is Sandoval compositions, although he also snuck in a Latinized "Groovin' High."

The Latin Train works much better. A special CD single that is included has Sandoval playing the schlocky "Dreams So Real" (from a Walt Disney cartoon), but the main CD is filled with often-ferocious gems. "The Latin Trane" is an Afro-Cuban race through the "Giant Steps" chord changes, Joe Williams has a guest vocal on "I Can't Get Started," Dizzy's "Be-Bop" is taken at a roaring tempo, and the originals are generally pretty spirited, too. Sandoval utilizes his "Latin Train Band," a group featuring Kenny Anderson on reeds, pianist Otmaro Ruiz, bassist David Enos, drummer Aaron Serfaty, and percussionist Manuel Castrillo. In addition, there are guest percussionists and some background vocalists, Ed Calle helps out on tenor and baritone, and guitarist Rene Toledo is heard from. *Swingin'* dispenses with the Afro-Cuban rhythms and lives up to its name. Tenor great Michael Brecker matches wits with Sandoval on three numbers (including John Coltrane's "Moment's Notice"), clarinetist Eddie Daniels challenges the trumpeter on "Swingin'" and "Dizzy Atmosphere," Clark Terry sits in on "Mack the Knife," and the other musicians include Ed Calle, pianist Joey Calderazzo, guitarist Mike Stern, bassist John Patitucci, and drummer Greg Hutchinson. In addition to the songs mentioned, Sandoval pays tribute to Woody Shaw, John Coltrane, and Dizzy Gillespie, plays piano on "Streets of Desire, uses a plunger mute to humorous effect on "It Never Gets Old," and makes the impossible melody of "Real McBop" sound effortless.

Arturo Sandoval always wanted to lead a big band that reflected his roots in Cuban music. *Hot House* (which is also the name of his orchestra) is a fun effort even if commercial elements occasionally get in the way, including a forgettable Patti Austin vocal on "Only You." Michael Brecker and Tito

Puente (on timbales) make cameos, the big band itself is quite solid, and there are some good moments along the way (including a rendition of "Hot House") plus a well intentioned if confusing "Cuban American Medley." This orchestra should really be recorded again.

JACK SHELDON

b. Nov. 30, 1931, Jacksonville, FL

Jack Sheldon, a hilarious (if frequently tasteless) comedian and an underrated singer, is also a Bebop-oriented trumpeter who is flexible enough to fit into Cool Jazz, swing, and even Dixieland settings. He started playing trumpet when he was 12, working in public within a year. After moving to Los Angeles in 1947, he attended Los Angeles City College, was in the Air Force, and (starting in 1952) became part of the local jazz scene. Sheldon was a friend of trumpeter Chet Baker's and played and recorded with Jack Montrose, Jimmy Giuffre, Dexter Gordon, Wardell Gray, Art Pepper, Herb Geller, and the Dave Pell Octet. He was part of bassist Curtis Counce's underrated quintet (recording several albums) and had stints with Stan Kenton (1958) and Benny Goodman (1959).

Sheldon has since had countless gigs in the Los Angeles area, working in the studios and also playing bit parts in several movies. He was the star of the short-lived television series *Run Buddy Run* (1964–65), appeared as a comedy foil on *The Merv Griffin Show,* and had reunions with Benny Goodman, including at BG's 1978 Carnegie Hall concert. Jack Sheldon, who developed a great deal as a singer in the 1990s, has led a swing-oriented big band (with arrangements by Tom Kubis) for a decade and also heads freewheeling combos that often feature pianist Ross Tompkins.

8   *The Quartet & the Quintet / 1954–Nov. 18, 1955 / Pacific Jazz 93160*

8   *Playing for Change / May 24–25, 1986 / Uptown 82743*

9   *Hollywood Heroes / Sept. 1987 / Concord Jazz 4339*

8   *On My Own / Sept. 12, 1991 / Concord Jazz 4529*

7   *Jack Sheldon Sings / Sept. 1, 1992 / Butterfly 7701*

5   *Jack Is Back / 1995 / Butterfly 7702*

Jack Sheldon's first three sessions as a leader are on *The Quartet & the Quintet.* The trumpeter is heard on three numbers leading a quintet with altoist Joe Maini, Kenny Drew, bassist Leroy Vinnegar, and drummer Lawrence Marable, playing eight songs with pianist Walter Norris, bassist

Ralph Pena, and drummer Gene Gammage, and on eight selections with Zoot Sims, Norris, bassist Bob Whitlock, and Marable. Originals by Drew, Norris, Pena, Whitlock, and Sheldon ("Groovus Mentus") alternate with such standards as "It's Only a Paper Moon," "What Is There to Say?" and "I'm Getting Sentimental Over You."

Through the years Sheldon has also led dates for GNP, Reprise, Capitol (including a couple of comedy records), Dot, Beez, Atlas, Real Time, and Phontastic. *Playing for Change* is one of his strongest instrumental dates, although the music was not initially released until 1997. Sheldon interacts and swings with altoist Jerry Dodgion, Barry Harris, bassist Rufus Reid, and drummer Ben Riley on a variety of modern jazz tunes (including "Angel Eyes," "Along Came Betty," Tadd Dameron's "The Chase," and "Trane's Strain") plus a few complementary originals.

Of his three albums for Concord, two are available on CD. *Hollywood Heroes* is a particularly fun outing, with "Rosetta" having some of Sheldon's crazy ad-libs. The trumpeter and occasional singer is assisted by guitarist Doug MacDonald, pianist Ray Sherman, bassist Dave Stone, and drummer Gene Estes on such songs as "The Joint Is Jumpin'," "Poor Butterfly," and "I Thought About You." *On My Own* is much more sober as Sheldon plays and sings a set of duets with pianist Ross Tompkins. The material is mostly from the 1930s and '40s, including "Ac-Cent-Tchu-Ate the Positive," "How About You," "Opus One," and "Avalon."

In recent years, Sheldon has recorded for his own Butterfly label. *Jack Sheldon Sings* naturally features plenty of his vocalizing, but there are also some fine trumpet solos as Sheldon is featured with his big band, including on "Don't Worry 'Bout Me," "There Will Never Be Another You," "That Old Black Magic," and "Just Friends." *Jack Is Back* is not quite as good, due to the inclusion of too many warhorses ("New York, New York," "Satin Doll," and "Here's That Rainy Day" among them) and a dumb comedy number with Merv Griffin and Pat McCormick on "How About You?" But even this relatively weak program has a few worthwhile moments.

LPS TO SEARCH FOR

Jack Sheldon and His All Star Band (GNP Crescendo 9036), from 1957–59, features the trumpeter with a ten-piece band arranged by Lennie Niehaus (valve trombonist Stu Williamson, pianist Pete Jolly, and baritonist Billy Root have their spots) and on another date in which pianist Paul Moer did the writing and the sidemen include trumpeter

Chet Baker, Art Pepper, Herb Geller, and Harold Land. High-quality West Coast jazz. *Singular* (Beez 2), from 1979, is a fine all-round effort in which Sheldon is joined by cornetist Bill Berry, guitarist Mundell Lowe, pianist Dave Frishberg, Ray Brown, and drummer Nick Ceroli. Sheldon plays quite well (on such numbers as "Tenderly," Lanny Morgan's "Friends Again," and "Lester Leaps In") and jokes around a bit, including on "Yo Momma," "There's No Fool," and a brief comedy routine. *Angel Wings* (Atlas 27-1001), from 1980, is an obscure Japanese LP with Art Pepper, pianist Milcho Leviev, bassist Tony Dumas, and drummer Carl Burnett. The instrumental date features six standards (including "Softly As in a Morning Sunrise," "Broadway," and "Minority" plus "Jack's Blues." *Playin' It Straight* (Real Time 303) is a Boppish outing from 1980 with members of the Tonight Show band (Pete Christlieb, altoist Tommy Newsom, pianist Alan Broadbent, guitarist Mundell Lowe, bassist Joel Di Bartolo, and drummer Ed Shaughnessy) that was recorded direct-to-disc and consists of Charlie Parker's "Steeplechase," Sheldon's "Playin' It Straight," and six swinging standards. The one Concord album that has not been reissued yet, *Stand By for the Jack Sheldon Quartet* (Concord Jazz 229), has Sheldon in 1983 jamming and singing ten standards with Ross Tompkins, Ray Brown, and drummer Jake Hanna, including "I Love You," "Bye Bye Blackbird," "The Very Thought of You," and "The Shadow of Your Smile."

FILMS

Jack Sheldon acted in *Run Buddy Run,* the 1973–74 television series *The Girl with Something Extra, Freaky Friday* (1976), and *For the Boys.* His trumpet is heard on Johnny Mandel's "The Shadow of Your Smile" throughout *The Sandpiper* (1965). He can be seen as well as heard on 1962's *Stan Kenton* (Vintage Jazz Classics 2007) and *Jack Sheldon in New Orleans* (Leisure Video), a joyous set from 1989 that also features pianist Dave Frishberg.

IDREES SULIEMAN

b. Aug. 27, 1923, St. Petersburg, FL

A superior trumpeter, Idrees Sulieman (who was born Leonard Graham) never gained fame above the journeyman level, but his playing was always a strong asset to Bop dates. After studying at Boston Conservatory, he played with the Carolina Cotton Pickers and the Earl Hines Orchestra (1943–44), including during the period that Charlie Parker

and Dizzy Gillespie were with Hines. Sulieman worked with Mary Lou Williams, Thelonious Monk (1947), Cab Calloway, Count Basie, Illinois Jacquet, and Lionel Hampton. Perhaps his first notable recording was on a Coleman Hawkins date in 1957, during which he displayed his wide range and appealing tone along with some circular breathing (holding one note for several choruses). Sulieman mostly freelanced in the 1950s, including working with pianist Randy Weston (1958–59). In 1961 he toured Europe with Oscar Dennard and decided to settle in Stockholm; he moved to Copenhagen in 1964. Sulieman worked with radio orchestras and the Kenny Clarke-Francy Boland Big Band, keeping busy but becoming largely forgotten in the United States. Idrees Sulieman, who along the way appeared as a sideman on records by Gene Ammons, John Coltrane, Tommy Flanagan, Donald Byrd, Max Roach, Mal Waldron, Don Byas (with Bud Powell), Eric Dolphy, Dexter Gordon, Horace Parlan, and Thad Jones in addition to Monk, Hawkins, Weston, the Clarke-Boland band, and others, recorded as a leader for Swedish Columbia (1964) and Steeplechase (1976 and 1985). In the 1990s he resettled in his native Florida, where he sometimes plays locally.

LPS TO SEARCH FOR

Now Is the Time (Steeplechase 1052), from 1976, consists of "Now's the Time" and originals performed by Sulieman, pianist Cedar Walton, bassist Sam Jones, and drummer Billy Higgins. *Bird's Grass* (Steeplechase 1202), with tenor saxophonist Per Goldschmidt, Horace Parlan, Niels Pedersen, and Kenny Clarke, has two Bop classics (Denzil Best's "Wee" and "Billie's Bounce"), Michel Legrand's "The Summer Knows," Sulieman's ballad "All Your Words," and a Goldschmidt original. Nine years later, Sulieman, Goldschmidt, and Parlan reunited for *Groovin'* (Steeplechase 1218). Joined by bassist Mads Vinding and drummer Billy Hart, the quintet performs two obscurities, three originals, and "Groovin' High." Idrees Sulieman, who would be turning 62 soon, still sounded in fine form at this point. All three of his Steeplechase LPs will hopefully be reissued on CD eventually.

SUPERSAX

Back in 1947 on "I've Got News for You," the saxophone section of Woody Herman's Second Herd played part of Charlie Parker's recorded solo from "Dark Shadows," harmonized for five reeds. In 1972 altoist Med Flory and bassist

Buddy Clark formed Supersax, a nonet with five saxophones that was dedicated to performing Bird's best solos in similar fashion. Parker's improvisations (harmonized for the group) were played rather than the melodies of songs, and it resulted in some remarkably tight ensembles (particularly on uptempo pieces such as "Ko Ko") and a renaissance of interest in Charlie Parker's music.

In concerts, Supersax featured individual solos from the saxophonists, but on their records the only solos were by the other horn player (either Conte Candoli or Carl Fontana) and the pianist (often Lou Levy). Clark left the band in 1975, but Supersax (which now includes Lanny Morgan in its personnel) has continued on a part-time basis ever since, sometimes utilizing the L. A. Voices and even recording one album with strings. Supersax's recordings have been made for Capitol, Verve, MPS, and Columbia, the last one in 1989.

LPS TO SEARCH FOR

Supersax's recordings are long overdue to be reissued on CD. *Supersax Plays Bird* (Capitol 11177), from 1972, was their debut and found the group (which included Conte Candoli and pianist Ronnell Bright) reviving such Bird solos as "Ko Ko," "Just Friends," "Parker's Mood," and "Lady Be Good." *Salt Peanuts* (Capitol 11271), which alternates Candoli and Carl Fontana on different tracks along with Lou Levy and Walter Bishop Jr. on piano, has the sax section of altoists Med Flory and Joe Lopes, Jay Migliori and Warne Marsh on tenors, and baritonist Jack Nimitz. Among the famous Parker performances heard are "Yardbird Suite," "Embraceable You," "Confirmation," and "Salt Peanuts." *Supersax Plays Bird with Strings* (Capitol 11371) (which utilizes a full string section) is highlighted by "April in Paris," "Blue 'n Boogie," "Ornithology," and "Cool Blues."

Chasin' the Bird (MPS 99430), from 1977, differed from the preceding sets in that these renditions (with one exception) were solos taken from Parker's live performances, including "A Night in Tunisia," "Oop Bop Sh'Bam," and "Now's the Time." Since they were running out of material by their fifth record, *Dynamite* (MPS 68210) has the band getting away from their original concept, performing three Bud Powell songs, two Flory originals, Jobim's "Wave," "Gloomy Sunday," and just two Parker tunes. Candoli, Rosolino, and Levy have solos, but the saxophone section (altoists Flory and Lanny Morgan, Migliori and Don Menza on tenors, and baritonist Nimitz) sticks to ensemble work with no individual solos, a practice that seemed a bit

pointless. *Supersax & L. A. Voices Vols. 1–3* (Columbia 39140, 39925, and 40547) have the five-piece "L. A. Voices" (including Sue Raney and Med Flory) joining Supersax for both Charlie Parker standards and other Boppish material. After the release of the movie *Bird*, Supersax returned to its original concept for *Stone Bird* (Columbia 44436) in 1989, performing nine Charlie Parker solos, including a few that had been cut earlier. The concept still sounded fresh, but there have been no further recordings by this unusual group since.

LEW TABACKIN

b. May 26, 1940, Philadelphia, PA

Lew Tabackin has two different musical personalities. On tenor, his exciting and extroverted thick-toned solos are strongly touched by Sonny Rollins, Don Byas, and Ben Webster. On flute, Tabackin sounds like a master of Asian classical music, very expressive and haunting.

Tabackin studied flute at the Philadelphia Conservatory (1958–62). After a period in the Army, in 1965 he moved to New York where he quickly found work, including with Maynard Ferguson, the Thad Jones–Mel Lewis Orchestra, Joe Henderson, Donald Byrd, Duke Pearson, Elvin Jones, and the Tonight Show band. After spending 1968–69 as a soloist with the Danish Radio Orchestra, he married the Bud Powell–influenced pianist Toshiko Akiyoshi. They toured Japan during 1970–71 and in 1972 settled in Los Angeles. Soon they were co-leading a swinging big band that was most notable for Akiyoshi's superb arrangements and Tabackin's spectacular solos. After a decade, Tabackin and Akiyoshi moved to New York, and their big band (which is now billed under just the arranger's name) has continued on a part-time basis up to the present time. Lew Tabackin sounds just as skilled in combos as with the orchestra, and he has played in countless settings during the past 20 years, adding fire and sensitivity to every session in which he appears.

7 *Pyramid / Apr. 29, 1988 – June 8, 1994 / Koch 6917*
8 *Desert Lady / Dec. 1989 / Concord Jazz 4411*
9 *I'll Be Seeing You / Apr. 16–17, 1992 / Concord Jazz 4528*
8 *What a Little Moonlight Can Do / Apr. 4–5, 1994 / Concord Jazz 4617*

8 *Live at Vartan Jazz / Sept. 8–10, 1994 / Vartan Jazz 003*

10 *Tenority / June 11–12, 1996 / Concord Jazz 4733*

Lew Tabackin's earlier dates as a leader, for Japanese RCA (1974, 1976, and 1978), Inner City (1976–77), Insight (1979), Ascent (1979), Discomate (1980), Eastworld (a duet set with John Lewis from 1981 plus two from 1983–84), and Atlas (1982) are all quite difficult to find. *Pyramid* has Tabackin showcased as the main soloist with the Netherlands Metropole Orchestra (under the direction of Rob Pronk, who wrote most of the arrangements) on four occasions in 1988, 1990, 1991, and 1994. Among the nine veteran songs (plus his own "Broken Dreams") that Tabackin explores (as usual alternating between tenor and flute) are Duke Ellington's "Battle Royal," "Night and Day," and "Yesterdays." *Desert Lady,* the first of Tabackin's four Concord releases, has him joined by Hank Jones, bassist Dave Holland, and drummer Victor Lewis for a high-quality set of tunes, including "Hot House," Ellington's "Serenade to Sweden," his own "A Bit Byas'd," and a version of "You Leave Me Breathless" that does just that! *I'll Be Seeing You* is particularly unusual in that the title cut and the opening "I Surrender Dear," which are usually ballads, are played as heated cookers, and the transformation works quite well. Also on this typically strong set are tunes by Charlie Parker (a duet version of "Perhaps" with bassist Peter Washington), Thelonious Monk, Duke Ellington, John Coltrane (a flute feature on the haunting "Wise One"), and Toshiko Akiyoshi.

Tabackin liked the trio that he used on *I'll Be Seeing You* (pianist Benny Green, bassist Washington, and drummer Lewis Nash) so much that two years later he had a reunion with them for *What a Little Moonlight Can Do.* In the repertoire are three Billie Holiday–associated songs (including "I Wished on the Moon," which is turned into a tango), "Love Letters," "Poinciana," "This Time the Dream's On Me," a couple of obscurities, and a romp through Miles Davis's "Dig." *Live at Vartan Jazz* differs from his previous releases in that Tabackin is joined by just bassist Kenny Walker and drummer Bill Goodwin. All but one of the seven selections that he performs (four Monk tunes and three songs by Ellington or Strayhorn) are over nine minutes long and the focus is on Tabackin throughout. His tenor and flute do not wear out their welcome, and Tabackin never seems to run out of ideas on such tunes as "Bemsha Swing," "Cotton Tail," and "Hackensack."

Tenority is a classic. Tabackin (who sticks exclusively to tenor on this set) performs four songs (including "Autumn Nocturne" and "Me and My Shadow") with pianist Don Friedman, bassist Peter Washington, and drummer Mark Taylor. Trumpeter Randy Brecker joins up for the heated "Chasin' the Carrot." Brecker is also present on "Sentimental Journey" (which is treated in rather humorous fashion) and Monk's "Trinkle Tinkle" while Friedman drops out. Tabackin romps through "The Best Thing for You" and "You Stepped Out of a Dream" with just Washington and Taylor as his backup and the closing "You Don't Know What Love Is" is a brilliant unaccompanied tenor solo that wraps up this gem perfectly. Everything works on this CD, and Lew Tabackin shows throughout that he is one of jazz's finest tenors. Essential music.

LPS TO SEARCH FOR

A trio of albums for Inner City (recorded during 1976–77) were last available in the early 1980s: *Dual Nature* (Inner City 1028), which Tabackin splits between tenor and flute, *Tenor Gladness* (Inner City 6048), a two-tenor showdown with Warne Marsh in a pianoless quartet, and the flute-only *Rites of Pan* (Inner City 6052). *Black and Tan Fantasy* (Ascent 1001) from 1979 was the initial release from Toshiko Akiyoshi's private label, and it has two virtuosic flute and five memorable tenor features, with backing from bassist John Heard and drummer Billy Higgins.

FILMS

Lew Tabackin is featured with the Toshiko Akiyoshi Jazz Orchestra on 1993's *Strive for Jive* (View Video 1336).

BILLY TAYLOR

b. July 24, 1921, Greenville, NC

Billy Taylor has been one of jazz's most articulate spokesmen, on television (most notably on the *CBS Sunday Morning* television series, where his profiles of jazz artists have been quite popular), on radio (including as a disc jockey), in the press, and as an educator. However, one should never overlook his consistently superb piano playing, which, although based in swing and Art Tatum, fits easily into Bebop and more modern jazz styles.

Taylor studied classical piano, graduated from Virginia State College in 1942, moved to New York, and was befriended by tenor saxophonist Ben Webster. The pianist played on 52nd Street with Webster, Slam Stewart, violinists

Eddie South and Stuff Smith, Dizzy Gillespie, and Billie Holiday, staying quite busy during the classic Bebop era. He visited Europe with Don Redman's big band in 1946, freelancing overseas for a year. Taylor led a quartet during 1949–50, which for a time was taken over by Artie Shaw. In 1951 he became the house pianist at Birdland, and he has led his own trio ever since, playing at all of the major jazz clubs. Taylor, who has recorded prolifically throughout his long career, was involved in television as early as the 1950s. In 1965 he founded the Jazzmobile (which has regularly brought jazz to the poor of New York City) and in 1969 became the first African American bandleader on a regular television variety series (*The David Frost Show*). Later on he founded and directed the National Public Radio series *Jazz Alive*. And throughout all of his activities, the tireless Dr. Billy Taylor has kept his Boppish and swinging piano style modern and fresh, making it difficult to believe that he is now nearing 80.

8 *Billy Taylor Trio / Nov. 18, 1952–Dec. 29, 1953 / Prestige 24154*

7 *Cross Section / May 7, 1953 + July 30, 1954 / Original Jazz Classics 1730*

7 *The Billy Taylor Trio with Candido / Sept. 7, 1954 / Original Jazz Classics 015*

9 *My Fair Lady Loves Jazz / Jan. 8, 1957–Feb. 5, 1957 / GRP/Impulse 141*

8 *With Four Flutes / July 20, 1959 / Original Jazz Classics 1830*

8 *Uptown / Feb. 4, 1960 / Original Jazz Classics 1901*
Billy Taylor first recorded as a leader for Savoy (1945 and 1949), Swing (1946), H. R. S. (1947), Atlantic (1951), and Roost (1951–52). Most of his slightly later work for Prestige and Riverside has fortunately come out on CD. Taylor's early 1950s trio with bassist Earl May and drummer Charlie Smith has had its recordings from two former LPs reissued in full on *Billy Taylor Trio*. The 20 selections are concise (all around three minutes apiece), but Taylor makes every swinging note count. *Cross Section* has four numbers in which Taylor, May, and Smith (switching to conga) are joined by three members of Machito's rhythm section, including Machito himself on maracas for such numbers as "Early Morning Mambo," "Mambo Azul," and "I Love to Mambo." The remainder of the date is straight-ahead Bop by Taylor's 1955 trio, featuring Earl May and drummer Percy Brice, alternating standards (including "Lullaby of Birdland") with catchy originals. The set with Candido (also

featuring May and Brice) finds the conga player fitting in quite smoothly with the trio. "Bit of Bedlam" is pure Bud Powell, and the music is essentially Latin Bop; pity that there is less than 32 minutes of music!

My Fair Lady Loves Jazz was recorded at a time when *My Fair Lady* was a major Broadway hit but before it became a film. On this superb outing, Taylor's trio (with May and Ed Thigpen) is joined by seven horns for eight of the songs from the show. In addition to Taylor, there are short solos for trumpeter Ernie Royal, Jimmy Cleveland, altoist Anthony Ortega, and baritonist Gerry Mulligan. The arrangements by Quincy Jones rank with his best, highly recommended. *Billy Taylor with Four Flutes* is a change of pace as Taylor's trio (with bassist Tommy Williams and Dave Bailey or Albert "Tootie" Heath on drums) is augmented by Chino Pozo on conga and the flutes of Frank Wess, Herbie Mann, Jerome Richardson, and Phil Bodner (with Billy Slapin, Jerry Sanfino, or Seldon Powell substituting on some tracks). Taylor wrote the arrangements, and there are opportunities for the flutists to solo. The repertoire includes such songs as "The Song Is Ended," "Oh, Lady Be Good," "How About You," and four Taylor tunes. In comparison, *Uptown* is more conventional. However, the live set by Taylor (with bassist Henry Grimes and drummer Ray Mosca) sounds inspired as the pianist digs into four of his songs (including "Cu-Blu") and such numbers as Erroll Garner's "La Petite Mambo," "Jordu," and "Moanin'."

7 *Where've You Been? / Dec. 1980 / Concord Jazz 4145*

8 *You Tempt Me / June 24, 1985 / Taylor Made 1004*

8 *White Nights / June 13–14, 1988 / Taylor-Made 1001*

9 *Solo / Aug. 1–2, 1988 / Taylor-Made 1002*

7 *The Jazzmobile All Stars / Apr. 5–6, 1989 / Taylor-Made 1003*

7 *Among Friends / Feb. 1991 / Harrison Digital Productions 235*
Billy Taylor's 1961–79 recordings (for Moodsville, Mercury, Sesac, Capitol, Tower, MPS, Bell, West 54, and Monmouth Evergreen) remain out of print. *Where've You Been?* is most notable for featuring the fine jazz violinist Joe Kennedy (a cousin of Benny Carter's), who spent most of his career teaching in the Richmond, Virginia, area. Together with bassist Victor Gaskin and drummer Keith Copeland, the quartet performs eight of Taylor's obscure originals, and the music is generally quite appealing; pity that Joe Kennedy did not record much more during his career. Frustrated by

His important careers as an educator, broadcaster, and jazz's top spokesman should never be allowed to overshadow Billy Taylor's brilliance as a Bop-based pianist.

the lack of opportunities to record (the Concord set was his only album as a leader for a decade), Billy Taylor started the Taylor-Made label in 1989, releasing four albums. *You Tempt Me* is a strong outing by his 1985 trio (with Victor Gaskin and drummer Curtis Boyd) that includes a slower-than-usual rendition of "Take the 'A' Train," two originals, and five songs that make up his "Let Us Make a Joyful Noise" jazz suite. The music is spiritual in spots, usually quite infectious, and typically well played. *White Nights* has Taylor, Gaskin, and drummer Bobby Thomas performing live from Leningrad in the Soviet Union. This time around, Taylor mostly sticks to standards ("C-A-G" is his only new song), including two of Clare Fischer's best-known tunes ("Pensativa" and "Morning"), "Secret Love," and "My Romance." A superior outing.

Many Bop-era pianists have difficulty playing sets of un-

accompanied solos. But since Billy Taylor's roots are in swing, he was able to excel on *Solo* while still sounding fairly modern. In fact, on "All the Things You Are" he plays the first three choruses with just his left hand! Also on this set is a remake of "Bit of Bedlam" (one of his seven originals), "Old Folks," "More Than You Know," and "Gone with the Wind." One of Dr. Taylor's best recordings. *The Jazzmobile All-Stars* has Taylor, Gaskin, and Thomas joined by guitarist Ted Dunbar, Frank Wess on tenor and soprano, and trumpeter Jimmy Owens. Owens often takes solo honors on the nine Taylor tunes and Lee Morgan's "Ceora," displaying a lot of potential that he has yet to really fulfill. *Among Friends* features the relatively unknown but talented tenor and soprano saxophonist Fred Tillis with the Taylor-Gaskin-Thomas trio. Other than Tillis's "The Holidays," most of the tunes are familiar, including "Confirmation,"

"When Lights Are Low," and "It Don't Mean a Thing." The set opens and closes with full-length versions of W. C. Handy's "Harlem Blues." A fine, if obscure, effort.

- **7** | *Dr. T* / 1992 / GRP 9692
- **7** | *It's a Matter of Pride* / 1993 / GRP 9753
- **8** | *Homage* / Oct. 10–11, 1994 / GRP 9806
- **10** | *Music Keeps Us Young* / Aug. 6–8, 1996 / Arkadia 71601
- **9** | *Ten Fingers—One Voice* / Aug. 6–8, 1996 / Arkadia 71602

It had been many years since Billy Taylor (despite his fame) had recorded for a major label when he signed with GRP. Although GRP was best known for its commercial crossover dates, there is no feeling of compromise on Taylor's sessions. Taylor, Gaskin, and Thomas are joined by baritonist Gerry Mulligan on three of the ten numbers on *Dr. T.* Taylor romps on such tunes as "I'll Remember April," "Line for Lyons," and Mulligan's "Rico Apollo." *It's a Matter of Pride* has ten Taylor compositions performed by the pianist with bassist Christian McBride, drummer Marvin "Smitty" Smith, Ray Mantilla on conga (for four songs), and (as a guest on three numbers) tenor saxophonist Stanley Turrentine; Grady Tate contributes two warm ballad vocals. A fine Boppish and swinging set. *Homage* has Taylor (along with bassist Chip Jackson and drummer Steve Johns) paying tribute to some of his early heroes, including Slam Stewart, Oscar Pettiford, Art Tatum, Stuff Smith, and Eddie South on the three-part "Homage," assisted by the Turtle Island String Quartet. In addition, the ten-part "Step Into My Dream," which is meant to be performed along with the Da-vid Parsons Dance Company, covers a variety of music, from stride piano and calypso to free form, Bop, and even a rap (which is fortunately brief). Also on the intriguing CD is a ballad and a brief "encore" piece with Turtle Island.

He may have turned 75 two weeks earlier, but Billy Taylor sounds quite ageless on his two Arkadia releases. *Music Keeps Us Young* (played with Chip Jackson and Steve Johns) has Taylor alternating heated pieces, ballads, originals (including his famous "I Wish I Knew How It Would Feel to Be Free"), and standards such as "Wouldn't It Be Lovely," "Caravan," and a 10½-minute version of "Body and Soul." Joyful (and surprisingly youthful) energy is displayed throughout this wonderful set. *Ten Fingers—One Voice* is from the same sessions but differs in that it finds Taylor sounding quite self-sufficient as a piano soloist. Highlights

of yet another highly recommended Billy Taylor date include "Wrap Your Troubles in Dreams," "Joy Spring," and "Tea for Two."

LPS TO SEARCH FOR

Evergreens (ABC-Paramount 112) is a scarce trio set (with Earl May and Percy Brice) from 1956. *I Wish I Knew How It Would Feel to Be Free* (Tower 5111), from 1967, has Taylor's instrumental version of his hit title cut, which Solomon Burke's vocal recording made famous during the era; otherwise this is a fairly conventional date with bassist Ben Tucker and drummer Grady Tate. *Sleeping Bee* (Pausa 7096) from 1969 finds the same trio playing mostly originals and obscurities (other than "There Will Never Be Another You" and "A Sleeping Bee"). *OK Billy!* (Bell 6049) is the one album recorded by Taylor with the 11-piece band that he led for *The David Frost Show*. *Jazz Alive* (Monmouth/Evergreen 7089) consists of a radio broadcast from 1977 with Taylor's trio of the time (Victor Gaskin and drummer Freddie Waits). One side of the LP is made up of six Duke Ellington songs and is titled "Echoes of Ellington." The flip side is a bit odd, for although it is called "Suite for Jazz Piano and Orchestra," it is actually performed only by the three musicians! Overall this is a strong outing that will hopefully re-emerge on CD someday.

CLARK TERRY

b. Dec. 14, 1920, St. Louis, MO

Clark Terry, whose joyous sound has always been instantly recognizable within two or three notes, has roots in both swing and Bop. The trumpeter (who switched to flugelhorn in the 1960s) was most influenced (particularly in the early days) by Dizzy Gillespie, was an early inspiration to Miles Davis, and has been able to fit in with the most modern soloists, even recording with avant-garde pianist Cecil Taylor in 1960. Terry worked in St. Louis in the early 1940s, served in the Navy (where he played with a dance band), and was featured with the orchestras of Lionel Hampton (1945), George Hudson, Charlie Barnet (his modern outfit of 1947–48), and Count Basie (1948–49). Terry stayed with Basie when he reluctantly cut back to a septet and then in 1951 joined Duke Ellington. During his eight years with Duke, Terry gained a strong reputation for his happy sound and high musicianship. He was featured on many recordings

("Perdido" was usually his showcase) and also began to lead record dates of his own.

When he left Ellington, it was to tour Europe with the Quincy Jones Orchestra (1959–60) as part of Harold Arlen's show *The Free and Easy*. Shortly after the production flopped, Terry returned to the United States to join the staff of NBC, where he was one of the first black studio musicians. In the 1960s, in addition to his studio work (and becoming a member of the Tonight Show Orchestra), Terry played regularly in jazz settings, including with the Gerry Mulligan Concert Jazz Band, co-leading a quintet with valve trombonist Bob Brookmeyer, and cutting a classic recording with the Oscar Peterson Trio. On the last, Terry sang "Mumbles," a somewhat incoherent vocal that made fun of the more primitive blues singers. "Mumbles" became so popular that Terry has since included similar nonsensical scat singing as a regular part of his performances.

The flugelhornist led a Boppish big band for a time in the 1970s but has appeared mostly with combos in the decades leading to the present time, spreading happiness to every session in which he performs. Clark Terry, who has also given countless clinics and is always enthusiastic about helping younger players, only began to show his age a little bit in his playing in the late 1990s, when he was nearing 80 and having some health problems. He was still very active as the 21st century began, constantly demonstrating that there was nothing wrong with being entertaining and having a good time while playing jazz.

8 *Serenade to a Bus Seat / Apr. 1957 / Original Jazz Classics 066*

8 *Duke with a Difference / July 29, 1957 + Sept. 6, 1957 / Original Jazz Classics 2219*

8 *In Orbit / May 1958 / Original Jazz Classics 302*

7 *Top and Bottom Brass / Feb. 24–26, 1959 / Original Jazz Classics 764*

Other than three selections made as V-Discs in 1947, Clark Terry first began leading his own record dates in 1955; there have been many ever since. During 1957–59 C.T. recorded four albums for the Riverside label, all of which are now available in the Original Jazz Classics series. *Serenade to a Bus Seat* matches Terry with Johnny Griffin, pianist Wynton Kelly, bassist Paul Chambers, and drummer Philly Joe Jones for five of his originals plus "Donna Lee" and two standards. *Duke with a Difference* has a set of tunes associated with Duke Ellington that were given fresh arrangements by

C.T. and Mercer Ellington. The solos by Terry, either Quentin Jackson or Britt Woodman on trombone, altoist Johnny Hodges, Paul Gonsalves, and Tyree Glenn on vibes and trombone are consistently rewarding while being concise. *In Orbit* is one of the few examples of Thelonious Monk's appearing as a sideman, being a measure of the great respect that the jazz world unanimously has had for Terry. Only one of the songs ("Let's Cool One") is a Monk tune, with most of the remainder being catchy numbers by C.T. (including "One Foot in the Gutter"). *Top and Bottom Brass* has Terry sharing the frontline with the tuba of Don Butterfield (who is well featured), with backing by pianist Jimmy Jones, bassist Sam Jones, and drummer Art Taylor.

8 *Daylight Express / July 26, 1957 + Aug. 6, 1957 / GRP/Chess 819*

6 *Mellow Moods / July 21, 1961–May 15, 1962 / Prestige 24136*

10 *Color Changes / Nov. 19, 1960 / Candid 79009*

9 *The Happy Horns of Clark Terry / Mar. 13, 1964 / GRP/Impulse 148*

8 *The Power of Positive Swinging / Mar. 1965 / Musical Heritage Society 513447*

Daylight Express has all of the music from an obscure Terry session for Argo (in a quintet with clarinetist Mike Simpson and pianist Willie Jones) and a Paul Gonsalves set in which Terry is a well-featured sideman. *Mellow Moods*, a single-CD "twofer" with all of the music from a pair of Terry's Moodsville albums, sticks mostly to ballads, with its second set having Oliver Nelson's arrangements for the forgotten songs of the play *All American*. In contrast, *Color Changes* is a classic. The arrangements of Yusef Lateef, Budd Johnson, and Al Cohn are colorful, Terry leads a high-quality octet (with trombonist Jimmy Knepper, Julius Watkins on French horn, Lateef on tenor, flute, oboe, and English horn, Seldon Powell on tenor and flute, Tommy Flanagan, bassist Joe Benjamin, and drummer Ed Shaughnessy), and the swinging originals contain more than their share of surprises. An inspiring set.

The Happy Horns has plenty of joyful moments. Terry's sextet consists of Phil Woods (doubling on clarinet), tenor saxophonist Ben Webster, pianist Roger Kellaway, bassist Milt Hinton, and drummer Walter Perkins. "Rockin' in Rhythm," Bix Beiderbecke's "In a Mist," the flugelhorn-drum duet "Return to Swahili," and a brief but effective Duke Ellington medley are among the highlights. *The Power of Positive Swinging* has a special group, Terry's quintet with valve trombonist Bob Brookmeyer, Kellaway, bassist Bill Crow, and drummer Dave Bailey. Terry and Brookmeyer bring out the best in each other on witty and swinging versions of "The King," "Ode to a Flugelhorn," and "Just an Old Manuscript."

8 *Big B-A-D Band Live! / Apr. 21, 1974 / Vanguard 79355*

8 *Swiss Radio Days Jazz Series, Vol. 8 / Dec. 16, 1978 / TCB 02082*

7 *Memories of Duke / Mar. 11, 1980 / Original Jazz Classics 604*

7 *Yes, the Blues / Jan. 19, 1981 / Original Jazz Classics 856*

8 *Portraits / Dec. 16, 1988 / Chesky 2*

9 *The Clark Terry Spacemen / Feb. 13, 1989 / Chiaroscuro 309*

Clark Terry led a big band on a part-time basis in the 1970s. Its appearance at the 1974 Wichita Jazz Festival is available on the Vanguard release, *Big B-A-D Band Live!,* featuring among its soloists Phil Woods, Jimmy Heath, and Duke Jordan. C.T.'s playing is well showcased on the TCB radio broadcast, *Swiss Radio Days Jazz Series, Vol. 8,* in a quintet with altoist Chris Woods and pianist Horace Parlan on such numbers as "The Hymn," "The Silly Samba," "On the Trail," and "Over the Rainbow." Terry revisits the Duke Ellington songbook on *Memories of Duke* with pianist Jack Wilson, Joe Pass, Ray Brown, and drummer Frank Severino, managing to sound enthusiastic on such overplayed songs as "Things Ain't What They Used to Be," "Cottontail," and "Sophisticated Lady."

Yes, the Blues has a matchup that should have happened much more often: Clark Terry and Eddie "Cleanhead" Vinson. This blues-oriented set puts the emphasis on their instrumental (rather than vocal) skills and has many happy moments. *Portraits* features Terry paying tribute to some of his favorite trumpeters, including Louis Armstrong ("When It's Sleepy Time Down South"), Roy Eldridge ("Little Jazz"), Dizzy Gillespie ("Ow"), and Miles Davis ("I Don't Wanna Be Kissed"), with the assistance of pianist Don Friedman, Victor Gaskin, and Lewis Nash. *The Clark Terry Spacemen* is a special date, for Terry is heard with a tentet that includes a couple of rarely featured Swing-era alumni (trombonist Britt Woodman and baritonist Haywood Henry), trumpeter Virgil Jones, Al Grey, Phil Woods, and Red Holloway. The music is full of spirit and hot riffs, and

there is also a 19-minute Terry "Jazzspeak" at the conclusion of the disc in which C.T. humorously tells his life story.

8 *Having Fun / Apr. 11–12, 1990 / Delos 4021*

7 *Live at the Village Gate / Nov. 19–20, 1990 / Chesky 49*

7 *The Second Set / Nov. 19–20, 1990 / Chesky 127*

9 *What a Wonderful World / Feb. 1, 1993 / Red Baron 53750*

7 *The Good Things in Life / Dec. 9, 1993 / Mons 874 437*

7 *Shades of Blues / May 13, 1994 / Challenge 70007*

7 *Remember the Time / Aug. 29–30, 1994 / Mons 874 762*

7 *Top and Bottom / Oct. 30, 1995–Nov. 2, 1995 / Chiaroscuro 347*

With the passing and decline of so many other veterans, the 1990s found Clark Terry in even greater demand than previously for record dates, both as a leader and as a sideman. *Having Fun* has plenty of good humor from Terry, Red Holloway, and the humming bassist Major Holley on such numbers as "Mumbles," "Meet the Flintstones," "The Snapper," "Mule's Soft Claw," and "Tee Pee Time." Although Terry was nearly 70 at the time, his flugelhorn playing is still heard in peak form on *Live at the Village Gate* and *The Second Set,* quintet performances with Jimmy Heath and Don Friedman. *What a Wonderful World,* a delightful meeting between Terry and Al Grey (and designed as a tribute to Louis Armstrong and Duke Ellington) has a hilarious ad-lib monologue on "Duke's Place" during which Terry talks about the virtues of the fictional establishment at great length, particularly its food and women. *The Good Things in Life* (quintet jams with altoist George Robert and pianist Dado Moroni), *Shades of Blues* (11 blues played by Terry and Al Grey in a drumless quartet), and *Remember the Time* (with Robert and trombonist Mark Nightingale) feature C.T. in exuberant form on standards and basic originals. Though Clark Terry was nearly 75 at the time of *Top and Bottom,* his trumpet chops were still in fine form as he plays typically spirited and hard-swinging music with Red Holloway, altoist David Glasser, and pianist Willie Pickens.

Clark Terry recordings do not require detailed analysis in order to recommend and enjoy!

LPS TO SEARCH FOR

Although there is no shortage of readily available Clark Terry CDs, there are also some worthy LPs that will be more difficult to find. *Paris 1960* (Swing 8406), from the time that he was overseas with Quincy Jones's orchestra, has combo numbers with Eric Dixon (on flute and tenor), trombonist Quentin Jackson, pianist Martial Solal (who contributed five numbers written for a French film and documented on this album), and Kenny Clarke prominent among the sidemen. *Tread Ye Lightly* (Cameo 1071) is one of Terry's best albums of the 1960s, a really fun set with spirited renditions of "Georgia on My Mind," "Lilies of the Field," "Tread Ye Lightly," and "Freedom Blues." The personnel include Seldon Powell on tenor, the harmonica of Budd Lucas, and a pianist listed as "Homer Fields" who is actually Ray Bryant. *Live 1964* (Emerald 1002) features Terry jamming on five standards and "Haig and Haig" with the Michael Abene Trio. *Clark Terry/Bob Brookmeyer* Quintet (Mainstream 320) has additional titles by the underrated quintet. Clark Terry leads an international big band in 1969 (with Ernie Wilkins arrangements) on *At the Montreux Jazz Festival* (Polydor 24-5002), and his Big B-A-D Band swings *Live! at Buddy's Place* (Vanguard 79373) in 1976. Terry meets tenor saxophonist Ernie Wilkins in a sextet on *The Globetrotter* (Vanguard 79393), teams up with bassist Red Mitchell, Kenny Drew, and Ed Thigpen in 1978's *Funk Dumplin's* (Matrix 1002), and has a set of high-quality flugelhorn-bass duets with Mitchell on *To Duke and Basie* (Enja 5011). Their vocal duet on "Hey Mr. Mumbles, What Did You Say?" is even funnier than one would expect.

FILMS

Clark Terry is featured with the Count Basie Septet (when it also included Wardell Gray and Buddy DeFranco) on a series of Snader Transcriptions made for television during 1950-51. Hopefully someday these will be fully released to the public.

TOOTS THIELEMANS

b. Apr. 29, 1922, Brussels, Belgium

It may be the most inexpensive of all instruments, but very few musicians have mastered the chromatic harmonica (as opposed to the blues harp). Jean "Toots" Thielemans has been at the top of his very small field for the past 45 years; practically his only predecessor was Larry Adler, who generally played classical and show music rather than jazz. Thielemans began on the accordion when he was three, started playing harmonica when he was 17, and did not pick up the guitar (which would be his main instrument until the

1960s) until he was 22, inspired by Django Reinhardt. He developed quickly, and Thielemans was a Bop guitarist by the mid-1940s. He visited the United States for the first time in 1947 and at the 1949 Paris Jazz Festival, Toots played with Charlie Parker. In 1950 Thielemans toured Europe with the Benny Goodman Sextet, moving to the United States the following year.

As a member of the George Shearing Quintet during 1953-59, Thielemans was featured mostly on guitar. However, he had first recorded on harmonica in 1950, and in 1955 he recorded his first full-length album on the small instrument, amazing listeners with his fluidity and ability to play like a Bop saxophonist. After leaving Shearing, Thielemans became a studio musician (on harmonica and guitar in addition to his expert whistling, which was usually done in unison with his guitar), first recording his hit song "Bluesette" in 1961. Since that time, Toots Thielemans has primarily been a leader (although making many guest shots on records), touring the world with small groups and even trading off with Oscar Peterson. Hendrik Meurkens's rise in the 1990s was the first time that a jazz harmonica player even came close to the effortless brilliance of Toots, whose harmonica playing is impossible to top.

6 *Jazz Masters 59 / Mar. 12, 1953-Apr. 4, 1991 / Verve 314 535 271*
8 *Man Bites Harmonica / Dec. 30, 1957 + Jan. 7, 1958 / Original Jazz Classics 1738*
9 *Images / Sept. 16, 1974 / Candid 71007*
9 *Live in the Netherlands / July 15, 1980 / Original Jazz Classics 930*
8 *Do Not Leave Me / June 19, 1986 / Stash 12*

Toots Thielemans first recorded as a leader back in 1949, and he recorded 28 selections during 1949-51 plus six others for MGM during 1952-53 before making albums. *Jazz Masters 59* has 16 selections (programmed in chronological order) that Thielemans cut through the years for labels now owned by Polygram. He is heard playing harmonica with George Shearing in 1953 ("Undecided" and "Body and Soul") and on two cuts from the 1960s, but otherwise the music dates from 1970-91. Most notable are Thielemans' appearances with the Quincy Jones Orchestra (including "Hummin'" and "Bluesette"). He is also heard on sets led by bassists Marc Johnson and Pierre Michelot plus a few items from his own dates. A decent if not essential sampler.

Man Bites Harmonica is the best available example of Thielemans' harmonica playing in the 1950s, although two of the eight songs actually have Toots heard exclusively on guitar. The fine Hard Bop date (five standards, two songs by Thielemans's, and one from Ray Bryant) features Toots in a group with baritonist Pepper Adams, Kenny Drew, bassist Wilbur Ware, and drummer Art Taylor.

Toots Thielemans recorded frequently in the 1960s, mostly for European labels, but those albums have not been made available in recent times. *Images* features Thielemans holding his own at a club with a modern rhythm section (pianist Joanne Brackeen, bassist Cecil McBee, and drummer Freddie Waits) on such songs as "Days of Wine and Roses," "Airegin," "Giant Steps," and Brackeen's "Snooze." Tricky chord changes never seem to cause any problem for the harmonica virtuoso. *Live in the Netherlands* was Thielemans's only Pablo date as a leader and it is a real gem. Toots is heard in a trio with Joe Pass and Niels Pedersen, playing pure Bebop on "Blues in the Closet," Duke Ellington's "The Mooche," "Thriving from a Riff," "Autumn Leaves," and "Someday My Prince Will Come," while his unaccompanied guitar solo on Duke Ellington's "The Mooche" is also memorable. *Do Not Leave Me,* a quartet date with pianist Fred Hersch, bassist Marc Johnson, and drummer Joey Baron, is also a strong outing. The highlight is a 19½-minute medley of "Blue 'n Green" and "All Blues."

8   *Only Trust Your Heart / Apr. 1988–May 1988 / Concord Jazz 4355*

7   *Footprints / Dec. 19–20, 1989 / Emarcy 846 650*

6   *For My Lady / 1991 / Emarcy 314 510 133*

8   *The Brasil Project / 1992 / Private Music 82101*

7   *The Brasil Project, Vol. II / 1993 / Private Music 82110*

5   *East Coast West Coast / 1994 / Private Music 82120*

The liner notes on *Only Trust Your Heart* state that his lone Concord date was his first jazz recording as a leader in more than a dozen years. Does that mean that his 14 European dates and albums for Stash and Pablo do not count? Thielemans is heard in excellent form with pianist Fred Hersch, Marc Johnson or Harvie Swartz on bass and drummer Joey Baron, digging into such numbers as Wayne Shorter's "Speak No Evil," "All of You," Benny Carter's title cut, and Thelonious Monk's "Little Rootie Tootie." *Footprints* is often quite relaxed, emphasizing ballads, other than the closing "C to G Jam Blues." What is unusual is that on several of the selections, Thielemans plays unaccompanied solo harmonica (including on "'Round Midnight"); the

other tunes add pianist Mulgrew Miller, bassist Rufus Reid, and drummer Louis Nash. Highlights include "Blues on Time," "If You Could See Me Now," and "Sultry Serenade." *For My Lady* is not quite as sparse, but it is another ballad set, with only "Blues in the Closet" generating much heat. Thielemans is joined by the Shirley Horn Trio for a dozen standards; the pianist takes a vocal on "Someone to Watch Over Me." Tasteful, if not too exciting.

The Brasil Project was a rather popular album when it came out. Toots Thielemans, who has always loved Brazilian music, performs with the who's who of Brazilian music of the early 1990s, including Ivan Lins, Djavan, Oscar Castro-Neves, Dori Caymmi, Ricardo Silveira, Joao Bosco, Gilberto Gil, Milton Nascimento, Luis Bonfa, and others plus a few flexible Americans (including guitarist Lee Ritenour and pianist Eliane Elias). *Vol. II* is more of the same and also includes a few numbers with strings. All of the songs (other than "Bluesette" from the first date) are Brazilian originals, mostly avoiding standards in favor of new material, although *Vol. II* is uplifted by the inclusion of "One Note Samba" and "Samba de Orfeu." An excellent way for jazz listeners to be introduced to Brazilian music.

East Coast West Coast, which should have been a superb jazz set (since it features separate all-star lineups in New York and Los Angeles), is a major disappointment. With such players as trumpeter Terence Blanchard and tenors Joshua Redman and Ernie Watts performing 13 standards, this project had great potential. But, other than two ballads, all of the performances are less than five minutes long, with the horn solos often being cut off after one chorus, even on tunes such as "In Walked Bud" and "Groovin' High"! Maybe the label was most concerned about radio airplay, but the overall results only hint at what should have taken place. Get one of Toots Thielemans's live recordings instead.

LPS TO SEARCH FOR

Toots Thielemans's first full album as a leader resulted in 1955's *The Sound* (Columbia 658), a variety of tunes, some of which have the leader and a rhythm section joined by four trombones or four woodwinds. This album helped publicize the fact that there was a remarkable jazz harmonica player around. *The Soul of Toots Thielemans* (Doctor Jazz 40550), from 1959–60, has not only some good harmonica solos from Toots but a few of his better spots on guitar and one of his first whistling solos (on "Brother John"). Thielemans is joined by pianist Ray Bryant, bassist Tom Bryant, and drummer Oliver Jackson on a wide-ranging set that includes "You Are My Sunshine," Django Reinhardt's "Nuages," and "Confirmation." *Yesterday and Today* (A&M 3613), from 1972, is an ok meeting between Thielemans and violinist Svend Asmussen; the music is rather commercial and the tunes are mostly forgettable, although the two lead voices have their moments. *Live* (Polydor 2491003) and *Live 2* (Polydor 2441063) feature Thielemans in superior form during 1974–75 with European rhythm sections (including, on *Live 2*, Niels Pedersen). The second set (which includes "Tenor Madness," "St. Thomas," and such vintage material as "Muskrat Ramble" and Duke Ellington's "Black Beauty") is a particularly strong effort.

ED THIGPEN

b. Dec. 28, 1930, Chicago, IL

Ed Thigpen can swing on drums at any speed, is a master with brushes, and can play with the very best, although his good taste and subtle nature have often led to his being underrated. His father, Ben Thigpen, was the drummer with Andy Kirk's orchestra in the 1930s. Ed Thigpen played with Candy Johnson and Cootie Williams (1951–52), served in the Army, and worked with Dinah Washington (1954), Lennie Tristano, Johnny Hodges, Jutta Hipp, Bud Powell, and Billy Taylor's trio (1956–59). He gained his greatest fame with the Oscar Peterson Trio (1959–65), playing alongside O.P. and Ray Brown as they recorded constantly and toured the world during a six-year period. The drummer followed up his association with Peterson by having two stints with Ella Fitzgerald (1966–67 and 1968–72). Ed Thigpen moved to Copenhagen in 1972 and since then has worked as an educator, written instructional books, and freelanced, visiting the United States on an occasional basis.

8   *Out of the Storm / Apr. 18–20, 1966 / Verve 314 557 100*

8   *Easy Flight / Nov. 13, 1989–Jan. 28, 1990 / Reckless 9902*

7   *Mr. Taste / Apr. 11, 1991–July 19, 1991 / Justin Time 79379*

Ed Thigpen's debut as a leader, *Out of the Storm* was made during the year after he left the Oscar Peterson Trio. Heading an all-star quintet that includes Clark Terry, guitarist Kenny Burrell, pianist Herbie Hancock, and bassist Ron Carter, the drummer performs three of his originals, one song by Burrell, the traditional "Cielito Lindo," the theme from the film *Harper,* and "Struttin' with Some Barbecue." Terry in particular is in top form, and Thigpen, although mostly in a supportive role, gives the music momentum, drive, and swing.

Thigpen led dates for GNP/Crescendo (1974) and Timeless (1989). *Easy Flight* is quite reminiscent of the Oscar Peterson Trio, since O.P. is the main influence on pianist Johnny O'Neal. Also in the quartet (playing nine jazz standards and two group originals) are guitarist Tony Purrone (best known for playing with the Heath Brothers) and bassist Marlene Rosenberg. Highlights of the straightahead date include "I Hear a Rhapsody," Horace Silver's "Strollin'," and "Just the Way You Look Tonight." *Mr. Taste* is in a similar if sparser vein, featuring Purrone, bassist Mads Vinding, and Thigpen as a trio that mixes together standards (including Jimmy Heath's "Ginger Bread Boy," "Dewey Square," and "'Round Midnight"), originals, and obscurities. The cool-toned music is Boppish, and Ed Thigpen lives up to the album's title.

MEL TORME

b. Sept. 13, 1925, Chicago, IL, d. June 5, 1999, Los Angeles, CA

Mel Torme always considered himself to be a swing singer, but he learned from Bebop, was a brilliant scatter, and continually improved as a jazz vocalist the older he became. More than just a singer, Torme was a composer (best known for "The Christmas Song" and "Born to Be Blue"), an arranger, an enthusiastic drummer, an actor (although his Hollywood career went nowhere), and a writer. Among his books are a colorful biography of Buddy Rich (*Traps, the Drum Wonder*), his autobiography (*It Wasn't All Velvet*), one about *The Judy Garland Show* (*The Other Side of the Rainbow*), and a discussion of some of his favorite vocalists (*My Singing Teachers*).

Mel Torme first sang in public on Monday nights with the Coon-Sanders Orchestra in 1929, when he was four! He was a child actor (appearing in radio soap operas), had a song published when he was 15, and in 1941 joined the Chico Marx Band (which was really run by Ben Pollack) as a drummer, vocal arranger, and singer. Torme wrote "The Christmas Song" in 1944, when he was 19, and two years later Nat King Cole's recording made it a standard. Torme and his vocal group, The Mel-Tones, recorded with Artie Shaw in

Has any singer, other than Mel Torme, actually improved in power, improvising skills, tone, and breath control while in their sixties?

1945, including a hip version of "What Is This Thing Called Love?" After beginning his solo career, Torme (who was given a nickname he disliked, "The Velvet Fog") recorded middle-of-the-road pop music and swinging standards, occasionally playing with his group on piano or drums. By the mid-1950s he was a superior jazz singer, as he showed on his collaborations with the Marty Paich Dek-tette. He had a hit in 1962 with "Comin' Home Baby," but bad record contracts resulted in his barely being on records during the next 15 years, and even then being cast by the unthinking labels mostly in the role of an aging teenager stuck recording other people's pop hits. Live at clubs, where he had control over his material, was a different matter, and Torme continually evolved as an improviser.

During 1983–96, Mel Torme recorded a series of consistently superb sets for the Concord label, showing that his voice was at its prime. In fact, his voice became stronger as he went through his sixties, which was rather unprecedented. Torme constantly performed in public, usually with a trio but sometimes teaming up with George Shearing or big bands (including Rob McConnell's Boss Brass and Marty Paich's Dek-tette). Mel Torme paid tribute to both swing and Bebop, and he was at the peak of his powers in 1996 when a stroke permanently ended his career.

* **The Mel Torme Collection** / 1944–Sept. 18, 1985 / Rhino 71589

10 **Lulu's Back in Town** / Jan. 1956 / Avenue Jazz / Bethlehem 75732

9 **Sings Fred Astaire** / Nov. 1956 / Bethlehem 20-30082

9 **Swings Schubert Alley** / Jan. 1960–Feb. 1960 / Verve 821 581

Because Mel Torme's recording career is covered in great depth in the book *Swing,* this section deals with only his more Bop-oriented recordings, primarily the mid- to late-1950s recordings with Marty Paich and his work for Concord. The four-CD Rhino box set does a fine job of hitting the high points of Torme's career prior to his signing with Concord. Included are numbers with the Mel-Tones, Torme overcoming middle-of-the-road pop string orchestras, small-group dates, selections with Marty Paich's Dektette, some so-so material in the 1960s, and then his re-emergence in the mid-1980s. The classic *Lulu's Back in Town* teams Torme with arranger Paich, whose charts, along with the soft tones of the soloists (including Don Fagerquist, valve trombonist Bob Enevoldsen, altoist Bud Shank, and Bob Cooper on tenor), perfectly fit the singer's voice, resulting in famous versions of "Lulu's Back in Town,"

"When the Sun Comes Out," "Fascinating Rhythm," "The Lady Is a Tramp," and "Lullaby of Birdland." The Torme/Paich combination also works very well on the Fred Astaire tribute (which includes "Something's Gotta Give," "A Fine Romance," "The Way You Look Tonight," and "They All Laughed") and *Swings Schubert Alley.* The latter has a dozen songs from Broadway shows, including "Too Close for Comfort," "On the Street Where You Live," "Old Devil Moon," and "Too Darn Hot."

9 *An Evening at Charlie's / Oct. 1983 / Concord Jazz 4248*

10 *Mel Torme/Rob McConnell and the Boss Brass / May 1986 / Concord Jazz 4306*

9 *A Vintage Year / Aug. 1987 / Concord Jazz 4341*

8 *Reunion / Aug. 1988 / Concord Jazz 4360*

10 *In Concert Tokyo / Dec. 11, 1988 / Concord Jazz 4382*

9 *Nights at the Concord Pavilion / Aug. 1990 / Concord Jazz 4433*

8 *Mel Torme/George Shearing "Do" World War II / Sept. 2–3, 1990 / Concord Jazz 4471*

10 *Fujitsu-Concord Jazz Festival in Japan '90 / Nov. 11, 1990 / Concord Jazz 4481*

When Mel Torme began recording for Concord, he was finally free to document whatever he wanted. His remarkable voice, high musicianship, and impeccable musical taste made this period the finest of his career. *An Evening at Charlie's* is one of several brilliant sets that team Torme with George Shearing (assisted this time around by bassist Don Thompson and drummer Donny Osborne); they interpret "Love Is Just Around the Corner," "Nica's Dream," and a couple of colorful medleys. Torme's project with Rob McConnell's Boss Brass is similar to his earlier matchups with Marty Paich and is of the same high quality. Among the gems are "Just Friends," "Don'cha Go Way Mad," "A House Is Not a Home," "The Song Is You," and a six-song Duke Ellington medley. *A Vintage Year,* by Torme and Shearing (with bassist John Leitham and Donny Osborne), is highlighted by "Someday I'll Find You," "The Way You Look Tonight," "When Sunny Gets Blue," and a funny "New York, New York Medley." *Reunion* shows that the combination of Torme and Marty Paich's Dek-tette was still quite magical. Other than a couple of forgettable Steely Dan tunes, this is a superb date, which includes "Sweet Georgia Brown," "The Blues," "More Than You Know," and a bossa nova medley. Torme and Paich reunited five months later for

In Concert Tokyo. This classic set includes "When the Sun Comes Out," "More Than You Know," "The Carioca," and "The Christmas Song"; Torme happily plays drums on "Cotton Tail."

Nights at the Concord Pavilion finds the nearly 65-year-old singer still getting better. Joined by his trio (pianist John Campbell, bassist Bob Maize, and Donny Osborne), Torme performs four songs (among them "Early Autumn" and "Day In, Day Out") and three medleys, highlighted by a spectacular grouping of songs from *Guys and Dolls.* A specially assembled big band co-led by Frank Wess and Harry "Sweets" Edison joins Torme for the last three numbers, including "You're Driving Me Crazy" and "Sent for You Yesterday." In 1990, Torme and Shearing came back together to perform songs made popular during World War II. Shearing has three instrumental features before the trio (with bassist Neil Swainson and Donny Osborne) accompanies Torme on vintage material, including a Duke Ellington medley, "Aren't You Glad You're You?" and a touching rendition of "We Mustn't Say Goodbye." At the 1990 Fujitsu-Concord Jazz Festival, Torme swings with his trio (John Campbell, Bob Maize, and Donny Osborne), with the Frank Wess Orchestra joining in on four songs. Highlights include Torme playing drums on "Swingin' the Blues," cooking on "Shine on Your Shoes," and showing how beautiful his voice still was on the ballads "A Nightingale Sang in Berkeley Square" and "Stardust."

3 *Nothing Without You / Mar. 12–13, 1991 / Concord Jazz 4515*

8 *The Great American Songbook / Oct. 7–8, 1992 / Telarc 83328*

8 *Sing, Sing, Sing / Nov. 1992 / Concord Jazz 4542*

5 *A Tribute to Bing Crosby / Mar. 12–17, 1994 / Concord Jazz 4614*

7 *Velvet & Brass / July 5–6, 1995 / Concord Jazz 4667*

8 *An Evening with Mel Torme / July 23, 1996 / Concord Jazz 4736*

A collaboration with singer Cleo Laine, *Nothing Without You* is a mess. The problem is that Laine cannot improvise, so she consistently gets in the way of Torme, weighing down and eventually sinking the effort. *The Great American Songbook* has Torme and his trio (pianist John Colianni, John Leitham, and Donny Osborne) augmented by a dozen horns. The singer plays drums on "Rockin' in Rhythm," wrote the majority of the 15 arrangements, and sounds at his best on a seven-song Duke Ellington miniset and a classic version of "Stardust." *Sing, Sing, Sing,* from the 1992 Fujitsu-Concord Festival, pays tribute to Benny Goodman. Torme's trio is joined by clarinetist Ken Peplowski and vibraphonist Peter Appleyard for swing-era standards, including a 14-minute Goodman medley. A fine version of "Sing, Sing, Sing" has Torme on drums.

Less successful is Torme's tribute to Bing Crosby. He performs mostly very straight ballads, and the charts for the 20-piece string orchestra are surprisingly dull. *Velvet & Brass,* a reunion with Rob McConnell's Boss Brass, is not quite at the same level as their previous meeting, but Torme's voice sounds quite beautiful on "If You Could See Me Now," "Autumn Serenade," "My Sweetie Went Away," and "I'm Glad There Is You." Torme's final recording, taken from a television special made a month before his stroke, finds the singer, at age 70, still at the peak of his powers. Assisted by pianist Mike Renzi, Leitham, and Osborne, Mel Torme sounds quite happy on some of his favorite songs, including "Pick Yourself Up," "Stardust," "Stairway to the Stars," and "Oh Lady Be Good." The last song that he ever recorded? "Ev'ry Time We Say Goodbye"!

LPS TO SEARCH FOR

'Round Midnight (Stash 252) features Torme on radio transcriptions with the Marty Paich Dek-tette in 1955–56 and with Shorty Rogers's Giants in 1962. *Together Again—For the First Time* (Gryphon 1100) from 1978, which has Torme singing with the Buddy Rich big band, contains an adventurous and memorable version of "Blues in the Night."

FILMS

A very young-looking Mel Torme sings four numbers in 1950 on *The Snader Telescriptions—The Vocalists* (Storyville 6007).

EDDIE "CLEANHEAD" VINSON

b. Dec. 18, 1917, Houston, TX, d. July 2, 1988, Los Angeles, CA

Eddie "Cleanhead" Vinson is best remembered as a likable blues singer who performed humorous, self-effacing blues, swing standards, and early R&B. But when he soloed on alto, he often sounded, in terms of tone, very close to Charlie Parker. Vinson started on alto when he was 16 and devel-

oped so quickly that within a year he was part of the Chester Boone Orchestra, a band that also included tenors Illinois Jacquet and Arnett Cobb. Vinson stayed with the big band (which was headed by Milt Larkins during 1936–40 and Floyd Ray afterward) for six years. He gained fame while with the Cootie Williams Big Band (1942–45), taking vocals on "Cherry Red" and "Somebody's Got to Go" that made him a popular attraction.

Vinson (whose "Cleanhead" nickname referred to his baldness) led a big band during 1946–47 before cutting back to a septet for many years. He wrote two future jazz standards ("Four" and "Tune Up") that Miles Davis later copyrighted under his own name. John Coltrane was Vinson's sideman for a period, and Trane originally switched from alto to tenor in order to join Cleanhead's band. Vinson faded into obscurity (although he still worked fairly regularly) for quite a few years after the mid-50s. But after he toured Europe with Jay McShann in 1969, he had a comeback, recording more often (including with Johnny Otis, Count Basie, and Roomful of Blues) and making some sessions for the Pablo label. Vinson appeared at both jazz and blues festivals in later years, staying active up until his death at the age of 70. Among his more popular songs were Bill Broonzy's "Just a Dream," "Kidney Stew," "Person to Person," "Old Maid Boogie," and "They Call Me Mr. Cleanhead." Although Eddie "Cleanhead" Vinson rarely played any Bebop standards, whenever he picked up his horn, the spirit of Charlie Parker was heard.

7 *Eddie Vinson Sings / Sept. 1957 / Bethlehem 20-4003*
8 *Kidney Stew Is Fine / Mar. 28, 1969 / Delmark 631*
8 *Jamming the Blues / July 2, 1974 / Black Lion 760188*
9 *I Want a Little Girl / Feb. 10, 1981 / Original Jazz Classics 868*

Eddie "Cleanhead" Vinson recorded as a leader as early as 1945 and would make a series of R&B-oriented sides for Mercury and King. But there would be only three albums during the 1956–68 period. *Eddie Vinson Sings* does indeed mostly feature his voice (on tunes such as "Cleanhead's Back in Town," "Kidney Stew," "Caldonia," and "Cherry Red"), with assistance from such Count Basie-associated players as trumpeter Joe Newman, pianist Nat Pierce, and tenors Frank Foster and Paul Quinichette. *Kidney Stew Is Fine* is notable for having blues guitarist T-Bone Walker, Jay

McShann, and tenorman Hal Singer in Vinson's backup group; highlights include "Just a Dream," "Old Maid Boogie," and "Wee Baby Blues." *Jamming the Blues,* from the 1974 Montreux Jazz Festival, has Vinson singing "Person to Person" and "Hold It Right There" but also playing instrumental versions of "Laura," "Now's the Time," and "C Jam Blues." *I Want a Little Girl* is blues-oriented, with Eddie "Cleanhead" Vinson (assisted by tenor saxophonist Rashid Ali, trumpeter Martin Banks, and a rhythm section) in infectious and joyous form. His singing and playing always made everyone feel good.

LPS TO SEARCH FOR

Cleanhead & Cannonball (Landmark 1309), from 1961–62, is an unusual set. Vinson is heard both as a vocalist with the Cannonball Adderley Quintet and taking Cannonball's place as an altoist on a few instrumental tunes. Unfortunately Vinson and Adderley never play alto together. *Kidney Stew* (Circle 57) puts Vinson in a Dixielandish setting in 1976 with Ted Easton's Dutch band. 1978's *The Clean Machine* (Muse 5116) splits its repertoire between Vinson vocals and instrumental features for Cleanhead's alto. From the same year, *Live at Sandy's* (Muse 5208) and *Hold It Right There* (Muse 5243) feature Vinson in top form at jam sessions with the Ray Bryant Trio; tenors Arnett Cobb and Buddy Tate make guest appearances.

BILL WATROUS

b. June 8, 1939, Middletown, CT

A brilliant technician with a beautiful tone, Bill Watrous is one of the finest trombonists to emerge since 1960. Watrous was introduced to jazz by his father, who was also a trombonist. He played in local bands as a teenager and studied with pianist-composer Herbie Nichols while in the military. After his release, Watrous played with Billy Butterfield and with Kai Winding's trombone groups (1962–67). He worked in the New York studios in the 1960s, and among his many sideman recordings were dates with the orchestras of Maynard Ferguson, Johnny Richards, and Woody Herman. Watrous also played with the television bands for the Merv Griffin and Dick Cavett shows and was on the staff of CBS.

The trombonist was with the jazz-rock group Ten Wheel Drive in 1971 and then led his Manhattan Wildlife Refuge (1973–77), an excellent big band that recorded two strong albums for Columbia. Bill Watrous moved to Los Angeles in the late 1970s, became a busy studio musician, and has since appeared at local clubs and jazz parties, occasionally leading a big band. In addition to his skills as a trombonist, he has developed into a virtuosic whistler and a good-natured singer.

6 *Someplace Else / 1986 / Soundwings 2100*
7 *Reflections / 1987 / Soundwings 2104*
9 *Bone-ified / 1992 / GNP/Crescendo 2211*
7 *A Time for Love / 1993 / GNP/Crescendo 2222*
9 *Space Available / Dec. 1996 / Double-Time 124*
7 *Live at the Blue Note / Mar. 30, 1998 / Half Note 15095-4204*

Bill Watrous's two Soundwings releases both have him joined by orchestras arranged by Patrick Williams. *Someplace Else* has a few standards (including "There Is No Greater Love" and a medley of "I'm Getting Sentimental Over You" and "Yesterdays") plus adaptations of a couple of classical works. Overall it is a middle-of-the-road date and, although Watrous's tone is typically lush, no real surprises occur. *Reflections* finds the trombonist joined by three trumpets (including Snooky Young), strings, and a rhythm section. Best are "Li'l Darlin'," "Cinnamon and Clove," and "Why Not." Watrous's decision to sing Dave Frishberg's "Dear Bix" is a mistake, but he compensates by contributing two hot whistling solos.

Bone-ified is a consistently brilliant date, a quartet performance with pianist Shelly Berg, bassist Lou Fischer, and Randy Drake or Tom Cummings on drums. Even with some overdubbing of extra trombones in a few of the ensembles and Berg sometimes adding synthesized strings, the music is quite Boppish and freewheeling. Best among the selections are "Day In, Day Out," "Indian Summer," "Change Partners," and "Just in Time." *A Time for Love* features Watrous joined by a big band for nine Johnny Mandel compositions, arranged by either Shelly Berg or Sammy Nestico. Other than one Ron Stout trumpet solo, all of the solo space is taken by Watrous and Berg. The music consists of ballads, with just a few cookers (especially "Low Life" and "Not Really the Blues"), so this is a laid-back rather than a hard-swinging session.

Ever since moving to Los Angeles, Bill Watrous has led a part-time big band. In late 1996, the orchestra finally had an opportunity to record. With arrangements by Tom Kubis, Shelly Berg, Gordon Goodwin, Ken Kaplan, and Frank Perowsky, the band swings through eight numbers on *Space*

Available. Watrous and Berg are the main soloists, but there is also space for tenors Gene Burkurt and Bill Liston, trumpeters Bob Summers and Steve Huffsteter, and altoist Sal Lozano. Highlights include "Space Available," "My Foolish Heart," "Mama Llama Samba," "My Romance," and "Village Dance." Making a rare trip back to New York, Watrous is well showcased on *Live at the Blue Note* in a quartet also including pianist Derek Smith, bassist Russell George, and drummer Joe Ascione. The great trombonist really stretches out on seven standards ("Just in Time," at 8:59, is the briefest cut), showing off his strong chops and quick ideas on "Smiles," "Blue Monk," and "I Want to Be Happy," although the so-so recording quality muffles Watrous's usually beautiful tone a bit.

LPS TO SEARCH FOR

Manhattan Wildlife Refuge (Columbia 33090) and *The Tiger of San Pedro* (Columbia 33701) are both exciting sets by the 1974–75 Bill Watrous big band; trumpeter Danny Stiles was a major asset to the orchestra. Watrous also recorded a series of now-scarce combo dates for the Famous Door label, including *Bone Straight Ahead* (Famous Door 101), *Watrous in Hollywood* (Famous Door 127), *I'll Play for You* (Famous Door 134), *Coronary Trombossa* (Famous Door 136), and *Roarin' Back into New York, New York* (Famous Door 144), that put the emphasis on standards and long, flowing solos by Watrous's trombone. Also worth picking up is *Bill Watrous in London* (Mole 7), a quartet set with the Brian Dee Trio that has lengthy workouts on four standards, including "Straight, No Chaser" and "Diane."

CARLA WHITE

b. Sept. 15, 1951, Oakland, CA

Carla White initially was known for her brilliant scat singing, but she has developed into a superior interpreter of lyrics too. White was raised in New York and hoped to become an improvising dancer but instead became a singer and actress while in high school. She studied at the Webber-Douglas Academy of Dramatic Art in London (1969–71), traveled overseas, and in New York studied for four years with Lennie Tristano and Warne Marsh. She co-led a band with trumpeter Manny Duran for several years starting in the late 1970s; they recorded together for Stash in 1983. Since then, Carla White (one of the best Bop-oriented singers of the past 20 years) has worked mostly on the East Coast, recording for Milestone, Evidence and Vartan Jazz.

8 *Listen Here / Sept. 4–5, 1991 / Evidence 22109*
8 *Live at Vartan Jazz / Apr. 21–22, 1996 / Vartan Jazz 016*

Listen Here is an excellent all-round showcase for Carla White, who is joined by Lew Tabackin on tenor and flute, pianist Peter Madsen, bassist Dean Johnson, and drummer Lewis Nash. The repertoire consists of mostly veteran standards (other than Dave Frishberg's little-known title cut), but there is a lot of variety, including such numbers as "Devil May Care," "Harlem Nocturne" (which is rarely ever sung), "Lotus Blossom," and a calypso version of "It's Only a Paper Moon" that is a vocal duet with bassist Johnson. Just as valuable is her 1996 live set in Denver, *Live at Vartan Jazz,* on which she is accompanied by pianist Mark Soskin, guitarist Jerry Hahn, bassist Harvie Swartz, and drummer Joe LaBarbera. Carla White digs into and uplifts such numbers as Charlie Parker's "Bloomdido," "I Hear Music," "The End of a Love Affair," and "It Might As Well Be Spring." Both CDs are easily recommended.

LPS TO SEARCH FOR

Andruline (Stash 237), from 1983, puts the emphasis on Carla White's scat singing. Her recording debut finds her co-leading a quintet with trumpeter Manny Duran (they are joined by Peter Madsen, bassist Ed Howard, and drummer Taro Okamoto), with Carla stretching out on Miles Davis's "Dig," "Lover Man," "Good Morning Heartache," and Fats Navarro's "Fat's Flats" plus two originals. *Orient Express* (Milestone 9147), recorded in 1985–86, has White mostly showing off her interpretative skill with lyrics on such tunes as "Something to Live For," "Detour Ahead," and "Snuggled on Your Shoulder," although she also scats quite expertly on "You'd Be So Nice to Come Home To" and the title cut. She is joined by Madsen, Howard, and drummer Tim Horner, with trumpeter Duran making a guest appearance on "The Man with the Horn." *Mood Swings* (Milestone 9159), from 1988, was the best of the singer's early efforts as White uplifts and swings "If Dreams Come True," "The Gentleman Is a Dope," "Yardbird Suite," and Bob Dorough's "Love Came on Stealthy Fingers." In addition to Madsen, bassist Phil Bowler, and Horner, Lew Tabackin plays tenor or flute on five numbers and guitarist Joshua Breakstone helps out on four.

GERALD WIGGINS

b. May 12, 1922, New York, NY

Most inspired by Erroll Garner and Art Tatum, Gerald Wiggins has long had his own sound on piano, whether romping with his trio, riffing insistently behind another soloist, or backing a singer. His style falls between swing and Bop. He began piano lessons when he was four and started to play jazz as a teenager. Wiggins (later known affectionately as "The Wig") doubled on bass while attending the High School of Music & Art, was an accompanist for Stepin Fetchit in some shows, and gained experience playing with the big bands of Les Hite, Louis Armstrong, and Benny Carter (1943). While in the military (1944–46), he was stationed near Seattle and often had the chance to work in local clubs. In 1946 Wiggins permanently moved to Los Angeles. Through the years he accompanied with many singers, including Lena Horne, Helen Humes, Ella Mae Morse, Eartha Kitt, Nat King Cole, Kay Starr, Lou Rawls, Ernie Andrews, Linda Hopkins, Joe Williams, and even Marilyn Monroe (in his role as a vocal coach for Hollywood film studios).

Wiggins has led trios since the 1950s and for a long time had a popular unit that included the late bassist Andy Simpkins and drummer Paul Humphrey. He became the pianist with the Juggernaut in the 1990s after Nat Pierce's death and sometimes plays with Mainstream swing artists who visit Los Angeles, including tenor saxophonist Scott Hamilton. He has not recorded enough as a leader through the years, although he has been a sideman on many sessions, including with Benny Carter, Milt Jackson, Art Pepper, Illinois Jacquet, King Pleasure, Joe Pass, Red Holloway, Frank Capp, and Scott Hamilton. Gerald Wiggins's Concord dates of the 1990s offer listeners definitive examples of "The Wig's" joyful music. His son, J. J. Wiggins, is an excellent bassist.

5 *Music from "Around the World in 80 Days" / 1956–1957 / Original Jazz Classics 1761*

7 *Reminiscin' with Wig / Feb. 1957 / Fresh Sound 47*

7 *The King and I / 1958 / Fresh Sound 53*

6 *Wiggin' Out / Sept. 1960 / Original Jazz Classics 1034*

8 *Relax and Enjoy It / 1961 / Original Jazz Classics 173*

Gerald Wiggins first led his own record dates back in 1950 for Swing and Vogue, but he has headed relatively few sessions through the years. *Music from "Around the World in 80 Days"* finds Wiggins, bassist Eugene Wright, and drummer Bill Douglass doing their best to uplift the rather weak and forgettable themes from the film of the same name; the total amount of music is under a half-hour. *Reminiscin' with Wig,* a CD reissue of music originally put out by the tiny Motif label, features Wiggins, Wright, and Douglass playing music from the early part of the 20th century. Their renditions of such songs as "Three O'Clock in the Morning," "Oh, You Beautiful Doll," "Ma, He's Making Eyes at Me," and "In My Merry Oldsmobile" are lightly swinging and often filled with sly wit. The same trio interprets eight songs from the score of *The King and I,* including "Shall We Dance," "We Kiss in a Shadow," and "Getting to Know You." The performances are fine and the songs are flexible enough to retain their personalities in a jazz setting. But with less than 31 minutes of music, this is another chintzy CD.

Wiggin' Out is a trio date from 1960 that finds Wiggins switching to organ and joined by tenor saxophonist Harold Land and drummer Jackie Mills. The material (two originals and four standards, including "Teach Me Tonight," "A Night in Tunisia," and "Without a Song") is fine, but Wiggins displays less personality on organ (an instrument he has rarely recorded on) than he has on piano. On a higher level is *Relax and Enjoy It.* Wiggins is back on piano, where he belongs, in a trio with bassist Joe Comfort and drummer Jackie Mills, playing standards that suit his style (including "The Lady Is a Tramp," "My Heart Stood Still," and "Serenade in Blue"), with the playing time being over 40 minutes for a change. Overall, this is the best recording from Gerald Wiggins's early years.

8 *Live at Maybeck Recital Hall, Vol. 8 / Aug. 1990 / Concord Jazz 4450*

9 *Soulidarity / Aug. 23-24, 1995 / Concord Jazz 4706*

Gerald Wiggins was in his playing prime throughout the 1990s. The Maybeck Recital Hall concert is a set of unaccompanied solos, and, although Wig is at his best in trios, his background in swing makes these performances sound quite complete. Among the highlights are "Yesterdays," "Night Mist Blues," "Body and Soul," "You're Mine You," and "Take the 'A' Train." The best overall Gerald Wiggins recording is *Soulidarity,* which features his longtime group with bassist Andy Simpkins and drummer Paul Humphrey. The musical communication among the three musicians is almost telepathic at times, and Wiggins's sly humor is very much in evidence. Among the more memorable selections are "The Way You Look Tonight," "Surprise Blues," "What Is There to Say," and "Lover."

LPS TO SEARCH FOR

The Gerald Wiggins Trio (V.S.O.P. 28), from 1956, has Wiggins, Joe Comfort, and Bill Douglass jamming on two originals and seven standards, including "Love for Sale," "Surrey with the Fringe on Top," and "Three Little Words."

PHIL WOODS

b. Nov. 2, 1931, Springfield, MA

Phil Woods is a brilliant altoist who mastered Bebop early in his career. His later work (starting with his move to Europe in 1968) will be covered in the Hard Bop book in this series. Woods's first alto was left to him by an uncle, and the youth began seriously practicing when he was 12. After working locally in Massachusetts, Woods moved to New York in 1948. He studied with Lennie Tristano and attended both the Manhattan School of Music and Juilliard. Woods began to emerge as a player in 1954, playing with Charlie Barnet and leading his first record dates. The altoist worked with the groups of guitarist Jimmy Raney and George Wallington, was part of the Dizzy Gillespie big band, and had stints with Buddy Rich (1958–59), Quincy Jones's orchestra (1959–61), and the Benny Goodman big band that toured the Soviet Union in 1962. But more important were his many recordings of the era and his own club dates with his quartet. He also co-led a group for a time with fellow altoist Gene Quill that was called "Phil & Quill." A certain amount of jealousy from other musicians resulted in Woods's being underrated and put down as a "Bird imitator," particularly after he married Chan Parker (becoming the stepfather to future singer Kim Parker) and inherited Bird's horn. But in reality, from the start, Woods had his own sound.

In the 1960s Phil Woods (who by then was occasionally doubling on clarinet) freelanced, working in the studios, appearing on Benny Carter's *Further Definitions* album, and touring Europe in 1967 with the Thelonious Monk Nonet. Frustrated with the jazz situation in the United States, in 1968 he moved to France, staying overseas for the next four years. During this period Woods explored avant-garde jazz with his adventurous European Rhythm Machine. After returning to the United States and leading a short-lived electric jazz group with keyboardist Pete Robinson, Woods formed a quintet with pianist Mike Melillo, bassist Steve

Gilmore, drummer Bill Goodwin, and guitarist Harry Leahey. Since that time the band (which temporarily became a quartet when Leahey dropped out) has been a constant in Phil Woods's life. It resumed being a quintet during the periods of trumpeter Tom Harrell (1983–89), trombonist Hal Crook (1989–92), and trumpeter Brian Lynch, with the piano slot being filled by Hal Galper (1980–90), Jim McNeely (1990–95), and Bill Charlap; Gilmore and Goodwin have remained with Woods up to the present time. The music of the Phil Woods Quartet/Quintet is an extension of Bop and Hard Bop, a perfect vehicle for the exciting altoist.

7 *Early Quintets / Aug. 11, 1954 + Mar. 3, 1959 / Original Jazz Classics 1865*
   Pot Pie, with Jon Eardley / Oct. 12, 1954 + Feb. 4, 1955 / Original Jazz Classics 1881
7 *Woodlore / Nov. 25, 1955 / Original Jazz Classics 052*
7 *Pairing Off / June 15, 1956 / Original Jazz Classics 092*
7 *The Young Bloods / Nov. 2, 1956 / Original Jazz Classics 1732*

Phil Woods largely had his sound and concept together at the time of the August 11, 1954, date that opens *Early Quintets*. That session, which was actually led by guitarist Jimmy Raney, also includes trumpeter John Wilson, bassist Bill Crow, and drummer Joe Morello. The later set on the CD (from 1959) teams Woods with Howard McGhee, pianist Dick Hyman (the leader of that date), bassist Teddy Kotick, and Roy Haynes. The CD (which is 37 minutes long) has its moments, including fine versions of "Stella by Starlight" and George Wallington's "Lemon Drop." *Pot Pie* is more exciting, seven group originals plus the standard "Mad About the Boy" played in frequently heated fashion by Woods, trumpeter Jon Eardley, pianist George Syran, Teddy Kotick, and drummer Nick Stabulas. *Woodlore*, an excellent quartet showcase for Woods (with a quiet rhythm section comprised of pianist John Williams, Kotick, and Stabulas), would have a higher rating if it were longer than 33 minutes! The altoist swings hard on "Slow Boat to China," "Get Happy," two other standards, and a pair of originals. *Pairing Off* is essentially a jam session, with three Woods songs and the ballad "Suddenly It's Spring" explored by a pair of trumpeters (Donald Byrd and Kenny Dorham), two altos (Woods and Gene Quill), plus a fine rhythm section (Tommy Flanagan, bassist Doug Watkins, and drummer

PHOTO BY SUSAN ROSMARIN

Whether it be Bop, Hard Bop, fresh versions of standards,
or swinging originals, Phil Woods has always kept alive the
spirit of the Bebop pioneers.

Philly Joe Jones). There is plenty of youthful energy on this
enjoyable set. *The Young Bloods* has Byrd and Woods as the
lead voices in a quintet with Al Haig, Teddy Kotick, and
drummer Charlie Persip. Woods (who contributed four of
the six songs) consistently steals solo honors, and it is a pleasure to hear Haig sounding so strong during an era when he
was largely neglected.

6 *Four Altos / Feb. 9, 1957 / Original Jazz Classics
   1734*
8 *Phil & Quill with Prestige / Mar. 29, 1957 /
   Original Jazz Classics 215*
8 *Sugan / July 19, 1957 / Original Jazz Classics 1841*

10 *Right of Swing / Jan. 26, 1961 + Feb. 10, 1961 /
   Candid 79016*

Four Altos suffers from having the four altoists (Woods,
Gene Quill, Sahib Shihab, and Hal Stein) sounding so similar. The Charlie Parker influence is so strong that, at least on
this date, there is not much individuality to be heard. Accompanied by pianist Mal Waldron, Tommy Potter, and
drummer Louis Hayes, the saxophonists play well on five
obscurities and "Don't Blame Me," but no one stands out.

Although Phil Woods and Gene Quill did sound pretty
similar in 1957, their competitiveness and mutual respect
are felt throughout *Phil & Quill.* They battle it out on six
swinging originals, Miles Davis's "Solar," and Sonny Rol-

lins's "Airegin," backed by a tasteful rhythm section (pianist George Syran, Teddy Kotick, and Nick Stabulas). *Sugan* is a fine Bebop jam session featuring Woods, trumpeter Ray Copeland, Red Garland, and, once again, Kotick and Stabulas. The quintet romps through three Woods pieces and a trio of Charlie Parker songs: "Au Privave," "Steeplechase," and "Scrapple from the Apple."

Phil Woods did not record as a leader during 1958–60. However, his last set during his early classic period is a real gem. *Rights of Swing* utilizes an octet comprising trumpeter Benny Bailey, trombonist Curtis Fuller, Julius Watkins on French horn, baritonist Sahib Shihab, Tommy Flanagan, bassist Buddy Catlett, and drummer Osie Johnson. Woods's five-part "Right of Swing" suite has colorful tone colors (helped greatly by the presence of Watkins), strong themes, impressive variety, and meaningful and concise solos. This is one of the finest recordings of Phil Woods's career, allowing him to be more than just a hot alto soloist.

But strangely enough, the concept was never repeated, and Woods led only one more set before moving to Europe in 1968, an odd album for Impulse with Greek musicians called *Greek Cooking*!

LPS TO SEARCH FOR

Bird Calls, Vol. 1 (Savoy 1179) has four selections from 1955 with pianist Hall Overton, Teddy Kotick, and Nick Stabulas

(including "Pennies from Heaven" and "It's Only a Paper Moon") and three numbers from a date with George Wallington in 1957 that also includes trumpeter Donald Byrd, bassist Knobby Totah, and Stabulas. This last is highlighted by a version of Bud Powell's "Dance of the Infidels" and a lengthy rendition of Dizzy Gillespie's "Ow." *Phil Talks with Quill* (Columbia 36806) is a Woods and Quill date from 1957 (with pianist Bob Corwin, bassist Sonny Dallas, and Stabulas) that has heated jams on five Bop standards (including "A Night in Tunisia" and two versions of "Doxy") plus Woods's "Hymn for Kim." Partly recorded on the same day, *Warm Woods* (Portrait 44408) uses the identical group except without Quill. Woods sounds lyrical on the ballad-oriented set, which includes Dave Brubeck's "In Your Own Sweet Way," "Like Someone in Love," and his own "Waltz for a Lovely Wife."

FILMS

Phil Woods appears briefly in one scene of *The Hustler* (1961). He is interviewed and plays "Last Night When We Were Young" in the 1978 documentary *Jazz in Exile* (Rhapsody Films). His 1979 group is featured on *Jazz at the Maintenance Shop* (Shanachie 6305) and *Phil Woods Quartet* (Rhapsody 9037). In addition, Woods is the main soloist during *In Concert with Joe Sudler's Swing Machine* (View Video 1312), and his 1990 quartet is featured for two numbers on *A Tribute to Charlie Parker, Vol. 2* (Storyville 6049).

VARIOUS ARTISTS

This section features samplers, all-star leaderless dates, and special concerts that include some intriguing Bebop-oriented performances.

7 *All-Star Jam Sessions: Ow! / 1954–1955 / Moon 075*
The music on this European CD is taken from two Jazz at the Philharmonic performances. Both Buddy Rich and Louie Bellson have drum spectaculars, and trumpeter Roy Eldridge has the brief "Willow Weep for Me" (which might have been part of a ballad medley) as his feature. But best are the lengthy "Jazz Concert Blues" and "The Challengers," which have exciting solos by Eldridge, Dizzy Gillespie, Bill Harris, Ben Webster, and Flip Phillips with the Oscar Peterson Quartet. There are some fiery moments, although this set falls short of classic. When will Verve take control of the situation and reissue the complete JATP output of the 1950s?

8 *Americans in Europe / Jan. 3, 1963 / GRP/Impulse 150*
Producer-writer Joachim Berendt put together a concert in West Germany in early 1963 that showcased some of the major American jazz musicians who were living overseas. Originally 13 selections were released as two LPs; however, this single-CD just has eight of the cuts, leaving out selections by clarinetist Albert Nicholas and blues performers Champion Jack Dupree and Curtis Jones. What is on this set is quite impressive, particularly two selections featuring Don Byas ("All the Things You Are" and "I Remember Clifford") and showcases for Idrees Sulieman ("I Can't Get Started") and Bud Powell ("'Round Midnight"). The remainder of the intriguing concert has two numbers apiece by a trio headed by Kenny Clarke (with guitarist Jimmy Gourley and organist Lou Bennett) and a quintet led by clarinetist Bill Smith that features Herb Geller. Overall the performances are Bop-oriented, with Byas stealing the show.

* *Bebop in Britain / Jan. 13, 1948–Apr. 13, 1953 / Esquire 100–4*
By 1948, when this four-CD set begins, Bebop was becoming an international language and the music was clearly here to stay, at least as a major influence on other styles. The first disc has some of the earlier British Bop dates, all from 1948 and featuring such notable players as tenor saxophonist Ronnie Scott and pianist Ralph Sharon (heard with the Es-

quire Five), a date led by Victor Feldman (who at the time was a 13-year-old drummer!) with clarinetist John Dankworth, an "All-Star Sextet" with trumpeter Reg Arnold and Aubrey Frank on tenor, and a few jam session numbers. Ronnie Scott and Johnny Dankworth (on alto) are showcased on a CD apiece (with such sidemen as trumpeter Jimmy Deuchar, the young Spike Robinson on alto, Victor Feldman in 1951 on piano, altoist Derek Humble, and tenor saxophonist Don Rendell). The final disc (from 1951–52) has a potpourri of items, including selections by tenor saxophonist Kenny Graham's Afro-Cubists, drummer Norman Burns's quintet, accordionist Tito Burn's sextet, and Victor Lewis. Overall the music is historic and rare, showing that Great Britain was an unexpected haven of Bebop.

9 *Be Bop Revisited, Vol. 1 / Jan. 11, 1946–Nov. 22, 1950 / EPM/Xanadu*
Drawn from the Xanadu catalog, this European CD contains five very interesting Bop-era sessions; all but the Bird date were last out in the *Bebop Revisited* LP series. Charlie Parker is heard on four numbers in Sweden with local musicians, including Rolf Ericson. Aaron Sachs and Terry Gibbs are showcased in a quintet (with Gene DiNovi, bassist Clyde Lombardi, and Tiny Kahn) that greatly updates the Benny Goodman-Lionel Hampton clarinet-vibes tradition, and Teddy Edwards leads a Los Angeles quintet (which includes Hampton Hawes and Roy Porter) in 1948. In addition, Chubby Jackson's Fifth Dimensional Jazz Group (a sextet with Conte Candoli, tenor saxophonist Frank Socolow, Lou Levy, Terry Gibbs, and Denzil Best) romps on six numbers (including "Lemon Drop" and "Dee Dee's Dance"), and Lucky Thompson is heard on four selections with Dodo Marmarosa, Ray Brown, and drummer Jackie Mills. Overall the music (recorded in Sweden, Los Angeles, and New York) is high-quality classic Bebop, and these obscure sessions hold their own with their more famous counterparts.

8 *The Bebop Singers / Sept. 16, 1950–Mar. 28, 1973 / Prestige 24216*
Most of the music on this disc is available elsewhere, but this CD does offer listeners a strong sampling of Bop and vo-

calese singing including most of the genre's "greatest hits." Included are performances by King Pleasure (including "Red Top," "Parker's Mood," and "Moody's Mood for Love"), Dizzy Gillespie ("She's Gone Again"), Eddie Jefferson, Annie Ross ("Twisted," "Farmer's Market," and "Jackie"), Jon Hendricks, and Joe Carroll. Not for completists, but a fine overview of the field.

7 Birdland All Stars at Carnegie Hall / Sept. 25, 1954–Dec. 1, 1954 / Roulette 98660

This very interesting twofer, taken mostly from a single night's concert, features several major artists at intriguing points in their career. The Count Basie Orchestra, which has seven features (including "Blues Backstage," "Perdido," and "Two Franks"), was on the brink of great success, although Joe Williams had not joined up yet. Their great former tenor, Lester Young, sits in on exciting versions of "Pennies from Heaven" (which is quite emotional) and "Jumpin' at the Woodside" in one of his infrequent reunions with his former musical home. Charlie Parker is heard on one of his final recordings (less than six months before his death), playing three so-so numbers with a quartet. Billie Holiday sounds somewhat out of it as she runs through six tunes with the Basie band. But in contrast, Sarah Vaughan is in typically wondrous form on 13 songs, including "Perdido," "East of the Sun," "Polka Dots and Moonbeams," and "Tenderly." The twofer concludes with five selections from a later concert by the Count Basie band, with tenor saxophonist Stan Getz happily starring on three numbers (including "Little Pony"). Get this for Basie, Pres, and especially Sassy.

7 Birdland Stars 1956 / Feb. 27, 1956 / Bluebird 66159

The "Birdland Stars" consist of Kenny Dorham, Conte Candoli, Phil Woods, tenorman Al Cohn, Hank Jones, bassist John Simmons, and Kenny Clarke (shortly before he left for Europe). The odd part about the dozen songs they perform is that, instead of jamming standards, the septet performs six originals apiece by Ernie Wilkins and Manny Albam, none of which were destined to catch on. The most intriguing song title is Albam's "Conte's Condolences"! All of the musicians play up to their usual level, although there are no unexpected fireworks. This could have benefited from the competitiveness of Jazz at the Philharmonic.

8 Birdology / June 7, 1989 / Verve 841 132

The Paris concert on this CD features an all-star group performing Jackie McLean's "Bird Lives" and five songs associated with Charlie Parker, including "Yardbird Suite," "Chasin' the Bird," and "Donna Lee." Trumpeter Don Sickler provided the arrangements and transcriptions (some of which are recorded solos by Parker and Duke Jordan), and there are many fine solos from the septet, which is made up of Sickler, altoist McLean, Johnny Griffin, Cecil Payne, Duke Jordan, bassist Ron Carter, and Roy Haynes. A spirited set.

* Classic Capitol Jazz Sessions / June 5, 1942–Dec. 11, 1953 / Mosaic 12-170

This perfectly done 12-CD box has only a touch of Bebop (dates by Red Norvo and Stan Hasselgard), but it is well worth mentioning anyway. All of the 65 Capitol sessions are complete, with the styles ranging from Dixieland and big bands to Bop, with many obscurities included among the 245 selections. Since it is a limited-edition release and most of the performances have consistently eluded reissue programs, this box is a must for jazz collectors. Along with Dixieland-oriented sides by former Bob Crosby sidemen, Wingy Manone, and Bud Freeman, there are performances by drummer Big Sid Catlett (with Illinois Jacquet and trumpeter Gerald Wilson), Anita O'Day, Benny Carter (his 1943–45 big band, which includes J.J. Johnson), the 1945–46 Cootie Williams Orchestra, and Louie Bellson's Just Jazz All-Stars of 1952 with Wardell Gray and Clark Terry.

* Central Avenue Sounds / June 21, 1922–Feb. 6, 1956 / Rhino 75872

Although it is tempting to believe that most significant jazz emanates from New York, other cities (including Los Angeles) have also been the home for major jazz artists through the decades. In fact, the Central Avenue scene of the mid- to late 1940s was a competitor to (and actually outlived) New York's 52nd Street. This four-CD set celebrates vintage jazz in Los Angeles with recordings from a 34-year period starting with Kid Ory's Sunshine Orchestra of 1922. By the 16th of the 91 selections, the chronology is already into the 1940s, with Bebop very much under way by the 40th selection. There are many rarities on this set (which draws its material partly from radio broadcasts and obscurities from tiny L.A. labels). In addition to such prebop greats as Jelly Roll Morton, Louis Armstrong, Art Tatum, Lester Young, and Nat King Cole, there are titles from Slim Gaillard, the Gerald Wilson Orchestra, Charlie Parker, Baron Mingus's Octet, Lucky Thompson, Howard McGhee, Dexter Gordon, Teddy Edwards, Roy Porter's 17 Beboppers, and Frank Morgan. The 92-page booklet is also a major plus.

6 *Crazy Rhythms / June 12, 1945 + Aug. 28, 1945 / Savoy 0195*

The early 1990s Savoy reissue program conducted by Japanese Nippon tended to be ill conceived, with exact replicas of LPs being reissued on CD despite the brief playing time and countless errors. This disc is somewhat valuable, for it has all of the titles from Charlie Kennedy's only date as a leader. Unfortunately the quintet outing features Kennedy on tenor (rather than his more distinctive alto), but he plays well on five standards with a quintet that also includes solo space for pianist Johnny Guarnieri and Bill DeArango. Also on this CD is a lesser-known quartet date by Charlie Ventura including "Dark Eyes" (which is listed as one of his compositions!).

7 *First Ladies of Jazz / Jan. 26, 1940–Feb. 1954 / Savoy 1202*

This CD has three completely unrelated sessions featuring female pianists. Mary Lou Williams is heard back in her swing-oriented days of 1940 leading a septet taken from Andy Kirk's orchestra, including tenor saxophonist Dick Wilson. Six songs have German pianist Jutta Hipp in Munich with a 1952 quartet that includes tenor saxophonist Hans Koller, performing Boppish versions of swing standards. In addition, there are three tunes by pianist Beryl Booker in France from 1954 with a quartet that stars Don Byas. This 1989 CD comes from the period when the Savoy label was administered by Muse, and the reissue is well done.

8 *From the Newport Jazz Festival / July 1964 + Feb. 15, 1967 / Bluebird 6457*

The first part of this CD is taken from the 1964 Newport Jazz Festival, a half-hour of music dedicated to Charlie Parker. Howard McGhee, J. J. Johnson, Sonny Stitt (on tenor), pianist Harold Mabern, bassist Arthur Harper, and Max Roach perform spirited versions of "Buzzy," "Now's the Time," and "Wee." Making the occasion more historic is the fact that the set's MC (Father Norman O'Connor) gets the musicians to say a few words about Bird before the audience. Wrapping up the CD are unrelated but passionate renditions of "Embraceable You" and "Old Folks" played by altoist Jackie McLean in 1967 with his quartet. McLean pays tribute to Parker by playing in his own modern style.

8 *Giants of Jazz in Berlin '71 / Nov. 5, 1971 / Emarcy 834 567*

The Giants of Jazz existed for a year (1971–72) and were a good excuse for Dizzy Gillespie, Sonny Stitt, Kai Winding,

Thelonious Monk, Al McKibbon, and Art Blakey (taking a vacation from his Jazz Messengers) to tour the world while playing Bebop standards. It was particularly unusual to have Monk as a sideman in the group, and, although there was no official leader, Gillespie often assumed that role. They recorded a double LP for Atlantic that unfortunately has not been reissued on CD. This 1988 CD features different versions of six of the nine songs on the twofer, with the only "fresh" material being "Lover Man." The Giants' renditions of "Blue 'n Boogie," "Tour de Force," and "A Night in Tunisia" are generally memorable and find the musicians (particularly Stitt) in top form.

9 *Jazz in Los Angeles: the 1940s / Sept. 1, 1941–1949 / KLON 1*

This 1992 CD was released in anticipation of a planned Hollywood Jazz Festival by radio station KLON; however, the L.A. riots of that year resulted in the whole thing being cancelled. This will be a difficult disc to find (perhaps it is available through the station), but the music is quite worthwhile. Duke Ellington and the Jump for Joy Choir play a medley from the short-lived *Jump for Joy* show, and there are broadcast appearances by Lester Young, the Cee Pee Johnson Orchestra, Benny Carter, Dizzy Gillespie with Charlie Parker, and the Boyd Raeburn Orchestra (playing George Handy's four-part "Jazz Symphony"). In addition, there are studio and radio features for Lucky Thompson, Gerald Wilson's Big Band, the Nat King Cole Trio, the orchestras of Earle Spencer and Lyle Griffin, Howard McGhee, Dexter Gordon and Wardell Gray ("The Chase"), Teddy Edwards, and Charles Mingus. The underrated richness of the L.A. scene of the 1940s is well displayed throughout this CD.

10 *The Jazz Scene / Mar. 1946–Feb. 4, 1955 / Verve 314 521 661*

In 1949, producer Norman Granz put together a prestigious album of 78s that included many special works which summed up the jazz scene of the time. Baritonist Harry Carey was featured on two numbers with strings, Neal Hefti, George Handy, and Ralph Burns wrote some complex arrangements, Lester Young, Charlie Parker, Bud Powell, Machito ("Tanga"), and altoist Willie Smith had features, and Coleman Hawkins took "Picasso" as a historic unaccompanied tenor solo. In 1994, all of the music plus a lot more was reissued as this deluxe two-CD set, which is accompanied by many pictures and historic liner notes. In addition to all of the mentioned selections, there are some alternate takes plus additional music by Billy Strayhorn,

Lester Young, Willie Smith, Coleman Hawkins, Flip Phillips, and Ralph Burns (with the JATP All-Stars and Roy Eldridge). A remarkable reissue that is essential for serious Bebop collections.

* *The 1940s Mercury Sessions / Sept. 25, 1945–Oct. 27, 1951 / Mercury 314 525 609*

The packing of this limited-edition seven-CD set is wonderful, for it looks like an old radio. The radio box, which has the accurate subtitle of "Blues, Boogie & Bop," covers those styles quite well and includes many rarely reissued sessions. Of greatest interest from the Bop standpoint are a dozen titles from Buddy Rich's Bebop orchestra and ten by Cootie Williams's bands (including his hit version of "Gator Tail" featuring the screaming tenor of Willis Jackson). Also included are 34 tunes from boogie-woogie pianist Albert Ammons (including his one date with his son, Gene Ammons), 16 songs featuring singer Helen Humes, 24 by Jay McShann during his post-Charlie Parker era, 30 from Eddie "Cleanhead" Vinson, nine by New Orleans R&B pioneer Professor Longhair, and four tunes apiece from cornetist Rex Stewart and singers Julia Lee and Myra Taylor. The seventh disc is filled with previously unreleased alternate takes from most of these performers plus two formerly unknown numbers by Mary Lou Williams. All of the sessions are issued complete; get this valuable set while you can!

8 *The 1940s: Small Groups—New Directions / Mar. 8, 1945–Nov. 3, 1947 / Columbia 44222*

Three different groups are featured on this CD, all of strong interest. Woody Herman's 1946 Woodchoppers (which has the main players from the First Herd, including Sonny Berman, Bill Harris, Flip Phillips, and Red Norvo) is showcased on ten numbers, including "Igor," "Fan It," and "Four Men on a Horse." The Gene Krupa Trio (with Charlie Ventura and pianist Teddy Napoleon) romps on "Dark Eyes" and four previously unreleased performances. And in the biggest surprise, swing trumpet great Harry James performs "Pagan Love Song" and a very Boppish version of "Tuxedo Junction" that shows that he was quite familiar with Dizzy Gillespie; his solo on the latter ranks with his very best.

7 *Prestige First Sessions, Vol. 1 / July 2, 1949–July 20, 1950 / Prestige 24114*
7 *Prestige First Sessions, Vol. 3 / Feb. 7, 1950–Oct. 5, 1951 / Prestige 24116*

Part of a three-CD series (*Vol. 2* comprises Sonny Stitt recordings and is reviewed under his name), these discs include most of the first sessions recorded by the Prestige label, from the tail end of the classic Bebop era. *Vol. 1* has all of Don Lanphere's early dates as a leader (including his famous session with Fats Navarro) along with outings headed by Leo Parker and Al Haig. *Vol. 3* includes some early R&Bish tenor by Eddie "Lockjaw" Davis, a little known four-song Dizzy Gillespie date (cut shortly after he broke up his big band), and sessions led by Red Rodney and Bennie Green. Although not entirely essential, these CDs contain many little-known three-minute gems that could help fill a lot of gaps for collectors.

8 *RCA Victor 80th Anniversary—Vol. 3—1940–1949 / Jan. 3, 1940–Nov. 14, 1949 / RCA 68779*

In 1997 RCA celebrated the 80th anniversary of the first jazz recording with the release of eight single CDs that were also available as one large set, each disc covering a decade. *Vol. 3*, which goes through the 1940s in chronological order, begins with swing performances, including selections by Coleman Hawkins, Duke Ellington, Artie Shaw's Gramercy Five, Benny Carter, Tommy Dorsey, and John Kirby's sextet. After ten selections from 1940–42, the disc jumps to 1946 and Dizzy Gillespie's "Night in Tunisia." Later numbers feature the 52nd Street All-Stars, Kenny Clarke, Art Tatum, Errol Garner, the Metronome All-Stars, and Oscar Peterson, among others (including Art Tatum, Lennie Tristano, and Louis Armstrong). A fine sampler of an intriguing decade.

7 *Saturday Night Swing Session / Mar. 1947–May 1947 / Original Jazz Classics 1915*

The music on this former LP is taken from a couple of broadcasts from the WNEW *Saturday Night Swing Session* radio series. Reflecting the time period, the music heard is often Bop-oriented swing. Four numbers feature Roy Eldridge and Flip Phillips with a sextet that includes guitarist Al Casey, Ed Safranski, and sometimes Mel Torme (who has a silly vocal with Eldridge on "Honeysuckle Rose" and also sits in on drums). "Buck Still Jumps" is an Al Casey feature. The final two numbers are much more Boppish, an octet composed of Fats Navarro, Charlie Ventura, Allen Eager, Bill Harris, Ralph Burns, guitarist Al Valente, Chubby Jackson, and Buddy Rich that performs Ventura's "High on an Open Mike" and "Sweet Georgia Brown."

9 *The Savoy Story: Volume One—Jazz / Apr. 17, 1944– May 21, 1959 / Savoy 92856*

This three-CD set is a well-conceived overview of the Savoy label. The first disc mostly features advanced swing (including Ben Webster, Lester Young, trumpeter Hot Lips Page, tenor saxophonist Ike Quebec, Erroll Garner, Illinois Jacquet, and finally Charlie Parker, Dexter Gordon, and Boyd Raeburn). Disc two sticks mostly to the Bop years (J. J. Johnson, the Bebop Boys, Fats Navarro, Serge Chaloff, more Bird and Dexter, George Shearing, Red Norvo, and Dizzy Gillespie), while disc three traces the music's gradual evolution into Hard Bop (J. J. Johnson and Kai Winding, Cannonball Adderley, Milt Jackson, flutist Herbie Mann, Curtis Fuller, and others). Although most of the music is available elsewhere, listening to the three-CD set straight through lets collectors and jazz fans hear many of the high points of Savoy's rich catalog during this important period.

8 *Stars of Birdland on Tour / 1955 / Jazz Classics 5015*

The Birdland club sponsored several national tours of some of its most popular attractions in elaborate shows during the 1950s. This two CD set, recorded in Topeka, Kansas, features the Count Basie Orchestra on a few numbers and backing such top artists as Lester Young, Joe Williams, Stan Getz, and Sarah Vaughan (in typically exciting form). In addition, there are rare live minisets from Erroll Garner's trio and George Shearing's quintet. The recording quality is decent, and the performances (particularly by Vaughan and Shearing) are quite exciting and swinging.

9 *Sunset Swing / Mar. 1, 1945–Nov. 12, 1945 / Black Lion 760171*

The 22 selections on this CD are mostly transitional music between swing and Bebop from the important year of 1945. Among the musicians heard in the eight different groups represented (all of the music was originally made for the Sunset label) are Howard McGhee, Charlie Ventura, pianist Andre Previn, Lucky Thompson, Harry "Sweets" Edison, and Dodo Marmarosa. Even though the music is technically swing, it is fascinating to hear how the new Bebop style was affecting the older idiom. The overall results are consistently swinging, and there are many rewarding moments.

8 *An Unforgettable Session / Apr. 29, 1947 / Giants of Jazz 53097*

The music from this all-star Pasadena Civic Auditorium concert has been reissued in piecemeal and fragmented fashion on budget labels through the years, so it is a joy finally to have it all together. In addition to a version of "Lover" by Erroll Garner in a quartet, four other overlapping all-star groups are featured on a variety of standards, including

"Just You, Just Me," "Perdido," "Groovin' High," "Hot House," and "How High the Moon." The top-notch musicians include trumpeters Howard McGhee, Charlie Shavers, and Chuck Peterson, trombonist Vic Dickenson, altoists Benny Carter, Sonny Criss, and Willie Smith, the tenors of Charlie Barnet, Wardell Gray, and Stan Getz, pianists Dodo Marmarosa, Garner, and Nat Cole, vibraphonist Red Norvo, guitarists Irving Ashby and Oscar Moore, bassists Red Callender and Johnny Miller, and drummers Jackie Mills and Louie Bellson. Practically everyone has his moments, and the net results are well worth getting!

7 *USA All Stars in Berlin / Feb. 1955 / Jazz Band 2113*

Although it does not say Jazz at the Philharmonic anywhere on this British CD, the music is taken from the 1955 tour of JATP. Best are two jam session numbers featuring Dizzy Gillespie, Roy Eldridge, Bill Harris, Flip Phillips, the Oscar Peterson Trio, and Louie Bellson. There is also a four-song ballad medley, a drum feature for Bellson, two numbers ("Easy Does It" and "Seven Come Eleven") by the Peterson-Herb Ellis-Ray Brown trio, an opportunity for Buddy DeFranco to stretch out on "Billie's Bounce," and two swinging vocals by Ella Fitzgerald including "Perdido." The music is high quality if a bit typical, easily recommended for JATP fans.

LPS TO SEARCH FOR

Battle of the Tenor Saxes (IAJRC 15) consists of recordings from 1945–51 that have spots for such tenors as Coleman Hawkins, Ben Webster, Gene Ammons, Ike Quebec, Paul Gonsalves, Illinois Jacquet, Lester Young, Dexter Gordon, Allen Eager, Warne Marsh, James Moody, and Wardell Gray. Although some of the performances have since been reissued on CD, quite a few are still rare.

The Bebop Boys (Savoy 2225) has a variety of notable recordings from 1946–52, including eight selections by the Bebop Boys (featuring Kenny Dorham, Sonny Stitt, and Bud Powell), a Ray Brown date with Dizzy Gillespie, Gil Fuller heading the Gillespie big band in 1949, vocal numbers from Kenny Hagood, Babs Gonzales, and Eddie Jefferson, plus a couple of Leo Parker dates with such sidemen as trumpeter Joe Newman, J. J. Johnson, and Dexter Gordon. Savoy is long overdue to make most of this material more readily available.

The Be-Bop Era (RCA Vintage 519) was one of the very best overviews of classic Bebop that was available in the 1960s. Included are one selection apiece by Coleman Hawkins with Allen Eager, Illinois Jacquet, Lucky Thompson, Charlie Ventura, the 1949 Metronome All-Stars, and Count Basie's sextet plus multiple titles from Kenny Clarke's 52nd Street Boys and Dizzy Gillespie's orchestra. Hearing Dizzy Gillespie, Fats Navarro, and Miles Davis trade off on "Overtime" (all sounding close to identical) with the Metronome All-Stars is a definite high point.

The six volumes of *Bebop Revisited* (Xanadu 120, 124, 172, 197, 205, and 208) made available a variety of rather rare sessions, mostly from the classic Bebop era; some of the music has become more common with time. *Vol. 1* has two songs and a pair of alternate takes from Dexter Gordon with trombonist Melba Liston, a Don Lanphere date with Fats Navarro and singer Earl Coleman (best are two instrumental versions of "Move"), and a Chubby Jackson sextet session from 1947. All of the music has since been reissued. *Vol. 2* has three songs by a big band led by Oscar Pettiford that includes Dizzy Gillespie and Don Byas but mostly backs singer Rubberlegs Williams, very early combo dates headed by Kai Winding and J. J. Johnson, and a matchup by Terry Gibbs and Aaron Sachs. *Vol. 3* is from 1951–53 and consists of a Kai Winding-Warne Marsh quintet, trumpeter Tony Fruscella playing cool-toned Bop with a septet that includes Herb Geller, and a pioneering jazz flute date by Sam Most that also includes Doug Mettome and Bob Dorough on piano. *Vol. 4* has two of James Moody's early sessions (from 1948 and 1950), including such titles as "A Lesson in Bopology" and "Honeysuckle Bop"; in addition there are four songs from Bernie Green in 1950 with Budd Johnson. *Vol. 5* includes a rare quartet set from 1964 by Kenny Dorham with Barry Harris and two long performances by Conte Candoli in a quintet with tenor saxophonist Richie Kamuca, pianist Dick Shreve, bassist Red Mitchell, and drummer Stan Levey. *Vol. 6* contains some of the most valuable performances in the series, including quartet/quintet dates led by tenors John Hardee, Eddie "Lockjaw" Davis, and Paul Quinichette during 1947–52. Most interesting are the three songs recorded on May 2, 1945, by tenorman Frankie Socolow in a quintet using Bud Powell (on one of his first dates) and the legendary and shadowy trumpeter Freddy Webster, who takes a couple of his best recorded solos.

The Bop Session (Sonet 692) is a typical Bebop jam session date from 1975 featuring Dizzy Gillespie, Sonny Stitt, John Lewis, or Hank Jones on piano, Percy Heath, and Max Roach. They happily jam through six Bop standards (including "Confirmation" and "Groovin' High") with the only song close to an obscurity being "Lady Bird"; Dizzy still sounded strong at this point.

Central Avenue Breakdown, Volume 1 (Onyx 212) features Dodo Marmarosa in 1946 (including on one date with Lucky Thompson), Teddy Edwards's 1948 quintet with Hampton Hawes, and pianist-arranger George Handy in a quartet led by bassist Vivian Garry. *Central Avenue Breakdown, Volume 2* (Onyx 215) has a session by jokester-guitarist Slim Gaillard (a quartet that includes Marmarosa), Barney Kessel's debut as a leader (from 1945), and eight songs from a 1947 session by Teddy Edwards that features trumpeter Benny Bailey.

The 1970 Charlie Parker Memorial Concert (Cadet 60002) is a two-LP set that features performances by such notables as Dexter Gordon with Red Rodney and tenor saxophonist Von Freeman, Kenny Dorham (in one of his last recordings) with Ray Nance on trumpet and violin, Howard McGhee with altoist Vi Redd, and Lee Konitz interacting with trumpeter Arthur Hoyle; Eddie Jefferson is featured on "Disappointed." Although there are some long-winded solos (particularly by Gordon), this historic event (celebrating what would have been Charlie Parker's 50th birthday) is well worth being reissued on CD someday.

Harry Lim during 1944–47 recorded one classic after another for his Keynote label, documenting virtually every top small-group swing player and some emerging Bop musicians. The remarkable 21-LP box *The Complete Keynote Collection* (Polygram/Keynote 18PJ-1051-71) has all of the music (including alternate takes) recorded by Lim for the Keynote label, 334 performances in all, including 115 alternate takes! Most of the music is late-period swing (including famous sessions by Lester Young, Coleman Hawkins, Earl Hines, and Benny Carter) plus Dixieland, but there are also sets headed by Chubby Jackson, Bill Harris, Lennie Tristano, Dave Lambert & Buddy Stewart, and Red Rodney. However, this will be a difficult box to find, and only some of the music has thus far been reissued on CD.

Cool Whalin' (Spotlite 135) has rare and previously unissued material from several Bop-oriented vocalists. Joe Carroll sings with Howard McGhee's band in 1970, Kenny "Pancho" Hagood is heard in 1948 and 1967, Babs Gonzales jams in 1952, and Earl Coleman is featured in 1948. Most interesting are the earliest examples of Eddie Jefferson on record (from 1949–50) and two songs by Frankie Passions in which he is backed by Thelonious Monk's group.

The music on *The East/West Controversy* (Xanadu 104) is

far from controversial. Included are Hampton Hawes's first date as a leader (six trio numbers from 1951 with bassist Harper Cosby and drummer Lawrence Marable) and seven rare numbers from a session by bassist Paul Chambers with a 1957 quintet featuring tenors Jack Montrose and Bill Perkins.

The Giants of Jazz (Atlantic 2–905) documents the all-star sextet (Dizzy Gillespie, Sonny Stitt, Kai Winding, Thelonious Monk, Al McKibbon, and Art Blakey) during 1971–72, and this two-LP set is the best existing document of the super group. Stitt (who is showcased on "Everything Happens to Me") in particular is in fine form, and the highlights include "A Night in Tunisia," "Tour de Force," "Allen's Alley," and "Blue 'n Boogie."

The two-LP *I Remember Bebop* (Columbia 35381) is a celebration of Bop from 1977 that has solo piano numbers by Al Haig, Duke Jordan, John Lewis, Sadik Hakim, Walter Bishop Jr., Barry Harris, Tommy Flanagan, and Jimmie Rowles. All of those musicians were still in their prime at the time but, considering that Bebop pianists usually played in trios, it is surprising that what is heard are unaccompanied solos.

The two-LP *Masters of the Modern Piano* (Verve 2514) has performances by Bud Powell (the most common tracks on the twofer), avant-gardist Cecil Taylor (at the 1957 Newport Jazz Festival), Mary Lou Williams (with Dizzy Gillespie's big band), Paul Bley, Wynton Kelly, and Bill Evans. *The Modern Jazz Piano Album* (Savoy 2247), also a twofer, has trio sessions by pianists Lennie Tristano, Dodo Marmarosa, and George Wallington, an obscure quartet outing from Herbie Nichols, three of the titles of the Bebop Boys with Kenny Dorham, Sonny Stitt, and Bud Powell, and a hard Bop outing from 1956 with pianist Horace Silver and trumpeter Donald Byrd.

The New York Scene in the '40s (CBS 65392), a French CBS release, has some of the finest Bop recordings in Co-lumbia's archives. The Cootie Williams Orchestra's 1942 version of "Epistrophy" is here, along with two early cuts by Dizzy Gillespie (including a radical transformation of "I Can't Get Started"), two numbers from the 1950 Metronome All-Stars, and three of Gil Evans's more Boppish charts for Claude Thornhill's orchestra. In addition, there are four numbers apiece from Chubby Jackson's 1949 big band and Sarah Vaughan's classic 1950 session with Miles Davis.

Okeh Jazz (Epic 37315) is a two-LP set consisting of sessions from 1947–54 led by tenor saxophonist Arnett Cobb, "Little" Johnny Griffin in 1954, Red Rodney in 1952, the early Ahmad Jamal Trio, organist Wild Bill Davis, and singer Mary Ann McCall.

The Tempo Jazzmen/The Hermanites (Spotlite 132) combines all of the takes from two historic Bop dates. Dizzy Gillespie is heard on February 6, 1946, with the Tempo Jazzmen, the band he led in Los Angeles with Charlie Parker; unfortunately Bird did not show up for this date. Dizzy performs such numbers as "Confirmation" and "'Round Midnight" with Lucky Thompson, Milt Jackson, Al Haig, Ray Brown, and drummer Stan Levey. In addition, the ill-fated trumpeter Sonny Berman teams up with other Woody Herman sidemen (including Bill Harris, Flip Phillips, future Hermanite Serge Chaloff, and Ralph Burns) in 1946, taking a particularly haunting solo on "Nocturne."

V.S.O.P. Album (Mercury 824 116) celebrated the 40th anniversary of the Mercury label in 1985 with a four-LP set of previously unreleased material (some alternate takes, some completely different titles) dating from 1945–65. Included are recordings by Erroll Garner, Gene Ammons, Jay McShann, Arnett Cobb, Clark Terry, Dinah Washington, Paul Quinichette, pianist Junior Mance, Clifford Brown, Cannonball Adderley, the Quincy Jones Orchestra, Billy Taylor, Dizzy Gillespie's 1965 quintet, and others.

Hopefully five years from now, virtually all of the music in this section will be available on CD.

RECOMMENDED BEBOP BOOKS

There have been many books written through the years on Bebop and its musicians, singers, and personalities, with new ones coming out on a regular basis. Here are 53 of the best, all well worth acquiring and savoring:

Biographies

Serge Chaloff
Serge Chaloff by Vladimir Simosko (Scarecrow Press, 1998)

Buddy DeFranco
Buddy DeFranco—A Biographical Portrait and Discography by John Kuehn and Arne Astrup (Scarecrow Press, 1993)

Ella Fitzgerald
Ella Fitzgerald by Stuart Nicholson (Da Capo Press, 1993)
The Ella Fitzgerald Companion edited by Leslie Gourse (Schirmer Books, 1998)

Dizzy Gillespie
Groovin' High by Alyn Shipton (Oxford University Press, 1999)

Coleman Hawkins
The Song of the Hawk by John Chilton (University of Michigan Press, 1990)

Woody Herman
Blue Flame by Robert Kriebel (Purdue University Press, 1995)
Chronicles of the Herds by Williams Clancy and Audree Coke Kenton (Schirmer Books,1995)

Stan Kenton
The Man and His Music by Lillian Arganian (Artistry Press, 1989)
Stan Kenton by Carol Easton (Da Capo Press, 1973)

Thelonious Monk
Straight No Chaser by Leslie Gourse (Schirmer Books, 1997)
Thelonious Monk by Thomas Fitterling (Berkley Hills Books, 1997)

Charlie Parker
Bird Lives by Ross Russell (Quartet Books, 1972)
Bird—The Legend of Charlie Parker edited by Robert Reisner (Da Capo Press, 1962)
Celebrating Bird by Gary Giddins (Beechtree Books, 1987)
The Charlie Parker Companion edited by Carl Woideck (Schirmer Books, 1998)
Charlie Parker—His Music And Life by Carl Woideck (University of Michigan Press, 1996)
Cool Blues by Mark Miller (Nightwood Editions, 1989)

Oscar Peterson
Oscar Peterson by Gene Lees (Prima Publishing, 1990)

Bud Powell
Bouncing with Bud by Carl Smith (Biddle Publishing Company, 1997)
Dance of the Infidels by Francis Paudras (Biddle Publishers, 1998)

Buddy Rich
Traps—The Boy Wonder by Mel Torme (Oxford University Press, 1991)

Art Tatum
Too Marvelous for Words by James Lester (Oxford University Press, 1994)

Sarah Vaughan
Sassy by Leslie Gourse (Charles Scribner & Sons, 1993)

Mary Lou Williams
Morning Glory by Linda Dahl (Pantheon Books, 1999)

Lester Young
A Lester Young Reader edited by Louis Porter (Smithsonian Institution Press, 1991)
You Just Fight for Your Life by Frank Buchmann-Moller (Greenwood Press, 1990)

Autobiographies

Charlie Barnet

Those Swinging Years with Stanley Dance (Louisiana State
University Press, 1984)

Red Callender

Unfinished Dream with Elaine Cohen (Quartet Jazz, 1985)

Dizzy Gillespie

To Be or Not to Bop with Al Fraser (Doubleday, 1979)

Babs Gonzales

I Paid My Dues (Expubidence Publishing Corp., 1967)

Hampton Hawes

Raise Up Off Me with Don Asher (Da Capo Press, 1974)

Anita O'Day

High Times, Hard Times with George Eells (G. E.
Putnam & Sons, 1981)

Art Pepper

Straight Life with Laurie Pepper (Da Capo Press, 1979)

Producer Teddy Reig

Reminiscing in Tempo with Edward Berge (Scarecrow
Press, 1990)

Other Bebop Topics

All Music Guide to Jazz, 3rd edition ed. by Scott Yanow,
Michael Erlewine, Chris Woodstra, and Vladimir
Bogdanov (Miller Freeman, 1998)

American Musicians II by Whitney Balliett (Oxford
University Press, 1996)

Barney, Bradley and Max—16 Portraits in Jazz by Whitney
Balliett (Oxford University Press, 1989)

Bebop—The Music and the Players by Thomas Owens
(Oxford University Press, 1995)

The Biographical Encyclopedia of Jazz by Leonard Feather
and Ira Gitler (Oxford University Press, 1999)

The Birth of Bebop by Scott DeVeaux (University of
California Press, 1997)

Central Avenue—Its Rise and Fall by Bette Yarbrough Cox
(Beem Publications, 1996)

Central Avenue Sounds edited by Clora Bryant, Buddy
Collette, Steven Isoardi, Gerald Wilson, and others
(University of California Press, Berkeley, 1998)

Drummin' Men by Burt Korall (Schirmer Books, 1990)

52nd Street by Arnold Shaw (Da Capo Press, 1971)

From Satchmo to Miles by Leonard Feather (Da Capo
Press, 1972)

Hear Me Talkin' to Ya edited by Nat Hentoff and Nat
Shapiro (Peer Davies, 1955)

Inside Jazz by Leonard Feather (Da Capo Press, 1949)

The Jazz Life by Nat Hentoff (Da Capo Press, 1961)

Jazz Masters of the Forties by Ira Gitler (Da Capo Press,
1966)

Jazz Singing by Will Friedwald (Charles Scribner & Sons,
1990)

My Singing Teachers by Mel Torme (Oxford University
Press, 1994)

Swing to Bop by Ira Gitler (Oxford University Press, 1985)

THE FUTURE OF BEBOP

Although the classic Bebop era unofficially ended by 1950, the music has lived on ever since. The next two jazz styles to rise to prominence, Cool Jazz (also known as West Coast Jazz) and Hard Bop, both owed their existence to the innovations of Bop. In fact, they overlapped with the once-radical music. Cool Jazz was really a conservative step forward, consolidating the harmonic innovations of Bop but with quieter and lighter rhythms, more of an emphasis on arrangements (even many of the improvised ensembles tended to sound arranged) and a stronger focus on tones (looking back toward the swing era). Hard Bop brought back the fire of Bop while mixing in gospel and soul influences, as did Soul Jazz of the 1960s. When one realizes that Charlie Parker for a month on the West Coast in 1952 used Cool Jazz trumpeter Chet Baker in his band, that Dexter Gordon was considered one of the top Hard Bop tenors of the 1960s, and that Lou Donaldson was one of the most popular attractions of Soul Jazz, the connections between those later styles and Bebop is obvious.

In 1946 Benny Goodman (who was 37) and Louis Armstrong (45) were considered "old-timers" while Dizzy Gillespie (at 29) was practically the elder statesman of the Bebop movement. But because the evolution of jazz moved so quickly between 1920 and 1975, by 1960 (when Gillespie was 43) Bebop was considered old hat by many. With the arrival of altoist Ornette Coleman in New York, playing unisons with cornetist Don Cherry that owed a lot to Bird and Diz, but then improvising freely without any chord changes, the former Bebop radicals were now thought of as conservatives in comparison! Free (or avant-garde) Jazz was "liberating" jazz from the "tyranny" of repeating chord changes, and, although the late Charlie Parker was considered a folk hero, it was time for jazz to move ahead. The former challengers of the mainstream had succeeded so well in taking over jazz that now it was time for the Beboppers (seen as traditionalists and the establishment) to be tossed out as time moved on.

The 1960s were an increasingly rough time for the surviving Bop players. The rise of avant-garde jazz (which never caught on with the general public) started to give jazz a bad name to listeners unprepared for the sound explorations. And while jazz had been able to coexist with rock and roll in the 1950s, the emergence of the Beatles and the takeover of the music industry by rock a decade later resulted in there being many fewer work opportunities for jazz musicians. By the late 1960s, when quite a few veteran players had at least temporarily moved to Europe, Bebop no longer had much of a presence in the United States other than a few celebrities (particularly Dizzy Gillespie and Thelonious Monk). The rise of fusion in the late '60s seemed to seal Bop's fate.

But by the mid-1970s, things began to change. Up until then, new styles of jazz were thought of as "improvements" and replacements of the older styles as jazz rushed to complete freedom. But with the evolution of the music starting to run out of gas after Free Jazz and fusion, straightahead acoustic jazz began to make a comeback. The rise of tenor saxophonist Scott Hamilton later in the decade and trumpeter Wynton Marsalis in the early 1980s helped start a movement in which surviving veterans were celebrated for their accomplishments and all styles of jazz were welcome as long as the music was played creatively and not just a re-creation of the past. Richie Cole and Jon Faddis had already emerged as Bebop's new heroes, and now such veterans as Dizzy Gillespie, Red Rodney, J.J. Johnson, Buddy De-Franco, Sonny Stitt, Jimmy Heath, Dexter Gordon (whose return to the United States was historic), Milt Jackson, Oscar Peterson, Ray Brown, and Max Roach were being properly recognized as classic greats who should be treasured.

Unlike with swing, which had a Retro Swing movement in the 1990s, there has not been a rush to revive classic Bebop, but perhaps that is because the music has remained such an important part of jazz's foundation. Although most of the giants from the classic Bebop era have since passed on, the music still lives, both as a historic turning point for jazz (when it was first thought of as a very significant art form rather than just being entertainment) and as a challenging style that most young players strive to master before developing their own individual voice.

Perhaps the best summation of the music's longevity, and its timeless viability, can be summed up in the graffiti that appeared shortly after Charlie Parker's death: Bird Lives!

ABOUT THE AUTHOR

Scott Yanow has been writing about jazz since 1975. Jazz editor of *Record Review* during its entire publishing history (1976–84), he has written for *Downbeat*, *Jazz Times*, *Jazz Forum*, *Jazz News*, and *Strictly Jazz* magazines. Yanow currently is a regular contributor to *Cadence*, *Jazziz*, *Coda*, *L.A. Jazz Scene*, *Mississippi Rag*, *Jazz Improv*, *Jazz Now*, *Jazz Report*, and *Planet Jazz*. He also compiles the jazz listings for the *Los Angeles Times*. Editor of the *All Music Guide to Jazz*, Yanow is the author of *Duke Ellington* and *Swing* as well as the forthcoming *Afro-Cuban Jazz* guide, which joins the *Third Ear—The Essential Listening Companion* series. Yanow has also written over 200 album liner notes.

INDEX

Kirby, John, 82, 180, 370
  career of, 28–29
  CDs of, 28–29
  films and, 29
  sextet of, 28, 36, 55, 88, 137
Kirk, Andy, 46, 82, 85, 130
  orchestra of, 5, 137
Konitz, Lee, 84, 150, 163, 176, 186, 289
Krupa, Gene, 1, 3, 5–6, 16, 27, 30, 35, 42–43, 122, 124–125, 166, 168, 179, 180, 199, 205, 214, 268
  band of, 16, 86, 95–96, 124–125, 142, 178, 228
  career of, 228
  CDs of, 228–229
  films and, 229
  LPs of, 229
  trio of, 120, 124–125, 205, 228–229, 370

L

Lambert, Dave, 42, 49, 172, 180, 209, 228–229, 261, 291–292, 300–301, 342
  career of, 177
Lambert, Hendricks, and Ross, 303, 338, 343
  career of, 301–302
  CDs of, 302
  LPs of, 302
Lamond, Don, 218, 224, 231
  career of, 170
  CDs of, 170
  films and, 170
Lanphere, Don, 85, 219, 221, 370, 372
  career of, 117
  CDs of, 117–118
Leonard, Harlan, 46
  orchestra of, 9
Levy, John, 132, 143
Levy, Lou, 121, 129, 161, 193, 208, 218, 247, 251, 264, 310, 317, 348, 367
  career of, 140–141
  CDs of, 141
  films of, 141
  quartet of, 19
  trio of, 179
Lewis, John, 40, 47, 51, 54, 56, 76, 77–78, 89, 90, 96–98, 156, 169, 193–194, 196, 244, 332, 340, 372, 373
  career of, 141
  CDs of, 141–142
  films and, 142
  LPs of, 142
Lunceford, Jimmie, 1, 87, 125, 186–187, 212, 278

M

Machito, 187–188, 350, 369
  band of, 229
  career of, 229
  CDs of, 229–230
  LPs of, 230

Mangione, Chuck, 185
  career of, 302–303
  CDs of, 303
Manhattan Transfer, 302, 336
  career of, 303
  CDs of, 303–304
Manne, Shelly, 22, 71, 84, 95–96, 116, 124, 138, 141, 152–53, 156, 166, 197, 203, 218, 226–228, 231, 241, 246, 261, 264, 268, 274, 286–287, 323, 341
  career of, 170–171
Margolis, Kitty
  career of, 304
  CDs of, 304
Marmarosa, Dodo, 20, 29, 40, 42, 46, 48, 82, 105, 115–116, 151, 201, 203, 209, 229, 231, 234–236, 367, 371, 372–373
  career of, 142–143
  CDs of, 142–143
McConnell, Rob
  career of, 304
  CDs of, 305–306
  LPs of, 306
McGhee, Howard, 5, 15, 20, 22–23, 42, 46, 48, 51, 74, 80, 85, 94, 98, 106, 114, 116, 119, 121, 125, 137, 142–143, 161, 164, 166, 169, 171, 193, 205, 207–209, 229–230, 261, 268, 364, 368–369, 371–372
  band of, 107–108, 285
  career of, 82
  CDs of, 82–84
  films and, 84
  LPs of, 84
McKibbon, Al, 55, 70, 73, 76, 93, 143–144, 369, 373
  career of, 161–162
  CDs of, 162
McKinley, Ray
  band of, 230
  career of, 230
  CDs, 230
  films and, 230
  LPs of, 230
McPartland, Marian, 145, 170
  career of, 306
  CDs of, 306–308
  films and, 308
  LPs of, 308
McPherson, Charles, 87, 99, 156, 284–285
  career of, 308
  CDs of, 309–310
  films and, 310
  LPs of, 310
McRae, Carmen, 50, 145
  career of, 310
  CDs of, 310–313
  films and, 313
  LPs of, 313
McShann, Jay, 20, 36, 37, 45–46, 98, 173, 370, 373
  band of, 5, 46–48, 230–231

Third Ear

**Fresh perspectives,
new discoveries,
great music.**

Third Ear—The Essential Listening Companion is a new series of music guides exploring some of the most compelling genres in popular music. Each guide is written or edited by a leading authority in the field, who provides uncommon insight into the music. These books offer informed histories, anecdotal artist biographies, and incisive reviews and ratings of recordings. In-depth essays explore the roots and branches of the music. Easy to use and fun to browse, ***Third Ear*** guides are visually inviting as well, with evocative artist photos.

Swing
By Scott Yanow

Swing explores the musical phenomenon that has younger listeners up and dancing, and older ones fondly looking back. From the 1930s' classic sound of Duke Ellington through today's Retro-Swing movement with Big Bad Voodoo Daddy, this guide covers every era of swing. It profiles over 500 band leaders, players, vocalists, sidemen and composers, and the recordings that make (or don't make) the cut. Plus—it covers swing in the movies, books, hard-to-find recordings, and more.
Softcover, 514 pages, ISBN 0-87930-600-9, $22.95

Alternative Rock
By Dave Thompson

Alternative Rock looks inside the music that transformed the soundscape of the late '70s, '80s and '90s, and is still evolving today. Detailed essays delve into the meaning of "alternative," exploring topics ranging from primary musical influences to cultural trends, sampling, lo-fi, and more. Featured artists include The Beastie Boys, The Clash, The Cure, Green Day, PJ Harvey, Jane's Addiction, Nirvana, Smashing Pumpkins, The Smiths, Sonic Youth, and hundreds more.
Softcover, 800 pages, ISBN 0-87930-607-6, $24.95

Afro-Cuban Jazz
By Scott Yanow

This is the ultimate guide to the irresistible music that blends bebop with Cuban folk music and rhythms. Covering such early figures as Chano Pozo, Machito, Tito Puente, Cal Tjader and Willie Bobo, the book highlights today's leading artists— Poncho Sanchez, Chucho Valdes, Arturo Sandoval, Gato Barbieri, and many more. It also notes traditional jazz musicians who have frequently recorded Afro-Cuban jazz, and related strains of folk-influenced music by groups such as the Buena Vista Social Club.
Softcover, 240 pages, ISBN 0-87930-619-X, November 2000, $17.95

Celtic Music
Edited by Kenny Mathieson

Today's Celtic music hails from its traditional homelands but also embraces new fusions from around the globe. Featuring 100 color photos, this guide captures the flavor of this widely enjoyed music in all its forms—traditional, new Celtic, and Celtic-influenced music. It describes known and lesser-known solo artists, groups, singers and players, ranging from Irish piper Johnny Doran to the Chieftains. Plus—essays explore Celtic's regional variations and unique instrumentation such as harp, pipe, fiddle, and squeezebox.
Softcover, 192 pages, ISBN 0-87930-623-8, January 2001, $19.95

Available at fine book and music stores everywhere. Or contact:

MFI Miller Freeman Books

6600 Silacci Way, Gilroy, CA 95020 USA
Phone: (800) 848-5594 • **Fax:** (408) 848-5784
E-mail: mfi@rushorder.com • **Web:** www.books.mfi.com